PLAYFAIR
CRICKET ANNUAL 2010
63rd edition
EDITED BY IAN MARSHALL
All statistics by the Editor unless otherwise stated

Preface by Mike Atherton 2
Foreword and Acknowledgements 3

Test Cricket
England v Bangladesh – Series Records 5
England v Pakistan – Series Records 7
Australia, Bangladesh and Pakistan Registers 9
Statistical Highlights in 2009 11
Scorecards (December 2008–Jan... 15
England Averages in 2009 63
ICC Elite List of Ur 64
Current Career Ave 65
Test Match Records 75

County Cricket
County Register, 2009 89
First-Class Umpires 20 203
University Registers 206
Touring Teams Register 208
Statistical Highlights in 2 209
LV County Championship 214
Friends Provident Trophy 218
NatWest PRO 40 League 222
Twenty20 Cup 224
Cricketer of the Year Awards 227
First-Class Averages in 2009 229
First-Class Cricket Career Averages 245
Leading Current Players 263
Limited-Overs 'List A' Cricket Career Averages 264
First-Class Cricket Records 271

Limited-Overs and Twenty20 Internationals
England Limited-Overs Internationals in 2009 280
ICC World Twenty20 2009 283
Current Career Averages 285
Limited-Overs Internationals Records 298
Twenty20 Internationals Records 309

Other Cricket
Oxbridge Match Results and Records 314
IPL Twenty20 316
Champions League Twenty20 318
Women's Test Cricket Records 319
Women's Limited-Overs Records 323

2010 Fixtures
Principal Matches 326
Test Match Championship Schedule 332

Fillers/Miscellaneous
County Caps Awarded 2009 94
What is a Kolpak Registration? 219
Duckworth/Lewis – A Brief Explanation 333
Fielding Chart 335

PREFACE

A new decade begins with the world game looking very different from ten years ago. At the turn of the millennium, Twenty20 had not been invented (at least not as part of the professional game), player power was only just stirring, Australia were dominant, and private investors, if they looked at cricket at all, did so only as an enthusiasm rather than as a potential investment.

In the second half of the decade, Australia's demise was in relative rather than absolute terms. That they are no longer dominant now, though, seems to me to be an excellent portent for Test cricket over the next few years. There are four or five teams at the moment that could all beat each other, depending on which enjoys home advantage, so that the chances of competitive, rather than one-sided, cricket should be enhanced.

Two things, above all, will determine how well Test cricket survives the next ten years. The first is the nature of the competition, which, in the absence of a dominant team for the first time in two decades, is ensured. The second is the nature of the pitches that the players are asked to compete on. The recently concluded four-match series between England and South Africa showed the benefits of playing upon surfaces which offered at least something to the bowler.

The balance between bat and ball is absolutely critical to the future health of the longer game. If groundsmen – and this applies particularly to the sub-continent – continue to produce graveyard pitches, then interest will dwindle. Pace and bounce, or spin and bounce, are vital to protect the interests of bowlers at a time when, with changes to bat and boundary sizes, they are challenged like never before. The most thrilling moment in any day's play remains the fall of a wicket, not the blasting of a six.

How far technological changes affect the balance between bat and ball remains to be seen. There was early anecdotal evidence that the move to the Decision Review System (DRS) encouraged umpires to give more leg-before decisions to the spinners, which resulted, in turn, in batsmen playing more with bat rather than pad. This, though, was the only positive development from a system that, if not altered, will continue to dominate discussions unsatisfactorily. Players quickly realised that they could exploit the DRS in a tactical way, so that it became far removed from the original intention of simply stopping obvious blunders. If technology is to stay (and there is no going back now, sadly), then the umpires and not the players must remain in control of it. One of the core principles of the game is that the umpire's decision is final – something that the DRS undermines fundamentally, with the result that player behaviour at all levels is likely to decline.

Test cricket faces many challenges, from within and beyond its boundaries. Undoubtedly, the biggest challenge will come from the continued rise of franchise cricket, fuelled by private investors entering the game for profit. With the Indian Premier League looking to expand its borders into 'emerging markets', and needing the highest profile players to do so, the conflict between countries and franchises is likely to get more fraught, especially as players look to find ways of easing the burden on their tiring bodies. Against a punishing treadmill of international cricket, well-paid Twenty20 tournaments will look increasingly attractive.

It is not a good time, therefore, for the International Cricket Council to be more irrelevant than at any time in its recent history. Reform at the highest level is necessary, to put the game in the hands of people who can look beyond the narrow confines of national boundaries and beyond the need for cricket to constantly increase its revenues. It remains a game, not an industry.

MIKE ATHERTON

FOREWORD

Welcome to the 63rd edition of *Playfair Cricket Annual*. As all readers of this volume, not to mention many millions of other cricket fans around the world, must know, Bill Frindall passed away last year. His sudden death was a huge shock not just to the cricket world, but also to his family and friends. Having worked with Bill for almost 20 years, and published at least a book a year with him in that time, I was privileged to count myself among the latter group. While I was delighted to accept the offer to take over as the Editor, I wish that the circumstances could have been different. I am all too aware of what a daunting act I have to follow. I hope that some of what Bill taught me over the last two decades has filtered through, and will try my best to maintain the supreme standards that he set.

Although I am keen to maintain the traditions of *Playfair* that have made it such a success, I also realise that the book has to adapt to the changing world of cricket and, indeed, of life beyond. For this reason there are a few changes in this year's book, starting with Mike Atherton's excellent Preface, which assesses how recent developments in the game may evolve in the coming decade.

I have also decided to revise the ordering of the contents of *Playfair* in a way that I hope will make it simpler to use. The book is now divided into five sections as follows: Test match cricket, county cricket, international limited-overs cricket (including Twenty20), other cricket (IPL, Champions League, women's Test and limited-overs cricket, universities), and fixtures for the coming season. Each section, where appropriate, begins with a preview of forthcoming events, followed by a review of events during the previous season, then come the player records, and finally the records section.

The records sections now include matches involving multinational teams, and those where the sides tossed up but the players did not take the pitch. Bill argued that these matches should not count, and his records did not include them. However, until the ICC changes its mind on this matter, I have reluctantly decided that *Playfair*'s records should reflect those that exist elsewhere.

The changing nature of the sport, with ever-increasing amounts of cricket (England played 48 matches in 2009 for a scheduled total of 104 days), has also had an impact on the content of this book. Already in recent editions, the growth of Twenty20 cricket was filling an increasing amount of space. This trend has been continued again this year, with last summer's excellent ICC World Twenty20 given full coverage, an expanded section on the IPL and a new section on the inaugural Champions League. I have also expanded coverage of England's limited-overs performances, providing details of all matches played during 2009, rather than simply covering those matches played in England.

Echoing the Statistical Highlights of the English Season, a new section provides Test match highlights of the year. The fact that so many of the highlights are batting ones, rather than bowling ones (no one took ten wickets in a Test throughout the whole of 2009), provides proof for Mike Atherton's concerns that the balance of the game is tipping towards the bat. County cricket remains not only the bedrock of the domestic game, but also the key element of *Playfair*, and this part of the book remains unaltered.

However, these extra features have put pressure on the space available within the book, so a few familiar features have had to be dropped, such as the coverage of Minor Counties and 2nd XI cricket. For those who miss these sections of the book, I am delighted to announce the launch of a new *Playfair Cricket* website this year, www.playfaircricket.co.uk, which will continue to provide this information, as well as other useful material, and a means for contacting me if you have any suggestions you want to make for future editions. There are many excellent cricket websites already available, but I hope this one will provide something slightly different, as well as being a useful additional tool for all *Playfair* readers.

Ian Marshall
Eastbourne, March 2010

3

ACKNOWLEDGEMENTS AND THANKS

This book could not be written without the help of many people giving freely of their time and expertise, so I would like to thank the following for all they have done to help ensure this edition of *Playfair Cricket Annual* could be written:

First, I must thank Debbie Frindall, whose help in excavating Bill's records to save me from having to start the entire book from scratch was much appreciated, at a time when there were many other things for her to be thinking about.

At the counties, I would like to thank the following for their help over the last year: Derbyshire – Tom Holdcroft and John Brown; Durham – Brian Hunt (in what was his benefit year); Essex – Danny Macklin and Tony Choat; Glamorgan – Andrew Hignell; Gloucestershire – Lizzie Allen and Keith Gerrish; Hampshire – Tim Tremlett and Tony Weld; Kent – Carolyn Dunne and Jack Foley; Lancashire – Diana Lloyd and Alan West; Leicestershire – Elaine Pickering and Graham York; Middlesex – Rebecca Hart and Don Shelley; Northamptonshire – Tony Kingston; Nottinghamshire – Helen Palmer and Brian Hewes; Somerset – Guy Wolfenden and Gerald Stickley; Surrey – Steve Howes and Keith Booth; Sussex – Simon Dyke and Mike Charman; Warwickshire – Keith Cook and David Wainwright; Worcestershire – Joan Grundy and Neil Smith; Yorkshire – Janet Bairstow and John Potter.

At the universities, Cambridge – Tony Gibbs and Anthony Hyde; Durham – Graeme Fowler; Loughborough – Margaret Folwell; Oxford – Rajiv Sharma and Neil Harris. For the international umpires, thank you to Brent Silva and Vince van der Bijl; and Chris Kelly for the domestic umpires. To Alan Fordham, thank you for the principal fixtures. Philip Bailey, as ever, provided the first-class and List A career records, and, with his long experience in this field, was a most valuable help in compiling the book.

At Headline, my first thanks must go to David Wilson for giving me the opportunity to become only the fourth Editor of *Playfair* in its existence; Rhea Halford, already a veteran on her fourth edition, for her calm support; Louise Rothwell, for whom this was a first opportunity in six years to remind me that I was slipping slightly behind schedule, but who I know will ensure the book is produced on time; Sam Eades, for looking after the publicity; and Sam Habib, for setting up the *Playfair* website, work that I hope was a labour of love. John Skermer was meticulous in checking the proofs.

At Letterpart, the typesetter, Chris Leggett, Caroline Leggett, Lorraine Byfield and the rest of the team turned everything round with their customary speed and skill.

Finally, on a personal level, I would like to thank my parents, in whose house some of this volume was produced while we were between homes; my young daughters, Kiri and Sophia, who were so good at letting their daddy do his work, even if it meant missing *Ben and Holly's Little Kingdom*; and of course to my wife, Sugra, for smiling patiently now that I have even more reason for talking about cricket.

ENGLAND v BANGLADESH

SERIES RECORDS

2003-04 to 2005

HIGHEST INNINGS TOTALS

England	in England	528-3d		Lord's	2005
	in Bangladesh	326		Chittagong	2003-04
Bangladesh	in England	316		Chester-le-Street	2005
	in Bangladesh	255		Dhaka	2003-04

LOWEST INNINGS TOTALS

England	in England	447-3d		Chester-le-Street	2005
	in Bangladesh	295		Dhaka	2003-04
Bangladesh	in England	104		Chester-le-Street	2005
	in Bangladesh	138		Chittagong	2003-04

HIGHEST MATCH AGGREGATE 917 for 33 wickets Dhaka 2003-04
LOWEST MATCH AGGREGATE 795 for 23 wickets Lord's 2005

HIGHEST INDIVIDUAL INNINGS

England	in England	194	M.E.Trescothick	Lord's	2005
	in Bangladesh	113	M.E.Trescothick	Dhaka	2003-04
Bangladesh	in England	82*	Aftab Ahmed	Chester-le-Street	2005
	in Bangladesh	59	Hannan Sarkar	Dhaka	2003-04

HIGHEST AGGREGATE OF RUNS IN A SERIES

England	in England	345	(av 345.00)	M.E.Trescothick	2005
	in Bangladesh	208	(av 69.33)	M.P.Vaughan	2003-04
Bangladesh	in England	155	(av 38.75)	Javed Omar	2005
	in Bangladesh	114	(av 38.00)	Mushfiqur Rahman	2003-04

RECORD WICKET PARTNERSHIPS – ENGLAND

1st	148	M.E.Trescothick (194)/A.J.Strauss (69)	Lord's	2005
2nd	255	M.E.Trescothick (194)/M.P.Vaughan (120)	Lord's	2005
3rd	155	M.E.Trescothick (151)/I.R.Bell (162*)	Chester-le-Street	2005
4th	187*	I.R.Bell (162*)/G.P.Thorpe (66*)	Chester-le-Street	2005
5th	116	N.Hussain (76)/R.Clarke (55)	Chittagong	2003-04
6th	63	N.Hussain (76)/C.M.W.Read (37)	Chittagong	2003-04
7th	41	G.P.Thorpe (64)/G.J.Batty (19)	Dhaka	2003-04
8th	8	A.F.Giles (6)/R.L.Johnson (6)	Chittagong	2003-04
9th	5	A.F.Giles (6)/ M.J.Saggers (1)	Chittagong	2003-04
10th	28	A.F.Giles (19)/M.J.Hoggard (6*)	Dhaka	2003-04

RECORD WICKET PARTNERSHIPS – BANGLADESH

1st	50	Javed Omar (71)/Nafis Iqbal (15)	Chester-le-Street	2005
2nd	108	Hannan Sarkar (59)/Habibul Bashar (58)	Dhaka	2003-04
3rd	31	Javed Omar (22)/Aftab Ahmed (20)	Lord's	2005
4th	24	Javed Omar (71)/Habibul Bashar (63)	Chester-le-Street	2005
5th	70	Habibul Bashar (63)/Khaled Masud (25)	Chester-le-Street	2005
6th	60	Mushfiqur Rahman (34)/Khaled Masud (51)	Dhaka	2003-04
7th	29	Mushfiqur Rahman (46*)/Khaled Mahmud (18)	Dhaka	2003-04
8th	34	Khaled Masud (51)/Mohammad Rafique (32)	Dhaka	2003-04
9th	60	Aftab Ahmed (82*)/Tapash Baisya (18)	Chester-le-Street	2005
10th	13	Mohammad Rafique (12*)/Enamul Haque[2] (9)	Chittagong	2003-04

BEST INNINGS BOWLING ANALYSIS

England	in England	5-38	S.J.Harmison	Chester-le-Street	2005
	in Bangladesh	5-35	S.J.Harmison	Dhaka	2003-04
Bangladesh	in England	2-91	Mashrafe Mortaza	Chester-le-Street	2005
	in Bangladesh	4-60	Mashrafe Mortaza	Chittagong	2003-04

BEST MATCH BOWLING ANALYSIS

England	in England	8- 97	M.J.Hoggard	Chester-le-Street	2005
	in Bangladesh	9- 79	S.J.Harmison	Dhaka	2003-04
Bangladesh	in England	2- 91	Mashrafe Mortaza	Chester-le-Street	2005
	in Bangladesh	5-141	Mohammad Rafique	Dhaka	2003-04

HIGHEST AGGREGATE OF WICKETS IN A SERIES

England	in England	14	(av 12.92)	M.J.Hoggard	2005
	in Bangladesh	9	(av 8.77)	S.J.Harmison	2003-04
		9	(av 22.66)	M.J.Hoggard	2003-04
		9	(av 10.33)	R.L.Johnson	2003-04
Bangladesh	in England	4	(av 49.50)	Mashrafe Mortaza	2005
	in Bangladesh	10	(av 31.00)	Mohammad Rafique	2003-04

RESULTS SUMMARY

ENGLAND v BANGLADESH – IN ENGLAND

	Tests		Series			Lord's			Chester-le-Street	
		E	B	D	E	B	D	E	B	D
2005	2	2	–	–	1	–	–	1	–	–

ENGLAND v BANGLADESH – IN BANGLADESH

	Tests		Series			Dhaka			Chittagong	
		E	B	D	E	B	D	E	B	D
2003-04	2	2	–	–	1	–	–	1	–	–
Totals	4	4	–	–						

An updated version of these records will appear on www.playfaircricket.co.uk after the conclusion of England's tour of Bangladesh.

ENGLAND v PAKISTAN

SERIES RECORDS

1954 to 2006

HIGHEST INNINGS TOTALS

England	in England	558-6d	Nottingham	1954
	in Pakistan	546-8d	Faisalabad	1983-84
Pakistan	in England	708	The Oval	1987
	in Pakistan	636-8d	Lahore	2005-06

LOWEST INNINGS TOTALS

England	in England	130	The Oval	1954
	in Pakistan	130	Lahore	1987-88
Pakistan	in England	87	Lord's	1954
	in Pakistan	158	Kingston	2000-01

HIGHEST MATCH AGGREGATE 1553 for 40 wickets Leeds 2006
LOWEST MATCH AGGREGATE 509 for 28 wickets Nottingham 1967

HIGHEST INDIVIDUAL INNINGS

England	in England	278	D.C.S.Compton	Nottingham	1954
	in Pakistan	205	E.R.Dexter	Karachi	1961-62
Pakistan	in England	274	Zaheer Abbas	Birmingham	1971
	in Pakistan	223	Mohammad Yousuf	Lahore	2005-06

HIGHEST AGGREGATE OF RUNS IN A SERIES

England	in England	453	(av 90.60)	D.C.S.Compton	1954
	in Pakistan	449	(av 112.25)	D.I.Gower	1983-84
Pakistan	in England	631	(av 90.14)	Mohammad Yousuf	2006
	in Pakistan	431	(av 107.75)	Inzamam-ul-Haq	2005-06

RECORD WICKET PARTNERSHIPS – ENGLAND

1st	198	G.Pullar (165)/R.W.Barber (86)	Dacca	1961-62
2nd	248	M.C.Cowdrey (182)/E.R.Dexter (172)	The Oval	1962
3rd	267	M.P.Vaughan (120)/G.P.Thorpe (138)	Manchester	2001
4th	233	A.N.Cook (105)/P.D.Collingwood (186)	Lord's	2006
5th	192	D.C.S.Compton (278)/T.E.Bailey (36*)	Nottingham	1954
6th	166	G.P.Thorpe (118)/C.White (93)	Lahore	2000-01
7th	167	D.I.Gower (152)/V.J.Marks (83)	Faisalabad	1983-84
8th	99	P.H.Parfitt (119)/D.A.Allen (62)	Leeds	1962
9th	76	T.W.Graveney (153)/F.S.Trueman (29)	Lord's	1962
10th	79	R.W.Taylor (54)/R.G.D.Willis (28*)	Birmingham	1982

RECORD WICKET PARTNERSHIPS – PAKISTAN

1st	173	Mohsin Khan (104)/Shoaib Mohammed (80)	Lahore	1983-84
2nd	291	Zaheer Abbas (274)/Mushtaq Mohammed (100)	Birmingham	1971
3rd	363	Younis Khan (173)/Mohd Yousuf Youhana (192)	Leeds	2006
4th	322	Javed Miandad (153*)/Salim Malik (165)	Birmingham	1992
5th	197	Javed Burki (101)/Nasim-ul-Ghani (101)	Lord's	1962
6th	269	Mohammad Yousuf (223)/Kamran Akmal (154)	Lahore	2005-06
7th	112	Asif Mujtaba (51)/Moin Khan (105)	Leeds	1996
8th	130	Hanif Mohammed (187*)/Asif Iqbal (76)	Lord's	1967
9th	190	Asif Iqbal (146)/Intikhab Alam (51)	The Oval	1967
10th	62	Sarfraz Nawaz (53)/Asif Mahmood (4*)	Leeds	1974

BEST INNINGS BOWLING ANALYSIS

England	in England	8-34	I.T.Botham	Lord's	1978
	in Pakistan	7-66	P.H.Edmonds	Karachi	1977-78
Pakistan	in England	7-40	Imran Khan	Leeds	1987
	in Pakistan	9-56	Abdul Qadir	Lahore	1987-88

BEST MATCH BOWLING ANALYSIS

England	in England	13- 71	D.L.Underwood	Lord's	1974
	in Pakistan	11- 83	N.G.B.Cook	Karachi	1983-84
Pakistan	in England	12- 99	Fazal Mahmood	The Oval	1954
	in Pakistan	13-101	Abdul Qadir	Lahore	1987-88

HIGHEST AGGREGATE OF WICKETS IN A SERIES

England	in England	22	(av 19.95)	F.S.Trueman	1962
	in Pakistan	17	(av 24.11)	A.F.Giles	2000-01
Pakistan	in England	22	(av 25.31)	Waqar Younis	1992
	in Pakistan	30	(av 14.56)	Abdul Qadir	1987-88

RESULTS SUMMARY

ENGLAND v PAKISTAN – IN ENGLAND

	Tests	Series			Lord's			Nottingham			Manchester			The Oval			Birmingham			Leeds		
		E	P	D	E	P	D	E	P	D	E	P	D	E	P	D	E	P	D	E	P	D
1954	4	1	1	2	–	–	1	1	–	–	–	–	1	–	1	–	–	–	–	–	–	–
1962	5	4	–	1	1	–	–	–	–	1	–	–	–	1	–	–	1	–	–	1	–	–
1967	3	2	–	1	–	–	1	1	–	–	–	–	–	1	–	–	–	–	–	–	–	–
1971	3	1	–	2	–	–	1	–	–	–	–	–	–	–	–	–	–	–	1	1	–	–
1974	3	–	–	3	–	–	1	–	–	–	–	–	–	–	–	1	–	–	–	–	–	1
1978	3	2	–	1	1	–	–	–	–	–	–	–	–	–	–	–	1	–	–	–	–	1
1982	3	2	1	–	–	1	–	–	–	–	–	–	–	–	–	–	1	–	–	1	–	–
1987	5	–	1	4	–	–	1	–	–	–	–	–	1	–	–	1	–	–	1	–	1	–
1992	5	1	2	2	–	1	–	–	–	–	–	–	1	–	1	–	–	–	1	1	–	–
1996	3	–	2	1	–	1	–	–	–	–	–	–	–	–	1	–	–	–	–	–	–	1
2001	2	1	1	–	1	–	–	–	–	–	–	1	–	–	–	–	–	–	–	–	–	–
2006	4	3	–	1	–	–	1	–	–	–	1	–	–	1	–	–	–	–	–	1	–	–
	43	17	8	18	3	3	6	2	–	1	1	1	3	3	3	2	3	–	3	5	1	3

ENGLAND v PAKISTAN – IN PAKISTAN

	Tests	Series			Lahore			Dacca			Karachi			Hyderabad			Faisalabad			Multan		
		E	P	D	E	P	D	E	P	D	E	P	D	E	P	D	E	P	D	E	P	D
1961-62	3	1	–	2	1	–	–	–	–	1	–	–	1	–	–	–	–	–	–	–	–	–
1968-69	3	–	–	3	–	–	1	–	–	1	–	–	1	–	–	–	–	–	–	–	–	–
1972-73	3	–	–	3	–	–	1	–	–	–	–	–	1	–	–	1	–	–	–	–	–	–
1977-78	3	–	–	3	–	–	1	–	–	–	–	–	1	–	–	1	–	–	–	–	–	–
1983-84	3	–	1	2	–	–	1	–	–	–	–	1	–	–	–	–	–	–	1	–	–	–
1987-88	3	–	1	2	–	1	–	–	–	–	–	–	1	–	–	–	–	–	1	–	–	–
2000-01	3	1	–	2	–	–	1	–	–	–	1	–	–	–	–	–	–	–	1	–	–	–
2005-06	3	–	2	1	–	1	–	–	–	–	–	–	–	–	–	–	–	–	1	–	1	–
	24	2	4	18	1	2	5	–	–	2	1	1	5	–	–	2	–	–	4	–	1	–
Totals	67	19	12	36																		

TOURING TEAMS REGISTER 2010

Neither Bangladesh nor Pakistan had selected their 2010 touring teams at the time of going to press. Australia will play Pakistan in the UK during the summer, but were also yet to announce their team. The following players who had represented those teams in Test matches since 9 October 2008 were still available for selection:

AUSTRALIA

Full Names	Birthdate	Birthplace	Team	Type	F-C Debut
BOLLINGER, Douglas Erwin	24.07.81	Sydney	NSW	LHB/RFM	2002-03
CLARK, Stuart Rupert	28.09.75	Sydney	NSW	RHB/RFM	1997-98
CLARKE, Michael John	02.04.81	Liverpool	NSW	RHB/SLA	1999-00
HADDIN, Bradley James	23.10.77	Cowra	NSW	RHB/WK	1999-00
HAURITZ, Nathan Michael	18.10.81	Wondai	NSW	RHB/OB	2000-01
HILFENHAUS, Benjamin William	15.03.83	Ulverstone	Tasmania	RHB/RFM	2005-06
HUGHES, Phillip Joel	30.11.88	Macksville	NSW	LHB	2007-08
HUSSEY, Michael Edward Killeen	27.05.75	Morley	W Australia	LHB/RM	1994-95
JOHNSON, Mitchell Guy	02.11.81	Townsville	Queensland	LHB/LF	2001-02
KATICH, Simon Mathew	21.08.75	Middle Swan	NSW	LHB/SLC	1996-97
KREJZA, Jason John	14.01.83	Sydney	Tasmania	RHB/OB	2004-05
McDONALD, Andrew Barry	15.06.81	Wodonga	Victoria	RHB/RFM	2001-02
McGAIN, Bryce Edward	25.03.72	Mornington	Victoria	RHB/LBG	2001-02
McKAY, Clinton James	22.02.83	Melbourne	Victoria	RHB/RFM	2006-07
MANOU, Graham Allan	23.04.79	Modbury	S Australia	RHB/WK	1998-99
NORTH, Marcus James	28.07.79	Melbourne	W Australia	LHB/OB	1998-99
PONTING, Ricky Thomas	19.12.74	Launceston	Tasmania	RHB/RM	1992-93
SIDDLE, Peter Matthew	25.11.84	Traralgon	Victoria	RHB/RFM	2005-06
WATSON, Shane Robert	17.06.81	Ipswich	Queensland	RHB/RMF	2000-01
WHITE, Cameron Leon	18.08.83	Bairnsdale	Victoria	RHB/LBG	2000-01

BANGLADESH

Full Names	Birthdate	Birthplace	Team	Type	F-C Debut
ABDUR RAZZAK	15.06.82	Khulna	Khulna	LHB/SLA	2001-02
AFTAB AHMED	10.11.85	Chittagong	Chittagong	RHB/RM	2001-02
ENAMUL HAQUE[2]	05.12.86	Sylhet	Sylhet	RHB/SLA	2001-02
IMRUL KAYES	02.02.87	Kushtia	Khulna	LHB/WK	2006-07
JUNAID SIDDIQUE	30.10.87	Rajshahi	Rajshahi	LHB/OB	2003-04
MAHBUBUL ALAM	01.12.83	Dhaka	Dhaka	RHB/RMF	2003-04
MAHMUDULLAH	04.02.86	Mymensingh	Dhaka	RHB/OB	2004-05
MASHRAFE MORTAZA	05.10.83	Norail	Khulna	RHB/RFM	2001-02
MEHRAB HOSSAIN[2]	08.07.87	Dhaka	Dhaka	LHB/SLA	2004-05
MOHAMMAD ASHRAFUL	07.07.84	Dhaka	Dhaka	RHB/OB	2000-01
MUSHFIQUR RAHIM	01.09.88	Bogra	Sylhet	RHB/WK	2004-05
NAIM ISLAM	31.12.86	Gaibandha	Rajshahi	RHB/OB	2003-04
RAJIN SALEH	20.11.83	Sylhet	Sylhet	RHB/OB	2000-01
RAQIBUL HASAN	08.10.87	Jamalpur	Barisal	RHB/LBG	2004-05
RUBEL HOSSAIN	01.01.90		Chittagong	RHB/RMF	2007-08
SHAFIUL ISLAM	06.10.89	Bogra	Rajshahi	RHB/RFM	2007-08
SHAHADAT HOSSAIN	07.08.86	Dhaka	Dhaka	RHB/RMF	2003-04
SHAHRIAR NAFIS	25.01.86	Dhaka	Barisal	LHB	2003-04
SHAKIB AL HASAN	24.03.87	Magura	Khulna	LHB/SLA	2004-05
TAMIM IQBAL	20.03.89	Chittagong	Chittagong	LHB/SLA	2004-05

PAKISTAN

Full Names	Birthdate	Birthplace	Team	Type	F-C Debut
ABDUR RAUF	09.12.78	Renala Khurd	Lahore	RHB/RFM	1999-00
DANISH KANERIA	16.12.80	Karachi	Karachi	RHB/LBG	1998-99
FAISAL IQBAL	30.12.81	Karachi	Karachi	RHB/RM	1998-99
FAWAD ALAM	08.10.85	Karachi	National Bank	LHB/SLA	2003-04
IMRAN FARHAT	20.05.82	Lahore	Lahore	LHB/LBG	1998-99
KAMRAN AMKAL	13.01.82	Lahore	Punjab	RHB/WK	1997-98
KHURRAM MANZOOR	10.06.86	Karachi	Karachi	RHB/OB	2002-03
MISBAH-UL-HAQ	28.05.74	Mianwali	SNGPL	RHB/LBG	1998-99
MOHAMMAD AAMER	13.04.92	Gujjar Khan	National Bank	LHB/LFM	2008-09
MOHAMMAD ASIF	20.12.82	Sheikhupura	National Bank	LHB/RFM	2000-01
MOHAMMAD SAMI	24.02.81	Karachi	Karachi	RHB/RF	1999-00
MOHAMMAD TALHA	15.10.88	Faisalabad	National Bank	RHB/RMF	2007-08
MOHAMMAD YOUSUF	27.08.74	Lahore	WAPDA	RHB/OB	1996-97
SAEED AJMAL	14.10.77	Faisalabad	ZT Bank	RHB/OB	1996-97
SALMAN BUTT	07.10.84	Lahore	Lahore	LHB/OB	2000-01
SARFRAZ AHMED	22.05.87	Karachi	PIA	RHB/WK	2005-06
SHOAIB MALIK	01.02.82	Sialkot	PIA	RHB/OB	1997
SOHAIL KHAN	06.03.84	Malakand	SSGC	RHB/RFM	2007-08
UMAR AKMAL	26.05.90	Lahore	Punjab	RHB	2007-08
UMAR GUL	14.04.84	Peshawar	Habib Bank	RHB/RFM	2001-02
YASIR ARAFAT	12.03.82	Rawalpindi	KRL	RHB/RM	1997-98
YOUNUS KHAN	29.11.77	Mardan	Habib Bank	RHB/RM	1998-99

STATISTICAL HIGHLIGHTS IN 2009 TESTS

Including Tests from No. 1902 (Australia v South Africa, 3rd Test) and No. 1904 (Bangladesh v Sri Lanka, 2nd Test) to No. 1942 (South Africa v England, 2nd Test) and No. 1945 (Australia v Pakistan, 1st Test). († *National record*)

TEAM HIGHLIGHTS
HIGHEST INNINGS TOTALS

765-6d†	Pakistan v Sri Lanka	Karachi
760-7d	Sri Lanka v India	Ahmedabad
749-9d	West Indies v England	Bridgetown
726-9d†	India v Sri Lanka	Mumbai
674-6d	Australia v England	Cardiff
651	South Africa v Australia	Cape Town
644-7d	Sri Lanka v Pakistan	Karachi
642	India v Sri Lanka	Kanpur
619-9d	New Zealand v India	Napier
606	Sri Lanka v Pakistan	Lahore
600-6d	England v West Indies	Bridgetown

HIGHEST FOURTH INNINGS TOTALS

406	Australia (set 522) v England	Lord's

LOWEST INNINGS TOTALS

51	England v West Indies	Kingston
90	Pakistan v Sri Lanka	Colombo (PSS)
99	New Zealand v Pakistan	Wellington

MATCH AGGREGATES OF 1500 RUNS

1628-17	West Indies (749-9) v England (600-6, 279-2)	Bridgetown
1598-21	India (426 & 412-4) v Sri Lanka (760-7)	Ahmedabad
1553-18	Pakistan (765-6) v Sri Lanka (644-7 & 144-5)	Karachi

BATSMEN'S MATCH (Qualification: 1200 runs, average 70 per wicket)

95.76 (1628-17)	West Indies (749-9) v England (600-6, 279-2)	Bridgetown
86.27 (1553-18)	Pakistan (765-6) v Sri Lanka (644-7 & 144-5)	Karachi
76.09 (1598-21)	India (426 & 412-4) v Sri Lanka (760-7)	Ahmedabad

LARGE MARGINS OF VICTORY

Inns & 144 runs	India (642) beat Sri Lanka (229 & 269)	Kanpur
465 runs†	Sri Lanka (384 & 447-6) beat Bangladesh (208 & 158)	Chittagong

NARROW MARGINS OF VICTORY

32 runs	New Zealand (429 & 153) beat Pakistan (332 & 218)	Dunedin

FOUR HUNDREDS IN AN INNINGS

Australia (674-6d) v England	Cardiff

SIX FIFTIES IN AN INNINGS

India (726-9d) v Sri Lanka	Mumbai
Pakistan (455) v New Zealand	Napier

SIXTY EXTRAS IN AN INNINGS

	B	LB	W	NB		
74	35	12	11	16	West Indies (544) v England	Port-of-Spain
62	19	24	9	10	South Africa (651) v Australia	Cape Town
61	20	5	8	28	England (569-9d) v West Indies	Chester-le-St

BATTING HIGHLIGHTS
TRIPLE HUNDREDS

Younus Khan	313	Pakistan v Sri Lanka	Karachi

DOUBLE HUNDREDS

D.P.M.D.Jayawardena (2)	240	Sri Lanka v Pakistan	Karachi
	275	Sri Lanka v India	Ahmedabad
J.D.Ryder	201	New Zealand v India	Napier
T.T.Samaraweera (2)	231	Sri Lanka v Pakistan	Karachi
	214	Sri Lanka v Pakistan	Lahore
R.R.Sarwan	291	West Indies v England	Bridgetown
V.Sehwag	293	India v Sri Lanka	Mumbai

HUNDREDS IN THREE CONSECUTIVE INNINGS

R.S.Bopara (England)	104	v West Indies	Bridgetown
	143	v West Indies	Lord's
	108	v West Indies	Chester-le-St

HUNDRED IN EACH INNINGS OF A MATCH

T.M.Dilshan	162	143	Sri Lanka v Bangladesh	Chittagong
P.J.Hughes	115	160	Australia v South Africa	Durban

FASTEST HUNDRED

C.H.Gayle (102)	70 balls	West Indies v Australia	Perth

FASTEST DOUBLE HUNDRED

V.Sehwag (293)	168 balls	India v Sri Lanka	Mumbai

200 OR MORE RUNS IN A DAY

V.Sehwag	284	(0-284*) India v Sri Lanka	Mumbai

Third highest in Test match history, after D.G.Bradman (309) and W.R.Hammond (295).

200 RUNS FROM BOUNDARIES IN AN INNINGS

Runs	6s	4s			
202	7	40	V.Sehwag (293)	India v Sri Lanka	Mumbai

HUNDRED ON TEST DEBUT

Umar Akmal	129	Pakistan v New Zealand	Dunedin
Fawad Alam	168	Pakistan v Sri Lanka	Colombo (PSS)
A.B.Barath	104	West Indies v Australia	Brisbane
M.J.North	117	Australia v South Africa	Johannesburg
I.J.L.Trott	119	England v Australia	The Oval

CARRYING BAT THROUGH COMPLETED INNINGS

C.H.Gayle	165*	West Indies (317) v Australia	Adelaide
Imran Farhat	117*	Pakistan (223) v New Zealand	Napier

LONG INNINGS (Qualification: 600 mins and/or 400 balls)

Min	Balls			
760	568	Younus Khan (313)	Pakistan v Sri Lanka	Karachi
698	452	R.R.Sarwan (291)	West Indies v England	Bridgetown
643	436	G.Gambhir (137)	India v New Zealand	Napier
610	435	D.P.M.D.Jayawardena (275)	Sri Lanka v India	Ahmedabad
531	423	D.P.M.D.Jayawardena (240)	Sri Lanka v Pakistan	Karachi

NOTABLE PARTNERSHIPS

Qualifications: 1st-4th wkts: 250 runs; 5th-6th: 225; 7th: 200; 8th: 175; 9th: 150; 10th: 100.

Fourth Wicket

437†	D.P.M.D.Jayawardena/T.T.Samaraweera	Sri Lanka v Pakistan	Karachi
271†	L.R.P.L.Taylor/J.D.Ryder	New Zealand v India	Napier

Fifth Wicket

234	S.Chanderpaul/B.P.Nash	West Indies v England	Port-of-Spain

Sixth Wicket

351†	D.P.M.D.Jayawardena/ H.A.P.W.Jayawardena	Sri Lanka v India	Ahmedabad
261	R.R.Sarwan/D.Ramdin	West Indies v England	Bridgetown

BOWLING HIGHLIGHTS

SEVEN OR MORE WICKETS IN AN INNINGS

Danish Kaneria	7-168	Pakistan v New Zealand	Napier

TEN OR MORE WICKETS IN A MATCH

None. Best – Mohammad Asif   9-107   Pakistan v New Zealand   Wellington

FIVE WICKETS IN AN INNINGS ON DEBUT

Mahmudullah	5-51	Bangladesh v West Indies	Kingstown
G.Onions	5-38	England v West Indies	Lord's

200 RUNS CONCEDED IN AN INNINGS

A.Mishra	58-6-203-1	India v Sri Lanka	Ahmedabad
H.M.R.K.B.Herath	53.3-2-240-3	Sri Lanka v India	Mumbai

60 OVERS IN AN INNINGS

M.Muralitharan	65-14-172-1	Sri Lanka v Pakistan	Karachi

WICKET-KEEPING HIGHLIGHTS

SIX OR MORE WICKET-KEEPING DISMISSALS IN AN INNINGS

M.S.Dhoni	6ct†	India v New Zealand	Wellington

NINE OR MORE WICKET-KEEPING DISMISSALS IN A MATCH

B.B.McCullum	8ct, 1st†	New Zealand v Pakistan	Napier

NO BYES CONCEDED IN AN INNINGS OF 600 OR MORE

726-9	H.A.P.W.Jayawardena	Sri Lanka v India	Mumbai
644-7	Kamran Akmal	Pakistan v Sri Lanka	Karachi

LEADING TEST AGGREGATES IN 2009

1000 RUNS IN 2009

	M	I	NO	HS	Runs	Avge	100	50
T.T.Samaraweera (SL)	11	20	3	231	1234	72.58	4	4
D.P.M.D.Jayawardena (SL)	11	20	1	275	1194	62.84	3	3
A.J.Strauss (E)	14	24	2	169	1172	54.13	4	4
S.M.Katich (A)	13	23	–	122	1111	50.91	2	8
T.M.Dilshan (SL)	11	18	1	162	1097	64.52	6	1
K.C.Sangakkara (SL)	11	20	1	137	1083	57.00	4	5
M.J.Clarke (A)	13	23	4	138	1042	54.84	3	5

RECORD CALENDAR YEAR RUNS AGGREGATE

	M	I	NO	HS	Runs	Avge	100	50
Mohammad Yousuf (P) (2006)	11	19	1	202	1788	99.33	9	3

RECORD CALENDAR YEAR RUNS AVERAGE

	M	I	NO	HS	Runs	Avge	100	50
G.St A.Sobers (WI) (1958)	7	12	3	365*	1193	132.55	5	3

1000 RUNS IN DEBUT CALENDAR YEAR

	M	I	NO	HS	Runs	Avge	100	50
M.A.Taylor (A) (1989)	11	20	1	219	1219	64.15	4	5
A.N.Cook (E) (2006)	13	24	2	127	1013	46.04	4	3

50 WICKETS IN 2009

	M	O	R	W	Avge	Best	5wI	10wM
M.G.Johnson (A)	13	502.5	1728	63	27.42	5-69	2	–
G.P.Swann (E)	12	518.0	1508	54	27.92	5-54	4	–

RECORD CALENDAR YEAR WICKETS AGGREGATE

	M	O	R	W	Avge	Best	5wI	10wM
M.Muralitharan (SL) (2006)	11	588.4	1521	90	16.90	8-70	9	5
S.K.Warne (A) (2005)	14	691.4	2043	90	22.70	6-46	6	2

40 WICKET-KEEPING DISMISSALS IN 2009

	M	Dis	Ct	St
B.J.Haddin (A)	12	48	46	2

RECORD CALENDAR YEAR DISMISSALS AGGREGATE

	M	Dis	Ct	St
I.A.Healy (A) (1993)	16	67	58	9
M.V.Boucher (SA) (1998)	13	67	65	2

20 CATCHES BY FIELDERS IN 2009

	M	Ct
L.R.P.L.Taylor (NZ)	8	20
R.T.Ponting (A)	13	20

RECORD CALENDAR YEAR FIELDER'S AGGREGATE

	M	Ct
G.C.Smith (SA) (2008)	15	30

TEST MATCH SCORES
AUSTRALIA v SOUTH AFRICA (1st Test)

At WACA Ground, Perth, on 17, 18, 19, 20, 21 December 2008.
Toss: Australia. Result: **SOUTH AFRICA** won by six wickets.
Debuts: South Africa – J.P.Duminy.

AUSTRALIA

M.L.Hayden	c Smith b Ntini	12		c and b Steyn	4
S.M.Katich	lbw b Morkel	83		c Boucher b Kallis	37
*R.T.Ponting	c De Villiers b Ntini	0		c Boucher b Harris	32
M.E.K.Hussey	c De Villiers b Steyn	0		b Ntini	8
M.J.Clarke	c Smith b Harris	62		c Kallis b Steyn	25
A.Symonds	c McKenzie b Harris	57		c Smith b Harris	37
†B.J.Haddin	c Duminy b Ntini	46		st Boucher b Harris	94
B.Lee	c Duminy b Steyn	29		c De Villiers b Kallis	5
J.J.Krejza	not out	30		c De Villiers b Kallis	32
M.G.Johnson	lbw b Morkel	18		c Kallis b Morkel	21
P.M.Siddle	c Boucher b Ntini	23		not out	4
Extras	(LB 7, W 3, NB 5)	15		(B 4, LB 7, W 2, NB 7)	20
Total	**(98.5 overs; 435 mins)**	**375**		**(97 overs; 427 mins)**	**319**

SOUTH AFRICA

N.D.McKenzie	c Krejza b Johnson	2	(2)	c Haddin b Johnson	10
*G.C.Smith	b Johnson	48	(1)	lbw b Johnson	108
H.M.Amla	b Krejza	47		c Haddin b Lee	53
J.H.Kallis	c Haddin b Johnson	63		c Hussey b Johnson	57
A.B.de Villiers	c Haddin b Johnson	63		not out	106
J.P.Duminy	c Haddin b Johnson	1		not out	50
†M.V.Boucher	c Katich b Siddle	26			
M.Morkel	c Krejza b Johnson	1			
P.L.Harris	c Krejza b Johnson	0			
D.W.Steyn	c Haddin b Johnson	8			
M.Ntini	not out	5			
Extras	(LB 5, W 5, NB 7)	17		(B 13, LB 9, W 2, NB 6)	30
Total	**(89.5 overs; 387 mins)**	**281**		**(4 wkts; 119.2 overs; 517 mins)**	**414**

SOUTH AFRICA	O	M	R	W		O	M	R	W
Ntini	19.5	1	72	4	(2)	21	2	76	1
Steyn	23	4	81	2	(1)	19	3	81	2
Kallis	15	2	65	0	(4)	14	4	24	3
Morkel	20	1	80	2	(5)	16	4	42	1
Harris	21	2	70	2	(3)	27	3	85	3
AUSTRALIA									
Lee	21	3	59	0		27	4	73	1
Johnson	24	4	61	8		34.2	5	98	3
Krejza	25	2	102	1	(4)	24	2	102	0
Siddle	16.5	5	44	1	(3)	26	2	84	0
Symonds	3	1	10	0					
Clarke					(5)	8	0	35	0

FALL OF WICKETS

	A	SA	A	SA
Wkt	*1st*	*1st*	*2nd*	*2nd*
1st	14	16	25	19
2nd	14	106	59	172
3rd	15	110	88	179
4th	164	234	88	303
5th	166	237	148	–
6th	259	238	157	–
7th	298	241	162	–
8th	303	241	241	–
9th	341	256	278	–
10th	375	281	319	–

Umpires: Alim Dar (*Pakistan*) (53) and E.A.R.de Silva (*Sri Lanka*) (36).
Referee: R.S.Madugalle (*Sri Lanka*) (108). **Test No. 1900/78 (A702/SA339)**

AUSTRALIA v SOUTH AFRICA (2nd Test)

At Melbourne Cricket Ground, on 26, 27, 28, 29, 30 December 2008.
Toss: Australia. Result: **SOUTH AFRICA** won by nine wickets.
Debuts: None.

AUSTRALIA

M.L.Hayden	c Duminy b Ntini	8	c Duminy b Steyn		23
S.M.Katich	b Steyn	54	c Boucher b Steyn		15
*R.T.Ponting	c Amla b Harris	101	c Smith b Morkel		99
M.E.K.Hussey	c Boucher b Steyn	0	c Amla b Morkel		2
M.J.Clarke	not out	88	c McKenzie b Steyn		29
A.Symonds	c Kallis b Morkel	27	c Kallis b Steyn		0
†B.J.Haddin	c Smith b Ntini	40	c Kallis b Ntini		10
B.Lee	c Kallis b Steyn	21	b Kallis		8
M.G.Johnson	b Steyn	0	not out		43
N.M.Hauritz	c Smith b Steyn	12	b Kallis		3
P.M.Siddle	c De Villiers b Kallis	19	c Boucher b Steyn		6
Extras	(B 5, LB 12, NB 7)	24	(B 1, LB 3, NB 5)		9
Total	**(113.4 overs; 500 mins)**	**394**	**(84.2 overs; 370 mins)**		**247**

SOUTH AFRICA

*G.C.Smith	c Harris b Siddle	62	lbw b Hauritz		75
N.D.McKenzie	b Siddle	0	not out		59
H.M.Amla	c Symonds b Johnson	19	not out		30
J.H.Kallis	c Haddin b Hauritz	26			
A.B.de Villiers	b Siddle	5			
J.P.Duminy	c Siddle b Hauritz	166			
†M.V.Boucher	c Hussey b Hauritz	3			
M.Morkel	b Johnson	21			
P.L.Harris	c Johnson b Hussey	39			
D.W.Steyn	b Siddle	76			
M.Ntini	not out	2			
Extras	(B 5, LB 13, NB 15, Pen 5)	38	(LB 9, W 2, NB 8)		19
Total	**(153 overs; 615 mins)**	**459**	**(1 wkt; 48 overs; 204 mins)**		**183**

SOUTH AFRICA	O	M	R	W		O	M	R	W		FALL OF WICKETS				
Steyn	29	6	87	5		20.2	3	67	5			A	SA	A	SA
Ntini	27	7	108	2		14	1	26	1		*Wkt*	*1st*	*1st*	*2nd*	*2nd*
Kallis	18.4	4	55	1	(5)	14	1	57	2		1st	21	1	37	121
Morkel	22	3	89	1	(3)	15	2	46	2		2nd	128	39	40	–
Harris	17	3	38	1	(4)	21	1	47	0		3rd	143	102	49	–
											4th	184	126	145	–
AUSTRALIA											5th	223	132	145	–
Lee	13	2	68	0		10	0	49	0		6th	277	141	165	–
Siddle	34	9	81	4		14	5	34	0		7th	322	184	180	–
Johnson	39	6	127	2		11	1	36	0		8th	326	251	212	–
Hauritz	43	13	98	3		10	0	41	1		9th	352	431	231	–
Clarke	8	0	26	0		3	0	14	0		10th	394	459	247	–
Hussey	5	0	22	1											
Symonds	11	3	14	0											

Umpires: Alim Dar (*Pakistan*) (54) and B.R.Doctrove (*West Indies*) (22).
Referee: R.S.Madugalle (*Sri Lanka*) (109). **Test No. 1901/79 (A703/SA340)**

AUSTRALIA v SOUTH AFRICA (3rd Test)

At Sydney Cricket Ground, on 3, 4, 5, 6, 7 January 2009.
Toss: Australia. Result: **AUSTRALIA** won by 103 runs.
Debuts: Australia – D.E.Bollinger, A.B.McDonald.

AUSTRALIA

M.L.Hayden	b Steyn	31	b Morkel		39
S.M.Katich	c De Villiers b Kallis	47	lbw b Steyn		61
*R.T.Ponting	c Boucher b Morkel	0	b Morkel		53
M.E.K.Hussey	c Kallis b Harris	30	not out		45
M.J.Clarke	c and b Duminy	138	c Amla b Harris		41
A.B.McDonald	c Boucher b Ntini	15			
†B.J.Haddin	b Steyn	38			
M.G.Johnson	c Smith b Steyn	64			
N.M.Hauritz	c Duminy b Harris	41			
P.M.Siddle	lbw b Harris	23			
D.E.Bollinger	not out	0			
Extras	(LB 7, W 3, NB 8)	18	(B 8, LB 9, NB 1)		18
Total	**(136.2 overs; 583 mins)**	**445**	**(4 wkts dec; 67.3 overs; 289 mins)**		**257**

SOUTH AFRICA

N.D.McKenzie	lbw b Siddle	23	c Hussey b Bollinger		27
*G.C.Smith	retired hurt	30	(11) b Johnson		3
H.M.Amla	lbw b McDonald	51	c Katich b Hauritz		59
J.H.Kallis	c Hayden b Johnson	37	c and b McDonald		4
A.B.de Villiers	run out	11	b Siddle		56
J.P.Duminy	lbw b Johnson	13	lbw b Johnson		16
†M.V.Boucher	b Siddle	89	lbw b Siddle		4
M.Morkel	b Siddle	40	(2) c Johnson b Bollinger		28
P.L.Harris	lbw b Siddle	2	(8) lbw b Siddle		6
D.W.Steyn	b Siddle	6	(9) lbw b McDonald		28
M.Ntini	not out	0	(10) not out		28
Extras	(LB 12, W 9, NB 4)	25	(B 12, LB 18, W 4, NB 2, Pen 5)		41
Total	**(120.5 overs; 486 mins)**	**327**	**(114.2 overs; 442 mins)**		**272**

SOUTH AFRICA	O	M	R	W	O	M	R	W	FALL OF WICKETS				
										A	SA	A	SA
Steyn	27	5	95	3	13	1	60	1					
Ntini	29	5	102	1	12	1	66	0	*Wkt*	*1st*	*1st*	*2nd*	*2nd*
Morkel	27	3	89	1	12	2	38	2	1st	62	76	62	2
Kallis	20	6	54	1	10	5	13	0	2nd	63	131	134	68
Harris	29.2	6	84	3	20.3	1	63	1	3rd	109	161	181	91
Duminy	4	0	14	1					4th	130	166	257	110
									5th	162	193	–	166
AUSTRALIA									6th	237	308	–	172
Siddle	27.5	11	59	5	27	12	54	3	7th	379	310	–	190
Bollinger	23	4	78	0	21	5	53	2	8th	381	316	–	202
Johnson	28	6	69	2	23.2	7	49	2	9th	440	327	–	257
McDonald	22	8	41	1	13	6	32	2	10th	445	–	–	272
Hauritz	20	4	68	0	28	10	47	1					
Clarke					2	1	2	0					

Umpires: B.F.Bowden (*New Zealand*) (52) and E.A.R.de Silva (*Sri Lanka*) (37).
Referee: R.S.Madugalle (*Sri Lanka*) (110).
G.C.Smith retired hurt at 35-0 in South Africa's first innings.

Test No. 1902/80 (A704/SA341)

BANGLADESH v SRI LANKA (1st Test)

At Shere Bangla National Stadium, Mirpur, 26, 27, 28, 30, 31 December 2008.
Toss: Sri Lanka. Result: **SRI LANKA** won by 107 runs.
Debuts: None.

SRI LANKA

Batsman	1st innings		2nd innings	
M.G.Vandort	c Shakib b Shahadat	44	b Mortaza	6
B.S.M.Warnapura	lbw b Mortaza	14	lbw b Alam	8
K.C.Sangakkara	c Ashraful b Shakib	43	c Rahim b Mehrab	67
*D.P.M.D.Jayawardena	b Shakib	3	c Siddique b Mehrab	166
T.T.Samaraweera	c Siddique b Shakib	90	b Mortaza	62
T.M.Dilshan	b Shakib	14	c Rahim b Shakib	47
†H.A.P.W.Jayawardena	c Iqbal b Shahadat	6	not out	3
W.P.U.C.J.Vaas	c Rahim b Mortaza	37	not out	15
K.T.G.D.Prasad	lbw b Shakib	3		
H.M.R.K.B.Herath	run out	1		
M.Muralitharan	not out	0		
Extras	(B 4, LB 13, W12, NB 9)	38	(B 16, LB 5, W 2, NB 8)	31
Total	(89.4 overs; 405 mins)	293	(6 wkts dec; 108 overs)	405

BANGLADESH

Batsman	1st innings		2nd innings	
Tamim Iqbal	c Warnapura b Muralitharan	17	c H.A.P.W.Jayawardena b Prasad	47
Imrul Kayes	c H.A.P.W.Jayawardena b Vaas	33	run out	13
Junaid Siddique	b Muralitharan	29	c D.P.M.D.Jayawardena b Muralitharan	37
*Mohammad Ashraful	c Dilshan b Vaas	12	(5) lbw b Vaas	101
Raqibul Hasan	b Prasad	11	(4) b Muralitharan	24
Mehrab Hossain[2]	c D.P.M.D.Jayawardena b Herath	29	c sub (C.K.Kapugedera) b Muralitharan	23
Shakib Al Hasan	c D.P.M.D.Jayawardena b Muralitharan	26	b Prasad	96
†Mushfiqur Rahim	not out	12	c Dilshan b Muralitharan	61
Mashrafe Mortaza	lbw b Muralitharan	0	c H.A.P.W.Jayawardena b Prasad	2
Shahadat Hossain	st H.A.P.W.Jayawardena b Muralitharan	5	(11) not out	0
Mahbubul Alam	c Warnapura b Muralitharan	0	(10) run out	2
Extras	(B 4)	4	(LB 3, NB 4)	7
Total	(60 overs)	178	(126.2 overs; 485 mins)	413

BANGLADESH	O	M	R	W		O	M	R	W
Mashrafe Mortaza	18	2	67	2		21	4	59	2
Mahbubul Alam	19	4	56	0		17	1	62	1
Shahadat Hossain	16	2	55	2	(4)	14	1	66	0
Shakib Al Hasan	28.4	4	70	5	(3)	40	10	134	1
Mehrab Hossain[2]	6	1	22	0		10	0	37	2
Mohammad Ashraful	2	0	6	0	(7)	5	0	24	0
Raqibul Hasan					(6)	1	0	2	0
SRI LANKA									
Vaas	11	4	33	2		25	5	74	1
Prasad	13	0	61	1		25.2	5	105	3
Dilshan	2	0	2	0	(5)	2	0	4	0
Muralitharan	22	8	49	6	(3)	48	9	141	4
Herath	12	1	29	1	(4)	26	4	86	0

FALL OF WICKETS

	SL	B	SL	B
Wkt	1st	1st	2nd	2nd
1st	24	44	16	40
2nd	119	68	18	72
3rd	121	90	153	124
4th	135	95	291	144
5th	155	117	386	180
6th	171	158	388	292
7th	270	162	–	403
8th	285	162	–	409
9th	291	176	–	411
10th	293	178	–	413

Umpires: S.A.Bucknor (*West Indies*) (125) and N.J.Llong (*England*) (3).
Referee: J.J.Crowe (*New Zealand*) (29).   **Test No. 1903/11 (B58/SL181)**

BANGLADESH v SRI LANKA (2nd Test)

At Chittagong Divisional Stadium, 3, 4, 5, 6 January 2009.
Toss: Sri Lanka. Result: **SRI LANKA** won by 465 runs.
Debuts: None.

SRI LANKA

B.S.M.Warnapura	lbw b Ashraful	63	lbw b Shahadat		27
†H.A.P.W.Jayawardena	lbw b Mortaza	0	c Shakib b Ashraful		28
K.C.Sangakkara	b Mortaza	5	b Ashraful		54
*D.P.M.D.Jayawardena	c Rahim b Shakib	11	c Kayes b Haque		22
T.T.Samaraweera	b Shahadat	19	lbw b Shakib		77
T.M.Dilshan	b Haque	162	b Haque		143
C.K.Kapugedera	lbw b Shakib	96	not out		59
W.P.U.C.J.Vaas	lbw b Mortaza	3	not out		20
M.Muralitharan	lbw b Shakib	0			
B.A.W.Mendis	not out	6			
C.R.D.Fernando	lbw b Shakib	0			
Extras	(B 4, LB 8, W1, NB 6)	19	(B 3, LB 4, W 4, NB 6)		17
Total	**(94 overs; 400 mins)**	**384**	**(6 wkts dec; 127 overs; 495 mins)**		**447**

BANGLADESH

Tamim Iqbal	c H.A.P.W.Jayawardena b Vaas	0	c H.A.P.W.Jayawardena b Vaas		17
Imrul Kayes	lbw b Vaas	6	c D.P.M.D.Jayawardena b Mendis		5
Junaid Siddique	b Fernando	28	lbw b Mendis		4
Raqibul Hasan	lbw b Mendis	0	b Fernando		10
*Mohammad Ashraful	c H.A.P.W.Jayawardena b Muralitharan	45	c H.A.P.W.Jayawardena b Mendis		7
Mehrab Hossain[2]	b Mendis	18	(8) lbw b Dilshan		5
Shakib Al Hasan	b Mendis	0	st H.A.P.W.Jayawardena b Dilshan		46
†Mushfiqur Rahim	st H.A.P.W.Jayawardena b Mendis	21	(6) run out		43
Mashrafe Mortaza	c Dilshan b Muralitharan	63	c D.P.M.D.Jayawardena b Dilshan		0
Enamul Haque[2]	c H.A.P.W.Jayawardena b Muralitharan	4	(11) not out		0
Shahadat Hossain	not out	5	(10) b Dilshan		1
Extras	(B 5, LB 5, NB 8)	18	(B 4, LB 5, NB 11)		20
Total	**(76.2 overs; 315 mins)**	**208**	**(49.2 overs; 225 mins)**		**158**

BANGLADESH	O	M	R	W		O	M	R	W
Mashrafe Mortaza	22	7	58	3		15	3	53	0
Shahadat Hossain	14	0	80	1		28	3	92	1
Shakib Al Hasan	30	6	109	4		20	2	79	1
Enamul Haque[2]	19	3	70	1		36	2	109	2
Mehrab Hossain[2]	7	1	36	0	(6)	8	0	38	0
Mohammad Ashraful	2	0	19	1	(5)	17	1	56	2
Raqibul Hasan						1	0	3	0
Imrul Kayes						1	0	7	0
Tamim Iqbal						1	3	3	0

SRI LANKA									
Vaas	10	5	21	2		8	3	16	1
Fernando	18	4	44	1		12	4	36	1
Mendis	28	5	71	4		15	4	57	3
Muralitharan	20.2	6	62	3		10	0	30	0
Dilshan						4.2	1	10	4

FALL OF WICKETS

	SL	B	SL	B
Wkt	1st	1st	2nd	2nd
1st	1	0	55	18
2nd	7	26	55	22
3rd	39	33	123	32
4th	75	65	163	42
5th	194	90	310	52
6th	367	90	396	144
7th	376	122	–	154
8th	376	136	–	154
9th	384	145	–	156
10th	384	208	–	158

Umpires: S.A.Bucknor (*West Indies*) (126) and N.J.Llong (*England*) (4).
Referee: J.J.Crowe (*New Zealand*) (30).   **Test No. 1904/12 (B59/SL182)**

WEST INDIES v ENGLAND (1st Test)

At Sabina Park, Kingston, Jamaica, on 4, 5, 6, 7 February 2009.
Toss: England. Result: **WEST INDIES** won by an innings and 23 runs.
Debuts: None.

ENGLAND

*A.J.Strauss	c Ramdin b Taylor	7	c Ramdin b Taylor		9
A.N.Cook	c Sarwan b Powell	4	c Smith b Taylor		0
I.R.Bell	c Smith b Gayle	28	c Ramdin b Benn		4
K.P.Pietersen	c Ramdin b Benn	97	b Taylor		1
P.D.Collingwood	lbw b Benn	16	b Taylor		1
A.Flintoff	c Nash b Powell	43	b Edwards		24
†M.J.Prior	c and b Benn	64	b Taylor		0
S.C.J.Broad	c Benn b Taylor	4	c Marshall b Benn		0
R.J.Sidebottom	not out	26	lbw b Benn		6
S.J.Harmison	lbw b Taylor	7	b Benn		0
M.S.Panesar	lbw b Benn	0	not out		0
Extras	(B 7, LB 8, NB 7)	22	(B 2, NB 4)		6
Total	**(122.2 overs; 498 mins)**	**318**	**(33.2 overs; 155 mins)**		**51**

WEST INDIES

*C.H.Gayle	b Broad	104
D.S.Smith	lbw b Flintoff	6
R.R.Sarwan	b Flintoff	107
X.M.Marshall	lbw b Broad	0
S.Chanderpaul	lbw b Broad	20
B.P.Nash	c Prior b Broad	55
†D.Ramdin	c Collingwood b Panesar	35
J.E.Taylor	lbw b Harmison	8
S.J.Benn	c Cook b Broad	23
D.B.L.Powell	c Prior b Harmison	9
F.H.Edwards	not out	10
Extras	(B 6, LB 8, W 1)	15
Total	**(157.4 overs; 698 mins)**	**392**

WEST INDIES	O	M	R	W		O	M	R	W
Taylor	20	4	74	3		9	4	11	5
Edwards	14	1	58	0	(5)	1	0	1	1
Powell	20	5	54	2	(2)	7	3	5	0
Benn	44.2	13	77	4	(3)	14.2	2	31	4
Gayle	24	9	40	1	(4)	2	1	1	0

ENGLAND	O	M	R	W
Sidebottom	24	5	35	0
Flintoff	33	11	72	2
Harmison	20.4	4	49	2
Broad	29	7	85	5
Panesar	47	14	122	1
Pietersen	4	1	15	0

FALL OF WICKETS

	E	WI	E
Wkt	1st	1st	2nd
1st	8	18	1
2nd	31	220	11
3rd	71	220	12
4th	94	235	20
5th	180	254	23
6th	241	320	23
7th	256	341	26
8th	288	371	50
9th	313	376	51
10th	318	392	51

Umpires: A.L.Hill (*New Zealand*) (8) and R.E.Koertzen (*South Africa*) (98).
Referee: A.G.Hurst (*Australia*) (23).   **Test No. 1905/139 (WI451/E880)**

WEST INDIES v ENGLAND (2nd Test)

At Sir Vivian Richards Stadium, North Sound, Antigua, on 13 February 2009.
Toss: West Indies. Result: **MATCH DRAWN**.
Debuts: None.

ENGLAND

*A.J.Strauss	not out	6
A.N.Cook	not out	1
O.A.Shah		
K.P.Pietersen		
P.D.Collingwood		
A.Flintoff		
†M.J.Prior		
S.C.J.Broad		
R.J.Sidebottom		
M.S.Panesar		
J.M.Anderson		
Extras		0
Total	**(0 wkts; 1.4 overs; 14 mins)**	**7**

WEST INDIES

*C.H.Gayle
D.S.Smith
R.R.Sarwan
S.Chanderpaul
B.P.Nash
R.O.Hinds
†D.Ramdin
J.E.Taylor
S.J.Benn
D.B.L.Powell
F.H.Edwards
    Extras
    Total

WEST INDIES	O	M	R	W
Taylor	1	0	5	0
Edwards	0.4	0	2	0

FALL OF WICKETS

	E
Wkt	*1st*
1st	–
2nd	–
3rd	–
4th	–
5th	–
6th	–
7th	–
8th	–
9th	–
10th	–

Umpires: D.J.Harper (*Australia*) (78) and A.L.Hill (*New Zealand*) (9).
Referee: A.G.Hurst (*Australia*) (24).
The shortest Test match on record was abandoned after ten balls because the sandy
ground conditions, especially on the run-ups, made play too dangerous to continue.

Test No. 1906/140 (WI452/E881)

WEST INDIES v ENGLAND (3rd Test)

At Recreation Ground, St John's, Antigua, on 15, 16, 17, 18, 19 February 2009.
Toss: West Indies. Result: **MATCH DRAWN**.
Debuts: None.

ENGLAND

*A.J.Strauss	c and b Edwards	169		c Smith b Edwards	14
A.N.Cook	c Smith b Gayle	52		c Smith b Hinds	58
O.A.Shah	run out	57	(4)	b Powell	14
K.P.Pietersen	b Taylor	51	(5)	c Ramdin b Benn	32
J.M.Anderson	c Ramdin b Edwards	4	(3)	c Ramdin b Powell	20
P.D.Collingwood	c Smith b Hinds	113		b Hinds	34
A.Flintoff	b Taylor	0	(9)	c Hinds b Benn	0
†M.J.Prior	c Chanderpaul b Nash	39	(7)	not out	15
S.C.J.Broad	c Ramdin b Hinds	44	(8)	run out	1
G.P.Swann	not out	20	(10)	not out	7
S.J.Harmison					
Extras	(B 10, LB 1, W 1, NB 5)	17		(B 12, LB 3, W 5, NB 6)	26
Total	**(9 wkts dec; 165.2 overs; 680 mins)**	**566**		**(8 wkts dec; 50 overs)**	**221**

WEST INDIES

*C.H.Gayle	c Anderson b Harmison	30		lbw b Swann	46
D.S.Smith	b Swann	38		lbw b Harmison	21
D.B.L.Powell	c Collingwood b Swann	22	(10)	not out	22
R.R.Sarwan	c Flintoff b Swann	94	(3)	b Broad	106
R.O.Hinds	c Prior b Flintoff	27	(4)	c Shah b Broad	6
S.Chanderpaul	c Prior b Broad	1	(5)	c Prior b Broad	55
B.P.Nash	c Collingwood b Flintoff	18	(6)	lbw b Swann	23
†D.Ramdin	c and b Swann	0	(7)	b Anderson	21
J.E.Taylor	c and b Flintoff	19	(8)	c sub (I.R.Bell) b Anderson	11
S.J.Benn	lbw b Swann	0	(9)	lbw b Swann	21
F.H.Edwards	not out	0		not out	5
Extras	(B 17, LB 5, W 2, NB 11)	35		(B 21, LB 7, W 1, NB 4)	33
Total	**(89.2 overs; 410 mins)**	**285**		**(9 wkts; 128 overs)**	**370**

WEST INDIES	O	M	R	W		O	M	R	W
Taylor	28	7	73	2	(2)	9	2	34	0
Edwards	26	2	75	2	(1)	9	1	36	1
Powell	26	3	103	0		7	0	33	2
Gayle	13	1	41	1					
Benn	39	5	143	0	(4)	14	1	58	2
Hinds	22.2	4	86	2	(5)	11	1	45	2
Nash	11	2	34	1					

ENGLAND	O	M	R	W		O	M	R	W
Anderson	19	1	55	0		25	6	68	2
Flintoff	14.2	3	47	3	(5)	15	5	32	0
Harmison	12	3	44	1	(4)	22	3	54	1
Broad	14	4	24	1	(2)	21	3	69	3
Swann	24	7	57	5	(3)	39	12	92	3
Pietersen	2	0	14	0		3	0	15	0
Collingwood	4	0	22	0					
Shah					(7)	3	0	12	0

FALL OF WICKETS

	E	WI	E	WI
Wkt	1st	1st	2nd	2nd
1st	123	45	23	59
2nd	276	109	69	81
3rd	295	130	97	96
4th	311	200	145	244
5th	405	201	189	261
6th	405	251	195	287
7th	467	251	201	313
8th	529	278	206	322
9th	566	279	–	353
10th	–	285	–	–

Umpires: D.J.Harper (*Australia*) (79) and R.E.Koertzen (*South Africa*) (99).
Referee: A.G.Hurst (*Australia*) (25). **Test No. 1907/141 (WI453/E882)**

WEST INDIES v ENGLAND (4th Test)

At Kensington Oval, Bridgetown, Barbados, on 26, 27, 28 February, 1, 2 March 2009.
Toss: England. Result: **MATCH DRAWN**.
Debuts: None.

ENGLAND

*A.J.Strauss	b Powell	142	b Gayle		38
A.N.Cook	c Hinds b Taylor	94	not out		139
O.A.Shah	c Smith b Benn	7	lbw b Benn		21
K.P.Pietersen	lbw b Edwards	41	not out		72
P.D.Collingwood	c Nash b Edwards	96			
R.S.Bopara	c Taylor b Edwards	104			
†T.R.Ambrose	not out	76			
S.C.J.Broad	not out	13			
G.P.Swann					
J.M.Anderson					
R.J.Sidebottom					
Extras	(B 5, LB 3, W 11, NB 8)	27	(B 6, NB 3)		9
Total	**(6 wkts dec; 153.2 overs)**	**600**	**(2 wkts dec; 81 overs; 294 mins)**		**279**

WEST INDIES

D.S.Smith	lbw b Swann	55
*C.H.Gayle	lbw b Anderson	6
R.R.Sarwan	b Sidebottom	291
R.O.Hinds	lbw b Swann	15
S.Chanderpaul	lbw b Anderson	70
B.P.Nash	lbw b Swann	33
†D.Ramdin	b Swann	166
J.E.Taylor	b Swann	53
S.J.Benn	c Ambrose b Anderson	14
D.B.L.Powell	not out	13
F.H.Edwards		
Extras	(B 15, LB 11, W 1, NB 6)	33
Total	**(9 wkts dec; 194.4 overs)**	**749**

WEST INDIES	O	M	R	W		O	M	R	W
Taylor	29.2	7	107	1	(4)	4	0	15	0
Edwards	30	0	151	3	(1)	10	1	41	0
Powell	24	3	107	1	(2)	12	0	35	0
Benn	30	7	106	1	(3)	21	1	64	1
Gayle	15	4	28	0		17	5	46	1
Hinds	14	2	62	0		14	1	56	0
Nash	9	1	20	0					
Sarwan	2	0	11	0	(7)	3	0	16	0
ENGLAND									
Anderson	37	9	125	3					
Sidebottom	35	4	146	1					
Broad	32	4	113	0					
Swann	50.4	8	165	5					
Pietersen	9	1	38	0					
Bopara	13	0	66	0					
Collingwood	16	1	51	0					
Shah	2	0	19	0					

FALL OF WICKETS			
	E	WI	E
Wkt	1st	1st	2nd
1st	229	13	88
2nd	241	121	129
3rd	259	159	–
4th	318	281	–
5th	467	334	–
6th	580	595	–
7th	–	672	–
8th	–	701	–
9th	–	749	–
10th	–	–	–

Umpires: Alim Dar (*Pakistan*) (55) and R.B.Tiffin (*Zimbabwe*) (43).
Referee: A.G.Hurst (*Australia*) (26).   **Test No. 1908/142 (WI454/E883)**

WEST INDIES v ENGLAND (5th Test)

At Queen's Park Oval, Port-of-Spain, Trinidad, on 6, 7, 8, 9, 10 March 2009.
Toss: England. Result: **MATCH DRAWN**.
Debuts: West Indies – L.M.P.Simmons; England – A.Khan.

ENGLAND

*A.J.Strauss	b Edwards	142	c and b Gayle		14
A.N.Cook	c Ramdin b Powell	12	c Ramdin b Hinds		24
O.A.Shah	run out	33	c Ramdin b Baker		1
K.P.Pietersen	b Hinds	10	c sub (D.J.Bravo) b Edwards		102
P.D.Collingwood	lbw b Baker	161	b and b Hinds		9
†M.J.Prior	not out	131	b Baker		61
S.C.J.Broad	c Simmons b Baker	19	not out		13
G.P.Swann	not out	11			
J.M.Anderson					
M.S.Panesar					
A.Khan					
Extras	(B 8, LB 7, W 1, NB 11)	27	(B 2, LB 6, W 1, NB 4)		13
Total	(6 wkts dec; 158.5 overs; 632 mins)	546	(6 wkts dec; 38.4 overs; 201 mins)		237

WEST INDIES

*C.H.Gayle	c Strauss b Swann	102	(8) lbw b Panesar		4
D.S.Smith	b Panesar	28	(1) lbw b Swann		17
D.B.L.Powell	c Pietersen b Broad	0	(9) b Anderson		0
R.R.Sarwan	lbw b Khan	14	(3) c Collingwood b Swann		14
L.M.P.Simmons	lbw b Panesar	24	(2) c Collingwood b Anderson		8
S.Chanderpaul	not out	147	(5) lbw b Swann		6
B.P.Nash	c Collingwood b Broad	109	(6) lbw b Anderson		1
R.O.Hinds	st Prior b Swann	23	(4) c Collingwood b Panesar		20
†D.Ramdin	lbw b Anderson	15	(7) not out		17
F.H.Edwards	c Prior b Broad	8	not out		1
L.S.Baker	lbw b Swann	0			
Extras	(B 35, LB 12, W 11, NB 16)	74	(B 17, LB 6, W 1, NB 2)		26
Total	(178.4 overs; 751 mins)	544	(8 wkts; 65.5 overs; 268 mins)		114

WEST INDIES	O	M	R	W		O	M	R	W		FALL OF WICKETS			
Edwards	24	5	63	1		11.4	1	67	1			E	WI	E	WI
Powell	16	1	79	1							*Wkt*	*1st*	*1st*	*2nd*	*2nd*
Baker	23	4	77	2	(2)	8	1	39	2		1st	26	90	26	25
Nash	23	3	77	0	(6)	3	0	21	0		2nd	156	96	27	31
Gayle	26	1	80	0	(3)	3	0	16	1		3rd	263	118	72	58
Hinds	39.5	2	126	1	(4)	8	0	57	2		4th	268	203	101	80
Smith	1	0	3	0							5th	486	437	207	85
Simmons	1	0	26	0	(5)	5	0	29	0		6th	530	482	237	90
											7th	–	519	–	107
ENGLAND											8th	–	526	–	109
Anderson	32	7	70	1		16	7	24	3		9th	–	543	–	–
Broad	30	11	67	3		5	3	9	0		10th	–	544	–	–
Khan	25	1	111	1	(4)	4	0	11	0						
Swann	45.4	12	130	3	(3)	21	13	13	3						
Panesar	43	6	114	2		19.5	9	34	2						
Pietersen	3	0	5	0											

Umpires: D.J.Harper (*Australia*) (80) and R.B.Tiffin (*Zimbabwe*) (44).
Referee: A.G.Hurst (*Australia*) (27).
In the first innings O.A.Shah retired at 133-1 and resumed at 263-3; C.H.Gayle retired at 195 and resumed at 519.   **Test No. 1909/143 (WI455/E884)**

24

PAKISTAN v SRI LANKA (1st Test)

At National Stadium, Karachi, on 21, 22, 23, 24, 25 February 2009
Toss: Sri Lanka. Result: **MATCH DRAWN**.
Debuts: Pakistan – Khurram Manzoor, Sohail Khan; Sri Lanka – N.T.Paranavitana.

SRI LANKA

B.S.M.Warnapura	c Misbah b Arafat	59	(2) c Akmal b Gul		2
N.T.Paranavitana	c Misbah b Gul	0	(1) run out		9
K.C.Sangakkara	c Misbah b Kaneria	70	lbw b Kaneria		65
*D.P.M.D.Jayawardena	c Akmal b Malik	240	(5) c Iqbal b Kaneria		22
T.T.Samaraweera	b Kaneria	231	(6) not out		24
T.M.Dilshan	c Akmal b Malik	0	(4) c Iqbal b Gul		8
†H.A.P.W.Jayawardena	b Kaneria	18	not out		7
W.P.U.C.J.Vaas	not out	12			
C.R.D.Fernando					
B.A.W.Mendis					
M.Muralitharan					
Extras	(LB 4, W 1, NB 9)	14	(NB 7)		7
Total	(7 wkts; 155.2 overs; 654 mins)	**644**	(5 wkts; 31 overs; 154 mins)		**144**

PAKISTAN

Khurram Manzoor	c H.A.P.W.Jayawardena b Mendis	27
Salman Butt	c D.P.M.D.Jayawardena b Muralitharan	23
*Younus Khan	b Fernando	313
Shoaib Malik	run out	56
Misbah-ul-Haq	lbw b Fernando	42
Faisal Iqbal	lbw b D.P.M.D.Jayawardena	57
†Kamran Akmal	not out	158
Yasir Arafat	not out	50
Sohail Khan		
Umar Gul		
Danish Kaneria		
Extras	(B 4, LB 12, W 5, NB 18)	39
Total	(6 wkts dec; 248.5 overs; 993 mins)	**765**

PAKISTAN	O	M	R	W		O	M	R	W
Umar Gul	24	2	92	1		9	1	41	2
Sohail Khan	21	2	131	0		6	0	33	0
Yasir Arafat	26	2	90	1		6	0	32	0
Shoaib Malik	36	3	140	2	(5)	1	0	3	0
Danish Kaneria	46.2	5	170	3	(4)	9	1	35	2
Younis Khan	1	0	6	0					
Salman Butt	1	0	11	0					

SRI LANKA	O	M	R	W
Vaas	36	10	66	0
Fernando	39	2	124	2
Mendis	59	14	157	1
Muralitharan	65	14	172	1
Dilshan	19	3	82	0
Paranavitana	1	0	33	0
Sangakkara	10	0	34	0
D.P.M.D.Jayawardena	6.5	0	41	1
Warnapura	9	0	40	0

FALL OF WICKETS

	SL	P	SL
Wkt	1st	1st	2nd
1st	3	44	2
2nd	93	78	32
3rd	177	227	45
4th	614	357	103
5th	614	531	120
6th	614	596	–
7th	644		
8th			
9th			
10th			

Umpires: S.J.Davis (*Australia*) (16) and S.J.A.Taufel (*Australia*) (54).
Referee: B.C.Broad (*England*) (34).   Test No. 1910/33 (P336/SL183)

PAKISTAN v SRI LANKA (2nd Test)

At Gaddafi Stadium, Lahore, on 1, 2 March 2009
Toss: Pakistan. Result: **MATCH DRAWN**.
Debuts: Pakistan – Mohammad Talha

SRI LANKA

B.S.M.Warnapura	c Misbah b Gul	8
N.T.Paranavitana	c Malik b Gul	21
K.C.Sangakkara	c Akmal b Arafat	104
*D.P.M.D.Jayawardena	c Akmal b Gul	30
T.T.Samaraweera	run out	214
T.M.Dilshan	run out	145
†H.A.P.W.Jayawardena	c Akmal b Gul	15
T.Thushara	b Gul	10
M.Muralitharan	b Talha	22
B.A.W.Mendis	b Gul	0
C.R.D.Fernando	not out	14
Extras	(B 4, LB 1, W 5 NB 13)	23
Total	**(151 overs; 660 mins)**	**606**

PAKISTAN

Khurram Manzoor	not out	59
Salman Butt	run out	48
*Younus Khan		
Shoaib Malik		
Misbah-ul-Haq		
Faisal Iqbal		
†Kamran Akmal		
Yasir Arafat		
Mohammad Talha		
Umar Gul		
Danish Kaneria		
Extras	(NB 3)	3
Total	**(1 wkt; 23.4 overs; 98 mins)**	**110**

PAKISTAN	O	M	R	W		O	M	R	W
Umar Gul	37	2	135	6					
Mohammad Talha	17	0	88	1					
Yasir Arafat	20	2	106	1					
Danish Kaneria	47	5	183	0					
Shoaib Malik	28	3	80	0					
Younis Khan	2	0	9	0					
SRI LANKA									
Thushara	8	0	46	0					
Fernando	2	0	20	0					
Mendis	8	2	21	0					
Muralitharan	4.4	0	23	0					
Dilshan	1	1	0	0					

FALL OF WICKETS

Wkt	1st	1st
	SL	P
1st	16	110
2nd	35	–
3rd	96	–
4th	300	–
5th	507	–
6th	542	–
7th	566	–
8th	572	–
9th	572	–
10th	606	–

Umpires: S.J.Davis (*Australia*) (17) and S.J.A.Taufel (*Australia*) (55).
Referee: B.C.Broad (*England*) (35).
This Test was abandoned following a terrorist attack on the Sri Lankan team bus.

Test No. 1911/34 (P337/SL184)

SOUTH AFRICA v AUSTRALIA (1st Test)

At New Wanderers Stadium, Johannesburg, on 26, 27, 28 February, 1, 2 March 2009.
Toss: Australia. Result: **AUSTRALIA** won by 162 runs.
Debuts: Australia – B.W.Hilfenhaus, P.J.Hughes, M.J.North.

AUSTRALIA

Batsman	1st dismissal	1st	2nd dismissal	2nd
P.J.Hughes	c Boucher b Steyn	0	c De Villiers b Harris	75
S.M.Katich	c McKenzie b Steyn	3	c Boucher b Morkel	10
*R.T.Ponting	b Ntini	83	c Amla b Kallis	25
M.E.K.Hussey	c Kallis b Morkel	4	c Ntini b Kallis	0
M.J.Clarke	c Boucher b Steyn	68	c Kallis b Harris	0
M.J.North	st Boucher b Harris	117	b Kallis	5
†B.J.Haddin	c Harris b Ntini	63	c Boucher b Ntini	37
A.B.McDonald	c Kallis b Steyn	0	c Boucher b Ntini	7
M.G.Johnson	not out	96	c Kallis b Ntini	1
P.M.Siddle	c Kallis b Morkel	9	not out	22
B.W.Hilfenhaus	c De Villiers b Morkel	0	b Steyn	16
Extras	(B 6, LB 8, W 2, NB 7)	23	(LB 5, W 1, NB 3)	9
Total	**(125.4 overs; 576 mins)**	**466**	**(53.4 overs; 244 mins)**	**207**

SOUTH AFRICA

Batsman	1st dismissal	1st	2nd dismissal	2nd
N.D.McKenzie	lbw b Siddle	36	c Haddin b Johnson	35
*G.C.Smith	c Haddin b Johnson	0	c Johnson b Hilfenhaus	69
H.M.Amla	c Ponting b Hilfenhaus	1	c Hughes b Siddle	57
J.H.Kallis	c Hussey b Siddle	27	b Johnson	45
A.B.de Villiers	not out	104	lbw b McDonald	3
J.P.Duminy	c Haddin b Johnson	17	c Ponting b Siddle	29
†M.V.Boucher	c Haddin b Johnson	0	b Hilfenhaus	24
M.Morkel	c and b Siddle	2	(2) c Hughes b Johnson	2
P.L.Harris	lbw b North	1	(8) c Katich b Siddle	8
D.W.Steyn	c North b McDonald	17	(9) b Johnson	6
M.Ntini	b Johnson	1	(10) not out	0
Extras	(B 4, LB 6, NB 4)	14	(B 1, LB 6, W 2, NB 4)	13
Total	**(81.1 overs; 356 mins)**	**220**	**(119.2 overs; 515 mins)**	**291**

SOUTH AFRICA	O	M	R	W		O	M	R	W
Steyn	30	4	113	4		16.4	5	51	1
Ntini	27	6	71	2		11	3	52	3
Morkel	28.4	3	117	3		10	1	41	1
Kallis	8	0	33	0	(5)	5	0	22	3
Harris	18	2	64	1	(4)	11	0	36	2
Duminy	14	2	54	0					

AUSTRALIA	O	M	R	W	O	M	R	W
Johnson	18.1	7	25	4	34.2	2	112	4
Hilfenhaus	25	9	58	1	31	7	68	2
Siddle	21	1	76	3	25	8	46	3
McDonald	10	4	22	1	22	8	31	1
North	7	0	29	1	7	0	27	0

FALL OF WICKETS

	A	SA	A	SA
Wkt	1st	1st	2nd	2nd
1st	0	1	38	76
2nd	18	2	99	130
3rd	38	49	99	206
4th	151	93	99	229
5th	182	138	104	229
6th	295	138	138	268
7th	296	154	145	272
8th	413	156	147	284
9th	466	208	174	289
10th	466	220	207	291

Umpires: B.F.Bowden (*New Zealand*) (53) and S.A.Bucknor (*West Indies*) (127).
Referee: J.J.Crowe (*New Zealand*) (31). **Test No. 1912/81 (A705/SA342)**

SOUTH AFRICA v AUSTRALIA (2nd Test)

At Kingsmead, Durban, on 6, 7, 8, 9, 10 March 2009.
Toss: Australia. Result: **AUSTRALIA** won by 175 runs.
Debuts: None.

AUSTRALIA

P.J.Hughes	c McKenzie b Kallis	115	c Morkel b Ntini		160
S.M.Katich	c Smith b Steyn	108	c Harris b Kallis		30
*R.T.Ponting	c McKenzie b Harris	9	c McKenzie b Morkel		81
M.E.K.Hussey	b Morkel	50	c Kallis b Duminy		19
M.J.Clarke	b Harris	3	not out		23
M.J.North	c Steyn b Kallis	38	c De Villiers b Steyn		0
†B.J.Haddin	c Amla b Ntini	5			
A.B.McDonald	not out	4			
M.G.Johnson	lbw b Ntini	0			
P.M.Siddle	c Boucher b Steyn	0			
B.W.Hilfenhaus	c Smith b Steyn	0			
Extras	(B 6, LB 4, W 2, NB 8)	20	(B 12, LB 2, NB 4)		18
Total	**(107.4 overs; 483 mins)**	**352**	**(5 wkts dec; 94.4 overs; 385 mins)**		**331**

SOUTH AFRICA

N.D.McKenzie	c Haddin b Johnson	0	(2) c Haddin b Siddle		31
*G.C.Smith	retired hurt	2	absent hurt		–
H.M.Amla	lbw b Johnson	0	(1) c Ponting b Siddle		43
J.H.Kallis	c Ponting b McDonald	22	(3) c Ponting b Johnson		93
A.B.de Villiers	lbw b Hilfenhaus	3	(4) c Haddin b Siddle		84
J.P.Duminy	not out	73	(5) c Haddin b Hilfenhaus		17
†M.V.Boucher	b Johnson	1	(6) c and b North		25
P.L.Harris	b McDonald	4	(7) c Siddle b Katich		5
M.Morkel	b McDonald	2	(8) c Haddin b Katich		24
D.W.Steyn	c Haddin b Siddle	8	(9) st Haddin b Katich		7
M.Ntini	lbw b Siddle	0	(10) not out		4
Extras	(B 10, LB 12, NB 1)	23	(B 13, LB 11, W 3, NB 10)		37
Total	**(57.3 overs; 277 mins)**	**138**	**(132.2 overs; 549 mins)**		**370**

SOUTH AFRICA	O	M	R	W	O	M	R	W	FALL OF WICKETS
Steyn	25.4	3	83	3	15.4	1	75	1	A SA A SA
Ntini	19	4	58	2	15	2	55	1	*Wkt 1st 1st 2nd 2nd*
Morkel	24	4	81	1	14	1	60	1	1st 184 0 55 63
Kallis	15	4	49	2	8	0	21	1	2nd 208 0 219 80
Harris	21	5	66	2	31	8	68	0	3rd 259 6 260 267
Duminy	3	1	5	0	11	1	38	1	4th 266 62 330 279
									5th 329 104 331 299
AUSTRALIA									6th 348 104 – 307
Johnson	16	5	37	3	33	9	78	1	7th 348 106 – 345
Hilfenhaus	11	2	28	1	24	4	79	1	8th 348 138 – 363
McDonald	12	4	25	3	(4) 16	3	47	0	9th 352 138 – 370
Siddle	13.3	6	20	2	(3) 28	12	61	3	10th 352 – – –
North	4	3	6	0	20	6	36	1	
Clarke	1	1	0	0					
Katich					(6) 11.2	1	45	3	

Umpires: Asad Rauf (*Pakistan*) (23) and B.F.Bowden (*New Zealand*) (54).
Referee: J.J.Crowe (*New Zealand*) (32).
In the first innings G.C.Smith retired hurt at 3 and J.H.Kallis (22*) retired hurt at 56 and
resumed at 104-5. **Test No. 1913/82 (A706/SA343)**

SOUTH AFRICA v AUSTRALIA (3rd Test)

At Newlands, Cape Town, on 19, 20, 21, 22 March 2009.
Toss: Australia. Result: **SOUTH AFRICA** won by an innings and 20 runs.
Debuts: South Africa – I.Khan, J.A.Morkel; Australia – B.E.McGain.

AUSTRALIA

P.J.Hughes	lbw b Harris	33	c Kallis b Harris		32
S.M.Katich	c Khan b Harris	55	c Duminy b Harris		54
*R.T.Ponting	c Boucher b Morkel	0	c Boucher b Steyn		12
M.E.K.Hussey	b Steyn	20	c Duminy b Steyn		39
M.J.Clarke	b Steyn	0	b Steyn		47
†B.J.Haddin	lbw b Harris	42	c Duminy b Harris		18
A.B.McDonald	c Kallis b Ntini	13	c De Villiers b Harris		68
M.G.Johnson	c Prince b Steyn	35	not out		123
P.M.Siddle	c De Villiers b Ntini	0	c De Villiers b Harris		0
B.E.McGain	c De Villiers b Steyn	2	run out		0
B.W.Hilfenhaus	not out	0	c Prince b Harris		12
Extras	(LB 6, W 1, NB 2)	9	(B 8, LB 2, W 2 NB 5)		17
Total	**(72 overs; 327 mins)**	**209**	**(121.5 overs; 532 mins)**		**422**

SOUTH AFRICA

I.Khan	c and b Siddle	20
A.G.Prince	c Haddin b Hilfenhaus	150
H.M.Amla	c Haddin b Johnson	46
*J.H.Kallis	c and b Hilfenhaus	102
A.B.de Villiers	c McDonald b Katich	163
J.P.Duminy	b Johnson	7
†M.V.Boucher	c Ponting b Johnson	12
J.A.Morkel	b McDonald	58
P.L.Harris	c Haddin b Johnson	27
D.W.Steyn	c Clarke b Katich	0
M.Ntini	not out	4
Extras	(B 19, LB 24, W 9, NB 10)	62
Total	**(154.3 overs; 679 mins)**	**651**

SOUTH AFRICA	O	M	R	W		O	M	R	W
Steyn	16	5	56	4		27	5	96	3
Ntini	17	7	38	2		19	6	66	0
Kallis	10	2	31	0	(5)	10	4	21	0
Morkel	12	3	44	1	(3)	20	1	88	0
Harris	17	5	34	3	(4)	42.5	9	127	6
Duminy						3	1	14	0

AUSTRALIA	O	M	R	W
Johnson	37.3	5	148	4
Hilfenhaus	34	4	133	2
Siddle	35	15	67	1
McGain	18	2	149	0
McDonald	27	7	102	1
Katich	3	1	9	2

FALL OF WICKETS

	A	SA	A
Wkt	1st	1st	2nd
1st	58	65	57
2nd	59	162	76
3rd	81	322	138
4th	81	415	146
5th	152	443	191
6th	158	467	218
7th	190	591	381
8th	190	637	381
9th	209	637	388
10th	209	651	422

Umpires: Asad Rauf (*Pakistan*) (24) and S.A.Bucknor (*West Indies*) (128).
Referee: J.J.Crowe (*New Zealand*) (33).   **Test No. 1914/83 (A707/SA344)**

NEW ZEALAND v INDIA (1st Test)

At Seddon Park, Hamilton, on 18, 19, 20, 21 March 2009.
Toss: India. Result: **INDIA** won by ten wickets.
Debuts: New Zealand – M.J.Guptill.

NEW ZEALAND

T.G.McIntosh	c Sehwag b Sharma	12		c Tendulkar b Khan		0
M.J.Guptill	c Dravid b Khan	14		c Sehwag b Harbhajan		48
D.R.Flynn	c Dhoni b Khan	0		c Gambhir b Harbhajan		67
L.R.P.L.Taylor	b Sharma	18	(5)	c Sehwag b Patel		4
J.D.Ryder	c Laxman b Sharma	102	(6)	lbw b Harbhajan		21
J.E.C.Franklin	c Dhoni b Sharma	0	(7)	c Patel b Harbhajan		14
†B.B.McCullum	c Laxman b Patel	3	(8)	c Laxman b Yuvraj		84
*D.L.Vettori	c Dhoni b Patel	118	(9)	c Dhoni b Harbhajan		21
K.D.Mills	b Patel	0	(4)	lbw b Patel		2
I.E.O'Brien	st Dhoni b Harbhajan	8		c Laxman b Harbhajan		14
C.S.Martin	not out	0		not out		0
Extras	(LB 1, NB 3)	4		(B 1, LB 3)		4
Total	(78.2 overs; 345 mins)	279		(102.3 overs; 450 mins)		279

INDIA

G.Gambhir	c McCullum b Martin	72		not out	30
V.Sehwag	run out	24			
R.Dravid	b O'Brien	66	(2)	not out	8
S.R.Tendulkar	c Taylor b O'Brien	160			
V.V.S.Laxman	c Taylor b Martin	30			
Yuvraj Singh	b Martin	22			
*†M.S.Dhoni	c McCullum b O'Brien	47			
Harbhajan Singh	c Vettori b Mills	16			
Z.Khan	not out	51			
I.Sharma	c McCullum b Vettori	6			
M.M.Patel	c Martin b Vettori	9			
Extras	(B 6, LB 3, NB 8)	17		(B 1)	1
Total	(152.4 overs; 634 mins)	520		(0 wkts; 5.2 overs; 23 mins)	39

INDIA	O	M	R	W	O	M	R	W
Khan	16	3	70	2	28	7	79	1
Sharma	19.2	4	73	4	22	7	62	0
Patel	18	4	60	3	17	2	60	2
Harbhajan Singh	22	7	57	1	28	2	63	6
Sehwag	3	0	18	0				
Yuvraj Singh					(5) 7.3	2	11	1

NEW ZEALAND	O	M	R	W	O	M	R	W
Martin	30	9	98	3	3	0	17	0
Mills	22	4	98	1	2.2	0	21	0
O'Brien	33	7	103	3				
Franklin	23	1	98	0				
Vettori	35.4	8	90	2				
Ryder	9	5	24	0				

FALL OF WICKETS

	NZ	I	NZ	I
Wkt	1st	1st	2nd	2nd
1st	17	37	0	–
2nd	17	142	68	–
3rd	40	177	75	–
4th	51	238	110	–
5th	51	314	132	–
6th	60	429	154	–
7th	246	443	161	–
8th	246	457	199	–
9th	275	492	275	–
10th	279	520	279	–

Umpires: I.J.Gould (*England*) (3) and S.J.A.Taufel (*Australia*) (56).
Referee: A.G.Hurst (*Australia*) (28).   **Test No. 1915/45 (NZ349/I428)**

NEW ZEALAND v INDIA (2nd Test)

At McLean Park, Napier, on 26, 27, 28, 29, 30 March 2009.
Toss: New Zealand. Result: **MATCH DRAWN**.
Debuts: None.

NEW ZEALAND

T.G.McIntosh	c Karthik b Sharma	12
M.J.Guptill	c Sehwag b Khan	8
J.M.How	b Khan	1
L.R.P.L.Taylor	c Yuvraj b Harbhajan	151
J.D.Ryder	b Khan	201
J.E.C.Franklin	run out	52
†B.B.McCullum	c Tendulkar b Sharma	115
*D.L.Vettori	b Sharma	55
J.S.Patel	c Sharma b Harbhajan	1
I.E.O'Brien	not out	1
C.S.Martin		
Extras	(B 7, LB 8, NB 7)	22
Total	**(9 wkts dec; 154.4 overs; 650 mins)**	**619**

INDIA

G.Gambhir	c Vettori b Patel	16		lbw b Patel	137
*V.Sehwag	c McCullum b Vettori	34		lbw b Patel	22
R.Dravid	c McCullum b Ryder	83		c How b Vettori	62
I.Sharma	lbw b Vettori	0			
S.R.Tendulkar	c Taylor b Patel	49	(4)	c McCullum b Martin	64
V.V.S.Laxman	c McIntosh b Martin	76	(5)	not out	124
Yuvraj Singh	c McIntosh b Martin	0	(6)	not out	54
†K.D.Karthik	c Ryder b Martin	6			
Harbhajan Singh	c Martin b O'Brien	18			
Z.Khan	c Ryder b O'Brien	8			
M.M.Patel	not out	0			
Extras	(B 1, LB 7, NB 7)	15		(B 9, LB 1, NB 3)	13
Total	**(93.5 overs; 405 mins)**	**305**		**(4 wkts; 180 overs; 723 mins)**	**476**

INDIA	O	M	R	W		O	M	R	W
Khan	34	6	129	3					
Sharma	27	5	95	3					
Patel	28	3	128	0					
Harbhajan Singh	41.4	7	120	2					
Sehwag	12	0	73	0					
Yuvraj Singh	12	0	59	0					
NEW ZEALAND									
Martin	24	5	89	3		30	8	86	1
Franklin	15	4	34	0	(3)	21	5	48	0
Vettori	19	5	45	2	(6)	38	13	76	1
O'Brien	13.5	4	66	2	(2)	32	9	94	0
Patel	19	2	60	2	(4)	45	10	120	2
Ryder	3	1	3	1	(5)	11	5	38	0
Taylor						2	1	4	0
How						1	1	0	0

FALL OF WICKETS

	NZ	I	I
Wkt	1st	1st	2nd
1st	21	48	30
2nd	22	73	163
3rd	23	78	260
4th	294	165	356
5th	415	246	–
6th	477	253	–
7th	605	270	–
8th	618	291	–
9th	619	305	–
10th	–	305	–

Umpires: B.R.Doctrove (*West Indies*) (23) and I.J.Gould (*England*) (4).
Referee: A.G.Hurst (*Australia*) (29).   Test No. 1916/46 (NZ350/I429)

NEW ZEALAND v INDIA (3rd Test)

At Basin Reserve, Napier, on 3, 4, 5, 6, 7 April 2009.
Toss: New Zealand. Result: **MATCH DRAWN**.
Debuts: None.

INDIA

G.Gambhir	lbw b Franklin	23	lbw b O'Brien	167
V.Sehwag	c McCullum b O'Brien	48	c Taylor b Martin	12
R.Dravid	c Franklin b Martin	35	c McCullum b Vettori	60
S.R.Tendulkar	c McCullum b Martin	62	c Taylor b Vettori	9
V.V.S.Laxman	c McIntosh b Southee	4	b O'Brien	61
Yuvraj Singh	lbw b Ryder	9	c Taylor b Martin	40
*†M.S.Dhoni	c O'Brien b Southee	52	not out	56
Harbhajan Singh	c Vettori b Martin	60	c Southee b Martin	0
Z.Khan	c McCullum b O'Brien	33	not out	18
I.Sharma	c McCullum b Martin	18		
M.M.Patel	not out	15		
Extras	(B 2, LB 8, W 3, NB 7)	20	(LB 5, W 1, NB 5)	11
Total	(92.1 overs; 396 mins)	379	(7 wkts dec; 116 overs; 471 mins)	434

NEW ZEALAND

T.G.McIntosh	c Yuvraj b Khan	32	c Dravid b Khan	4
M.J.Guptill	b Khan	17	lbw b Harbhajan	49
D.R.Flynn	c Dhoni b Khan	2	b Khan	10
L.R.P.L.Taylor	c Dhoni b Harbhajan	42	b Harbhajan	107
J.D.Ryder	c Dhoni b Khan	3	c Dravid b Harbhajan	0
J.E.C.Franklin	c Sehwag b Harbhajan	15	lbw b Tendulkar	49
†B.B.McCullum	c Dhoni b Harbhajan	24	c Dravid b Tendulkar	6
*D.L.Vettori	c Dhoni b Sharma	11	not out	15
T.G.Southee	c and b Khan	16	c Dhoni b Harbhajan	3
I.E.O'Brien	c Dhoni b Patel	19	not out	19
C.S.Martin	not out	4		
Extras	(B 9, LB 3)	12	(B 10, LB 2, W 1, NB 6)	19
Total	(65 overs; 290 mins)	197	(8 wkts; 94.3 overs; 419 mins)	281

NEW ZEALAND	O	M	R	W	O	M	R	W		FALL OF	WICKETS		
										I	NZ	I	NZ
Martin	25.1	3	98	4	(2) 22	7	70	3	Wkt	1st	1st	2nd	2nd
Southee	18	1	94	2	(1) 12	2	58	0	1st	73	21	14	30
O'Brien	22	3	89	2	25	6	100	2	2nd	75	31	184	54
Franklin	14	4	38	1	16	3	72	0	3rd	165	80	208	84
Vettori	9	1	47	0	(6) 35	5	108	2	4th	173	98	314	84
Ryder	4	2	3	1	(5) 6	1	21	0	5th	182	120	319	226
									6th	204	125	397	244
INDIA									7th	283	138	397	253
Khan	18	2	65	5	19.3	6	57	2	8th	315	160	–	258
Sharma	14	3	47	1	(3) 12	2	57	0	9th	347	181	–	
Patel	8	2	20	1	(2) 13	4	22	0	10th	379	197	–	
Harbhajan Singh	23	4	43	3	33	8	59	4					
Yuvraj Singh	2	0	10	0	1	0	4	0					
Sehwag					7	0	25	0					
Tendulkar					9	0	45	2					

Umpires: D.J.Harper (*Australia*) (81) and S.J.A.Taufel (*Australia*) (57).
Referee: A.G.Hurst (*Australia*) (30).   Test No. 1917/47 (NZ351/I430)

ENGLAND v WEST INDIES (1st Test)

At Lord's, London, on 6, 7, 8 May 2009
Toss: West Indies. Result: **ENGLAND** won by 10 wickets.
Debuts: England – T.T.Bresnan, G.Onions.

ENGLAND

*A.J.Strauss	c Ramdin b Taylor	16	not out		14
A.N.Cook	b Edwards	35	not out		14
R.S.Bopara	c Nash b Taylor	143			
K.P.Pietersen	c Ramdin b Edwards	0			
P.D.Collingwood	c Smith b Edwards	8			
†M.J.Prior	c Simmons b Edwards	42			
S.C.J.Broad	c Taylor b Benn	38			
T.T.Bresnan	lbw b Benn	9			
G.P.Swann	not out	63			
J.M.Anderson	c Ramdin b Edwards	1			
G.Onions	b Edwards	0			
Extras	(B 1, LB 5, W 7, NB 9)	22	(NB 4)		4
Total	(111.3 overs; 500 mins)	377	(0 wkts; 6.1 overs; 29 mins)		32

WEST INDIES

*C.H.Gayle	b Broad	28	c Swann b Anderson		0
D.S.Smith	b Swann	46	b Onions		41
R.R.Sarwan	c Prior b Broad	13	b Anderson		1
L.M.P.Simmons	c Strauss b Onions	16	c Cook b Onions		21
S.Chanderpaul	c Collingwood b Swann	0	c Bopara b Swann		4
B.P.Nash	c Collingwood b Swann	4	c Cook b Broad		81
†D.Ramdin	lbw b Onions	5	b Broad		61
J.E.Taylor	c Prior b Onions	0	lbw b Swann		15
S.J.Benn	c Swann b Onions	2	b Swann		0
F.H.Edwards	not out	10	c Bresnan b Broad		2
L.S.Baker	lbw b Onions	17	not out		2
Extras	(LB 10, W 1)	11	(B 8, LB 18, W 2)		28
Total	(32.3 overs; 155 mins)	152	(72.2 overs; 325 mins)		256

WEST INDIES	O	M	R	W		O	M	R	W
Taylor	24	2	83	2	(2)	3	0	20	0
Edwards	26.3	4	92	6	(1)	3.1	0	12	0
Baker	24	5	75	0					
Benn	27	4	84	2					
Nash	2	1	2	0					
Simmons	5	1	24	0					
Gayle	3	0	11	0					
ENGLAND									
Broad	11	0	56	2	(2)	19.2	2	64	3
Swann	5	2	16	3	(4)	17	4	39	3
Anderson	7	0	32	0	(1)	15	6	38	2
Onions	9.3	1	38	5	(5)	12	2	64	2
Bresnan					(3)	7	3	17	0
Bopara						2	0	8	0

FALL OF WICKETS

	E	WI	WI	E
Wkt	1st	1st	2nd	2nd
1st	28	46	14	–
2nd	92	70	22	–
3rd	92	99	70	–
4th	109	99	75	–
5th	193	117	79	–
6th	262	117	222	–
7th	275	117	243	–
8th	368	119	246	–
9th	377	128	249	–
10th	377	152	256	–

Umpires: S.J.Davis (*Australia*) (18) and E.A.R.de Silva (*Sri Lanka*) (38).
Referee: A.J.Pycroft (*Zimbabwe*) (1).   **Test No. 1918/144 (E885/WI456)**

ENGLAND v WEST INDIES (2nd Test)

At Riverside Ground, Chester-le-Street, on 14, 15 (*no play*), 16, 17, 18 May 2009
Toss: England. Result: **ENGLAND** won by an innings and 83 runs.
Debuts: None.

ENGLAND

*A.J.Strauss	c Ramdin b Gayle	26
A.N.Cook	c Gayle b Benn	160
R.S.Bopara	b Baker	108
J.M.Anderson	b Edwards	14
K.P.Pietersen	c Simmons b Benn	49
P.D.Collingwood	not out	60
†M.J.Prior	c Benn b Simmons	63
S.C.J.Broad	not out	28
T.T.Bresnan		
G.P.Swann		
G.Onions		
Extras	(B 20, LB 5, W 8, NB 28)	61
Total	**(6 wkts dec; 147 overs; 616 mins)**	**569**

WEST INDIES

D.S.Smith	b Anderson	7	lbw b Swann	11
*C.H.Gayle	lbw b Anderson	19	c Strauss b Onions	54
R.R.Sarwan	c Bresnan b Broad	100	lbw b Onions	22
L.M.P.Simmons	c Strauss b Anderson	8	c sub (S.G.Borthwick) b Anderson	10
S.Chanderpaul	c Prior b Broad	23	c Collingwood b Anderson	47
B.P.Nash	b Anderson	10	c sub (S.G.Borthwick) b Bresnan	1
†D.Ramdin	c Swann b Anderson	55	c Anderson b Bresnan	0
J.E.Taylor	lbw b Onions	10	b Anderson	5
S.J.Benn	run out	35	b Anderson	0
F.H.Edwards	c Strauss b Broad	11	c sub (K.Turner) b Bresnan	4
L.S.Baker	not out	0	not out	4
Extras	(B 2, LB 21, W 2, NB 7)	32	(B 8, LB 5, W 5)	18
Total	**(84.3 overs; 380 mins)**	**310**	**(44 overs; 202 mins)**	**176**

WEST INDIES	O	M	R	W		O	M	R	W
Taylor	20	2	68	0					
Edwards	25	1	113	1					
Baker	30	3	119	1					
Gayle	14	2	31	1					
Benn	43	8	146	2					
Simmons	14	0	60	1					
Sarwan	1	0	7	0					

ENGLAND	O	M	R	W		O	M	R	W
Anderson	26.3	5	87	5		16	5	38	4
Broad	16	2	62	3		5	1	21	0
Onions	18	6	52	1	(4)	6	0	46	2
Bresnan	10	2	35	0	(5)	14	2	45	3
Swann	14	4	51	0	(3)	3	0	13	1

FALL OF WICKETS

	E	WI	WI
Wkt	1st	1st	2nd
1st	69	18	53
2nd	282	38	88
3rd	326	68	89
4th	410	167	141
5th	419	188	142
6th	513	205	146
7th	–	216	163
8th	–	286	167
9th	–	310	168
10th	–	310	176

Umpires: S.J.Davis (*Australia*) (19) and E.A.R.de Silva (*Sri Lanka*) (39).
Referee: A.J.Pycroft (*Zimbabwe*) (2).   **Test No. 1919/145 (E886/WI457)**

SRI LANKA v PAKISTAN (1st Test)

At Galle International Stadium on 4, 5, 6, 7 July 2009.
Toss: Pakistan. Result: **SRI LANKA** won by 50 runs.
Debuts: Sri Lanka – A.D.Mathews; Pakistan – Abdur Rauf, Mohammad Aamer, Saeed Ajmal.

SRI LANKA

B.S.M.Warnapura	b Aamer	2	(2) c Khan b Gul		0
N.T.Paranavitana	c Misbah b Rauf	72	(3) c Akmal b Aamer		49
*K.C.Sangakkara	c Malik b Rauf	9	(4) c Akmal b Aamer		14
D.P.M.D.Jayawardena	c Akmal b Rauf	30	(5) c Akmal b Aamer		0
T.T.Samaraweera	c Kamran b Khan	31	(6) c Misbah b Ajmal		34
†T.M.Dilshan	c Malik b Aamer	28	(7) c Manzoor b Khan		22
A.D.Mathews	c Akmal b Gul	42	(8) c Butt b Rauf		27
K.M.D.N.Kulasekara	c Akmal b Aamer	38	(9) lbw b Ajmal		25
H.M.R.K.B.Herath	not out	20	(1) lbw b Khan		15
T.Thushara	c Manzoor b Ajmal	10	not out		15
B.A.W.Mendis	st Akmal b Ajmal	5	b Ajmal		1
Extras	(B 1, LB 3, NB 1)	5	(LB 7, W 1, NB 7)		15
Total	**(80.2 overs; 353 mins)**	**292**	**(56.2 overs; 281 mins)**		**217**

PAKISTAN

Khurram Manzoor	lbw b Thushara	2	c Jayawardena b Mendis		15
Salman Butt	b Kulasekara	0	c Paranavitana b Herath		28
*Younus Khan	c Dilshan b Mathews	25	lbw b Mathews		3
Abdur Rauf	c Dilshan b Kulasekara	31	(4) c Jayawardena b Herath		13
Mohammad Yousuf	run out	112	(4) lbw b Herath		12
Misbah-ul-Haq	c Jayawardena b Herath	56	(5) run out		7
Shoaib Malik	b Kulasekara	38	(6) c Dilshan b Thushara		0
†Kamran Akmal	run out	31	(7) lbw b Thushara		6
Umar Gul	b Kulasekara	7	b Mendis		9
Mohammad Aamer	c Paranavitana b Thushara	4	c Dilshan b Herath		6
Saeed Ajmal	not out	4	not out		1
Extras	(B 12, LB 15, W 1, NB 7)	35	(B 13, LB 3, W 1)		17
Total	**(94 overs; 402 mins)**	**342**	**(44.3 overs; 202 mins)**		**117**

PAKISTAN	O	M	R	W		O	M	R	W
Umar Gul	14	3	45	1	(2)	10	2	62	1
Mohammad Aamer	19	3	74	3	(1)	11	2	38	3
Abdur Rauf	14	1	59	2		13	1	49	1
Younus Khan	7	2	23	2		10	1	27	2
Saeed Ajmal	23.2	4	79	2		12.2	0	34	3
Shoaib Malik	3	1	8	0					

SRI LANKA	O	M	R	W		O	M	R	W
Kulasekara	24	3	71	4		7	1	25	0
Thushara	21	3	77	2		12	4	21	2
Mendis	25	2	89	0	(4)	10	0	27	2
Mathews	8	2	26	1	(3)	4	0	13	1
Herath	16	2	52	1		11.3	5	15	4

FALL OF WICKETS

	SL	P	SL	P
Wkt	1st	1st	2nd	2nd
1st	3	1	0	36
2nd	21	5	68	39
3rd	96	55	86	71
4th	139	80	88	72
5th	160	219	101	72
6th	194	294	138	80
7th	241	303	156	85
8th	271	329	191	95
9th	282	339	211	110
10th	292	342	217	117

Umpires: I.J.Gould (*England*) (5) and D.J.Harper (*Australia*) (82).
Referee: A.G.Hurst (*Australia*) (31).   **Test No. 1920/35 (SL185/P338)**

35

SRI LANKA v PAKISTAN (2nd Test)

At P.Saravanamuttu Stadium, Colombo, on 12, 13, 14 July 2009.
Toss: Pakistan. Result: **SRI LANKA** won by seven wickets.
Debuts: Pakistan – Fawad Alam.

PAKISTAN

Batsman	First innings		Second innings	
Khurram Manzoor	c Dilshan b Kulasekara	3	c Dilshan b Herath	38
Fawad Alam	lbw b Mathews	16	c Warnapura b Herath	168
*Younus Khan	b Thushara	0	c Dilshan b Paranavitana	82
Mohammad Yousuf	c Herath b Kulasekara	10	lbw b Herath	6
Misbah-ul-Haq	c Dilshan b Kulasekara	0	lbw b Kulasekara	3
Shoaib Malik	not out	39	b Herath	6
†Kamran Akmal	c Dilshan b Thushara	9	lbw b Kulasekara	3
Abdur Rauf	lbw b Kulasekara	0	lbw b Kulasekara	0
Umar Gul	c Samaraweera b Mendis	1	lbw b Herath	2
Mohammad Aamer	lbw b Mendis	2	not out	1
Saeed Ajmal	lbw b Mendis	0	lbw b Kulasekara	0
Extras	(B 4, LB 2, W 2, NB 2)	10	(B 8, LB 1, W 1, NB 1)	11
Total	(36 overs; 167 mins)	90	(96.4 overs; 431 mins)	320

SRI LANKA

Batsman	First innings		Second innings	
B.S.M.Warnapura	lbw b Gul	11	c Akmal b Rauf	54
N.T.Paranavitana	c Akmal b Ajmal	26	b Ajmal	17
*K.C.Sangakkara	lbw b Gul	87	c Misbah b Malik	46
D.P.M.D.Jayawardena	c Manzoor b Ajmal	19	not out	37
T.T.Samaraweera	run out	21	not out	6
†T.M.Dilshan	c Akmal b Ajmal	20		
A.D.Mathews	c Yousuf b Ajmal	27		
K.M.D.N.Kulasekara	c Misbah b Gul	11		
H.M.R.K.B.Herath	c and b Gul	0		
T.Thushara	lbw b Rauf	1		
B.A.W.Mendis	not out	0		
Extras	(B 8, LB 1, NB 8)	17	(LB 7, NB 4)	11
Total	(80 overs; 359 mins)	240	(3 wkts; 31.5 overs; 146 mins)	171

SRI LANKA	O	M	R	W		O	M	R	W
Kulasekara	9	3	21	4		19.4	6	37	4
Thushara	8	3	23	2		13	0	48	0
Mendis	10	3	20	3	(4)	17	0	81	0
Mathews	3	0	15	1	(3)	6	0	20	0
Herath	6	3	5	0		35	5	99	5
Paranavitana						6	0	26	1

PAKISTAN	O	M	R	W		O	M	R	W
Umar Gul	18	1	43	4		6	0	38	0
Mohammad Aamer	13	2	36	0		6	0	33	0
Abdur Rauf	11	1	38	1	(4)	4	1	13	1
Saeed Ajmal	31	5	87	4	(3)	12	1	56	1
Younus Khan	7	1	27	0		2	0	11	0
Shoaib Malik						1.5	0	13	1

FALL OF WICKETS

	P	SL	P	SL
Wkt	1st	1st	2nd	2nd
1st	4	28	85	60
2nd	6	82	285	100
3rd	17	133	294	160
4th	19	177	303	–
5th	51	188	303	–
6th	67	203	306	–
7th	74	220	312	–
8th	80	220	316	–
9th	90	227	319	–
10th	90	240	320	–

Umpires: D.J.Harper (*Australia*) (83) and S.J.A.Taufel (*Australia*) (58).
Referee: A.G.Hurst (*Australia*) (32).   Test No. 1921/36 (SL186/P339)

SRI LANKA v PAKISTAN (3rd Test)

At Sinhalese Sports Club, Colombo, on 20, 21, 22, 23, 24 July 2009.
Toss: Sri Lanka. Result: **MATCH DRAWN**.
Debuts: None.

PAKISTAN

Khurram Manzoor	c Jayawardena b Vaas	93	b Herath		2
Fawad Alam	c Dilshan b Thushara	16	c and b Thushara		16
*Younus Khan	b Thushara	2	lbw b Kulasekara		19
Mohammad Yousuf	run out	90	c Sangakkara b Herath		23
Misbah-ul-Haq	c Dilshan b Kulasekara	27	c Sangakkara b Mathews		65
Shoaib Malik	lbw b Thushara	45	c sub (R.A.S.Lakmal) b Herath		134
†Kamran Akmal	b Thushara	1	c Jayawardena b Kulasekara		74
Umar Gul	b Kulasekara	2	c Vaas b Herath		46
Danish Kaneria	lbw b Kulasekara	1	c Thushara b Herath		5
Mohammad Aamer	not out	2	not out		22
Saeed Ajmal	b Thushara	8	not out		3
Extras	(B 10, NB 2)	12	(B 10, LB 2, W 2, NB 2)		16
Total	**(89.4 overs; 404 mins)**	**299**	**(9 wkts dec; 123 overs; 561 mins)**		**425**

SRI LANKA

B.S.M.Warnapura	b Gul	0	(2) c Malik b Kaneria		31
N.T.Paranavitana	b Khan	5	(1) c Alam b Malik		73
*K.C.Sangakkara	lbw b Ajmal	45	not out		130
D.P.M.D.Jayawardena	b Kaneria	79	c Akmal b Kaneria		2
T.T.Samaraweera	b Ajmal	6	c Akmal b Ajmal		73
A.D.Mathews	c Misbah b Kaneria	31	not out		64
W.P.U.C.J.Vaas	lbw b Kaneria	4			
†T.M.Dilshan	c Akmal b Kaneria	44			
K.M.D.N.Kulasekara	c Misbah b Ajmal	1			
H.M.R.K.B.Herath	lbw b Kaneria	7			
T.Thushara	not out	5			
Extras	(LB 2, NB 4)	6	(B 1, LB 7, W 1, NB 9)		18
Total	**(68.3 overs; 303 mins)**	**233**	**(4 wkts; 134 overs; 586 mins)**		**391**

SRI LANKA	O	M	R	W		O	M	R	W
Vaas	20	6	43	1	(4)	19	6	47	0
Kulasekara	16	2	47	3	(1)	20	5	55	2
Thushara	20.4	2	83	5	(2)	28	2	121	1
Herath	23	4	76	0	(3)	46	6	157	5
Mathews	8	2	31	0		10	1	33	1
Jayawardena	2	0	9	0					

PAKISTAN	O	M	R	W		O	M	R	W
Umar Gul	10	0	55	1		12	0	65	0
Mohammad Aamer	10	2	34	0		21	5	46	0
Younus Khan	3	1	10	1		8	0	25	0
Saeed Ajmal	25	5	70	3		43	9	95	1
Danish Kaneria	20.3	3	62	5	(6)	36	3	114	2
Shoaib Malik						14	1	38	1

FALL OF WICKETS

	P	SL	P	SL
Wkt	1st	1st	2nd	2nd
1st	34	0	16	83
2nd	36	23	22	139
3rd	203	63	54	155
4th	285	82	67	277
5th	285	153	186	–
6th	285	171	319	–
7th	287	174	371	–
8th	288	181	399	–
9th	289	204	405	–
10th	299	233	–	–

Umpires: I.J.Gould (*England*) (6) and S.J.A.Taufel (*Australia*) (59).
Referee: A.G.Hurst (*Australia*) (33).   **Test No. 1922/37 (SL187/P340)**

ENGLAND v AUSTRALIA (1st Test)

At Sophia Gardens, Cardiff, on 8, 9, 10, 11, 12 July 2009.
Toss: England. Result: **MATCH DRAWN**.
Debuts: None.

ENGLAND

*A.J.Strauss	c Clarke b Johnson	30	c Haddin b Hauritz		17
A.N.Cook	c Hussey b Hilfenhaus	10	lbw b Johnson		6
R.S.Bopara	c Hughes b Johnson	35	lbw b Hilfenhaus		1
K.P.Pietersen	c Katich b Hauritz	69	b Hilfenhaus		8
P.D.Collingwood	c Haddin b Hilfenhaus	64	c Hussey b Siddle		74
†M.J.Prior	b Siddle	56	c Clarke b Hauritz		14
A.Flintoff	b Siddle	37	c Ponting b Johnson		26
J.M.Anderson	c Hussey b Hauritz	26	(10) not out		21
S.C.J.Broad	b Johnson	19	(8) lbw b Hauritz		14
G.P.Swann	not out	47	(9) lbw b Hilfenhaus		31
M.S.Panesar	c Ponting b Hauritz	4	not out		7
Extras	(B 13, LB 11, W 2, NB 12)	38	(B 9, LB 9, W 4, NB 11)		33
Total	**(106.5 overs; 442 mins)**	**435**	**(9 wkts; 105 overs; 414 mins)**		**252**

AUSTRALIA

P.J.Hughes	c Prior b Flintoff	36
S.M.Katich	lbw b Anderson	122
*R.T.Ponting	b Panesar	150
M.E.K.Hussey	c Prior b Anderson	3
M.J.Clarke	c Prior b Broad	83
M.J.North	not out	125
†B.J.Haddin	c Bopara b Collingwood	121
M.G.Johnson		
N.M.Hauritz		
P.M.Siddle		
B.W.Hilfenhaus		
Extras	(B 9, LB 14, W 4, NB 7)	34
Total	**(6 wkts dec; 181 overs; 724 mins)**	**674**

AUSTRALIA	O	M	R	W		O	M	R	W	FALL OF WICKETS			
											E	A	E
Johnson	22	2	87	3		22	4	44	2	Wkt	1st	1st	2nd
Hilfenhaus	27	5	77	2		15	3	47	3	1st	21	60	13
Siddle	27	3	121	2		18	2	51	1	2nd	67	299	17
Hauritz	23.5	1	95	3		37	12	63	3	3rd	90	325	31
Clarke	5	0	20	0		3	0	8	0	4th	228	331	46
Katich	2	0	11	0	(7)	3	0	7	0	5th	241	474	70
North					(6)	7	4	14	0	6th	327	674	127
										7th	329	–	159
ENGLAND										8th	355	–	221
Anderson	32	6	110	2						9th	423	–	233
Broad	32	6	129	1						10th	435	–	–
Swann	38	8	131	0									
Flintoff	35	3	128	1									
Panesar	35	4	115	1									
Collingwood	9	0	38	1									

Umpires: Alim Dar (*Pakistan*) (56) and B.R.Doctrove (*West Indies*) (24).
Referee: J.J.Crowe (*New Zealand*) (34).   Test No. 1923/317 (E887/A708)

ENGLAND v AUSTRALIA (2nd Test)

At Lord's, London, on 16, 17, 18, 19, 20 July 2009.
Toss: England. Result: **ENGLAND** won by 115 runs.
Debuts: None.

ENGLAND

*A.J.Strauss	b Hilfenhaus	161	c Clarke b Hauritz		32
A.N.Cook	lbw b Johnson	95	lbw b Hauritz		32
R.S.Bopara	lbw b Hilfenhaus	18	c Katich b Hauritz		27
K.P.Pietersen	c Haddin b Siddle	32	c Haddin b Siddle		44
P.D.Collingwood	c Siddle b Clarke	16	c Haddin b Siddle		54
†M.J.Prior	b Johnson	8	run out		61
A.Flintoff	c Ponting b Hilfenhaus	4	not out		30
S.C.J.Broad	b Hilfenhaus	16	not out		0
G.P.Swann	c Ponting b Siddle	4			
J.M.Anderson	c Hussey b Johnson	29			
G.Onions	not out	17			
Extras	(B 15, LB 2, NB 8)	25	(B 16, LB 9, W 1, NB 5)		31
Total	**(101.4 overs; 425 mins)**	**425**	**(6 wkts dec; 71.2 overs; 317 mins)**		**311**

AUSTRALIA

P.J.Hughes	c Prior b Anderson	4	c Strauss b Flintoff		17
S.M.Katich	c Broad b Onions	48	c Pietersen b Flintoff		6
*R.T.Ponting	c Strauss b Anderson	2	b Broad		38
M.E.K.Hussey	b Flintoff	51	c Collingwood b Swann		27
M.J.Clarke	c Cook b Anderson	1	b Swann		136
M.J.North	b Anderson	0	b Swann		6
†B.J.Haddin	c Cook b Broad	28	c Collingwood b Flintoff		80
M.G.Johnson	c Cook b Broad	4	b Swann		63
N.M.Hauritz	c Collingwood b Onions	24	b Flintoff		1
P.M.Siddle	c Strauss b Onions	35	b Flintoff		7
B.W.Hilfenhaus	not out	6	not out		4
Extras	(B 4, LB 6, NB 2)	12	(B 5, LB 8, NB 8)		21
Total	**(63 overs; 267 mins)**	**215**	**(107 overs; 459 mins)**		**406**

AUSTRALIA	O	M	R	W		O	M	R	W
Hilfenhaus	31	12	103	4		19	5	59	0
Johnson	21.4	2	132	3		17	2	68	0
Siddle	20	1	76	2		15.2	4	64	2
Hauritz	8.3	1	26	0		16	1	80	3
North	16.3	2	59	0					
Clarke	4	1	12	1	(5)	4	0	15	0

ENGLAND									
Anderson	21	5	55	4		21	4	86	0
Flintoff	12	4	27	1		27	4	92	5
Broad	18	1	78	2	(4)	16	3	49	1
Onions	11	1	41	3	(3)	9	0	50	0
Swann	1	0	4	0		28	3	87	4
Collingwood						6	1	29	0

FALL OF WICKETS

	E	A	E	A
Wkt	1st	1st	2nd	2nd
1st	196	4	61	17
2nd	222	10	74	34
3rd	267	103	147	78
4th	302	111	174	120
5th	317	111	260	128
6th	333	139	311	313
7th	364	148	–	356
8th	370	152	–	363
9th	378	196	–	388
10th	425	215	–	406

Umpires: B.R.Doctrove (*West Indies*) (25) and R.E.Koertzen (*South Africa*) (100).
Referee: J.J.Crowe (*New Zealand*) (35).   **Test No. 1924/318 (E888/A709)**

ENGLAND v AUSTRALIA (3rd Test)

At Edgbaston, Birmingham, on 30, 31 July, 1, 2, 3 August 2009.
Toss: Australia. Result: **MATCH DRAWN**.
Debuts: Australia – G.A.Manou.

AUSTRALIA

S.R.Watson	lbw b Onions	62	c Prior b Anderson		53
S.M.Katich	lbw b Swann	46	c Prior b Onions		26
*R.T.Ponting	c Prior b Onions	38	b Swann		5
M.E.K.Hussey	b Onions	0	c Prior b Broad		64
M.J.Clarke	lbw b Anderson	29	not out		103
M.J.North	c Prior b Anderson	12	c Anderson b Broad		96
†G.A.Manou	b Anderson	8	not out		13
M.G.Johnson	lbw b Anderson	0			
N.M.Hauritz	not out	20			
P.M.Siddle	c Prior b Anderson	13			
B.W.Hilfenhaus	c Swann b Onions	20			
Extras	(B 5, LB 7, W 2, NB 1)	15	(B 4, LB 6, W 2, NB 3)		15
Total	**(70.4 overs; 319 mins)**	**263**	**(5 wkts; 112.2 overs; 466 mins)**		**375**

ENGLAND

*A.J.Strauss	c Manou b Hilfenhaus	69
A.N.Cook	c Manou b Siddle	0
R.S.Bopara	b Hilfenhaus	23
I.R.Bell	lbw b Johnson	53
P.D.Collingwood	c Ponting b Hilfenhaus	13
†M.J.Prior	c sub (P.J.Hughes) b Hilfenhaus	41
A.Flintoff	c Clarke b Hauritz	74
S.C.J.Broad	c and b Siddle	55
G.P.Swann	c North b Johnson	24
J.M.Anderson	c Manou b Hilfenhaus	1
G.Onions	not out	2
Extras	(B 2, LB 4, W 6, NB 9)	21
Total	**(93.3 overs; 399 mins)**	**376**

ENGLAND	O	M	R	W		O	M	R	W
Anderson	24	7	80	5		21	8	47	1
Flintoff	15	2	58	0		15	0	35	0
Onions	16.4	2	58	4		19	3	74	1
Broad	13	2	51	0	(5)	16	2	38	2
Swann	2	0	4	1	(4)	31	4	119	1
Bopara						8.2	1	44	0
Collingwood						2	0	8	0

AUSTRALIA	O	M	R	W
Hilfenhaus	30	7	109	4
Siddle	21.3	3	89	3
Hauritz	18	2	57	1
Johnson	21	1	92	2
Watson	3	0	23	0

FALL OF WICKETS

	A	E	A
Wkt	1st	1st	2nd
1st	85	2	47
2nd	126	60	52
3rd	126	141	137
4th	163	159	161
5th	193	168	346
6th	202	257	–
7th	202	309	–
8th	203	348	–
9th	229	355	–
10th	263	376	–

Umpires: Alim Dar (*Pakistan*) (57) and R.E.Koertzen (*South Africa*) (101).
Referee: J.J.Crowe (*New Zealand*) (36).   **Test No. 1925/319 (E889/A710)**

ENGLAND v AUSTRALIA (4th Test)

At Headingley, Leeds, on 7, 8, 9 August 2009.
Toss: England. Result: **AUSTRALIA** won by an innings and 80 runs.
Debuts: None.

ENGLAND

*A.J.Strauss	c North b Siddle	3		lbw b Hilfenhaus	32
A.N.Cook	c Clarke b Clark	30		c Haddin b Johnson	30
R.S.Bopara	c Hussey b Hilfenhaus	1		lbw b Hilfenhaus	0
I.R.Bell	c Haddin b Johnson	8		c Ponting b Johnson	3
P.D.Collingwood	c Ponting b Clark	0		lbw b Johnson	4
†M.J.Prior	not out	37	(7)	c Haddin b Hilfenhaus	22
S.C.J.Broad	c Katich b Clark	3	(8)	c Watson b Siddle	61
G.P.Swann	c Clarke b Siddle	0	(9)	c Haddin b Johnson	62
S.J.Harmison	c Haddin b Siddle	0	(10)	not out	19
J.M.Anderson	c Haddin b Siddle	3	(6)	c Ponting b Hilfenhaus	4
G.Onions	c Katich b Siddle	0		b Johnson	0
Extras	(B 5, LB 8, W 1, NB 3)	17		(B 5, LB 5, W 5, NB 11)	26
Total	**(33.5 overs; 163 mins)**	**102**		**(61.3 overs; 275 mins)**	**263**

AUSTRALIA

S.R.Watson	lbw b Onions	51
S.M.Katich	c Bopara b Harmison	0
*R.T.Ponting	lbw b Broad	78
M.E.K.Hussey	lbw b Broad	10
M.J.Clarke	lbw b Onions	93
M.J.North	c Anderson b Broad	110
†B.J.Haddin	c Bell b Harmison	14
M.G.Johnson	c Bopara b Broad	27
P.M.Siddle	b Broad	0
S.R.Clark	b Broad	32
B.W.Hilfenhaus	not out	0
Extras	(B 9, LB 14, W 4, NB 3)	30
Total	**(104.1 overs; 463 mins)**	**445**

AUSTRALIA	O	M	R	W		O	M	R	W
Hilfenhaus	7	0	20	1		19	2	60	4
Siddle	9.5	0	21	5		12	2	50	1
Johnson	7	0	30	1	(4)	19.3	3	69	5
Clark	10	4	18	3	(3)	11	1	74	0

ENGLAND	O	M	R	W
Anderson	18	3	89	0
Harmison	23	4	98	2
Onions	22	5	80	2
Broad	25.1	6	91	6
Swann	16	4	64	0

FALL OF WICKETS

	E	A	E
Wkt	1st	1st	2nd
1st	11	14	58
2nd	16	133	58
3rd	39	140	67
4th	42	151	74
5th	63	303	78
6th	72	323	86
7th	92	393	120
8th	98	394	228
9th	102	440	259
10th	102	445	263

Umpires: Asad Rauf (*Pakistan*) (25) and B.F.Bowden (*New Zealand*) (55).
Referee: R.S.Madugalle (*Sri Lanka*) (111).   **Test No. 1926/320 (E890/A711)**

ENGLAND v AUSTRALIA (5th Test)

At The Oval, London, on 20, 21, 22, 23 August 2009.
Toss: England. Result: **ENGLAND** won by 197 runs.
Debuts: England – I.J.L.Trott.

ENGLAND

*A.J.Strauss	c Haddin b Hilfenhaus	55	c Clarke b North		75
A.N.Cook	c Ponting b Siddle	10	c Clarke b North		9
I.R.Bell	b Siddle	72	c Katich b Johnson		4
P.D.Collingwood	c Hussey b Siddle	24	c Katich b Johnson		1
I.J.L.Trott	run out	41	c North b Clark		119
†M.J.Prior	c Watson b Johnson	18	run out		4
A.Flintoff	c Haddin b Johnson	7	c Siddle b North		22
S.C.J.Broad	c Ponting b Hilfenhaus	37	c Ponting b North		29
G.P.Swann	c Haddin b Siddle	18	c Haddin b Hilfenhaus		63
J.M.Anderson	lbw b Hilfenhaus	0	not out		15
S.J.Harmison	not out	12			
Extras	(B 12, LB 5, W 3, NB 18)	38	(B 1, LB 15, W 7, NB 9)		32
Total	**(90.5 overs; 414 mins)**	**332**	**(9 wkts dec; 95 overs; 408 mins)**		**373**

AUSTRALIA

S.R.Watson	lbw b Broad	34	lbw b Broad	40
S.M.Katich	c Cook b Swann	50	lbw b Swann	43
*R.T.Ponting	b Broad	8	run out	66
M.E.K.Hussey	lbw b Broad	0	c Cook b Swann	121
M.J.Clarke	c Trott b Broad	3	run out	0
M.J.North	lbw b Swann	8	st Prior b Swann	10
†B.J.Haddin	b Broad	1	c Strauss b Swann	34
M.G.Johnson	c Prior b Swann	11	c Collingwood b Harmison	0
P.M.Siddle	not out	26	c Flintoff b Harmison	10
S.R.Clark	c Cook b Swann	6	c Cook b Harmison	0
B.W.Hilfenhaus	b Flintoff	6	not out	4
Extras	(B 1, LB 5, NB 1)	7	(B 7, LB 7, NB 6)	20
Total	**(52.5 overs; 226 mins)**	**160**	**(102.2 overs; 431 mins)**	**348**

AUSTRALIA	O	M	R	W		O	M	R	W
Hilfenhaus	21.5	5	71	3		11	1	58	1
Siddle	21	6	75	4		17	3	69	0
Clark	14	5	41	0	(6)	12	2	43	1
Johnson	15	0	69	2		17	1	60	2
North	14	3	33	0	(3)	30	4	98	4
Watson	5	0	26	0					
Katich					(5)	5	2	9	0
Clarke					(7)	3	0	20	0

ENGLAND	O	M	R	W		O	M	R	W
Anderson	9	3	29	0		12	2	46	0
Flintoff	13.5	4	35	1		11	1	42	0
Swann	14	3	38	4	(4)	40.2	8	120	4
Harmison	4	1	15	0	(3)	16	5	54	3
Broad	12	1	37	5		22	4	71	1
Collingwood						1	0	1	0

FALL OF WICKETS

	E	A	E	A
Wkt	1st	1st	2nd	2nd
1st	12	73	27	86
2nd	114	89	34	90
3rd	176	93	39	217
4th	181	108	157	220
5th	229	109	168	236
6th	247	109	200	327
7th	268	111	243	327
8th	307	131	333	343
9th	308	143	373	343
10th	332	160	–	348

Umpires: Asad Rauf (*Pakistan*) (26) and B.F.Bowden (*New Zealand*) (56).
Referee: R.S.Madugalle (*Sri Lanka*) (112).   **Test No. 1927/321 (E891/A712)**

WEST INDIES v BANGLADESH (1st Test)

At Arnos Vale, Kingstown, St Vincent, on 9, 10, 11, 12, 13 July 2009.
Toss: Bangladesh. Result: **BANGLADESH** won by 95 runs.
Debuts: West Indies – R.A.Austin, T.M.Dowlin, N.O.Miller, O.J.Phillips, D.M.Richards, K.A.J.Roach, C.A.K.Walton; Bangladesh – Mahmudullah, Rubel Hossain.

BANGLADESH

Player	1st innings		2nd innings	
Tamim Iqbal	c Reifer b Best	14	c Dowlin b Bernard	128
Imrul Kayes	lbw b Sammy	33	c Roach b Austin	24
Junaid Siddique	c Dowlin b Bernard	27	c Richards b Sammy	78
Raqibul Hasan	c Sammy b Bernard	14	b Sammy	18
Mohammad Ashraful	c Walton b Best	6	lbw b Roach	3
Shakib Al Hasan	c Richards b Roach	17	c Austin b Sammy	30
†Mushfiqur Rahim	run out	36	b Roach	37
Mahmudullah	c Phillips b Roach	9	lbw b Roach	8
*Mashrafe Mortaza	c Walton b Roach	39	c Roach b Sammy	0
Shahadat Hossain	c Walton b Austin	33	not out	0
Rubel Hossain	not out	3	lbw b Sammy	1
Extras	(B 2, LB 2, W 1, NB 2)	7	(LB 9, W 2, NB 7)	18
Total	**(88.2 overs)**	**238**	**(120.1 overs)**	**345**

WEST INDIES

Player	1st innings		2nd innings	
D.M.Richards	lbw b Shakib	13	run out	14
O.J.Phillips	c Raqibul b Rubel	94	lbw b Shakib	14
R.A.Austin	c Kayes b Rubel	17	(9) lbw b Mahmudullah	0
T.M.Dowlin	lbw b Shakib	22	(3) c Kayes b Mahmudullah	19
*F.L.Reifer	c Shakib b Mahmudullah	25	(4) lhw b Mahmudullah	19
D.E.Bernard	c sub (Mehrab Hossain[2]) b Shahadat	53	(5) not out	52
†C.A.K.Walton	c Shakib b Mahmudullah	0	(6) lbw b Mahmudullah	10
D.J.G.Sammy	b Mahmudullah	48	(7) c Shahadat b Shakib	19
N.O.Miller	c Rahim b Rubel	0	(8) c Rahim b Ashraful	5
K.A.J.Roach	c sub (Mehrab Hossain[2]) b Ashraful	6	c Rahim b Mahmudullah	3
T.L.Best	not out	1	lbw b Shakib	9
Extras	(B 4, LB 3, W 2, NB 19)	28	(B 5, LB 5, W 2, NB 5)	17
Total	**(95.1 overs)**	**307**	**(70.1 overs)**	**181**

WEST INDIES	O	M	R	W		O	M	R	W
Best	17	4	58	2	(2)	13	3	49	0
Roach	23	11	46	3	(1)	26	4	67	3
Sammy	19	7	38	1	(4)	30.1	6	70	5
Bernard	11	2	30	2	(6)	4	0	32	1
Austin	13.2	5	35	1	(3)	30	4	78	1
Miller	5	1	27	0	(5)	17	4	40	0

BANGLADESH	O	M	R	W		O	M	R	W
Mashrafe Mortaza	6.3	0	26	0					
Shahadat Hossain	13	2	48	1	(1)	12	2	32	0
Shakib Al Hasan	35	10	76	2		28.1	11	39	3
Rubel Hossain	15	1	76	3	(2)	10	1	45	0
Mahmudullah	19.4	2	59	3	(4)	15	4	51	5
Mohammad Ashraful	6	0	15	1	(5)	5	1	4	1

	FALL OF WICKETS			
	B	WI	B	WI
Wkt	1st	1st	2nd	2nd
1st	45	15	82	20
2nd	49	94	228	33
3rd	79	142	258	69
4th	98	176	261	72
5th	100	227	267	82
6th	121	227	327	119
7th	149	267	342	151
8th	172	267	344	164
9th	207	306	344	172
10th	238	307	345	181

Umpires: E.A.R.de Silva (*Sri Lanka*) (40) and A.L.Hill (*New Zealand*) (10).
Referee: A.J.Pycroft (*Zimbabwe*) (3). **Test No. 1928/5 (WI458/B60)**

WEST INDIES v BANGLADESH (2nd Test)

At National Cricket Stadium, St George's, Grenada, on 17, 18, 19, 2o July 2009.
Toss: Bangladesh. Result: **BANGLADESH** won by four wickets.
Debuts: None.

WEST INDIES

D.M.Richards	c and b Mahmudullah	69	lbw b Shakib		12
O.J.Phillips	c Iqbal b Shakib	23	c Ashraful b Shakib		29
T.M.Dowlin	c Iqbal b Shakib	95	lbw b Haque		49
R.O.Hinds	c and b Mahmudullah	2	c Mahmudullah b Shakib		2
*F.L.Reifer	lbw b Mahmudullah	1	lbw b Mahmudullah		3
D.E.Bernard	c Ashraful b Shakib	17	st Rahim b Haque		69
D.J.G.Sammy	lbw b Haque	1	c Raqibul b Haque		22
†C.A.K.Walton	c Ashraful b Haque	2	c Mahmudullah b Shakib		1
R.A.Austin	hit wkt b Shahadat	19	c Iqbal b Shahadat		3
T.L.Best	b Haque	0	c Rahim b Shakib		12
K.A.J.Roach	not out	4	not out		1
Extras	(LB 1, NB 3)	4	(LB 2, NB 4)		6
Total	**(76.1 overs)**	**237**	**(70.5 overs)**		**209**

BANGLADESH

Tamim Iqbal	c Walton b Bernard	37	c Walton b Sammy		18
Imrul Kayes	c Walton b Sammy	14	c Sammy b Roach		8
Enamul Haque[2]	c Walton b Roach	13			
Junaid Siddique	b Austin	7	(3) c Reifer b Sammy		5
Raqibul Hasan	c Walton b Roach	44	(4) c and b Sammy		65
Mohammad Ashraful	c Sammy b Hinds	12	(5) c Walton b Sammy		3
*Shakib Al Hasan	c Austin b Roach	16	(6) not out		96
†Mushfiqur Rahim	c Walton b Roach	48	(7) c and b Sammy		12
Mahmudullah	c Austin b Roach	28	(8) not out		0
Shahadat Hossain	c Richards b Roach	0			
Rubel Hossain	not out	1			
Extras	(LB 2, W 3, NB 7)	12	(B 1, LB 3, W 2, NB 4)		10
Total	**(79.5 overs)**	**232**	**(6 wkts; 54.4 overs)**		**217**

BANGLADESH	O	M	R	W		O	M	R	W
Shahadat Hossain	9	2	30	1	(2)	4	0	18	1
Rubel Hossain	6	0	27	0	(1)	9	1	34	0
Enamul Haque[2]	24	2	62	3		17	3	48	3
Shakib Al Hasan	21.1	7	59	3		24.5	3	70	5
Mahmudullah	13	2	44	3		15	1	37	1
Mohammad Ashraful	3	0	14	0		1	1	0	0

WEST INDIES	O	M	R	W		O	M	R	W
Roach	23.5	8	48	6	(3)	13.4	4	68	1
Best	17	3	47	0	(1)	9	0	38	0
Sammy	15	3	45	1	(4)	16	1	55	5
Bernard	8	0	29	1	(2)	9	1	33	0
Austin	8	0	29	1		3	0	13	0
Hinds	8	1	32	1		4	0	6	0

FALL OF WICKETS

	WI	B	WI	B
Wkt	1st	1st	2nd	2nd
1st	60	26	20	27
2nd	104	51	72	29
3rd	106	75	84	49
4th	114	77	95	173
5th	157	106	110	173
6th	158	150	166	201
7th	160	157	167	–
8th	219	219	187	–
9th	220	223	201	–
10th	237	232	209	–

Umpires: E.A.R.de Silva (*Sri Lanka*) (41) and A.L.Hill (*New Zealand*) (11).
Referee: A.J.Pycroft (*Zimbabwe*) (4).   **Test No. 1929/6 (WI459/B61)**

44

SRI LANKA v NEW ZEALAND (1st Test)

At Galle International Stadium, on 18, 19, 20, 21, 22 August 2009.
Toss: New Zealand. Result: **SRI LANKA** won by 202 runs.
Debuts: None.

SRI LANKA

N.T.Paranavitana	c McCullum b Martin	0	c Taylor b O'Brien		5
T.M.Dilshan	b O'Brien	92	not out		123
*K.C.Sangakkara	c Flynn b Martin	8	run out		46
D.P.M.D.Jayawardena	c Taylor b O'Brien	114	c and b Patel		27
T.T.Samaraweera	c Patel b Vettori	159	c Taylor b Vettori		20
A.D.Mathews	c McCullum b Vettori	39			
†H.A.P.W.Jayawardena	c Flynn b Vettori	7	(6) not out		30
K.M.D.N.Kulasekara	c McCullum b Martin	18			
T.Thushara	c O'Brien b Vettori	0			
M.Muralitharan	c McCullum b Martin	8			
B.A.W.Mendis	not out	0			
Extras	(B 1, LB 2, W 2, NB 2)	7	(B 5, LB 3)		8
Total	**(117.4 overs; 468 mins)**	**452**	**(4 wkts dec; 49 overs; 208 mins)**		**259**

NEW ZEALAND

T.G.McIntosh	lbw b Muralitharan	69	(4) c Samaraweera b Thushara		0
M.J.Guptill	b Thushara	24	(1) b Thushara		18
D.R.Flynn	b Mendis	14	(2) c D.P.M.D.Jayawardena b Kulasekara		0
J.S.Patel	lbw b Muralitharan	26	(9) st H.A.P.W.Jayawardena b Muralitharan		22
L.R.P.L.Taylor	c H.A.P.W.Jayawardena b Thushara	35	(3) c H.A.P.W.Jayawardena b D.P.M.D.Jayawardena		16
J.D.Ryder	b Kulasekara	42	(7) c H.A.P.W.Jayawardena b Muralitharan		24
†B.B.McCullum	b Thushara	1	(8) run out		29
J.D.P.Oram	c sub (B.S.M.Warnapura) b Muralitharan	12	(5) lbw b Mendis		21
*D.L.Vettori	b Thushara	42	(6) c H.A.P.W.Jayawardena b Mendis		67
I.E.O'Brien	c H.A.P.W.Jayawardena b Muralitharan	9	c Paranavitana b Muralitharan		5
C.S.Martin	not out	2	not out		0
Extras	(B 6, LB 5, W 1, NB 11)	23	(B 4, LB 1, NB 3)		8
Total	**(116 overs; 451 mins)**	**299**	**(71.5 overs; 290 mins)**		**210**

NEW ZEALAND	O	M	R	W		O	M	R	W
Martin	23	5	77	4		5	1	25	0
O'Brien	21	1	125	2		8	12	45	1
Oram	7	1	25	0		5	0	31	0
Vettori	37.4	9	78	4		19	3	81	1
Patel	24	3	120	0		12	0	69	1
Ryder	5	1	24	0					

SRI LANKA	O	M	R	W		O	M	R	W
Kulasekara	10	2	41	1		8	2	20	1
Thushara	23	2	81	4		14	3	37	2
Mendis	39	8	85	1		18.5	4	50	2
Muralitharan	42	10	73	4		27	4	88	3
Paranavitana	2	0	8	0					
D.P.M.D.Jayawardena					(5)	4	1	10	1

FALL OF WICKETS

	SL	NZ	SL	NZ
Wkt	1st	1st	2nd	2nd
1st	0	45	19	1
2nd	16	80	120	37
3rd	134	129	174	39
4th	300	180	205	45
5th	386	188	—	86
6th	408	195	—	134
7th	444	223	—	167
8th	444	259	—	204
9th	452	290	—	210
10th	452	299	—	210

Umpires: D.J.Harper (*Australia*) (84) and N.J.Llong (*England*) (5).
Referee: A.J.Pycroft (*Zimbabwe*) (5).   Test No. 1930/25 (SL188/NZ352)

SRI LANKA v NEW ZEALAND (2nd Test)

At Sinhalese Sports Club, Colombo, on 26, 27, 28, 29, 30 August 2009.
Toss: Sri Lanka. Result: **SRI LANKA** won by 96 runs.
Debuts: None.

SRI LANKA

N.T.Paranavitana	c Taylor b Vettori	19	(2) c McCullum b Vettori		34
T.M.Dilshan	c and b O'Brien	29	(1) c Guptill b Patel		33
*K.C.Sangakkara	c Oram b Vettori	50	c Taylor b Patel		109
D.P.M.D.Jayawardena	c McCullum b O'Brien	92	c Taylor b O'Brien		96
T.T.Samaraweera	c McCullum b Patel	143	lbw b Vettori		25
C.K.Kapugedera	c Vettori b Patel	35	not out		7
†H.A.P.W.Jayawardena	c O'Brien b Martin	17			
K.T.G.D.Prasad	c Taylor b Patel	6			
H.M.R.K.B.Herath	lbw b Patel	0			
M.Muralitharan	not out	17			
T.Thushara	c Patel b Vettori	0			
Extras	(B 2, LB 5, NB 1)	8	(LB 1, W 2, NB 4)		7
Total	(130.3 overs; 549 mins)	416	(5 wkts dec; 85.2 overs; 352 mins)		311

NEW ZEALAND

T.G.McIntosh	lbw b Prasad	5	b Prasad		7
M.J.Guptill	c Muralitharan b Thushara	35	c H.A.P.W.Jayawardena b Herath		28
D.R.Flynn	c H.A.P.W.Jayawardena b Thushara	13	lbw b Herath		50
L.R.P.L.Taylor	c H.A.P.W.Jayawardena b Herath	81	c D.P.M.D.Jayawardena b Herath		27
J.D.Ryder	c Paranavitana b Herath	23	lbw b Herath		38
J.S.Patel	c D.P.M.D.Jayawardena b Muralitharan	1	(9) c Kapugedera b Muralitharan		12
†B.B.McCullum	c D.P.M.D.Jayawardena b Muralitharan	18	(6) b Muralitharan		13
J.D.P.Oram	c Kapugedera b Herath	24	(7) c Sangakkara b Dilshan		56
*D.L.Vettori	c Kapugedera b Dilshan	23	(8) c Herath b Muralitharan		140
I.E.O'Brien	lbw b Muralitharan	4	c H.A.P.W.Jayawardena b Herath		12
C.S.Martin	not out	0	not out		0
Extras	(LB 3, W 2, NB 2)	7	(LB 13, NB 1)		14
Total	(77.4 overs; 363 mins)	234	(123.5 overs; 475 mins)		397

NEW ZEALAND	O	M	R	W		O	M	R	W		FALL OF WICKETS				
												SL	NZ	SL	NZ
Martin	24	3	81	1	(3)	9	0	34	0		Wkt	1st	1st	2nd	2nd
O'Brien	22	4	73	2		15.2	1	77	1		1st	34	14	56	36
Vettori	40.3	12	104	3	(1)	24	4	62	2		2nd	75	49	89	41
Oram	21	7	56	0							3rd	115	63	262	97
Patel	20	3	78	4	(4)	34	2	122	2		4th	295	148	301	131
Ryder	3	1	17	0	(5)	3	0	15	0		5th	367	149	311	158
SRI LANKA											6th	389	183	–	176
Dilshan	3	0	12	1	(6)	6	0	15	1		7th	396	183	–	300
Thushara	9	2	37	2		23.3	1	78	0		8th	396	226	–	318
Prasad	6	0	41	1		15	1	56	1		9th	415	234	–	387
Herath	34	11	70	3		48	9	139	5		10th	416	234	–	397
Muralitharan	25.4	2	71	3		28.2	2	85	3						
Paranavitana					(1)	1	0	2	0						
Kapugedera						2	0	9	0						

Umpires: D.J.Harper (*Australia*) (85) and N.J.Llong (*England*) (6).
Referee: A.J.Pycroft (*Zimbabwe*) (6).   **Test No. 1931/26 (SL189/NZ353)**

INDIA v SRI LANKA (1st Test)

At Sardar Patel Stadium, Motera, Ahmedabad, on 16, 17, 18, 19, 20 November 2009.
Toss: India. Result: **MATCH DRAWN**.
Debuts: None.

INDIA

G.Gambhir	b Welegedara	1	c Prasad b Herath		114
V.Sehwag	lbw b Welegedara	16	c Mathews b Herath		51
R.Dravid	b Welegedara	177	lbw b Welegedara		38
S.R.Tendulkar	b Welegedara	4	(5) not out		100
V.V.S.Laxman	b Prasad	0	(6) not out		51
Yuvraj Singh	c Dilshan b Muralitharan	68			
*†M.S.Dhoni	c H.A.P.W.Jayawardena b Prasad	110			
Harbhajan Singh	b Muralitharan	22			
Z.Khan	lbw b Herath	12			
A.Mishra	not out	7	(4) c Dilshan b Mathews		24
I.Sharma	st H.A.P.W.Jayawardena b Muralitharan	0			
Extras	(B 2, LB 2, W 1, NB 4)	9	(B 12, LB 9, W 2, NB 11)		34
Total	**(104.5 overs; 460 mins)**	**426**	**(4 wkts; 129 overs)**		**412**

SRI LANKA

T.M.Dilshan	c Dravid b Khan	112
N.T.Paranavitana	c Dhoni b Sharma	35
*K.C.Sangakkara	c Tendulkar b Khan	31
D.P.M.D.Jayawardena	b Mishra	275
T.T.Samaraweera	c Yuvraj b Sharma	70
A.D.Mathews	c Gambhir b Harbhajan	17
†H.A.P.W.Jayawardena	not out	154
K.T.G.D.Prasad	c Mishra b Harbhajan	21
H.M.R.K.B.Herath		
M.Muralitharan		
U.W.M.B.C.A.Welegedara		
Extras	(B 5, LB 16, W 4, NB 20)	45
Total	**(7 wkts dec; 202.4 overs; 843 mins)**	**760**

SRI LANKA	O	M	R	W		O	M	R	W
Welegedara	22	4	87	4		21	1	76	1
Prasad	22	1	106	2		13	0	56	0
Mathews	12	1	50	0	(5)	15	6	29	1
Muralitharan	25.5	4	97	3		38	6	124	0
Herath	22	2	79	1	(3)	40	6	97	2
Dilshan	1	0	3	0		1	0	2	0
Paranavitana						1	0	7	0

INDIA	O	M	R	W
Khan	36	6	109	2
Sharma	33	0	135	2
Harbhajan Singh	48.4	4	189	2
Mishra	58	6	203	1
Yuvraj Singh	16	1	64	0
Tendulkar	7	0	20	0
Sehwag	4	1	19	0

FALL OF WICKETS

	I	SL	I
Wkt	1st	1st	2nd
1st	14	74	81
2nd	27	189	169
3rd	31	194	209
4th	32	332	275
5th	157	375	–
6th	381	726	–
7th	389	760	–
8th	414	–	–
9th	426	–	–
10th	426	–	–

Umpires: D.J.Harper (*Australia*) (86) and A.L.Hill (*New Zealand*) (12).
Referee: J.J.Crowe (*New Zealand*) (37). **Test No. 1932/30 (I431/SL190)**

INDIA v SRI LANKA (2nd Test)

At Green Park, Kanpur, on 24, 25, 26, 27 November 2009.
Toss: India. Result: **INDIA** won by an innings and 144 runs.
Debuts: India – P.P.Ojha.

INDIA

G.Gambhir	c and b Muralitharan	167
V.Sehwag	c Dilshan b Muralitharan	131
R.Dravid	run out	144
S.R.Tendulkar	c Samaraweera b Mendis	40
V.V.S.Laxman	c Dilshan b Herath	63
Yuvraj Singh	c Sangakkara b Mendis	67
*†M.S.Dhoni	b Herath	4
Harbhajan Singh	b Herath	5
Z.Khan	c D.P.M.D.Jayawardena b Herath	1
S.Sreesanth	lbw b Herath	0
P.P.Ojha	not out	1
Extras	(B 4, LB 11, NB 4)	19
Total	**(154 overs; 622 mins)**	**642**

SRI LANKA

T.M.Dilshan	c Ojha b Khan	0	(2) c Dhoni b Sreesanth		11
N.T.Paranavitana	c Dhoni b Sreesanth	38	(1) lbw b Sehwag		20
*K.C.Sangakkara	b Sreesanth	44	b Harbhajan		11
D.P.M.D.Jayawardena	c Tendulkar b Ojha	47	run out		10
T.T.Samaraweera	b Sreesanth	2	not out		78
A.D.Mathews	b Harbhajan	13	c Dravid b Khan		15
†H.A.P.W.Jayawardena	c Dhoni b Sreesanth	39	b Harbhajan		29
H.M.R.K.B.Herath	b Sreesanth	11	lbw b Harbhajan		13
M.Muralitharan	lbw b Ojha	6	b Ojha		29
U.W.M.B.C.A.Welegedara	lbw b Harbhajan	7	(11) c and b Ojha		4
B.A.W.Mendis	not out	6	(10) lbw b Yuvraj		27
Extras	(B 9, LB 2, NB 5)	16	(B 7, LB 1, NB 14)		22
Total	**(84 overs; 367 mins)**	**229**	**(65.3 overs; 294 mins)**		**269**

SRI LANKA	O	M	R	W	O	M	R	W
Welegedara	26	4	103	0				
Mathews	17	2	49	0				
Herath	33	2	121	5				
Mendis	38	3	162	2				
Muralitharan	37	0	175	2				
Dilshan	3	0	17	0				
INDIA								
Khan	17	5	51	1	11	0	63	1
Sreesanth	22	4	75	5	11	4	47	1
Harbhajan Singh	21	5	54	2	22	2	98	3
Ojha	23	12	37	2	15.3	4	36	2
Yuvraj Singh	1	0	1	0	(7) 2	0	7	1
Sehwag					(4) 3	0	4	1
Tendulkar					(6) 1	0	6	0

FALL OF WICKETS			
	I	SL	SL
Wkt	1st	1st	2nd
1st	233	0	13
2nd	370	82	37
3rd	464	101	54
4th	511	111	54
5th	613	134	79
6th	619	194	140
7th	639	204	154
8th	641	216	191
9th	641	219	264
10th	642	229	269

Umpires: A.L.Hill (*New Zealand*) (13) and N.J.Llong (*England*) (7).
Referee: J.J.Crowe (*New Zealand*) (38). **Test No. 1933/31 (I432/SL191)**

INDIA v SRI LANKA (3rd Test)

At Brabourne Stadium, Mumbai, 2, 3, 4, 5, 6 December 2009.
Toss: Sri Lanka. Result: **INDIA** won by an innings and 24 runs.
Debuts: None.

SRI LANKA

N.T.Paranavitana	c Dravid b Harbhajan	53	lbw b Sreesanth		54
T.M.Dilshan	c Vijay b Harbhajan	109	lbw b Harbhajan		16
*K.C.Sangakkara	c Dhoni b Ojha	18	c Dhoni b Khan		137
D.P.M.D.Jayawardena	c Sehwag b Sreesanth	29	c Dhoni b Khan		12
T.T.Samaraweera	c Vijay b Harbhajan	1	c Laxman b Khan		0
A.D.Mathews	run out	99	c Dhoni b Ojha		5
†H.A.P.W.Jayawardena	c Harbhajan b Ojha	43	lbw b Ojha		32
K.M.D.N.Kulasekara	c Dhoni b Ojha	12	c Laxman b Khan		19
H.M.R.K.B.Herath	c Dravid b Harbhajan	1	c Ojha b Khan		3
M.Muralitharan	not out	4	c Dhoni b Harbhajan		14
U.W.M.B.C.A.Welegedara	lbw b Ojha	8	not out		0
Extras	(B 4, LB 6, W 2, NB 4)	16	(B 12, LB 1, W 1, NB 3)		17
Total	**(94.4 overs; 415 mins)**	**393**	**(100.4 overs; 418 mins)**		**309**

INDIA

M.Vijay	lbw b Herath	87
V.Sehwag	c and b Muralitharan	293
R.Dravid	c H.A.P.W.Jayawardena b Welegedara	74
S.R.Tendulkar	b Kulasekara	53
V.V.S.Laxman	c Kulasekara b Muralitharan	62
Yuvraj Singh	c Mathews b Herath	23
*†M.S.Dhoni	not out	100
Harbhajan Singh	b Muralitharan	1
Z.Khan	c Kulasekara b Muralitharan	7
S.Sreesanth	lbw b Herath	8
P.P.Ojha	not out	5
Extras	(LB 3, NB 10)	13
Total	**(9 wkts dec; 163.3 overs; 705 mins)**	**726**

INDIA	O	M	R	W	O	M	R	W
Khan	19	2	70	1	(3) 21	5	72	5
Sreesanth	16	1	82	1	(4) 13	4	36	1
Harbhajan Singh	32	3	112	4	(1) 34.4	5	80	2
Ojha	23.4	1	101	3	(2) 23	4	84	2
Yuvraj Singh	4	0	18	0	9	2	24	0

SRI LANKA	O	M	R	W
Welegedara	30	3	131	1
Kulasekara	20	1	105	1
Herath	53.3	2	240	3
Muralitharan	51	4	195	4
Mathews	6	0	36	0
Dilshan	3	0	16	0

FALL OF WICKETS			
	SL	I	SL
Wkt	1st	1st	2nd
1st	93	221	29
2nd	128	458	119
3rd	187	487	135
4th	188	558	137
5th	262	591	144
6th	329	610	208
7th	359	615	278
8th	362	647	282
9th	379	670	307
10th	393	–	309

Umpires: D.J.Harper (*Australia*) (87) and N.J.Llong (*England*) (8).
Referee: J.J.Crowe (*New Zealand*) (39).   **Test No. 1934/32 (I433/SL192)**

NEW ZEALAND v PAKISTAN (1st Test)

At University Oval, Dunedin, on 24, 25, 26, 27, 28 November 2009.
Toss: Pakistan. Result: **NEW ZEALAND** won by 32 runs.
Debuts: Pakistan – Umar Akmal.

NEW ZEALAND

T.G.McIntosh	b Aamer	0	(2)	lbw b Asif	31
M.J.Guptill	c Alam b Aamer	60	(1)	b Aamer	0
D.R.Flynn	c Kamran Akmal b Asif	8		lbw b Aamer	0
L.R.P.L.Taylor	c Farhat b Ajmal	94		run out	59
P.G.Fulton	b Asif	29		lbw b Gul	0
G.D.Elliott	c Kamran Akmal b Asif	8		c Kamran Akmal b Gul	25
†B.B.McCullum	b Gul	78		c Kamran Akmal b Asif	0
*D.L.Vettori	c Kamran Akmal b Gul	99		c Alam b Asif	8
S.E.Bond	c Kamran Akmal b Asif	22		b Asif	7
I.E.O'Brien	not out	13		lbw b Gul	4
C.S.Martin	lbw b Ajmal	0		not out	1
Extras	(LB 14, W 1, NB 3)	18		(B 4, LB 5, W 1, NB 3, Pen 5)	18
Total	**(131.5 overs; 573 mins)**	**429**		**(67 overs; 310 mins)**	**153**

PAKISTAN

Khurram Manzoor	b Martin	6		c McCullum b Bond	4
Imran Farhat	lbw b Martin	22		c McIntosh b Martin	1
Fawad Alam	c McCullum b Bond	29		c Fulton b Bond	5
*Mohammad Yousuf	c and b Bond	17		c McCullum b Martin	41
Umar Akmal	c Fulton b Bond	129		c and b Bond	75
Shoaib Malik	b Bond	2		c McCullum b O'Brien	32
†Kamran Akmal	c Taylor b Vettori	82		lbw b O'Brien	27
Mohammad Aamer	c Vettori b Bond	26		c and b Vettori	15
Umar Gul	lbw b Vettori	6		c Vettori b O'Brien	4
Mohammad Asif	c McIntosh b Martin	10		c Taylor b Vettori	0
Saeed Ajmal	not out	1		not out	1
Extras	(NB 2)	2		(B 9, LB 1, W 2, NB 1)	13
Total	**(96.5 overs; 402 mins)**	**332**		**(76 overs; 323 mins)**	**218**

PAKISTAN	O	M	R	W	O	M	R	W
Mohammad Aamer	24	3	87	2	16	7	29	2
Mohammad Asif	34	6	108	4	20	6	43	4
Umar Gul	36	10	129	2	14	3	41	3
Saeed Ajmal	37.5	10	91	2	17	5	26	0

NEW ZEALAND	O	M	R	W	O	M	R	W
Bond	27.5	4	107	5	21	5	46	3
Martin	21	8	63	3	16	4	45	2
O'Brien	21	3	98	0	23	3	63	3
Vettori	27	7	64	2	14	1	51	2
Elliott					2	0	3	0

FALL OF WICKETS

	NZ	P	NZ	P
Wkt	1st	1st	2nd	2nd
1st	0	11	0	4
2nd	27	43	0	6
3rd	144	74	87	24
4th	192	79	91	95
5th	210	85	112	161
6th	211	261	115	195
7th	375	293	123	197
8th	402	302	143	203
9th	428	320	150	213
10th	429	332	153	218

Umpires: B.R.Doctrove (*West Indies*) (26) and S.J.A.Taufel (*Australia*) (60).
Referee: A.G.Hurst (*Australia*) (34).   **Test No. 1935/46 (NZ354/P341)**

NEW ZEALAND v PAKISTAN (2nd Test)

At Basin Reserve, Wellington, on 3, 4, 5, 6 December 2009.
Toss: New Zealand. Result: **PAKISTAN** won by 141 runs.
Debuts: None.

PAKISTAN

Imran Farhat	c Taylor b Vettori	32			c Fulton b O'Brien		35
Salman Butt	c Tuffey b O'Brien	29			c Taylor b O'Brien		18
Umar Akmal	b Tuffey	46	(5)		c Vettori b Martin		52
*Mohammad Yousuf	lbw b Vettori	0	(3)		lbw b Martin		83
Misbah-ul-Haq	lbw b Vettori	21	(4)		c McCullum b O'Brien		33
Shoaib Malik	c Vettori b Tuffey	9			c McCullum b Elliott		3
†Kamran Akmal	c Vettori b Tuffey	70			c McCullum b Elliott		0
Mohammad Aamer	c Taylor b Vettori	21			c Guptill b Martin		9
Umar Gul	c O'Brien b Tuffey	31			c Fulton b O'Brien		1
Mohammad Asif	c and b Vettori	4	(11)		not out		0
Danish Kaneria	not out	0	(10)		c Taylor b Martin		0
Extras	(W 1)	1			(B 4, LB 1)		5
Total	**(88.2 overs; 384 mins)**	**264**			**(86.3 overs; 361 mins)**		**239**

NEW ZEALAND

T.G.McIntosh	c Butt b Asif	4	(2)	lbw b Asif		2
M.J.Guptill	c Kamran Akmal b Aamer	0	(1)	b Asif		15
D.R.Flynn	lbw b Asif	29		c Kamran Akmal b Asif		20
L.R.P.L.Taylor	b Gul	30		c Misbah b Aamer		97
P.G.Fulton	lbw b Gul	0		c Kamran Akmal b Aamer		13
G.D.Elliott	c and b Kaneria	20		b Kaneria		6
†B.B.McCullum	c Malik b Asif	0		c Kamran Akmal b Kaneria		24
*D.L.Vettori	c Misbah b Kaneria	6		c Umar Akmal b Kaneria		40
D.R.Tuffey	c Yousuf b Asif	3		lbw b Kaneria		3
I.E.O'Brien	c Farhat b Kaneria	0		c Malik b Asif		31
C.S.Martin	not out	0		not out		0
Extras	(LB 7)	7		(B 6, LB 6)		12
Total	**(36.5 overs; 176 mins)**	**99**		**(82.5 overs; 370 mins)**		**263**

NEW ZEALAND	O	M	R	W	O	M	R	W	FALL OF WICKETS				
										P	NZ	P	NZ
Martin	20	2	64	0	19	4	52	4					
Tuffey	23.2	5	64	4	16	3	45	0	Wkt	1st	1st	2nd	2nd
O'Brien	23	4	78	2	(4) 21.3	6	64	4	1st	60	1	49	4
Vettori	22	6	58	4	(3) 25	11	63	0	2nd	66	5	54	36
Elliott					5	1	8	2	3rd	66	48	131	37
									4th	119	52	197	80
PAKISTAN									5th	131	85	210	108
Mohammad Aamer	11	2	25	1	16	3	64	2	6th	156	85	210	186
Mohammad Asif	12.5	2	40	4	23.5	9	67	5	7th	193	95	230	206
Umar Gul	7	2	21	2	(4) 11	2	41	0	8th	257	96	239	212
Danish Kaneria	6	2	6	3	(3) 31	6	74	3	9th	264	96	239	252
Shoaib Malik					1	0	5	0	10th	264	99	239	263

Umpires: R.E.Koertzen (*South Africa*) (102) and S.J.A.Taufel (*Australia*) (61).
Referee: A.G.Hurst (*Australia*) (35).   Test No. 1936/47 (NZ355/P342)

NEW ZEALAND v PAKISTAN (3rd Test)

At McLean Park, Napier, on 11, 12, 13, 14, 15 December 2009.
Toss: Pakistan. Result: **MATCH DRAWN**.
Debuts: New Zealand – B.J.Watling.

PAKISTAN

Imran Farhat	not out	117	c and b Guptill		61
Salman Butt	b Southee	9	c and b Guptill		66
Faisal Iqbal	c Guptill b O'Brien	6	c Taylor b Martin		67
*Mohammad Yousuf	c McIntosh b O'Brien	0	c McCullum b O'Brien		89
Umar Akmal	c Guptill b O'Brien	0	c McCullum b Southee		77
Misbah-ul-Haq	c McCullum b O'Brien	0	st McCullum b Vettori		7
†Kamran Akmal	c Guptill b Martin	22	not out		56
Mohammad Aamer	c McCullum b Tuffey	23	c Martin b Vettori		7
Umar Gul	c McCullum b Tuffey	24	c Flynn b O'Brien		0
Mohammad Asif	c McCullum b Tuffey	0	(11) lbw b Guptill		0
Danish Kaneria	c McCullum b Tuffey	16	(10) c McCullum b Southee		11
Extras	(LB 2, NB 4)	6	(B 3, LB 2, W 1, NB 3, Pen 5)		14
Total	**(64.3 overs; 286 mins)**	223	**(193.2 overs; 756 mins)**		455

NEW ZEALAND

T.G.McIntosh	c Kamran Akmal b Kaneria	74	not out	23
B.J.Watling	c Umar Akmal b Asif	18	not out	60
M.J.Guptill	lbw b Kaneria	13		
L.R.P.L.Taylor	c Yousuf b Kaneria	21		
D.R.Flynn	c Kamran Akmal b Kaneria	5		
*D.L.Vettori	c Umar Akmal b Asif	134		
†B.B.McCullum	c Iqbal b Gul	89		
D.R.Tuffey	not out	80		
T.G.Southee	lbw b Kaneria	0		
I.E.O'Brien	st Kamran Akmal b Kaneria	19		
C.S.Martin	lbw b Kaneria	0		
Extras	(B 8, LB 4, W 2, NB 4)	18	(B 2, LB 1, NB 4)	7
Total	**(139 overs; 606 mins)**	471	**(0 wkts; 19 overs; 86 mins)**	90

NEW ZEALAND	O	M	R	W	O	M	R	W	FALL OF WICKETS				
Martin	9	0	37	1	32	6	82	1		P	NZ	P	NZ
Southee	17	4	62	1	31	8	64	2	*Wkt*	*1st*	*1st*	*2nd*	*2nd*
O'Brien	15	5	35	4	40	6	108	2	1st	14	60	129	–
Tuffey	15.3	4	52	4	21	2	61	0	2nd	39	82	146	–
Vettori	8	0	35	0	56	25	93	2	3rd	43	118	274	–
Guptill					13.2	2	37	3	4th	51	136	333	–
									5th	51	145	361	–
									6th	90	321	397	–
PAKISTAN									7th	159	408	421	–
Mohammad Aamer	22	6	74	0	(2) 6	1	27	0	8th	194	409	423	–
Mohammad Asif	31	10	103	2	(1) 5	0	15	0	9th	194	471	449	–
Umar Gul	33	5	114	1	(4) 5	0	21	0	10th	223	471	455	–
Danish Kaneria	53	10	168	7	(3) 3	0	24	0					

Umpires: B.R.Doctrove (*West Indies*) (27) and R.E.Koertzen (*South Africa*) (103).
Referee: A.G.Hurst (*Australia*) (36).   **Test No. 1937/48 (NZ356/P343)**

AUSTRALIA v WEST INDIES (1st Test)

At Woolloongabba, Brisbane, on 26, 27, 28 November 2009.
Toss: Australia. Result: **AUSTRALIA** won by an innings and 65 runs.
Debuts: West Indies – A.B.Barath, R.Rampaul.

AUSTRALIA

S.R.Watson	lbw b Taylor	0
S.M.Katich	c Ramdin b Bravo	92
*R.T.Ponting	c Ramdin b Roach	55
M.E.K.Hussey	c and b Benn	66
M.J.Clarke	c Gayle b Bravo	41
M.J.North	c Ramdin b Bravo	79
†B.J.Haddin	c Ramdin b Rampaul	38
M.G.Johnson	c Ramdin b Benn	7
N.M.Hauritz	not out	50
P.M.Siddle	not out	20
B.W.Hilfenhaus		
Extras	(B 2, LB 9, W 1, NB 20)	32
Total	**(8 wkts dec; 135 overs; 632 mins)**	**480**

WEST INDIES

*C.H.Gayle	lbw b Hilfenhaus	31	lbw b Hilfenhaus	1
A.B.Barath	c Watson b Johnson	15	lbw b Watson	104
T.M.Dowlin	c Watson b Hauritz	62	b Hilfenhaus	4
S.Chanderpaul	lbw b Siddle	2	c Katich b Hilfenhaus	2
D.J.Bravo	c Watson b Johnson	0	c Hilfenhaus b Hussey	23
B.P.Nash	c Haddin b Watson	18	lbw b Hauritz	7
†D.Ramdin	c North b Johnson	54	c Haddin b Hauritz	16
S.J.Benn	c Siddle b Hilfenhaus	28	(9) not out	15
J.E.Taylor	c Katich b Hauritz	8	(8) c Hilfenhaus b Watson	0
K.A.J.Roach	c Clarke b Hauritz	0	c Hussey b Siddle	5
R.Rampaul	not out	1	c Haddin b Johnson	0
Extras	(B 1, LB 3, NB 5)	9	(LB 4, NB 6)	10
Total	**(63 overs; 280 mins)**	**228**	**(52.1 overs; 225 mins)**	**187**

WEST INDIES	O	M	R	W	O	M	R	W
Taylor	9	2	43	1				
Roach	25	4	76	1				
Rampaul	26	4	110	1				
Bravo	32	4	118	3				
Benn	34	5	86	2				
Gayle	9	0	36	0				

AUSTRALIA	O	M	R	W	O	M	R	W
Hilfenhaus	16	6	50	2	7	3	20	3
Siddle	13	4	51	1	10	3	41	1
Johnson	19	4	75	3	9.1	1	35	1
Watson	9	0	31	1	10	0	44	2
Hauritz	6	3	17	3	14	1	40	2
Hussey					2	0	3	1

FALL OF WICKETS

	A	WI	WI
Wkt	1st	1st	2nd
1st	0	49	6
2nd	126	49	18
3rd	200	58	39
4th	253	63	105
5th	287	96	141
6th	371	174	154
7th	386	212	158
8th	444	221	170
9th	–	221	187
10th	–	228	187

Umpires: Asad Rauf (*Pakistan*) (27) and I.J.Gould (*England*) (7).
Referee: B.C.Broad (*England*) (36). **Test No. 1938/106 (A713/WI460)**

AUSTRALIA v WEST INDIES (2nd Test)

At Adelaide Oval, on 4, 5, 6, 7, 8 December 2009.
Toss: West Indies. Result: **MATCH DRAWN**.
Debuts: None.

WEST INDIES

*C.H.Gayle	c Haddin b Bollinger	26		not out	165
A.B.Barath	c Hussey b Bollinger	3		run out	17
R.R.Sarwan	c Clarke b Johnson	28		c Haddin b Johnson	7
S.Chanderpaul	c Haddin b Watson	62		lbw b Bollinger	27
B.P.Nash	b Johnson	92		b Watson	24
D.J.Bravo	b Hauritz	104		c Hauritz b Johnson	22
†D.Ramdin	b Watson	4		b Johnson	0
D.J.G.Sammy	lbw b Siddle	44		c Ponting b Bollinger	10
S.J.Benn	lbw b Hauritz	17		c Siddle b Johnson	5
K.A.J.Roach	c Haddin b Johnson	2	(11)	c Ponting b Bollinger	8
R.Rampaul	not out	40	(10)	b Johnson	14
Extras	(B 5, LB 14, W 5, NB 5)	29		(B 8, LB 3, W 1, NB 6)	18
Total	**(124.1 overs; 542 mins)**	**451**		**(99.5 overs; 441 mins)**	**317**

AUSTRALIA

S.R.Watson	b Benn	96		c Bravo b Sammy	48
S.M.Katich	c Barath b Benn	80		c Barath b Bravo	21
*R.T.Ponting	c Bravo b Roach	36		b Rampaul	20
M.E.K.Hussey	c Ramdin b Roach	41		c Ramdin b Bravo	29
M.J.Clarke	c Sarwan b Benn	71		not out	61
M.J.North	c Bravo b Benn	16		c Sarwan b Bravo	2
†B.J.Haddin	not out	55		not out	21
M.G.Johnson	c Gayle b Sammy	7			
N.M.Hauritz	c Ramdin b Roach	17			
P.M.Siddle	c Bravo b Roach	0			
D.E.Bollinger	run out	0			
Extras	(LB 2, NB 18)	20		(B 1, LB 2, NB 7)	10
Total	**(131.1 overs; 533 mins)**	**439**		**(5 wkts; 76 overs)**	**212**

AUSTRALIA	O	M	R	W	O	M	R	W
Bollinger	25	3	67	2	(2) 17.5	3	50	3
Siddle	25	6	92	1	(4) 8	2	38	0
Johnson	26.1	3	105	3	(1) 22	1	103	5
Hauritz	36	5	111	2	(3) 27	4	68	0
Watson	12	2	57	2	(6) 11	5	15	1
North					(5) 14	2	42	0

WEST INDIES	O	M	R	W	O	M	R	W
Roach	25.1	3	93	3	16	3	66	0
Rampaul	14	1	52	0	9	2	22	1
Bravo	12	1	43	0	(4) 15	4	37	3
Sammy	18	2	79	1	(6) 5	0	21	1
Benn	53	8	155	5	(3) 27	10	51	0
Gayle	9	1	15	0	(5) 3	1	8	0
					1	0	4	0

FALL OF WICKETS

	WI	A	WI	A
Wkt	1st	1st	2nd	2nd
1st	26	174	45	33
2nd	39	193	61	68
3rd	84	233	133	114
4th	235	312	194	133
5th	239	353	251	139
6th	273	370	251	
7th	336	377	277	
8th	380	418	284	
9th	383	419	302	
10th	451	439	317	

Umpires: M.R.Benson (*England*) (28) and I.J.Gould (*England*) (8);
Asad Rauf (*Pakistan*) (28) deputised for M.R.Benson (ill) after the first day.
Referee: B.C.Broad (*England*) (37).
In the first innings Nash retired on 20 at 119-3 and resumed at 273-6.

Test No. 1939/107 (A714/WI461)

AUSTRALIA v WEST INDIES (3rd Test)

At WACA Ground, Perth, on 16, 17, 18, 19, 20 December 2009.
Toss: Australia. Result: **AUSTRALIA** won by 35 runs.
Debuts: Australia – C.J.McKay; West Indies – G.C.Tonge.

AUSTRALIA

S.R.Watson	c Ramdin b Roach	89		lbw b Tonge	30
S.M.Katich	c Roach b Benn	99		b Rampaul	10
*R.T.Ponting	retired hurt	23	(9)	c Dowlin b Roach	2
M.E.K.Hussey	c Ramdin b Rampaul	82		c Dowlin b Benn	17
M.J.Clarke	c Gayle b Deonarine	11	(3)	c Ramdin b Bravo	25
M.J.North	c and b Deonarine	68	(5)	c Ramdin b Bravo	1
†B.J.Haddin	c Ramdin b Roach	88	(6)	c Bravo b Benn	23
M.G.Johnson	c Benn b Bravo	35	(7)	c Nash b Bravo	5
N.M.Hauritz	not out	2	(8)	c Sarwan b Bravo	11
C.J.McKay				c Deonarine b Benn	10
D.E.Bollinger				not out	2
Extras	(B 4, LB 2, W 1, NB 16)	23		(B 9, LB 2, W 1, NB 2)	14
Total	**(7 wkts dec; 130.4 overs; 546 mins)**	**520**		**(51.3 overs; 230 mins)**	**150**

WEST INDIES

*C.H.Gayle	c Watson b Bollinger	102	c Haddin b Watson	21
T.M.Dowlin	c Hussey b Johnson	55	c Clarke b Bollinger	22
R.R.Sarwan	c Hussey b Bollinger	42	c Haddin b Hauritz	11
N.Deonarine	c Watson b Johnson	18	b Watson	82
B.P.Nash	c Clarke b Hauritz	44	b Bollinger	65
D.J.Bravo	c Haddin b Bollinger	26	c Hussey b Johnson	1
†D.Ramdin	b Bollinger	8	b McKay	14
S.J.Benn	c Haddin b Hauritz	3	c sub (T.P.Doropoulos) b Johnson	33
R.Rampaul	c Haddin b Hauritz	0	c McKay b Johnson	10
K.A.J.Roach	not out	0	c Haddin b Bollinger	17
G.C.Tonge	c Haddin b Bollinger	2	not out	23
Extras	(LB 5, W 1, NB 6)	12	(B 9, LB 9, W 1, NB 5)	24
Total	**(81 overs; 370 mins)**	**312**	**(94.3 overs; 395 mins)**	**323**

WEST INDIES	O	M	R	W		O	M	R	W
Roach	22	2	104	2		6	0	18	1
Rampaul	22	6	85	1		6	1	21	1
Tonge	18	1	85	0		10	2	28	1
Bravo	17.4	1	79	1	(5)	17.3	6	42	4
Benn	28	4	87	1	(6)	11	2	29	3
Deonarine	23	4	74	2	(4)	1	0	1	0
AUSTRALIA									
Bollinger	20	3	70	5		20.3	3	71	3
Johnson	18	3	92	2		16	5	67	3
McKay	14	3	45	0		14	2	56	1
Hauritz	17	1	66	3	(5)	23	7	61	1
Watson	12	3	34	0	(4)	14	5	30	2
North						7	1	20	0

FALL OF WICKETS

	A	WI	A	WI
Wkt	1st	1st	2nd	2nd
1st	132	136	15	35
2nd	260	175	66	52
3rd	277	214	81	68
4th	355	239	89	196
5th	444	285	109	197
6th	510	295	117	231
7th	520	310	125	245
8th	–	310	134	279
9th	–	310	146	279
10th	–	312	150	323

Umpires: B.F.Bowden (*New Zealand*) (57) and I.J.Gould (*England*) (9).
Referee: B.C.Broad (*England*) (38).
R.T.Ponting retired hurt at 175-1.

Test No. 1940/108 (A715/WI462)

SOUTH AFRICA v ENGLAND (1st Test)

At Centurion Park (Verwoerdburg), Pretoria, on 16, 17, 18, 19, 20 December 2009.
Toss: England. Result: **MATCH DRAWN**.
Debuts: South Africa – F.de Wet.

SOUTH AFRICA

*G.C.Smith	c Prior b Broad	0	(2) b Onions		12
A.G.Prince	c Collingwood b Swann	45	(1) b Anderson		0
H.M.Amla	c Collingwood b Onions	19	(4) b Anderson		100
J.H.Kallis	c Collingwood b Anderson	120	(5) c Cook b Broad		4
A.B.de Villiers	c Cook b Swann	32	(6) c Bell b Broad		64
J.P.Duminy	c Collingwood b Swann	56	(7) lbw b Anderson		11
†M.V.Boucher	c Cook b Swann	49	(8) not out		63
M.Morkel	c Prior b Onions	13	(9) not out		22
P.L.Harris	b Onions	38	(3) b Anderson		11
F.de Wet	lbw b Swann	20			
M.Ntini	not out	4			
Extras	(B 2, LB 15, W 5)	22	(LB 10, W 4)		14
Total	(153.2 overs; 640 mins)	418	(7 wkts dec; 85.5 overs; 368 mins)		301

ENGLAND

*A.J.Strauss	b Ntini	46	c Boucher b Morkel		1
A.N.Cook	c Boucher b De Wet	15	c Smith b Harris		12
I.J.L.Trott	b Harris	28	(4) c De Villiers b De Wet		69
K.P.Pietersen	b Morkel	40	(5) run out		81
P.D.Collingwood	c Kallis b Harris	50	(6) not out		26
I.R.Bell	b Harris	5	(7) c Boucher b De Wet		2
†M.J.Prior	c De Wet b Harris	4	(8) c Boucher b De Wet		0
S.C.J.Broad	lbw b Duminy	17	(9) c Boucher b Harris		0
G.P.Swann	c Smith b Harris	85	(10) lbw b Morkel		2
J.M.Anderson	c Morkel b Ntini	29	(3) c Boucher b De Wet		10
G.Onions	not out	4	not out		1
Extras	(B 8, LB 8, W 5, NB 12)	33	(B 10, LB 3, NB 11)		24
Total	(104 overs; 472 mins)	356	(9 wkts; 96 overs; 432 mins)		228

ENGLAND	O	M	R	W		O	M	R	W
Anderson	37	9	104	1		20.5	1	73	4
Broad	32	8	74	1	(3)	16	5	58	2
Onions	30	5	86	3	(2)	16	3	50	1
Swann	45.2	10	110	5		27	3	91	0
Collingwood	7	1	18	0		6	1	19	0
Trott	2	0	9	0					

SOUTH AFRICA	O	M	R	W		O	M	R	W
Ntini	23	4	78	2		18	7	41	0
De Wet	20	3	72	1	(4)	23	8	55	4
Morkel	21	0	60	1	(2)	18	3	46	2
Harris	37	10	123	5	(3)	26	11	51	2
Duminy	3	0	7	1		8	2	17	0
Kallis						3	1	5	0

FALL OF WICKETS

Wkt	1st SA	1st E	2nd SA	2nd E
1st	1	25	2	5
2nd	51	98	20	16
3rd	93	119	34	27
4th	159	168	46	172
5th	283	189	165	205
6th	316	211	191	207
7th	341	221	266	208
8th	377	242	-	209
9th	414	348	-	218
10th	418	356	-	-

Umpires: Alim Dar (*Pakistan*) (58) and S.J.Davis (*Australia*) (20).
Referee: R.S.Mahanama (*Sri Lanka*) (25). Test No. 1941/135 (SA345/E892)

SOUTH AFRICA v ENGLAND (2nd Test)

At Kingsmead, Durban, on 26, 27, 28, 29, 30 December 2009.
Toss: South Africa. Result: **ENGLAND** won by an innings and 98 runs.
Debuts: None.

SOUTH AFRICA

*G.C.Smith	run out	75	(2)	lbw b Swann	22
A.G.Prince	c Swann b Anderson	2	(1)	c Bell b Swann	16
H.M.Amla	lbw b Broad	2		b Swann	6
J.H.Kallis	c Collingwood b Swann	75		b Broad	3
A.B.de Villiers	c Prior b Broad	50		lbw b Broad	2
J.P.Duminy	lbw b Onions	4		b Broad	0
†M.V.Boucher	lbw b Swann	39		c Prior b Broad	29
M.Morkel	lbw b Swann	23		lbw b Swann	15
P.L.Harris	lbw b Swann	2		c Broad b Anderson	36
D.W.Steyn	c Prior b Anderson	47		lbw b Swann	3
M.Ntini	not out	6		not out	1
Extras	(B 1, LB 17)	18			-
Total	**(108.3 overs; 474 mins)**	**343**		**(50 overs; 215 mins)**	**133**

ENGLAND

*A.J.Strauss	b Morkel	54
A.N.Cook	c Kallis b Morkel	118
I.J.L.Trott	c Boucher b Morkel	18
K.P.Pietersen	lbw b Harris	31
P.D.Collingwood	c Boucher b Duminy	91
I.R.Bell	c Boucher b Steyn	140
†M.J.Prior	b Duminy	60
S.C.J.Broad	c Kallis b Duminy	20
G.P.Swann	c Prince b Steyn	22
J.M.Anderson	not out	1
G.Onions	not out	2
Extras	(LB 10, W 6, NB 1)	17
Total	**(9 wkts dec; 170 overs; 724 mins)**	**574**

ENGLAND	O	M	R	W		O	M	R	W
Anderson	23.3	4	75	2		8	2	24	1
Onions	23	6	62	1		4	1	12	0
Broad	20	6	44	2	(4)	17	3	43	4
Swann	35	3	110	4	(3)	21	3	54	5
Trott	4	0	19	0					
Pietersen	2	0	7	0					
Collingwood	1	0	8	0					

SOUTH AFRICA	O	M	R	W
Steyn	34	6	94	2
Ntini	29	4	114	0
Morkel	31	6	78	3
Kallis	14	1	43	0
Harris	38	4	146	1
Duminy	24	1	89	3

FALL OF WICKETS			
	SA	E	SA
Wkt	1st	1st	2nd
1st	3	71	27
2nd	10	104	37
3rd	160	155	40
4th	166	297	44
5th	170	365	44
6th	233	477	50
7th	269	536	86
8th	280	564	108
9th	285	568	129
10th	343	-	133

Umpires: Alim Dar (*Pakistan*) (59) and A.M.Saheba (*India*) (3).
Referee: R.S.Mahanama (*Sri Lanka*) (26).   **Test No. 1942/136 (SA346/E893)**

SOUTH AFRICA v ENGLAND (3rd Test)

At Newlands, Cape Town, on 3, 4, 5, 6, 7 January 2010.
Toss: England. Result: **MATCH DRAWN**.
Debuts: None.

SOUTH AFRICA

*G.C.Smith	c Prior b Anderson	30	(2) c Collingwood b Onions		183
A.G.Prince	c Prior b Anderson	0	(1) lbw b Swann		15
H.M.Amla	lbw b Onions	14	c Cook b Swann		95
J.H.Kallis	c Prior b Onions	108	c Prior b Anderson		46
A.B.de Villiers	c Strauss b Swann	36	c Broad b Anderson		34
J.P.Duminy	c Prior b Swann	0	c Prior b Anderson		36
†M.V.Boucher	lbw b Broad	51	c Bell b Swann		15
D.W.Steyn	c Trott b Anderson	26	not out		1
M.Morkel	c Swann b Anderson	0			
P.L.Harris	not out	10			
F.de Wet	lbw b Anderson	0			
Extras	(B 1, LB 13, W 1, NB 1)	16	(B 8, LB 7, NB 2, Pen 5)		22
Total	**(86.1 overs; 362 mins)**	**291**	**(7 wkts dec; 111.2 overs; 507 mins)**		**447**

ENGLAND

*A.J.Strauss	c Boucher b Morkel	2	c Amla b Harris		45
A.N.Cook	c Prince b Morkel	65	c Boucher b De Wet		55
I.J.L.Trott	b Steyn	20	b Steyn		42
K.P.Pietersen	c and b Steyn	0	lbw b Steyn		6
P.D.Collingwood	lbw b Morkel	19	(6) c Kallis b Duminy		40
I.R.Bell	c Duminy b Kallis	48	(7) c Smith b Morkel		78
†M.J.Prior	b Steyn	76	(8) c De Villiers b Duminy		4
S.C.J.Broad	b Steyn	25	(9) c De Villiers b Harris		2
G.P.Swann	c Smith b Morkel	5	(10) not out		10
J.M.Anderson	c Smith b Morkel	0	(5) c Prince b Harris		9
G.Onions	not out	4	not out		0
Extras	(LB 6, W 2, NB 1)	9	(B 1, LB 4, W 1, NB 1)		7
Total	**(88 overs; 405 mins)**	**273**	**(9 wkts; 141 overs; 606 mins)**		**296**

ENGLAND	O	M	R	W		O	M	R	W		FALL OF WICKETS			
Anderson	21.1	1	63	5		22.2	1	98	3			SA	E	SA	E
Onions	20	4	69	2		22	4	87	1		*Wkt*	*1st*	*1st*	*2nd*	*2nd*
Broad	19	6	54	1	(4)	22	4	79	0		1st	1	2	31	101
Swann	22	1	74	2	(3)	37	5	127	3		2nd	46	36	261	107
Pietersen	4	0	17	0		3	0	6	0		3rd	51	36	346	129
Trott						5	0	30	0		4th	127	73	376	153
											5th	127	133	401	160
SOUTH AFRICA											6th	216	174	442	272
Morkel	22	4	75	5		28	9	51	1		7th	280	225	447	278
De Wet	16	3	36	0	(3)	12	5	23	1		8th	280	241	-	286
Steyn	22	5	74	4	(2)	35	11	74	2		9th	281	241	-	290
Kallis	14	2	27	1	(5)	14	4	28	0		10th	291	273	-	-
Harris	9	0	39	0	(4)	40	14	85	3						
Duminy	5	0	16	0		12	3	30	2						

Umpires: D.J.Harper (*Australia*) (88) and A.L.Hill (*New Zealand*) (14).
Referee: R.S.Mahanama (*Sri Lanka*) (27). **Test No. 1943/137 (SA347/E894)**

SOUTH AFRICA v ENGLAND (4th Test)

At New Wanderers Stadium, Johannesburg, on 14, 15, 16, 17 January 2010.
Toss: England. Result: **SOUTH AFRICA** won by an innings and 74 runs.
Debuts: South Africa – R.McLaren, W.D.Parnell.

ENGLAND

*A.J.Strauss	c Amla b Steyn	0	lbw b Parnell	22
A.N.Cook	lbw b Morkel	21	c Smith b Morkel	1
I.J.L.Trott	lbw b Morkel	5	c De Villiers b Steyn	8
K.P.Pietersen	c Parnell b Morkel	7	c Boucher b Parnell	12
P.D.Collingwood	c Duminy b McLaren	47	c Morkel b Duminy	71
I.R.Bell	b Steyn	35	c Kallis b Morkel	5
†M.J.Prior	c Boucher b Steyn	14	c Smith b Morkel	0
S.C.J.Broad	c Morkel b Kallis	13	c Boucher b Morkel	1
G.P.Swann	c Boucher b Steyn	27	c De Villiers b Steyn	20
R.J.Sidebottom	c Boucher b Steyn	0	b Duminy	15
J.M.Anderson	not out	6	not out	1
Extras	(LB 2, W 3)	5	(LB 6, W 1, NB 6)	13
Total	(47.5 overs; 228 mins)	180	(42.5 overs; 213 mins)	169

SOUTH AFRICA

*G.C.Smith	c Strauss b Sidebottom	105
A.G.Prince	c Swann b Broad	19
H.M.Amla	c Prior b Broad	75
J.H.Kallis	c Anderson b Sidebottom	7
A.B.de Villiers	c Collingwood b Broad	58
J.P.Duminy	c Collingwood b Swann	7
†M.V.Boucher	c Trott b Swann	95
R.McLaren	not out	33
D.W.Steyn	not out	1
M.Morkel		
W.D.Parnell		
Extras	(B 8, LB 9, W 5, NB 1)	23
Total	(7 wkts dec; 119 overs; 531 mins)	423

SOUTH AFRICA	O	M	R	W		O	M	R	W
Steyn	13.5	1	51	5		14	1	64	2
Morkel	11	1	39	3		16	5	59	4
McLaren	10	3	30	1	(4)	3	1	13	0
Parnell	3	0	18	0	(3)	8	1	17	2
Kallis	10	3	40	1					
Duminy					(5)	1.5	0	10	2

ENGLAND	O	M	R	W
Anderson	30	4	111	0
Sidebottom	31	6	98	2
Broad	29	4	83	3
Swann	23	0	93	2
Collingwood	6	1	21	0

FALL OF WICKETS

	E	SA	E
Wkt	1st	1st	2nd
1st	0	36	6
2nd	7	201	21
3rd	32	217	48
4th	39	217	84
5th	115	235	103
6th	133	355	103
7th	136	419	104
8th	148	-	134
9th	155	-	154
10th	180	-	169

Umpires: S.J.Davis (*Australia*) (21) and A.L.Hill (*New Zealand*) (15).
Referee: R.S.Mahanama (*Sri Lanka*) (28).   **Test No. 1944/138 (SA348/E895)**

AUSTRALIA v PAKISTAN (1st Test)

At Melbourne Cricket Ground, on 26, 27, 28, 29, 30 December 2009.
Toss: Australia. Result: **AUSTRALIA** won by 170 runs.
Debuts: None.

AUSTRALIA

S.R.Watson	run out	93		not out	120
S.M.Katich	c Butt b Asif	98		c Kamran Akmal b Asif	2
*R.T.Ponting	c Misbah b Asif	57		c Butt b Aamer	12
M.E.K.Hussey	lbw b Ajmal	82		lbw b Aamer	4
N.M.Hauritz	lbw b Rauf	75	(9)	st Kamran Akmal b Ajmal	8
M.J.Clarke	not out	28	(5)	c Kamran Akmal b Aamer	37
M.J.North			(6)	b Aamer	8
†B.J.Haddin			(7)	c Kamran Akmal b Aamer	0
M.G.Johnson			(8)	run out	22
D.E.Bollinger					
P.M.Siddle					
Extras	(B 2, LB 12, NB 7)	21		(LB 2, W 3, NB 7)	12
Total	**(5 wkts dec; 128 overs; 536 mins)**	**454**		**(8 wkts dec; 73.1 overs; 335 mins)**	**225**

PAKISTAN

Imran Farhat	lbw b Johnson	9		lbw b Bollinger	12
Salman Butt	lbw b Watson	45		lbw b Johnson	33
Faisal Iqbal	c Clarke b Hauritz	15		b Hauritz	48
*Mohammad Yousuf	c Haddin b Siddle	22		c Katich b Hauritz	61
Umar Akmal	c Ponting b Johnson	51		c Haddin b Johnson	27
Mohammad Aamer	c North b Bollinger	15	(8)	c Katich b Hauritz	0
Misbah-ul-Haq	not out	65	(6)	c Haddin b Johnson	0
†Kamran Akmal	c Haddin b Bollinger	12	(7)	st Haddin b Hauritz	30
Abdur Rauf	c North b Bollinger	3		b Bollinger	5
Mohammad Asif	c Watson b Siddle	0	(11)	not out	1
Saeed Ajmal	b Johnson	4	(10)	c Watson b Hauritz	10
Extras	(B 4, LB 3, W 1, NB 9)	17		(B 13, LB 4, W 2, NB 5)	24
Total	**(99 overs; 443 mins)**	**258**		**(72 overs; 329 mins)**	**251**

PAKISTAN	O	M	R	W	O	M	R	W
Mohammad Asif	27	5	86	2	16	3	38	1
Mohammad Aamer	27	7	101	0	24	6	79	5
Abdur Rauf	23	4	86	1	(4) 10	3	33	0
Saeed Ajmal	46	3	150	1	(3) 23.1	1	73	1
Imran Farhat	5	0	17	0				

AUSTRALIA	O	M	R	W	O	M	R	W
Bollinger	20	6	50	3	15	5	42	2
Siddle	24	7	77	2	13	5	32	0
Hauritz	20	3	58	1	24	4	101	5
Johnson	22	10	36	3	18	6	46	3
Watson	13	3	30	1				
Katich					2	0	13	0

FALL OF WICKETS

	A	P	A	P
Wkt	1st	1st	2nd	2nd
1st	182	26	15	18
2nd	233	59	32	80
3rd	291	84	40	116
4th	382	109	143	171
5th	454	159	161	214
6th	-	203	161	214
7th	-	215	198	221
8th	-	219	225	250
9th	-	220	-	250
10th	-	258	-	251

Umpires: B.R.Doctrove (*West Indies*) (28) and R.E.Koertzen (*South Africa*) (104).
Referee: R.S.Madugalle (*Sri Lanka*) (113). **Test No. 1945/53 (A716/P344)**

AUSTRALIA v PAKISTAN (2nd Test)

At Sydney Cricket Ground, on 3, 4, 5, 6 January 2010.
Toss: Australia. Result: **AUSTRALIA** won by 36 runs.
Debuts: None.

AUSTRALIA

S.R.Watson	c Kamran Akmal b Sami	6	c Iqbal b Gul	97
P.J.Hughes	c Iqbal b Sami	0	c and b Kaneria	37
*R.T.Ponting	c Gul b Sami	0	c Iqbal b Gul	11
M.E.K.Hussey	c Misbah b Asif	28	not out	134
M.J.Clarke	b Asif	3	lbw b Asif	21
M.J.North	c Kamran Akmal b Asif	10	c Iqbal b Kaneria	2
†B.J.Haddin	c Yousuf b Asif	6	lbw b Kaneria	15
M.G.Johnson	c Farhat b Asif	38	b Kaneria	3
N.M.Hauritz	b Asif	21	c Misbah b Gul	4
P.M.Siddle	not out	1	c Misbah b Asif	38
D.E.Bollinger	b Gul	9	b Kaneria	0
Extras	(B 1, LB 2, W 1, NB 1)	5	(B 6, LB 5, W 3, NB 5)	19
Total	**(44.2 overs; 224 mins)**	**127**	**(125.4 overs; 570 mins)**	**381**

PAKISTAN

Imran Farhat	c Haddin b Hauritz	53	c Johnson b Bollinger	22
Salman Butt	c Haddin b Johnson	71	c Haddin b Johnson	21
Faisal Iqbal	c Watson b Siddle	27	c Haddin b Johnson	7
*Mohammad Yousuf	c Haddin b Johnson	46	c and b Hauritz	19
Umar Akmal	lbw b Bollinger	49	c Johnson b Bollinger	49
Misbah-ul-Haq	c Haddin b Bollinger	11	c Hussey b Hauritz	0
†Kamran Akmal	c Watson b Bollinger	14	c Haddin b Johnson	11
Mohammad Sami	c Haddin b Watson	13	c Haddin b Hauritz	0
Umar Gul	c Bollinger b Watson	12	c Siddle b Hauritz	6
Danish Kaneria	c Hussey b Bollinger	4	c Watson b Hauritz	0
Mohammad Asif	not out	0	not out	0
Extras	(B 2, LB 16, W 5, NB 10)	33	(W 1, NB 1)	2
Total	**(96.5 overs; 437 mins)**	**333**	**(38 overs; 178 mins)**	**139**

PAKISTAN	O	M	R	W		O	M	R	W
Mohammad Asif	20	6	41	6		27	8	53	2
Mohammad Sami	12	4	27	3		19.5	4	74	0
Umar Gul	10.2	0	38	1	(4)	28	4	83	3
Danish Kaneria	2	0	18	0	(3)	47.5	3	151	5
Imran Farhat						3	0	9	0

AUSTRALIA	O	M	R	W		O	M	R	W
Bollinger	21.5	5	72	4		12	3	32	2
Siddle	22	4	62	1		4	1	27	0
Johnson	20	2	64	2	(4)	10	2	27	3
Watson	17	4	40	2					
Hauritz	16	3	77	1	(3)	12	1	53	5

FALL OF WICKETS

	A	P	A	P
Wkt	1st	1st	2nd	2nd
1st	2	109	105	34
2nd	2	144	144	50
3rd	10	205	159	51
4th	36	237	217	77
5th	51	277	226	77
6th	51	286	246	103
7th	62	295	252	133
8th	106	323	257	133
9th	117	331	380	135
10th	127	333	381	139

Umpires: E.A.R.de Silva (*Sri Lanka*) (42) and B.R.Doctrove (*West Indies*) (29).
Referee: R.S.Madugalle (*Sri Lanka*) (114).   **Test No. 1946/54 (A717/P345)**

61

AUSTRALIA v PAKISTAN (3rd Test)

At Bellerive Oval, Hobart, on 14, 15, 16, 17, 18 January 2010.
Toss: Australia. Result: **AUSTRALIA** won by 231 runs.
Debuts: Pakistan – Sarfraz Ahmed.

AUSTRALIA

Batsman	1st innings		2nd innings	
S.R.Watson	c Farhat b Gul	29	c Yousuf b Aamer	1
S.M.Katich	lbw b Asif	11	c Malikneria	100
*R.T.Ponting	c Yousuf b Aamer	209	c Ahmed b Malik	89
M.E.K.Hussey	c Ahmed b Aamer	6	not out	13
M.J.Clarke	b Kaneria	166		
M.J.North	c Ahmed b Asif	21		
†B.J.Haddin	c Gul b Kaneria	41	(5) run out	8
M.G.Johnson	c Ahmed b Kaneria	8	(6) c Farhat b Malik	0
N.M.Hauritz	not out	12		
P.M.Siddle				
D.E.Bollinger				
Extras	(B 1, LB 3, W 5, NB 7)	16	(B 4, LB 4)	8
Total	**(8 wkts dec; 142.5 overs; 617 mins)**	**519**	**(5 wkts dec; 48.4 overs; 208 mins)**	**219**

PAKISTAN

Batsman	1st innings		2nd innings	
Imran Farhat	c Haddin b Siddle	38	c Haddin b Siddle	14
Salman Butt	c Clarke b Katich	102	b Bollinger	8
Khurram Manzoor	c Ponting b Siddle	0	c Haddin b Hauritz	77
*Mohammad Yousuf	run out	7	lbw b Watson	23
Umar Akmal	run out	8	lbw b Watson	15
Shoaib Malik	c Bollinger b Hauritz	58	c Haddin b Siddle	19
†Sarfraz Ahmed	c Clarke b Katich	1	c Clarke b Hauritz	5
Mohammad Aamer	c Watson b Katich	4	not out	30
Umar Gul	not out	38	c Clarke b Hauritz	0
Danish Kaneria	c Ponting b Hauritz	0	(11) b Siddle	1
Mohammad Asif	c Hussey b Hauritz	29	(10) b Johnson	0
Extras	(B 2, LB 2, W 2, NB 2)	8	(B 10, LB 3, NB 1)	14
Total	**(105.4 overs; 405 mins)**	**301**	**(86.2 overs; 360 mins)**	**206**

PAKISTAN	O	M	R	W	O	M	R	W
Mohammad Asif	36	8	104	2	9	0	48	0
Mohammad Aamer	31	7	97	2	12	2	46	1
Umar Gul	25	4	98	1	10	0	45	0
Danish Kaneria	42.5	2	189	3	14	2	56	1
Shoaib Malik	8	0	27	0	3.4	0	16	2

AUSTRALIA	O	M	R	W	O	M	R	W
Bollinger	15	6	35	0	13	4	31	1
Siddle	20	8	39	2	15.2	7	25	3
Johnson	20	2	76	0	21	4	59	1
Hauritz	33.4	9	96	3	(5) 17	6	30	3
Watson	7	2	17	0	(4) 17	4	38	2
Katich	10	3	34	3	3	1	10	0

FALL OF WICKETS

	A	P	A	P
Wkt	1st	1st	2nd	2nd
1st	28	63	1	11
2nd	52	63	192	29
3rd	71	74	202	61
4th	423	84	213	83
5th	443	213	219	104
6th	498	215	-	123
7th	499	219	-	189
8th	519	227	-	191
9th	-	248	-	192
10th	-	301	-	206

Umpires: E.A.R.de Silva (*Sri Lanka*) (43) and R.E.Koertzen (*South Africa*) (105).
Referee: R.S.Madugalle (*Sri Lanka*) (115).   **Test No. 1947/55 (A718/P346)**

ENGLAND TEST MATCH AVERAGES 2009

These averages cover the 16 Tests played by England included in this book, against West Indies away then home, Australia at home and South Africa away.

BATTING AND FIELDING

	M	I	NO	HS	Runs	Avge	100	50	Ct/St
A.J.Strauss	16	28	2	169	1241	47.73	4	4	11
P.D.Collingwood	16	25	2	161	1092	47.47	2	8	22
R.S.Bopara	7	10	–	143	460	46.00	3	–	4
A.N.Cook	16	28	3	160	1100	44.00	3	6	14
M.J.Prior	15	24	3	131*	834	39.71	1	7	32/2
G.P.Swann	14	18	5	85	514	39.53	–	4	8
K.P.Pietersen	13	21	1	102	785	39.25	1	5	2
I.J.L.Trott	5	9	–	119	350	38.88	1	1	3
I.R.Bell	8	14	–	140	485	34.64	1	3	4
A.Flintoff	7	11	1	74	267	26.70	–	1	3
S.C.J.Broad	16	25	4	61	470	22.38	–	2	3
O.A.Shah	4	6	–	57	133	22.16	–	1	1
R.J.Sidebottom	4	4	1	26*	47	15.66	–	–	–
S.J.Harmison	4	6	3	19*	45	15.00	–	–	–
J.M.Anderson	15	19	5	29	194	13.85	–	–	5
G.Onions	8	10	7	17*	30	10.00	–	–	–
T.T.Bresnan	2	1	–	9	9	9.00	–	–	2
M.S.Panesar	4	4	2	7*	11	5.50	–	–	–

Also played (one Test): T.R.Ambrose 76* (1 ct); A.Khan did not bat.

BOWLING

	O	M	R	W	Avge	Best	5wI	10wM
G.P.Swann	600	117	1802	61	29.54	5-54	4	–
S.C.J.Broad	491.3	98	1549	51	30.37	6-91	3	–
G.Onions	238.1	43	869	28	31.03	5-38	1	–
T.T.Bresnan	31	7	97	3	32.33	3-45	–	–
J.M.Anderson	514.2	106	1627	48	33.89	5-63	3	–
S.J.Harmison	97.4	20	314	9	34.88	3-54	–	–
A.Flintoff	191.1	37	568	13	43.69	5-92	–	–
R.J.Sidebottom	90	15	279	3	93.00	2-98	–	–
M.S.Panesar	144.5	33	385	6	64.16	2-34	–	–

Also bowled: R.S.Bopara 23.2-1-118-0; P.D.Collingwood 58-5-215-1; A.Khan 29-1-122-1; K.P.Pietersen 30-2-117-0; O.A.Shah 5-0-31-0; I.J.L.Trott 11-0-58-0.

INTERNATIONAL UMPIRES AND REFEREES 2010

ELITE PANEL OF UMPIRES 2010

The Elite Panel of ICC Umpires and Referees was introduced in April 2002 to raise standards and guarantee impartial adjudication. Two umpires from this panel stand in Test matches while one officiates with a home umpire from the Supplementary International Panel in limited-overs internationals.

Full Names	Birthdate	Birthplace	Tests	Debut	LOI	Debut
ALIM Sarwar DAR	06.06.68	Jhang, Pakistan	59	2003-04	127	1999-00
ASAD RAUF	12.05.56	Lahore, Pakistan	27	2004-05	69	1999-00
BOWDEN, Brent Fraser	11.04.63	Auckland, New Zealand	59	1999-00	141	1994-95
DAVIS, Stephen James	09.04.52	London, England	23	1997-98	94	1992-93
DE SILVA, E.Asoka Ranjit	28.03.56	Kalutara, Sri Lanka	43	2000	100	1999-00
DOCTROVE, Billy Raymond	03.07.55	Marigot, Dominica	29	2000	89	1997-98
GOULD, Ian James	19.08.57	Taplow, England	11	2008-09	44	2006
HARPER, Daryl John	23.10.51	Adelaide, Australia	88	1998-99	161	1993-94
HILL, Anthony Lloyd	26.06.51	Auckland, New Zealand	15	2001-02	75	1997-98
KOERTZEN, Rudolf Eric ('Rudi')	26.03.49	Knysna, South Africa	106	1992-93	202	1992-93
TAUFEL, Simon James Arthur	21.01.71	Sydney, Australia	61	2000-01	147	1998-99

ELITE PANEL OF REFEREES 2010

Full Names	Birthdate	Birthplace	Tests	Debut	LOI	Debut
BROAD, Brian Christopher	29.09.57	Bristol, England	38	2003-04	161	2003-04
CROWE, Jeffrey John	14.09.58	Auckland, New Zealand	38	2004-05	114	2003-04
HURST, Alan George	15.07.50	Melbourne, Australia	37	2004-05	84	2004-05
MADUGALLE, Ranjan Senerath	22.04.59	Kandy, Sri Lanka	115	1993-94	246	1993-94
MAHANAMA, Roshan Siriwardena	31.05.66	Colombo, Sri Lanka	28	2004	132	2004
PYCROFT, Andrew John	06.06.56	Harare, Zimbabwe	10	2009	15	2009
SRINATH, Javagal	31.08.69	Mysore, India	13	2006	79	2006-07

INTERNATIONAL UMPIRES PANEL 2010

Nominated by their respective cricket boards, members from this panel officiate in home LOI and supplement the Elite Panel for Test matches. Specialist third umpires have been selected to undertake adjudication involving television replays. The number of Test matches/LOI in which they have stood is shown in brackets.

			Third Umpire
Australia	B.N.J.Oxenford (-/12)	R.J.Tucker (1/12)	P.R.Reiffel (-/3)
Bangladesh	Nadir Shah (-/32)	Enamal Haque (-/24)	Sharfuddoula (-/2)
England	R.A.Kettleborough (-/5)	N.J.Llong (8/32)	R.K.Illingworth (-/-)
India	A.M.Saheba (3/39)	S.K.Tarapore (-/12)	S.S.Hazare (-/4)
New Zealand	G.A.V.Baxter (-/28)	C.B.Gaffaney (-/-)	E.A.Watkin (2/23)
Pakistan	Zamir Haider (-/10)	Nadeem Ghauri (5/42)	Ahsan Raza (-/2)
South Africa	M.Erasmus (2/16)	B.G.Jerling (4/82)	J.D.Cloete (-/1)
Sri Lanka	H.D.P.K.Dharmasena (-/8)	T.H.Wijewardene (4/48)	R.Martinesz (-/-)
West Indies	C.R.Duncan (2/18)	N.A.Malcolm (-/7)	C.E.Mack (-/1)
	G.E.Greaves (-/-)		
Zimbabwe	K.C.Barbour (4/51)	R.B.Tiffin (44/111)	O.Chirombe (-/-)

Test Match statistics to 20 February 2010; LOI statistics to 27 February 2010.

TEST MATCH CAREER RECORDS

These records, complete to 20 February 2010, contain all players registered for county cricket in 2010 at the time of going to press, plus those who have played Test cricket since 9 October 2008 (Test No. 1886). The figures for the Australia v ICC 'Test' of 2005-06 are included.

ENGLAND – BATTING AND FIELDING

	M	I	NO	HS	Runs	Avge	100	50	Ct/St
U.Afzaal	3	6	1	54	83	16.60	–	1	–
K.Ali	1	2	–	9	10	5.00	–	–	–
T.R.Ambrose	11	16	1	102	447	29.80	1	3	31
J.M.Anderson	46	63	30	34	468	14.18	–	–	18
G.J.Batty	7	8	1	38	144	20.57	–	–	3
I.R.Bell	53	95	9	199	3457	40.19	9	22	48
I.D.Blackwell	1	1	–	4	4	4.00	–	–	–
R.S.Bopara	10	15	–	143	502	33.46	3	–	5
T.T.Bresnan	2	1	–	9	9	9.00	–	–	2
S.C.J.Broad	26	38	6	76	843	26.34	–	5	7
R.Clarke	2	3	–	55	96	32.00	–	1	1
P.D.Collingwood	57	100	10	206	3909	43.43	9	19	75
A.N.Cook	52	94	5	160	3796	42.65	10	22	48
D.G.Cork	37	56	8	59	864	18.00	–	3	18
R.D.B.Croft	21	34	8	37*	421	16.19	–	–	10
R.K.J.Dawson	7	13	3	19*	114	11.40	–	–	3
A.Flintoff	79	130	9	167	3845	31.77	5	26	52
J.S.Foster	7	12	3	48	226	25.11	–	–	17/1
S.J.Harmison	63	86	23	49*	743	11.79	–	–	7
M.J.Hoggard	67	92	27	38	473	7.27	–	–	24
G.O.Jones	34	53	4	100	1172	23.91	1	6	128/5
S.P.Jones	18	18	5	44	205	15.76	–	–	4
R.W.T.Key	15	26	1	221	775	31.00	1	3	11
A.Khan	1	–	–	–	–	–	–	–	–
R.J.Kirtley	4	7	1	12	32	5.33	–	–	3
J.Lewis	1	2	–	20	27	13.50	–	–	–
A.McGrath	4	5	–	81	201	40.20	–	2	3
D.L.Maddy	3	4	–	24	46	11.50	–	–	4
S.I.Mahmood	8	11	1	34	81	8.10	–	–	–
G.Onions	8	10	7	17*	30	10.00	–	–	–
M.S.Panesar	39	51	17	26	187	5.50	–	–	9
D.J.Pattinson	1	2	–	13	21	10.50	–	–	–
K.P.Pietersen	58	104	4	226	4824	48.24	16	16	32
L.E.Plunkett	9	13	2	44*	126	11.45	–	–	3
M.J.Prior	27	44	7	131*	1484	40.10	2	12	63/2
M.R.Ramprakash	52	92	6	154	2350	27.32	2	12	39
C.M.W.Read	23	23	4	55	360	18.94	–	1	48/6
C.P.Schofield	2	3	–	57	67	22.33	–	1	–
O.A.Shah	6	10	–	88	269	26.90	–	2	2
R.J.Sidebottom	22	31	11	31	313	15.65	–	–	5
A.J.Strauss	71	130	5	177	5436	43.48	18	18	77
G.P.Swann	16	21	5	85	525	32.81	–	4	10
C.T.Tremlett	3	5	1	25*	50	12.50	–	–	1
M.E.Trescothick	76	143	10	219	5825	43.79	14	29	95
I.J.L.Trott	5	9	–	119	350	38.88	1	1	3
S.D.Udal	4	7	1	33*	109	18.16	–	–	1

TEST   **ENGLAND – BOWLING**

	O	M	R	W	Avge	Best	5wI	10wM
U.Afzaal	9	0	49	1	49.00	1- 49	–	–
K.Ali	36	5	136	5	27.20	3- 80	–	–
J.M.Anderson	1571.4	322	5431	156	34.81	7- 43	8	–
G.J.Batty	232.2	34	733	11	66.63	3- 55	–	–
I.R.Bell	18	3	76	1	76.00	1- 33	–	–
I.D.Blackwell	19	2	71	0	–	–	–	–
R.S.Bopara	49.2	7	199	1	199.00	1- 39	–	–
T.T.Bresnan	31	7	97	3	32.33	3- 45	–	–
S.C.J.Broad	852.5	170	2725	77	35.38	6- 91	3	–
R.Clarke	29	11	60	4	15.00	2- 7	–	–
P.D.Collingwood	274.5	43	912	15	60.80	3- 23	–	–
A.N.Cook	1	0	1	0	–	–	–	–
D.G.Cork	1279.4	264	3906	131	29.81	7- 43	5	–
R.D.B.Croft	769.5	195	1825	49	37.24	5- 95	1	–
R.K.J.Dawson	186	20	677	11	61.54	4-134	–	–
A.Flintoff	2491.5	507	7410	226	32.78	5- 58	3	–
S.J.Harmison	2229.1	431	7192	226	31.82	7- 12	8	1
M.J.Hoggard	2318.1	493	7564	248	30.50	7- 61	7	1
S.P.Jones	470.1	78	1666	59	28.23	6- 53	3	–
A.Khan	29	1	122	1	122.00	1-111	–	–
R.J.Kirtley	179.5	50	561	19	29.52	6- 34	1	–
J.Lewis	41	9	122	3	40.66	3- 68	–	–
A.McGrath	17	1	56	4	14.00	3- 16	–	–
D.L.Maddy	14	1	40	0	–	–	–	–
S.I.Mahmood	188.2	25	762	20	38.10	4- 22	–	–
G.Onions	238.1	43	869	28	31.03	5- 38	1	–
M.S.Panesar	1507	308	4331	126	34.37	6- 37	8	1
D.J.Pattinson	30.1	2	96	2	48.00	2- 95	–	–
K.P.Pietersen	131.5	9	548	4	137.00	1- 0	–	–
L.E.Plunkett	256.2	39	916	23	39.82	3- 17	–	–
M.R.Ramprakash	149.1	16	477	4	119.25	1- 2	–	–
C.P.Schofield	18	2	73	0	–	–	–	–
O.A.Shah	5	0	31	0	–	–	–	–
R.J.Sidebottom	802	188	2231	79	28.24	7- 47	5	1
G.P.Swann	700.3	133	2118	69	30.69	5- 54	4	–
C.T.Tremlett	143.1	36	386	13	29.69	3- 12	–	–
M.E.Trescothick	50	6	155	1	155.00	1- 34	–	–
I.J.L.Trott	11	0	58	0	–	–	–	–
S.D.Udal	99.2	13	344	8	43.00	4- 14	–	–

TEST **AUSTRALIA – BATTING AND FIELDING**

	M	I	NO	HS	Runs	Avge	100	50	Ct/St
D.E.Bollinger	6	5	2	9	11	3.66	–	–	2
S.R.Clark	24	26	7	39	248	13.05	–	–	4
M.J.Clarke	58	94	12	166	4116	50.19	13	17	56
A.C.Gilchrist	96	137	20	204*	5570	47.60	17	26	379/37
B.J.Haddin	25	42	4	169	1474	38.78	2	5	101/2
N.M.Hauritz	13	18	4	75	317	22.64	–	2	3
M.L.Hayden	103	184	14	380	8625	50.73	30	29	128
B.W.Hilfenhaus	9	11	5	20	68	11.33	–	–	3
B.J.Hodge	6	11	2	203*	503	55.88	1	2	9
P.J.Hughes	6	11	–	160	509	46.27	2	1	3
M.E.K.Hussey	48	83	11	182	3819	53.04	11	19	45
P.A.Jaques	11	19	–	150	902	47.47	3	6	7
M.G.Johnson	32	43	8	123*	924	26.40	1	4	8
S.M.Katich	48	83	5	157	3503	44.91	9	20	36
J.J.Krejza	2	4	1	32	71	23.66	–	–	4
B.Lee	76	90	18	64	1451	20.15	–	5	23
A.B.McDonald	4	6	1	68	107	21.40	–	1	2
B.E.McGain	1	2	–	2	2	1.00	–	–	–
C.J.McKay	1	1	–	10	10	10.00	–	–	1
G.A.Manou	1	2	1	13*	21	21.00	–	–	3
M.J.North	13	21	1	125*	734	36.70	3	3	8
R.T.Ponting	142	240	27	257	11859	55.67	39	51	164
C.J.L.Rogers	1	2	–	15	19	9.50	–	–	1
P.M.Siddle	17	22	6	38	256	16.00	–	–	10
A.Symonds	26	41	5	162*	1462	40.61	2	10	22
S.W.Tait	3	5	2	8	20	6.66	–	–	1
S.R.Watson	17	29	1	120*	1106	39.50	1	8	13
C.L.White	4	7	2	46	146	29.20	–	–	1

AUSTRALIA – BOWLING

	O	M	R	W	Avge	Best	5wI	10wM
D.E.Bollinger	224.1	50	651	27	24.11	5- 70	1	–
S.R.Clark	857.4	230	2243	94	23.86	5- 32	2	–
M.J.Clarke	256.4	42	755	19	39.73	6- 9	1	–
N.M.Hauritz	517	108	1551	53	29.26	5- 53	2	–
M.L.Hayden	9	0	40	0	–	–	–	–
B.W.Hilfenhaus	328.5	75	1040	34	30.58	4- 60	–	–
B.J.Hodge	2	0	8	0	–	–	–	–
M.E.K.Hussey	30	4	103	2	51.50	1- 3	–	–
M.G.Johnson	1268.5	231	4069	143	28.45	8- 61	4	1
S.M.Katich	168.1	21	617	21	29.38	6- 65	1	–
J.J.Krejza	123.5	8	562	13	43.23	8-215	1	1
B.Lee	2755.1	547	9554	310	30.81	5- 30	10	–
A.B.McDonald	122	40	300	9	33.33	3- 25	–	–
B.E.McGain	18	2	149	0	–	–	–	–
C.J.McKay	28	5	101	1	101.00	1- 56	–	–
M.J.North	126.3	25	364	6	60.66	4- 98	–	–
R.T.Ponting	89.5	23	242	5	48.40	1- 0	–	–
P.M.Siddle	627.1	163	1892	60	31.53	5- 21	2	–
A.Symonds	349	81	896	24	37.33	3- 50	–	–
S.W.Tait	69	6	302	5	60.40	3- 97	–	–
S.R.Watson	291.4	56	883	27	32.70	4- 42	–	–
C.L.White	93	8	342	5	68.40	2- 71	–	–

TEST

SOUTH AFRICA – BATTING AND FIELDING

	M	I	NO	HS	Runs	Avge	100	50	Ct/St
H.M.Amla	43	75	6	253*	3261	47.26	10	16	36
N.Boje	43	62	10	85	1312	25.23	–	4	18
M.V.Boucher	131	186	22	125	5068	30.90	5	32	472/22
Z.de Bruyn	3	5	1	83	155	38.75	–	1	–
A.B.de Villiers	58	99	8	217*	3902	42.87	9	21	82/1
F.de Wet	2	2	–	20	20	10.00	–	–	1
J.P.Duminy	12	20	2	166	518	28.77	1	3	12
H.H.Gibbs	90	154	7	228	6167	41.95	14	26	94
A.J.Hall	21	33	4	163	760	26.20	1	3	16
P.L.Harris	29	40	5	46	406	11.60	–	–	13
C.W.Henderson	7	7	–	30	65	9.28	–	–	2
J.H.Kallis	137	231	33	189*	10843	54.76	34	52	155
I.Khan	1	1	–	20	20	20.00	–	–	1
N.D.McKenzie	58	94	7	226	3253	37.39	5	16	54
R.McLaren	1	1	1	33*	33	–	–	–	–
J.A.Morkel	1	1	–	58	58	58.00	–	1	–
M.Morkel	23	29	3	40	359	13.80	–	–	7
A.Nel	36	42	8	34	337	9.91	–	–	16
M.Ntini	101	116	45	32*	699	9.84	–	–	25
W.D.Parnell	3	2	–	22	34	17.00	–	–	1
A.N.Petersen	1	2	–	100	121	60.50	1	–	–
R.J.Peterson	6	7	1	61	163	27.16	–	1	5
A.G.Prince	54	87	12	162*	3195	42.60	11	8	34
J.A.Rudolph	35	63	7	222*	2028	36.21	5	8	22
G.C.Smith	83	145	9	277	6799	49.99	20	26	112
D.W.Steyn	38	49	11	76	477	12.55	–	1	10
M.van Jaarsveld	9	15	2	73	397	30.53	–	3	11
C.M.Willoughby	2	–	–	–	–	–	–	–	–
M.Zondeki	6	5	–	59	82	16.40	–	1	1

SOUTH AFRICA – BOWLING

	O	M	R	W	Avge	Best	5wI	10wM
H.M.Amla	7	0	28	0	–	–	–	–
N.Boje	1436.4	292	4265	100	42.65	5- 62	3	–
M.V.Boucher	1.2	0	6	1	6.00	1- 6	–	–
Z.de Bruyn	36	7	92	3	30.66	2- 32	–	–
A.B.de Villiers	33	6	99	2	49.50	2- 49	–	–
F.de Wet	71	19	186	6	31.00	4- 55	–	–
J.P.Duminy	111.5	11	408	11	37.09	3- 89	–	–
H.H.Gibbs	1	0	4	0	–	–	–	–
A.J.Hall	500.1	95	1617	45	35.93	3- 1	–	–
P.L.Harris	1101.4	234	3056	87	35.12	6-127	3	–
C.W.Henderson	327	79	928	22	42.18	4-116	–	–
J.H.Kallis	2925	739	8237	261	31.55	6- 54	5	–
N.D.McKenzie	15	0	68	0	–	–	–	–
R.McLaren	13	4	43	1	43.00	1- 30	–	–
J.A.Morkel	32	4	132	1	132.00	1- 44	–	–
M.Morkel	725.5	106	2566	78	32.89	5- 50	2	–
A.Nel	1271.4	280	3919	123	31.86	6- 32	3	1
M.Ntini	3472.2	759	11242	390	28.82	7- 37	18	4
W.D.Parnell	51	5	227	5	45.40	2- 17	–	–
R.J.Peterson	159.5	41	497	14	35.50	5- 33	1	–
A.G.Prince	16	1	47	1	47.00	1- 2	–	–
J.A.Rudolph	110.4	13	432	4	108.00	1- 1	–	–
G.C.Smith	219.5	28	801	8	100.12	2-145	–	–
D.W.Steyn	1296.2	236	4609	196	23.51	7- 51	13	4
M.van Jaarsveld	7	0	28	0	–	–	–	–
C.M.Willoughby	50	18	125	1	125.00	1- 47	–	–
M.Zondeki	130	25	480	19	25.26	6- 39	1	–

TEST

WEST INDIES – BATTING AND FIELDING

	M	I	NO	HS	Runs	Avge	100	50	Ct/St
R.A.Austin	2	4	–	19	39	9.75	–	–	3
L.S.Baker	4	6	4	17	23	11.50	–	–	1
A.B.Barath	2	4	–	104	139	34.75	1	–	2
S.J.Benn	12	20	2	35	251	13.94	–	–	6
D.E.Bernard	3	6	1	69	202	40.40	–	3	–
T.L.Best	14	23	3	27	196	9.80	–	–	1
D.J.Bravo	34	63	1	113	2009	32.40	3	11	35
G.R.Breese	1	2	–	5	5	2.50	–	–	1
S.Chanderpaul	123	210	32	203*	8669	48.70	21	53	50
S.Chattergoon	4	7	–	46	127	18.14	–	–	4
C.D.Collymore	30	52	27	16*	197	7.88	–	–	6
N.Deonarine	5	8	1	82	207	29.57	–	1	4
T.M.Dowlin	4	8	–	95	328	41.00	–	3	4
F.H.Edwards	43	69	21	21	248	5.16	–	–	7
C.H.Gayle	85	150	6	317	5848	40.61	12	31	82
R.O.Hinds	15	25	1	84	505	21.04	–	2	7
X.M.Marshall	7	12	–	85	243	20.25	–	2	7
N.O.Miller	1	2	–	5	5	2.50	–	–	–
B.P.Nash	12	19	–	109	747	39.31	1	6	4
O.J.Phillips	2	4	–	94	160	40.00	–	1	1
D.B.L.Powell	37	57	5	36*	407	7.82	–	–	8
D.Ramdin	39	68	7	166	1419	23.26	1	8	116/2
R.Rampaul	3	6	2	40*	65	16.25	–	–	–
F.L.Reifer	6	12	–	29	111	9.25	–	–	6
D.M.Richards	2	4	–	69	108	27.00	–	1	3
K.A.J.Roach	5	10	3	17	46	6.57	–	–	3
D.J.G.Sammy	8	15	–	48	291	19.40	–	–	8
R.R.Sarwan	83	146	8	291	5759	41.73	15	31	50
L.M.P.Simmons	3	6	–	24	87	14.50	–	–	5
D.R.Smith	10	14	1	105*	320	24.61	1	–	9
D.S.Smith	31	55	2	108	1315	24.81	1	4	27
J.E.Taylor	29	46	6	106	629	15.72	1	1	5
G.C.Tonge	1	2	1	10*	14	14.00	–	–	1
C.A.K.Walton	2	4	–	10	13	3.25	–	–	10

WEST INDIES – BOWLING

	O	M	R	W	Avge	Best	5wI	10wM
R.A.Austin	54.2	9	155	3	51.66	1- 29	–	–
L.S.Baker	110	16	395	5	79.00	2- 39	–	–
A.B.Barath	1	0	4	0	–	–	–	–
S.J.Benn	532.4	90	1586	35	45.31	5-155	1	–
D.E.Bernard	43	4	185	4	46.25	2- 30	–	–
T.L.Best	364.3	48	1363	28	48.67	4- 46	–	–
D.J.Bravo	950.4	177	3090	81	38.14	6- 55	2	–
G.R.Breese	31.2	3	135	2	67.50	2-108	–	–
S.Chanderpaul	280	50	845	8	105.62	1- 2	–	–
C.D.Collymore	1056.1	245	3004	93	32.30	7- 57	4	1
N.Deonarine	80.5	21	226	4	56.50	2- 74	–	–
F.H.Edwards	1209.5	141	4811	122	39.43	7- 87	8	–
C.H.Gayle	1138.5	223	2988	71	42.08	5- 34	2	–
R.O.Hinds	290.3	53	870	13	66.92	2- 45	–	–
X.M.Marshall	2	2	0	0	–	–	–	–
N.O.Miller	22	5	67	0	–	–	–	–
B.P.Nash	55	9	178	1	178.00	1- 34	–	–
D.B.L.Powell	1179.3	219	4068	85	47.85	5- 25	1	–
R.Rampaul	77	14	290	4	72.50	1- 21	–	–
K.A.J.Roach	180.4	39	586	20	29.30	6- 48	1	–
D.J.G.Sammy	243.4	44	749	27	27.74	7- 66	3	–
R.R.Sarwan	337	33	1163	23	50.56	4- 37	–	–
L.M.P.Simmons	30	1	139	1	139.00	1- 60	–	–
D.R.Smith	108.3	20	344	7	49.14	3- 71	–	–
D.S.Smith	1	0	3	0	–	–	–	–
J.E.Taylor	822.3	150	2923	82	35.64	5- 11	3	–
G.C.Tonge	28	3	113	1	113.00	1- 28	–	–

TEST   **NEW ZEALAND – BATTING AND FIELDING**

	M	I	NO	HS	Runs	Avge	100	50	Ct/St
A.R.Adams	1	2	–	11	18	9.00	–	–	1
S.E.Bond	18	20	7	41*	168	12.92	–	–	8
G.D.Elliott	5	9	1	25	86	10.75	–	–	2
D.R.Flynn	16	29	5	95	689	28.70	–	4	7
J.E.C.Franklin	26	36	6	122*	644	21.46	1	2	11
P.G.Fulton	10	16	1	75	314	20.93	–	1	12
M.R.Gillespie	3	5	1	16*	25	6.25	–	–	–
M.J.Guptill	9	16	1	189	574	38.26	1	2	8
J.M.How	19	35	1	92	772	22.70	–	4	18
P.J.Ingram	1	2	–	42	55	27.50	–	–	–
B.B.McCullum	50	83	5	185	2678	34.33	4	15	158/10
T.G.McIntosh	11	21	2	136	568	29.89	1	3	8
H.J.H.Marshall	13	19	2	160	652	38.35	2	2	1
C.S.Martin	54	77	40	12*	83	2.24	–	–	12
K.D.Mills	19	30	5	57	289	11.56	–	1	4
I.E.O'Brien	22	34	5	31	219	7.55	–	–	7
J.D.P.Oram	33	59	10	133	1780	36.32	5	6	15
J.S.Patel	10	13	3	27*	143	14.30	–	–	5
A.J.Redmond	7	14	1	83	299	23.00	–	2	5
J.D.Ryder	11	20	2	201	898	49.88	2	4	8
T.G.Southee	7	10	2	77*	127	15.87	–	1	1
L.R.P.L.Taylor	23	42	1	154*	1735	42.31	4	9	44
D.R.Tuffey	25	34	9	80*	380	15.20	–	1	15
D.L.Vettori	98	148	23	140	3802	30.41	5	21	55
B.J.Watling	2	4	1	60*	92	30.66	–	1	1

NEW ZEALAND – BOWLING

	O	M	R	W	Avge	Best	5wI	10wM
A.R.Adams	31.4	5	105	6	17.50	3- 44	–	–
S.E.Bond	562	113	1922	87	22.09	6- 51	5	1
G.D.Elliott	47	9	140	4	35.00	2- 8	–	–
J.E.C.Franklin	733.1	134	2612	80	32.65	6-119	3	–
M.R.Gillespie	86	15	380	11	34.54	5-136	1	–
M.J.Guptill	13.2	2	37	3	12.33	3- 37	–	–
J.M.How	2	1	4	0	–	–	–	–
H.J.H.Marshall	1	0	4	0	–	–	–	–
C.S.Martin	1782.5	376	6081	180	33.78	6- 54	8	1
K.D.Mills	483.4	118	1453	44	33.02	4- 16	–	–
I.E.O'Brien	732.2	158	2429	73	33.27	6- 75	1	–
J.D.P.Oram	827.2	240	1983	60	33.05	4- 41	–	–
J.S.Patel	453	104	1417	35	40.48	5-110	1	–
A.J.Redmond	12.3	2	62	3	20.66	2- 47	–	–
J.D.Ryder	63	19	212	4	53.00	2- 7	–	–
T.G.Southee	229.3	45	804	19	42.31	5- 55	1	–
L.R.P.L.Taylor	5.2	1	14	0	–	–	–	–
D.R.Tuffey	790.5	202	2396	77	31.11	6- 54	2	–
D.L.Vettori	4058.4	1017	10688	318	33.61	7- 87	18	3

TEST

INDIA – BATTING AND FIELDING

	M	I	NO	HS	Runs	Avge	100	50	Ct/St
S.Badrinath	2	3	–	56	63	21.00	–	1	2
P.P.Chawla	2	2	–	4	5	2.50	–	–	–
M.S.Dhoni	43	66	9	148	2428	42.59	4	17	113/20
R.S.Dravid	139	240	28	270	11395	53.75	29	58	193
G.Gambhir	31	.55	4	206	2798	54.86	9	11	25
S.C.Ganguly	113	188	17	239	7212	42.17	16	35	71
Harbhajan Singh	83	114	20	66	1585	16.86	–	7	40
K.D.Karthik	23	37	1	129	1000	27.77	1	7	51/5
M.Kartik	8	10	1	43	88	9.77	–	–	2
Z.Khan	72	94	22	75	969	13.45	–	5	18
A.Kumble	132	173	32	110*	2506	17.77	1	5	60
V.V.S.Laxman	110	181	28	281	7136	46.64	15	43	115
A.Mishra	9	12	2	50	165	16.50	–	1	5
P.P.Ojha	3	3	3	5*	7	–	–	–	3
M.M.Patel	12	13	5	15*	56	7.00	–	–	6
W.P.Saha	1	2	–	36	36	18.00	–	–	–
V.Sehwag	76	130	5	319	6691	53.52	19	21	60
I.Sharma	23	30	.15	23	163	10.86	–	–	7
S.Sreesanth	17	24	7	35	226	13.29	–	–	2
S.R.Tendulkar	166	271	29	248*	13447	55.56	47	54	104
M.Vijay	5	7	–	87	234	33.42	–	1	5
Yuvraj Singh	33	50	6	169	1582	35.95	3	8	30

INDIA – BOWLING

	O	M	R	W	Avge	Best	5wI	10wM
P.P.Chawla	34.1	6	137	3	45.66	2- 66	–	–
M.S.Dhoni	2	0	14	0	–	–	–	–
R.S.Dravid	20	4	39	1	39.00	1- 18	–	–
S.C.Ganguly	519.3	108	1681	32	52.53	3- 28	–	–
Harbhajan Singh	3900.1	738	10985	355	30.94	8- 84	24	5
M.Kartik	322	74	820	24	34.16	4- 44	–	–
Z.Khan	2402.5	484	7983	242	32.98	7- 87	9	1
A.Kumble	6808.2	1576	18355	619	29.65	10- 74	35	8
V.V.S.Laxman	54	12	126	2	63.00	1- 2	–	–
A.Mishra	415.4	68	1242	32	38.81	5- 71	1	–
P.P.Ojha	123.1	26	384	13	29.53	3-101	–	–
M.M.Patel	399	83	1230	34	36.17	4- 25	–	–
V.Sehwag	464.1	67	1405	32	43.90	5-104	1	–
I.Sharma	704	127	2306	66	34.93	5-118	1	–
S.Sreesanth	564.1	126	1921	60	32.01	5- 40	2	–
S.R.Tendulkar	665.4	81	2299	44	52.25	3- 10	–	–
Yuvraj Singh	125.1	13	431	86	53.87	2- 9	–	–

TEST

PAKISTAN – BATTING AND FIELDING

	M	I	NO	HS	Runs	Avge	100	50	Ct/St
Abdur Rauf	3	6	–	31	52	8.66	–	–	–
Azhar Mahmood	21	34	4	136	900	30.00	3	1	14
Danish Kaneria	58	79	32	29	306	6.51	–	–	18
Faisal Iqbal	26	44	2	139	1124	26.76	1	8	22
Fawad Alam	3	6	–	168	250	41.66	1	–	3
Imran Farhat	33	63	2	128	2071	33.95	3	13	35
Kamran Akmal	48	82	6	158*	2550	33.55	6	12	159/22
Khurram Manzoor	7	12	1	93	326	29.63	–	3	3
Misbah-ul-Haq	19	33	3	161*	1008	33.60	2	4	24
Mohammad Aamer	8	16	4	30*	187	15.58	–	–	–
Mohammad Asif	17	28	10	29	104	5.77	–	–	2
Mohammad Sami	34	53	13	49	473	11.82	–	–	7
Mohammad Talha	1	–	–	–	–	–	–	–	–
Mohammad Yousuf	88	152	12	223	7431	53.07	24	32	65
Saeed Ajmal	5	10	5	10	29	5.80	–	–	–
Salman Butt	27	50	–	122	1548	30.96	3	8	12
Sarfraz Ahmed	1	2	0	5	6	3.00	–	–	4
Shahid Afridi	26	46	1	156	1683	37.40	5	8	10
Shoaib Malik	29	48	6	148*	15172	36.11	2	8	16
Sohail Khan	1	–	–	–	–	–	–	–	–
Umar Akmal	6	12	–	129	578	48.16	1	4	3
Umar Gul	26	36	3	46	325	9.84	–	–	7
Yasir Arafat	3	3	1	50*	94	47.00	–	1	–
Younus Khan	63	112	7	313	5260	50.09	16	21	67

PAKISTAN – BOWLING

	O	M	R	W	Avge	Best	5wI	10wM
Abdur Rauf	75	11	278	6	46.33	2- 59	–	–
Azhar Mahmood	502.3	111	1402	39	35.94	4- 50	–	–
Danish Kaneria	2859.3	506	8705	254	34.27	7- 77	15	2
Faisal Iqbal	1	0	7	0	–	–	–	–
Imran Farhat	57.1	3	244	3	81.33	2- 69	–	–
Mohammad Aamer	269	58	890	21	42.38	5- 79	1	–
Mohammad Asif	650.4	154	1926	83	23.20	6- 41	6	1
Mohammad Sami	1195.5	191	4262	84	50.73	5- 36	2	–
Mohammad Talha	17	0	88	1	88.00	1- 88	–	–
Mohammad Yousuf	1	0	3	0	–	–	–	–
Saeed Ajmal	270.4	43	761	18	42.27	4- 87	–	–
Salman Butt	22.5	1	106	1	106.00	1- 36	–	–
Shahid Afridi	515.2	69	1640	47	34.89	5- 52	1	–
Shoaib Malik	347.4	45	1201	19	63.21	4- 42	–	–
Sohail Khan	27	2	164	0	–	–	–	–
Umar Gul	919.2	141	3324	96	34.62	6-135	4	–
Yasir Arafat	104.3	12	438	9	48.66	5-161	1	–
Younus Khan	90	12	341	7	48.71	2- 23	–	–

TEST **SRI LANKA – BATTING AND FIELDING**

	M	I	NO	HS	Runs	Avge	100	50	Ct/St
C.M.Bandara	8	11	3	43	124	15.50	–	–	4
T.M.Dilshan	60	95	10	168	3691	43.42	11	13	70
C.R.D.Fernando	33	40	13	36*	198	7.33	–	–	10
H.M.R.K.B.Herath	21	27	4	33*	207	9.00	–	–	4
D.P.M.D.Jayawardena	110	182	13	374	9120	53.96	27	35	152
H.A.P.W.Jayawardena	30	40	6	154*	1044	30.70	2	2	61/20
C.K.Kapugedera	8	15	3	96	418	34.83	–	4	6
K.M.D.N.Kulasekara	11	16	1	64	245	16.33	–	1	4
A.D.Mathews	7	11	1	99	379	37.90	–	2	2
B.A.W.Mendis	10	11	4	27	64	9.14	–	–	1
M.Muralitharan	132	163	55	67	1256	11.62	–	1	72
N.T.Paranavitana	10	18	–	73	530	29.44	–	4	4
K.T.G.D.Prasad	4	4	–	36	66	16.50	–	–	1
T.T.Samaraweera	57	90	13	231	3938	51.14	11	21	36
K.C.Sangakkara	88	147	10	287	7549	55.10	21	32	157/20
T.Thushara	9	13	2	15*	90	8.18	–	–	3
W.P.U.C.J.Vaas	111	162	35	100*	3089	24.32	1	13	31
M.G.Vandort	20	33	2	140	1144	36.90	4	4	6
B.S.M.Warnapura	14	24	1	120	821	35.69	2	7	14
U.W.M.B.C.A.Welagedara	4	4	1	8	19	6.33	–	–	1

SRI LANKA – BOWLING

	O	M	R	W	Avge	Best	5wI	10wM
C.M.Bandara	192	29	633	16	39.56	3- 84	–	–
T.M.Dilshan	154.2	31	471	13	36.23	4- 10	–	–
C.R.D.Fernando	854.2	129	3072	88	34.90	5- 42	3	–
H.M.R.K.B.Herath	852.1	155	2568	70	36.68	5- 99	4	–
D.P.M.D.Jayawardena	91.1	18	292	6	48.66	2- 32	–	–
C.K.Kapugedera	2	0	9	0	–	–	–	–
K.M.D.N.Kulasekara	268.4	51	862	25	34.48	4- 21	–	–
A.D.Mathews	89	14	302	5	60.40	1- 13	–	–
B.A.W.Mendis	431	69	1298	44	29.50	6-117	2	1
M.Muralitharan	7278.1	1786	17989	792	22.71	9- 51	66	22
N.T.Paranavitana	15	0	76	1	76.00	1- 26	–	–
K.T.G.D.Prasad	122.2	7	567	13	43.61	3- 82	–	–
T.T.Samaraweera	215.1	36	679	14	48.50	4- 49	–	–
K.C.Sangakkara	11	0	38	0	–	–	–	–
T.Thushara	257	31	961	28	34.32	5- 83	1	–
W.P.U.C.J.Vaas	3906.2	895	10501	355	29.58	7- 71	12	2
B.S.M.Warnapura	9	0	40	0	–	–	–	–
U.W.M.B.C.A.Welagedara	121	14	473	10	47.30	4- 87	–	–

TEST **ZIMBABWE – BATTING AND FIELDING**

	M	I	NO	HS	Runs	Avge	100	50	Ct/St
S.M.Ervine	5	8	–	86	261	32.62	–	3	7
G.W.Flower	67	123	6	201*	3457	29.54	6	15	43
M.W.Goodwin	19	37	4	166*	1414	42.84	3	8	10

ZIMBABWE – BOWLING

	O	M	R	W	Avge	Best	5wI	10wM
S.M.Ervine	95	18	388	9	43.11	4-116	–	–
G.W.Flower	563	122	1537	25	61.48	4- 41	–	–
M.W.Goodwin	19.5	3	69	0			–	–

BANGLADESH – BATTING AND FIELDING

	M	I	NO	HS	Runs	Avge	100	50	Ct/St
Abdur Razzak	5	9	3	33	129	21.50	–	–	2
Aftab Ahmed	15	29	3	82*	555	21.34	–	1	6
Enamul Haque[2]	14	24	15	13	53	5.88	–	–	3
Imrul Kayes	9	18	–	33	247	13.72	–	–	8
Junaid Siddique	14	27	–	78	617	22.85	–	5	7
Mahbubul Alam	4	7	3	2	5	1.25	–	–	–
Mahmudullah	5	10	2	115	387	48.37	1	2	5
Mashrafe Mortaza	36	67	5	79	797	12.85	–	3	9
Mehrab Hossain[2]	7	13	1	83	243	20.25	–	1	2
Mohammad Ashraful	53	103	4	158*	2256	22.78	5	7	24
Mushfiqur Rahim	19	37	3	101	893	26.26	1	4	29/4
Naeem Islam	2	4	–	19	44	11.00	–	–	1
Rajin Saleh	24	46	2	89	1141	25.93	–	7	15
Raqibul Hasan	7	14	–	65	268	19.14	–	1	7
Rubel Hossain	5	9	4	4*	13	2.60	–	–	2
Shafiul Islam	3	6	1	13	48	9.60	–	–	–
Shahadat Hossain	26	49	14	40	344	9.82	–	–	6
Shahriar Nafees	16	32	–	138	835	26.09	1	4	12
Shakib Al Hasan	17	32	2	100	977	32.56	1	4	8
Tamim Iqbal	15	28	–	151	940	33.57	2	4	7

BANGLADESH – BOWLING

	O	M	R	W	Avge	Best	5wI	10wM
Abdur Razzak	188	27	561	7	80.14	3- 93	–	–
Aftab Ahmed	56.2	8	235	5	47.00	2- 31	–	–
Enamul Haque[2]	531.3	94	1609	41	39.24	7- 95	3	1
Imrul Kayes	1	0	7	0			–	–
Junaid Siddique	3	0	11	0			–	–
Mahbubul Alam	97.5	19	314	5	62.80	2- 62	–	–
Mahmudullah	119.4	10	443	16	27.68	5- 51	1	–
Mashrafe Mortaza	998.2	202	3239	78	41.52	4- 60	–	–
Mehrab Hossain[2]	67.5	3	281	4	70.25	2- 29	–	–
Mohammad Ashraful	263.1	11	1175	20	58.75	2- 42	–	–
Naeem Islam	20	2	46	1	46.00	1- 11	–	–
Rajin Saleh	73	5	268	2	134.00	1- 9	–	–
Raqibul Hasan	3	1	5	1	5.00	1- 0	–	–
Rubel Hossain	134	5	641	9	71.22	5-166	1	–
Shafiul Islam	92	7	372	5	74.40	3- 86	–	–
Shahadat Hossain	648.2	66	2699	60	44.98	6- 27	1	–
Shakib Al Hasan	641.4	132	1782	58	30.72	7- 36	6	–
Tamim Iqbal	2	0	4	0			–	–

INTERNATIONAL TEST MATCH RESULTS

Matches completed by 20 February 2010.

| Opponents | Tests | Won by | | | | | | | | | | Tied | Drawn |
		E	A	SA	WI	NZ	I	P	SL	Z	B		
England Australia	321	99	132	–	–	–	–	–	–	–	–	–	90
South Africa	138	56	–	29	–	–	–	–	–	–	–	–	53
West Indies	145	43	–	–	53	–	–	–	–	–	–	–	49
New Zealand	94	45	–	–	–	8	–	–	–	–	–	–	41
India	99	34	–	–	–	–	19	–	–	–	–	–	46
Pakistan	67	19	–	–	–	–	–	12	–	–	–	–	36
Sri Lanka	21	8	–	–	–	–	–	–	6	–	–	–	7
Zimbabwe	6	3	–	–	–	–	–	–	–	0	–	–	3
Bangladesh	4	4	–	–	–	–	–	–	–	–	0	–	–
Australia South Africa	83	–	47	18	–	–	–	–	–	–	–	–	18
West Indies	108	–	52	–	32	–	–	–	–	–	–	1	23
New Zealand	48	–	24	–	–	7	–	–	–	–	–	–	17
India	76	–	34	–	–	–	18	–	–	–	–	1	23
Pakistan	55	–	27	–	–	–	–	11	–	–	–	–	17
Sri Lanka	20	–	13	–	–	–	–	–	1	–	–	–	6
Zimbabwe	3	–	3	–	–	–	–	–	–	0	–	–	–
Bangladesh	4	–	4	–	–	–	–	–	–	–	0	–	–
South Africa West Indies	22	–	–	14	3	–	–	–	–	–	–	–	5
New Zealand	35	–	–	20	–	4	–	–	–	–	–	–	11
India	24	–	–	11	–	–	6	–	–	–	–	–	7
Pakistan	16	–	–	8	–	–	–	3	–	–	–	–	5
Sri Lanka	17	–	–	8	–	–	–	–	4	–	–	–	5
Zimbabwe	7	–	–	6	–	–	–	–	–	0	–	–	1
Bangladesh	8	–	–	8	–	–	–	–	–	–	0	–	–
West Indies New Zealand	37	–	–	–	10	9	–	–	–	–	–	–	18
India	82	–	–	–	30	–	11	–	–	–	–	–	41
Pakistan	44	–	–	–	14	–	–	15	–	–	–	–	15
Sri Lanka	12	–	–	–	3	–	–	–	6	–	–	–	3
Zimbabwe	6	–	–	–	4	–	–	–	–	–	–	–	2
Bangladesh	6	–	–	–	3	–	–	–	–	–	2	–	1
New Zealand India	47	–	–	–	–	9	15	–	–	–	–	–	23
Pakistan	48	–	–	–	–	7	–	22	–	–	–	–	19
Sri Lanka	26	–	–	–	–	9	–	–	7	–	–	–	10
Zimbabwe	13	–	–	–	–	7	–	–	–	0	–	–	6
Bangladesh	9	–	–	–	–	8	–	–	–	–	0	–	1
India Pakistan	59	–	–	–	–	–	9	12	–	–	–	–	38
Sri Lanka	32	–	–	–	–	–	13	–	5	–	–	–	14
Zimbabwe	11	–	–	–	–	–	7	–	–	2	–	–	2
Bangladesh	7	–	–	–	–	–	6	–	–	–	0	–	1
Pakistan Sri Lanka	37	–	–	–	–	–	–	15	9	–	–	–	13
Zimbabwe	14	–	–	–	–	–	–	8	–	2	–	–	4
Bangladesh	6	–	–	–	–	–	–	6	–	–	0	–	–
Sri Lanka Zimbabwe	15	–	–	–	–	–	–	–	10	0	–	–	5
Bangladesh	12	–	–	–	–	–	–	–	12	–	0	–	–
Zimbabwe Bangladesh	8	–	–	–	–	–	–	–	–	4	1	–	3
	1952	311	336	122	152	68	104	104	60	8	3	2	682

	Tests	Won	Lost	Drawn	Tied	Toss Won
England	895	311	259	325	–	433
Australia	718	336	186	194	2	361
South Africa	350	122	123	105	–	167
West Indies	462	152	152	157	1	242
New Zealand	357	68	143	146	–	181
India	437	104	137	195	1	224
Pakistan	346	104	95	147	–	163
Sri Lanka	192	60	69	63	–	97
Zimbabwe	83	8	49	26	–	49
Bangladesh	64	3	57	6	–	33

INTERNATIONAL TEST CRICKET RECORDS

(To 20 February 2010)

TEAM RECORDS

HIGHEST INNINGS TOTALS

952-6d	Sri Lanka v India	Colombo (RPS)	1997-98
903-7d	England v Australia	The Oval	1938
849	England v West Indies	Kingston	1929-30
790-3d	West Indies v Pakistan	Kingston	1957-58
765-6d	Pakistan v Sri Lanka	Karachi	2008-09
760-7d	Sri Lanka v India	Ahmedabad	2009-10
758-8d	Australia v West Indies	Kingston	1954-55
756-5d	Sri Lanka v South Africa	Colombo (SSC)	2006
751-5d	West Indies v England	St John's	2003-04
749-9d	West Indies v England	Bridgetown	2008-09
747	West Indies v South Africa	St John's	2004-05
735-6d	Australia v Zimbabwe	Perth	2003-04
729-6d	Australia v England	Lord's	1930
726-9d	India v Sri Lanka	Mumbai	2009-10
713-3d	Sri Lanka v Zimbabwe	Bulawayo	2003-04
708	Pakistan v England	The Oval	1987
705-7d	India v Australia	Sydney	2003-04
701	Australia v England	The Oval	1934
699-5	Pakistan v India	Lahore	1989-90
695	Australia v England	The Oval	1930
692-8d	West Indies v England	The Oval	1995
687-8d	West Indies v England	The Oval	1976
682-6d	South Africa v England	Lord's	2003
681-8d	West Indies v England	Port-of-Spain	1953-54
679-7d	Pakistan v India	Lahore	2005-06
676-7	India v Sri Lanka	Kanpur	1986-87
675-5d	India v Pakistan	Multan	2003-04
674-6	Pakistan v India	Faisalabad	1984-85
674-6d	Australia v England	Cardiff	2009
674	Australia v India	Adelaide	1947-48
671-4	New Zealand v Sri Lanka	Wellington	1990-91
668	Australia v West Indies	Bridgetown	1954-55
664	India v England	The Oval	2007
660-5d	West Indies v New Zealand	Wellington	1994-95
659-8d	Australia v England	Sydney	1946-47

658-8d	England v Australia	Nottingham	1938
658-9d	South Africa v West Indies	Durban	2003-04
657-7d	India v Australia	Calcutta	2000-01
657-8d	Pakistan v West Indies	Bridgetown	1957-58
656-8d	Australia v England	Manchester	1964
654-5	England v South Africa	Durban	1938-39
653-4d	England v India	Lord's	1990
653-4d	Australia v England	Leeds	1993
652-7d	England v India	Madras	1984-85
652-7d	Australia v South Africa	Johannesburg	2001-02
652-8d	West Indies v England	Lord's	1973
652	Pakistan v India	Faisalabad	1982-83
651	South Africa v Australia	Cape Town	2008-09
650-6d	Australia v West Indies	Bridgetown	1964-65

The highest for Zimbabwe is 563-9d (v WI, Harare, 2001), and for Bangladesh 488 (v Z, Chittagong, 2004-05).

LOWEST INNINGS TOTALS

† One batsman absent

26	New Zealand v England	Auckland	1954-55
30	South Africa v England	Port Elizabeth	1895-96
30	South Africa v England	Birmingham	1924
35	South Africa v England	Cape Town	1898-99
36	Australia v England	Birmingham	1902
36	South Africa v Australia	Melbourne	1931-32
42	Australia v England	Sydney	1887-88
42	New Zealand v Australia	Wellington	1945-46
42†	India v England	Lord's	1974
43	South Africa v England	Cape Town	1888-89
44	Australia v England	The Oval	1896
45	England v Australia	Sydney	1886-87
45	South Africa v Australia	Melbourne	1931-32
46	England v West Indies	Port-of-Spain	1993-94
47	South Africa v England	Cape Town	1888-89
47	New Zealand v England	Lord's	1958
47	West Indies v England	Kingston	2003-04

The lowest for Pakistan is 53† (v A, Sharjah, 2002-03), for Sri Lanka 71 (v P, Kandy, 1994-95), for Zimbabwe 54 (v SA, Cape Town, 2004-05), and for Bangladesh 62 (v SL, Colombo PPS, 2006-07).

BATTING RECORDS

5000 RUNS IN A TEST CAREER

Runs			M	I	NO	HS	Avge	100	50
13447	S.R.Tendulkar	I	166	271	29	248*	55.56	47	54
11953	B.C.Lara	WI/ICC	131	232	6	400*	52.88	34	48
11859	R.T.Ponting	A	142	240	27	257	55.67	39	51
11395	R.Dravid	I/ICC	139	240	28	270	53.75	29	58
11174	A.R.Border	A	156	265	44	205	50.56	27	63
10927	S.R.Waugh	A	168	260	46	200	51.06	32	50
10843	J.H.Kallis	SA/ICC	137	231	33	189*	54.76	34	52
10122	S.M.Gavaskar	I	125	214	16	236*	51.12	34	45
9120	D.P.M.D.Jayawardena	SL	110	182	13	374	53.96	27	35
8900	G.A.Gooch	E	118	215	6	333	42.58	20	46
8832	Javed Miandad	P	124	189	21	280*	52.57	23	43
8830	Inzamam-ul-Haq	P/ICC	120	200	22	329	49.60	25	46

Runs			M	I	NO	HS	Avge	100	50
8669	S.Chanderpaul	WI	123	210	32	203*	48.70	21	53
8625	M.L.Hayden	A	103	184	14	380	50.73	30	29
8540	I.V.A.Richards	WI	121	182	12	291	50.23	24	45
8463	A.J.Stewart	E	133	235	21	190	39.54	15	45
8231	D.I.Gower	E	117	204	18	215	44.25	18	39
8114	G.Boycott	E	108	193	23	246*	47.72	22	42
8032	G.St A.Sobers	WI	93	160	21	365*	57.78	26	30
8029	M.E.Waugh	A	128	209	17	153*	41.81	20	47
7728	M.A.Atherton	E	115	212	7	185*	37.70	16	46
7696	J.L.Langer	A	105	182	12	250	45.27	23	30
7624	M.C.Cowdrey	E	114	188	15	182	44.06	22	38
7558	C.G.Greenidge	WI	108	185	16	226	44.72	19	34
7549	K.C.Sangakkara	SL	88	147	10	287	55.10	21	32
7525	M.A.Taylor	A	104	186	13	334*	43.49	19	40
7515	C.H.Lloyd	WI	110	175	14	242*	46.67	19	39
7487	D.L.Haynes	WI	116	202	25	184	42.29	18	39
7431	Mohammad Yousuf	P	88	152	12	223	53.07	24	32
7422	D.C.Boon	A	107	190	20	200	43.65	21	32
7289	G.Kirsten	SA	101	176	15	275	45.27	21	34
7249	W.R.Hammond	E	85	140	16	336*	58.45	22	24
7212	S.C.Ganguly	I	113	188	17	239	42.17	16	35
7172	S.P.Fleming	NZ	111	189	10	274*	40.06	9	46
7136	V.V.S.Laxman	I	110	181	28	281	46.64	15	43
7110	G.S.Chappell	A	87	151	19	247*	53.86	24	31
6996	D.G.Bradman	A	52	80	10	334	99.94	29	13
6973	S.T.Jayasuriya	SL	110	188	14	340	40.07	14	31
6971	L.Hutton	E	79	138	15	364	56.67	19	33
6868	D.B.Vengsarkar	I	116	185	22	166	42.13	17	35
6806	K.F.Barrington	E	82	131	15	256	58.67	20	35
6799	G.C.Smith	SA/ICC	83	145	9	277	49.99	20	26
6744	G.P.Thorpe	E	100	179	28	200*	44.66	16	39
6691	V.Sehwag	I/ICC	76	130	5	319	53.52	19	21
6361	P.A.de Silva	SL	93	159	11	267	42.97	20	22
6227	R.B.Kanhai	WI	79	137	6	256	47.53	15	28
6215	M.Azharuddin	I	99	147	9	199	45.03	22	21
6167	H.H.Gibbs	SA	90	154	7	228	41.95	14	26
6149	R.N.Harvey	A	79	137	10	205	48.41	21	24
6080	G.R.Viswanath	I	91	155	10	222	41.93	14	35
5949	R.B.Richardson	WI	86	146	12	194	44.39	16	27
5848	C.H.Gayle	WI	85	150	6	317	40.61	12	31
5825	M.E.Trescothick	E	76	143	10	219	43.79	14	29
5807	D.C.S.Compton	E	78	131	15	278	50.06	17	28
5768	Salim Malik	P	103	154	22	237	43.69	15	29
5764	N.Hussain	E	96	171	16	207	37.19	14	33
5762	C.L.Hooper	WI	102	173	15	233	36.46	13	27
5759	R.R.Sarwan	WI	83	146	8	291	41.73	15	31
5719	M.P.Vaughan	E	82	147	9	197	41.44	18	18
5570	A.C.Gilchrist	A	96	137	20	204*	47.60	17	26
5502	M.S.Atapattu	SL	90	156	15	249	39.02	16	17
5444	M.D.Crowe	NZ	77	131	11	299	45.36	17	18
5436	A.J.Strauss	E	71	130	5	177	43.48	18	18
5410	J.B.Hobbs	E	61	102	7	211	56.94	15	28
5357	K.D.Walters	A	74	125	14	250	48.26	15	33
5345	I.M.Chappell	A	75	136	10	196	42.42	14	26
5334	J.G.Wright	NZ	82	148	7	185	37.82	12	23
5312	M.J.Slater	A	74	131	7	219	42.84	14	21

Runs			M	I	NO	HS	Avge	100	50
5260	Younus Khan	P	63	112	7	313	50.09	16	21
5248	Kapil Dev	I	131	184	15	163	31.05	8	27
5234	W.M.Lawry	A	67	123	12	210	47.15	13	27
5200	I.T.Botham	E	102	161	6	208	33.54	14	22
5138	J.H.Edrich	E	77	127	9	310*	43.54	12	24
5105	A.Ranatunga	SL	93	155	12	135*	35.69	4	38
5068	M.V.Boucher	SA/ICC	131	186	22	125	30.90	5	32
5062	Zaheer Abbas	P	78	124	11	274	44.79	12	20

The most for Zimbabwe is 4794 (63 innings) by A.Flower, and for Bangladesh 3026 by Habibul Bashar (99 innings).

750 RUNS IN A SERIES

Runs			Series	M	I	NO	HS	Avge	100	50
974	D.G.Bradman	A v E	1930	5	7	–	334	139.14	4	–
905	W.R.Hammond	E v A	1928-29	5	9	1	251	113.12	4	–
839	M.A.Taylor	A v E	1989	6	11	1	219	83.90	2	5
834	R.N.Harvey	A v SA	1952-53	5	9	–	205	92.66	4	3
829	I.V.A.Richards	WI v E	1976	4	7	–	291	118.42	3	2
827	C.L.Walcott	WI v A	1954-55	5	10	–	155	82.70	5	2
824	G.St A.Sobers	WI v P	1957-58	5	8	2	365*	137.33	3	3
810	D.G.Bradman	A v E	1936-37	5	9	–	270	90.00	3	1
806	D.G.Bradman	A v SA	1931-32	5	5	1	299*	201.50	4	–
798	B.C.Lara	WI v E	1993-94	5	8	–	375	99.75	2	2
779	E.de C.Weekes	WI v I	1948-49	5	7	–	194	111.28	4	2
774	S.M.Gavaskar	I v WI	1970-71	4	8	3	220	154.80	4	3
765	B.C.Lara	WI v E	1995	6	10	1	179	85.00	3	3
761	Mudassar Nazar	P v I	1982-83	5	8	2	231	126.83	4	1
758	D.G.Bradman	A v E	1934	5	8	–	304	94.75	2	1
753	D.C.S.Compton	E v SA	1947	5	8	–	208	94.12	4	2
752	G.A.Gooch	E v I	1990	3	6	–	333	125.33	3	2

HIGHEST INDIVIDUAL INNINGS

400*	B.C.Lara	WI v E	St John's	2003-04
380	M.L.Hayden	A v Z	Perth	2003-04
375	B.C.Lara	WI v E	St John's	1993-94
374	D.P.M.D.Jayawardena	SL v SA	Colombo (SSC)	2006
365*	G.St A.Sobers	WI v P	Kingston	1957-58
364	L.Hutton	E v A	The Oval	1938
340	S.T.Jayasuriya	SL v I	Colombo (RPS)	1997-98
337	Hanif Mohammed	P v WI	Bridgetown	1957-58
336*	W.R.Hammond	E v NZ	Auckland	1932-33
334*	M.A.Taylor	A v P	Peshawar	1998-99
334	D.G.Bradman	A v E	Leeds	1930
333	G.A.Gooch	E v I	Lord's	1990
329	Inzamam-ul-Haq	P v NZ	Lahore	2001-02
325	A.Sandham	E v WI	Kingston	1929-30
319	V.Sehwag	I v SA	Chennai	2007-08
317	C.H.Gayle	WI v SA	St John's	2004-05
313	Younus Khan	P v SL	Karachi	2008-09
311	R.B.Simpson	A v E	Manchester	1964
310*	J.H.Edrich	E v NZ	Leeds	1965
309	V.Sehwag	I v P	Multan	2003-04
307	R.M.Cowper	A v E	Melbourne	1965-66
304	D.G.Bradman	A v E	Leeds	1934
302	L.G.Rowe	WI v E	Bridgetown	1973-74

299*	D.G.Bradman	A v SA	Adelaide	1931-32
299	M.D.Crowe	NZ v SL	Wellington	1990-91
293	V.Sehwag	I v SL	Mumbai	2009-10
291	I.V.A.Richards	WI v E	The Oval	1976
291	R.R.Sarwan	WI v E	Bridgetown	2008-09
287	R.E.Foster	E v A	Sydney	1903-04
287	K.C.Sangakkara	SL v SA	Colombo (SSC)	2006
285*	P.B.H.May	E v WI	Birmingham	1957
281	V.V.S.Laxman	I v A	Calcutta	2000-01
280*	Javed Miandad	P v I	Hyderabad	1982-83
278	D.C.S.Compton	E v P	Nottingham	1954
277	B.C.Lara	WI v A	Sydney	1992-93
277	G.C.Smith	SA v E	Birmingham	2003
275*	D.J.Cullinan	SA v NZ	Auckland	1998-99
275	G.Kirsten	SA v E	Durban	1999-00
275	D.P.M.D.Jayawardena	SL v I	Ahmedabad	2009-10
274*	S.P.Fleming	NZ v SL	Colombo (SSC)	2002-03
274	R.G.Pollock	SA v A	Durban	1969-70
274	Zaheer Abbas	P v E	Birmingham	1971
271	Javed Miandad	P v NZ	Auckland	1988-89
270*	G.A.Headley	WI v E	Kingston	1934-35
270	D.G.Bradman	A v E	Melbourne	1936-37
270	R.Dravid	I v P	Rawalpindi	2003-04
270	K.C.Sangakkara	SL v Z	Bulawayo	2003-04
268	G.N.Yallop	A v P	Melbourne	1983-84
267*	B.A.Young	NZ v SL	Dunedin	1996-97
267	P.A.de Silva	SL v NZ	Wellington	1990-91
267	Younus Khan	P v I	Bangalore	2004-05
266	W.H.Ponsford	A v E	The Oval	1934
266	D.L.Houghton	Z v SL	Bulawayo	1994-95
262*	D.L.Amiss	E v WI	Kingston	1973-74
262	S.P.Fleming	NZ v SA	Cape Town	2005-06
261*	R.R.Sarwan	WI v B	Kingston	2004
261	F.M.M.Worrell	WI v E	Nottingham	1950
260	C.C.Hunte	WI v P	Kingston	1957-58
260	Javed Miandad	P v E	The Oval	1987
259	G.M.Turner	NZ v WI	Georgetown	1971-72
259	G.C.Smith	SA v E	Lord's	2003
258	T.W.Graveney	E v WI	Nottingham	1957
258	S.M.Nurse	WI v NZ	Christchurch	1968-69
257*	Wasim Akram	P v Z	Sheikhupura	1996-97
257	R.T.Ponting	A v I	Melbourne	2003-04
256	R.B.Kanhai	WI v I	Calcutta	1958-59
256	K.F.Barrington	E v A	Manchester	1964
255*	D.J.McGlew	SA v NZ	Wellington	1952-53
254	D.G.Bradman	A v E	Lord's	1930
254	V.Sehwag	I v P	Lahore	2005-06
253*	H.M.Amla	SA v I	Nagpur	2009-10
253	S.T.Jayasuriya	SL v P	Faisalabad	2004-05
251	W.R.Hammond	E v A	Sydney	1928-29
250	K.D.Walters	A v NZ	Christchurch	1976-77
250	S.F.A.F.Bacchus	WI v I	Kanpur	1978-79
250	J.L.Langer	A v E	Melbourne	2002-03

The highest for Bangladesh is 158* by Mohammad Ashraful (v I, Chittagong, 2004-05).

20 HUNDREDS

					Opponents								
			200	Inn	E	A	SA	WI	NZ	I	P	SL	Z	B
47	S.R.Tendulkar	I	4	271	7	10	5	3	4	–	2	8	3	5
39	R.T.Ponting	A	5	240	8	–	8	7	2	6	5	1	1	1
34	S.M.Gavaskar	I	4	214	4	8	–	13	2	–	5	2	–	–
34	B.C.Lara	WI	8	232	7	9	4	–	1	2	4	5	1	1
34	J.H.Kallis	SA	–	231	7	4	–	7	5	3	4	–	3	1
32	S.R.Waugh	A	1	260	10	–	2	7	2	2	3	3	1	2
30	M.L.Hayden †	A	2	184	5	–	6	5	1	6	1	3	2	–
29	D.G.Bradman	A	12	80	19	–	4	2	–	4	–	–	–	–
29	R.Dravid	I	5	240	4	3	1	3	4	–	5	3	3	3
27	A.R.Border	A	2	265	8	–	–	3	5	4	6	1	–	–
27	D.P.M.D.Jayawardena	SL	6	182	6	1	5	1	3	5	1	–	1	4
26	G.St A.Sobers	WI	2	160	10	4	–	–	1	8	3	–	–	–
25	Inzamam-ul-Haq	P	2	200	5	1	–	4	3	3	–	5	2	2
24	G.S.Chappell	A	4	151	9	–	5	3	2	1	6	–	–	–
24	I.V.A.Richards	WI	3	182	8	5	–	1	8	2	–	–	–	–
24	Mohammad Yousuf	P	4	152	6	1	–	7	1	4	–	1	2	2
23	J.L.Langer	A	3	182	5	–	2	3	4	3	4	–	1	–
23	Javed Miandad	P	6	189	2	6	–	2	7	5	4	1	–	–
22	W.R.Hammond	E	7	140	–	9	6	1	4	2	–	–	–	–
22	M.Azharuddin	I	–	147	6	2	4	–	2	–	3	1	2	–
22	M.C.Cowdrey	E	–	188	–	5	3	6	2	3	3	–	–	–
22	G.Boycott	E	1	193	–	7	1	5	2	4	3	–	–	–
21	R.N.Harvey	A	2	137	6	–	8	3	–	4	–	–	–	–
21	G.Kirsten	SA	3	176	5	2	–	3	2	3	2	1	1	2
21	D.C.Boon	A	1	190	7	–	3	3	6	1	1	–	–	–
21	S.Chanderpaul	WI	1	210	5	4	4	–	1	5	1	–	–	1
21	K.C.Sangakkara	SL	6	147	1	1	2	2	3	3	5	–	2	2
20	K.F.Barrington	E	1	131	–	5	2	3	3	3	4	–	–	–
20	P.A.de Silva	SL	2	159	2	1	–	2	5	8	–	1	1	1
20	M.E.Waugh	A	–	209	6	–	4	4	1	1	3	–	–	–
20	G.A.Gooch	E	2	215	–	4	5	3	4	5	1	1	–	–
20	G.C.Smith	SA	4	145	6	1	3	–	1	–	2	–	1	3

† Includes century scored for Australia v ICC in 2005-06.

The most for New Zealand is 17 by M.D.Crowe (131 innings), for Zimbabwe 12 by A.Flower (112), and for Bangladesh 5 by Mohammad Ashraful (103 innings).

The most double hundreds by batsmen not included above are 6 by M.S.Atapattu (16 hundreds for Sri Lanka), 6 by V.Sehwag (19 hundreds for India), 4 by L.Hutton (19 for England), 4 by C.G.Greenidge (19 for West Indies), 4 by Zaheer Abbas (12 for Pakistan).

HIGHEST PARTNERSHIP FOR EACH WICKET

1st	415	N.D.McKenzie/G.C.Smith	SA v B	Chittagong	2007-08
2nd	576	S.T.Jayasuriya/R.S.Mahanama	SL v I	Colombo (RPS)	1997-98
3rd	624	K.C.Sangakkara/D.P.M.D.Jayawardena	SL v SA	Colombo (SSC)	2006
4th	437	D.P.M.D.Jayawardena/T.T.Samaraweera	SL v P	Karachi	2008-09
5th	405	S.G.Barnes/D.G.Bradman	A v E	Sydney	1946-47
6th	351	D.P.M.D.Jayawardena/H.A.P.W.Jayawardena	SL v I	Ahmedabad	2009-10
7th	347	D.St E.Atkinson/C.C.Depeiza	WI v A	Bridgetown	1954-55
8th	313	Wasim Akram/Saqlain Mushtaq	P v Z	Sheikhupura	1996-97
9th	195	M.V.Boucher/P.L.Symcox	SA v P	Johannesburg	1997-98
10th	151	B.F.Hastings/R.O.Collinge	NZ v P	Auckland	1972-73
	151	Azhar Mahmood/Mushtaq Ahmed	P v SA	Rawalpindi	1997-98

BOWLING RECORDS
200 WICKETS IN TESTS

Wkts			M	Balls	Runs	Avge	5 wI	10 wM
792	M.Muralitharan	SL/ICC	132	43669	17989	22.71	66	22
708	S.K.Warne	A	145	40705	17995	25.41	37	10
619	A.Kumble	I	132	40850	18355	29.65	35	8
563	G.D.McGrath	A	124	29248	12186	21.64	29	3
519	C.A.Walsh	WI	132	30019	12688	24.44	22	3
434	Kapil Dev	I	131	27740	12867	29.64	23	2
431	R.J.Hadlee	NZ	86	21918	9612	22.30	36	9
421	S.M.Pollock	SA	108	24453	9733	23.11	16	1
414	Wasim Akram	P	104	22627	9779	23.62	25	5
405	C.E.L.Ambrose	WI	98	22104	8500	20.98	22	3
390	M.Ntini	SA	101	20834	11242	28.82	18	4
383	I.T.Botham	E	102	21815	10878	28.40	27	4
376	M.D.Marshall	WI	81	17584	7876	20.94	22	4
373	Waqar Younis	P	87	16224	8788	23.56	22	5
362	Imran Khan	P	88	19458	8258	22.81	23	6
355	D.K.Lillee	A	70	18467	8493	23.92	23	7
355	W.P.U.C.J.Vaas	SL	111	23438	10501	29.58	12	2
355	Harbhajan Singh	I	83	23401	10985	30.94	24	5
330	A.A.Donald	SA	72	15519	7344	22.25	20	3
325	R.G.D.Willis	E	90	17357	8190	25.20	16	–
318	D.L.Vettori	NZ/ICC	98	24352	10688	33.61	18	3
310	B.Lee	A	76	16531	9554	30.81	10	–
309	L.R.Gibbs	WI	79	27115	8989	29.09	18	2
307	F.S.Trueman	E	67	15178	6625	21.57	17	3
297	D.L.Underwood	E	86	21862	7674	25.83	17	6
291	C.J.McDermott	A	71	16586	8332	28.63	14	2
266	B.S.Bedi	I	67	21364	7637	28.71	14	1
261	J.H.Kallis	SA/ICC	137	17550	8237	31.55	5	–
259	J.Garner	WI	58	13169	5433	20.97	7	–
259	J.N.Gillespie	A	71	14234	6770	26.13	8	–
254	Danish Kaneria	P	58	17157	8705	34.27	15	2
252	J.B.Statham	E	70	16056	6261	24.84	9	1
249	M.A.Holding	WI	60	12680	5898	23.68	13	2
248	R.Benaud	A	63	19108	6704	27.03	16	1
248	M.J.Hoggard	E	67	13909	7564	30.50	7	1
246	G.D.McKenzie	A	60	17681	7328	29.78	16	3
242	B.S.Chandrasekhar	I	58	15963	7199	29.74	16	2
242	Z.Khan	I	72	14417	7983	32.98	9	1
236	A.V.Bedser	E	51	15918	5876	24.89	15	5
236	Abdul Qadir	P	67	17126	7742	32.80	15	5
236	J.Srinath	I	67	15104	7196	30.49	10	1
235	G.St A.Sobers	WI	93	21599	7999	34.03	6	–
234	A.R.Caddick	E	62	13558	6999	29.91	13	1
229	D.Gough	E	58	11821	6503	28.39	9	–
228	R.R.Lindwall	A	61	13650	5251	23.03	12	–
226	S.J.Harmison	E/ICC	63	13375	7192	31.82	8	1
226	A.Flintoff	E/ICC	79	14951	7410	32.78	3	–
218	C.L.Cairns	NZ	62	11698	6410	29.40	13	1
216	C.V.Grimmett	A	37	14513	5231	24.21	21	7
216	H.H.Streak	Z	65	13559	6079	28.14	7	–
212	M.G.Hughes	A	53	12285	6017	28.38	7	1
208	S.C.G.MacGill	A	44	11237	6038	29.02	12	2
208	Saqlain Mushtaq	P	49	14070	6206	29.83	13	3
202	A.M.E.Roberts	WI	47	11136	5174	25.61	11	2
202	J.A.Snow	E	49	12021	5387	26.66	8	1
200	J.R.Thomson	A	51	10535	5601	28.00	8	–

The most for Bangladesh 100 in 33 Tests by Mohammad Rafique.

35 WICKETS IN A SERIES

Wkts		Series	M	Balls	Runs	Avge	5 wI	10 wM
49	S.F.Barnes	E v SA	1913-14	4	1356	536	10.93	7	3
46	J.C.Laker	E v A	1956	5	1703	442	9.60	4	2
44	C.V.Grimmett	A v SA	1935-36	5	2077	642	14.59	5	3
42	T.M.Alderman	A v E	1981	6	1950	893	21.26	4	–
41	R.M.Hogg	A v E	1978-79	6	1740	527	12.85	5	2
41	T.M.Alderman	A v E	1989	6	1616	712	17.36	6	1
40	Imran Khan	P v I	1982-83	6	1339	558	13.95	4	2
40	S.K.Warne	A v E	2005	5	1517	797	19.92	3	2
39	A.V.Bedser	E v A	1953	5	1591	682	17.48	5	1
39	D.K.Lillee	A v E	1981	6	1870	870	22.30	2	1
38	M.W.Tate	E v A	1924-25	5	2528	881	23.18	5	1
37	W.J.Whitty	A v SA	1910-11	5	1395	632	17.08	2	–
37	H.J.Tayfield	SA v E	1956-57	5	2280	636	17.18	4	1
36	A.E.E.Vogler	SA v E	1909-10	5	1349	783	21.75	4	1
36	A.A.Mailey	A v E	1920-21	5	1465	946	26.27	4	2
36	G.D.McGrath	A v E	1997	6	1499	701	19.47	2	–
35	G.A.Lohmann	E v SA	1895-96	3	520	203	5.80	4	2
35	B.S.Chandrasekhar	I v E	1972-73	5	1747	662	18.91	4	–
35	M.D.Marshall	WI v E	1988	5	1219	443	12.65	3	1

The most for New Zealand is 33 by R.J.Hadlee (3 Tests v A, 1985-86), for Sri Lanka 30 by M.Muralitharan (3 Tests v Z, 2001-02), for Zimbabwe 22 by H.H.Streak (3 Tests v P, 1994-95), and for Bangladesh 18 by Enamul Haque[2] (2 Tests v Z, 2004-05).

15 WICKETS IN A TEST († On debut)

19- 90	J.C.Laker	E v A	Manchester	1956
17-159	S.F.Barnes	E v SA	Johannesburg	1913-14
16-136†	N.D.Hirwani	I v WI	Madras	1987-88
16-137†	R.A.L.Massie	A v E	Lord's	1972
16-220	M.Muralitharan	SL v E	The Oval	1998
15- 28	J.Briggs	E v SA	Cape Town	1888-89
15- 45	G.A.Lohmann	E v SA	Port Elizabeth	1895-96
15- 99	C.Blythe	E v SA	Leeds	1907
15-104	H.Verity	E v A	Lord's	1934
15-123	R.J.Hadlee	NZ v A	Brisbane	1985-86
15-124	W.Rhodes	A v E	Melbourne	1903-04
15-217	Harbhajan Singh	I v A	Madras	2000-01

The best analysis for South Africa is 13-132 by M.Ntini (v WI, Port-of-Spain, 2004-05), for West Indies 14-149 by M.A.Holding (v E, The Oval, 1976), for Pakistan 14-116 by Imran Khan (v SL, Lahore, 1981-82), for Zimbabwe 11-257 by A.G.Huckle (v NZ, Bulawayo, 1997-98), and for Bangladesh 12-200 by Enamul Haque[2] (v Z, Dhaka, 2004-05).

NINE WICKETS IN AN INNINGS

10-53	J.C.Laker	E v A	Manchester	1956
10-74	A.Kumble	I v P	Delhi	1998-99
9-28	G.A.Lohmann	E v SA	Johannesburg	1895-96
9-37	J.C.Laker	E v A	Manchester	1956
9-51	M.Muralitharan	SL v Z	Kandy	2001-02
9-52	R.J.Hadlee	NZ v A	Brisbane	1985-86
9-56	Abdul Qadir	P v E	Lahore	1987-88
9-57	D.E.Malcolm	E v SA	The Oval	1994
9-65	M.Muralitharan	SL v E	The Oval	1998
9-69	J.M.Patel	I v A	Kanpur	1959-60
9-83	Kapil Dev	I v WI	Ahmedabad	1983-84
9-86	Sarfraz Nawaz	P v A	Melbourne	1978-79

9- 95	J.M.Noreiga	WI v I	Port-of-Spain	1970-71
9-102	S.P.Gupte	I v WI	Kanpur	1958-59
9-103	S.F.Barnes	E v SA	Johannesburg	1913-14
9-113	H.J.Tayfield	SA v E	Johannesburg	1956-57
9-121	A.A.Mailey	A v E	Melbourne	1920-21

The best analysis for Zimbabwe is 8-109 by P.A.Strang (v NZ, Bulawayo, 2000-01), and for Bangladesh 7-95 by Enamul Haque[2] (v Z, Dhaka, 2004-05).

HAT-TRICKS

F.R.Spofforth	Australia v England	Melbourne	1878-79
W.Bates	England v Australia	Melbourne	1882-83
J.Briggs[7]	England v Australia	Sydney	1891-92
G.A.Lohmann	England v South Africa	Port Elizabeth	1895-96
J.T.Hearne	England v Australia	Leeds	1899
H.Trumble	Australia v England	Melbourne	1901-02
H.Trumble	Australia v England	Melbourne	1903-04
T.J.Matthews (2)[2]	Australia v South Africa	Manchester	1912
M.J.C.Allom[1]	England v New Zealand	Christchurch	1929-30
T.W.J.Goddard	England v South Africa	Johannesburg	1938-39
P.J.Loader	England v West Indies	Leeds	1957
L.F.Kline	Australia v South Africa	Cape Town	1957-58
W.W.Hall	West Indies v Pakistan	Lahore	1958-59
G.M.Griffin[7]	South Africa v England	Lord's	1960
L.R.Gibbs	West Indies v Australia	Adelaide	1960-61
P.J.Petherick[1/7]	New Zealand v Pakistan	Lahore	1976-77
C.A.Walsh[7]	West Indies v Australia	Brisbane	1988-89
M.G.Hughes[3/7]	Australia v West Indies	Perth	1988-89
D.W.Fleming[1]	Australia v Pakistan	Rawalpindi	1994-95
S.K.Warne	Australia v England	Melbourne	1994-95
D.G.Cork	England v West Indies	Manchester	1995
D.Gough[1]	England v Australia	Sydney	1998-99
Wasim Akram[4]	Pakistan v Sri Lanka	Lahore	1998-99
Wasim Akram[4]	Pakistan v Sri Lanka	Dhaka	1998-99
D.N.T.Zoysa[5]	Sri Lanka v Zimbabwe	Harare	1999-00
Abdul Razzaq	Pakistan v Sri Lanka	Galle	2000-01
G.D.McGrath	Australia v West Indies	Perth	2000-01
Harbhajan Singh	India v Australia	Calcutta	2000-01
Mohammad Sami[7]	Pakistan v Sri Lanka	Lahore	2001-02
J.J.C.Lawson[7]	West Indies v Australia	Bridgetown	2002-03
Alok Kapali[7]	Bangladesh v Pakistan	Peshawar	2003
A.M.Blignaut	Zimbabwe v Bangladesh	Harare	2003-04
M.J.Hoggard	England v West Indies	Bridgetown	2003-04
J.E.C.Franklin	New Zealand v Bangladesh	Dhaka	2004-05
I.K.Pathan[6/7]	India v Pakistan	Karachi	2005-06
R.J.Sidebottom[7]	England v New Zealand	Hamilton	2007-08

[1] On debut. [2] Hat-trick in each innings. [3] Involving both innings. [4] In successive Tests. [5] His first 3 balls (second over of the match). [6] The fourth, fifth and sixth balls of the match. [7] On losing side.

84

WICKET-KEEPING RECORDS
100 DISMISSALS IN TESTS

Total			Tests	Ct	St
494	M.V.Boucher	South Africa/ICC	131	472	22
416	A.C.Gilchrist	Australia	96	379	37
395	I.A.Healy	Australia	119	366	29
355	R.W.Marsh	Australia	96	343	12
270†	P.J.L.Dujon	West Indies	79	265	5
269	A.P.E.Knott	England	95	250	19
241†	A.J.Stewart	England	82	227	14
228	Wasim Bari	Pakistan	81	201	27
219	R.D.Jacobs	West Indies	65	207	12
219	T.G.Evans	England	91	173	46
201†	A.C.Parore	New Zealand	67	194	7
198	S.M.H.Kirmani	India	88	160	38
189	D.L.Murray	West Indies	62	181	8
187	A.T.W.Grout	Australia	51	163	24
181	Kamran Akmal	Pakistan	48	159	22
176	I.D.S.Smith	New Zealand	63	168	8
174	R.W.Taylor	England	57	167	7
167	B.B.McCullum	New Zealand	50	157	10
165	R.C.Russell	England	54	153	12
152	D.J.Richardson	South Africa	42	150	2
151†	A.Flower	Zimbabwe	55	142	9
151†	K.C.Sangakkara	Sri Lanka	48	131	20
147†	Moin Khan	Pakistan	66	127	20
141	J.H.B.Waite	South Africa	49	124	17
133	M.S.Dhoni	India	43	113	20
133	G.O.Jones	England	34	128	5
130	Rashid Latif	Pakistan	37	119	11
130	K.S.More	India	49	110	20
130	W.A.S.Oldfield	Australia	54	78	52
119	R.S.Kaluwitharana	Sri Lanka	49	93	26
118	D.Ramdin	West Indies	39	116	2
112†	J.M.Parks	England	43	101	11
107	N.R.Mongia	India	44	99	8
104	Salim Yousuf	Pakistan	32	91	13
103	B.J.Haddin	Australia	25	101	2
101†	J.R.Murray	West Indies	31	98	3

The most for Bangladesh is 87 (78 ct, 9 st) by Khaled Masud in 44 Tests.
† Excluding catches taken in the field

25 DISMISSALS IN A SERIES

28	R.W.Marsh	Australia v England	1982-83
27 (inc 2st)	R.C.Russell	England v South Africa	1995-96
27 (inc 2st)	I.A.Healy	Australia v England (6 Tests)	1997
26 (inc 3st)	J.H.B.Waite	South Africa v New Zealand	1961-62
26	R.W.Marsh	Australia v West Indies (6 Tests)	1975-76
26 (inc 5st)	I.A.Healy	Australia v England (6 Tests)	1993
26 (inc 1st)	M.V.Boucher	South Africa v England	1998
26 (inc 2st)	A.C.Gilchrist	Australia v England	2001
26 (inc 2st)	A.C.Gilchrist	Australia v England	2006-07
25 (inc 2st)	I.A.Healy	Australia v England	1994-95
25 (inc 2st)	A.C.Gilchrist	Australia v England	2002-03
25	A.C.Gilchrist	Australia v India	2007-08

TEN DISMISSALS IN A TEST

11	R.C.Russell	England v South Africa	Johannesburg	1995-96
10	R.W.Taylor	England v India	Bombay	1979-80
10	A.C.Gilchrist	Australia v New Zealand	Hamilton	1999-00

SEVEN DISMISSALS IN AN INNINGS

7	Wasim Bari	Pakistan v New Zealand	Auckland	1978-79
7	R.W.Taylor	England v India	Bombay	1979-80
7	I.D.S.Smith	New Zealand v Sri Lanka	Hamilton	1990-91
7	R.D.Jacobs	West Indies v Australia	Melbourne	2000-01

FIVE STUMPINGS IN AN INNINGS

5	K.S.More	India v West Indies	Madras	1987-88

FIELDING RECORDS
100 CATCHES IN TESTS

Total			Tests	Total			Tests
193	R.Dravid	India/ICC	139	120	M.C.Cowdrey	England	114
181	M.E.Waugh	Australia	128	115	C.L.Hooper	West Indies	102
171	S.P.Fleming	New Zealand	111	115	V.V.S.Laxman	India	110
164	B.C.Lara	West Indies/ICC	131	112	G.C.Smith	South Africa/ICC	83
164	R.T.Ponting	Australia	142	112	S.R.Waugh	Australia	168
157	M.A.Taylor	Australia	104	110	R.B.Simpson	Australia	62
156	A.R.Border	Australia	156	110	W.R.Hammond	England	85
155	J.H.Kallis	South Africa/ICC	137	109	G.St A.Sobers	West Indies	93
152	D.P.M.D.Jayawardena	Sri Lanka	110	108	S.M.Gavaskar	India	125
128	M.L.Hayden	Australia	103	105	I.M.Chappell	Australia	75
125	S.K.Warne	Australia	145	105	M.Azharuddin	India	99
122	G.S.Chappell	Australia	87	105	G.P.Thorpe	England	100
122	I.V.A.Richards	West Indies	121	104	S.R.Tendulkar	India	166
120	I.T.Botham	England	102	103	G.A.Gooch	England	118

The most for Pakistan is 93 by Javed Miandad (124), for Zimbabwe 60 by A.D.R.Campbell (60) and for Bangladesh 24 by Mohammad Ashraful (53).

15 CATCHES IN A SERIES

15	J.M.Gregory	Australia v England	1920-21

SEVEN CATCHES IN A TEST

7	G.S.Chappell	Australia v England	Perth	1974-75
7	Yajurvindra Singh	India v England	Bangalore	1976-77
7	H.P.Tillekeratne	Sri Lanka v New Zealand	Colombo (SSC)	1992-93
7	S.P.Fleming	New Zealand v Zimbabwe	Harare	1997-98
7	M.L.Hayden	Australia v Sri Lanka	Galle	2003-04

FIVE CATCHES IN AN INNINGS

5	V.Y.Richardson	Australia v South Africa	Durban	1935-36
5	Yajurvindra Singh	India v England	Bangalore	1976-77
5	M.Azharuddin	India v Pakistan	Karachi	1989-90
5	K.Srikkanth	India v Australia	Perth	1991-92
5	S.P.Fleming	New Zealand v Zimbabwe	Harare	1997-98

100 TEST MATCH APPEARANCES

Opponents

			E	A	SA	WI	NZ	I	P	SL	Z	B
168	S.R.Waugh	Australia	46	–	16	32	23	18	20	8	3	2
166	S.R.Tendulkar	India	24	29	22	16	19	–	18	22	9	7
156	A.R.Border	Australia	47	–	6	31	23	20	22	7	–	–
145†	S.K.Warne	Australia	36	–	24	19	20	14	15	13	1	2
142†	R.T.Ponting	Australia	31	–	21	21	13	23	13	12	3	4
139†	R.Dravid	India/ICC	17	26	18	17	12	–	15	17	9	7
137†	J.H.Kallis	South Africa/ICC	28	23	–	21	14	13	13	12	6	6
133	A.J.Stewart	England	–	33	23	24	16	9	13	9	6	–
132	A.Kumble	India	19	20	21	17	11	–	15	18	7	4
132†	M.Muralitharan	Sri Lanka	16	12	15	12	14	21	16	–	14	11
132	C.A.Walsh	West Indies	36	38	10	–	10	15	18	3	2	–
131†	M.V.Boucher	South Africa	25	18	–	21	14	11	13	14	6	8
131	Kapil Dev	India	27	20	4	25	10	–	29	14	2	–
131†	B.C.Lara	West Indies	30	30	18	–	11	17	12	8	2	2
128	M.E.Waugh	Australia	29	–	18	28	14	14	15	9	1	–
125	S.M.Gavaskar	India	38	20	–	27	9	–	24	7	–	–
124†	G.D.McGrath	Australia	30	–	17	23	14	11	17	8	1	2
124	Javed Miandad	Pakistan	22	24	–	17	18	28	–	12	3	–
123	S.Chanderpaul	West Indies	30	17	18	–	13	18	13	4	6	4
121	I.V.A.Richards	West Indies	36	34	–	–	7	28	16	–	–	–
120†	Inzamam-ul-Haq	Pakistan/ICC	19	13	13	15	12	10	–	20	11	6
119	I.A.Healy	Australia	33	–	12	28	11	9	14	11	1	–
118	G.A.Gooch	England	–	42	3	26	15	19	10	3	–	–
117	D.I.Gower	England	–	42	–	19	13	24	17	2	–	–
116	D.L.Haynes	West Indies	36	33	14	–	10	19	16	1	–	–
116	D.B.Vengsarkar	India	26	24	–	25	11	–	22	8	–	–
115	M.A.Atherton	England	–	33	18	27	11	7	11	4	4	–
114	M.C.Cowdrey	England	–	43	14	21	18	8	10	–	–	–
113	S.C.Ganguly	India	12	24	17	12	8	–	12	14	9	5
111	S.P.Fleming	New Zealand	19	14	15	11	–	13	9	13	11	6
111	W.P.U.C.J.Vaas	Sri Lanka	15	12	11	9	10	14	18	–	15	7
110	S.T.Jayasuriya	Sri Lanka	14	13	15	10	13	10	17	–	13	5
110	D.P.M.D.Jayawardena	Sri Lanka	16	10	12	9	11	15	18	–	8	11
110	V.V.S.Laxman	India	13	24	16	16	7	–	15	10	6	3
110	C.H.Lloyd	West Indies	34	29	–	–	8	28	11	–	–	–
108	G.Boycott	England	–	38	7	29	15	13	6	–	–	–
108	C.G.Greenidge	West Indies	29	32	–	–	10	23	14	–	–	–
108	S.M.Pollock	South Africa	23	13	–	16	11	12	12	13	5	3
107	D.C.Boon	Australia	31	–	6	22	17	11	11	9	–	–
105†	J.L.Langer	Australia	21	–	11	18	14	14	13	8	3	2
104	M.A.Taylor	Australia	33	–	11	20	11	9	12	8	–	–
104	Wasim Akram	Pakistan	18	13	4	17	9	12	–	19	10	2
103†	M.L.Hayden	Australia	20	–	19	15	11	18	6	7	2	4
103	Salim Malik	Pakistan	19	15	1	7	18	22	–	15	6	–
102	I.T.Botham	England	–	36	–	20	15	14	14	3	–	–
102	C.L.Hooper	West Indies	24	25	10	–	2	19	14	6	2	–
101	G.Kirsten	South Africa	22	18	–	13	13	10	11	9	3	2
101	M.Ntini	South Africa	18	15	–	15	11	10	9	12	3	8
100	G.P.Thorpe	England	–	36	2	20	15	4	5	2	–	–

† Includes appearance in the Australia v ICC 'Test' in 2005-06. The most for Zimbabwe is 67 by G.W.Flower, and for Bangladesh 53 by Mohammad Ashraful.

100 CONSECUTIVE TEST APPEARANCES

153	A.R.Border	Australia	March 1979 to March 1994
107	M.E.Waugh	Australia	June 1993 to October 2002
106	S.M.Gavaskar	India	January 1975 to February 1987

50 TESTS AS CAPTAIN

			Won	Lost	Drawn	Tied
93	A.R.Border	Australia	32	22	38	1
80	S.P.Fleming	New Zealand	28	27	25	–
75	G.C.Smith	South Africa	35	23	17	–
74	C.H.Lloyd	West Indies	36	12	26	–
67	R.T.Ponting	Australia	44	11	12	–
57	S.R.Waugh	Australia	41	9	7	–
56	A.Ranatunga	Sri Lanka	12	19	25	–
54	M.A.Atherton	England	13	21	20	–
53	W.J.Cronje	South Africa	27	11	15	–
51	M.P.Vaughan	England	26	11	14	–
50	I.V.A.Richards	West Indies	27	8	15	–
50	M.A.Taylor	Australia	26	13	11	–

The most for India is 49 by S.C.Ganguly, for Pakistan 48 by Imran Khan, for Zimbabwe 21 by A.D.R.Campbell and H.H.Streak, and for Bangladesh 18 by Habibul Bashar.

50 TEST UMPIRING APPEARANCES

128	S.A.Bucknor	(West Indies)	28.04.1989 to 22.03.2009
106	R.E.Koertzen	(South Africa)	26.12.1992 to 19.02.2010
92	D.R.Shepherd	(England)	01.08.1985 to 07.06.2005
88	D.J.Harper	(Australia)	28.11.1998 to 07.01.2010
78	D.B.Hair	(Australia)	25.01.1992 to 08.06.2008
73	S.Venkataraghavan	(India)	29.01.1993 to 20.01.2004
66	H.D.Bird	(England)	05.07.1973 to 24.06.1996
61	S.J.A.Taufel	(Australia)	26.12.2000 to 06.12.2009
59	Alim Dar	(Pakistan)	21.10.2003 to 30.12.2009
59	B.F.Bowden	(New Zealand)	11.03.2000 to 27.01.2010

THE FIRST-CLASS COUNTIES REGISTER, RECORDS AND 2009 AVERAGES

Career statistics are to the end of February 2010.
Test Match and LOI career bests have been updated to 20 and 27 February 2010 respectively.

ABBREVIATIONS – General

*	not out/unbroken partnership	IT20	International Twenty20
b	born	l-o	limited-overs
BB	Best innings bowling analysis	LOI	Limited-Overs Internationals
Cap	Awarded 1st XI County Cap	Tests	International Test Matches
f-c	first-class	F-c Tours	Overseas tours involving first-class
HS	Highest Score		appearances

Awards

PCA 2009	Professional Cricketer's Association Player of 2009
Wisden 2008	One of *Wisden Cricketers' Almanack's* Five Cricketers of 2008
YC 2009	Cricket Writers' Club Young Cricketer of 2009

ECB Competitions

BHC	Benson & Hedges Cup (1972-2002)
CC	LV County Championship
CGT	Cheltenham & Gloucester Trophy (2001-06)
FPT	Friends Provident Trophy
NL	National League (1999-2005)
NWT	NatWest Trophy (1981-2000)
P40	NatWest PRO 40 League
SL	Sunday League (1969-98)
T20	Twenty20 Competition

Education

ARU	Anglia Ruskin University
BHS	Boys' High School
C	College
CFE	College of Further Education
CHE	College of Higher Education
CS	Comprehensive School
GS	Grammar School
HS	High School
I	Institute
IHE	Institute of Higher Education
RGS	Royal Grammar School
S	School
SFC	Sixth Form College
SM	Secondary Modern School
SS	Secondary School
TC	Technical College
T(H)S	Technical (High) School
U	University
UMIST	University of Manchester Institute of Science and Technology
UWIC	University of Wales Institute, Cardiff

Playing Categories

LBG	Bowls right-arm leg-breaks and googlies
LF	Bowls left-arm fast
LFM	Bowls left-arm fast-medium
LHB	Bats left-handed
LM	Bowls left-arm medium pace
LMF	Bowls left-arm medium fast
OB	Bowls right-arm off-breaks
RF	Bowls right-arm fast
RFM	Bowls right-arm fast-medium

RHB	Bats right-handed
RM	Bowls right-arm medium pace
RMF	Bowls right-arm medium-fast
RSM	Bowls right-arm slow-medium
SLA	Bowls left-arm leg-breaks
SLC	Bowls left-arm 'Chinamen'
WK	Wicket-keeper

Teams (see also p 228)

ACT	Australian Capital Territory
ADBP	Agricultural Development Bank of Pakistan
B	Bangladesh
CD	Central Districts
EL	England Lions
EP	Eastern Province
FS	Free State
GW	Griqualand West
HK	Hong Kong
K	Kenya
KRL	Khan Research Laboratories
MWR	Mid West Rhinos
NBP	National Bank of Pakistan
ND	Northern Districts
NSW	New South Wales
NT	Northern Transvaal
NW	North West
(O)FS	(Orange) Free State
PIA	Pakistan International Airlines
PNSC	Pakistan National Shipping Corporation
PTC	Pakistan Telecommunication Co
Q	Queensland
REDCO	Really Efficient Development Co
SAU	South African Universities
SNGPL	Sui Northern Gas Pipelines Limited
SR	Southern Rocks
SSGC	Sui Southern Gas Corporation
Tas	Tasmania
T&T	Trinidad & Tobago
UP	Uttar Pradesh
Vic	Victoria
WA	Western Australia
WAPDA	Water & Power Development Auth.
WP	Western Province

DERBYSHIRE

Formation of Present Club: 4 November 1870
Inaugural First-Class Match: 1871
Colours: Chocolate, Amber and Pale Blue
Badge: Rose and Crown
County Champions: (1) 1936
Gillette/NatWest/C&G/FP Trophy Winners: (1) 1981
Benson and Hedges Cup Winners: (1) 1993
Pro 40/National League (Div 1) Winners: (0); best – 4th
(Div 2) 2002
Sunday League Winners: (1) 1990
Twenty20 Cup Winners: (0) best – Quarter-Finalist 2005

Chief Executive: Keith Loring, Derbyshire County Cricket Club, Grandstand Road, Derby DE21 6AF • Tel: 01332 388101 • Fax: 0844 500 8322 • Email: info@derbyshireccm.com • Web: www. derbyshireccm.com

Head of Cricket: J.E.Morris. **Assistant Coach:** Andy Brown. **Captain:** C.J.L.Rogers. **Vice-Captain:** None. **Overseas Player:** C.J.L.Rogers. **2010 Beneficiary:** None. **Head Groundsman:** Neil Godrich. **Scorer:** John M.Brown. ‡ New registration. ^{NQ} Not qualified for England.

BORRINGTON, Paul Michael (Repton S; Chellarton S; Loughborough U), b Nottingham 24 May 1988. Son of A.J.Borrington (Derbyshire 1971-80). 5'10". RHB, OB. Debut (Derbyshire) 2005. Loughborough UCCE 2008-09. HS 105 LU v Hants (Southampton) 2009. De HS 85 v Worcs (Worcester) 2008. BB – . LO HS 25 v Glam (Derby) 2009 (P40).

CLARE, Jonathan Luke (St Theodore's HS), b Burnley, Lancs 14 Jun 1986. 6'4". RHB, RMF. Lancashire 2nd XI. Derbyshire 2nd XI 2006-07. Debut (Derbyshire) 2007, taking 5-90 v Notts (Chesterfield). HS 129* and BB 7-74 v Northants (Northampton) 2008. LO HS 34 v Kent (Chesterfield) 2009 (P40). LO BB 3-39 v Scotland (Derby) 2008 (FPT). T20 HS 4*. T20 BB 2-20.

‡FOOTITT, Mark Harold Alan (Carlton le Willows S; West Notts C), b Nottingham 25 Nov 1985. 6'2". RHB, LFM. Nottinghamshire 2005-09. MCC 2006. No f-c appearances in 2008. HS 19* Nt v Hants (Southampton) 2005. BB 5-45 Nt v West Indies A (Nottingham) 2006. CC BB 5-59 Nt v Essex (Nottingham) 2007. LO HS – and BB – . T20 HS – . T20 BB – .

‡GODDARD, Lee James (Batley GS; Huddersfield TC; Loughborough U), b Dewsbury, Yorks 22 Oct 1982. 5'10". RHB, WK. Loughborough UCCE 2003. Derbyshire 2004, 2006. Durham 2007. No f-c appearances for Du in 2008-09. HS 91 v Surrey (Derby) 2006. LO HS 36 v Kent (Canterbury) 2006 (P40). T20 HS – .

GROENEWALD, Timothy Duncan (Maritzburg C; South Africa U), b Pietermaritzburg, South Africa 10 Jan 1984. 6'0". RHB, RFM. Debut Cambridge UCCE 2006. Warwickshire 2006-08. Derbyshire debut 2009. HS 78 Wa v Bangladesh A (Birmingham) 2008. CC HS 76 Wa v Durham (Chester-le-St) 2006. De HS 50 v Northants (Chesterfield) 2009. BB 6-50 v Surrey (Croydon) 2009. LO HS 36 Wa v Lancs (Manchester) 2007 (FPT). LO BB 3-25 Wa v Worcs (Birmingham) 2007 (P40). T20 HS 41. T20 BB 3-40.

‡**HUGHES, Chesney** Francis, b Anguilla 20 January 1991. 6'2". LHB, SLA. British passport. Derbyshire 2nd XI 2009 – awaiting f-c debut. LO HS 31 and BB 1-17 WI U19s v Leeward Is (Enmore) 2007-08. T20 HS 20. T20 BB – .

HUNTER, Ian David (Fyndoune Community C, Sacriston; New C, Durham), b Durham City 11 Sep 1979. 6'2". RHB, RMF. Durham 2000-03. Derbyshire debut 2004. HS 65 Du v Northants (Northampton) 2002. De HS 48 v Somerset (Taunton) 2006. BB 5-46 v Essex (Chelmsford) 2009. LO HS 39 Du v Leics (Leicester) 2002 (BHC). LO BB 4-29 Du v Essex (Ilford) 2000 (NL). T20 HS 25*. T20 BB 3-26.

JONES, Edward Peter (Trentham HS; Stoke-on-Trent SFC; Derby U), b Stoke-on-Trent, Staffs 23 Oct 1989. 6'4" RHB, RMF. Derbyshire 2nd XI debut 2007. Staffordshire 2007-08. Summer contract – awaiting 1st XI debut.

‡**JONES, Philip Steffan** (Stradey CS, Llanelli; Neath TC; Loughborough U; Homerton C, Cambridge), b Llanelli, Carms, Wales 9 Feb 1974. 6'2". RHB, RMF. Cambridge U 1997; blue 1997. Somerset 1997-2003, 2007-08; cap 2001. Northamptonshire 2004-05. Derbyshire 2006, 2009 to date. Kent 2009. Wales MC 1994-97. HS 114 Sm v Leics (Leicester) 2007. De HS 54* v Middx (Derby) 2009. 50 wkts (2); most – 59 (2001, 2006). BB 6-25 v Glamorgan (Cardiff) 2006. LO HS 42 Sm v Glamorgan (Taunton) 2008 (FPT). LO BB 6-56 Nh v Ire (Clontarf) 2004 (CGT). T20 HS 24*. T20 BB 3-26.

LUNGLEY, Tom (St John Houghton SS; SE Derbyshire C), b Derby 25 Jul 1979. 6'1". LHB, RM. Debut (Derbyshire) 2000; cap 2007. HS 50 v Warwks (Derby) 2008. 50 wkts (1): 59 (2007). BB 5-20 v Leics (Derby) 2007. LO HS 45 v Essex (Chelmsford) 2001 (NL). LO BB 4-28 v Essex (Derby) 2001 (NL). T20 HS 25. T20 BB 5-27 v Leics (Leicester) 2009 – De record.

‡**NOMADSEN, Wayne** Lee (Kearsney C, Durban; U of South Africa), b Durban, South Africa 2 Jan 1984. Nephew of M.B.Madsen (Natal 1967-68 to 1978-79), T.R.Madsen (Natal 1976-77 to 1989-90) and H.R.Fotheringham (Natal, Transvaal 1971-72 to 1989-90) and cousin of G.S.Fotheringham (KwaZulu-Natal 2008-09 to date). 5'11". RHB, OB. KwaZulu-Natal 2003-04 to 2007-08. Dolphins 2006-07 to 2007-08. Derbyshire debut 2009. HS 170* v Glos (Cheltenham) 2009 – on De debut. BB 3-45 KZ-Natal v EP (Pt Elizabeth) 2007-08. LO HS 55* KZ-Natal v KZ-Natal Inland (Pietermaritzburg) 2006-07. LO BB 2-18 v Glamorgan (Derby) 2009 (P40).

NEEDHAM, Jake (Nottingham Bluecoat S, Aspley), b Portsmouth, Hants 30 Sep 1986. 6'1". RHB, OB. Debut (Derbyshire) 2005. HS 48 v Notts (Chesterfield) 2007. BB 6-49 v Leics (Leicester) 2008. LO HS 42 and BB 2-36 v Somerset (Taunton) 2007 (P40). T20 HS 7*. T20 BB 4-21.

PARK, Garry Terence (Eshowe HS, Natal; Anglia Ruskin U), b Empangeni, Zululand, South Africa 19 Apr 1983. 5'7". RHB, WK, RM. Cambridge UCCE 2003-05. Durham 2006-08. Derbyshire debut 2009. Cambridgeshire 2005. 1000 runs (1): 1059 (2009). HS 178* v Kent (Derby) 2009. BB 3-25 v Surrey (Derby) 2009. LO HS 64 v Surrey (Croydon) 2009 (P40). LO BB 2-40 v Middx (Uxbridge) 2009 (P40). T20 HS 50. T20 BB 3-23.

‡**NQPETERSON, Robin** John, b Pt Elizabeth, South Africa 4 Aug 1979. LHB, SLA. E Province 1998-99 to 2003-04. Warriors 2004-05 to 2008-09. Cape Cobras 2009-10. Kolpak registration. **Tests** (SA): 6 (2003 to 2007-08); HS 61 v B (Dhaka) 2003 – on debut; BB 5-33 v B (Chittagong) 2007-08. **LOI** (SA): 35 (2002-03 to 2006-07); HS 36 v WI (Centurion) 2003-04; BB 2-26 v P (Faisalabad) 2003-04. F-c Tours (SA): E 2003; WI 2000-01 (SA A); P 2003-04; B 2003, 2007-08. HS 130 EP v Gauteng (Johannesburg) 2002-03. BB 6-67 EP v Border (East London) 1999-00. LO HS 101 EP v Border (Pt Elizabeth) 2001-02. LO BB 7-24 Warriors v Eagles (East London) 2007-08. IT20 HS 34. IT20 BB 3-30. T20 HS 72*. T20 BB 3-24.

POYNTON, Thomas (John Taylor HS, Barton-under-Needwood; Repton S), b Burton upon Trent, Staffs 25 Nov 1989. 5'10". RHB, WK. Debut (Derbyshire) 2007. No f-c appearances in 2009. HS 14 v Bangladesh A (Derby) 2008. CC HS 2 v Glamorgan (Derby) 2007. LO HS 24 v Warwicks (Birmingham) 2009 (P40). T20 HS 3.

REDFERN, Daniel James (Adam's GS, Newport, Shropshire), b Shrewsbury, Shropshire 18 Apr 1990. 5'9". LHB, OB. Debut (Derbyshire) 2007. HS 95 v Northants (Northampton) 2009. BB 1-7. LO HS 57* v Yorkshire (Derby) 2007 (P40). T20 HS 9.

NQROGERS, Christopher John Llewellyn (Wesley C, Perth; Curtin U, Perth), b St George, Sydney, Australia 31 Aug 1977. Son of W.J.Rogers (NSW 1968-69 to 1969-70). 5'10". LHB, LBG. W Australia 1998-99 to 2007-08. Derbyshire debut 2004; cap 2008; captain 2008 (*part*) to date. Leicestershire 2005. Northamptonshire 2006. Victoria 2008-09 to date. Shropshire 2003. Wiltshire 2005. **Tests** (A): 1 (2007-08); HS 15 v I (Perth) 2007-08 – on debut. F-c Tour (Aus A): P 2007-08. 1000 runs (3+2); most – 1461 (2009). HS 319 Nh v Glos (Northampton) 2006. De HS 248* v Warwks (Birmingham) 2008. BB 1-16 Nh v Leics (Northampton) 2006. LO HS 140 Vic v S Aus (Melbourne) 2009-10. BB 2-22 Nh v Durham (Northampton) 2006. T20 HS 58.

SADLER, John Leonard (St Thomas A'Becket S, Sandal), b Dewsbury, Yorks 19 Nov 1981. 5'11". LHB, LBG. Leicestershire 2003-07. Derbyshire debut 2008. 1000 runs (1): 1024 (2006). HS 145 Le v Surrey (Leicester) 2003 and 145 Le v Sussex (Hove) 2003. De HS 50 v Bangladesh A (Derby) 2008. BB 1-5 v Middlesex (Southgate) 2007. De BB 1-57 v Essex (Derby) 2008. LO HS 113* Le v Derbys (Leicester) 2002 (FPT). LO BB 1-33 Le v Yorks (Leeds) 2007 (FPT). T20 HS 73. T20 BB – .

NQSMITH, Gregory Marc (St Stithins C), b Johannesburg, South Africa 20 Apr 1983. 5'9". RHB, RM/OB. Debut (SA Academy) 2003-04. Griqualand West 2003-04. Derbyshire debut 2006 (Kolpak registration); cap 2009. HS 126 v Glos (Cheltenham) 2009. BB 5-65 v Middx (Uxbridge) 2009. LO HS 88 v Kent (Derby) 2007 (P40). LO BB 4-53 v Lancs (Derby) 2009 (P40). T20 HS 100* v Yorks (Leeds) 2008 – De record. T20 BB 5-27.

WAGG, Graham Grant (Ashlawn S, Rugby), b Rugby, Warwks 28 Apr 1983. 6'0". RHB, LM. Warwickshire 2002-04; contract terminated after ECB imposed a 15-month ban, expiring 1 Jan 2006, for taking cocaine. Derbyshire debut 2006; cap 2007. F-c Tour (Eng A): I 2003-04. HS 108 v Northants (Northampton) 2008. 50 wkts (2); most – 59 (2008). BB 6-35 v Surrey (Derby) 2009. LO HS 45 Eng A v Karnataka (Bangalore) 2003-04 and v Yorks (Derby) 2007. LO BB 4-35 v Durham (Derby) 2008 (FPT). T20 HS 62. T20 BB 3-23.

WHITELEY, Ross Andrew (Repton S), b Sheffield, Yorks 13 Sep 1988. RHB, WK. Derbyshire 2nd XI 2006-08. Debut (Derbyshire) 2008. No f-c appearances in 2009. HS 27 v Leics (Leicester) 2008 – on debut. LO HS 24 v Glamorgan (Cardiff) 2008.

RELEASED/RETIRED
(Having made a County First-Class or List A appearance in 2009)

NQHAYWARD, Mornantu ('*Nantie*') (Daniel Pienaar THS), Uitenhage, South Africa 6 Mar 1977. RHB, RF. E Province 1995-96 to 2003-04. Worcestershire 2003. Middlesex 2004-05. Warriors 2004-05 and 2006-07 to 2007-08. Dolphins 2005-06. Hampshire 2008. Derbyshire 2009. **Tests** (SA): 16 (1999-00 to 2004); HS 14 v A (Melbourne) 2001-02; BB 5-56 v P (Durban) 2002-03. **LOI** (SA): 21 (1998 to 2001-02); HS 4; BB 4-31 v I (Sharjah) 1999-00. F-c Tours (SA): A 2001-02; I 1999-00; SL 2000-01, 2004. HS 55* EP v Boland (Pt Elizabeth) 1997-98. CC HS 28 Wo v Durham (Stockton) 2003. De HS 6 v Middx (Derby) 2009. 50 wkts (1): 67 (2003). BB 6-31 (12-94 match) EP v Easterns (Pt Elizabeth) 1999-00. CC BB 5-46 Wo v Somerset (Worcester) 2003. De BB 4-99 v Northants (Northampton) 2009. LO HS 19* EP v WP (Cape Town) 1996-97. LO BB 5-37 EP v KZ-Natal (Durban) 1998-99. T20 HS 5. T20 BB 3-21.

NQHINDS, Wavell Wayne (Camperdown HS), b Kingston, Jamaica 7 Sep 1976. 6'0". LHB, RM. Jamaica 1995-96 to date. Derbyshire 2008-09 (Kolpak registration); cap 2009. **Tests** (WI): 45 (1999-00 to 2005-06); HS 213 v SA (Georgetown) 2004-05; BB 3-79 v SA (Johannesburg) 2003-04. **LOI** (WI): 114 (1999 to 2006-07); HS 127* v Z (Harare) 2003-04; BB 3-24 v E (Oval) 2004. F-c Tours (WI): A 2000-01, 2005-06; SA 1997-98, 2003-04; NZ 1999-00; I 1998-99, 2002-03; P (Sharjah) 2001-02; Z 2001, 2003-04; B 1998-99, 2002-03. HS 213 (*see Tests*). De HS 148 v Northants (Northampton) 2009. BB 3-9 WI B v Jamaica (Montego Bay) 2000-01. De BB 3-22 v Middlesex (Derby) 2008. LO HS 127* (*see LOI*). LO BB 4-35 WI v Zim A (Kwekwe) 2003-04. IT20 HS 14. T20 HS 72*. T20 BB 2-14.

KLOKKER, Frederik Andreas (Hindsholm S), b Odense, Denmark 13 Mar 1983. LHB, WK. Warwickshire 1 match) 2006. Derbyshire 2007-09, scoring 100* v CU (Cambridge) on debut. Denmark (not f-c) 1999-00 to 2005. MCC YC 2002-05. HS 103* v Warwks (Derby) 2008. BB – . LO HS 138* Denmark v USA (Armagh) 2005.

LAW, Stuart Grant (Craigslea State HS), b Herston, Brisbane, Australia 18 Oct 1968. 6'1". RHB, RM/LBG. Queensland 1988-89 to 2003-04; captain 1994-95 to 1996-97, 1999-00 to 2001-02. Essex 1996-2001; cap 1996. Lancashire 2002-08; cap 2002; benefit 2007; captain 2008. Derbyshire 2009. *Wisden* 1997. PCA 1999. British Citizenship after 2004 season. **Tests** (A): 1 (1995-96); HS 54* v SL (Perth) 1995-96. **LOI** (A): 54 (1994-95 to 1998-99); HS 110 v Z (Hobart) 1994-95; BB 2-22 v P (Sydney) 1996-97. F-c Tours: E 1995 (Young A); Z 1991-92 (Aus B). 1000 runs (9+2); most – 1833 (1999). HS 263 Ex v Somerset (Chelmsford) 1999. De HS 29 v Essex (Chelmsford) 2009. BB 5-39 Q v Tasmania (Brisbane) 1995-96. CC BB 3-27 Ex v Worcs (Chelmsford) 1997. LO HS 163 Young A v Surrey (Oval) 1995. LO BB 5-26 Q v SL (Cairns) 1995-96. T20 HS 101.

LAWSON, Mark Anthony Kenneth (Castle Hall Language C, Mirfield), b Leeds, Yorks 24 Oct 1985. 5'8". RHB, LB. Yorkshire 2004-07. Middlesex (1 match) 2008. Derbyshire 2008-09. HS 44 Y v Hants (Southampton) 2006. De HS 24* v Glamorgan (Cardiff) 2009. BB 6-88 Y v Middlesex (Scarborough) 2006. De BB 2-20 v Leics (Leicester) 2009. LO HS 20 Y v Warwks (Birmingham) 2005 (NL). LO BB 2-36 v Glamorgan (Derby) 2009 (FPT). T20 HS 4*. T20 BB 2-20.

PIPE, David James (Queensbury S, Bradford), b Bradford, Yorks 16 Dec 1977. 5'11". RHB, WK. Worcestershire 1998-2005. Derbyshire 2006-09; cap 2007. HS 133* v Essex (Chelmsford) 2007. LO HS 83 v Leics (Leicester) 2007 (FPT). Held 8 catches Wo v Herts (Hertford) 2001 (CGT) to equal l-o record. T20 HS 45.

STUBBINGS, Stephen David (Frankston HS, Aus; Swinburne U, Aus), b Huddersfield, Yorks 31 Mar 1978. 6'3". LHB, OB. Derbyshire 1997-2009; cap 2001; benefit 2008. 1000 runs (3); most – 1126 (2005). HS 151 v Somerset (Taunton) 2005. LO HS 110 v Northants (Northampton) 2006 (CGT). T20 HS 57.

NQTELO, Filipe Dominic (Wynberg BHS; Unitek C), b Cape Town, South Africa 4 Mar 1986. 5'6". RHB, OB. Western Province 2005-06 to date. Cape Cobras 2005-06 to 2007-08. SA Academy 2006 to 2006-07. Derbyshire 2008 (Kolpak registration), no f-c appearances in 2009. HS 134* WP v Boland (Paarl) 2007-08. De HS 6 v Essex (Chelmsford) 2008. BB 1-36 v Essex (Derby) 2008. LO HS 90 WP v Border (East London) 2005-06. T20 HS 48.

D.J.Birch left the staff without making a County First-Class or List A appearance for Derbyshire in 2009.

COUNTY CAPS AWARDED IN 2009

Derbyshire	W.W.Hinds, G.M.Smith
Durham	–
Essex	–
Glamorgan	G.P.Rees
Gloucestershire	G.M.Hussain
Hampshire	D.G.Cork, Imran Tahir
Kent	–
Lancashire	V.V.S.Laxman
Leicestershire	T.J.New, J.W.A.Taylor
Middlesex	S.T.Finn
Northamptonshire	A.J.Hall, D.S.Lucas, J.J.van der Wath
Nottinghamshire	A.D.Brown
Somerset	C.Kieswetter, A.V.Suppiah
Surrey	U.Afzaal
Sussex	P.P.Chawla, E.C.Joyce
Warwickshire	C.R.Woakes
Worcestershire (colours)	M.Ahmed, O.B.Cox, A.N.Kervezee, A.A.Noffke, J.D.Shantry, D.A.Wheeldon
Yorkshire	–

Durham abolished their capping system after 2005. Gloucestershire award caps on first-class debut. Worcestershire award club colours on Championship debut. Glamorgan's capping system is now based on a player's number of appearances and not on his performances.

DERBYSHIRE 2009

RESULTS SUMMARY

	Place	Won	Lost	Tied	Drew	NR
County Championship (2nd Division)	6th	2	3		11	
All First-Class Matches		2	3		11	
FP Trophy (Group D)	3rd	3	4			1
Pro40 League (2nd Division)	7th	2	4			2
Twenty20 Cup (North Division)	6th	3	7			

LV COUNTY CHAMPIONSHIP AVERAGES

BATTING AND FIELDING

Cap		M	I	NO	HS	Runs	Avge	100	50	Ct/St
2008	C.J.L.Rogers	13	21	1	222	1461	73.05	6	4	21
	J.L.Sadler	3	4	3	27*	71	71.00	–	–	3
	W.L.Madsen	9	16	2	170*	809	57.78	3	3	8
2009	G.M.Smith	16	27	4	126	977	42.47	1	6	5
	G.T.Park	16	27	2	178*	1059	42.36	2	8	14
2007	D.J.Pipe	14	18	5	64*	493	37.92	–	3	36/2
2009	W.W.Hinds	16	26	2	148	841	35.04	2	2	7
	P.S.Jones	9	9	3	54*	199	33.16	–	2	4
	I.D.Hunter	7	7	3	47	129	32.25	–	–	2
	D.J.Redfern	14	23	1	95	668	30.36	–	5	8
2001	S.D.Stubbings	7	11	1	83	296	29.60	–	1	4
	M.A.K.Lawson	6	5	2	24*	75	25.00	–	–	3
2007	G.G.Wagg	14	14	1	71	273	21.00	–	1	4
2007	T.Lungley	4	4	1	33	62	20.66	–	–	2
	T.D.Groenewald	9	11	1	50	194	19.40	–	–	2
	F.A.Klokker	2	4	1	32*	53	17.66	–	–	3
	J.Needham	5	7	3	20	55	13.75	–	–	3
	S.G.Law	2	4	–	29	39	9.75	–	–	2
	M.Hayward	5	5	2	6	14	4.66	–	–	1
	J.L.Clare	5	5	–	6	13	2.60	–	–	1

BOWLING

	O	M	R	W	Avge	Best	5wI	10wM
T.D.Groenewald	273.2	49	921	34	27.08	6-50	2	–
I.D.Hunter	181.4	33	593	21	28.23	5-46	2	–
P.S.Jones	318	65	970	30	32.33	5-35	1	–
G.M.Smith	330.2	64	1098	32	34.31	5-65	1	–
G.G.Wagg	521.3	85	1773	47	37.72	6-35	3	–
J.L.Clare	119	27	407	10	40.70	3-64	–	–
M.Hayward	123.2	19	472	11	42.90	4-99	–	–
Also bowled:								
G.T.Park	90.3	8	311	7	44.42	3-25	–	–
T.Lungley	92.5	8	392	8	49.00	3-56	–	–
J.Needham	101.4	11	353	7	50.42	3-47	–	–

W.W.Hinds 60-6-181-4; M.A.K.Lawson 105-15-333-4; W.L.Madsen 18-2-67-0; D.J.Pipe 1-0-5-0; D.J.Redfern 32-3-117-2.

The First-Class Averages (pp 228–244) give the records of Derbyshire players in all first-class county matches, with the exception of P.S.Jones and T.Lungley, whose first-class figures for Derbyshire are as above.

DERBYSHIRE RECORDS

FIRST-CLASS CRICKET

Highest Total	For 801-8d		v	Somerset	Taunton	2007
	V 662		by	Yorkshire	Chesterfield	1898
Lowest Total	For 16		v	Notts	Nottingham	1879
	V 23		by	Hampshire	Burton upon T	1958
Highest Innings	For 274	G.A.Davidson	v	Lancashire	Manchester	1896
	V 343*	P.A.Perrin	for	Essex	Chesterfield	1904

Highest Partnership for each Wicket

1st	322	H.Storer/J.Bowden	v	Essex	Derby	1929
2nd	417	K.J.Barnett/T.A.Tweats	v	Yorkshire	Derby	1997
3rd	316*	A.S.Rollins/K.J.Barnett	v	Leics	Leicester	1997
4th	328	P.Vaulkhard/D.Smith	v	Notts	Nottingham	1946
5th	302*†	J.E.Morris/D.G.Cork	v	Glos	Cheltenham	1993
6th	212	G.M.Lee/T.S.Worthington	v	Essex	Chesterfield	1932
7th	258	M.P.Dowman/D.G.Cork	v	Durham	Derby	2000
8th	198	K.M.Krikken/D.G.Cork	v	Lancashire	Manchester	1996
9th	283	A.Warren/J.Chapman	v	Warwicks	Blackwell	1910
10th	132	A.Hill/M.Jean-Jacques	v	Yorkshire	Sheffield	1986

† 346 runs were added for this wicket in two separate partnerships

Best Bowling	For 10- 40	W.Bestwick	v	Glamorgan	Cardiff	1921
(Innings)	V 10- 45	R.L.Johnson	for	Middlesex	Derby	1994
Best Bowling	For 17-103	W.Mycroft	v	Hampshire	Southampton	1876
(Match)	V 16-101	G.Giffen	for	Australians	Derby	1886

Most Runs – Season	2165	D.B.Carr	(av 48.11)	1959
Most Runs – Career	23854	K.J.Barnett	(av 41.12)	1979-98
Most 100s – Season	8	P.N.Kirsten		1982
Most 100s – Career	53	K.J.Barnett		1979-98
Most Wkts – Season	168	T.B.Mitchell	(av 19.55)	1935
Most Wkts – Career	1670	H.L.Jackson	(av 17.11)	1947-63
Most Career W-K Dismissals	1304	R.W.Taylor	(1157 ct; 147 st)	1961-84
Most Career Catches in the Field	563	D.C.Morgan		1950-69

LIMITED-OVERS CRICKET

Highest Total	FPT	365-3		v	Cornwall	Derby	1986
	P40	304-3		v	Kent	Maidstone	2005
	T20	195-8		v	Yorkshire	Leeds	2005
Lowest Total	FPT	79		v	Surrey	The Oval	1967
	P40	60		v	Kent	Canterbury	2008
	T20	98		v	Lancashire	Manchester	2005
Highest Innings	FPT	173*	M.J.Di Venuto	v	Derbys CB	Derby	2000
	P40	141*	C.J.Adams	v	Kent	Chesterfield	1992
	T20	100*	G.M.Smith	v	Yorkshire	Leeds	2008
Best Bowling	FPT	8-21	M.A.Holding	v	Sussex	Hove	1988
	P40	6- 7	M.Hendrick	v	Notts	Nottingham	1972
	T20	5-27	T.Lungley	v	Leicestershire	Leicester	2009

DURHAM

Formation of Present Club: 23 May 1882
Inaugural First-Class Match: 1992
Colours: Navy Blue, Yellow and Maroon
Badge: Coat of Arms of the County of Durham
County Champions: (2) 2008, 2009
Gillette/NatWest/C&G/FP Trophy Winners: (1) 2007
Benson and Hedges Cup Winners: (0); best –
Quarter-Finalist 1998, 2000, 2001
Pro 40/National League (Div 1) Winners: (0); best – 6th
(Div 1) 2009
Sunday League Winners: (0); best – 7th 1993
Twenty20 Cup Winners: (0); best – Semi-Finalist 2008

Chief Executive: David Harker, County Ground, Riverside, Chester-le-Street, Co Durham DH3 3QR • Tel: 0191 387 1717 • Fax: 0191 387 1616 • Email: marketing@durham-ccc.co.uk • Web: www.durhamccc.co.uk

Director of Cricket: G.Cook. **Assistant Coaches:** J.J.B.Lewis and A.Walker. **Captain:** W.R.Smith. **Vice-Captain:** none. **Overseas Player:** none. **2010 Beneficiary:** none. **Head Groundsman:** David Measor. **Scorer:** Brian Hunt. ‡ New registration. NQ Not qualified for England.

Durham initially awarded caps immediately after their players joined the staff but revised this policy in 1998, again capping players on merit, past 'awards' having been nullified. Durham abolished both their capping and 'awards' systems after the 2005 season.

BENKENSTEIN, Dale Martin (Durban HS; Michaelhouse HS), b Salisbury, Rhodesia 9 Jun 1974. Son of M.M.Benkenstein (Rhodesia, Natal B 1970-71 to 1980-81); brother of twins B.R. (Natal B 1993-94) and B.N. Benkenstein (Natal B, GW 1994-95 to 1996-97). 5'9". RHB, RM/OB. Natal/KwaZulu-Natal 1993-94 to 2003-04. Dolphins 2004-05 to 2007-08. MCC 2004. British passport. Durham debut/cap 2005; captain 2006-08. *Wisden* 2008. **LOI** (SA): 23 (1998-99 to 2002-03); HS 69 v WI (Cape Town) 1998-99; BB 3-5 v Kenya (Colombo) 2002-03. F-c Tours (SA A): WI 2000; NZ 1998-99 (SA); SL 1995 (SA U-24), 1998. 1000 (4); most – 1500 (2006). HS 259 KZ-Natal v Northerns (Durban) 2001-02. Du HS 181 v Somerset (Taunton) 2009. BB 4-16 Dolphins v Warriors (Durban) 2005-06. Du BB 4-29 v Northants (Northampton) 2005. LO HS 107* Natal v North West (Fochville) 1997-98. LO BB 4-16 v Surrey (Chester-le-St) 2005. T20 HS 56*. T20 BB 3-10.

BLACKWELL, Ian David (Brookfield Community S), b Chesterfield, Derbys 10 Jun 1978. 6'2". LHB, SLA. Derbyshire 1997-99. Somerset 2000-08; cap 2001; captain 2006 (*part*). Durham debut 2009. **Tests:** 1 (2005-06); HS 4 and BB- v I (Nagpur) 2005-06. **LOI:** 34 (2002-03 to 2005-06); HS 82 v I (Colombo) 2002-03; BB 3-26 v A (Adelaide) 2002-03. F-c Tour: I 2005-06. 1000 runs (3); most – 1256 (2005). HS 247* Sm v Derbys (Taunton) 2003 – off 156 balls and including 204 off 98 balls in reduced post-lunch session. Won Walter Lawrence Trophy 2005 for 67-ball hundred v Derbys (Taunton). Du HS 158 v Warwks (Birmingham) 2009. BB 7-85 v Lancs (Manchester) 2008. LO HS 134* Sm v Sussex (Taunton) 2005 (NL). LO BB 5-26 Sm v Derbys (Taunton) 2005 (NL). T20 HS 82. T20 BB 4-26.

BORTHWICK, Scott George (Farringdon Community Sports C, Sunderland), b Sunderland 19 Apr 1990. 5'9". LHB, LBG. Debut (Durham) 2009. Durham 2nd XI debut 2006. England U19 2008-09 to 2009. HS 26* and BB 3-95 v Hampshire (Southampton) 2009 – on debut. LO HS 3* v Somerset (Taunton) 2009 (P40). LO BB 2-11 v Worcs (Chester-le-St) 2009 (P40). T20 HS – . T20 BB 3-23.

BREESE, Gareth Rohan (Wolmer's BHS, Kingston; Kingston U of Technology, Jamaica), b Montego Bay, Jamaica 9 Jan 1976. 5'7". RHB, OB. Jamaica 1995-96 to 2005-06; captain/overseas player 2003-04 to 2005-06. British passport (Welsh father). Durham debut 2004; cap 2005. **Tests** (WI): 1 (2002-03); HS 5 and BB 2-108 v I (Madras) 2002-03. F-c Tours (WI): E 2002 (WI A); I 2002-03. HS 165* v Somerset (Taunton) 2004. BB 7-60 Jamaica v Barbados (Bridgetown) 2000-01. Du BB 5-41 (10-151 match) v Yorks (Scarborough) 2004 – scored 35 and 68 to complete match double. LO HS 68* v Notts (Chester-le-St) 2007 (FPT). LO BB 5-41 v Derbys (Chester-le-St) 2008 (FPT). T20 HS 37. T20 BB 4-14.

CLAYDON, Mitchell Eric (Westfield Sports HS, Sydney), b Fairfield, NSW, Australia 25 Nov 1982. 6'4". LHB, RMF. Yorkshire 2005-06. Durham debut 2007. HS 40 v Lancs (Manchester) 2008. BB 4-90 v Sussex (Hove) 2009. LO HS 19 v Glos (Bristol) 2009 (FPT). LO BB 3-31 v Bangladesh A (Chester-le-St) 2008. T20 HS 12*. T20 BB 5-26.

COETZER, Kyle James (Aberdeen GS), b Aberdeen, Scotland 14 Apr 1984. 5'11". RHB, RM. Debut (Durham) 2004. Scotland 2004, 2009-10. **LOI** (Scot): 4 (2008 to 2008-09); HS 44 v Afghanistan (Benoni) 2008-09. F-c Tour (Scot): Kenya 2009-10. HS 153* v DU (Durham) 2007. CC HS 142 v Warwks (Chester-le-St) 2007. BB 2-16 Scot v Kenya (Nairobi) 2009-10. LO HS 127 Scot v Oman (Johannesburg) 2008-09. LO BB – . IT20 HS 48*. IT20 BB 3-25. T20 HS 64. T20 BB 3-25.

COLLINGWOOD, Paul David (Blackfyne CS; Derwentside C), b Shotley Bridge 26 May 1976. 5'11". RHB, RM. Debut (Durham) 1996 v Northants (Chester-le-St) taking wicket of D.J.Capel with his first ball before scoring 91 and 16; cap 1998; benefit 2007. MBE 2005. *Wisden* 2007. **ECB central contract 2009-10. Tests**: 57 (2003-04 to 2009-10); HS 206 v A (Adelaide) 2006-07; BB 3-23 v NZ (Wellington) 2007-08. **LOI**: 173 (2001 to 2009-10, 25 as captain); HS 120* v A (Melbourne) 2006-07; BB 6-31 v B (Nottingham) 2005 – first to score a hundred (112*) and take six wickets in same LOI. F-c Tours: A 2006-07; SA 2009-10; WI 2003-04, 2008-09; NZ 2007-08; I 2005-06, 2008-09; P 2005-06; SL 2003-04, 2007-08; B 2009-10. 1000 runs (2); most – 1120 (2005), inc six hundreds (Du record). HS 206 (*see Tests*). Du HS 190 v SL (Chester-le-St) 2002 and 190 v Derbys (Derby) 2005, sharing Du record 4th wkt partnership of 250 with D.M.Benkenstein. BB 5-52 v Somerset (Stockton) 2005. LO HS 120* (*see LOI*). LO BB 6-31 (*see LOI*). IT20 HS 79. IT20 BB 4-22. T20 HS 79. T20 BB 5-14 v Derbys (Chester-le-St) 2008 – Du record.

DAVIES, Anthony Mark (Northfield CS, Billingham; Stockton SFC), b Stockton-on-Tees 4 Oct 1980. 6'3". RHB, RMF. Debut (Durham) 2002; cap 2005. Nottinghamshire 2007 (on loan). F-c Tour (Eng A): NZ 2008-09. HS 62 v Somerset (Stockton) 2005. 50 wkts (1): 50 (2004). BB 8-24 (11-75 match) v Hampshire (Basingstoke) 2008. LO HS 31* v Warwks (Chester-le-St) 2002 (NL). LO BB 4-13 v Sussex (Chester-le-St) 2001 (NL). T20 HS 6. T20 BB 2-14.

^{NQ}**Di VENUTO, Michael** James (St Virgil's C; Hobart), b Hobart, Australia 12 Dec 1973. 6'0". LHB, RM/LBG. Tasmania 1991-92 to 2007-08. Sussex 1999; cap 1999. Derbyshire 2000-06; cap 2000; appointed captain for 2004 but missed entire season – back surgery. Durham debut 2007, carrying his bat for 155* v Worcs (Worcester) on debut. Italian passport 2008. **LOI** (A): 9 (1996-97 to 1997-98); HS 89 v SA (Johannesburg) 1996-97. F-c Tours: Z 1995-96 (Tas); Scotland/Ireland 1998 (Aus A). 1000 runs (9); most – 1654 (2009), inc six hundreds (Du record). HS 254* v Sussex (Chester-le-St) 2009. BB 1-0 Tas v Q (Brisbane) 1999-00. UK BB 1-3 Sx v Somerset (Taunton) 1999. LO HS 173* v Derbys CB (Derby) 2000 (NWT). LO BB 1-10 Tas v Q (Hobart) 1995-96. T20 HS 95*. T20 BB 3-19.

EVANS, Luke (St Aidan's S, Sunderland), b Sunderland 26 Apr 1987. 6'7". RHB, RMF. Debut (Durham) 2007 – awaiting CC debut. No 1st XI appearances in 2008. HS 1 and BB 2-39 v SL A (Chester-le-St) 2007. LO HS 0 v Yorks (Leeds) 2009 (FPT). LO BB 2-53 v Notts (Chester-le-St) 2009 (P40).

GIDMAN, William Robert Simon (Wycliffe C; Berkshire C of Agriculture), b High Wycombe, Bucks 14 Feb 1985. Younger brother of A.P.R.Gidman (*see GLOUCESTER-SHIRE*). 6'2". LHB, RM. Debut (Durham) 2007 (awaiting CC debut). No f-c appearances in 2008 and 2009. MCC YC 2004-06. HS 8 and BB 3-37 v SL A (Chester-le-St) 2007. LO HS 21 MCC v Bangladesh A (Durham) 2008. LO BB 2-21 v Bangladesh A (Chester-le-St) 2008.

HARMISON, Ben William (Ashington HS), b Ashington, Northumb 9 Jan 1986. Younger brother of S.J.Harmison. 6'5". LHB, RMF. Debut (Durham) 2006, scoring 110 v OU (Oxford). Scored 105 in his second match (v West Indies A) to emulate A.Fairbairn (Middlesex 1947) in scoring hundreds in first two f-c matches, those matches being in England. HS 110 (*see above*). CC HS 101 v Warwks (Chester-le-St) 2007. LO HS 67 v Notts (Chester-le-St) 2009 (P40). LO BB 3-43 v Scotland (Chester-le-St) 2008 (FPT). T20 HS 21. T20 BB 3-20.

HARMISON, Stephen James (Ashington HS), b Ashington, Northumb 23 Oct 1978. Elder brother of B.W.Harmison. 6'4". RHB, RF. Debut (Durham) 1996; cap 1999. Lions 2007-08. MCC 2007. *Wisden* 2004. MBE 2005. **Tests**: 63 (2002 to 2009); HS 49* v SA (Oval) 2008; BB 7-12 (9-73 match) v WI (Kingston) 2003-04. **LOI**: 58 (2002-03 to 2008-09); HS 18* v WI (Providence) 2006-07; BB 5-33 v A (Bristol) 2005; hat-trick v I (Nottingham) 2004. F-c Tours: A 2002-03, 2005-06 (RW), 2006-07; SA 1998-99 (Eng A), 2004-05; WI 2003-04, 2008-09; NZ 2007-08; I 2005-06, 2008-09; P 2005-06; SL 2007-08; Z 1998-99 (Eng A); B 2003-04. HS 49* (*see Tests*). Du HS 36* v Hampshire (Chester-le-St) 2008. 50 wkts (6); most – 65 (2008). BB 7-12 (*see Tests*). Du BB 6-20 v Notts (Nottingham) 2009. Hat-tricks (2): v Worcs (Chester-le-St) 2005 and v Sussex (Hove) 2008. LO HS 25* v Somerset (Chester-le-St) 2008 (P40). LO BB 5-33 (*see LOI*). IT20 HS – . IT20 BB 1-13. T20 HS 6. T20 BB 4-38.

HINDMARCH, Paul Robert (Keswick S), b Carlisle, Cumbria 8 Feb 1988. 6'2". RHB, RMF. Durham 2nd XI debut 2006. Cumberland 2006. Development contract – awaiting 1st XI debut.

KILLEEN, Neil (Greencroft CS; Derwentside C; Teesside U), b Shotley Bridge 17 Oct 1975. 6'2". RHB, RMF. Debut (Durham) 1995; cap 1999; benefit 2006. MCC 1999-2000. No f-c appearances in 2009. Tour (MCC): B 1999-00. HS 48 v Somerset (Chester-le-St) 1995. 50 wkts (1): 58 (1999). BB 7-70 v Hants (Chester-le-St) 2003. LO HS 32 v Middlesex (Lord's) 1996 (SL). LO BB 6-31 v Derbys (Derby) 2000 (NL) – Du l-o record. T20 HS 17*. T20 BB 4-7.

MUCHALL, Gordon James (Durham S), b Newcastle upon Tyne, Northumb 2 Nov 1982. Elder brother of P.B.Muchall (*see below*). 6'0". RHB, RM. Northumberland 1999. Debut (Durham) 2002; cap 2005. F-c Tours (E): NZ 2007-08; SL 2002-03 (ECB Acad), 2007-08. HS 219 v Kent (Canterbury) 2006, sharing Du record 6th wkt partnership of 249 with P.Mustard (*see below*). BB 3-26 v Yorks (Leeds) 2003. LO HS 101* v Yorks (Leeds) 2005 (NL). LO BB 1-15 v Sussex (Hove) 2003 (NL). T20 HS 64*. T20 BB 1-8.

MUSTARD, Philip (Usworth CS), b Sunderland 8 Oct 1982. 5'11". LHB, WK. Debut (Durham) 2002. **LOI**: 10 (2007-08); HS 83 v NZ (Napier) 2007-08. HS 130 v Kent (Canterbury) 2006. LO HS 108 v Northants (Northampton) 2007 (FPT). IT20 HS 40. T20 HS 67* v Derbys (Chester-le-St) 2006 – Du record.

ONIONS, Graham (St Thomas More RC S, Blaydon), b Gateshead 9 Sep 1982. 6'1". RHB, RFM. Debut (Durham) 2004. MCC 2007-08. **ECB central contract 2009-10. Tests:** 8 (2009 to 2009-10); HS 17* v A (Lord's) 2009; BB 5-38 v WI (Lord's) 2009 – on debut. **LOI:** 4 (2009 to 2009-10); HS 1 v A (Centurion) 2009-10; BB 2-58 v SL (Johannesburg) 2009-10. F-c Tours: SA 2009-10; I 2007-08 (Eng L); B 2006-07 (Eng A), 2009-10. HS 41 v Yorks (Leeds) 2007. 50 wkts (2); most – 69 (2009). BB 8-101 v Warwks (Birmingham) 2007. LO HS 19 v Derbys (Derby) 2008 (FPT). LO BB 3-39 v Derbys (Derby) 2005 (NL). T20 HS 31. T20 BB 3-25.

PLUNKETT, Liam Edward (Nunthorpe SS; Teesside Tertiary C), b Middlesbrough, Yorks 6 Apr 1985. 6'3". RHB, RFM. Debut (Durham) 2003. Dolphins 2007-08. **Tests:** 9 (2005-06 to 2007); HS 44* v WI (Leeds) 2007; BB 3-17 v SL (Birmingham) 2006. **LOI:** 27 (2005-06 to 2007); HS 56 v P (Lahore) 2005-06; BB 3-24 v A (Sydney) 2006-07. F-c Tours: NZ 2008-09 (Eng L); I 2005-06, 2007-08 (Eng L); P 2005-06; B 2006-07. HS 94* v Sussex (Hove) 2009. 50 wkts (3); most – 60 (2009). BB 6-63 (11-119) v Worcs (Chester-le-St) 2009. LO HS 72 v Somerset (Chester-le-St) 2008 (P40). LO BB 4-15 v Essex (Chester-le-St) 2007 (FPT). IT20 HS – . IT20 BB 1-37. T20 HS 13*. T20 BB 3-16.

‡**RICHARDSON, Michael** John (Stonyhurst C, Nottingham U), b Pt Elizabeth, South Africa 4 Oct 1986. Son of D.J.Richardson (South Africa, EP and NT 1977-78 to 1997-98), grandson of J.H.Richardson (NE Transvaal and Transvaal B 1952-53 to 1960-61), nephew of R.P.Richardson (WP 1984-85 to 1988-89). RHB, WK. MCC Young Cricketer 2008-09. Awaiting 1st XI debut.

SMITH, William Rew (Bedford S; Collingwood C, Durham), b Luton, Beds 28 Sep 1982. 5'9". RHB, OB. Nottinghamshire 2002-06. Durham UCCE 2003-05; captain 2004-05. British U 2004-05. Durham debut 2007; captain 2009 to date. Notts 2nd XI debut 1999 when aged 16y 309d. Bedfordshire 1999-2002. HS 201* v Surrey (Guildford) 2008. BB 3-34 DU v Leics (Leicester) 2005. CC BB 1-5 v Lancs (Chester-le-St) 2007. LO HS 103 v Worcs (Chester-le-St) 2007 (FPT). LO BB 1-6 v Derbys (Chester-le-St) 2008 (FPT). T20 HS 55. T20 BB 1-31.

‡**STOKES, Benjamin** Andrew ('**Ben**') (Cockermouth S), b Christchurch, Canterbury, New Zealand 4 Jun 1991. 6'0". LHB, RM. Durham 2nd XI debut 2007 when aged 16y 99d. England U19s 2009 to 2009-10. Awaiting f-c debut. LO HS 11* and BB 2-22 v Surrey (Oval) 2009 (FPT).

STONEMAN, Mark Daniel (Whickham CS), b Newcastle upon Tyne, Northumb 26 Jun 1987. 5'11". LHB, RM. Debut (Durham) 2007. HS 101 v Sussex (Chester-le-St) 2007. LO HS 21 v Bangladesh A (Chester-le-St) 2008.

THORP, Callum David (Servite C, Tuart Hill, Perth), b Mount Lawley, Perth, Australia 11 Feb 1975. 6'3". British passport (English parents). RHB, RMF. W Australia 2002-03 to 2003-04. Durham debut 2005. HS 75 v Hants (Southampton) 2006. 50 wkts (1): 50 (2008). BB 7-88 v Kent (Canterbury) 2008. LO HS 52 v B (Chester-le-St) 2005. LO BB 6-17 v Scotland (Edinburgh) 2006 (CGT). T20 HS 13. T20 BB 2-32.

TURNER, Karl (Deerness Valley CS, Ushaw Moor), b Dryburn, Durham 29 Nov 1987. 5'10". LHB, RM. Durham 2nd XI debut 2005. Development contract – awaiting 1st XI debut.

^{NQ}**CHANDERPAUL, Shivnarine** (Cove and John SS, Unity Village), b Unity Village, Demerara, Guyana 16 Aug 1974. 5'6". LHB, LB. Guyana 1991-92 to date. Durham 2007-09. **Tests** (WI): 123 (1993-94 to 2009-10, 14 as captain); HS 203* v SA (Georgetown) 2004-05; BB 1-2 v A (Adelaide) 1996-97. **LOI** (WI): 252 (1994-95 to 2009, 16 as captain); HS 150 v SA (E London) 1998-99; BB 3-18 v I (Sharjah) 1997-98. F-c Tours (WI) (C=Captain): E 1995, 2000, 2004, 2007, 2009; A 1995-96, 1996-97, 2000-01, 2005-06C, 2009-10; SA 1998-99, 2003-04, 2007-08; NZ 1994-95, 1999-00, 2005-06C, 2008-09; I 1994-95, 2002-03; P 1997-98, 2001-02 (Sharjah), 2006-07; SL 2005C; Z 2001, 2003-04; B 1999-00, 2002-03; K 2001. 1000 runs (1+1); most – 1107 (2004-05). HS 303* Guyana v Jamaica (Kingston) 1995-96. Du HS 201* v Worcs (Worcester) 2009. BB 4-48 v Leeward Is (Basseterre) 1992-93. Du BB – . LO HS 150 (*see LOI*). LO BB 4-22 Guyana v Trinidad (Hampton Court) 1995-96. IT20 HS 41. T20 HS 48.

GODDARD, L.J. – *see DERBYSHIRE.*

P.B.Muchall, D.A.Warner and P.J.Wiseman left the staff without making a County First-Class or List A appearance in 2009.

DURHAM 2009

RESULTS SUMMARY

	Place	Won	Lost	Tied	Drew	NR
County Championship (1st Division)	1st	8			8	
All First-Class Matches		9			9	
FP Trophy (Group C)	5th	3	5			
Pro40 League (1st Division)	6th	4	4			
Twenty20 Cup (North Division)	QF	5	5			1

LV COUNTY CHAMPIONSHIP AVERAGES

BATTING AND FIELDING

Cap		M	I	NO	HS	Runs	Avge	100	50	Ct/St
	S.Chanderpaul	5	6	4	201*	472	236.00	3	–	3
	M.J.Di Venuto	16	26	6	254*	1601	80.05	6	5	23
2005	D.M.Benkenstein	16	22	–	181	1155	52.50	5	4	10
	L.E.Plunkett	12	12	3	94*	400	44.44	–	3	12
	P.Mustard	16	20	6	94*	592	42.28	–	5	61/1
	I.D.Blackwell	16	22	2	158	801	40.05	1	6	4
	K.J.Coetzer	6	9	1	107	284	35.50	1	–	7
	W.R.Smith	15	23	2	150	700	33.33	2	3	6
	G.J.Muchall	11	17	2	106*	497	33.13	1	2	13
	M.D.Stoneman	11	18	–	64	376	20.88	–	1	10
	C.D.Thorp	12	12	–	42	207	17.25	–	–	15
	M.E.Claydon	10	11	1	38	110	11.00	–	–	3
2005	A.M.Davies	9	8	4	16*	37	9.25	–	–	2
	G.Onions	7	8	4	12*	25	6.25	–	–	3
1999	S.J.Harmison	13	10	1	10*	16	1.77	–	–	2

Also batted: (one match each): S.G.Borthwick 26*; G.R.Breese (cap 2005) 48 (2 ct).

BOWLING

	O	M	R	W	Avge	Best	5wI	10wM
G.Onions	248.5	61	688	45	15.28	7-38	4	–
S.J.Harmison	412.2	109	1154	51	22.62	6-20	4	–
I.D.Blackwell	430.1	121	1012	43	23.53	7-85	3	–
L.E.Plunkett	346.2	65	1217	49	24.83	6-63	3	1
C.D.Thorp	307.5	89	831	30	27.70	5-49	2	–
A.M.Davies	217.1	60	562	19	29.57	4-87	–	–
M.E.Claydon	210	40	734	22	33.36	4-90	–	–
Also bowled:								
D.M.Benkenstein	42	10	150	8	18.75	3-20	–	–

S.G.Borthwick 27-2-95-3; G.R.Breese 17-6-50-0; W.R.Smith 10-2-31-0.

The First-Class Averages (pp 228–244) give the records of Durham players in all first-class county matches (Durham's other opponents being MCC and Durham UCCE), with the exception of S.Chanderpaul, whose first-class figures for Durham are as above, and:

    S.J.Harmison 14-11-2-25*-41-4.55-0-0-2ct. 428.2-115-1201-52-23.09-6/20-4-0.

    G.Onions 8-8-4-12*-25-6.25-0-0-3ct. 262.5-63-730-46-15.86-7/38-4-0.

    L.E.Plunkett 14-13-3-94*-408-40.80-0-3-13ct. 381.2-73-1318-55-23.96-6/63-3-1.

DURHAM RECORDS

FIRST-CLASS CRICKET

Highest Total	For 648-5d		v	Notts	Chester-le-St[2]	2009
	V 810-4d		by	Warwicks	Birmingham	1994
Lowest Total	For 67		v	Middlesex	Lord's	1996
	V 56		by	Somerset	Chester-le-St[2]	2003
Highest Innings	For 273	M.L.Love	v	Hampshire	Chester-le-St[2]	2003
	V 501*	B.C.Lara	for	Warwicks	Birmingham	1994

Highest Partnership for each Wicket

1st	334*	S.Hutton/M.A.Roseberry	v	Oxford U	Oxford	1996
2nd	258	J.J.B.Lewis/M.L.Love	v	Notts	Chester-le-St[2]	2001
3rd	205	G.Fowler/S.Hutton	v	Yorkshire	Leeds	1993
4th	250	P.D.Collingwood/D.M.Benkenstein	v	Derbyshire	Derby	2005
5th	222	D.M.Benkenstein/G.R.Breese	v	Middlesex	Lord's	2006
6th	249	G.J.Muchall/P.Mustard	v	Kent	Canterbury	2006
7th	315	D.M.Benkenstein/O.D.Gibson	v	Yorkshire	Leeds	2006
8th	147	P.Mustard/L.E.Plunkett	v	Yorkshire	Leeds	2009
9th	127	D.G.C.Ligertwood/S.J.E.Brown	v	Surrey	Stockton	1996
10th	103	M.M.Betts/D.M.Cox	v	Sussex	Hove	1996

Best Bowling	For 10- 47	O.D.Gibson	v	Hampshire	Chester-le-St[2]	2007
(Innings)	V 9- 36	M.S.Kasprowicz	for	Glamorgan	Cardiff	2003
Best Bowling	For 14-177	A.Walker	v	Essex	Chelmsford	1995
(Match)	V 13-110	M.S.Kasprowicz	for	Glamorgan	Chester-le-St[2]	2003

Most Runs – Season	1654	M.J.Di Venuto	(av 78.76)	2009
Most Runs – Career	7854	J.J.B.Lewis	(av 31.41)	1997-2006
Most 100s – Season	6	P.D.Collingwood		2005
	6	M.J.Di Venuto		2009
Most 100s – Career	16	D.M.Benkenstein		2005-09
Most Wkts – Season	80	O.D.Gibson	(av 20.75)	2007
Most Wkts – Career	518	S.J.E.Brown	(av 28.30)	1992-2002
Most Career W-K Dismissals	359	P.Mustard	(346 ct; 13 st)	2002-09
Most Career Catches in the Field	123	P.D.Collingwood		1996-2008

LIMITED-OVERS CRICKET

Highest Total	FPT	332-4	v	Worcs	Chester-le-St[2]	2007
	P40	319-3	v	Worcs	Worcester	2004
	T20	181-4	v	Lancashire	Manchester	2008
Lowest Total	FPT	82	v	Worcs	Chester-le-St[1]	1968
	P40	72	v	Warwicks	Birmingham	2002
	T20	93	v	Kent	Canterbury	2009
Highest Innings	FPT	138	M.J.Di Venuto	v	Derbyshire	Chester-le-St[2]	2008
	P40	131*	W.Larkins	v	Hampshire	Portsmouth	1994
	T20	67*	P.Mustard	v	Derbyshire	Chester-le-St[2]	2006
Best Bowling	FPT	7-32	S.P.Davis	v	Lancashire	Chester-le-St[1]	1983
	P40	6-31	N.Killeen	v	Derbyshire	Derby	2000
	T20	5-14	P.D.Collingwood	v	Derbyshire	Chester-le-St[2]	2008

[1] Chester-le-Street CC (Ropery Lane) [2] Riverside Ground

ESSEX

Formation of Present Club: 14 January 1876
Inaugural First-Class Match: 1894
Colours: Blue, Gold and Red
Badge: Three Seaxes above Scroll bearing 'Essex'
County Champions: (6) 1979, 1983, 1984, 1986, 1991, 1992
Gillette/NatWest/C&G/FP Trophy Winners: (3) 1985, 1997, 2008
Benson and Hedges Cup Winners: (2) 1979, 1998
Pro 40/National League (Div 1) Winners: (2) 2005, 2006
Sunday League Winners: (3) 1981, 1984, 1985
Twenty20 Cup Winners: (0); best – Semi-Finalist 2006, 2008

Chief Executive: David E.East, County Ground, New Writtle Street, Chelmsford CM2 0PG • Tel: 01245 252420 • Fax: 01245 254030 • Email: administration.essex@ecb.co.uk • Web: www.essexcricket.org.uk

First Team Coach: A.P.Grayson. **Batting Coach**: G.A.Gooch. **Bowling Coach**: C.E.W.Silverwood. **Captain**: M.L.Pettini. **Vice-Captain**: J.S.Foster. **Overseas Player**: Danish Kaneria. **2010 Beneficiary**: none. **Head Groundsman**: Stuart Kerrison. **Scorer**: A.E. (Tony) Choat. ‡ New registration. NQ Not qualified for England.

BOPARA, Ravinder Singh (Brampton Manor S; Barking Abbey Sports C), b Newham, London 4 May 1985. 5'8". RHB, RM. Debut (Essex) 2002; cap 2005. Auckland 2009-10. MCC 2006, 2008. YC 2008. **Tests**: 10 (2007-08 to 2009); HS 143 v WI (Lord's) 2009; BB 1-39 v SL (Galle) 2007-08. **LOI**: 50 (2006-07 to 2009-10); HS 60 v I (Kanpur) 2008-09. BB 2-43 v Canada (Gros Islet, St Lucia) 2006-07. F-c Tours: WI 2008-09; SL 2007-08. 1000 runs (1): 1256 (2008). HS 229 v Northants (Chelmsford) 2007. BB 5-75 v Surrey (Chelmsford) 2006. LO HS 201* v Leics (Leicester) 2008 (FPT) – Ex record. LO BB 4-52 v Derbys (Derby) 2008 (P40). IT20 HS 55. T20 HS 84. T20 BB 3-18.

CHAMBERS, Maurice Anthony (Homerton TC; Sir George Monoux C), b Port Antonio, Portland, Jamaica 14 Sep 1987. 6'3". RHB, RFM. Debut (Essex) 2005. No f-c appearances 2006-07 – stress fracture of the back. MCC YC 2004. HS 8* v Middx (Chelmsford) 2009. BB 4-62 v WI (Chelmsford) 2009. CC BB 3-30 v Glos (Bristol) 2009. LO HS 1* v Leics (Leicester) 2008 (P40). LO BB 1-26 v Yorkshire (Chelmsford) 2008. T20 HS 10*. T20 BB 3-31.

‡COMBER, Michael Andrew (Clacton County HS), b Colchester 26 Oct 1989. 6'3". RHB, RMF. Essex 2nd XI debut 2007. Awaiting 1st XI debut.

COOK, Alastair Nathan (Bedford S), b Gloucester 25 Dec 1984. 6'3". LHB, OB. Debut (Essex) 2003; cap 2005. MCC 2004-07. Essex 2nd XI debut 2000 when aged 15y 235d. England U19 captain 2003-04. YC 2005. **ECB central contract 2009-10. Tests**: 52 (2005-06 to 2009-10); HS 160 v WI (Chester-le-St) 2009. Scored 60 and 104* v I (Nagpur) 2005-06 on debut. Third, after D.G.Bradman and S.R.Tendulkar, to score seven Test hundreds before his 23rd birthday. Second, after M.A.Taylor, to score 1000 runs in the calendar year of his debut. BB – . **LOI**: 23 (2006 to 2008-09); HS 102 v I (Southampton) 2007. F-c Tours (C=captain): A 2006-07; SA 2009-10; WI 2005-06; NZ 2007-08; I 2005-06, 2008-09; SL 2004-05 (Eng A), 2007-08; B 2009-10C. 1000 runs (4); most – 1466 (2005). HS 195 v Northants (Northampton) 2005. Scored 214 v Australians (Chelmsford) 2005 in 2-day non-f-c match. BB 3-13 v Northants (Chelmsford) 2005. LO HS 125 v Surrey (Croydon) 2007 (FPT). BB – . IT20 HS 26. T20 HS 100*.

104

^{NQ}**DANISH** Parabha Shanker **KANERIA** (St Patrick's HS; Government Islamia C), b Karachi, Pakistan 16 Dec 1980. 6'1". Cousin of Anil Dalpat (Pakistan) and second Hindu to represent Pakistan. RHB, LBG. Debut (PNSC) 1998-99. Karachi Whites/Blues/Harbour 1998-99 to 2006-07. Habib Bank 2000-01 to date. Essex debut 2004; cap 2004. Sind 2007-08. **Tests** (P): 58 (2000-01 to 2009-10); HS 29 v E (Leeds) 2006; BB 7-77 v B (Dhaka) 2001-02. **LOI** (P): 18 (2001-02 to 2006-07); HS 6*; BB 3-31 v NZ (Dambulla) 2003. F-c Tours (P): E 2006; A 2004-05, 2009-10; SA 2006-07; WI 2004-05; NZ 2003-04, 2009-10; I 2004-05, 2007-08; SL 2001 (Pak A), 2005-06, 2009; B 2001-02; K 2000 (Pak A). HS 65 v Notts (Nottingham) 2007. 50 wkts (3+1); most – 75 (2009). BB 8-59 (13-81 match) Habib Bank v SSGC (Karachi) 2008-09. UK BB 8-116 (12-203 match) v Leics (Chelmsford) 2009. Hat-trick v Derbys (Derby) 2009. LO HS 64 Habib Bank v KRL (Rawalpindi) 2009-10. LO BB 5-21 Habib Bank v Customs (Karachi) 2005-06. T20 HS 12. T20 BB 4-22.

^{NQ}**FLOWER, Grant** William (St George's C), b Salisbury, Rhodesia 20 Dec 1970. 5'10". Younger brother of A.Flower (Mashonaland, Essex, S Australia and Zimbabwe 1986-87 to 2006). RHB, SLA. Debut (Zimbabwe) 1989-90. Mashonaland U24/Young Mashonaland 1993-94 to 1995-96. Mashonaland 1994-95 to 2003-04. MCC 1996-97. Leicestershire 2002 (one match); cap 2002. Essex debut/cap 2005 (Kolpak registration). **Tests** (Z): 67 (1992-93 to 2003-04); HS 201* v P (Harare) 1994-95 sharing with A.Flower in 4th wicket partnership of 269, the highest stand between brothers in Test cricket; BB 4-41 (8-104 match) v B (Chittagong) 2001-02. **LOI** (Z): 219 (1992-93 to 2003-04, 1 as captain); HS 142* v B (Bulawayo) 2000-01; BB 4-32 v Kenya (Dhaka) 1998-99. F-c Tours (Z): E 1990, 2000; A 1994-95; SA 1999-00; WI 1999-00; NZ 1995-96, 1997-98, 2000-01; I 1992-93, 2000-01, 2001-02; P 1993-94, 1996-97, 1998-99; SL 1996-97, 1997-98, 2001-02; B 2001-02. HS 243* Mashonaland v Matabeleland (Harare) 1996-97. UK HS 203 v Northants (Chelmsford) 2007. BB 7-31 Z v Lahore (Lahore) 1998-99. UK BB 4-66 Le v Warwks (Birmingham) 2002. Two BB 3-28 v Glos (Bristol) 2006. LO HS 148* Mashonaland v Midlands (Kwekwe) 2002-03. LO BB 4-32 (*see LOI*). T20 HS 61. T20 BB 3-30.

FOSTER, James Savin (Forest S, Snaresbrook; Collingwood C, Durham U), b Whipps Cross 15 Apr 1980. 6'0". RHB, WK. British U 2000-01. Essex debut 2000; cap 2001. Durham UCCE 2001. MCC 2004, 2008, 2009. **Tests**: 7 (2001-02 to 2002-03); HS 48 v I (Bangalore) 2001-02. **LOI**: 11 (2001-02); HS 13 v I (Bombay) 2001-02. F-c Tours: A 2002-03; WI 2000-01 (Eng A); NZ 2001-02; I 2001-02, 2007-08 (Eng A). 1000 runs (1): 1037 (2004). HS 212 v Leics (Chelmsford) 2004. BB 1-122 v Northants (Northampton) 2008 – in contrived circumstances. LO HS 83* v Durham, inc 5 sixes in 5 balls off S.G.Borthwick (Chester-le-St) 2009 (P40). T20 HS 62*.

‡**GODLEMAN, Billy** Ashley (Islington Green S), b Islington, London 11 Feb 1989. 6'3". LHB, LB. Middlesex 2005-09. England U19s 2006 to 2007-08. HS 113* M v Somerset (Taunton) 2007 – on CC debut. BB – . LO HS 82 M v Scotland (Lord's) 2009 (FPT). T20 HS 69.

MASTERS, David Daniel (Fort Luton HS; Mid Kent CHE), b Chatham, Kent 22 Apr 1978. Son of K.D.Masters (Kent 1983-84). 6'4". RHB, RMF. Kent 2000-02. Leicestershire 2003-07; cap 2007. Essex debut 2008. HS 119 Le v Sussex (Hove) 2003. Ex HS 67 v Leics (Chelmsford) 2009. BB 6-24 v Leics (Chelmsford) 2008. LO HS 39 Le v Glos (Cheltenham) 2006 (P40). LO BB 5-17 v Surrey (Oval) 2008 (FPT). T20 HS 14. T20 BB 3-7.

MAUNDERS, John Kenneth (Ashford HS; Spelthorne C), b Ashford, Middlesex 4 Apr 1981. 5'10". LHB, RM. Middlesex 1999 (one non-CC match); 2nd XI debut aged 16 years 19 days. Leicestershire 2003-07. Essex debut 2008. Shropshire 2008. HS 180 Le v Glos (Cheltenham) 2006. Ex HS 150 v Leics (Chelmsford) 2009. BB 4-15 Le v Worcs (Worcester) 2006. LO HS 109* Le v Derbys (Leicester) 2007 (FPT). LO BB 2-16 Le v Warwks (Birmingham) 2005 (CGT). T20 HS 10. T20 BB 2-14.

MICKLEBURGH, Jaik Charles (Bungay HS), b Norwich, Norfolk 30 Mar 1990. RHB, RM. Norfolk 2007. Debut (Essex) 2008. Essex 2nd XI debut aged 16 years 160 days. England U19s 2008-09 to 2009. HS 72 v Warwks (Chelmsford) 2008. BB – .

NAPIER, Graham Richard (The Gilberd S, Colchester), b Colchester 6 Jan 1980. 5'9½". RHB, RM. Debut (Essex) 1997; cap 2003. MCC 2004. Wellington 2008-09. F-c Tour (Eng A): I 2003-04. HS 125 v Notts (Chelmsford) 2007. BB 6-103 v Glamorgan (Southend) 2008. LO HS 79 Essex CB v Lancs CB (Chelmsford) 2000 (NWT). LO BB 6-29 v Worcs (Chelmsford) 2001 (NL). T20 HS 152* v Sussex (Chelmsford) 2008 – record T20 Cup score (58b, 10 fours, 16 sixes); 2nd highest score in all T20. T20 BB 4-10 v Northants (Chelmsford) 2008 – Ex record.

‡**OSBORNE, Max** (Sawyers Hall C), b Orsett 21 Nov 1990. 6'3". RHB, RMF. Essex 2nd XI debut 2009. Awaiting 1st XI debut.

PALLADINO, Antonio Paul (Cardinal Pole SS; Anglia Polytechnic U), b Tower Hamlets, London 29 Jun 1983. 6'0". RHB, RMF. Cambridge UCCE 2003-05. Essex debut 2003. Namibia 2009-10. HS 53* Namibia v Boland (Windhoek) 2009-10. UK HS 41 v Notts (Nottingham) 2004. BB 6-41 v Kent (Canterbury) 2003. LO HS 31 Namibia v Boland (Windhoek) 2009-10. LO BB 3-32 v Glamorgan (Chelmsford) 2003 (NL). T20 HS 8*. T20 BB 4-21.

PETTINI, Mark Lewis (Comberton Village C; Hills Road SFC, Cambridge; Cardiff U), b Brighton, Sussex 7 Aug 1983. RHB. Debut (Essex) 2001; cap 2006; captain 2007 (*part*) to date. MCC 2005. 1000 runs (1): 1218 (2006). HS 208* v Derbys (Chelmsford) 2006. BB – . LO 144 v Surrey (Oval) 2007 (FPT). T20 HS 87.

PHILLIPS, Timothy James (Felsted S; St Hild & St Bede C, Durham U), b Cambridge 13 Mar 1981. 6'1". LHB, SLA. Essex 1999, 2001-02, 2005 to date; cap 2006. Durham UCCE 2001-02. HS 89 v Worcs (Worcester) 2005. BB 5-41 v Derbys (Chelmsford) 2006. LO HS 41 v Somerset (Taunton) 2009 (P40). LO BB 5-34 v Lancs (Chelmsford) 2006 (P40). T20 HS 31. T20 BB 2-11.

^{NQ}**Ten DOESCHATE, Ryan** Neil (Fairbairn C; Cape Town U), b Port Elizabeth, South Africa 30 Jun 1980. 5'10½". RHB, RMF. Debut (Essex) 2003; cap 2006. EU passport – Dutch ancestry. Netherlands 2005 to date. **LOI** (Ne): 26 (2006 to 2009-10); HS 109* v Bermuda (Nairobi) 2006-07; BB 4-31 v Canada (Nairobi) 2006-07. F-c Tours (Ne): SA 2006-07, 2007-08; K 2005-06, 2009-10; Ireland 2005. HS 259* and BB 6-20 (9-112 match) Netherlands v Canada (Pretoria) 2006. Ex HS 159* v Surrey (Guildford) 2009. Ex BB 6-57 v NZ (Chelmsford) 2008. CC BB 5-58 v Leics (Chelmsford) 2008. LO HS 134* Ne v Namibia (Benoni) 2008-09. LO BB 5-50 v Glos (Bristol) 2007 (FPT). IT20 HS 56. IT20 BB 3-23. T20 HS 56. T20 BB 4-24.

WALKER, Matthew Jonathan (King's S, Rochester), b Gravesend, Kent 2 Jan 1974. Grandson of Jack Walker (Kent 1949). 5'8". LHB, RM. Kent 1992-93 (Z tour) to 2008; UK debut 1994; cap 2000; benefit 2008. Essex debut 2009. F-c Tour: Z 1992-93 (K). 1000 runs (4); most – 1419 (2006). HS 275* K v Somerset (Canterbury) 1996. Ex HS 150 v Middx (Lord's) 2009. BB 2-21 K v Middlesex (Canterbury) 2004. LO HS 117 K v Warwks (Canterbury) 1997 (BHC). LO BB 4-24 K v Yorks (Leeds) 2001 (NL). T20 HS 58*.

WESTFIELD, Mervyn Simon (Barking C), b Romford 5 May 1988. 6'1". RHB, RFM. Debut (Essex) 2005. No 1st XI appearances in 2008. England U19s 2006-07. HS 32 and BB 4-72 v Somerset (Southend) 2006. LO HS 17 v Notts (Southend) 2009 (P40). LO BB 2-32 v Hampshire (Chelmsford) 2009 (P40).

WESTLEY, Thomas (Linton Village C; Hills Road SFC), b Cambridge 13 March 1989. 6'2". RHB, OB. Debut (Essex) 2007. MCC 2007, 2009. Essex 2nd XI debut 2004 when aged 15 years 88 days. Cambridgeshire 2005. HS 132 v Derbys (Derby) 2009. BB 2-33 v Glamorgan (Cardiff) 2009. CC BB – . LO HS 36 v Worcs (Chelmsford) 2007 (P40).

WHEATER, Adam (Millfield S), b Whipps Cross 13 Feb 1990. RHB, WK. Debut (Essex) 2008. Essex 2nd XI debut when aged 16 years 190 days. HS 36 v Cambridge UCCE (Cambridge) 2009. CC HS 22 v Derbys (Derby) 2008 – on debut. T20 HS 4.

WRIGHT, Christopher Julian Clement (Eggars S, Alton; Anglia Ruskin U), b Chipping Norton, Oxon 14 Jul 1985. 6'3". RHB, RFM. Cambridge UCCE 2004-05. Middlesex 2004-07. Tamil Union 2005-06. Essex debut 2008. HS 76 CU v Essex (Cambridge) 2005. CC HS 71* v Middx (Chelmsford) 2008. BB 6-22 v Leics (Leicester) 2008. LO HS 23 v Kent (Chelmsford) 2008 (FPT). LO BB 3-3 v Northants (Southend) 2008. T20 HS 6*. T20 BB 4-24.

RELEASED/RETIRED
(Having made a County First-Class or List A appearance in 2009)

AHMED, Jahid Sheikh (St Peter's HS, Burnham-on-Crouch; East London U), b Chelmsford 20 Feb 1986. 5'11". RHB, RMF. Essex 2005-09. MCC YC 2004. HS 16* and BB 3-42 v Glos (Bristol) 2008. LO HS 1* v Hants (Southampton) 2007 (P40). LO BB 4-32 v SL (Chelmsford) 2006. T20 HS – . T20 BB 1-25.

AMLA, H.M. – *see NOTTINGHAMSHIRE.*

CHOPRA, V. – *see WARWICKSHIRE.*

GALLIAN, Jason Edward Riche (Pittwater House S, Sydney; Keble C, Oxford), b Manly, Sydney, Australia 25 Jun 1971. Qualified for England 1994. 6'0". RHB, RM. Lancashire 1990-97, taking wicket of D.A.Hagan (OU) with his first ball; cap 1994. Oxford U 1992-93; blue 1992-93; captain 1993. Combined U 1992-93. Nottinghamshire 1998-2007; cap 1998; captain 1998 (*part*) to 2004; benefit 2005. Essex 2008-09; cap 2008. Captained Australia YC v England YC 1989-90, scoring 158* in 1st 'Test'. **Tests:** 3 (1995 to 1995-96); HS 28 v SA (Pt Elizabeth) 1995-96. F-c Tours: A 1996-97 (Eng A); WI 1995-96 (La); SA 1995-96 (*part*); I 1994-95 (Eng A); P 1995-96 (Eng A). 1000 runs (6); most – 1220 (2005). HS 312 La v Derbys (Manchester) 1996 (record score at Old Trafford). Ex HS 171 v Northants (Chelmsford) 2008 – on Ex CC debut. BB 6-115 La v Surrey (Southport) 1996. Ex BB – . LO HS 134 La v Notts (Manchester) 1995 (BHC). LO BB 5-15 La v Minor C (Leek) 1995 (BHC). T20 HS 62.

MIDDLEBROOK, J.D. – *see NORTHAMPTONSHIRE.*

ESSEX 2009

RESULTS SUMMARY

	Place	Won	Lost	Tied	Drew	NR
County Championship (2nd Division)	2nd	6	3		7	
All First-Class Matches		6	3		9	
FP Trophy (Group D)	QF	5	3			1
Pro40 League (1st Division)	4th	5	3			
Twenty20 Cup (South Division)	4th	5	4			1

LV COUNTY CHAMPIONSHIP AVERAGES

BATTING AND FIELDING

Cap		M	I	NO	HS	Runs	Avge	100	50	Ct/St
2005	R.S.Bopara	2	4	2	201	269	134.50	1	1	2
	H.M.Amla	3	5	1	181	410	102.50	2	1	2
2006	R.N.ten Doeschate	14	22	4	159*	823	45.72	2	2	5
	T.Westley	6	11	2	132	383	42.55	1	1	3
2006	M.L.Pettini	15	28	6	101*	870	39.54	1	4	10
2001	J.S.Foster	15	24	1	103*	905	39.34	1	6	57/4
2005	A.N.Cook	8	15	1	87	493	35.21	–	4	11
2003	G.R.Napier	10	16	6	64*	348	34.80	–	2	3
	M.J.Walker	16	29	2	150	933	34.55	2	2	12
	J.K.Maunders	10	17	–	150	560	32.94	1	2	12
2006	T.J.Phillips	3	4	–	69	111	27.75	–	1	2
2008	D.D.Masters	15	16	1	67	341	22.73	–	2	7
	V.Chopra	10	18	–	85	385	21.38	–	3	6
	M.A.Chambers	5	7	6	8*	19	19.00	–	–	–
	J.C.Mickleburgh	4	8	–	62	138	17.25	–	1	2
2003	J.D.Middlebrook	6	8	2	19	96	16.00	–	–	1
	C.J.C.Wright	14	16	7	24*	130	14.44	–	–	2
2008	J.E.R.Gallian	5	10	1	44*	120	13.33	–	–	2
2004	Danish Kaneria	11	15	2	37	158	12.15	–	–	5

Also batted: A.P.Palladino (3 matches) 5, 0; A.J.Wheater (1) 0 (4 ct).

BOWLING

	O	M	R	W	Avge	Best	5wI	10wM
Danish Kaneria	597.5	124	1777	75	23.69	8-116	6	2
D.D.Masters	557.2	184	1212	45	26.93	5- 65	1	–
G.R.Napier	271.3	55	1005	29	34.65	4- 32	–	–
C.J.C.Wright	437.1	67	1538	40	38.45	4- 43	–	–
M.A.Chambers	117.4	13	438	10	43.80	3- 30	–	–
R.N.ten Doeschate	246	32	970	22	44.09	5- 62	1	–
Also bowled:								
A.P.Palladino	82	19	258	7	36.85	4- 68	–	–
J.D.Middlebrook	99	16	345	9	38.33	3- 87	–	–
T.J.Phillips	105	23	279	6	46.50	3- 61	–	–

R.S.Bopara 8-3-30-0; V.Chopra 8.1-1-27-0; A.N.Cook 10-0-51-2; J.C.Mickleburgh 7.5-1-28-0; M.L.Pettini 6.5-0-62-0; M.J.Walker 3.2-0-22-0; T.Westley 29-2-104-2.

The First-Class Averages (pp 228–244) give the records of Essex players in all first-class county matches (Essex's other opponents being the West Indians and Cambridge UCCE), with the exception of R.S.Bopara, whose first-class figures for Essex are as above, and:

A.N.Cook 9-17-2-87-613-40.86-0-5-11ct. 10-0-51-2-25.50-1/3-0-0.

J.S.Foster 16-26-2-103*-976-40.66-1-6-60ct/4st.

T.Westley 7-12-2-132-387-38.70-1-1-3ct. 29-2-104-2-52.00-0/33-0-0.

ESSEX RECORDS

FIRST-CLASS CRICKET

Highest Total	For 761-6d		v	Leics	Chelmsford	1990
	V 803-4d		by	Kent	Brentwood	1934
Lowest Total	For 30		v	Yorkshire	Leyton	1901
	V 14		by	Surrey	Chelmsford	1983
Highest Innings	For 343*	P.A.Perrin	v	Derbyshire	Chesterfield	1904
	V 332	W.H.Ashdown	for	Kent	Brentwood	1934

Highest Partnership for each Wicket

1st	316	G.A.Gooch/P.J.Prichard	v	Kent	Chelmsford	1994
2nd	403	G.A.Gooch/P.J.Prichard	v	Leics	Chelmsford	1990
3rd	347*	M.E.Waugh/N.Hussain	v	Lancashire	Ilford	1992
4th	314	Salim Malik/N.Hussain	v	Surrey	The Oval	1991
5th	316	N.Hussain/M.A.Garnham	v	Leics	Leicester	1991
6th	206	J.W.H.T.Douglas/J.O'Connor	v	Glos	Cheltenham	1923
	206	B.R.Knight/R.A.G.Luckin	v	Middlesex	Brentwood	1962
7th	261	J.W.H.T.Douglas/J.Freeman	v	Lancashire	Leyton	1914
8th	263	D.R.Wilcox/R.M.Taylor	v	Warwicks	Southend	1946
9th	251	J.W.H.T.Douglas/S.N.Hare	v	Derbyshire	Leyton	1921
10th	218	F.H.Vigar/T.P.B.Smith	v	Derbyshire	Chesterfield	1947

Best Bowling	For 10- 32	H.Pickett	v	Leics	Leyton	1895
(Innings)	V 10- 40	E.G.Dennett	for	Glos	Bristol	1906
Best Bowling	For 17-119	W.Mead	v	Hampshire	Southampton	1895
(Match)	V 17- 56	C.W.L.Parker	for	Glos	Gloucester	1925

Most Runs – Season	2559	G.A.Gooch	(av 67.34)		1984
Most Runs – Career	30701	G.A.Gooch	(av 51.77)		1973-97
Most 100s – Season	9	J.O'Connor			1929, 1934
	9	D.J.Insole			1955
Most 100s – Career	94	G.A.Gooch			1973-97
Most Wkts – Season	172	T.P.B.Smith	(av 27.13)		1947
Most Wkts – Career	1610	T.P.B.Smith	(av 26.68)		1929-51
Most Career W-K Dismissals	1231	B.Taylor	(1040 ct; 191 st)		1949-73
Most Career Catches in the Field	519	K.W.R.Fletcher			1962-88

LIMITED-OVERS CRICKET

Highest Total	FPT	391-5	v	Surrey	The Oval	2008
	P40	316-4	v	Glamorgan	Chelmsford	2004
	T20	242-3	v	Sussex	Chelmsford	2008
Lowest Total	FPT	57	v	Lancashire	Lord's	1996
	P40	69	v	Derbyshire	Chesterfield	1974
	T20	99	v	Kent	Chelmsford	2007
Highest Innings	FPT	201* R.S.Bopara	v	Leics	Leicester	2008
	P40	176 G.A.Gooch	v	Glamorgan	Southend	1983
	T20	152* G.R.Napier	v	Sussex	Chelmsford	2008
Best Bowling	FPT	5- 8 J.K.Lever	v	Middlesex	Westcliff	1972
		5- 8 G.A.Gooch	v	Cheshire	Chester	1995
	P40	8-26 K.D.Boyce	v	Lancashire	Manchester	1971
	T20	4-10 G.R.Napier	v	Northants	Chelmsford	2008

GLAMORGAN

Formation of Present Club: 6 July 1888
Inaugural First-Class Match: 1921
Colours: Blue and Gold
Badge: Gold Daffodil
County Champions: (3) 1948, 1969, 1997
Gillette/NatWest/C&G/FP Trophy Winners: (0); best – Finalist 1977
Benson and Hedges Cup Winners: (0); best – Finalist 2000
Pro 40/National League (Div 1) Winners: (2) 2002, 2004
Sunday League Winners: (1) 1993
Twenty20 Cup Winners: (0); best – Semi-Finalist 2004

Chief Executive: A.D.Hamer, SWALEC Stadium, Cardiff, CF11 9XR • Tel: 0871 282 3401 • Fax: 0871 282 3405 • email: info@glamorgancricket.co.uk • Web: www.glamorgancricket.com

Cricket Director: M.P.Maynard. **Assistant Coaches:** R.V.Almond and S.L.Watkin. **Captain:** J.W.M.Dalrymple. **Vice-Captain:** M.A.Wallace. **Overseas Player:** M.J.Cosgrove and S.W.Tait. **2010 Beneficiary:** DA.Cosker. **Head Groundsman:** Keith Exton. **Scorer:** Andrew K.Hignell. ‡ New registration. ^NQ Not qualified for England.

‡**ALLENBY, James** (Christ Church GS, Perth), b Perth, W Australia 12 Sep 1982. 6'0". RHB, RM. Leicestershire 2006-09. Glamorgan debut 2009. Western Australia (T20) 2006-07. HS 138* Le v Bangladesh A (Leicester) 2008. CC HS 137 v Surrey (Oval) 2009. BB 5-125 Le v Glos (Bristol) 2007 – his first five f-c wickets. LO HS 91* Le v Middlesex (Lord's) 2007 (P40). LO BB 5-43 Le v Derbys (Leicester) 2007 (FPT). T20 HS 110. T20 BB 5-21 v Lancashire (Manchester) 2008 – Le record, inc 4 wkts in 4 balls.

ASHLING, Christopher Paul (Millfield S, UWIC), b Manchester 26 Nov 1988. 5'7". RHB/RFM. Lancashire 2nd XI debut 2005. Cardiff UCCE 2008. Wales MC 2008-09. HS 12 and BB 2-66 v Leics (Leicester) 2009 – only f-c game. LO HS 6* v Leics (Leicester) 2009 (P40). LO BB 2-33 v Lancs (Cardiff) 2009 (P40).

BRAGG, William David (Rougemont S, Newport; UWIC), b Newport, Monmouthshire 24 Oct 1986. 5'9". LHB, WK. Debut (Glamorgan) 2007. No f-c appearances in 2008. Wales MC 2004-09. HS 92 v Glos (Bristol) 2009. LO HS 78 v Leics (Leicester) 2009.

‡**BROWN, David** Owen (Queen Elizabeth GS, Blackburn; Collingwood C, Durham U), b Burnley, Lancs 8 Dec 1982. Younger brother of M.J.Brown (*see SURREY*). RHB, RM. 6'0". Durham UCCE 2003-05. British U 2005. Gloucestershire 2006-08; cap 2006. HS 83 Gs v Worcs (Cheltenham) 2008. BB 5-38 Gs v Derbys (Derby) 2008. LO HS 63* Gs v Surrey (Bristol) 2006 (CGT) – on debut. LO BB 3-29 Gs v Glamorgan (Colwyn Bay) 2007 (FPT). T20 HS 56. T20 BB 1-11.

^NQ**COSGROVE, Mark** James, b Elizabeth, Adelaide, S Australia 14 Jun 1984. 5'10". LHB/RM. S Australia 2002-03 to date. Glamorgan debut 2006 – scoring 114 v Derbys (Cardiff). **LOI** (A): 3 (2005-06 to 2006-07); HS 74 v B (Fatullah) 2005-06 – on debut; BB 1-1 v WI (Kuala Lumpur) 2006-07. HS 233 v Derbys (Derby) 2006. BB 3-3 S Aus v Tas (Adelaide) 2006-07. Gm BB 3-30 v Derbys (Derby) 2009. LO HS 121 S Aus v WA (Perth) 2005-06. LO BB 2-21 S Aus v Q (Brisbane) 2005-06. T20 HS 52. T20 BB 2-11.

COSKER, Dean Andrew (Millfield S), b Weymouth, Dorset 7 Jan 1978. 5'11". RHB, SLA. Debut (Glamorgan) 1996; cap 2000; benefit 2010. F-c Tours (Eng A): SA 1998-99; SL 1997-98; Z 1998-99; K 1997-98. HS 52 v Glos (Bristol) 2005. BB 6-91 (11-126 match) v Essex (Cardiff) 2009. LO HS 50* v Northants (Northampton) 2009 (FPT). LO BB 5-54 v Essex (Chelmsford) 2003 (NL). T20 HS 16*. T20 BB 3-18.

CROFT, Robert Damien Bale (St John Lloyd Catholic CS, Llanelli; Neath Tertiary C; W Glamorgan IHE), b Morriston, Swansea 25 May 1970. 5'10½". RHB, OB. Debut (Glamorgan) 1989; cap 1992; benefit 2000; captain 2003 (*part*) to 2006 (*part*). MCC 1996. **Tests**: 21 (1996 to 2001); HS 37* v SA (Manchester) 1998; BB 5-95 v NZ (Christchurch) 1996-97. **LOI**: 50 (1996 to 2001); HS 32 v SL (Perth) 1998-99; BB 3-51 v SA (Oval) 1998. F-c Tours: A 1998-99; SA 1993-94 (Eng A), 1995-96 (Gm); WI 1991-92 (Eng A), 1997-98; NZ 1996-97; SL 2000-01, 2003-04; Z 1990-91 (Gm), 1994-95 (Gm), 1996-97. HS 143 v Somerset (Taunton) 1995. 50 wkts (10); most – 76 (1996). Took 1,000th f-c wicket 2007. BB 8-66 (14-169 match) v Warwks (Swansea) 1992. LO HS 143 v Lincs (Lincoln) 2004 (CGT). LO BB 6-20 v Worcs (Cardiff) 1994 (SL). T20 HS 62*. T20 BB 3-12.

DALRYMPLE, James William Murray (Radley C; St Peter's C, Oxford), b Nairobi, Kenya 21 Jan 1981. Brother of S.H.Dalrymple (Oxford U 2002-04). 5'11". RHB, OB. Oxford UCCE/U 2001-03; captain 2002; blue 2001-02-03. British U 2001-02. Middlesex 2001-07; cap 2004. Glamorgan debut 2008; captain 2009 to date. **LOI**: 27 (2006 to 2006-07); HS 67 v SL (Lord's) 2006; BB 2-5 v I (Jaipur) 2006-07. F-c Tour (Eng A): WI 2005-06. 1000 runs (1): 1009 (2009). HS 244 M v Surrey (Oval) 2004. Gm HS 128 v Derbys (Derby) 2009. BB 5-49 OU v CU (Cambridge) 2003. CC BB 4-53 M v Hants (Southgate) 2005. Gm BB 3-11 v Leics (Colwyn Bay) 2009. LO HS 107 M v Glamorgan (Lord's) 2004 (CGT). LO BB 4-14 M v Essex (Southgate) 2001 (NL). IT20 HS 32. IT20 BB 1-10. T20 HS 63. T20 BB 2-8.

‡**GLOVER, John** Charles (Llantarnam CS; St Aidan's C, Durham U), b Cardiff 29 Aug 1989. 6'4". RHB, RMF. Durham UCCE 2008-09. Wales MC 2008-09. HS 14 and BB 5-38 DU v Durham (Durham) 2009. Awaiting 1st XI debut. Development contract.

HARRIS, James Alexander Russell (Pontardulais CS; Gorseinon C), b Morriston 16 May 1990. 6'0". RHB, RFM. Debut (Glamorgan) 2007 – aged 16 years 351 days – youngest Glamorgan player to take a first-class wicket. Glamorgan 2nd XI debut 2005 when aged 14 years 353 days. Wales MC 2005-08. England U19s 2007 to 2008. HS 87* v Notts (Swansea) 2007. BB 7-66 (12-118) v Glos (Bristol) 2007 – youngest (17 years 3 days) to take 10 wickets in any CC match. LO HS 21 v Derbys (Derby) 2009 (FPT). LO BB 4-48 v Kent (Canterbury) 2008 (P40). T20 HS 11. T20 BB 4-23.

HARRISON, David Stuart (W Monmouth CS; Usk C, Pontypool), b Newport, Monmouthshire 30 Jul 1981. Elder brother of A.J.Harrison (Glamorgan 2005-06); son of S.C.Harrison (Glamorgan 1971-77). 6'4". RHB, RMF. Debut (Glamorgan) 1999; cap 2006. No appearances 2007. MCC 2005. HS 88 v Essex (Chelmsford) 2004. 50 wkts (1): 57 (2004). BB 5-48 v Somerset (Swansea) 2004. LO HS 37* and LO BB 5-26 v Yorks (Leeds) 2002 (NL). T20 HS 4*. T20 BB 2-17.

‡**JAMES, Nicholas** Alexander (King Edward VI S, Aston), b Sandwell, Birmingham 17 Sep 1986. 5'9". LHB, SLA. Warwickshire 2008. Staffordshire 2006-07. England U19 2005 to 2005-06. HS 34 and BB 1-6 Wa v Cambridge U (Cambridge) 2008 – only f-c game. LO HS 30 Wa v Worcs (Birmingham) 2006 (CGT) on Wa debut. LO BB 2-34 Wa v Notts (Birmingham) 2006 (CGT). T20 HS 12*.

JONES, Alexander John (Cowbridge CS), b Bridgend 10 Nov 1988. RHB, LM. Glamorgan 2nd XI debut 2008. Wales MC 2007-09. Cardiff UCCE 2009. Awaiting 1st XI debut.

MAYNARD, Thomas Lloyd (Millfield S; Whitchurch HS, Cardiff), b Cardiff 25 Mar 1989. Son of M.P.Maynard (Glamorgan and England 1985-2005). 6'3". RHB, OB. Debut (Glamorgan) 2007. Wales MC 2006-08. HS 51* v Derbys (Cardiff) 2009. BB – . LO HS 108 v Northants (Colwyn Bay) 2009 (P40). T20 HS 49*.

‡NORMAN, Aneurien John, b Cardiff 22 Mar 1991. RHB, RM. Glamorgan 2nd XI debut 2008. Wales MC 2008-09. Awaiting 1st XI debut. Development contract.

OWEN, William Thomas (Prestatyn HS; UWIC), b St Asaph, Flintshire 2 Sep 1988. 6'0". RHB, RMF. Debut (Glamorgan) 2007. Wales MC 2007-09. HS – v Glos (Cardiff) 2007 – only 1st XI appearance.

POWELL, Michael John (Crickhowell SS; Pontypool CFE), b Abergavenny, Monmouthshire 3 Feb 1977. 6'1". RHB, OB, occ WK. Debut (Glamorgan) 1997 scoring 200* v OU (Oxford); cap 2000. 1000 runs (5); most – 1327 (2006). HS 299 v Glos (Cheltenham) 2006 – record score for Glamorgan in England. BB 2-39 v OU (Oxford) 1999. CC BB – . LO HS 114* v Hants (Cardiff) 2008 (FPT). LO BB 1-26 (CGT). T20 HS 68*.

‡REED, Michael Thomas, b Leicester 10 Sep 1988. RHB, RFM. Glamorgan 2nd XI debut 2009. Wales MC 2009. Awaiting 1st XI debut. Development contract.

REES, Gareth Peter (Coedcae CS; Bath U), b Swansea 8 Apr 1985. 6'1". LHB, LM. Wales MC 2003-05. Debut (Glamorgan) 2006; cap 2009. 1000 runs (2); most – 1088 (2008). HS 154 v Surrey (Oval) 2008. LO HS 123* v Essex (Chelmsford) 2009 (FPT). T20 HS 15.

SHANTRY, Adam John (Priory S; Shrewsbury SFC), b Bristol 13 Nov 1982. 6'2½". Son of B.K.Shantry (Gloucestershire 1978-79), brother of J.D.Shantry (*see WORCESTERSHIRE*). LHB, LFM. Northamptonshire 2003-04. Warwickshire 2006-07. Glamorgan debut 2008. Shropshire 2001. HS 100 v Leics (Colwyn Bay) 2009. BB 5-49 Wa v West Indies A (Birmingham) 2006. Gm BB 5-52 (10-129 match) v Warwks (Birmingham) 2008. LO HS 19* v Northants (Northampton) 2009 (FPT). LO BB 5-37 Nh v NZ (Northampton) 2004. T20 HS – . T20 BB – .

‡NQTAIT, Shaun William (Oakbank Area S, S Aus), b Bedford Park, Adelaides 22 Feb 1983. RHB, RF. S Australia 2002-03 to date. Durham 2004. **Tests** (A): 3 (2005 to 2007-08); HS 8 v I (Perth) 2007-08; BB 3-97 v E (Nottingham) 2005. **LOI** (A): 22 (2006-07 to 2008-09); HS 11 v E (Sydney) 2006-07; BB 4-39 v SA (Gros Islet) 2006-07. F-c Tour (A): E 2005. HS 68 S Aus v Vic (Adelaide) 2005-06. CC HS 4. BB 7-29 (10-98 match) S Aus v Q (Brisbane) 2007-08. CC BB – . LO HS 22* Aus A v Z (Perth) 2003-04. LO BB 8-43 inc hat-trick S Aus v Tas (Adelaide) 2003-04, 8th best analysis in all 1-o cricket. IT20 HS 1*. IT20 BB 3-13. T20 HS 14*. T20 BB 4-14.

WALLACE, Mark Alexander (Crickhowell HS), b Abergavenny, Monmouthshire 19 Nov 1981. 5'9". LHB, WK. Debut (Glamorgan) 1999; cap 2003. F-c Tour (ECB Acad): SL 2002-03. HS 139 v Surrey (Oval) 2009. LO HS 85 v Surrey (Cardiff) 2008 (P40). T20 HS 35*.

WATERS, Huw Thomas (Llantaram CS; Monmouth S), b Cardiff 26 Sep 1986. 6'2". RHB, RMF. Debut (Glamorgan) 2005. No f-c appearances in 2009. Wales MC 2004-07. HS 34 v Kent (Canterbury) 2005. BB 5-86 v Somerset (Taunton) 2006. LO HS 8 v Hants (Swansea) 2007 (FPT). LO BB 3-47 v Durham (Chester-le-St) 2007 (P40).

WRIGHT, Ben James (Cowbridge CS), b Preston, Lancs 5 Dec 1987. 5'9". RHB, RM. Debut (Glamorgan) 2006. No f-c appearances in 2008. HS 108 v Leics (Leicester) 2007. BB 1-14 v Essex (Chelmsford) 2007. LO HS 65 v Derbys (Cardiff) 2009 (FPT). LO BB 1-19 v Derbys (Derby) 2009 (FPT). T20 HS 55*. T20 BB 1-16.

GIBBS, H.H. – *see YORKSHIRE.*

NO**KRUGER, Garnett** John-Peter (Gelvandale HS; Russel Road C), b Port Elizabeth, South Africa 5 Jan 1977. RHB, RMF. E Province 1997-98 to 2002-03. Gauteng 2003-04. Lions 2004-05 to 2008-09. Leicestershire 2007-08. Glamorgan 2009 (Kolpak registration). Warriors 2009-10. **LOI** (SA): 3 (2005-06); HS 0*; BB 1-43 v A (Brisbane) 2005-06 – on debut. F-c Tours (SA A): WI 2000-01; SL 2005-06; Z 2004. HS 58 South Africa A v Windward Is (Kingstown) 2000-01. UK HS 28* v Essex (Chelmsford) 2009. BB 8-112 Lions v Dolphins (Durban) 2005-06. UK BB 6-93 (9-121 match) v Surrey (Oval) 2009. LO HS 24* Warriors v Cobras (Cape Town) 2009-10. LO BB 6-23 EP v NW (Port Elizabeth) 1999-00. IT20 HS 3. IT20 BB – . T20 HS 19*. T20 BB 4-10.

O'SHEA, Michael Peter (Barry CS; Millfield S), b Cardiff 4 Sep 1987. 5'11". RHB, OB. Glamorgan 2005-09; no f-c appearances 2006, 2008. Wales MC 2005-08. England U19s 2004-05 to 2006. HS 50 v Kent (Canterbury) 2009. LO HS 49 v Durham (Chester-le-St) 2007 (P40). LO BB 2-37 v Hants (Swansea) 2007 (FPT). T20 HS 5.

WATKINS, Ryan Edward (Pontllanfraith CS; Cross Keys TC), b Abergavenny, Monmouthshire 9 Jun 1983. 6'0". LHB, RM. Glamorgan 2005-08. Wales MC 2004-06. HS 87 v Essex (Cardiff) 2006. BB 4-40 v Worcs (Worcester) 2006. LO HS 39 v Derbys (Derby) 2007 (P40). LO BB 2-25 v Warwks (Colwyn Bay) 2006 (P40). T20 HS 18. T20 BB 5-16 v Glos (Cardiff) 2009 – Gm record.

WHARF, Alexander George (Buttershaw Upper S; Thomas Danby C), b Bradford, Yorks 4 Jun 1975. 6'5". RHB, RMF. Yorkshire 1994-97. Nottinghamshire 1998-99. Glamorgan 2000-08, scoring 100* v OU (Oxford) on debut; cap 2000; benefit 2009. **LOI**: 13 (2004 to 2004-05); HS 9; BB 4-24 v Z (Harare) 2004-05. F-c Tour (Eng A): WI 2005-06. HS 128* v Glos (Bristol) 2007. 50 wkts (1): 52 (2003). BB 6-59 v Glos (Bristol) 2005. LO HS 72 v Lancs (Manchester) 2004 (NL). LO BB 6-5 v Kent (Cardiff) 2004 (NL). T20 HS 19. T20 BB 4-39.

GLAMORGAN 2009

RESULTS SUMMARY

	Place	Won	Lost	Tied	Drew	NR
County Championship (2nd Division)	5th	2	2		12	
All First-Class Matches		2	2		13	
FP Trophy (Group D)		2	5			1
Pro40 League (2nd Division)	6th	2	4			2
Twenty20 Cup (Midlands/West/Wales Division)	6th	2	8			

LV COUNTY CHAMPIONSHIP AVERAGES

BATTING AND FIELDING

Cap		M	I	NO	HS	Runs	Avge	100	50	Ct/St
	M.J.Cosgrove	9	14	2	175	757	63.08	3	5	4
	J.W.M.Dalrymple	16	23	3	128	1009	50.45	3	5	17
2009	G.P.Rees	16	24	1	154	1028	44.69	3	4	13
2000	M.J.Powell	16	24	1	108	934	40.60	2	7	7
	J.Allenby	5	8	–	137	299	37.37	1	2	6
	H.H.Gibbs	5	7	–	96	259	37.00	–	2	7
1992	R.D.B.Croft	16	21	4	121	574	33.76	1	1	4
	W.D.Bragg	9	12	–	92	367	30.58	–	2	4
2003	M.A.Wallace	16	22	–	139	645	29.31	2	–	30/6
	A.J.Shantry	12	17	3	100	314	22.42	1	–	–
	B.J.Wright	8	13	–	81	271	20.84	–	1	3
	J.A.R.Harris	13	16	3	76*	256	19.69	–	1	1
2006	D.S.Harrison	7	7	2	51	98	19.60	–	1	2
	T.L.Maynard	5	7	1	51*	115	19.16	–	1	5
	G.J-P.Kruger	13	13	7	28*	91	15.16	–	–	2
2000	D.A.Cosker	8	11	3	46*	107	13.37	–	–	5

Also batted (1 match each): C.P.Ashling 12; M.P.O'Shea 50, 25.

BOWLING

	O	M	R	W	Avge	Best	5wI	10wM
D.A.Cosker	312.1	83	769	26	29.57	6-91	2	1
R.D.B.Croft	720	152	1681	56	30.01	5-65	1	–
A.J.Shantry	266	46	867	27	32.11	5-62	1	–
J.A.R.Harris	425.2	83	1441	41	35.14	4-69	–	–
J.W.M.Dalrymple	224.2	27	709	20	35.45	3-11	–	–
D.S.Harrison	194.1	29	732	19	38.52	4-60	–	–
G.J-P.Kruger	353.4	59	1283	33	38.87	6-93	1	–
Also bowled:								
J.Allenby	78	19	209	6	34.83	2-34	–	–
M.J.Cosgrove	51	7	188	5	37.60	3-30	–	–

C.P.Ashling 28-3-116-3; W.D.Bragg 5-0-23-0; B.J.Wright 8-0-41-0.

The First-Class Averages (pp 228–244) give the records of Glamorgan players in all first-class county matches (Glamorgan's other opponents being Oxford UCCE), with the exception of J.Allenby, whose first-class figures for Glamorgan are as above.

GLAMORGAN RECORDS

FIRST-CLASS CRICKET

Highest Total	For 718-3d		v	Sussex	Colwyn Bay	2000
	V 712		by	Northants	Northampton	1998
Lowest Total	For 22		v	Lancashire	Liverpool	1924
	V 33		by	Leics	Ebbw Vale	1965
Highest Innings	For 309*	S.P.James	v	Sussex	Colwyn Bay	2000
	V 322*	M.B.Loye	for	Northants	Northampton	1998

Highest Partnership for each Wicket

1st	374	M.T.G.Elliott/S.P.James	v	Sussex	Colwyn Bay	2000
2nd	252	M.P.Maynard/D.L.Hemp	v	Northants	Cardiff	2002
3rd	313	D.E.Davies/W.E.Jones	v	Essex	Brentwood	1948
4th	425*	A.Dale/I.V.A.Richards	v	Middlesex	Cardiff	1993
5th	264	M.Robinson/S.W.Montgomery	v	Hampshire	Bournemouth	1949
6th	240	J.Allenby/M.A.Wallace	v	Surrey	The Oval	2009
7th	211	P.A.Cottey/O.D.Gibson	v	Leics	Swansea	1996
8th	202	D.Davies/J.J.Hills	v	Sussex	Eastbourne	1928
9th	203*	J.J.Hills/J.C.Clay	v	Worcs	Swansea	1929
10th	143	T.Davies/S.A.B.Daniels	v	Glos	Swansea	1982

Best Bowling	For 10- 51	J.Mercer	v	Worcs	Worcester	1936
(Innings)	V 10- 18	G.Geary	for	Leics	Pontypridd	1929
Best Bowling	For 17-212	J.C.Clay	v	Worcs	Swansea	1937
(Match)	V 16- 96	G.Geary	for	Leics	Pontypridd	1929

Most Runs – Season	2276	H.Morris	(av 55.51)	1990
Most Runs – Career	34056	A.Jones	(av 33.03)	1957-83
Most 100s – Season	10	H.Morris		1990
Most 100s – Career	54	M.P.Maynard		1985-2005
Most Wkts – Season	176	J.C.Clay	(av 17.34)	1937
Most Wkts – Career	2174	D.J.Shepherd	(av 20.95)	1950-72
Most Career W-K Dismissals	933	E.W.Jones	(840 ct; 93 st)	1961-83
Most Career Catches in the Field	656	P.M.Walker		1956-72

LIMITED-OVERS CRICKET

Highest Total	FPT	429	v	Surrey	The Oval	2002
	P40	305-6	v	Worcs	Cardiff	2001
	T20	206-6	v	Somerset	Taunton	2006
Lowest Total	FPT	76	v	Northants	Northampton	1968
	P40	42	v	Derbyshire	Swansea	1979
	T20	112-9	v	Somerset	Cardiff	2009
Highest Innings	FPT	162* I.V.A.Richards	v	Oxfordshire	Swansea	1993
	P40	155* J.H.Kallis	v	Surrey	Pontypridd	1999
	T20	116* I.J.Thomas	v	Somerset	Taunton	2004
Best Bowling	FPT	5-13 R.J.Shastri	v	Scotland	Edinburgh	1988
	P40	7-16 S.D.Thomas	v	Surrey	Swansea	1998
	T20	5-16 R.E.Watkins	v	Glos	Cardiff	2009

GLOUCESTERSHIRE

Formation of Present Club: 1871
Inaugural First-Class Match: 1870
Colours: Blue, Gold, Brown, Silver, Green and Red
Badge: Coat of Arms of the City and County of Bristol
County Champions (since 1890): (0); best – 2nd 1930, 1931, 1947, 1959, 1969, 1986
Gillette/NatWest/C&G/FP Trophy Winners: (5) 1973, 1999, 2000, 2003, 2004
Benson and Hedges Cup Winners: (3) 1977, 1999, 2000
Pro 40/National League (Div 1) Winners: (1) 2000
Sunday League Winners: (0); best – 2nd 1988
Twenty20 Cup Winners: (0); best – Finalist 2007

Chief Executive: Tom E.M.Richardson, County Ground, Nevil Road, Bristol BS7 9EJ • Tel: 0117 910 8000 • Fax: 0117 924 1193 • Email: info@glosccc.co.uk • Web: www.glosccc.co.uk

Director of Cricket: J.G.Bracewell. **Assistant Coach:** S.N.Barnes. **Captain:** A.P.R.Gidman. **Vice-Captain:** tbc. **Overseas Player:** J.E.C.Franklin. **2010 Beneficiary:** none. **Head Groundsman:** Sean Williams. **Scorer:** Keith T.Gerrish. ‡ New registration. ^{NQ} Not qualified for England.

Gloucestershire revised their capping policy in 2004 and now award players with their County Caps when they make their first-class debut.

ALI, Kadeer (Handsworth GS), b Moseley, Birmingham 7 Mar 1983. 6'1". Brother of M.M.Ali (*see WORCESTERSHIRE*), cousin of Kabir Ali (*see HAMPSHIRE*). RHB, RM/LB. Worcestershire 2000-04. Gloucestershire debut/cap 2005. F-c Tour (Eng A): I 2003-04. HS 161 v Northants (Bristol) 2008. BB 1-4 v Glamorgan (Bristol) 2005. LO HS 114 v Hants (Southampton) 2007 (P40). LO BB 1-4 Wo v Worcs CB (Worcester) 2003 (CGT). T20 HS 53.

BANERJEE, Vikram (King Edward's S, Birmingham; Downing C, Cambridge), b Bradford, Yorks 20 Mar 1984. 6'0". LHB, SLA. Cambridge UCCE 2004-06; blue 2004-05-06. Gloucestershire debut/cap 2006. HS 29 CU v OU (Cambridge) 2005. Gs HS 16 v Surrey (Oval) 2009 and v Northants (Northampton) 2009. BB 4-38 v Northants (Gloucester) 2007. LO HS 6 v Surrey (Bristol) 2009 (FPT). LO BB 3-47 v Sussex (Bristol) 2009 (FPT). T20 HS 5*. T20 BB 2-30.

‡BATTY, Jonathan Neil (Wheatley Park S, Oxon; Repton S; Durham U; Keble C, Oxford), b Chesterfield, Derbys 18 Apr 1974. 5'10". RHB, WK. Comb U 1994-95. Oxford U 1996; blue 1996. Surrey 1997-2009; cap 2001; captain 2004; benefit 2009. Oxfordshire 1993-96. Minor C 1996. 1000 runs (1): 1025 (2006). HS 168* Sy v Essex (Chelmsford) 2003. BB 1-21 Sy v Lancs (Manchester) 2000. LO HS 158* Sy v Hants (Oval) 2005 (CGT). T20 HS 59.

DAWSON, Richard Kevin James (Batley GS; Exeter U), b Doncaster, Yorks 4 Aug 1980. 6'3". RHB, OB. British U 2000. Yorkshire 2001-06; cap 2004. MCC 2002. Northamptonshire 2007. Gloucestershire debut/cap 2008. Devon 1999-2000. **Tests:** 7 (2001-02 to 2002-03); HS 19* v A (Perth) 2002-03; BB 4-134 v I (Chandigarh) 2001-02 – on debut. F-c Tours: A 2002-03; NZ 2001-02; I 2001-02; SL 2002-03 (ECB Acad), 2004-05 (Eng A). HS 87 Y v Kent (Canterbury) 2002. Gs HS 50 and BB 4-76 v Glamorgan (Cardiff) 2009. BB 6-82 Y v Glamorgan (Scarborough) 2001. LO HS 41 Y v Leics (Scarborough) 2002 (NL). LO BB 4-13 Y v Derbys (Derby) 2002 (BHC). T20 HS 27*. T20 BB 3-24.

‡DENT, Christopher David James (Backwell CS; Alton C), b Bristol 20 Jan 1991. 5'9".
LHB, WK, occ SLA. Gloucestershire 2nd XI debut 2007, aged 16y 80d. England U19s
2009-10. LO HS – . Awaiting f-c debut.

‡^{NQ}FRANKLIN, James Edward Charles (Wellington C; Victoria U), Wellington, New
Zealand 7 Nov 1960. 6'4½". LHB, LFM. Wellington 1998-99 to date. Gloucestershire
debut/cap 2004. Glamorgan 2006. **Tests** (NZ): 26 (2000-01 to 2008-09); HS 122* v SA
(Cape Town) 2006-07; BB 6-119 v A (Auckland) 2004-05. Hat-trick v B (Dhaka) 2004-05.
LOI (NZ): 72 (2000-01 to 2009-10); HS 45* v SL (Queenstown) 2006-07; BB 5-42 v E
(Chester-le-St) 2004. F-c Tours (NZ): E 2004; A 2004-05; SA 2004-05 (NZ A), 2005-06; Z
2005; B 2004-05. HS 219 Wellington v Auckland (Auckland) 2008-09. UK/Gs HS 109 v
Derbys (Cheltenham) 2009; became only the second man for Gs to score a hundred and take
a hat-trick in the same match. BB 7-30 Wellington v CD (Wellington) 2005-06. UK/Gs BB
7-60 v Lancs (Cheltenham) 2004. Hat-trick (*see above*). LO HS 87* Wellington v Otago
(Invercargill) 2008-09. LO BB 5-42 (*see LOI*). IT20 HS 20. IT20 BB 3-23. T20 HS 72. T20
BB 3-23.

GIDMAN, Alex Peter Richard (Wycliffe C), b High Wycombe, Bucks 22 Jun 1981. Elder
brother of W.R.S.Gidman (*see DURHAM*). 6'3". RHB, RM. Debut (Gloucestershire) 2002;
cap 2004; captain 2009 to date. MCC YC 2001. MCC 2004, 2007. Otago 2007-08. F-c Tour
(Eng A): SL 2004-05. Appointed captain of Eng A tour to India 2003-04 but withdrew
because of hand injury. 1000 runs (4); most – 1244 (2006). HS 176 v Surrey (Bristol) 2009.
BB 4-47 v Glamorgan (Cardiff) 2005. LO HS 116 v Sussex (Hove) 2009 (FPT). LO BB
5-42 Eng A v Bangladesh A (Mirpur) 2006-07. T20 HS 64. T20 BB 2-24.

‡HUSSAIN, Gemaal Maqsood (Top Valley CS, Nottingham; High Pavement SFC, Nottingham), b Whipps Cross, London, 10 Oct 1983. 6'5". RHB, RMF. Debut (Gloucestershire)
2009; cap 2009. Bradford/Leeds UCCE 2003. HS 8 (twice) and BB 2-73 v Kent (Beckenham) 2009 – only f-c match. LO HS– and BB 2-17 v Notts (Nottingham) 2009 (P40). T20
HS 8. T20 BB 3-22.

^{NQ}IRELAND, Anthony John (Plumtree HS), b Masvingo, Zimbabwe 30 Aug 1984. RHB,
RM. Midlands 2002-03 to 2004-05. Gloucestershire debut/cap 2007 (Kolpak registration).
LOI (Z): 26 (2005-06 to 2006-07); HS 8* v K (Bulawayo) 2005-06; BB 3-41 v B (Harare)
(twice) – 2006 and 2006-07. HS 16* v Middlesex (Bristol) 2008. BB 7-36 Zimbabwe A v
Bangladesh A (Mirpur) 2006-07. Gs BB 6-31 v Leics (Bristol) 2009. LO HS 17 Midlands v
Matabeleland (Harare) 2005-06. LO BB 4-16 Zimbabwe A v Kenya (Harare) 2005-06. IT20
HS 2*. IT20 BB 1-33. T20 HS 8*. T20 BB 3-10.

KIRBY, Steven Paul (Elton HS; Bury C), b Ainsworth, nr Bolton, Lancs 4 Oct 1977. 6'3½".
RHB, RFM. Leicestershire staff 1998 – no f-c appearances. Yorkshire 2001-04, debut as sub
for M.J.Hoggard (England duty) taking 7-50; cap 2003. Gloucestershire debut/cap 2005.
MCC 2008. F-c Tour (Eng A): I 2003-04 (*part*). HS 57 Y v Hants (Leeds) 2002. Gs HS 37
v Northants (Northampton) 2007. 50 wkts (2); most – 67 (2003). BB 8-80 (13-154 match) Y
v Somerset (Taunton) 2003. Gs BB 5-41 v Essex (Southend) 2007. LO HS 15 Y v Leics
(Leicester) 2003 (NL). LO BB 5-36 v Middlesex (Lord's) 2007 (FPT). T20 HS 25. T20 BB
3-29.

LEWIS, Jonathan (Churchfields S, Swindon; Swindon C), b Aylesbury, Bucks 26 Aug 1975. 6'2". RHB, RMF. Debut (Gloucestershire) 1995; cap 1998; captain 2006-08; benefit 2007. MCC 2005. Wiltshire 1993, 1995. Northamptonshire staff 1994. **Tests**: 1 (2006); HS 20 and BB 3-68 v SL (Nottingham) 2006. **LOI**: 13 (2005 to 2007); HS 17 v I (Leeds) 2007; BB 4-36 v A (Brisbane) 2006-07. F-c Tours (Eng A): WI 2000-01; SL 2004-05. HS 62 v Worcs (Cheltenham) 1999. 50 wkts (7); most – 74 (2003). BB 8-95 v Z (Gloucester) 2000. CC BB 7-38 (10-75 match) v Somerset (Bristol) 2006. Hat-trick v Notts (Nottingham) 2000. LO HS 54 v Durham (Cheltenham) 2009 (P40). LO BB 5-19 v Hants (Southampton) 2005 (NL). IT20 HS 1. IT20 BB 4-24. T20 HS 43. T20 BB 4-24.

NQ**MARSHALL, Hamish** John Hamilton (Mahurangi C, Warkworth; King C, Auckland), b Warkworth, New Zealand 15 Feb 1979. Twin brother of J.A.H.Marshall (ND and NZ 1997-98 to date). Irish passport. 5'9". RHB, RM. N Districts 1998-99 to date. Gloucestershire debut 2006 (scoring 102 v Worcs on UK debut); cap 2006; Kolpak registration 2008-10. Buckinghamshire 2003. **Tests** (NZ): 13 (2000-01 to 2005-06); HS 160 v SL (Napier) 2004-05. **LOI** (NZ): 66 (2003-04 to 2006-07); HS 101* v P (Faisalabad) 2003-04. F-c Tours (NZ): A 2004-05; SA 2000-01, 2005-06; Z 2005; B 2004-05. 1000 runs (1): 1218 (2006). HS 168 v Leics (Cheltenham) 2006. BB 4-24 v Leics (Leicester) 2009. LO HS 122 v Sussex (Hove) 2007 (P40). LO BB 2-21 v Hampshire (Southampton) 2009 (P40). IT20 HS 8. T20 HS 100.

‡**PAYNE, David** Alan (Lytchett Minster S), b Poole, Dorset, 15 Feb 1991. 6'2". RHB, LMF. Gloucestershire 2nd XI debut 2008. Dorset 2009. England U19s 2009 to 2009-10. Awaiting f-c debut. LO HS 3* v Hampshire (Southampton) 2009 (P40). LO BB 3-10 v Notts (Nottingham) 2009 (P40).

NQ**PORTERFIELD, William** Thomas Stuart (Strabane GS; Leeds Met U), b Londonderry, N.Ireland 6 Sep 1984. 5'11". LHB, OB. Debut (Ireland) 2006. MCC 2007. Gloucestershire debut/cap 2008. Captained Ireland in ICC Intercontinental Cup in Africa in 2008-09. **LOI** (Ire): 37 (2006 to 2009); HS 112* v Bermuda (Nairobi) 2006-07. F-c Tours (Ire, C=captain): E 2007; SL 2009-10C; Scot 2006; UAE 2006-07. HS 166 Ireland v Bermuda (Dublin) 2007. Gs HS 93 v Glamorgan (Cardiff) 2008. BB 1-57 v LU (Bristol) 2008. LO HS 112* (*see LOI*). IT20 HS 46. T20 HS 62.

SAXELBY, Ian David (Oakham S), b Nottingham 22 May 1989. 6'2". RHB, RMF. Nephew of K.Saxelby (Nottinghamshire 1978-90) and M.Saxelby (Notts, Durham and Derbys 1989-2000). Debut (Gloucestershire) 2008; cap 2008. Nottinghamshire 2nd XI debut 2006. England U19s 2008. HS 60* v Northants (Northampton) 2009. BB 3-31 v Essex (Southend) 2009 and v Leics (Leicester) 2009. LO HS 7* and BB 4-31 v Surrey (Bristol) 2009 (FPT). T20 HS 2. T20 BB 2-32.

SNELL, Stephen David (Sandown HS), b Winchester, Hampshire 27 Feb 1983. 6'0". RHB, WK. Debut (Gloucestershire)/cap 2005. MCC YC 2002-04. HS 127 v Worcs (Worcester) 2008. LO HS 19 v Notts (Bristol) 2009 (FPT). T20 HS 11.

TAYLOR, Christopher Glyn (Colston's Collegiate S), b Southmead, Bristol 27 Sep 1976. 5'7". RHB, OB. Debut (Gloucestershire) 2000, scoring 104 v Middlesex – first to score a hundred at Lord's in a Championship match on his first-class debut; cap 2001. Gloucestershire cap 2004-05. 1000 runs (2); most – 1101 (2003). HS 196 v Notts (Nottingham) 2001. BB 4-52 v Northants (Northampton) 2007. LO HS 93 v Warwks (Bristol) 2002 (BHC). LO BB 2-5 v Northants (Northampton) 2004 (NL). T20 HS 83. T20 BB 1-22.

WOODMAN, Robert James (Castle S, Taunton; Richard Huish C), b Taunton, Somerset 12 Oct 1986. 5'11". LHB, LMF. Somerset 2005. Gloucestershire debut/cap 2008. Devon 2006-07. HS 46* Sm v Worcs (Worcester) 2005 – on debut. Gs HS 32 v Surrey (Bristol) 2009. BB 4-65 v Essex (Bristol) 2008. LO HS 14 MCC v Bangladesh A (Durham) 2008. LO BB 1-38 Sm v Durham (Taunton) 2005. T20 HS 1*. T20 BB 2-37.

RELEASED/RETIRED
(Having made a County First-Class or List A appearance in 2009)

ADSHEAD, Stephen John (Bridley Moor HS, Redditch), b Redditch 29 Jan 1980. 5'9". RHB, WK. Herefordshire 1999. Leicestershire 2000 (1 non-CC match). Worcestershire 2003 (2 matches). Gloucestershire 2004-09; cap 2004. HS 156* v Essex (Southend) 2009. LO HS 87 v Durham (Chester-le-St) 2009 (FPT). T20 HS 81.

BROWN, D.O. – *see GLAMORGAN.*

HODNETT, Grant Phillip (Durban Preparatory HS; Northwood HS), b Johannesburg, South Africa 17 Aug 1982. 6'4". RHB, LB. Gloucestershire 2005-09; cap 2005 (Kolpak registration). HS 168 v Derbys (Bristol) 2007. BB 2-91 v LU (Bristol) 2008. CC BB – . LO HS 50 v Somerset (Bristol) 2007 (FPT). T20 HS 60.

SPEARMAN, Craig Murray (Kelston HS, Auckland; Massey U, Palmerston North), b Auckland, New Zealand 4 Jul 1972. RHB. Auckland 1993-94 to 1994-95. Central Districts 1996-97 to 2003-04. Gloucestershire 2002-09; cap 2002; benefit 2008. Qualified for England 2005. **Tests** (NZ): 19 (1995-96 to 2000-01); HS 112 v Z (Auckland) 1995-96. **LOI** (NZ): 51 (1995-96 to 2000-01); HS 86 v Z (Harare) 2000-01. F-c Tours (NZ): SA 2000-01; WI 1995-96; I 1999-00; P 1996-97; SL 1998; Z 1997-98, 2000-01. 1000 runs (3); most – 1462 (2004). HS 341 v Middlesex (Gloucester) 2004 – record Gs score. BB 1-37 CD v Wellington (New Plymouth) 1999-00. LO HS 153 v Warwks (Gloucester) 2003 (NL) – record Gs 40-over score. LO BB – . T20 HS 88.

STAYT, Thomas Patrick (Lavington S, Market Lavington; St Augustine's C, Trowbridge; Exeter U), b Salisbury, Wilts 20 Jan 1986. 6'2". RHB, RMF. Gloucestershire 2007-09; cap 2007. No f-c appearances in 2008. HS 36 v Leics (Bristol) 2009. BB 3-51 v Middlesex (Lord's) 2007 – on debut. LO HS 1. LO BB 2-51 v Yorkshire (Leeds) 2009 (FPT).

M.T.Gitsham left the staff without making a County First-Class or List A appearance in 2009.

GLOUCESTERSHIRE 2009

RESULTS SUMMARY

	Place	Won	Lost	Tied	Drew	NR
County Championship (2nd Division)	4th	6	6		4	
All First-Class Matches		6	6		4	
FP Trophy (Group C)	SF	6	3			1
Pro40 League (1st Division)	8th	2	5			1
Twenty20 Cup (Midlands/Wales/West Division)	5th	2	8			

LV COUNTY CHAMPIONSHIP AVERAGES

BATTING AND FIELDING

Cap†		M	I	NO	HS	Runs	Avge	100	50	Ct/St
2004	J.E.C.Franklin	14	22	4	109	904	50.22	3	4	6
2004	A.P.R.Gidman	15	23	–	176	1028	44.69	4	4	9
2004	S.J.Adshead	7	10	1	156*	367	40.77	2	–	22/1
2006	H.J.H.Marshall	16	26	2	158	844	35.16	1	5	13
2005	Kadeer Ali	16	28	4	90	834	34.75	–	4	10
2001	C.G.Taylor	15	22	1	111	705	33.57	1	5	11
2008	R.K.J.Dawson	7	10	–	50	254	25.40	–	1	12
2002	C.M.Spearman	6	9	–	57	206	22.88	–	1	9
2008	W.T.S.Porterfield	9	16	1	81	341	22.73	–	2	17
1998	J.Lewis	15	22	6	61*	358	22.37	–	2	5
2008	I.D.Saxelby	9	13	3	60*	168	16.80	–	1	5
2005	S.D.Snell	9	14	1	85	215	16.53	–	1	28/2
2008	R.J.Woodman	6	10	1	32	144	16.00	–	–	3
2005	S.P.Kirby	16	22	8	27	157	11.21	–	–	2
2006	V.Banerjee	7	12	3	16	71	7.88	–	–	2
2007	A.J.Ireland	7	7	2	16	21	4.20	–	–	3

Also batted (1 match each): G.P.Hodnett (cap 2005) 31; G.M.Hussain (cap 2009) 8, 8 (1 ct);
T.P.Stayt (cap 2007) 36.

BOWLING

	O	M	R	W	Avge	Best	5wI	10wM
J.Lewis	426.3	110	1146	57	20.10	5-73	1	–
S.P.Kirby	472.4	107	1420	64	22.18	5-44	1	–
H.J.H.Marshall	104	24	360	16	22.50	4-24	–	–
J.E.C.Franklin	292.4	63	904	31	29.16	5-30	1	–
I.D.Saxelby	185.2	30	620	20	31.00	3-31	–	–
A.J.Ireland	167	34	664	21	31.61	6-31	1	–
V.Banerjee	200.3	38	667	21	31.76	4-58	–	–
R.K.J.Dawson	158.4	13	610	12	50.83	4-76	–	–

Also bowled:
| C.G.Taylor | 86.2 | 22 | 242 | 6 | 40.33 | 1- 6 | – | – |

Kadeer Ali 4-0-15-0; A.P.R.Gidman 59.1-13-162-4; G.P.Hodnett 6-0-41-1; G.M.Hussain
22-1-107-2; T.P.Stayt 34-7-77-2; R.J.Woodman 5-3-8-1.

Gloucestershire played no first-class fixtures outside the County Championship in 2009. The
First-Class Averages (pp 228–244) give the records of their players in all first-class county
matches.

   † Gloucestershire revised their capping policy in 2004 and now award players with their
County Caps when they make their first-class debut.

GLOUCESTERSHIRE RECORDS

FIRST-CLASS CRICKET

Highest Total	For 695-9d		v	Middlesex	Gloucester	2004
	V 774-7d		by	Australians	Bristol	1948
Lowest Total	For 17		v	Australians	Cheltenham	1896
	V 12		by	Northants	Gloucester	1907
Highest Innings	For 341	C.M.Spearman	v	Middlesex	Gloucester	2004
	V 319	C.J.L.Rogers	for	Northants	Northampton	2006

Highest Partnership for each Wicket

1st	395	D.M.Young/R.B.Nicholls	v	Oxford U	Oxford	1962
2nd	256	C.T.M.Pugh/T.W.Graveney	v	Derbyshire	Chesterfield	1960
3rd	336	W.R.Hammond/B.H.Lyon	v	Leics	Leicester	1933
4th	321	W.R.Hammond/W.L.Neale	v	Leics	Gloucester	1937
5th	261	W.G.Grace/W.O.Moberley	v	Yorkshire	Cheltenham	1876
6th	320	G.L.Jessop/J.H.Board	v	Sussex	Hove	1903
7th	248	W.G.Grace/E.L.Thomas	v	Sussex	Hove	1896
8th	239	W.R.Hammond/A.E.Wilson	v	Lancashire	Bristol	1938
9th	193	W.G.Grace/S.A.P.Kitcat	v	Sussex	Bristol	1896
10th	131	W.R.Gouldsworthy/J.G.Bessant	v	Somerset	Bristol	1923

Best Bowling	For 10-40	E.G.Dennett	v	Essex	Bristol	1906
(Innings)	V 10-66	A.A.Mailey	for	Australians	Cheltenham	1921
	10-66	K.Smales	for	Notts	Stroud	1956
Best Bowling	For 17-56	C.W.L.Parker	v	Essex	Gloucester	1925
(Match)	V 15-87	A.J.Conway	for	Worcs	Moreton-in-M	1914

Most Runs – Season	2860	W.R.Hammond	(av 69.75)	1933
Most Runs – Career	33664	W.R.Hammond	(av 57.05)	1920-51
Most 100s – Season	13	W.R.Hammond		1938
Most 100s – Career	113	W.R.Hammond		1920-51
Most Wkts – Season	222	T.W.J.Goddard	(av 16.80)	1937
	222	T.W.J.Goddard	(av 16.37)	1947
Most Wkts – Career	3170	C.W.L.Parker	(av 19.43)	1903-35
Most Career W-K Dismissals	1054	R.C.Russell	(950 ct; 104 st)	1981-2004
Most Career Catches in the Field	719	C.A.Milton		1948-74

LIMITED-OVERS CRICKET

Highest Total	FPT	401-7		v	Bucks	Wing	2003
	P40	344-6		v	Northants	Cheltenham	2001
	T20	227-4		v	Somerset	Bristol	2006
Lowest Total	FPT	82		v	Notts	Bristol	1987
	P40	49		v	Middlesex	Bristol	1978
	T20	93		v	Worcs	Bristol	2008
Highest Innings	FPT	177	A.J.Wright	v	Scotland	Bristol	1997
	P40	153	C.M.Spearman	v	Warwicks	Gloucester	2003
	T20	100*	I.J.Harvey	v	Warwicks	Birmingham	2003
Best Bowling	FPT	6-21	C.A.Walsh	v	Kent	Bristol	1990
		6-21	C.A.Walsh	v	Cheshire	Bristol	1992
	P40	6-52	J.N.Shepherd	v	Kent	Bristol	1983
	T20	4-22	I.D.Fisher	v	Somerset	Bristol	2004

HAMPSHIRE

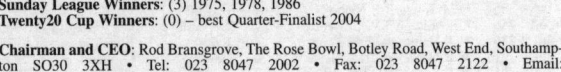

Formation of Present Club: 12 August 1863
Inaugural First-Class Match: 1864
Colours: Blue, Gold and White
Badge: Tudor Rose and Crown
County Champions: (2) 1961, 1973
Gillette/NatWest/C&G/FP Trophy Winners: (3) 1991, 2005, 2009
Benson and Hedges Cup Winners: (2) 1988, 1992
Pro 40/National League (Div 1) Winners: (0); best – 2nd 2008
Sunday League Winners: (3) 1975, 1978, 1986
Twenty20 Cup Winners: (0) – best Quarter-Finalist 2004

Chairman and CEO: Rod Bransgrove, The Rose Bowl, Botley Road, West End, Southampton SO30 3XH • Tel: 023 8047 2002 • Fax: 023 8047 2122 • Email: enquiries@rosebowlplc.com • Web: www.rosebowlplc.com

Cricket Secretary and Director of Rose Bowl Plc: T.M.Tremlett. **First XI Manager:** G.W.White. **Captain:** A.D.Mascarenhas. **Vice-Captain:** N.Pothas. **Overseas Players:** Shahid Afridi and B.A.W.Mendis. **2010 Beneficiary:** B.V.Taylor (testimonial). **Head Groundsman:** Nigel Gray. **Scorer:** A.E. (Tony) Weld. ‡ New registration. NQ Not qualified for England.

ADAMS, James Henry Kenneth (Sherborne S; University C, London; Loughborough U), b Winchester 23 Sep 1980. 6'2". LHB, LM. British U 2002-04. Hampshire debut 2002; cap 2006. Loughborough UCCE 2003-04 – scoring 107 v Somerset (Taunton) on debut. Dorset 1998. 1000 runs (2); most – 1351 (2009). HS 262* v Notts (Nottingham) 2006. BB 2-16 v Durham (Chester-le-St) 2004. LO HS 90 v Durham (Southampton) 2008 (P40). LO BB 1-34 v Essex (Chelmsford) 2007 (FPT). T20 HS 68*. T20 BB – .

‡ALI, Kabir (Moseley CS and SFC), b Moseley, Birmingham, Warwks 24 Nov 1980. 6'0". Cousin of Kadeer Ali (*see GLOUCESTERSHIRE*) and M.M.Ali (*see WORCESTERSHIRE*). RHB, RMF. Worcestershire 1999-2009. Rajasthan 2006-07. **Tests:** 1 (2003); HS 9 and BB 3-80 v SA (Leeds) 2003. **LOI:** 14 (2003 to 2006); HS 39* v P (Rawalpindi) 2005-06; BB 4-45 v I (Delhi) 2005-06. F-c Tours (Eng A): WI 2005-06; SL 2002-03 (ECB Acad). HS 84* Wo v Durham (Stockton) 2003. 50 wkts (5); most – 71 (2002). BB 8-50 Wo v Lancs (Manchester) 2007. Took 8-53 before lunch first day Wo v Yorks (Scarborough) 2003. LO HS 92 Wo v Essex (Worcester) 2003 (NL). LO BB Wo 5-36 v Yorks (Leeds) 2002 (NL). T20 HS 49. T20 BB 4-44.

BALCOMBE, David John (St John's S, Leatherhead; St Hild & St Bede C, Durham), b City of London 24 Dec 1984. 6'4". RHB, RFM. Durham UCCE 2005-07. British U 2006. Hampshire debut 2007. HS 73 DU v Leics (Leicester) 2005. H HS 29 v Kent (Southampton) 2007. BB 5-112 DU v Durham (Durham) 2005. H BB 3-58 v Yorks (Leeds) 2007. LO HS 2 (twice). LO BB 2-39 v Somerset (Taunton) 2008. T20 HS 3. T20 BB – .

‡BATES, Alexander **Michael**, b Portsmouth 10 Oct 1990. RHB, WK. Hampshire 2nd XI debut 2007. England U19s 2009-10. Awaiting 1st XI debut.

BENHAM, Christopher Charles (Yately CS; Loughborough U), b Frimley, Surrey 24 Mar 1983. 6'1". RHB, RM/OB. Loughborough UCCE 2004. Hampshire debut 2004. HS 111 v LU (Southampton) 2009. CC HS 95 v Warwks (Southampton) 2006. BB – . LO HS 158 v Glamorgan (Southampton) 2006. T20 HS 59.

‡**BRIGGS, Danny** Richard (Isle of Wight C), b Newport, IoW, 30 Apr 1991. 6'2". RHB, SLA. Debut (Hampshire) 2009. Hampshire 2nd XI debut 2007, aged 16y 120d. HS 36 and BB 3-62 v Somerset (Southampton) 2009 – on debut. LO HS 4 v Worcs (Worcester) 2009 (FPT). LO BB 2-36 v Notts (Southampton) 2009 (P40).

CARBERRY, Michael Alexander (St John Rigby Catholic C), b Croydon, Surrey 29 Sep 1980. 6'0". LHB, OB. Surrey 2001-02. Kent 2003-05. Hampshire debut/cap 2006. MCC 2008. F-c Tours: B 2006-07 (Eng A), 2009-10. 1000 runs (2); most – 1251 (2009). HS 204 v Warwks (Southampton) 2009. BB 2-85 v Durham (Chester-le-St) 2006. LO HS 121* v Ireland (Southampton) 2009 (FPT). LO BB 2-11 v Notts (Nottingham) 2009 (FPT). T20 HS 90. T20 BB 1-16.

CORK, Dominic Gerald (St Joseph's C, Stoke-on-Trent; Newcastle CFE), b Newcastle-under-Lyme, Staffs 7 Aug 1971. 6'2". RHB, RFM. Derbyshire 1990-2003; cap 1993; captain 1998-2002; benefit 2001. Lancashire 2004-08; cap 2004. Hampshire debut/cap 2009. *Wisden* 1995. PCA 1995. Staffordshire 1989-90. **Tests**: 37 (1995 to 2002); HS 59 v NZ (Auckland) 1996-97; BB 7-43 v WI (Lord's) 1995 – on debut (record England analysis by Test match debutant); hat-trick v WI (Manchester) 1995 – the first in Test history to occur in the opening over of a day's play. **LOI**: 32 (1992 to 2002-03); HS 31* v NZ (Napier) 1996-97; BB 3-27 v WI (Lord's) 1995. F-c Tours: A 1992-93 (Eng A), 1998-99; SA 1993-94 (Eng A), 1995-96; WI 1991-92 (Eng A); NZ 1996-97; I 1994-95 (Eng A); P 2000-01 (*part*). HS 200* De v Durham (Derby) 2000. H HS 52 v Somerset (Southampton) 2009. 50 wkts (7); most – 90 (1995). BB 9-43 (13-93 match) De v Northants (Derby) 1995. H BB 5-14 v Worcs (Worcester) 2009. Took 8-53 before lunch on his 20th birthday for De v Essex (Derby) 1991. 2 hat-tricks: 1994 and 1995 (*see Tests*). LO HS 93 De v Derbys CB (Derby) 2000 (NWT). LO BB 6-21 De v Glamorgan (Chesterfield) 1997 (SL). T20 HS 28. T20 BB 4-16.

DAWSON, Liam Andrew (John Bentley S, Calne), b Swindon, Wilts 1 Mar 1990. 5'8". RHB, SLA. Debut (Hampshire) 2007. England U19s 2006-07 to 2008-09. Wiltshire 2006-07. HS 100* v Notts (Nottingham) 2008. BB 2-3 v Sussex (Southampton) 2009. LO HS 69* v Essex (Chelmsford) 2009 (P40). BB 4-45 v Middlesex (Lord's) 2008 (P40). T20 HS 23. T20 BB 3-25.

^NQ**ERVINE, Sean** Michael (Lomagundi C, Chinhoyi), b Harare, Zimbabwe 6 Dec 1982. Elder brother of C.R.Ervine (Midlands, SR 2003-04 to date); son of R.M.Ervine (Rhodesia 1977-78); grandson of M.A.Den (Rhodesia 1935-36); nephew of N.B.Ervine (Rhodesia 1977-78) and G.M.Den (Rhodesia and Eastern Province 1963-64 to 1969-70). Irish passport. 6'2". LHB, RM. CFX Academy 2000-01 to 2001. Midlands 2001-02 to 2003-04. Hampshire debut/cap 2005 (Kolpak registration). Western Australia 2006-07 to 2007-08. Southern Rocks 2009-10. **Tests** (Z): 5 (2003 to 2003-04); HS 86 v B (Harare) 2003-04; BB 4-146 v A (Perth) 2003-04. **LOI** (Z): 42 (2001-02 to 2004-04); HS 100 v I (Adelaide) 2003-04; BB 3-29 v P (Sharjah) 2001-02. F-c Tours (Z): E 2003; A 2003-04. HS 208 SR v MWR (Masvingo) 2009-10, scoring 160 in 2nd innings. H HS 114 v Lancs (Southampton) 2009. BB 6-82 Midlands v Mashonaland (Kwekwe) 2002-03. H BB 5-60 v Glamorgan (Cardiff) 2005. LO HS 167* v Ireland (Southampton) 2009. LO BB 5-50 v Glamorgan (Cardiff) 2005 (CGT). T20 HS 56*. T20 BB 4-16.

GRIFFITHS, David Andrew (Sandown HS, IoW), b Newport, IoW 10 Sep 1985. 6'1". LHB, RFM. Debut (Hampshire) 2006. HS 31* v Surrey (Southampton) 2007. BB 4-46 v Durham (Chester-le-St) 2007 – on CC debut. H HS 3* v Worcs (Worcester) 2008 (FPT). LO BB 4-29 v Glos (Southampton) 2009 (P40). T20 HS 4*. T20 BB 3-13.

HOWELL, Benny Alexander Cameron (The Oratory S), b Bordeaux, France 5 Oct 1988. Son of J.B.Howell (Warwickshire 2nd XI 1978). 5'11". RHB, RM. Awaiting 1st XI debut. Hampshire 2nd XI debut 2005. Berkshire 2007.

‡**JONES, Simon** Philip (Coedcae CS; Millfield S), b Morriston, Swansea 25 Dec 1978. Son of I.J.Jones (Glamorgan and England 1960-68). 6'3½". LHB, RFM. Glamorgan 1998-2007; cap 2002. Worcestershire 2008 (no 1st XI appearances in 2009). MCC 2002-04. MBE 2005. *Wisden* 2005. **Tests**: 18 (2002 to 2005); HS 44 v I (Lord's) 2002 – on debut; BB 6-53 v A (Manchester) 2005. **LOI**: 8 (2004-05 to 2005); HS 1; BB 2-43 v Z (Bulawayo) 2004-05 – on debut. F-c Tours: A 2002-03 (*part*); SA 2004-05; WI 2003-04; I 2003-04 (Eng A – *part*). HS 46 Gm v Yorks (Scarborough) 2001. BB 6-45 Gm v Derbys (Cardiff) 2002. LO HS 26 Gm v Hants (Swansea) 2007 (FPT). LO BB 5-32 Wo v Hampshire (Worcester) 2008 (FPT). T20 HS 11*. T20 BB 1-36.

LUMB, Michael John (St Stithians C, Johannesburg), b Johannesburg, South Africa 12 Feb 1980. Son of R.G.Lumb (Yorkshire 1970-84); nephew of A.J.S.Smith (SAU and Natal 1972-73 to 1983-84). 6'0". LHB, RM. Yorkshire 2000-06; ECB qualified and CC debut 2001; cap 2003. Hampshire debut 2007; cap 2008. F-c Tour (Eng A): I 2003-04. 1000 runs (2); most – 1038 (2003). HS 219 v Notts (Nottingham) 2009. BB 2-10 Y v Kent (Canterbury) 2001. H BB – . LO HS 110 EL v Pakistan A (Dubai) 2009-10. T20 HS 124* v Essex (Southampton) 2009 – H record. T20 BB 3-32.

‡^NQ**McKENZIE, Neil** Douglas (King Edward VII HS; Rand Afrikaans U), b Johannesburg, South Africa 24 Nov 1975. 5'9½". Son of K.A.McKenzie (N-E Transvaal and Transvaal 1966-67 to 1986-87). RHB, RM. Transvaal/Gauteng 1994-95 to 1998-99. Northerns 1999-00 to 2003-04. Lions 2004-05 to date; captain 2004-05 to 2009-10 (*part*). Somerset 2007. Durham 2008 (*part*). Joins Hampshire in 2010 as a Kolpak registration. *Wisden* 2008. **Tests** (SA): 58 (2000 to 2008-09); HS 226 v B (Chittagong) 2007-08, sharing Test record 1st wkt partnership of 415 with G.C.Smith; BB – . **LOI** (SA): 64 (1999-00 to 2008-09); HS 131* v Kenya (Cape Town) 2001-02; BB – . F-c Tours (SA): E 2003, 2008; A 2001-02, 2008-09; WI 2000-01; NZ 2003-04; I 2007-08; P 2003-04; SL 2000; Z 2001-02, 2004 (SA A); B 2003, 2007-08. HS 226 (*see Tests*). UK HS 138 SA v E (Lord's) 2008. CC HS 84 Sm v Glamorgan (Taunton) 2007. BB 2-13 Lions v Eagles (Kimberley) 2007-08. LO HS 131* (*see LOI*). LO BB 2-19 Gauteng v GW (Kimberley) 1997-98. IT20 HS 7*. T20 HS 85*. T20 BB – .

MASCARENHAS, Adrian Dimitri (Trinity C, Perth, Australia), b Hammersmith, London 30 Oct 1977. 6'2". Resident in Australia 1979-96. RHB, RMF. Debut (Hampshire) 1996, taking 6-88 v Glamorgan (Southampton); took 16 wickets in first two CC matches; cap 1998; benefit 2007; captain 2008 to date. Dorset 1996. **LOI**: 20 (2007 to 2009); HS 52 v I (Bristol) 2007; hit sixes off five successive balls from Yuvraj Singh v I (Oval) 2007; BB 3-23 v I (Lord's) 2007. HS 131 v Kent (Canterbury) 2006. 50 wkts (1): 56 (2004). BB 6-25 v Derbys (Southampton) 2004. LO HS 79 v Worcs (Southampton) 1999 (NL) and 79 v Kent (Canterbury) 2004 (NL). LO BB 5-27 v Glos (Southampton) 2002 (NL). IT20 HS 31. IT20 BB 3-18. T20 HS 57*. T20 BB 5-14 v Sussex (Hove) 2004 – H record.

‡^NQ**MENDIS, Balapuwaduge Ajantha** Winslo, b Moratuwa, Sri Lanka, 11 March 1985. RHB, LBG. Sri Lanka Army 2006-07 to date. **Tests** (SL): 10 (2008 to 2009-10); HS 27 v I (Kanpur) 2009-10; BB 6-117 (match 10-209) v I (Galle) 2008. **LOI** (SL): 38 (2007-08 to 2009-10); HS 15* v B (Lahore) 2008 and v UAE (Lahore) 2008; BB 6-13 v I (Karachi) 2008. HS 37 SL Army v SL Air Force (Colombo) 2006-07. BB 7-37 SL Army v Lankan (Panagoda) 2007-08. LO HS 71* SL Army v Kurunegala Youth (Welisara) 2006-07. LO BB 6-13 (*see LOI*). IT20 HS 4*. IT20 BB 4-15. T20 HS 9. T20 BB 4-15.

PIETERSEN, Kevin Peter (Maritzburg C; Natal U), b Pietermaritzburg, South Africa 27 Jun 1980. British passport (English mother) – qualified for England Oct 2004. 6'4". RHB, OB. MBE 2005. *Wisden* 2005. Natal/KwaZulu-Natal 1997-98 to 1999-00. Nottinghamshire 2001-04; cap 2002. MCC 2004. Hampshire debut/cap 2005 (no f-c appearances 2006-07, 2009). **ECB central contract 2009-10. Tests**: 58 (2005 to 2009-10, 3 as captain); HS 226 v WI (Leeds) 2007; BB 1-0 v SA (Lord's) 2008. **LOI**: 95 (2004-05 to 2009-10, 12 as captain); HS 116 v SA (Pretoria) 2004-05; scored 454 runs (av 151.33) in 7-match series, including fastest England 100 off 69 balls (E London), v SA 2004-05; BB 2-22 v SA (Leeds) 2008. F-c Tours: A 2006-07; SA 2009-10; WI 2008-09; NZ 2007-08; I 2003-04 (Eng A), 2005-06, 2008-09 (Captain); P 2005-06; SL 2007-08; B 2009-10. 1000 runs (3); most – 1546 (2003). HS 254* Nt v Middlesex (Nottingham) 2002. H HS 126 v Glamorgan (Southampton) 2005. BB 4-31 Nt v DU (Nottingham) 2003. CC BB 3-72 Nt v Hants (Nottingham) 2004. H BB – . LO HS 147 Nt v Somerset (Taunton) 2002 (NL). LO BB 3-14 Nt v Middlesex (Lord's 2004 (NL). IT20 HS 79. IT20 BB 1-27. T20 HS 79. T20 BB 3-33.

POTHAS, Nic (King Edward VII S; Rand Afrikaans U), b Johannesburg, South Africa 18 Nov 1973. ECB qualified – EU (Greek) passport. 6'3". RHB, WK, occ RM. Transvaal 1993-94 to 1996-97. Gauteng 1997-98 to 2000-01. Hampshire debut 2002; cap 2003. **LOI** (SA): 3 (2000-01); HS 24 v P (Singapore) 2000 – on debut. F-c Tours (SA): E 1996 (SA A); WI 2000 (SA A); SL 1998. HS 165 Gauteng v KZ-Natal (Johannesburg) 1998-99. H HS 146* v Worcs (Worcester) 2003. BB 1-16 v Middlesex (Lord's) 2006. Held 7 catches in an innings v Lancs (Manchester) 2006. LO HS 114* v Glamorgan (Cardiff) 2005 (CGT). T20 HS 59.

RIAZUDDIN, Hamza (Bradfield C), b Chelsea, London 19 Dec 1989. 5'11". RHB, RMF. HS 4 and BB 1-21 v Somerset (Taunton) 2008 – on debut. Berkshire 2008. LO HS 2* v Worcs (Worcester) 2009 (P40). LO BB 2-47 v Somerset (Southampton) 2009 (P40). T20 HS 13*. T20 BB 3-15.

‡NQ**SHAHID** Khan **AFRIDI**, Sahibzaha Mohammad (Ibrahim Alibhai S; Islamia Science C, Karachi) b Kohat, Pakistan, 1 Mar 1980. Brother of Tariq Afridi (Karachi 1999-00) and Ashfaq Afridi (Karachi Blues 2008-09). RHB, LBG. Debut Combined XI v Eng A 1995-96. Karachi 1995-96 to 2003-04. Habib Bank 1997-98 to 2008-09. Leicestershire 2001; cap 2001. Derbyshire 2003. GW 2003-04. Sind 2007-08 to 2008-09. T20 contract for 2010. **Tests** (P): 26 (1998-99 to 2006); HS 156 v I (Faisalabad) 2005-06; BB 5-52 v A (Karachi) 1998-99 – on debut. **LOI** (P): 293 (1996-97 to 2009-10, 2 as captain); HS 109 v I (Toronto) 1998-99; BB 6-38 v A (Dubai) 2009. Scored a 37-ball hundred (*LOI record*) which included then joint record 11 sixes v SL (Nairobi) 1996-97 in his first LOI innings. F-c Tours (P): E 2006; A 1996-97, 2004-05; WI 1999-00, 2005; I 1998-99, 2004-05; SL 2005-06; Z 2002-03; B 1998-99. HS 164 Le v Northants (Northampton) 2001. BB 6-101 Habib Bank v KRL (Rawalpindi) 1997-98. UK BB 5-84 Le v Essex (Chelmsford) 2001. LO HS 114 Sind v Baluchistan (Karachi) 2008-09. LO BB 6-38 (*see LOI*). IT20 HS 54*. IT20 BB 4-11. T20 HS 54*. T20 BB 4-11.

TOMLINSON, James Andrew (Harrow Way S, Andover; Cardiff U), b Winchester 12 Jun 1982. 6'1". LHB, LMF. British U 2002-03. Hampshire debut 2002; cap 2008. Wiltshire 2001. HS 35* v Lancs (Southampton) 2008. 50 wkts (1): 67 (2008). BB 8-46 (10-194 match) v Somerset (Taunton) 2008. LO HS 6 v Surrey (Oval) 2002 (NL). LO BB 4-47 v Glamorgan (Southampton) 2006 (CGT). T20 HS 5. T20 BB 1-20.

VINCE, James Michael (Warminster S), b Cuckfield, Sussex 14 Mar 1991. 6'2". RHB, RM. Debut (Hampshire) 2009. Hampshire 2nd XI debut 2006. Wiltshire 2007-08. HS 75 v Notts (Southampton) 2009 – on CC debut. BB – . LO HS 93 v Essex (Chelmsford) 2009 (P40).

‡**WOOD, Christopher** Philip, b Basingstoke 27 June 1990. RHB, LM. Hampshire 2nd XI debut 2007. England U19s 2008-09 to 2009. Awaiting 1st XI debut.

BURROWS, Thomas George (Reading GS; Southampton Solent U), b Wokingham, Berkshire 5 May 1985. 5'8". RHB, WK. Hampshire 2005-09. Berkshire 2001-03. HS 42 v Kent (Canterbury) 2005 – on debut. LO HS 25 v Worcs (Worcester) 2009 (FPT). T20 HS 0.

CRAWLEY, John Paul (Manchester GS; Trinity C, Cambridge), b Maldon, Essex 21 Sep 1971. Younger brother of M.A.Crawley (Oxford U, Lancs and Notts 1987-94) and P.M.Crawley (Cambridge U 1992). 6'1". RHB, RM, occ WK. Lancashire 1990-2001; cap 1994; captain 1999-2001. Cambridge U 1991-93; blue 1991-92-93; captain 1992-93. Hampshire 2002-09; cap 2002; captain 2003; benefit 2007. YC 1994. **Tests**: 37 (1994 to 2002-03); HS 156* v SL (Oval) 1998. **LOI**: 13 (1994-95 to 1998-99); HS 73 v Z (Harare) 1996-97. F-c Tours: A 1994-95, 1998-99, 2002-03; SA 1993-94 (Eng A), 1995-96; WI 1995-96 (La), 1997-98, 2000-01 (Eng A); NZ 1996-97; Z 1996-97. 1000 runs (10); most – 1851 (1998). HS 311* v Notts (Southampton) 2005. BB 1-7 v Surrey (Oval) 2005. LO HS 114 La v Notts (Manchester) 1995 (BHC). T20 HS 23.

IMRAN TAHIR – see *WARWICKSHIRE*.

[NQ]**NORTH, Marcus** James (Kent Street Sr HS), b Pakenham, Melbourne, Australia 28 Jul 1979. 6'1". LHB, OB. Debut (Aus Academy in Zim) 1998-99. W Australia 1999-00 to date; captain 2007-08 to date. Durham 2004. Lancashire 2005. Derbyshire 2006. Gloucestershire 2007-08; cap 2007. Hampshire 2009 (one match only). **Tests** (A): 13 (2008-09 to 2009-10); scored 117 v SA (Johannesburg) 2008-09 – on debut; HS 125* v E (Cardiff) 2009; BB 4-98 v E (Oval) 2009. **LOI** (A): 2 (2009); HS 5 v P (Abu Dhabi) 2009; BB – . F-c Tours (A): E 2009; SA 2008-09 (Aus A); Z 1998-99 (Aus Acad). 1000 runs (0+1): 1074 (2003-04). HS 239* WA v Vic (Perth) 2006-07. UK HS 219 Du v Glamorgan (Cardiff) 2004. BB 6-69 A v SAB President's XI (Potchefstroom) 2008-09. UK BB 4-16 Du v DU (Chester-le-St) 2004 – on Du debut. CC BB 3-53 Gs v Leics (Bristol) 2007. LO HS 134* WA v Q (Perth) 2004-05. LO BB 4-26 Durham CB v Bucks (Beaconsfield) 2001 (CGT). IT20 HS 20. T20 HS 59. T20 BB 2-19.

PARSONS, Thomas William (Maidstone GS; Rutherford Hall, Loughborough U), b Melbourne, Australia 2 May 1987. 6'3". RHB, RFM. Loughborough UCCE 2007-08. Kent 2007 – l-o only, no f-c appearances. Hampshire 2009 (one non-CC f-c appearance). HS 12 LU v Worcs (Kidderminster) 2008. BB 3-39 v LU (Southampton) 2009. LO HS – and BB 2-41 K v Sri Lanka A (Canterbury) 2007.

TAYLOR, Billy Victor (Bitterne Park S, Southampton), b Southampton 11 Jan 1977. Younger brother of J.L.Taylor (Wiltshire 1998-2002). 6'3". LHB, RMF. Sussex 1999-2003. Hampshire 2004-09; cap 2006; testimonial 2010. No f-c appearances 2007-08. Wiltshire 1996-98. HS 40 v Essex (Southampton) 2004. BB 6-32 v Middlesex (Southampton) 2006 (inc hat-trick). LO HS 21* Sx v Notts (Cleethorpes) 1999 (NL). LO BB 5-28 Sx v Middlesex (Lord's) 2002 (BHC). T20 HS 12*. T20 BB 2-9.

TREMLETT, C.T. – see *SURREY*.

C.G.W.Morgan left the staff, without making a County First-Class or List A appearance in 2009.

HAMPSHIRE 2009

RESULTS SUMMARY

	Place	Won	Lost	Tied	Drew	NR
County Championship (1st Division)	6th	3	3		10	
All First-Class Matches		3	3		11	
FP Trophy (Group A)	Winners	8	2			1
Pro40 League (1st Division)	5th	4	4			
Twenty20 Cup (South Division)	QF	6	5			

LV COUNTY CHAMPIONSHIP AVERAGES

BATTING AND FIELDING

Cap		M	I	NO	HS	Runs	Avge	100	50	Ct/St
2003	N.Pothas	11	15	4	122*	816	74.18	1	6	24
2006	M.A.Carberry	12	21	3	204	1251	69.50	4	8	6
2006	J.H.K.Adams	16	28	4	147	1280	53.33	3	9	16
2005	S.M.Ervine	15	22	2	114	832	41.60	3	3	6
2008	M.J.Lumb	15	23	1	219	834	37.90	1	5	8
	C.C.Benham	5	8	2	100	205	34.16	1	1	5
	L.A.Dawson	14	21	4	69	536	31.52	–	4	10
1998	A.D.Mascarenhas	10	11	2	108	254	28.22	1	–	4
	J.M.Vince	8	11	–	75	282	25.63	–	1	2
2002	J.P.Crawley	7	12	2	81*	240	24.00	–	1	6
2009	D.G.Cork	12	15	2	52	290	22.30	–	1	18
2009	Imran Tahir	12	15	4	77*	206	18.72	–	1	4
2008	J.A.Tomlinson	12	14	7	23	92	13.14	–	–	3
2004	C.T.Tremlett	7	8	–	36	75	9.37	–	–	2
	T.G.Burrows	5	6	1	20	46	9.20	–	–	13/1
	D.A.Griffiths	9	12	3	20*	36	4.00	–	–	–

Also played: D.J.Balcombe (2 matches) 10, 0; D.R.Briggs (3) 36, 0, 1 (1 ct); M.J.North (1) 15; B.V.Taylor (1 – cap 2006) did not bat.

BOWLING

	O	M	R	W	Avge	Best	5wI	10wM
D.G.Cork	287	69	767	27	28.40	5- 14	1	–
Imran Tahir	487.4	81	1711	52	32.90	7-140	4	–
D.A.Griffiths	255	47	949	28	33.89	4- 48	–	–
J.A.Tomlinson	318.1	58	1193	30	39.76	3- 53	–	–
C.T.Tremlett	173	34	564	14	40.28	4- 49	–	–
A.D.Mascarenhas	241	70	618	13	47.53	2- 46	–	–
S.M.Ervine	233.3	55	793	13	61.00	3- 22	–	–
Also bowled:								
D.R.Briggs	85.4	13	295	8	36.87	3- 62	–	–
L.A.Dawson	73	9	312	7	44.57	2- 3	–	–

J.H.K.Adams 15-0-66-1; D.J.Balcombe 44-7-174-4; M.A.Carberry 43.1-3-242-2; B.V.Taylor 21-4-52-1; J.M.Vince 10-0-37-0.

The First-Class Averages (pp 228–244) give the records of Hampshire players in all first-class county matches (Hampshire's other opponents being Loughborough UCCE), with the exception of M.J.North, whose first-class figures for Hampshire are as above.

HAMPSHIRE RECORDS

FIRST-CLASS CRICKET

Highest Total	For 714-5d		v	Notts	Southampton	2005
	V 742		by	Surrey	The Oval	1909
Lowest Total	For 15		v	Warwicks	Birmingham	1922
	V 23		by	Yorkshire	Middlesbrough	1965
Highest Innings	For 316	R.H.Moore	v	Warwicks	Bournemouth	1937
	V 303*	G.A.Hick	for	Worcs	Southampton	1997

Highest Partnership for each Wicket

1st	347	V.P.Terry/C.L.Smith	v	Warwicks	Birmingham	1987
2nd	321	G.Brown/E.I.M.Barrett	v	Glos	Southampton	1920
3rd	344	G.Brown/C.P.Mead	v	Yorkshire	Portsmouth	1927
4th	263	R.E.Marshall/D.A.Livingstone	v	Middlesex	Lord's	1970
5th	235	G.Hill/D.F.Walker	v	Sussex	Portsmouth	1937
6th	411	R.M.Poore/E.G.Wynyard	v	Somerset	Taunton	1899
7th	325	G.Brown/C.H.Abercrombie	v	Essex	Leyton	1913
8th	257	N.Pothas/A.J.Bichel	v	Glos	Cheltenham	2005
9th	230	D.A.Livingstone/A.T.Castell	v	Surrey	Southampton	1962
10th	192	H.A.W.Bowell/W.H.Livsey	v	Worcs	Bournemouth	1921

Best Bowling	For	9- 25	R.M.H.Cottam	v	Lancashire	Manchester	1965
(Innings)	V	10- 46	W.Hickton	for	Lancashire	Manchester	1870
Best Bowling	For	16- 88	J.A.Newman	v	Somerset	Weston-s-Mare	1927
(Match)	V	17-103	W.Mycroft	for	Derbyshire	Southampton	1876

Most Runs – Season	2854	C.P.Mead	(av 79.27)	1928
Most Runs – Career	48892	C.P.Mead	(av 48.84)	1905-36
Most 100s – Season	12	C.P.Mead		1928
Most 100s – Career	138	C.P.Mead		1905-36
Most Wkts – Season	190	A.S.Kennedy	(av 15.61)	1922
Most Wkts – Career	2669	D.Shackleton	(av 18.23)	1948-69
Most Career W-K Dismissals	700	R.J.Parks	(630 ct; 70 st)	1980-92
Most Career Catches in the Field	629	C.P.Mead		1905-36

LIMITED-OVERS CRICKET

Highest Total	FPT	371-4		v	Glamorgan	Southampton	1975
	P40	353-8		v	Middlesex	Lord's	2005
	T20	225-2		v	Middlesex	Southampton	2006
Lowest Total	FPT	75		v	Essex	Chelmsford	2007
	P40	43		v	Essex	Basingstoke	1972
	T20	85		v	Essex	Southampton	2008
Highest Innings	FPT	177	C.G.Greenidge	v	Glamorgan	Southampton	1975
	P40	172	C.G.Greenidge	v	Surrey	Southampton	1987
	T20	124*	M.J.Lumb	v	Essex	Southampton	2009
Best Bowling	FPT	7-30	P.J.Sainsbury	v	Norfolk	Southampton	1965
	P40	6-20	T.E.Jesty	v	Glamorgan	Cardiff	1975
	T20	5-14	A.D.Mascarenhas	v	Sussex	Hove	2004

KENT

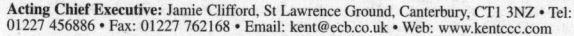

Formation of Present Club: 1 March 1859
Substantial Reorganisation: 6 December 1870
Inaugural First-Class Match: 1864
Colours: Maroon and White
Badge: White Horse on a Red Ground
County Champions: (6) 1906, 1909, 1910, 1913, 1970, 1978
Joint Champions: (1) 1977
Gillette/NatWest/C&G/FP Trophy Winners: (2) 1967, 1974
Benson and Hedges Cup Winners: (3) 1973, 1976, 1978
Pro 40/National League (Div 1) Winners: (1) 2001
Sunday League Winners: (4) 1972, 1973, 1976, 1995
Twenty20 Cup Winners: (1) 2007

Acting Chief Executive: Jamie Clifford, St Lawrence Ground, Canterbury, CT1 3NZ • Tel: 01227 456886 • Fax: 01227 762168 • Email: kent@ecb.co.uk • Web: www.kentccc.com

Head Coach: P.Farbrace. **Captain:** R.W.T.Key. **Vice-Captain:** M.van Jaarsveld. **Overseas Players:** C.M.Bandara and S.R.Clark. **2010 Beneficiary:** None. **Head Groundsman:** Andrew Peirson. **Scorer:** Jack C.Foley. ‡ New registration. NQ Not qualified for England.

NQ**AZHAR MAHMOOD** Sagar (F.G. No. 1 HS, Islamabad), b Rawalpindi, Pakistan 28 Feb 1975. 5'11". RHB, RFM. Islamabad 1993-94 to 1997-98, 2001-02 to 2006-07. United Bank 1995-96 to 1996-97. Rawalpindi 1998-99 to 2004-05. MCC 2001. PIA 2001-02. Surrey 2002-07; cap 2004. Habib Bank 2006-07. Kent debut 2008 (British passport holder) scoring 116 v Notts (Canterbury); cap 2008. **Tests** (P): 21 (1997-98 to 2001); HS 136 v SA (Johannesburg) 1997-98; BB 4-50 v E (Lord's) 2001. Scored 128* and 50* v SA (Rawalpindi) 1997-98 on debut. **LOI** (P): 143 (1996-97 to 2006-07); HS 67 v I (Adelaide) 1999-00; BB 6-18 vs WI (Sharjah) 1999-00. F-c Tours (P): E 1997 (Pak A), 2001; A 1999-00; SA 1997-98; I 1998-99; SL 2000; Z 1997-98. HS 204* Sy v Middlesex (Oval) 2005. K HS 116 (*see above*). 50 wkts (0+1): 59 (1996-97). BB 8-61 Sy v Lancs (Oval) 2002. K BB 6-55 v Yorkshire (Canterbury) 2008. LO HS 101* Sy v Glamorgan (Oval) 2006 (CGT). LO BB 6-18 (*see LOI*). T20 HS 65*. T20 BB 4-20.

‡**BALL, Adam** James, b Greenwich, London, 1 March 1993. RHB, LFM. Kent 2nd XI debut 2009, aged 16y 117d. England U19s 2009. Awaiting 1st XI debut.

‡NQ**BANDARA**, Herath Mudiyanselage Charitha **Malinga**, b Nagoda, Sri Lanka, 31 Dec 1979. 5'8". RHB, LBG. Kalutara Town 1996-97. Nondescripts 1998-99 to 2002-03. Tamil Union 2003-04. Southern Province 2003-04. Galle 2004-05. Gloucestershire 2005; cap 2005. Ragama 2006-07 to date. Basnahira 2008-09. **Tests** (SL): 8 (1998 to 2005-06); HS 43 v P (Kandy) 2005-06; BB 3-84 v I (Ahmedabad) 2005-06. **LOI** (SL): 31 (2005-06 to 2009-10); HS 31 v P (Colombo) 2009; BB 4-31 v SA (Hobart) 2005-06. F-c Tours (SL): E 1999 (SL A), 2006; A 2007-08; SA 2008-09 (SL A): WI 2006-07 (SL A); I 2005-06; B 2005-06. HS 79 SL A v Pakistan A (Dambulla) 2004-05. CC HS 70 and CC BB 5-71 Gs v Middx (Bristol) 2005. BB 8-49 SL A v England A (Colombo) 2004-05. UK BB 5-45 Gs v Bangladesh A (Bristol) 2005. LO HS 64 Ragama v Tamil Union (Colombo) 2008-09. LO BB 5-22 Nondescripts v Sebastianites (Colombo) 1999-00. IT20 HS 7. IT20 BB 3-32. T20 HS 31*. T20 BB 3-18.

BLAKE, Alexander ('**Alex**') James (Hayes SS; Leeds Met U), b Farnborough 25 Jan 1989. 6'1". LHB, RMF. Debut (Kent) 2008. Kent 2nd XI debut 2005. Leeds/Bradford UCCE 2009. England U19s 2006-07. HS 47 v Glos (Bristol) 2009. BB –. LO HS 80 v Derbys (Chesterfield) 2009 (P40). LO BB 1-25 v Glamorgan (Cardiff) 2007 (P40).

‡**NQCLARK, Stuart** Rupert (Woolooware HS; Sydney U), b Caringbah, Sydney, Australia 28 Sep 1975. 6'5". RHB, RMF. NSW 1997-98 to date. Middlesex 2004-05. Hampshire 2007; cap 2007. **Tests** (A): 24 (2005-06 to 2009); HS 39 v E (Brisbane) 2006-07; BB 5-32 v WI (Kingston) 2008. **LOI** (A): 39 (2005-06 to 2009); HS 16* v SA (Durban) 2005-06; BB 4-54 v NZ (Sydney) 2006-07. F-c Tours (A): E 2009; SA 2005-06; WI 2008; I 2008-09; P 2005-06 (Aus A); B 2005-06. HS 62 NSW v S Aus (Adelaide) 2006-07. CC HS 34 M v Northants (Northampton) 2004 – on debut. BB 8-58 NSW v WA (Perth) 2006-07, inc hat-trick. CC BB 7-82 H v Lancashire (Southampton) 2007. LO HS 29 NSW v Tas (Launceston) 2009-10. LO BB 6-27 H v Surrey (Southampton) 2007. IT20 HS – . IT20 BB 4-20. T20 HS 0*. T20 BB 4-20.

COLES, Matthew Thomas (Maplesden Noakes S; Mid-Kent C), b Maidstone 26 May 1990. 6'3". RHB, RMF. Debut (Kent) 2009. Kent 2nd XI debut 2007. HS 16 and BB 2-130 v Glos (Bristol) 2009. LO HS 5 (twice) 2009 (P40). LO BB 3-50 v Middx (Canterbury) 2009 (P40).

COOK, Simon James (Matthew Arnold S), b Oxford 15 Jan 1977. 6'4". RHB, RMF. Middlesex 1999-2004; cap 2003. Kent debut 2005; cap 2007. HS 93* M v Notts (Lord's) 2001. K HS 71 v Yorks (Leeds) 2006. BB 8-63 M v Northants (Northampton) 2002. K BB 6-35 v Sussex (Canterbury) 2007. LO HS 67* M v Durham (Lord's) 2003 (NL). LO BB 6-37 M v Leics (Leicester) 2004 (NL). T20 HS 25*. T20 BB 3-14.

DENLY, Joseph Liam (Chaucer TC), b Canterbury 16 Mar 1986. 6'0". RHB, LB. Debut (Kent) 2004; cap 2008. **LOI**: 9 (2009 to 2009-10); HS 67 v Ireland (Belfast) 2009 – on debut. F-c Tours (Eng A): NZ 2008-09; I 2007-08. 1000 runs (1): 1003 (2007). HS 149 v Somerset (Tunbridge Wells) 2008. BB 2-13 v Surrey (Canterbury) 2007. LO HS 115 v Warwks (Birmingham) 2009 (FPT). LO BB 1-20 E XI x SA A (Potchefstroom) 2009-10. IT20 HS 14. T20 HS 91. T20 BB 1-9.

DIXEY, Paul Garrod (King's S, Canterbury; Hatfield C, Durham U), b Canterbury 2 Nov 1987. 5'8". RHB, WK. Debut (Kent) 2005; awaiting CC debut – no f-c appearances for K 2007-09. MCC 2007. Durham UCCE 2007-09. HS 103 DU v Lancashire (Durham) 2009. K HS 24 v Bangladesh A (Canterbury) 2005 – on debut. LO HS 16 v Northants (Canterbury) 2009 (P40).

EDWARDS, Philip Duncan (Borden GS; Anglia Ruskin U, Cambridge), b Minster, Isle of Sheppey, 16 Apr 1984. 6'4". RHB, RMF. Cambridge UCCE 2004-05. Kent debut 2009. Suffolk 2002-08. HS 43 CU v Middx (Cambridge) 2004. K HS 5 v Derbys (Derby) 2009. BB 3-72 v Surrey (Canterbury) 2009. LO HS 2* v Lancs (Manchester) 2009 (P40). LO BB 3-57 v Derbys (Chesterfield) 2009 (P40).

FERLEY, Robert Steven (King Edward VII HS; Sutton Valence S; Grey C, Durham U), b Norwich, Norfolk 4 Feb 1982. 5'8". RHB, SLA. Durham UCCE 2001-03. British U 2001-03. Kent 2003-06. Nottinghamshire 2007-08. Norfolk 1998. HS 78* DU v Durham (Chester-le-St) 2003. CC HS 43* Nt v Essex (Chelmsford) 2007 – on Notts debut. K HS 29 v Surrey (Canterbury) 2004. BB 6-136 v Middlesex (Canterbury) 2006. LO HS 42 v Lancs (Manchester) 2004 (NL). LO BB 4-33 v Yorks (Scarborough) 2006 (P40). T20 HS 16*. T20 BB 3-17.

GOODMAN, James Elliot (St Olave's GS), b Farnborough 19 Nov 1990. 5'10". RHB, RM. Kent l-o debut 2007 – awaiting f-c debut. Kent 2nd XI debut 2006, aged 15y 194d. England U19s 2007-08 to 2009-10. LO HS 26* v Surrey (Canterbury) 2009 (P40).

HOCKLEY, James Bernard (Kelsey Park S, Beckenham), b Beckenham 16 Apr 1979. 6'2". RHB, OB. Kent 1998-2002, 2009 to date. HS 74 v Z (Canterbury) 2000. CC HS 72 v Essex (Chelmsford) 2009. BB 1-21 v Glamorgan (Maidstone) 2001. LO HS 121 v Warwks (Canterbury) 2002 (CGT). LO BB 2-32 v Northants (Canterbury) 2009 (P40). T20 HS 14.

130

JONES, Geraint Owen (Harristown State HS, Toowoomba and MacGregor State HS, Brisbane, Australia), b Kundiawa, Papua New Guinea 14 Jul 1976. Welsh parents. 5'10". RHB, WK. Debut (Kent) 2001; cap 2003. MBE 2005. **Tests**: 34 (2003-04 to 2006-07); HS 100 v NZ (Leeds) 2004. **LOI**: 49 (2004 to 2006); HS 80 v Z (Bulawayo) 2004-05. F-c Tours: A 2006-07; SA 2004-05; WI 2003-04; I 2005-06; P 2005-06; SL 2003-04. 1000 runs (1): 1345 (2009). HS 156 v Surrey (Canterbury) 2009. LO HS 86 v Surrey (Oval) 2008. IT20 HS 19. T20 HS 56.

JOSEPH, Robert ('Robbie') Hartman (Sutton Valence S; St Mary's C, Twickenham), b Antigua 20 Jan 1982. Resided in England since 1997. 6'1". RHB, RFM. Debut (First-Class Counties XI v NZ) 2000. Kent debut 2004. Leeward Is 2008-09. F-c Tour (Eng Lions): NZ 2008-09. HS 36* v Sussex (Hove) 2007. 50 wkts (1): 55 (2008). BB 6-32 (9-62 match) v Durham (Chester-le-St) 2008. LO HS 15 v Derbys (Canterbury) 2005 (NL). LO BB 5-13 v Derbys (Canterbury) 2008 (P40). T20 HS 1*. T20 BB 2-14.

KEY, Robert William Trevor (Colfe's S), b East Dulwich, London 12 May 1979. 6'1". RHB, RM/OB. Debut (Kent) 1998; cap 2001, captain 2006 to date. MCC 2002-04, 2009. *Wisden* 2004. **Tests**: 15 (2002 to 2004-05); HS 221 v WI (Lord's) 2004. **LOI**: 5 (2003 to 2004); HS 19 v WI (Lord's) 2004. F-c Tours: A 2002-03; SA 1998-99 (Eng A), 2004-05; NZ 2008-09 (Eng A – captain); SL 2002-03 (ECB Acad); Z 1998-99 (Eng A). 1000 runs (6); most – 1896 (2004). HS 270* v Glamorgan (Cardiff) 2009. BB 1-14 v Northants (Canterbury) 2009. LO HS 120* v Essex (Canterbury) 2008 (P40). IT20 HS 10*. T20 HS 68*.

KHAN, Amjad (Skolenpa Duevej, Denmark), b Copenhagen, Denmark 14 Oct 1980. 6'0". RHB, RFM. Debut (Kent) 2001. Denmark 1998-2000. Qualified for England Dec 2006. Missed 2007 season following reconstructive knee surgery. **Tests**: 1 (2008-09); HS – and BB 1-111 v WI (Port-of-Spain) 2008-09. F-c Tours: WI 2008-09 (*part*); NZ 2008-09 (Eng A – *part*). HS 78 v Middx (Lord's) 2003. 50 wkts (2); most – 63 (2002). BB 6-52 v Yorks (Canterbury) 2002. LO HS 65* Denmark v Ireland (Harare) 1999-00. LO BB 4-26 v Leics (Leicester) 2003 (NL). IT20 HS 2. IT 20 BB 2-34. T20 HS 15. T20 BB 3-11.

LEE, Warren Wain (Eaglesfield S, Shooters Hill), b New Delhi, India 28 Jul 1987. RHB, RM. Kent 2nd XI debut 2005. Awaiting f-c debut. LO HS 0. LO BB 3-39 v Middx (Canterbury) 2009 (P40).

NORTHEAST, Sam Alexander (Harrow S), b Ashford 16 Oct 1989. 5'11". RHB, OB. Debut (Kent) 2007. No 1st XI appearances in 2008. England U19s 2006-07 to 2009. HS 128* v Glos (Bristol) 2009. BB – . LO HS 69 v Surrey (Canterbury) 2009.

STEVENS, Darren Ian (Hinckley C), b Leicester 30 Apr 1976. 5'11". RHB, RM. Leicestershire 1997-2004; cap 2002. MCC 2002. Kent debut/cap 2005. F-c Tour (ECB Acad): SA 2002-03. 1000 runs (2); most – 1277 (2005). HS 208 v Glamorgan (Canterbury) 2005 and v Middx (Uxbridge) 2009. BB 4-36 v Yorks (Canterbury) 2006. LO HS 133 Le v Northumb (Jesmond) 2000 (NWT). LO BB 5-32 v Scotland (Edinburgh) 2005 (NL). T20 HS 77. T20 BB 4-14 v Essex (Chelmsford) 2007 – K record.

TREDWELL, James Cullum (Southlands Community CS, New Romney), b Ashford 27 Feb 1982. 6'0". LHB, OB. Debut (Kent) 2001; cap 2007. MCC 2004, 2008. F-c Tours: I 2003-04 (Eng A, captain); B 2009-10. HS 123* v NZ (Canterbury) 2008. CC HS 116* v Yorks (Tunbridge Wells) 2007. 50 wkts (1): 69 (2009). BB 8-66 (11-120 match) v Glamorgan (Canterbury) 2009. LO HS 88 v Surrey (Oval) 2007. LO BB 4-7 v Middx (Southgate) 2009 (FPT). T20 HS 34. T20 BB 4-21.

NQVAN JAARSVELD, Martin (Warmbaths S; Pretoria U), b Klerksdorp, South Africa 18 Jun 1974. 6'2". RHB, OB. N Transvaal/Northerns 1994-95 to 2003-04. Northamptonshire 2004. Titans 2004-05 to 2008-09. Kent debut/cap 2005 (Kolpak registration) scoring 118 and 111 v Warwicks (Canterbury) – second player after C.W.G.Bassano (Derbyshire) to score two hundreds on a county debut. PCA 2008. **Tests** (SA): 9 (2002-03 to 2004-05); HS 73 v WI (Johannesburg) 2003-04. **LOI** (SA): 11 (2002-03 to 2004); HS 45 v E (Birmingham) 2003; BB 1-0. Took wickets with his first and third balls in LOI. F-c Tours (SA): A 2002-03 (SA A); NZ 2003-04; I 2004-05; SL 1998-99 (SA A), 2004; Z 1998-99 (SA Acad). 1000 runs (5+1); most – 1509 (2009). HS 262* v Glamorgan (Cardiff) 2005. BB 5-33 v Surrey (Oval) 2008. LO HS 132* Titans v Eagles (Bloemfontein) 2008-09 and v Somerset (Canterbury) 2009 (FPT). LO BB 3-13 Titans v Cape Cobras (Centurion) 2008-09. T20 HS 76*. T20 BB 2-19.

RELEASED/RETIRED
(Having made a County First-Class or List A appearance in 2009)

NQKEMP, Justin Miles (Queens C; Port Elizabeth U), b Queenstown, Cape Province, South Africa 2 Oct 1977. Son of J.W.Kemp (Border 1975-76 to 1976-77); grandson of J.M.Kemp (Border 1947-48). RHB, RFM. E Province 1996-97 to 2002-03. Worcestershire 2003. Northerns 2003-04 to 2004-05. Titans 2004-05 to 2006-07. Kent 2005-06; cap 2006. Cape Cobras 2007-08 to date (missed 2008-09 season); captain 2007-08 to date. **Tests** (SA): 4 (2000-01 to 2005-06); HS 55 v A (Perth) 2005-06; BB 3-33 v SL (Pretoria) 2000-01 on debut. **LOI** (SA): 85 (2000-01 to 2007-08); HS 100* v I (Cape Town) 2006-07; BB 3-20 v I (Durban) 2001-02. F-c Tours (SA): A 2002-03 (SA A), 2005-06; WI 2000 (SA A), 2000-01; Z 1998-99 (SA Acad). HS 188 EP v North West (Port Elizabeth) 2000-01. CC HS 183 v Surrey (Oval) 2009. BB 6-56 EP v Border (Port Elizabeth) 2000-01. CC BB 5-48 Wo v Glamorgan (Cardiff) 2003 – on Worcs debut. K BB 3-12 v Derbys (Canterbury) 2009. LO HS 107* Northerns v GW (Centurion) 2003-04. LO BB 6-20 EP v FS (Port Elizabeth) 2000-01. IT20 HS 89*. IT20 BB – . T20 HS 89*. T20 BB 3-19.

NQMcLAREN, Ryan (Grey C, Bloemfontein; Free State U), b Kimberley, South Africa 9 Feb 1983. 6'4". Son of P.McLaren (GW 1977-78 to 1994-95). Nephew of Keith McLaren (GW 1971-72 to 1984-85). Cousin of A.P.McLaren (GW 1998-99 to date, Eagles 2007-08 to date). LHB, RMF. Free State 2003-04 to 2004-05. Eagles 2004-05 to date. Kent 2007-09 (Kolpak registration); cap 2007. **Tests** (SA): 1 (2009-10); HS 33* and BB 1-30 v E (Johannesburg) 2009-10. **LOI** (SA): 5 (2009-10); HS 6* and BB 3-51 v Z (Benoni) 2009-10 – on debut. HS 140 Eagles v Warriors (Bloemfontein) 2005-06. K HS 65* v Durham (Canterbury) 2008. 50 wkts (2); most – 54 (2006-07). BB 8-38 Eagles v Cape Cobras (Stellenbosch) 2006-07. K BB 6-75 v Notts (Nottingham) 2008. LO HS 82* Eagles v Dolphins (Durban) 2007-08. LO BB 5-46 v Surrey (Oval) 2008 (FPT). IT20 HS 1*. IT20 BB 3-33. T20 HS 46*. T20 BB 4-37.

NQPARNELL, Wayne Dillon (Grey HS), b Port Elizabeth, South Africa, 30 Jul 1989. 6'1". LHB, LFM. Eastern Province 2006-07. Warriors 2008-09 to date. Kent 2009. **Tests** (SA): 3 (2009-10); HS 22 v I (Kolkata) 2009-10; BB 2-17 v E (Johannesburg) 2009-10 – on debut. **LOI** (SA): 11 (2008-09 to 2009-10); HS 49 v I (Jaipur) 2009-10; BB 5-48 v E (Cape Town) 2009-10. HS 90 v Glamorgan (Canterbury) 2009. BB 4-7 EP v KwaZulu Natal (Port Elizabeth) 2006-07. K BB 4-78 v Essex (Chelmsford) 2009. LO HS 49 (*see LOI*). LO BB 5-48 (*see LOI*). IT20 HS – . IT20 BB 4-13. T20 HS 11*. T20 BB 4-13.

SAGGERS, Martin John (Springwood HS; King's Lynn; Huddersfield U), b King's Lynn, Norfolk 23 May 1972. 6'2". RHB, RMF. Durham 1996-98. Kent 1999-2009; cap 2001; benefit 2009. MCC 2004. Essex 2007 (on loan). Norfolk 1995-96. **Tests**: 3 (2003-04 to 2004); HS 1 and BB 2-29 v B (Chittagong) 2003-04 – on debut. F-c Tour: B 2003-04. HS 64 v Worcs (Canterbury) 2004. 50 wkts (4); most – 83 (2002). BB 7-79 v Durham (Chester-le-St) 2000. LO HS 34* Minor C v Leics (Jesmond) 1996 (BHC). LO BB 5-22 v Glos (Canterbury) 2001 (NL). T20 HS 5. T20 BB 2-14.

C.R.Hemphrey and J.A.Iles left the staff, without making a County First-Class or List A appearance in 2009.

KENT 2009

RESULTS SUMMARY

	Place	Won	Lost	Tied	Drew	NR
County Championship (2nd Division)	1st	8	3		5	
All First-Class Matches		8	3		6	
FP Trophy (Group B)	4th	3	4	1		
Pro40 League (2nd Division)	3rd	4	3			1
Twenty20 Cup (South Division)	SF	8	3			1

LV COUNTY CHAMPIONSHIP AVERAGES
BATTING AND FIELDING

Cap		M	I	NO	HS	Runs	Avge	100	50	Ct/St
2005	M.van Jaarsveld	15	24	3	182	1475	70.23	7	7	30
2001	R.W.T.Key	14	24	3	270*	1145	54.52	4	3	15
2003	G.O.Jones	16	25	–	156	1291	51.64	5	5	41/3
2006	J.M.Kemp	14	21	3	183	780	43.33	2	2	30
2008	J.L.Denly	9	14	1	123	542	41.69	3	1	5
2005	D.I.Stevens	16	23	2	208	857	40.80	3	2	11
	S.A.Northeast	10	18	2	128*	603	37.68	1	2	10
	W.D.Parnell	5	6	1	90	183	36.60	–	2	–
	J.B.Hockley	4	7	1	72	185	30.83	–	1	5
2007	J.C.Tredwell	16	21	5	86*	484	30.25	–	4	12
	A.J.Blake	4	5	–	47	125	25.00	–	–	1
2007	S.J.Cook	13	13	4	60*	220	24.44	–	1	–
2007	R.McLaren	7	8	1	44	127	18.14	–	–	1
	A.Khan	11	12	3	62*	153	17.00	–	1	2
2008	Azhar Mahmood	4	6	–	35	78	13.00	–	–	–
	P.S.Jones	3	4	–	16	26	6.50	–	–	1
	R.H.Joseph	4	5	2	9*	11	3.66	–	–	–
	P.D.Edwards	4	4	2	5	5	2.50	–	–	1
2001	M.J.Saggers	4	4	2	5*	5	2.50	–	–	–

Also batted: M.T.Coles (1 match) 14, 16; R.S.Ferley (2) 17 (1 ct).

BOWLING

	O	M	R	W	Avge	Best	5wI	10wM
Azhar Mahmood	130.3	38	382	21	18.19	5- 39	1	–
M.J.Saggers	108.5	34	264	10	26.40	3- 45	–	–
J.C.Tredwell	681.5	178	1838	69	26.63	8- 66	4	2
S.J.Cook	374.1	88	1047	34	30.79	5- 22	3	–
R.H.Joseph	97.2	9	373	12	31.08	6- 55	1	–
W.D.Parnell	166.3	35	529	17	31.11	4- 78	–	–
A.Khan	339.1	65	1146	36	31.83	5-113	1	–
R.McLaren	164.5	38	608	19	32.00	4- 51	–	–
Also bowled:								
R.S.Ferley	75	15	189	7	27.00	3- 73	–	–
P.D.Edwards	95	18	325	7	46.42	3- 72	–	–
J.M.Kemp	165.5	35	568	8	71.00	3- 12	–	–

A.J.Blake 4-0-15-0; M.T.Coles 17.4-0-130-2; J.L.Denly 25-7-60-0; P.S.Jones 80-19-240-4; R.W.T.Key 22-5-59-1; S.A.Northeast 1-0-2-0; D.I.Stevens 68-13-256-2; M.van Jaarsveld 71.1-10-241-4.

The First-Class Averages (pp 228–244) give the records of Kent players in all first-class county matches (Kent's other opponents being Loughborough UCCE), with the exception of P.S.Jones, whose first-class figures for Kent are as above, and:
J.L.Denly 10-15-1-123-578-41.29-3-1-5ct. 25-7-60-0.
R.W.T.Key 15-25-3-270*-1171-53.23-4-3-15ct. 22-5-59-1-59.00-1/14-0-0.

KENT RECORDS

FIRST-CLASS CRICKET

Highest Total	For 803-4d		v	Essex	Brentwood	1934
	V 676		by	Australians	Canterbury	1921
Lowest Total	For 18		v	Sussex	Gravesend	1867
	V 16		by	Warwicks	Tonbridge	1913
Highest Innings	For 332	W.H.Ashdown	v	Essex	Brentwood	1934
	V 344	W.G.Grace	for	MCC	Canterbury	1876

Highest Partnership for each Wicket

1st	300	N.R.Taylor/M.R.Benson	v	Derbyshire	Canterbury	1991
2nd	366	S.G.Hinks/N.R.Taylor	v	Middlesex	Canterbury	1990
3rd	323	R.W.T.Key/M.van Jaarsveld	v	Surrey	Tunbridge W	2005
4th	368	P.A.de Silva/G.R.Cowdrey	v	Derbyshire	Maidstone	1995
5th	277	F.E.Woolley/L.E.G.Ames	v	New Zealand	Canterbury	1931
6th	315	P.A.de Silva/M.A.Ealham	v	Notts	Nottingham	1995
7th	248	A.P.Day/E.Humphreys	v	Somerset	Taunton	1908
8th	177	G.O.Jones/Yasir Arafat	v	Warwicks	Canterbury	2007
9th	171	M.A.Ealham/P.A.Strang	v	Notts	Nottingham	1997
10th	235	F.E.Woolley/A.Fielder	v	Worcs	Stourbridge	1909

Best Bowling	For 10- 30	C.Blythe	v	Northants	Northampton	1907
(Innings)	V 10- 48	C.H.G.Bland	for	Sussex	Tonbridge	1899
Best Bowling	For 17- 48	C.Blythe	v	Northants	Northampton	1907
(Match)	V 17-106	T.W.J.Goddard	for	Glos	Bristol	1939

Most Runs – Season	2894	F.E.Woolley	(av 59.06)	1928
Most Runs – Career	47868	F.E.Woolley	(av 41.77)	1906-38
Most 100s – Season	10	F.E.Woolley		1928, 1934
Most 100s – Career	122	F.E.Woolley		1906-38
Most Wkts – Season	262	A.P.Freeman	(av 14.74)	1933
Most Wkts – Career	3340	A.P.Freeman	(av 19.04)	1914-36
Most Career W-K Dismissals	1253	F.H.Huish	(901 ct; 352 st)	1895-1914
Most Career Catches in the Field	773	F.E.Woolley		1906-38

LIMITED-OVERS CRICKET

Highest Total	FPT	384-6	v	Berkshire	Finchampstead	1994
	P40	327-6	v	Leics	Canterbury	1993
	T20	204-5	v	Essex	Beckenham	2008
Lowest Total	FPT	60	v	Somerset	Taunton	1979
	P40	83	v	Middlesex	Lord's	1984
	T20	91	v	Surrey	The Oval	2006
Highest Innings	FPT	136* C.L.Hooper	v	Berkshire	Finchampstead	1994
	P40	146 A.Symonds	v	Lancs	Tunbridge Wells	2004
	T20	112 A.Symonds	v	Middlesex	Maidstone	2004
Best Bowling	FPT	8-31 D.L.Underwood	v	Scotland	Edinburgh	1987
	P40	6- 9 R.A.Woolmer	v	Derbyshire	Chesterfield	1979
	T20	4-14 D.I.Stevens	v	Essex	Chelmsford	2007

LANCASHIRE

Formation of Present Club: 12 January 1864
Inaugural First-Class Match: 1865
Colours: Red, Green and Blue
Badge: Red Rose
County Champions (since 1890): (7) 1897, 1904, 1926,
1927, 1928, 1930, 1934
Joint Champions: (1) 1950
Gillette/NatWest/C&G/FP Trophy Winners: (7) 1970, 1971,
1972, 1975, 1990, 1996, 1998
Benson and Hedges Cup Winners: (4) 1984, 1990, 1995,
1996
Pro 40/National League (Div 1) Winners: (1) 1999.
Sunday League Winners: (4) 1969, 1970, 1989, 1998
Twenty20 Cup Winners: (0); best – Finalist 2005

Chief Executive: Jim Cumbes, Old Trafford, Manchester M16 0PX • Tel: 0161 282 4000 •
Fax: 0161 282 4100 • Email: enquiries@lccc.co.uk • Web: www.lccc.co.uk

Director of Cricket: M.Watkinson. **Head Coach:** Peter Moores. **Captain:** G.Chapple.
Vice-Captain: none. **Overseas Players:** D.B.L.Powell, A.G.Prince and K.C.Sangakkara.
2010 Beneficiary: none. **Head Groundsman:** Matthew Merchant. **Scorer:** Alan West.
‡ New registration. ^{NQ} Not qualified for England.

ANDERSON, James Michael (St Theodore RC HS and SFC, Burnley), b Burnley 30 Jul
1982. 6'2". LHB, RFM. Debut (Lancashire) 2002; cap 2003. YC 2003. *Wisden* 2008. **ECB
central contract 2009-10. Tests:** 46 (2003 to 2009-10); HS 34 v SA (Leeds) 2008; BB 7-43
v NZ (Nottingham) 2008. **LOI:** 120 (2002-03 to 2009-10); HS 15 v A (Jaipur) 2006-07; BB
5-23 v SA (Port Elizabeth) 2009-10. Hat-trick v P (Oval) 2003 – 1st for Eng in 373 LOI. F-c
Tours: A 2006-07; SA 2004-05, 2009-10; WI 2003-04, 2005-06 (Eng A) (*part*), 2008-09;
NZ 2007-08; I 2005-06 (*part*), 2008-09; SL 2003-04, 2007-08. HS 37* v Durham
(Manchester) 2005. 50 wkts (2); most – 60 (2005). BB 7-43 (*see Tests*). La BB 6-23 v Hants
(Southampton) 2002. Hat-trick v Essex (Manchester) 2003. LO HS 15 (*see LOI*). LO BB
5-23 (*see LOI*). IT20 HS 1*. IT20 BB 3-23. T20 HS 16. T20 BB 3-23.

BROWN, Karl Robert (Hesketh Fletcher HS, Atherton), b Bolton 17 May 1988. 5'10".
RHB, RMF. Debut (Lancashire) 2006. HS 40 v Kent (Liverpool) 2008. BB 2-30 v Notts
(Nottingham) 2009. LO HS 41 v Notts (Nottingham) 2008 (P40).

CHAPPLE, Glen (West Craven HS; Nelson & Colne C), b Skipton, Yorks 23 Jan 1974.
6'1". RHB, RMF. Debut (Lancashire) 1992; cap 1994; benefit 2004; captain 2009 to date.
LOI: 1 (2006); HS 14 and BB – v Ireland (Belfast) 2006. F-c Tours (Eng A): A 1996-97; WI
1995-96 (La); I 1994-95. HS 155 v Somerset (Manchester) 2001. Scored 100 off 27 balls in
contrived circumstances v Glamorgan (Manchester) 1993. 50 wkts (4); most – 55 (1994).
BB 7-53 v Durham (Blackpool) 2007. LO HS 81* v Derbys (Manchester) 2002 (CGT). LO
BB 6-18 v Essex (Lord's) 1996 (NWT) – La record. T20 HS 55*. T20 BB 2-11.

CHEETHAM, Steven Philip (Bury GS; Holy Cross SFC), b Oldham 5 Sep 1987. 6'5".
RHB, RFM. Debut (Lancashire) 2007. Awaiting CC debut; no f-c appearances in 2008 and
2009. HS – and BB 1-44 v DU (Durham) 2007. LO HS 3* v Derbys (Derby) 2008. LO BB
3-25 v Bangladesh A (Alderley Edge) 2008.

135

CHILTON, Mark James (Manchester GS; Durham U), b Sheffield, Yorks 2 Oct 1976. 6'3". RHB, RM. Debut (Lancashire) 1997; cap 2002; captain 2005-07. British U 1998. 1000 runs (1): 1154 (2003). HS 131 v Kent (Manchester) 2006. BB 2-3 v Durham UCCE (Durham) 2009. CC BB 1-1 (twice). LO HS 115 v Surrey (Croydon) 2004 (NL). LO BB 5-26 Brit U v Sussex (Cambridge) 1997 (BHC). T20 HS 38.

CROFT, Steven John (Highfield HS, Blackpool; Myerscough C), b Blackpool 11 Oct 1984. 5'10". RHB, RMF. Debut (Lancashire) 2005. Auckland 2008-09. HS 122 v Notts (Manchester) 2008. BB 4-51 v Notts (Nottingham) 2008. LO HS 70 v Hampshire (Southampton) 2008 (P40) and v Warwks (Manchester) 2009 (P40). LO BB 4-24 v Scotland (Manchester) 2008 (FPT). T20 HS 83*. T20 BB 3-6.

CROSS, Gareth David (Moorside S; Eccles C), b Bury 20 Jun 1984. 5'9". RHB, RMF, WK. Debut (Lancashire) 2005. No f-c appearances in 2009. HS 72 v Kent (Canterbury) 2006. LO HS 76 v Warwks (Birmingham) 2007 (P40). LO BB 2-26 v Durham (Chester-le-St) 2008 (FPT). T20 HS 62.

FLINTOFF, Andrew (Ribbleton Hall HS), b Preston 6 Dec 1977. 6'4". RHB, RF. Debut (Lancashire) 1995; cap 1998; benefit 2006. YC 1998. *Wisden* 2003. PCA 2004, 2005. MBE 2005. BBC Sports Personality of 2005. **Tests**: 79 (1998 to 2009, 11 as captain); HS 167 v WI (Birmingham) 2004; BB 5-58 v WI (Bridgetown) 2003-04. **LOI**: 141 (1998-99 to 2008-09, 14 as captain); HS 123 v WI (Lord's) 2004; BB 5-19 v WI (Gros Islet) 2008-09. F-c Tours (Eng) (C=Captain): A 2002-03 (*part*), 2006-07C; SA 1998-99 (Eng A), 1999-00, 2004-05; WI 2003-04, 2008-09; NZ 2001-02; I 2001-02, 2005-06C, 2008-09; P 2000-01 (*part*), 2005-06; SL 1997-98 (Eng A), 2003-04; Z 1998-99 (Eng A). K 1997-98 (Eng A). HS 167 (*see Tests*). La HS 160 v Yorkshire (Manchester) 1999. BB 5-24 v Hants (Southampton) 1999. LO HS 143 (off 66 balls) v Essex (Chelmsford) 1999 (NL) – La record. LO BB 5-19 (*see LOI*). IT20 HS 31. IT20 BB 2-23. T20 HS 93. T20 BB 4-12 v Durham (Chester-le-St) 2008 – La record.

HOGG, Kyle William (Saddleworth HS), b Birmingham, Warwks 2 Jul 1983. Son of W.Hogg (Lancashire and Warwickshire 1976-83); grandson of S.Ramadhin (Trinidad, Lancashire and West Indies 1949-50 to 1964). 6'4". LHB, RFM. Debut (Lancashire) 2001. Otago 2006-07. Worcestershire 2007 (on loan). Nottinghamshire 2007 (on loan). F-c Tour (ECB Acad): SL 2002-03. HS 71 Otago v CD (Napier) 2006-07. La HS 70 v Middlesex (Lord's) 2006. BB 5-48 v Leics (Manchester) 2002 – on CC debut. LO HS 66* v Scotland (Manchester) 2008 (FPT). LO BB 4-20 v Hants (Southampton) 2002 (NL). T20 HS 44. T20 BB 2-10.

HORTON, Paul James (St Margaret's HS, Liverpool), b Sydney, Australia 20 Sep 1982. 5'10". RHB, RM. UK resident since 1997. Debut (Lancashire) 2003; cap 2007. 1000 runs (2); most – 1116 (2007). HS 173 v Somerset (Taunton) 2009. LO HS 111* v Derbyshire (Manchester) 2009 (FPT). T20 HS 41.

KEEDY, Gary (Garforth CS), b Wakefield, Yorks 27 Nov 1974. 6'0". LHB, SLA. Yorkshire 1994 (one match). Lancashire debut 1995; cap 2000; benefit 2009. F-c Tour: WI 1995-96 (La). HS 64 v Sussex (Hove) 2003. 50 wkts (3); most – 72 (2004). BB 7-95 (14-227 match) v Glos (Manchester) 2004. LO HS 33 v Derbys (Derby) 2008. LO BB 5-30 v Sussex (Manchester) 2000 (NL). T20 HS 9*. T20 BB 4-15.

KERRIGAN, Simon Christopher (Corpus Christi RC HS, Preston), b Preston, 10 May 1989. RHB, SLA. Lancashire 2nd XI debut 2007. Awaiting 1st XI debut.

MAHMOOD, Sajid Iqbal (North C, Bolton), b Bolton 21 Dec 1981. 6'4". RHB, RF. Debut (Lancashire) 2002; cap 2007. MCC 2005, 2009. **Tests**: 8 (2006 to 2006-07); HS 34 and BB 4-22 v P (Leeds) 2006. **LOI**: 26 (2004 to 2009-10); HS 22* v P (Birmingham) 2006; BB 4-50 v SL (North Shore, Antigua) 2006-07. F-c Tours (Eng A): A 2006-07 (Eng); WI 2005-06; NZ 2008-09; I 2003-04; SL 2004-05. HS 94 v Sussex (Manchester) 2004. BB 6-30 v Durham (Chester-le-St) 2009. LO HS 29 v Staffs (Stone) 2004 (CGT). LO BB 5-16 v Sri Lanka A (Liverpool) 2007. IT20 HS 1*. IT20 BB 1-31. T20 HS 21. T20 BB 4-29.

‡**MONTGOMERY, Gary** Stephen (Warwick S; Henley C, Coventry), b Leamington Spa, Warwks, 8 Oct 1982. 6'2". RHB, LMF. Lancashire 2nd XI debut 2009. Has played goalkeeper in Football League for Kidderminster Harriers, Coventry City, Rotherham United and Grimsby Town. Awaiting 1st XI debut.

‡**MOORE, Stephen** Colin (St Stithian's C, Johannesburg; Exeter U), b Johannesburg, South Africa 4 Nov 1980. 6'1". RHB, RM. Worcestershire 2003-09. MCC 2009. F-c Tour (Eng A): NZ 2008-09. 1000 runs (3); most – 1451 (2008). HS 246 Wo v Derbys (Worcester) 2005. BB 1-13 Wo v Lancs (Worcester) 2004. LO HS 105* Wo v Leics (Leicester) 2006 (P40). LO BB 1-1 Wo v Scotland (Worcester) 2004 (NL). T20 HS 62*.

NEWBY, Oliver James (Ribblesdale HS; Myerscough C), b Blackburn 26 Aug 1984. 6'5". RHB, RMF. Debut (Lancashire) 2003. Nottinghamshire 2005 (on loan). Gloucestershire (on loan) 2008; cap 2008. HS 38* Nt v Kent (Nottingham) 2005 – on Notts debut. La HS 26 v Warwks (Manchester) 2007. BB 5-69 Gs v Northants (Bristol) 2008. La BB 4-21 v Durham UCCE (Durham) 2009. LO HS 12* v Derbyshire (Derby) 2009 (FPT). LO BB 4-41 v Glamorgan (Cardiff) 2009 (FPT). T20 HS 6*. T20 BB 2-34.

PARRY, Stephen David (Audenshaw S), b Manchester 12 Jan 1986. 5'11". RHB, SLA. Debut (Lancashire) 2007 taking 5-23 v Durham UCCE (Durham). No 1st XI appearances in 2008. Cumberland 2005-06. HS 2 and CC BB 2-51 v Durham (Manchester) 2009. BB 5-23 (*see above*). LO HS 31 v Essex (Chelmsford) 2009 (FPT). LO BB 2-12 v Northants (Northampton) 2009 (P40). T20 HS 4. T20 BB 3-20.

‡**NOPOWELL, Daren** Brent-Lyle (St Alban's S; St Elizabeth Technical HS), b Malvenn, St Elizabeth, Jamaica 15 Apr 1978. 6'0". RHB, RFM. Jamaica 2000-01 to date. Gauteng 2003-04. Derbyshire 2004. Hampshire 2007. **Tests** (WI): 37 (2002 to 2008-09); HS 36* v E (Lord's) 2007; BB 5-25 v SL (Kandy) 2005. **LOI** (WI): 55 (2002-03 to 2008-09); HS 48* v SA (St George's) 2006-07; BB 4-27 v I (Cuttack) 2006-07. F-c Tours (WI): E 2002 (WI A), 2006 (WI A), 2007; A 2005-06; SA 2007-08; NZ 2005-06, 2008-09; I 2002-03; P 2006-07; SL 2005; B 2002-03. HS 69 Jamaica v Barbados (Bridgetown) 2008-09. UK HS 62 West Indies A v Durham (Chester-le-St) 2006. CC HS 25 H v Surrey (Southampton) 2007. BB 6-49 De v DU (Derby) 2004. CC BB 4-8 H v Worcs (Southampton) 2007. LO HS (*see LOI*). LO BB 5-23 Jamaica v T&T (Discovery Bay) 2002-03. IT20 HS 1*. IT20 BB 1-6. T20 HS 1*. T20 BB 2-15.

NOPRINCE, Ashwell Gavin (St Thomas Senior SS, UPE), b Port Elizabeth, South Africa, 28 May 1977. LHB, OB. Eastern Province 1995-96 to 1997-98. Western Province 1997-98 to 2003-04. Western Province Boland 2004-05. Cape Cobras 2005-06 to 2007-08. Nottinghamshire 2008. Warriors 2008-09 to date. Lancashire debut 2009. **Tests** (SA): 54 (2001-02 to 2009-10, 2 as captain); HS 162* v B (Centurion) 2008-09; BB 1-2 v NZ (Cape Town) 2006. **LOI** (SA): 52 (2002-03 to 2007); HS 89* v WI (Port of Spain) 2005; BB – . F-c Tours (SA): E 2008; A 2005-06; WI 2000 (SA A), 2005; I 2007-08, 2009-10; P 2007-08; SL 2006; Z 2007 (SA A); B 2007-08. HS 254 Warriors v Titans (Centurion) 2008-09; CC HS 135* v Notts (Manchester) 2009. BB 2-11 SA v Middlesex (Uxbridge) 2008; CC BB – . LO HS 128 Warriors v Dolphins (East London) 2009-10. LO BB – . IT20 HS 5. T20 HS 46. T20 BB – .

‡**PROCTER, Luke** Anthony (Counthill S, Oldham), b Oldham 24 June 1988. 5'11". LHB, RM. Lancashire 2nd XI debut 2006. Cumberland 2007. Awaiting f-c debut. LO HS 2 v Warwks (Manchester) 2009 (P40).

‡**NOSANGAKKARA, Kumar** Chokshanada (Trinity C, Kandy; Colombo U), b Matale, Sri Lanka, 27 Oct 1977. 5'11". LHB, WK, occ OB. Nondescripts 1997-98 to 2007-08. Central Province 2003-04 to 2004-05. Warwickshire 2007; cap 2007. **Tests** (SL): 88 (2000 to 2009-10); HS 287 v SA (Colombo, SSC) 2006, sharing in world record f-c partnership for any wkt of 624 with D.P.M.D.Jayawardena; BB – . **LOI** (SL): 267 (2000 to 2009-10); HS 138* v I (Jaipur) 2005-06. F-c Tours (SL): E 2002, 2006; A 2004, 2007-08; SA 1999-00 (SL A), 2000-01, 2002-03; WI 2003, 2007-08; NZ 2004-05, 2006-07; I 2005-06, 2009-10; P 2001-02, 2004-05, 2008-09; Z 2004, 2008-09; B 2005-06, 2008-09. 1000 runs (0+1): 1191 (2003-04). HS 287 (*see Tests*). CC HS 149 Wa v Durham (Birmingham) 2007. BB 1-13 SL v Zim A (Harare) 2004. LO HS 156* SL A v Zim A (Moratuwa) 1999-00. IT20 HS 78. T20 HS 94.

SHANKAR, Adrian (Bedford S; Queens C, Cambridge U), b Ascot, Berks 7 May 1982. RHB, OB. Cambridge U 2002-05; blue 2002-03-04-05. Lancashire 2nd XI debut 2008. Bedfordshire 2000-06. Awaiting La 1st XI debut. HS 143 CU v OU (Oxford) 2002. LO HS 27 Beds v Sussex (Luton) 2005 (CGT).

SMITH, Thomas Christopher (Parkland HS, Chorley; Runshaw C, Leyland), b Liverpool 26 Dec 1985. 6'3". LHB, RMF. Debut (Lancashire) 2005. Leicestershire (on loan) 2008. F-c Tour (Eng A): B 2006-07. HS 104* v Durham UCCE (Durham) 2009. CC HS 95 v Hampshire (Southampton) 2009. BB 6-46 v Yorkshire (Manchester) 2009. LO HS 87* v Glamorgan (Cardiff) 2009 (FPT). LO BB 3-8 v Leics (Manchester) 2006 (CGT). T20 HS 57*. T20 BB 3-15.

SUTTON, Luke David (Millfield S; Durham U), b Keynsham, Somerset 4 Oct 1976. 5'11". RHB, WK. Somerset 1997-98. Derbyshire 2000-05; cap 2002; captain 2004-05. Lancashire debut 2006; cap 2007. HS 151* v Yorks (Manchester) 2006. LO HS 83 De v Lancs (Derby) 2003 (NL). T20 HS 61*.

RELEASED/RETIRED
(Having made a County First-Class or List A appearance in 2009)

NODu PLESSIS, Francois (*'Faf'*) (Affies BS, Pretoria), b Pretoria, South Africa 13 Jul 1984. 6'0". RHB, LB. Northerns 2003-04 to 2005-06. Titans 2005-06 to date. Lancashire 2008-09 (Kolpak registration). HS 176 Titans v Lions (Centurion) 2008-09. La HS 86* v Hampshire (Southampton) 2009. BB 4-39 Northerns v Free State (Pretoria) 2004-05. La BB 3-61 v Yorkshire (Manchester) 2008. LO HS 114* Titans v Eagles (Bloemfontein) 2008-09. LO BB 4-47 Northerns v Easterns (Pretoria) 2005-06. T20 HS 78*. T20 BB 3-18.

NOLAXMAN, Vangipurapu Venkata Sai (*'VVS'*) (Little Flower S; Osmania U, Hyderabad), b Hyderabad, India 1 Nov 1974. 6'1". RHB, OB. Hyderabad 1992-93 to date. South Zone 1994-95 to date. Lancashire 2007, 2009. Otago 2008-09. *Wisden* 2001. **Tests** (I): 110 (1996-97 to 2009-10); HS 281 v A (Calcutta) 2000-01; BB 1-2 v P (Calcutta) 2007-08. **LOI** (I): 86 (1997-98 to 2006-07); HS 131 v Z (Adelaide) 2003-04; BB – . F-c Tours (I): E 2002, 2007; A 1999-00, 2003-04, 2007-08; SA 1996-97, 2001-02, 2006-07; WI 1996-97, 2001-02, 2002-03 (Ind A – Capt), 2006; NZ 1998-99, 2002-03, 2008-09; P 2003-04, 2005-06; SL 1998-99, 2008; Z 2001, 2005-06; B 2004-05, 2008-09. 1000 runs (0+4); most – 1432 (1999-00). HS 353 Hyderabad v Karnataka (Bangalore) 1999-00. La HS 135 v Hampshire (Southampton) 2009. BB 3-11 Hyderabad v Railways (Delhi) 1999-00. La BB 1-13 v Durham (Manchester) 2009. LO HS 131 (*see LOI*). LO BB 2-42 Hyderabad v Tamil Nadu (Madras) 2000-01. T20 HS 78*.

LOYE, M.B. – *see NORTHAMPTONSHIRE.*

MULLANEY, S.J. – *see NOTTINGHAMSHIRE.*

LANCASHIRE 2009

RESULTS SUMMARY

	Place	Won	Lost	Tied	Drew	NR
County Championship (1st Division)	4th	4	2		10	
All First-Class Matches		5	2		10	
FP Trophy (Group D)	SF	7	3			
Pro40 League (2nd Division)	5th	3	3			2
Twenty20 Cup (North Division)	QF	8	2			1

LV COUNTY CHAMPIONSHIP AVERAGES

BATTING AND FIELDING

Cap		M	I	NO	HS	Runs	Avge	100	50	Ct/St
2009	V.V.S.Laxman	11	16	3	135	857	65.92	4	4	15
	A.G.Prince	5	10	2	135*	497	62.12	1	3	8
2003	M.B.Loye	13	21	3	151*	983	54.61	2	6	4
2002	M.J.Chilton	15	22	6	111*	777	48.56	1	6	14
1994	G.Chapple	11	14	2	89	390	32.50	–	3	3
	S.J.Croft	8	12	2	79	317	31.70	–	2	6
	F.du Plessis	13	20	3	86*	531	31.23	–	5	8
2007	P.J.Horton	16	29	2	173	776	28.74	1	4	16
	K.W.Hogg	13	13	1	69	307	25.58	–	2	2
2007	L.D.Sutton	16	21	6	45*	377	25.13	–	–	53/3
	T.C.Smith	8	13	1	95	235	19.58	–	1	5
1998	A.Flintoff	2	4	–	54	69	17.25	–	1	3
2007	S.I.Mahmood	11	12	1	30*	100	9.09	–	–	6
2000	G.Keedy	16	16	7	18	63	7.00	–	–	–
	O.J.Newby	12	11	1	15	64	6.40	–	–	2

Also batted: J.M.Anderson (1 match – cap 2003) 9* (1 ct); K.R.Brown (1) 3, 19;
T.Lungley (2) 27*, 10 (2 ct); S.D.Parry (2) 2, 1 (1 ct).

BOWLING

	O	M	R	W	Avge	Best	5wI	10wM
J.M.Anderson	51	15	109	11	9.90	6- 56	2	1
G.Chapple	335.4	87	884	35	25.25	6- 19	2	–
S.I.Mahmood	306.3	59	1118	38	29.42	6- 30	2	1
K.W.Hogg	319.2	83	965	30	32.16	4- 74	–	–
G.Keedy	487.5	83	1457	42	34.69	6- 50	3	–
O.J.Newby	274.1	35	1058	25	42.32	4-105	–	–
T.C.Smith	181	41	572	13	44.00	6- 46	1	–

Also bowled:
A.Flintoff	51.3	15	149	8	18.62	4- 47	–	–
T.Lungley	40	8	139	5	27.80	3- 85	–	–

K.R.Brown 8-0-37-2; S.J.Croft 16-3-83-2; F.du Plessis 54.1-1-199-4; P.J.Horton 2-1-10-0;
V.V.S.Laxman 13-4-26-1; S.D.Parry 68-10-210-4.

The First-Class Averages (pp 228–244) give the records of Lancashire players in all
first-class county matches (Lancashire's other opponents being Durham UCCE), with the
exception of J.M.Anderson, A.Flintoff, T.Lungley and S.I.Mahmood, whose first-class
figures for Lancashire are as above.

LANCASHIRE RECORDS

FIRST-CLASS CRICKET

Highest Total	For 863		v	Surrey	The Oval	1990
	V 707-9d		by	Surrey	The Oval	1990
Lowest Total	For 25		v	Derbyshire	Manchester	1871
	V 22		by	Glamorgan	Liverpool	1924
Highest Innings	For 424	A.C.MacLaren	v	Somerset	Taunton	1895
	V 315*	T.W.Hayward	for	Surrey	The Oval	1898

Highest Partnership for each Wicket

1st	368	A.C.MacLaren/R.H.Spooner	v	Glos	Liverpool	1903
2nd	371	F.B.Watson/G.E.Tyldesley	v	Surrey	Manchester	1928
3rd	364	M.A.Atherton/N.H.Fairbrother	v	Surrey	The Oval	1990
4th	358	S.P.Titchard/G.D.Lloyd	v	Essex	Chelmsford	1996
5th	360	S.G.Law/C.L.Hooper	v	Warwicks	Birmingham	2003
6th	278	J.Iddon/H.R.W.Butterworth	v	Sussex	Manchester	1932
7th	248	G.D.Lloyd/I.D.Austin	v	Yorkshire	Leeds	1997
8th	158	J.Lyon/R.M.Ratcliffe	v	Warwicks	Manchester	1979
9th	142	L.O.S.Poidevin/A.Kermode	v	Sussex	Eastbourne	1907
10th	173	J.Briggs/R.Pilling	v	Surrey	Liverpool	1885

Best Bowling	For	10-46	W.Hickton	v	Hampshire	Manchester	1870
(Innings)	V	10-40	G.O.B.Allen	for	Middlesex	Lord's	1929
Best Bowling	For	17-91	H.Dean	v	Yorkshire	Liverpool	1913
(Match)	V	16-65	G.Giffen	for	Australians	Manchester	1886

Most Runs – Season	2633	J.T.Tyldesley	(av 56.02)	1901
Most Runs – Career	34222	G.E.Tyldesley	(av 45.20)	1909-36
Most 100s – Season	11	C.Hallows		1928
Most 100s – Career	90	G.E.Tyldesley		1909-36
Most Wkts – Season	198	E.A.McDonald	(av 18.55)	1925
Most Wkts – Career	1816	J.B.Statham	(av 15.12)	1950-68
Most Career W-K Dismissals	925	G.Duckworth	(635 ct; 290 st)	1923-38
Most Career Catches in the Field	556	K.J.Grieves		1949-64

LIMITED-OVERS CRICKET

Highest Total	FPT	381-3		v	Herts	Radlett	1999
	P40	310-7		v	Somerset	Taunton	2003
	T20	220-5		v	Derbyshire	Derby	2009
Lowest Total	FPT	59		v	Worcs	Worcester	1963
	P40	68		v	Yorkshire	Leeds	2000
		68		v	Surrey	The Oval	2002
	T20	91		v	Derbyshire	Manchester	2003
Highest Innings	FPT	162*	A.R.Crook	v	Bucks	Wormsley	2005
	P40	143	A.Flintoff	v	Essex	Chelmsford	1999
	T20	102*	L.Vincent	v	Derbyshire	Manchester	2008
Best Bowling	FPT	6-18	G.Chapple	v	Essex	Lord's	1996
	P40	6-25	G.Chapple	v	Yorkshire	Leeds	1998
	T20	4-12	A.Flintoff	v	Durham	Chester-le-St	2008

LEICESTERSHIRE

Formation of Present Club: 25 March 1879
Inaugural First-Class Match: 1894
Colours: Dark Green and Scarlet
Badge: Gold Running Fox on Green Ground
County Champions: (3) 1975, 1996, 1998
Gillette/NatWest/C&G/FP Trophy Winners: (0); best –
Finalist 1992, 2001
Benson and Hedges Cup Winners: (3) 1972, 1975, 1985
Pro 40/National League (Div 1) Winners: (0); best – 2nd
2001
Sunday League Champions: (2) 1974, 1977
Twenty20 Cup Winners: (2) 2004, 2006

Chief Executive: David Smith, County Ground, Grace Road, Leicester LE2 8AD • Tel:
0871 282 1879 • Fax: 0871 282 1873 • Email: enquiries@leicestershireccc.co.uk • Web:
www.leicestershireccc.co.uk

Senior Coach: Tim Boon. **Head Coach/Academy Director:** Phil Whitticase. **Captain:**
M.J.Hoggard. **Vice-Captain:** tba. **Overseas Players:** A.B.McDonald and B.J.Hodge (T20
only). **2010 Beneficiary:** none. **Head Groundsman:** Andrew Ward. **Scorer:** Graham
A.York. ‡ New registration. [NQ] Not qualified for England.

‡**BENNING, James** Graham Edward (Beacon S; Chesham S; Caterham S), b Mill Hill, N
London 4 May 1983. 6'0". RHB, RM. Surrey 2003-09. Leicestershire debut 2009. Buckinghamshire 2000-01. HS 128 Sy v OU (Oxford) 2004. CC HS 112 Sy v Glos (Oval) 2006. Le
HS 72 v Northants (Northampton) 2009. BB 3-43 v Glamorgan (Leicester) 2009. LO HS
189* Sy v Glos (Bristol) 2006 (CGT). LO BB 4-43 Sy v Leics (Oval) 2003 (NL). T20 HS
88. T20 BB 1-7.

BOYCE, Matthew Andrew Golding (Oakham S; Nottingham U), b Cheltenham, Glos
13 Aug 1985. 5'9". LHB, RM. Debut (Leicestershire) 2006. HS 106 v Warwks (Birmingham) 2008. BB – . LO HS 80 v Hampshire (Leicester) 2009 (FPT). T20 HS 34.

BUCK, Nathan Liam (Newbridge HS; Ashby S), b Leicester 26 Apr 1991. 6'2" RHB, RMF.
Leicestershire 2nd XI debut 2007. England U19s 2008-09 to 2009-10. HS 24* v Derbys
(Leicester) 2009. BB 1-35 v Loughborough UCCE (Leicester) 2009. CC BB 1-73 v Surrey
(Oval) 2009. LO HS 21 and BB 2-38 v Glamorgan (Leicester) 2009 (P40).

CLIFF, Samuel James (Colonel Frank Seely S, Calverton, Notts), b Nottingham 3 Oct
1987. 6'2". RHB, RMF. Debut (Leicestershire) 2007. HS 26 v Northants (Leicester) 2009.
BB 4-42 v Derbys (Leicester) 2008. LO HS 9 v Notts (Nottingham) 2009 (FPT). LO BB
4-26 v Derbys (Leicester) 2008 (P40). T20 HS 4. T20 BB 1-24.

COBB, Joshua James (Oakham S), b Leicester 17 Aug 1990. 5'11½". Son of R.A.Cobb
(Leics and N Transvaal 1980-89). RHB, LB. Debut (Leicestershire) 2007. England U19s
2008-09 to 2009. HS 148* v Middlesex (Lord's) 2008. BB 2-11 v Glos (Leicester) 2008. LO
HS 43 v Northants (Northampton) 2009 (P40). T20 HS 2*.

Du TOIT, Jacques (Elspark S; Oosterlig C; Pretoria U), b Port Elizabeth, South Africa
2 Jan 1980. RHB, RMF. British passport. Easterns 1998-99 to 2004-05. Leicestershire debut
2008. HS 103 v Northants (Leicester) 2008. BB 3-31 v Glos (Leicester) 2008. LO HS 144 v
Glamorgan (Colwyn Bay) 2008 (P40). LO BB 2-30 Easterns v KZ-Natal (Benoni) 2004-05.
T20 HS 39. T20 BB 2-15.

141

GURNEY, Harry Frederick (Garendon HS; Loughborough GS; Leeds U), b Nottingham 25 Oct 1986. 6'2". RHB, LMF. Bradford/Leeds UCCE 2006-07 (not f-c). Debut (Leicestershire) 2007. HS 24* v Middx (Leicester) 2009. BB 5-82 v Surrey (Leicester) 2009. LO HS 0. LO BB 1-16 v Northants (Northampton) 2009 (P40). T20 HS – . T20 BB 3-21.

HARRIS, Andrew James (Hadfield CS; Glossopdale Community C), b Ashton-under-Lyne, Lancs 26 Jun 1973. 6'1". RHB, RM. Derbyshire 1994-99; cap 1996. Nottinghamshire 2000-08; cap 2000; benefit 2008. Gloucestershire (1 match) 2008. Worcestershire (2 matches) 2008. Leicestershire debut 2009. F-c Tour (Eng A): A 1996-97. HS 41* Nt v Northants (Northampton) 2002. Le HS 22* v Kent (Canterbury) 2009. Dismissed 'Timed Out' v DU (Nottingham) 2003 – third instance in f-c cricket. 50 wkts (2); most – 67 (2002). BB 7-54 (11-122 match) Nt v Northants (Nottingham) 2002. Le BB 5-26 v Glos (Leicester) 2009. LO HS 34 Nt v Durham (Nottingham) 2006 (CGT). LO BB Nt 5-35 v Hants (Nottingham) 2000 (NL). T20 HS 6*. T20 BB 2-13.

^{NQ}HENDERSON, Claude William (Worcester HS), b Worcester, Cape Province, South Africa 14 Jun 1972. Elder brother of J.M.Henderson (Boland, Transvaal, North West, Free State and Eagles 1994-95 to 2005-06). 6'1½". RHB, SLA. Boland 1990-91 to 1997-98. W Province 1998-99 to 2003-04. Leicestershire debut/cap 2004 (the first Kolpak registration). Lions 2005-06 to 2007-08. Cape Cobras 2008-09. **Tests** (SA): 7 (2001-02 to 2002-03); HS 30 and BB 4-116 v A (Adelaide) 2001-02. **LOI** (SA): 4 (2001-02); HS – ; BB 4-17 v Z (Harare) 2001-02. F-c Tours (SA): A 2001-02; SL 1998 (SA A); Z 2001-02. HS 81 v Glos (Leicester) 2007. BB 7-57 Boland v EP (Paarl) 1994-95. Le BB 7-74 v Durham (Leicester) 2004. LO HS 45 Lions v Eagles (Johannesburg) 2006-07. LO BB 6-29 Boland v Easterns (Paarl) 1997-98. T20 HS 16. T20 BB 3-23.

‡^{NQ}HODGE, Bradley John (St Bede's C, Mentone; Deakin U), b Sandringham, Victoria, Australia 29 Dec 1974. 5'8". RHB, OB. Victoria 1993-94 to date. Durham 2002. Leicestershire 2003-04; cap 2003; captain 2004 (*part*). Lancashire 2005-08; cap 2006. Signed for 2010 for T20 only. **Tests** (A): 6 (2005-06 to 2008); HS 203* v SA (Perth) 2005-06. BB – . **LOI** (A): 25 (2005-06 to 2007-08); HS 123 v Netherlands (Basseterre, St Kitts) 2006-07; BB 1-17 v Scotland (Basseterre) 2006-07. F-c Tours (A): I 2004-05; WI 2008; P 2005-06 (Aus A); Z 1998-99 (Aus Acad). 1000 runs (2+3); most – 1548 (2004). HS 302* v Notts (Nottingham) 2003. BB 4-17 Aus A v WI (Hobart) 2000-01. CC BB 3-21 La v Warwks (Birmingham) 2006. Le BB 3-35 v LU (Leicester) 2003. LO HS 164 Aus A v SA A (Perth) 2002-03. LO BB 5-28 Aus A v SA A (Canberra) 2002-03. IT20 HS 36. IT20 BB – . T20 HS 106. T20 BB 4-17.

‡HOGGARD, Matthew James (Grangefield S, Pudsey), b Leeds, Yorkshire 31 Dec 1976. 6'2". RHB, RMF. Yorkshire 1996-2009; cap 2000; benefit 2008. Free State 1998-99 to 1999-00. Joins Leicestershire in 2010 as captain. MCC 2004-07. MBE 2005. *Wisden* 2005. **Tests**: 67 (2000 to 2007-08); HS 38 v WI (Oval) 2004; BB 7-61 (12-205 match) v SA (Johannesburg) 2004-05; hat-trick v WI (Bridgetown) 2003-04. **LOI**: 26 (2001-02 to 2005-06); HS 7 v I (Cochin) 2005-06; BB 5-49 v Z (Harare) 2001-02. F-c Tours: A 2002-03, 2006-07; SA 2004-05; WI 2003-04; NZ 2001-02, 2007-08; I 2001-02, 2005-06; P 2000-01, 2005-06; SL 2000-01, 2003-04, 2007-08; B 2003-04. HS 89* Y v Glamorgan (Leeds) 2004. 50 wkts (2); most – 50 (2000, 2005). BB 7-49 Y v Somerset (Leeds) 2003. Hat-tricks (2): (see *Tests*) and v Sussex (Hove) 2009. LO HS 7* (*twice*). LO BB 5-28 Y v Leics (Leicester) 2000 (NL). T20 HS 18. T20 BB 3-23.

‡JEFFERSON, William Ingleby (Beeston Hall S, Norfolk; Oundle S; St Hild & St Bede C, Durham U), b Derby 25 Oct 1979. Son of R.I.Jefferson (Cambridge U and Surrey 1961-66); grandson of J.Jefferson (Army 1919, Comb Services 1922). 6'10". RHB, RMF. British U 2000-02. Essex 2000-06; cap 2002. Durham UCCE 2001-02. Nottinghamshire 2007-09. F-c Tour (Eng A): B 2006-07. 1000 runs (1): 1555 (2004). HS 222 Ex v Hants (Southampton) 2004. BB 1-16 Ex v Yorks (Leeds) 2005. LO HS 132 Ex v Essex CB (Chelmsford) 2003 (CGT). LO BB 2-9 Ex v Worcs (Worcester) 2005 (NL). T20 HS 75.

142

‡**NQMcDONALD, Andrew** Barry, b Wodonga, Victoria, Australia, 15 Jun 1981. 6'4". RHB, RFM. Victoria 2001-02 to date. **Tests** (A): 4 (2008-09); HS 68 v SA (Cape Town) 2008-09; BB 3-25 v SA (Durban) 2008-09). F-c Tours (A): E 2009; SA 2008-09. HS 150* Vic v NSW (Melbourne) 2006-07. BB 6-34 Vic v Q (Brisbane) 2006-07. LO HS 67 Vic v WA (Melbourne) 2008-09. LO BB 4-50 Vic v Q (Brisbane) 2009-10. T20 HS 43. T20 BB 4-21.

MALIK, Muhammad Nadeem (Wilford Meadows CS; Bilborough C), b Nottingham 6 Oct 1982. 6'5". RHB, RFM. Nottinghamshire 2001-03, 2007 – on loan. Worcestershire 2004-07. Leicestershire debut 2008, taking 5-51 (8-119 match) v Middlesex (Leicester). Notts 2nd XI debut 1999 when aged 16y 337d. HS 41 v Essex (Leicester) 2008. BB 6-46 v Essex (Chelmsford) 2008. LO HS 11 Nt v Worcs (Nottingham) 2002 (NL). LO BB 4-42 Wo v Sussex (Worcester) 2004 (NL). T20 HS 3*. T20 BB 4-16.

‡**MASTERS, Daniel** (Medway Community C), b Chatham, Kent, 7 Dec 1986. Son of K.D.Masters (Kent 1983-84), younger brother of D.D.Masters (*see ESSEX*). 6'0". RHB, RFM. Awaiting f-c debut. LO BB 1-49 v Warwks (Birmingham) 2009 (P40) – only 1st XI appearance.

NAIK, Jigar Kumar Hakumatrai (Rushey Mead SS; Gateway SFC; Nottingham Trent U; Loughborough U), b Leicester 10 Aug 1984. 6'2". RHB, OB. Debut (Leicestershire) 2006. Loughborough UCCE 2007. HS 109* v Derbys (Leicester) 2009. BB 3-70 v Bangladesh A (Leicester) 2008. CC BB 2-32 v Glos (Leicester) 2009. LO HS 18 v Derbys (Derby) 2009 (P40). LO BB 3-21 v Lancashire (Leicester) 2009 (P40). T20 HS 7*. T20 BB 2-22.

NEW, Thomas James (Quarrydale S), b Sutton in Ashfield, Notts 18 Jan 1985. 5'10". LHB, RM, WK. Debut (Leicestershire) 2004; cap 2009. Derbyshire 2008 – on loan. HS 125 v OU (Oxford) 2007. CC HS 109 v Middlesex (Leicester) 2008. BB 2-18 v Glos (Leicester) 2007. LO HS 68 v Northants (Oakham) 2006 (CGT). T20 HS 18.

NIXON, Paul Andrew (Ullswater HS, Penrith), b Carlisle, Cumberland 21 Oct 1970. 6'0". LHB, WK, occ RM. Leicestershire 1989-99, 2003 to date; cap 1994; benefit 2007; captain 2007 (*part*) to 2009 (*part*). MCC 1999-00. Kent 2000-02; cap 2000. Cumberland 1987. **LOI**: 19 (2006-07); HS 49 v NZ (Perth) 2006-07. F-c Tours: SA 1996-97 (Le); I 1994-95 (Eng A); P 2000-01; B 1999-00 (MCC). 1000 runs (1): 1046 (1994). HS 173* v Kent (Canterbury) 2009. LO HS 101 v Sri Lanka A (Galle) 1998-99. IT20 HS 31*. T20 HS 65.

POPE, Joel Ian (Whitton S), b Ashford, Middlesex 23 Oct 1988. Nephew of B.J.M.Scott (*see MIDDLESEX*). 5'6". RHB, WK. Middlesex 2nd XI 2006. MCC YC 2007. Leicestershire 2nd XI debut 2007. Awaiting f-c debut. LO HS 9 v Derbys (Leicester) 2008 (P40) – on debut.

SMITH, Gregory Philip (Oundle S; St Hild & St Bede C, Durham U), b Leicester 16 Nov 1988. 6'0". RHB, LBG. Debut (Leicestershire) 2008. England U19s 2008. HS 54 v Derbys (Leicester) 2008. BB 1-64 v Glos (Leicester) 2008. LO HS 58 v Surrey (Oval) 2008 (P40).

TAYLOR, James William Arthur (Shrewsbury S), b Nottingham 6 Jan 1990. RHB, LB. Debut (Leicestershire) 2008; cap 2009. Shropshire 2007. England U19s 2007-08 to 2009. YC 2009. 1000 runs (1): 1207 (2009). HS 207* v Surrey (Oval) 2009. BB – . LO HS 101 v Worcs (Worcester) 2009 (FPT). LO BB – . T20 HS 41*. T20 BB 1-10.

WHITE, Wayne Andrew (John Port S, Etwall; Nottingham Trent U), b Derby 22 Apr 1985. 6'2". RHB, RMF. Derbyshire 2005-08. Leicestershire debut 2009. HS 68 v Glamorgan (Leicester) 2009. BB 5-87 De v Northants (Northampton) 2007. Le BB 3-91 v Kent (Canterbury) 2009. LO HS 46* and BB 4-36 v Glamorgan (Leicester) 2009 (P40). T20 HS 12. T20 BB 3-27.

WYATT, Alexander Charles Frederick (Oakham S), b Roehampton 23 Jul 1990. 6'7". RHB, RMF. Debut (Leicestershire) 2009. Leicestershire 2nd XI debut 2007. HS 3 and BB 3-42 v West Indians (Leicester) 2009. CC HS 1 and BB 2-44 v Glos (Bristol) 2009. LO HS – . LO BB 1-31 (twice) 2009 (FPT). T20 HS – . T20 BB 3-14.

RELEASED/RETIRED
(Having made a County First-Class or List A appearance in 2009)

NQ**ACKERMAN, Hylton** Deon ('**HD**') (Rondebosch BHS), b Cape Town, South Africa 14 Feb 1973. 5'11". Son of H.M.Ackerman (Border, NE Transvaal, Northants, Natal, W Province 1963-64 to 1981-82). RHB, RM. W Province 1993-94 to 2002-03. Gauteng 2003-04. Lions 2004-05. Leicestershire 2005-09; captain/cap 2005 (Kolpak registration). Cape Cobras 2005-06. Warriors 2006-07 to 2007-08. Dolphins 2008-09 to date. **Tests** (SA): 4 (1997-98); HS 57 v P (Durban) 1997-98 – on debut. F-c Tours (SA): E 1996 (SA A); A 1995-96 (WP); SL 1995 (SA U-24), 1998; Z 1996-97 (WP). 1000 runs (3+1); most – 1808 (2006). HS 309* v Glamorgan (Cardiff) 2006 – Le record f-c score. BB – . LO HS 139 v Northants (Northampton) 2008 (FPT). BB – . T20 HS 87.

ALLENBY, J. – *see GLAMORGAN.*

NQ**DIPPENAAR, Hendrik Human ('Boeta')** (Grey C, Bloemfontein; UNISA), Kimberley, South Africa 14 Jun 1977. 5'10½". RHB, OB. Free State 1995-96 to 2003-04. Eagles 2004-05 to date; captain 2007-08 to date. Leicestershire 2008-09; cap 2008; captain 2009 (*part*). Kolpak registration 2009. **Tests** (SA): 38 (1999-00 to 2006-07); HS 177* v B (Chittagong) 2002-03. **LOI** (SA): 107 (1999-00 to 2007); HS 125* v SL (Adelaide) 2005-06. F-c Tours (SA) (C=Captain): E 2003; A 2001-02; WI 1996-97 (FS), 2000-01, 2004-05; I 2004-05, 2007-08C (SA A); P 2003-04; SL 2004, 2006; Z 1999-00, 2001-02, 2007C (SA A); B 2003. 1000 runs (1+1); most – 1121 (2009). HS 250* Eagles v Warriors (Kimberley) 2006-07. Le HS 143 v Surrey (Leicester) 2009. BB 1-6 v West Indians (Leicester) 2009. LO HS 125* (*see LOI*). LO BB 1-5 v Lancashire (Leicester) 2009 (P40). IT20 HS 1. T20 HS 63.

O'BRIEN, I.E. – *see MIDDLESEX.*

LEICESTERSHIRE 2009

RESULTS SUMMARY

	Place	Won	Lost	Tied	Drew	NR
County Championship (2nd Division)	9th	2	3		11	
All First-Class Matches		2	3		13	
FP Trophy (Group A)	4th	2	4			2
Pro40 League (2nd Division)	8th	2	5			1
Twenty20 Cup (North Division)	3rd	5	5			

LV COUNTY CHAMPIONSHIP AVERAGES

BATTING AND FIELDING

Cap		M	I	NO	HS	Runs	Avge	100	50	Ct/St
2009	J.W.A.Taylor	15	25	7	207*	1184	65.77	3	6	8
	J.Allenby	.5	8	2	96	328	54.66	–	4	3
2008	H.H.Dippenaar	15	28	4	143	1074	44.75	2	8	4
2005	H.D.Ackerman	11	20	1	180	741	39.00	1	4	5
	C.D.Crowe	2	4	2	41*	76	38.00	–	–	–
1994	P.A.Nixon	9	17	2	173*	531	35.40	1	2	10
2009	T.J.New	16	27	4	85*	800	34.78	–	6	28/1
	J.G.E.Benning	5	9	2	72	241	34.42	–	1	2
	J.K.H.Naik	5	8	2	109*	184	30.66	1	–	1
	M.A.G.Boyce	14	27	2	98	638	25.52	–	4	4
2004	C.W.Henderson	10	13	2	79*	241	21.90	–	1	1
	J.J.Cobb	12	23	–	95	445	19.34	–	3	4
	G.P.Smith	5	10	1	46	174	19.33	–	–	2
	W.A.White	10	16	1	68	242	16.13	–	1	5
	N.L.Buck	3	4	2	24*	29	14.50	–	–	–
	I.E.O'Brien	7	9	1	31	110	13.75	–	–	1
	H.F.Gurney	8	9	5	24*	53	13.25	–	–	2
	A.J.Harris	16	19	3	22*	143	8.93	–	–	–
	G.W.Walker	3	4	–	13	21	5.25	–	–	–

Also batted: S.J.Cliff (1 match) 26; J.du Toit (2) 100*, 42, 0 (1 ct); C.E.J.Thompson (1) 0, 16; A.C.F.Wyatt (1) 1*, 0

BOWLING

	O	M	R	W	Avge	Best	5wI	10wM
J.Allenby	101.3	29	238	10	23.80	3- 70	–	–
I.E.O'Brien	181.2	38	547	21	26.04	6- 39	2	–
W.A.White	170.3	18	728	18	40.44	3- 91	–	–
A.J.Harris	395.1	79	1439	35	41.11	5- 26	1	–
C.W.Henderson	394.5	70	1044	23	45.39	6-152	1	–
H.F.Gurney	189.5	30	726	15	48.40	5- 82	1	–
Also bowled:								
J.K.H.Naik	104	16	334	8	41.75	2- 32	–	–
J.G.E.Benning	112	20	384	7	54.85	3- 43	–	–

N.L.Buck 74-13-241-2; S.J.Cliff 23-2-92-2; J.J.Cobb 10-1-31-1; C.D.Crowe 66-11-249-3; H.H.Dippenaar 8-0-35-0; J.du Toit 19-1-89-0; T.J.New 8-1-36-0; P.A.Nixon 1.1-0-9-0; J.W.A.Taylor 19-1-82-0; C.E.J.Thompson 15.2-2-45-1; G.W.Walker 50-8-159-2; A.C.F.Wyatt 27-6-83-2.

The First-Class Averages (pp 228–244) give the records of Leicestershire players in all first-class county matches (Leicestershire's other opponents being Loughborough UCCE and the West Indians), with the exception of J.G.E.Benning and G.P.Smith, whose first-class figures for Leicestershire are as above, and:

J.Allenby 7-10-2-96-363-45.37-0-4-4ct. 112.4-33-262-11-23.82-3/70-0-0.

LEICESTERSHIRE RECORDS

FIRST-CLASS CRICKET

Highest Total	For	701-4d		v	Worcs	Worcester	1906
	V	761-6d		by	Essex	Chelmsford	1990
Lowest Total	For	25		v	Kent	Leicester	1912
	V	24		by	Glamorgan	Leicester	1971
		24		by	Oxford U	Oxford	1985
Highest Innings	For	309*	H.D.Ackerman	v	Glamorgan	Cardiff	2006
	V	341	G.H.Hirst	for	Yorkshire	Leicester	1905

Highest Partnership for each Wicket

1st	390	B.Dudleston/J.F.Steele	v	Derbyshire	Leicester	1979
2nd	289*	J.C.Balderstone/D.I.Gower	v	Essex	Leicester	1981
3rd	436*	D.L.Maddy/B.J.Hodge	v	L'boro UCCE	Leicester	2003
4th	290*	P.Willey/T.J.Boon	v	Warwicks	Leicester	1984
5th	322	B.F.Smith/P.V.Simmons	v	Notts	Worksop	1998
6th	284	P.V.Simmons/P.A.Nixon	v	Durham	Chester-le-St	1996
7th	219*	J.D.R.Benson/P.Whitticase	v	Hampshire	Bournemouth	1991
8th	195	J.W.A.Taylor/J.K.H.Naik	v	Derbyshire	Leicester	2009
9th	160	R.T.Crawford/W.W.Odell	v	Worcs	Leicester	1902
10th	228	R.Illingworth/K.Higgs	v	Northants	Leicester	1977

Best Bowling	For	10- 18	G.Geary	v	Glamorgan	Pontypridd	1929
(Innings)	V	10- 32	H.Pickett	for	Essex	Leyton	1895
Best Bowling	For	16- 96	G.Geary	v	Glamorgan	Pontypridd	1929
(Match)	V	16-102	C.Blythe	for	Kent	Leicester	1909

Most Runs – Season		2446	L.G.Berry	(av 52.04)	1937
Most Runs – Career		30143	L.G.Berry	(av 30.32)	1924-51
Most 100s – Season		7	L.G.Berry		1937
		7	W.Watson		1959
		7	B.F.Davison		1982
Most 100s – Career		45	L.G.Berry		1924-51
Most Wkts – Season		170	J.E.Walsh	(av 18.96)	1948
Most Wkts – Career		2131	W.E.Astill	(av 23.18)	1906-39
Most Career W-K Dismissals		905	R.W.Tolchard	(794 ct; 111 st)	1965-83
Most Career Catches in the Field		426	M.R.Hallam		1950-70

LIMITED-OVERS CRICKET

Highest Total	FPT	406-5		v	Berkshire	Leicester	1996
	P40	344-4		v	Durham	Chester-le-St	1996
	T20	221-3		v	Yorkshire	Leeds	2004
Lowest Total	FPT	56		v	Northants	Leicester	1964
	P40	36		v	Sussex	Leicester	1973
	T20	97-9		v	Durham	Leicester	2004
Highest Innings	FPT	201	V.J.Wells	v	Berkshire	Leicester	1996
	P40	154*	B.J.Hodge	v	Sussex	Horsham	2004
	T20	111	D.L.Maddy	v	Yorkshire	Leeds	2004
Best Bowling	FPT	6-16	C.M.Willoughby	v	Somerset	Leicester	2005
	P40	6-17	K.Higgs	v	Glamorgan	Leicester	1973
	T20	5-21	J.Allenby	v	Lancashire	Manchester	2008

MIDDLESEX

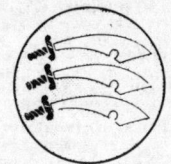

Formation of Present Club: 2 February 1864
Inaugural First-Class Match: 1864
Colours: Blue
Badge: Three Seaxes
County Champions (since 1890): (10) 1903, 1920, 1921,
1947, 1976, 1980, 1982, 1985, 1990, 1993
Joint Champions: (2) 1949, 1977
Gillette/NatWest/C&G/FP Trophy Winners: (4) 1977,
1980, 1984, 1988
Benson and Hedges Cup Winners: (2) 1983, 1986
Pro 40/National League (Div 1) Winners: (0); best – 1st
(Div 2) 2004
Sunday League Winners: (1) 1992
Twenty20 Cup Winners: (1) 2008

Secretary: Vincent J.Codrington, Lord's Cricket Ground, London NW8 8QN • Tel: 020
7289 1300 • Fax: 020 7289 5831 • Email: enquiries@middlesexccc.com • Web:
www.middlesexccc.com

Director of Cricket: Angus R.C.Fraser. **Head Coach:** Richard J.Scott. **Assistant Coach:**
Richard L.Johnson. **Captain:** S.D.Udal. **Vice-Captain:** tba. **Overseas Player:** A.C.Gilchrist
and I.E.O'Brien. **2010 Beneficiary:** none. **Head Groundsman:** Mick Hunt. **Scorer:** Don
K.Shelley. ‡ New registration. ᴺᵠ Not qualified for England.

BERG, Gareth Kyle (South African College S), b Cape Town, South Africa 18 Jan 1981.
6'0". RHB, RMF. England qualified through residency. Debut (Middlesex) 2008. Western
Province Academy (1999-00) and WP B (2001-02 to 2002-03). Northants 2nd XI 2004.
Middlesex 2nd XI 2007 (Kolpak registration). HS 98 v Kent (Canterbury) 2009. BB 5-55 v
Glos (Lord's) 2009. LO HS 65 v Surrey (Lord's) 2008 (FPT). LO BB 4-50 v Surrey (Oval)
2008. T20 HS 33. T20 BB 2-31.

BURTON, David Alexander (Sacred Heart RC SS; Lambeth C), b Dulwich, London 23 Aug
1985. 5'11". RHB, RMF. Gloucestershire 2006; cap 2006. Middlesex debut 2008. MCC YC
2006. HS 52* Gs v Glamorgan (Cardiff) 2006 – on debut. M HS 2* v Derbys (Uxbridge)
2009. BB 5-68 v Glos (Bristol) 2009. LO HS 2 v Kent (Canterbury) 2009 (P40). LO BB
1-26 v Leics (Lord's) 2009 (P40). T20 HS – . T20 BB 2-13.

‡DAVEY, Joshua Henry ('**Josh**') (Culford S), b Aberdeen, Scotland 3 Aug 1990. RHB, RM.
Middlesex 2nd XI debut 2008. Suffolk 2009. Awaiting 1st XI debut.

ᴺᵠDEXTER, Neil John (Northwood HS, Durban; Varsity C; U of South Africa), b
Johannesburg, South Africa 21 Aug 1984. 6'0". RHB, RM. Kent 2005-08. Essex 2008.
Middlesex debut 2009 (Kolpak registration). HS 146 (and 118) v Kent (Uxbridge) 2009. BB
2-37 v Glamorgan (Lord's) 2009 – on M debut. LO HS 135* K v Glamorgan (Cardiff) 2006
(CGT). LO BB 3-17 K v Leics (Canterbury) 2006 (P40). T20 HS 73. T20 BB 3-27.

EVANS, Daniel (Brierton CS, Hartlepool), b Hartlepool, Co Durham 24 Jul 1987. 6'5".
RHB, RFM. Debut (Middlesex) 2007. Durham 2nd XI 2004-06. HS 12* v Worcs (Lord's)
2008. BB 6-35 v Essex (Chelmsford) 2008. LO HS 1* v Warwks (Birmingham) 2009 (FPT).
LO BB 3-36 v Surrey (Oval) 2008. T20 HS 5*. T20 BB – .

FINN, Steven Thomas (Parmiter's S, Garston), b Watford, Herts 4 Apr 1989. 6'5½". RHB,
RFM. Debut (Middlesex) 2005; cap 2009. F-c Tour: B 2009-10. HS 26* v Worcs
(Kidderminster) 2008. 50 wkts (1): 53 (2009). BB 5-57 v Essex (Chelmsford) 2009. LO HS
13 v Kent (Southgate) 2009 (FPT). LO BB 3-23 v Somerset (Taunton) 2007 (P40). T20 HS
8. T20 BB 3-22.

147

‡^{NQ}**GILCHRIST, Adam** Craig, b Bellingen, NSW, Australia 14 Nov 1971. 6'1". LHB, occ OB, WK. NSW 1992-93 to 1993-94. WA 1994-95 to 2007-08. Middlesex T20 contract for summer 2010. **Tests** (A): 96 (1999-00 to 2007-08); HS 204* v SA (Johannesburg) 2001-02. **LOI** (A): 287 (1996-97 to 2007-08); HS 172 v Z (Hobart) 2003-04. F-c Tours: E 1995 (Young A), 1997, 2001, 2005; SA 2001-02, 2005-06; WI 2002-03; NZ 1999-00, 2004-05; I 2000-01, 2004-05; SL/UAE 2002-03; SL 2003-04; B 2005-06. HS 204* (*see Tests*). LO HS 172 (*see LOIs*). LO BB – . IT20 HS 48. T20 HS 109*.

HOUSEGO, Daniel Mark (Oratory S, Reading), b Windsor, Berkshire 12 Oct 1988. RHB, LB. Debut (Middlesex) 2008. Middlesex 2nd XI debut 2005. Berkshire 2006. England U19s 2007. HS 36 v Derbys (Derby) 2008 – on debut. BB – . T20 HS 18.

LONDON, Adam Brian (Bishop Wand S, Sunbury), b Ashford 12 Oct 1988. 5'8". LHB, OB. Debut (Middlesex) 2009. Middlesex 2nd XI debut 2006. HS 68 v Glos (Lord's) 2009 – on debut. BB – . LO HS and BB – .

MALAN, Dawid Johannes (Paarl HS), b Roehampton, Surrey 3 Sep 1987. Son of D.J.Malan (WP B and Transvaal B 1978-79 to 1981-82), elder brother of C.C.Malan (Loughborough UCCE 2009). LHB, LB. Boland 2005-06. MCC YC 2006-07. Middlesex debut 2008. HS 132* v Northants (Uxbridge) 2008 – on M debut. BB 2-21 v Leics (Southgate) 2009. LO HS 60 v Surrey (Oval) 2009 (P40). LO BB 2-4 v Scotland (Edinburgh) 2009 (FPT). T20 HS 103 v Lancashire (Oval) 2008 – M record. T20 BB 2-10.

MORGAN, Eoin Joseph Gerard (Catholic University S), b Dublin, Ireland 10 Sep 1986. 6'0". LHB, RM. British passport. Ireland 2004 to 2007-08. Middlesex debut 2006; cap 2008. **LOI** (E/Ire): 38 (23 for Ire 2006 to 2008-09; 15 for E 2009 to 2009-10); HS 115 Ire v Canada (Nairobi) 2006-07. F-c Tours (Ire): NZ 2008-09 (Eng A); Namibia 2005-06; UAE 2006-07, 2007-08. 1000 runs (1): 1085 (2008). HS 209* Ire v UAE (Abu Dhabi) 2006-07. CC HS 137* v Glos (Bristol) 2008. BB 2-24 v Notts (Lord's) 2007. LO HS 161 v Kent (Canterbury) 2009 (FPT). LO BB – . IT20 HS 85* v SA (Johannesburg) 2009-10 – E record. T20 HS 85*.

MURTAGH, Timothy James (John Fisher S; St Mary's C), b Lambeth, London 2 Aug 1981. Elder brother of C.P.Murtagh (*see SURREY*); nephew of A.J.Murtagh (Hampshire and E Province 1973-77). 6'0". LHB, RFM. British U 2000-03. Surrey 2001-06. Middlesex debut 2007; cap 2008. HS 74* Sy v Middlesex (Oval) 2004 and 74* Sy v Warwks (Croydon) 2005. M HS 51* v Leics (Southgate) 2009. 50 wkts (2); most – 64 (2008). BB 7-82 v Derbys (Derby) 2009. LO HS 35* v Surrey (Lord's) 2008 (FPT). LO BB 4-14 Sy v Derbys (Derby) 2005 (NL). T20 HS 40*. T20 BB 6-24 Sy v Middlesex (Lord's) 2005 – Sy record and 2nd best UK figs.

‡**NEWMAN, Scott** Alexander (Trinity S, Croydon; Coulsdon C; Brighton U), b Epsom, Surrey 3 Nov 1979. 6'2". LHB, RM. Surrey 2002-09, scoring 99 v Hampshire on debut; cap 2005. Nottinghamshire 2009 (on loan). F-c Tour (Eng A): I 2003-04. 1000 runs (4); most – 1404 (2006). HS 219 (and 117) Sy v Glamorgan (Oval) 2005. LO HS 177 v Yorks (Oval) 2009 (FPT). T20 HS 81*.

‡^{NQ}**O'BRIEN, Iain** Edward, b Lower Hutt, Wellington, New Zealand 10 Jul 1976. RHB, RFM. Wellington 2000-01 to date. Leicestershire 2009. **Tests** (NZ): 22 (2004-05 to 2009-10); HS 31 v P (Wellington) 2009-10; BB 6-75 v WI (Napier) 2008-09. **LOI** (NZ): 10 (2007-08 to 2008-09); HS 3* v I (Napier) 2008-09; BB 3-68 v A (Sydney) 2008-09. F-c Tours (NZ): E 2008; A 2008-09; SA 2007-08; SL 2005-06 (NZ A), 2009; B 2008-09. HS 44 Wellington v Canterbury (Wellington) 2006-07. CC HS 31 Le v Glos (Bristol) 2009. BB 8-55 (13-117 match) Wellington v Auckland (Wellington) 2006-07. CC BB 6-39 Le v Middx (Leicester) 2009. LO HS 19* Wellington v Canterbury (Christchurch) 2008-09. LO BB 5-35 Wellington v CD (Wellington) 2004-05. IT20 HS – . IT20 BB 2-30. T20 HS 3*. T20 BB 5-23.

^{NQ}**ROBSON, Sam** David (Marcellin C, Randwick), b Paddington, Sydney, NSW, Australia 1 Jul 1989. RHB, LBG. Debut (Middlesex) 2009. Middlesex 2nd XI debut 2008. Australia U19s 2007 to 2007-08. HS 110 v Essex (Lord's) 2009. BB – . LO HS 48 v Hampshire (Southampton) 2009 (FPT).

‡**ROLAND-JONES, Tobias** Skelton ('*Toby*'), b Ashford 29 Jan 1988. 6'4" RHB, RMF. Middlesex 2nd XI debut 2008. Leeds/Bradford UCCE 2009. Awaiting 1st XI debut.

SCOTT, Ben James Matthew (Whitton S, Richmond; Richmond C), b Isleworth 4 Aug 1981. Uncle of J.I.Pope (*see LEICESTERSHIRE*). 5'8". RHB, WK. Surrey 2003. Middlesex debut 2004; cap 2007. MCC YC 2000. On loan to Worcestershire for first part of 2010 season. F-c Tour (Eng A): NZ 2008-09. HS 164* v Northants (Uxbridge) 2008. BB – . LO HS 73* v Surrey (Southgate) 2006 (CGT). T20 HS 32*.

SHAH, Owais Alam (Isleworth & Syon S), b Karachi, Pakistan 22 Oct 1978. 6'0". RHB, OB. Debut (Middlesex) 1996; cap 2000; captain 2004 (*part*); benefit 2008. MCC 2002-08. YC 2001. **Tests**: 6 (2005-06 to 2008-09); HS 88 v I (Bombay) 2005-06. **LOI**: 71 (2001 to 2009-10); HS 107* v I (Oval) 2007; BB 3-15 v Ire (Belfast) 2009. F-c Tours (Eng A): A 1996-97; WI 2005-06 (*part*), 2008-09 (Eng); I 2005-06 (Eng – *part*); SL 1997-98, 2004-05, 2007-08 (Eng). 1000 runs (8); most – 1728 (2005). HS 203 v Derbys (Southgate) 2001. BB 3-33 v Glos (Bristol) 1999. LO HS 134 v Sussex (Arundel) 1999 (NL). LO BB 4-11 v Leics (Lord's) 2009 (P40). IT20 HS 55*. T20 HS 79. T20 BB 1-10.

SIMPSON, John Andrew (St Gabriel's RC HS), b Bury, Lancs 13 Jul 1988. 5'10". LHB, WK. Debut (Middlesex) 2009. Lancashire 2nd XI debut 2004. Cumberland 2007. MCC YCs 2008. England U19s 2004-05 to 2006. HS 87 v Northants (Northampton) 2009 – on debut. LO HS 32 v Northants (Uxbridge) 2009 (P40). T20 HS 13.

‡**SMITH, Thomas** Michael John (Seaford Head Community C; Sussex Downs C), b Eastbourne, Sussex 22 Aug 1987. 5'9". RHB, SLA. Sussex 2007-09. No f-c appearances in 2008. Surrey 2009 (l-o only). HS 10 Sx v Lancs (Hove) 2009. BB 1-52 Sx v Sri Lanka A (Hove) 2007 – on debut. LO HS 65 Sy v Leics (Leicester) 2009 (P40). BB 2-45 Sx v Durham (Chester-le-St) 2006 (P40). T20 HS 3*. T20 BB – .

‡^{NO}**STIRLING, Paul** Robert, b Ireland 3 Sep 1990. RHB, OB. Ireland 2007-08 to date. **LOI** (Ire): 6 (2008 to 2009); HS 84 v Kenya (Dublin) 2009. HS 100 Ire v Kenya (Eglinton) 2009. BB – . LO HS 84 (*see LOI*). IT20 HS 17. T20 HS 20.

STRAUSS, Andrew John (Radley C; Durham U), b Johannesburg, South Africa 2 Mar 1977. 5'11". LHB, LM. Debut (Middlesex) 1998; cap 2001; captain 2002 (*part*) to 2004 (*part*); benefit 2009. MCC 2002. Northern Districts 2007-08. Oxfordshire 1996. British U (List A) 1997-98. *Wisden* 2004. MBE 2005. **ECB central contract 2009-10. Tests**: 71 (2004 to 2009-10, 21 as captain); HS 177 v NZ (Napier) 2007-08. Scored 112 & 83 (run out) v NZ (Lord's) on debut and 126 & 94* v SA (Pt Elizabeth) 2004-05 on his debut overseas. **LOI**: 99 (2003-04 to 2009-10, 34 as captain); HS 152 v B (Nottingham) 2005; BB – . F-c Tours (C=captain): A 2006-07; SA 2004-05, 2009-10C; WI 2008-09C; NZ 2007-08; I 2005-06, 2008-09; P 2005-06. 1000 runs (4); most – 1529 (2003). HS 177 (*see Tests*). M HS 176 v Durham (Lord's) 2001. BB 1-16 v Notts (Lord's) 2007. LO HS 163 v Surrey (Oval) 2008 (FPT) – M record. BB – . IT20 HS 33. T20 HS 60.

TOOR, Kabir Singh (John Lyon S, Harrow), b Northwood, Herts 30 Apr 1990. RHB, LB. Middlesex 2nd XI debut 2006, when aged 16 years 87 days. Awaiting f-c debut. LO HS 5 v Northants (Uxbridge) 2009 (P40). LO BB 1-25 v Derbys (Uxbridge) 2009 (P40).

UDAL, Shaun David (Cove CS), b Cove, Farnborough, Hants 18 Mar 1969. Grandson of G.F.U.Udal (Middlesex and RAF 1932; Leics 1946); great great grandson of J.S.Udal (MCC 1871-75; Fiji 1894-95). 6'2". RHB, OB. Hampshire 1989-2007; cap 1992; benefit 2002. Middlesex debut/cap 2008; captain 2009 to date. **Tests**: 4 (2005-06); HS 33* v P (Faisalabad) 2005-06; BB 4-14 v I (Bombay) 2005-06. **LOI**: 11 (1994 to 2005-06); HS 11* v Z (Brisbane) 1994-95; BB 2-37 v A (Sydney) 1994-95. F-c Tours: A 1994-95; I 2005-06; P 1995-96 (Eng A); 2005-06. HS 117* H v Warwks (Southampton) 1997. M HS 91 v Worcs (Lord's) 2008. 50 wkts (7); most – 74 (1993). BB 8-50 H v Sussex (Southampton) 1992. M BB 6-36 (10-95 match) v Glamorgan (Swansea) 2009. LO HS 79* v Scotland (Edinburgh) 2009 (FPT). LO BB 5-43 H v Surrey (Oval) 1998 (SL). T20 HS 40*. T20 BB 3-19.

WILLIAMS, Robert Edward Morgan (Marlborough C; St Mary's C, Durham U); b Pembury, Kent 19 Jan 1987. 6'0". RHB, RMF. Durham UCCE 2007-09. MCC 2007. Middlesex debut 2007; no 1st XI appearances in 2008 after a stress fracture in his back. HS 15 and M BB 5-112 v Essex (Chelmsford) 2007 – on M debut. BB 5-70 DU v Lancs (Durham) 2007. LO HS – and BB – .

COMPTON, N.R.D. – *see SOMERSET.*

GODLEMAN, B.A. – *see ESSEX.*

^NQ^**HENDERSON, Tyron** (Durban HS), b Durban, Natal, South Africa 1 Aug 1974. Grandson of J.K.Henderson (N.E.Transvaal 1950-51). Great nephew of W.A.Henderson (N.E.Transvaal 1937-38 to 1946-47). 6'2". RHB, RFM. Border 1998-99 to 2003-04. Warriors 2004-05 to 2005-06. Kent 2006. Lions 2006-07. Cape Cobras 2007-08. Boland 2007-08. No f-c appearances for Middlesex 2008-09; cap 2008 (Kolpak registration). Berkshire 2002-03. F-c Tours (SA A): SL 2005-06; Ire/Scot 1999 (SA Acad). HS 81 Border v Gauteng (Johannesburg) 1999-00. UK HS 59 K v Hampshire (Canterbury) 2006. BB 7-67 (10-115 match) Boland v WP (Paarl) 2007-08. UK BB 5-44 SA Acad v Scotland (Linlithgow) 1999. CC BB 4-29 K v Lancashire (Canterbury) 2006. LO HS 126* Border v GW (Kimberley) 2003-04. LO BB 5-5 Border v WP (E London) 1998-99. IT20 HS 0. IT20 BB – . T20 HS 85. T20 BB 4-29.

^NQ^**HUGHES, Phillip** Joel, Macksville, NSW, Australia 30 Nov 1988. LHB, OB. NSW 2007-08 to date. Middlesex 2009, scoring 118 and 65* on debut. **Tests** (A): 6 (2008-09 to 2009-10); HS 160 and 115) v SA (Durban) 2008-09. F-c Tours (A): E 2009; SA 2008-09; I 2008-09 (Aus A). HS 198 NSW v S Australia (Adelaide) 2008-09. M HS 195 v Surrey (Oval) 2009. LO HS 119 v Somerset (Lord's) 2009 (FPT). T20 HS 83.

KARTIK, M. – *see SOMERSET.*

NASH, David Charles (Sunbury Manor S; Malvern C), b Chertsey, Surrey 19 Jan 1978. 5'8". RHB, occ LB, WK. Middlesex 1997-2009; cap 2000; benefit 2007. F-c Tour (Eng A): SL 1997-98. HS 114 v Somerset (Lord's) 1998. BB 1-8 v Essex (Chelmsford) 1997. LO HS 67 v Sussex (Lord's) 2002 (BHC).

RICHARDSON, A. – *see WORCESTERSHIRE.*

SILVERWOOD, Christopher Eric Wilfred (Garforth CS), b Pontefract, Yorks 5 Mar 1975. 6'1". RHB, RFM. Yorkshire 1993-2005; cap 1996; benefit 2004. MCC 1996. Middlesex 2006-09; cap 2006. Mashonaland Eagles 2009-10. YC 1996. **Tests**: 6 (1996-97 to 2002-03); HS 10 v A (Perth) 2002-03; BB 5-91 v SA (Cape Town) 1999-00. **LOI**: 7 (1996-97 to 2001-02); HS 12 v NZ (Auckland) 1996-97; BB 3-43 v Z (Bulawayo) 2001-02. F-c Tours: A 2002-03 (*part*); SA 1999-00 (*part*); WI 1997-98, 2000-01 (Eng A); NZ 1996-97; Z 1995-96 (Y), 1996-97. HS 80 Y v Durham (Chester-le-St) 2005. M HS 50 v Sussex (Horsham) 2006. 50 wkts (3); most – 63 (2006). BB 7-93 (12-148 match) Y v Kent (Leeds) 1997. M BB 6-49 v Somerset (Lord's) 2007. LO HS 61 Y v Northants (Northampton) 2002 (CGT). LO BB 5-28 Y v Scot (Leeds) 1996 (BHC). T20 HS 18*. T20 BB 2-22.

MIDDLESEX 2009

RESULTS SUMMARY

	Place	Won	Lost	Tied	Drew	NR
County Championship (2nd Division)	8th	2	7		7	
All First-Class Matches		2	7		7	
FP Trophy (Group B)	QF	4	5			
Pro40 League (2nd Division)	2nd	5	1			2
Twenty20 Cup (South Division)	6th	2	8			

LV COUNTY CHAMPIONSHIP AVERAGES
BATTING AND FIELDING

Cap		M	I	NO	HS	Runs	Avge	100	50	Ct/St
	P.J.Hughes	3	5	1	195	574	143.50	3	2	4
2001	A.J.Strauss	3	5	–	150	295	59.00	1	1	2
2000	O.A.Shah	8	16	2	159	591	42.21	2	2	5
	N.J.Dexter	10	19	2	146	709	41.70	2	5	15
	D.J.Malan	15	28	3	88	930	37.20	–	8	19
	S.D.Robson	7	13	–	110	441	33.92	1	2	12
2006	N.R.D.Compton	14	28	2	178	860	33.07	2	3	8
	G.K.Berg	13	23	2	98	668	31.80	–	7	9
	J.A.Simpson	3	6	–	87	170	28.33	–	1	5
	A.B.London	4	8	1	68	190	27.14	–	2	1
2008	E.J.G.Morgan	10	18	1	114*	413	24.29	1	1	12
2007	M.Kartik	10	19	5	62*	336	24.00	–	2	11
2008	S.D.Udal	14	24	4	55	398	19.90	–	1	4
2000	D.C.Nash	5	8	–	43	152	19.00	–	–	16
2008	T.J.Murtagh	13	20	6	51*	249	17.78	–	1	2
	B.A.Godleman	5	9	–	48	160	17.77	–	–	3
2006	C.E.W.Silverwood	5	8	1	46	113	16.14	–	–	2
	D.M.Housego	3	6	–	34	86	14.33	–	–	2
2005	A.Richardson	6	7	4	18*	40	13.33	–	–	5
2007	B.J.M.Scott	8	14	1	44	167	12.84	–	–	18/2
2009	S.T.Finn	14	22	4	24*	107	5.94	–	–	4
	D.A.Burton	2	4	2	2*	3	1.50	–	–	–

Also played: D.Evans (1 match) did not bat.

BOWLING

	O	M	R	W	Avge	Best	5wI	10wM
M.Kartik	317.1	103	755	33	22.87	5-65	1	–
T.J.Murtagh	443	81	1521	60	25.35	7-82	3	–
S.D.Udal	368.5	67	1007	37	27.21	6-36	2	1
S.T.Finn	418.3	64	1624	53	30.64	5-57	1	–
G.K.Berg	249.1	46	886	23	38.52	5-55	2	–
A.Richardson	222.2	53	618	11	56.18	3-52	–	–
Also bowled:								
D.A.Burton	53.2	3	249	8	31.12	5-68	1	–
N.J.Dexter	88	25	266	6	44.33	2-37	–	–
D.J.Malan	96.4	10	358	7	51.14	2-21	–	–

N.R.D.Compton 2-0-5-0; D.Evans 42-3-190-3; D.M.Housego 1.1-0-17-0; P.J.Hughes 3-0-9-0;
A.B.London 8-0-39-0; S.D.Robson 2-0-5-0; O.A.Shah 1-0-1-0; C.E.W.Silverwood
115-21-355-4; A.J.Strauss 2-1-10-0.

Middlesex played no first-class fixtures outside the County Championship in 2009. The
First-Class Averages (pp 228–244) give the records of Middlesex players in all first-class
county matches, with the exception of P.J.Hughes, E.J.G.Morgan and A.J.Strauss, whose
first-class figures for Middlesex are as above.

MIDDLESEX RECORDS

FIRST-CLASS CRICKET

Highest Total	For	642-3d		v	Hampshire	Southampton	1923
	V	850-7d		by	Somerset	Taunton	2007
Lowest Total	For	20		v	MCC	Lord's	1864
	V	31		by	Glos	Bristol	1924
Highest Innings	For	331*	J.D.B.Robertson	v	Worcs	Worcester	1949
	V	341	C.M.Spearman	for	Glos	Gloucester	2004

Highest Partnership for each Wicket

1st	372	M.W.Gatting/J.L.Langer	v	Essex	Southgate	1998
2nd	380	F.A.Tarrant/J.W.Hearne	v	Lancashire	Lord's	1914
3rd	424*	W.J.Edrich/D.C.S.Compton	v	Somerset	Lord's	1948
4th	325	J.W.Hearne/E.H.Hendren	v	Hampshire	Lord's	1919
5th	338	R.S.Lucas/T.C.O'Brien	v	Sussex	Hove	1895
6th	270	J.D.Carr/P.N.Weekes	v	Glos	Lord's	1994
7th	271*	E.H.Hendren/F.T.Mann	v	Notts	Nottingham	1925
8th	182*	M.H.C.Doll/H.R.Murrell	v	Notts	Lord's	1913
9th	160*	E.H.Hendren/T.J.Durston	v	Essex	Leyton	1927
10th	230	R.W.Nicholls/W.Roche	v	Kent	Lord's	1899

Best Bowling	For	10- 40	G.O.B.Allen	v	Lancashire	Lord's	1929
(Innings)	V	9- 38	R.C.R.Glasgow†	for	Somerset	Lord's	1924
Best Bowling	For	16-114	G.Burton	v	Yorkshire	Sheffield	1888
(Match)		16-114	J.T.Hearne	v	Lancashire	Manchester	1898
	V	16-100	J.E.B.B.P.Q.C.Dwyer	for	Sussex	Hove	1906

Most Runs – Season		2669	E.H.Hendren	(av 83.41)	1923
Most Runs – Career		40302	E.H.Hendren	(av 48.81)	1907-37
Most 100s – Season		13	D.C.S.Compton		1947
Most 100s – Career		119	E.H.Hendren		1907-37
Most Wkts – Season		158	F.J.Titmus	(av 14.63)	1955
Most Wkts – Career		2361	F.J.Titmus	(av 21.27)	1949-82
Most Career W-K Dismissals		1223	J.T.Murray	(1024 ct; 199 st)	1952-75
Most Career Catches in the Field		561	E.H.Hendren		1907-37

LIMITED-OVERS CRICKET

Highest Total	FPT	341-7		v	Somerset	Lord's	2009
	P40	337-5		v	Somerset	Southgate	2003
	T20	210-6		v	Hampshire	Southampton	2005
Lowest Total	FPT	41		v	Essex	Westcliff	1972
	P40	23		v	Yorkshire	Leeds	1974
	T20	104-6		v	Kent	Canterbury	2009
Highest Innings	FPT	163	A.J.Strauss	v	Surrey	The Oval	2008
	P40	147*	M.R.Ramprakash	v	Worcs	Lord's	1990
	T20	103	D.J.Malan	v	Lancashire	The Oval	2008
Best Bowling	FPT	6-15	W.W.Daniel	v	Sussex	Hove	1980
	P40	6- 6	R.W.Hooker	v	Surrey	Lord's	1969
	T20	5-13	M.Kartik	v	Essex	Lord's	2007

† R.C.Robertson-Glasgow

NORTHAMPTONSHIRE

Formation of Present Club: 31 July 1878
Inaugural First-Class Match: 1905
Colours: Maroon
Badge: Tudor Rose
County Champions: (0); best – 2nd 1912, 1957, 1965, 1976
Gillette/NatWest/C&G/FP Trophy Winners: (2) 1976, 1992
Benson and Hedges Cup Winners: (1) 1980
Pro 40/National League (Div 1) Winners: (0); best – 2nd 2006, 2007
Sunday League Winners: (0); best – 3rd 1991
Twenty20 Cup Winners: (0); best – Semi-Finalist 2009

Chief Executive: Mark J.Tagg, County Ground, Wantage Road, Northampton, NN1 4TJ •
Tel: 01604 514455 • **Fax:** 01604 609288 • **Email:** post@nccc.co.uk • **Web:** www.nccc.co.uk

First XI Coach: David J.Capel. **Captain:** N.Boje. **Vice-Captain:** none. **Overseas Player:** none. **2010 Beneficiary:** none. **Head Groundsman:** Paul Marshall. **Scorer:** A.C. (Tony) Kingston. ‡ New registration. ^{NQ} Not qualified for England.

^{NQ}**BOJE,** Nico ('*Nicky*') (Grey C, Bloemfontein), b Bloemfontein, South Africa 20 Mar 1973. 5'10". Brother of E.H.L.Boje (OFS 1989-1990 to 1990-91). LHB, SLA. (Orange) Free State 1990-91 to 2001-02. Nottinghamshire 2002. Eagles 2004-05 to 2006-07. Northamptonshire debut 2007 (Kolpak registration); cap 2008; captain 2008 to date. Tests (SA): 43 (1999-00 to 2006); HS 85 v I (Bangalore) 1999-00; BB 5-62 v SL (Colombo) 2000-01. LOI (SA): 115 (1995-96 to 2005-06); HS 129 v NZ (Pretoria) 2000-01; BB 5-21 v A (Cape Town) 2001-02. Tours (SA): E 1996 (SA A); A 2001-02, 2002-03 (SA A), 2005-06; WI 2000-01, 2004-05; NZ 1998-99, 2003-04; I 1996-97, 1999-00; SL 1995 (SA U-24), 1998 (SA A), 2000, 2004, 2006; Z 1994-95. HS 226* v Worcs (Northampton) 2008. BB 8-93 Eagles v Dolphins (Durban) 2004-05. Nh BB 6-110 v Leics (Leicester) 2007. LO HS 129 (*see LOI*). LO BB 5-21 (*see LOI*). IT20 HS – . IT20 BB 1-27. T20 HS 58*. T20 BB 3-10.

BROOKS, Jack Alexander (Wheatley Park S), b Oxford 4 Jun 1984. 6'2". RHB, RFM. Debut Oxfordshire 2009. Oxfordshire 2004-09. HS 10* v Australians (Northampton) and v Glam (Northampton) 2009. BB 4-76 v Derbys (Chesterfield) 2009. LO HS 10 v Middlesex (Uxbridge) 2009 (P40). LO BB – .

DAGGETT, Lee Martin (Woodhey HS, and Holy Cross C, Bury; Durham U) b Bury, Lancs 1 Oct 1982. 6'0". RHB, RFM. Durham UCCE 2003-05. British U 2004. Warwickshire 2006-08. Leicestershire 2008. Northamptonshire debut 2009. HS 33 Wa v Durham (Chester-le-St) 2007. Nh HS 2 v Essex (Chelmsford) 2009. BB 8-94 DU v Durham (Chester-le-St) 2004. CC BB 6-30 Wa v Durham (Birmingham) 2006. Nh BB 3-39 v Surrey (Oval) 2009. LO HS 14* and BB 4-51 v Derbys (Northampton) 2009 (FPT). T20 HS 3*. T20 BB 2-19.

^{NQ}**HALL,** Andrew James (Alberton HS), b Alberton, Johannesburg, South Africa 31 Jul 1975. 6'0". RHB, RFM. Transvaal/Gauteng 1995-96 to 2000-01. Easterns 2001-02 to 2003-04. Worcestershire 2003-04. Lions 2004-05 to 2005-06. Kent 2005-07; cap 2005. Northamptonshire debut 2008 (Kolpak registration); cap 2009. Dolphins 2009-10. Durham CB 1999. Suffolk 2002. Tests (SA): 21 (2001-02 to 2006-07); HS 163 v I (Kanpur) 2004-05; BB 3-1 v SL (Johannesburg) 2002-03. LOI (SA): 88 (1998-99 to 2007); HS 81 v SL (Galle) 2006-07; BB 5-18 v E (Bridgetown) 2006-07. F-c Tours (SA): E 2003; WI 2004-05; I 2004-05; SL 2006; Z 1995-96 (Transvaal B), 2007-08 (SA A). 1000 runs (1): 1161 (2009). HS 163 (*see Tests*). UK HS 159 v Leics (Northampton) 2009. BB 6-77 (11-99 match) Easterns v WP (Port Elizabeth) 2002-03. UK BB 5-29 v Essex (Northampton) 2009. LO HS 129* Gauteng v Border (E London) 1999-00. LO BB 5-18 (*see LOI*). IT20 HS 11. IT20 BB 3-22. T20 HS 66* and T20 BB 6-21 v Worcs (Northampton) 2008 (Nh record analysis, and 1st man in UK to score 50 and take 5 wkts in a game).

HARRISON, Paul William (Forest S and Collyer's C, Horsham; Loughborough U), b Cuckfield, Sussex 22 May 1984. 6'2". RHB, RM, WK. Loughborough UCCE 2004-06. Warwickshire (one non-CC match) 2005. British U 2006. Leicestershire 2006-07. Northamptonshire debut 2009. HS 54 LU v Notts (Nottingham) 2005. Nh and CC HS 32 v Essex (Chelmsford) 2009. LO HS 61 Le v Yorks (Scarborough) 2006 (P40). T20 HS 26.

HOWGEGO, Benjamin Henry Nicholas (*'Ben'*) (King's S, Ely; Stowe S; Exeter U), b King's Lynn, Norfolk 3 Mar 1988. 5'11". LHB, RM. Debut (Northamptonshire) 2008. Northamptonshire 2nd XI debut 2005. HS 47 v Middx (Lord's) 2009. LO HS 7 v Middx (Uxbridge) 2009 (P40).

‡**LOYE, Malachy** Bernhard (Moulton S), b Northampton 27 Sep 1972. 6'2". RHB, OB. Northamptonshire 1991-2002; cap 1994. PCA 1998. Lancashire 2003-09, scoring 126 v Surrey (Oval) and 113 v Notts (Manchester) in his first two innings; cap 2003; benefit 2008. Auckland 2006-07. **LOI:** 7 (2006-07); HS 45 v A (Sydney) 2006-07. F-c Tours (Eng A): SA 1993-94, 1998-99; Z 1994-95 (Nh), 1998-99. 1000 runs (6); most – 1296 (2006). HS 322* v Glamorgan (Northampton) 1998 – record Nh score until 2001. BB 1-8 La v Kent (Blackpool) 2003. Nh BB – . LO HS 127 La v Durham (Manchester) 2006 (CGT). T20 HS 100.

LUCAS, David Scott (Djanogly CTC, Nottingham), b Nottingham 19 Aug 1978. 6'2". RHB, LMF. Nottinghamshire 1999-2002. Yorkshire 2005. Northamptonshire debut 2007; cap 2009. Lincolnshire 2006. HS 55* v Essex (Chelmsford) 2009. 50 wkts (1): 60 (2009). BB 7-24 (12-73 match) v Glos (Cheltenham) 2009. LO HS 32* v Lancs (Manchester) 2009 (FPT). LO BB 4-27 Nt v Derbys (Derby) 2000 (NL). T20 HS 5*. T20 BB 2-37.

‡**MIDDLEBROOK, James** Daniel (Pudsey Crawshaw S), b Leeds, Yorks 13 May 1977. 6'1". RHB, OB. Yorkshire 1998-2001. Essex 2002-09; cap 2003. HS 127 Ex v Middx (Lord's) 2007. 50 wkts (1): 56 (2003). BB 6-82 (10-170 match) Y v Hampshire (Southampton) 2000 – including 4 wickets in 5 balls. Hat-trick Ex v Kent (Canterbury) 2003. LO HS 47 Ex v Worcs (Worcester) 2004 (CGT). LO BB 4-27 Ex v Somerset (Taunton) 2006 (CGT). T20 HS 43. T20 BB 3-13.

MURPHY, David (Richard Hale S, Hertford; Loughborough U), b Welwyn Garden City, Herts 24 June 1989. 5'11". RHB, WK. Loughborough UCCE 2009. Northamptonshire debut 2009. Northamptonshire 2nd XI debut 2007. HS 69* LU v Leics (Leicester) 2009 – on debut. Nh HS 14 v Surrey (Northampton) 2009.

O'BRIEN, Niall John (Marian C, Dublin), b Dublin, Ireland 8 Nov 1981. 5'6". Son of B.A.O'Brien (Ireland 1966-81); elder brother of K.J.O'Brien (*see NOTTINGHAMSHIRE*). LHB, WK. Kent 2004-06. Ireland 2005-06 to 2008-09. Northamptonshire debut 2007. **LOI** (Ire): 33 (2006 to 2009); HS 72 v Scotland (Belfast) 2007. HS 176 Ireland v UAE (Windhoek) 2005. Nh HS 168 v Glamorgan (Northampton) 2008. BB 1-4 K v CU (Cambridge) 2006 – his only f-c spell. LO HS 95 v Leics (Northampton) 2008. IT20 HS 50. T20 HS 84.

PETERS, Stephen David (Coopers Coborn & Co S), b Harold Wood, Essex 10 Dec 1978. 5'11". RHB, occ LB. Essex 1996-2001, scoring 110 and 12* v CU (Cambridge) on debut. Worcestershire 2002-05. Northamptonshire debut 2006; cap 2007. 1000 runs (3); most – 1177 (2003). HS 178 v Essex (Northampton) 2006. BB 1-19 Ex v OU (Chelmsford) 1999. LO HS 107 v Yorks (Leeds) 2007 (FPT). T20 HS 61*.

SALES, David John Grimwood (Caterham S; Cumnor House S), b Carshalton, Surrey 3 Dec 1977. 6'0". RHB, RM. Debut (Northamptonshire) 1996 v Worcs (Kidderminster) scoring 0 and 210* – record Championship score on f-c debut; youngest (18 years 237 days) to score 200 in a Championship match; cap 1999; captain 2004-07; benefit 2007. Wellington 2001-02. F-c Tours (Eng A): NZ 1999-00; SL 1997-98; K 1997-98; B 1999-00. Sustained severe knee injury prior to start of England A tour of WI 2000-01 – no f-c appearances 2001. Missed entire 2009 season with knee injury. 1000 runs (6); most – 1384 (2007). HS 303* v Essex (Northampton) 1999 – youngest Englishman (21 years 240 days) to score a f-c 300. BB 4-25 v SL A (Northampton) 1999. CC BB 2-7 v Yorks (Scarborough) 1999. LO HS 161 v Yorks (Northampton) 2006 (CGT) – Nh record. T20 HS 78*. T20 BB 1-10.

WAKELY, Alexander George (Bedford S), b Hammersmith, London 3 Nov 1988. 6'2". RHB, OB. Debut (Northamptonshire) 2007. Bedfordshire 2004-05. Northamptonshire 2nd XI debut when aged 15 years 295 days. HS 113* v Glamorgan (Cardiff) 2009. BB 2-62 v Somerset (Taunton) 2007 – on debut. LO HS 32 v Lancs (Manchester) 2009 (FPT). BB 2-14 v Lancs (Northampton) 2007 (P40). T20 HS 29*.

WHITE, Robert Allan (Stowe S; Durham U; Loughborough U), b Chelmsford, Essex 15 Oct 1979. 5'11". RHB, LB. Debut (Northamptonshire) 2000; cap 2008. Loughborough UCCE 2003. British U 2003. 1000 runs (1): 1037 (2008). HS 277 and BB 2-30 v Glos (Northampton) 2002 – highest maiden f-c hundred in UK; included 107 before lunch on first day. LO HS 111 v Warwks (Northampton) 2008 (FPT). LO BB 2-18 v Sussex (Northampton) 2002 (NL). T20 HS 94*.

WIGLEY, David Harry (St Mary's RCS, Menston, Ilkley; Loughborough U), b Bradford, Yorks 26 Oct 1981. 6'4". RHB, RFM. Yorkshire 2002 (one match). Loughborough UCCE 2003-04. British U 2004. Worcestershire 2003, 2005. Northamptonshire debut 2006. Gloucestershire 2008; cap 2008 (1 match). HS 70 v Middx (Northampton) 2007. BB 6-72 v Glos (Northampton) 2009. LO HS 10 v Middx (Southgate) 2007 (P40). LO BB 4-37 Wo v Leics (Worcester) 2004 (NL). T20 HS 1. T20 BB 1-8.

WILLEY, David Jonathan (Northampton S), b Northampton 28 Feb 1990. Son of P.Willey (Northants, Leics, England 1966-91). 6'1". LHB, LFM. Debut (Northamptonshire) 2009. Bedfordshire 2008. England U19s 2009. HS 60 v Leics (Leicester) 2009. BB 2-21 v Kent (Canterbury) 2009. LO HS 21 v Middx (Uxbridge) 2009 (P40). LO BB 2-44 v Derbys (Northampton) 2009 (FPT). T20 HS 18*. T20 BB 3-9.

RELEASED/RETIRED
(Having made a County First-Class or List A appearance in 2009)

CROOK, Steven Paul (Rostrevor C; Magill U), b Modbury, S Australia 28 May 1983. Younger brother of A.R.Crook (S Australia, Aus Academy, Lancashire, Northamptonshire 1998-99 to 2008). 5'11". RHB, RMF. British passport. Lancashire 2003-05. Northamptonshire 2005-09. Aus Academy 2001-02. HS 97 v Yorks (Northampton) 2005. BB 5-71 v Essex (Northampton) 2009. LO HS 72 v Essex (Chelmsford) 2009 (FPT). LO BB 4-20 v Sussex (Northampton) 2006 (P40). T20 HS 27. T20 BB 2-24.

CUMMINS, Ryan Anthony Gilbert (Wallington CGS; Loughborough U), b Sutton, Surrey 14 Apr 1984. Great-grandson of G.M.Reay (Surrey 1913-23). 6'4". RHB, RM. Loughborough UCCE 2003-05. Leicestershire 2005-08. HS 34* Le v OU (Oxford) 2007. CC HS 26* Le v Glos (Leicester) 2007. BB 5-60 Le v Northants (Leicester) 2007. LO HS 12* v Glamorgan (Northampton) 2009 (FPT). LO BB 3-21 Le v Warwks (Birmingham) 2008 (FPT). T20 HS – . T20 BB – .

NELSON, Mark Anthony George (Lord Grey S, Milton Keynes; Stowe S), b Milton Keynes, Bucks 24 Sep 1986. 5'11". LHB, RM. Northamptonshire 2007-09. HS 42 v Warwks (Birmingham) 2008. BB 2-62 v Middx (Northampton) 2007 – on debut. LO HS 74 v Derbys (Northampton) 2009 (FPT). LO BB 1-26 v Derbys (Northampton) 2008 (P40). T20 HS 13.

PANESAR, M.S. – *see SUSSEX.*

^{NQ}**VAN DER WATH, Johannes** Jacobus (Ermelo HS), b Newcastle, Natal, South Africa 10 Jan 1978. RHB, RFM. Easterns 1996-97. Free State 1997-98 to 2003-04. Eagles 2004-05 to date. Sussex 2005. Northamptonshire 2007-09; cap 2009. Kolpak registration. **LOI** (SA): 10 (2005-06 to 2007-08); HS 37* v A (Sydney) 2005-06; BB 2-21 v .SA (Melbourne) 2005-06 – on debut. F-c Tour (SA A): SL 2005-06. HS 113* FS v KZ-Natal (Bloemfontein) 2001-02. UK HS 94 v Essex (Northampton) 2007. 50 wkts (1): 50 (2009). BB 7-60 (12-128 match) v Middx (Uxbridge) 2008. LO HS 91 FS v GW (Bloemfontein) 2000-01. LO BB 4-31 SA A v NZ (Potchefstroom) 2005-06. IT20 HS 21. IT20 BB 2-31. T20 HS 48*. T20 BB 3-23.

^{NQ}**WESSELS, Mattheus Hendrik ('Riki')** (Woodridge C, Pt Elizabeth; Northampton U), b Marogudoore, Queensland, Australia 12 Nov 1985. Left Australia when 2 months old. Son of K.C.Wessels (OFS, Sussex, WP, NT, Q, EP, GW, Australia and South Africa 1973-74 to 1999-00). 5'11". RHB, WK. MCC 2004. Northamptonshire 2005-09 (Kolpak registration). Nondescripts (Sri Lanka) 2007-08. Mid West Rhinos 2009-10. HS 114 and BB 1-10 MWR v Matabeleland Tuskers (Bulawayo) 2009-10. Nh HS 109 v Surrey (Oval) 2009. Nh BB – . LO HS 100 v Surrey (Oval) 2008. LO BB 1-0 MWR v Matabeleland Tuskers (Bulawayo) 2009-10. T20 HS 86*.

WHITE, G.G. – *see NOTTINGHAMSHIRE.*

S.P.Bailey left the staff without making a County First-Class or List A appearance in 2009.

NORTHAMPTONSHIRE 2009

RESULTS SUMMARY

	Place	Won	Lost	Tied	Drew	NR
County Championship (2nd Division)	3rd	6	4	6		
All First-Class Matches		6	5	6		
FP Trophy (Group D)	5th	1	4	3		
Pro40 League (2nd Division)	4th	3	2	1	2	
Twenty20 Cup (Midlands/Wales/West Division)	SF	8	3	1		

LV COUNTY CHAMPIONSHIP AVERAGES
BATTING AND FIELDING

Cap		M	I	NO	HS	Runs	Avge	100	50	Ct/St
2009	A.J.Hall	16	25	2	159	1161	50.47	2	6	16
2007	S.D.Peters	14	25	1	175	1050	43.75	3	5	12
2008	N.Boje	15	25	5	98	801	40.05	–	8	7
2008	R.A.White	16	29	4	193	986	39.44	1	7	11
	M.H.Wessels	14	23	–	109	804	34.95	1	6	25/1
2009	J.J.van der Wath	13	19	1	85	452	25.11	–	3	4
	N.J.O'Brien	8	14	–	128	346	24.71	1	–	32/1
	A.G.Wakely	11	18	1	113*	394	23.17	1	1	9
	D.J.Willey	9	15	1	60	310	22.14	–	1	2
	B.H.N.Howgego	5	9	1	47	164	20.50	–	–	3
2009	D.S.Lucas	15	23	7	55*	290	18.12	–	1	5
	M.A.G.Nelson	3	5	–	38	88	17.60	–	–	2
2006	M.S.Panesar	13	20	5	38	182	12.13	–	–	5
	D.H.Wigley	11	14	8	10*	58	9.66	–	–	5
	L.M.Daggett	5	4	–	2	3	0.75	–	–	1

Also batted: J.A.Brooks (2 matches) 0*, 10* (1 ct); S.P.Crook (2) 16, 55, 13 (2 ct); P.W.Harrison (2) 32, 3, 18; D.Murphy (2) 14, 14, 2 (7 ct); G.G.White (1) 0, 29*.

BOWLING

	O	M	R	W	Avge	Best	5wI	10wM
D.S.Lucas	393.3	83	1224	58	21.10	7-24	3	1
A.J.Hall	310.2	76	911	40	22.77	5-29	1	–
J.J.van der Wath	364.3	75	1237	50	24.74	5-71	1	–
N.Boje	311	81	891	30	29.70	4-59	–	–
D.H.Wigley	284.1	54	1090	30	36.33	6-72	2	–
M.S.Panesar	412.1	89	1070	18	59.44	3-55	–	–
Also bowled:								
J.A.Brooks	50	5	184	7	26.28	4-76	–	–
S.P.Crook	48	8	193	6	32.16	5-71	1	–
L.M.Daggett	88	15	311	8	38.87	3-39	–	–

A.G.Wakely 11-0-64-0; M.H.Wessels 1-1-0-0; G.G.White 4-0-13-0; D.J.Willey 42.4-4-185-4.

The First-Class Averages (pp 228–244) give the records of Northamptonshire players in all first-class county matches (Northamptonshire's other opponents being the Australians), with the exception of D.Murphy and M.S.Panesar, whose first-class figures for Northamptonshire are as above.

NORTHAMPTONSHIRE RECORDS

FIRST-CLASS CRICKET

Highest Total	For 781-7d		v	Notts	Northampton	1995
	V 673-8d		by	Yorkshire	Leeds	2003
Lowest Total	For 12		v	Glos	Gloucester	1907
	V 33		by	Lancashire	Northampton	1977
Highest Innings	For 331*	M.E.K.Hussey	v	Somerset	Taunton	2003
	V 333	K.S.Duleepsinhji	for	Sussex	Hove	1930

Highest Partnership for each Wicket

1st	375	R.A.White/M.J.Powell	v	Glos	Northampton	2002
2nd	344	G.Cook/R.J.Boyd-Moss	v	Lancashire	Northampton	1986
3rd	393	A.Fordham/A.J.Lamb	v	Yorkshire	Leeds	1990
4th	370	R.T.Virgin/P.Willey	v	Somerset	Northampton	1976
5th	401	M.B.Loye/D.Ripley	v	Glamorgan	Northampton	1998
6th	376	R.Subba Row/A.Lightfoot	v	Surrey	The Oval	1958
7th	293	D.J.G.Sales/D.Ripley	v	Essex	Northampton	1999
8th	164	D.Ripley/N.G.B.Cook	v	Lancashire	Manchester	1987
9th	156	R.Subba Row/S.Starkie	v	Lancashire	Northampton	1955
10th	148	B.W.Bellamy/J.V.Murdin	v	Glamorgan	Northampton	1925

Best Bowling	For	10-127	V.W.C.Jupp	v	Kent	Tunbridge W	1932
(Innings)	V	10- 30	C.Blythe	for	Kent	Northampton	1907
Best Bowling	For	15- 31	G.E.Tribe	v	Yorkshire	Northampton	1958
(Match)	V	17- 48	C.Blythe	for	Kent	Northampton	1907

Most Runs – Season	2198	D.Brookes	(av 51.11)		1952
Most Runs – Career	28980	D.Brookes	(av 36.13)		1934-59
Most 100s – Season	8	R.A.Haywood			1921
Most 100s – Career	67	D.Brookes			1934-59
Most Wkts – Season	175	G.E.Tribe	(av 18.70)		1955
Most Wkts – Career	1102	E.W.Clark	(av 21.26)		1922-47
Most Career W-K Dismissals	810	K.V.Andrew	(653 ct; 157 st)		1953-66
Most Career Catches in the Field	469	D.S.Steele			1963-84

LIMITED-OVERS CRICKET

Highest Total	FPT	360-2		v	Staffs	Northampton	1990
	P40	319-7		v	Scotland	Northampton	2003
	T20	224-5		v	Glos	Milton Keynes	2005
Lowest Total	FPT	62		v	Leics	Leicester	1974
	P40	41		v	Middlesex	Northampton	1972
	T20	102-9 (20)		v	Warwicks	Milton Keynes	2008
Highest Innings	FPT	161	D.J.G.Sales	v	Yorkshire	Northampton	2006
	P40	172*	W.Larkins	v	Warwicks	Luton	1983
	T20	111*	L.Klusener	v	Worcs	Kidderminster	2007
Best Bowling	FPT	7-10	C.Pietersen	v	Denmark	Brondby	2005
	P40	7-39	A.Hodgson	v	Somerset	Northampton	1976
	T20	6-21	A.J.Hall	v	Worcs	Northampton	2008

NOTTINGHAMSHIRE

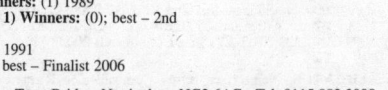

Formation of Present Club: March/April 1841
Substantial Reorganisation: 11 December 1866
Inaugural First-Class Match: 1864
Colours: Green and Gold
Badge: Badge of City of Nottingham
County Champions (since 1890): (5) 1907, 1929, 1981, 1987, 2005
Gillette/NatWest/C&G/FP Trophy Winners: (1) 1987
Benson and Hedges Cup Winners: (1) 1989
Pro 40/National League (Div 1) Winners: (0); best – 2nd 2007
Sunday League Winners: (1) 1991
Twenty20 Cup Winners: (0); best – Finalist 2006

Chief Executive: Derek Brewer, Trent Bridge, Nottingham NG2 6AG • Tel: 0115 982 3000 • Fax: 0115 945 5730 • Email: administration@nottsccc.co.uk • Webs: www.nottsccc.co.uk • www.trentbridge.co.uk

Director of Cricket: Mick Newell. **Club Coach:** Paul Johnson. **Captain:** C.M.W.Read. **Vice-Captain:** P.J.Franks. **Overseas Players:** H.M.Amla and D.J.Hussey. **2010 Beneficiary:** R.J.Sidebottom. **Head Groundsman:** Steve Birks. **Scorer:** L. Brian Hewes. ‡ New registration. NQ Not qualified for England.

NQ**ADAMS, Andre** Ryan (Westlake BHS, Auckland), b Mangere, Auckland, New Zealand 17 Jul 1975. 5'9". RHB, RMF. Auckland 1997-98 to 2007-08. Essex 2004-06; cap 2004. Nottinghamshire debut/cap 2007 (Kolpak registration). Herefordshire 2001. **Tests** (NZ): 1 (2001-02); HS 11 and BB 3-44 v E (Auckland) 2001-02 – on debut. **LOI** (NZ): 42 (2000-01 to 2006-07); HS 45 v P (Rawalpindi) 2001-02; BB 5-22 v I (Queenstown) 2002-03. HS 124 Ex v Leics (Leicester) 2004 (91 balls, 7 sixes, 13 fours; 100 off 80 balls) on UK debut. Nt HS 84 and joint Nt BB 4-39 v Yorks (Scarborough) 2009. BB 6-25 Auckland v Wellington. UK BB 5-60 Ex v Durham (Southend) 2005. Nt BB 4-39 v Somerset (Taunton) 2008. Hat-trick Ex v Somerset (Taunton) 2005. LO HS 90* N Is Selection XI v SL (New Plymouth) 2000-01. LO BB 5-7 Auckland v ND (Auckland) 1999-00. T20 HS 54*. T20 BB 3-35.

‡NQ**AMLA, Hashim** Mahomed, b Durban, South Africa 31 Mar 1983. Younger brother of A.M.Amla (Natal B, KwaZulu-Natal, Dolphins 1997-98 to date). RHB, RM/OB. KwaZulu-Natal 1999-00 to 2003-04. Dolphins 2004-05 to date. Essex 2009. **Tests** (SA): 43 (2004-05 to 2009-10); HS 253* v I (Nagpur) 2009-10; BB – . **LOI** (SA): 24 (2007-08 to 2009-10); HS 140 v B (Benoni) 2008-09. F-c Tours: SA: E 2008; A 2008-09; I 2004-05, 2007-08 (SA A), 2007-08, 2009-10; P 2007-08; SL 2005-06 (SA A), 2006; Z 2004 (SA A), 2007 (SA A); B 2007-08. HS 253* (see Tests). CC HS 181 Ex v Glamorgan (Chelmsford) 2009 – on debut. BB 1-10 SA A v India A (Kimberley) 2001-02. LO HS 140 (see LOI). IT20 HS 26. T20 HS 57.

BROAD, Stuart Christopher John (Oakham S), b Nottingham 24 Jun 1986. 6'5". LHB, RFM. Son of B.C.Broad (Glos, Notts, OFS and England 1979-94). Debut (Leicestershire) 2005; cap 2007. Nottinghamshire debut 2008. YC 2006. **ECB central contract 2009-10. Tests:** 26 (2007-08 to 2009-10); HS 76 v SA (Lord's) 2008; BB 6-91 v A (Leeds) 2009. **LOI:** 57 (2006 to 2009-10); HS 45* v I (Manchester) 2007; BB 5-23 v SA (Nottingham) 2008. F-c Tours: SA 2009-10; WI 2005-06 (Eng A), 2008-09; NZ 2007-08; I 2008-09; SL 2007-08; B 2006-07 (Eng A). HS 91* Le v Derbys (Leicester) 2007. Nt HS 60 and Nt BB 5-79 v Worcs (Nottingham) 2009. BB 6-91 (see Tests). CC BB 5-67 Le v Derbys (Leicester) 2007. LO HS 45* (see LOI). LO BB 5-23 (see LOI). IT20 HS 10*. IT20 BB 3-17. T20 HS 10*. T20 BB 3-13.

BROWN, Alistair Duncan (Caterham S), b Beckenham, Kent 11 Feb 1970. 5'10". RHB, OB, occ WK. Surrey 1992-2008; cap 1994; benefit 2002. Nottinghamshire debut/cap 2009. TCCB XI 1996. Walter Lawrence Trophy for fastest f-c hundred 1998. **LOI**: 16 (1996 to 2001); HS 118 v I (Manchester) 1996. 1000 runs (8); most – 1382 (1993). HS 295* Sy v Leics (Oakham) 2000 – record score (all levels) in Rutland. Nt HS 148 v Hampshire (Southampton) 2009. BB 3-25 Sy v Somerset (Guildford) 2006. Nt BB 1-16 v Yorks (Nottingham) 2009. LO HS 268 Sy v Glamorgan (Oval) 2002 (CGT) – world record l-o score (160 balls, 12 sixes, 30 fours). LO BB 3-39 Sy v Notts (Nottingham) 2000 (NL). T20 HS 83.

CARTER, Andrew (Lincoln C), b Lincoln 27 Aug 1988. RHB, RM. Debut (Nottinghamshire) 2009. Nottinghamshire 2nd XI debut 2006. Lincolnshire 2007-08. HS 4 and CC BB 1-28 v Worcs (Worcester) 2009. BB 1-27 v OU (Oxford) 2009. LO HS 12 v Sussex (Hove) 2009 (P40). LO BB 3-32 v Essex (Southend) 2009 (P40).

‡**EDWARDS, Neil** James (Cape Cornwall CS; Richard Huish C), b Treliske, Truro, Cornwall 14 Oct 1983. 6'3". LHB, RM. Somerset 2002-08. Cornwall 2000-06. 1000 runs (1): 1251 (2007). HS 212 Sm v LU (Taunton) 2007. CC HS 160 Sm v Hampshire (Taunton) 2003. BB 1-16 Sm v Derbys (Taunton) 2004. LO HS 65 Sm v Yorks (Taunton) 2006 (P40). T20 HS 1.

FLETCHER, Luke Jack (Henry Mellish S, Nottingham), b Nottingham 18 Sep 1988. 6'6". RHB, RMF. Debut (Nottinghamshire) 2008. Nottinghamshire 2nd XI debut 2007. HS 92 v Hampshire (Southampton) 2009. BB 4-38 v Somerset (Nottingham) 2009. LO HS 40* v Durham (Chester-le-St) 2009 (P40). LO BB 2-35 v Worcs (Nottingham) 2009 (FPT). T20 HS 1*. T20 BB 2-23.

FRANKS, Paul John (Southwell Minster CS), b Mansfield 3 Feb 1979. 6'2". LHB, RMF. Debut (Nottinghamshire) 1996; cap 1999; benefit 2007. Canterbury 2002-03. YC 2000. **LOI**: 1 (2000); HS 4 v WI (Nottingham) 2000. F-c Tours (Eng A): SA 1998-99; WI 2000-01; NZ 1999-00; SL 2004-05; B 1999-00. HS 123* v Leics (Leicester) 2003. 50 wkts (2); most – 63 (1999). BB 7-56 v Middlesex (Lord's) 2000. Hat-trick v Warwks (Nottingham) 1997. LO HS 84* v Lincs (Lincoln) 2003 (CGT). LO BB 6-27 v Durham (Chester-le-St) 2000 (NL). T20 HS 29*. T20 BB 2-12.

HALES, Alexander Daniel (Chesham S), b Hillingdon, Middlesex 3 Jan 1989. 6'5". RHB, RM, occ WK. Debut (Nottinghamshire) 2008. Nottinghamshire 2nd XI debut 2007. Buckinghamshire 2006-07. MCC YC 2006-07. England U19s 2008. HS 78 v Durham (Chester-le-St) 2009. BB 2-63 v Yorks (Nottingham) 2009. LO HS 150* v Worcs (Nottingham) 2009 (P40). T20 HS 15.

^NQ**HUSSEY, David** John (Prendiville Catholic C; Edith Cowan U), b Morley, Perth, Australia 15 Jul 1977. Younger brother of M.E.K.Hussey (WA, Northants, Glos, Durham and Australia 1994-95 to date). 5'11". RHB, OB. Victoria 2002-03 to date. Nottinghamshire debut/cap 2004, scoring 107* v OU (Oxford) – LV debut. Sussex CB (List A) 2001. **LOI** (A): 23 (2008 to 2009); HS 111 and BB 1-6 v Scotland (Edinburgh) 2009. F-c Tour (Aus A): P 2007-08. 1000 runs (4+1); most – 1315 (2004). HS 275 v Essex (Nottingham) 2007. Scored 170, 116 and 140 in successive innings 2004. BB 4-105 v Hampshire (Nottingham) 2005. LO HS 130 Vic v Q (Brisbane) 2005-06. LO BB 3-26 v Northants (Northampton) 2007 (P40). T20 HS 100*. T20 BB 2-10.

‡**MULLANEY, Steven** John (St Mary's RC S, Astley), b Warrington, Cheshire 19 Nov 1986. 5'9". RHB, RM. Lancashire 2006-08. No f-c appearances in 2009. HS 165* La v DU (Durham) 2007. CC HS 15 La v Notts (Nottingham) 2008. LO HS 12 La v Notts (Nottingham) 2007 (FPT). LO BB 3-13 La v Derbys (Derby) 2007 (FPT). T20 HS 5.

‡NQNANNES, Dirk Peter (Wesley C and Monash U, Melbourne), b Mount Waverley, Victoria, Australia 16 May 1976. 6'3". RHB, LFM. Victoria 2005-06 to date. Middlesex 2008; cap 2008. Dutch passport. LOI (A): 1 (2009) HS 1 and BB 1-20 v Scotland (Edinburgh) 2009. HS 31* Vic v S Australia (Adelaide) 2007-08. CC HS 5 and BB 6-32 M v Worcs (Kidderminster) 2008. LO HS 5* M v Somerset (Lord's) 2008. LO BB 4-38 M v Worcs (Kidderminster) 2008 (P40). IT20 HS 6. IT20 BB 3-21. T20 HS 6. T20 BB 4-11.

NQO'BRIEN, Kevin Joseph, b Dublin, Ireland 4 Mar 1984. Son of B.A.O'Brien (Ireland 1966-81) and younger brother of N.J.O'Brien (see NORTHAMPTONSHIRE). Ireland 2006-07 to date. Nottinghamshire debut 2009. LOI (Ire): 35 (2006 to 2009); HS 142 v Kenya (Nairobi) 2006-07; BB 3-30 v Netherlands (Dublin) 2008. HS 171* Ire v Kenya (Nairobi) 2008-09. Nt HS 13 and Nt BB 1-9 v OU (Oxford) 2009. BB 4-38 Ire v Scotland (Belfast) 2007. LO HS 142 (see LOI). LO BB 4-31 Ire v Notts (Dublin) 2008 (FPT). IT20 HS 39*. IT20 BB 2-15. T20 HS 39*. T20 BB 2-14.

‡PATEL, Akhil (Kimberley CS, Nottingham), b Nottingham 18 Jun 1990. Younger brother of S.R.Patel (below). 5'10". LHB, SLC. Derbyshire 2007. Nottinghamshire debut 2009, scoring 69* v OU (Oxford). CC HS 37 v Sussex (Nottingham) 2009. BB 1-34 v OU (Oxford) 2009. LO HS 41 v Glos (Nottingham) 2009 (P40). LO BB 2-34 v Hampshire (Southampton) 2009 (P40).

PATEL, Samit Rohit (Worksop C), b Leicester 30 Nov 1984. 5'8". Elder brother of A.Patel (above). RHB, SLA. Debut (Nottinghamshire) 2002; cap 2008. Nottinghamshire 2nd XI debut 1999, when aged 14 years 274 days. LOI: 11 (2008 to 2008-09); HS 31 and BB 5-41 v SA (Oval) 2008. F-c Tour: NZ 2008-09 (Eng A). HS 176 v Glos (Nottingham) 2007. BB 6-84 (9-124 match) v Sussex (Nottingham) 2009. LO HS 114 v Durham (Chester-le-St) 2008 (FPT). LO BB 6-13 v Ireland (Dublin) 2009 (FPT). T20 HS 84*. T20 BB 3-11.

PATTINSON, Darren John, b Grimsby, Lincs 2 Sep 1979. Elder brother of J.L.Pattinson (Victoria 2008-09 to date). RHB, RFM. Victoria 2006-07 to date. Nottinghamshire debut 2008 taking 5-22 (8-85 match) v Kent (Canterbury); cap 2008. Tests: 1 (2008); HS 13 and BB 2-95 v SA (Leeds) 2008. HS 59 v Durham (Chester-le-St) 2009. BB 6-30 v Lancs (Nottingham) 2008. LO HS 13* v Lancs (Nottingham) 2008. LO BB 4-29 v Warwks (Nottingham) 2008. T20 HS 5. T20 BB 3-18.

READ, Christopher Mark Wells (Torquay GS; Bath U), b Paignton, Devon 10 Aug 1978. 5'8". RHB, WK. Gloucestershire (l-o only) 1997. Debut 1997-98 for England A in Kenya. Nottinghamshire debut 1998; cap 1999; captain 2008 to date; benefit 2009. MCC 2002. Devon 1995-97. Tests: 15 (1999 to 2006-07); HS 55 v P (Leeds) 2006. Made six dismissals twice in successive innings 2006-07 to establish an Ashes record. LOI: 36 (1999-00 to 2006-07); HS 30* v SA (Manchester) 2003. F-c Tours: A 2006-07; SA 1998-99 (Eng A), 1999-00; WI 2000-01 (Eng A), 2003-04, 2005-06 (Eng A); SL 1997-98 (Eng A), 2002-03 (ECB Acad), 2003-04; Z 1998-99 (Eng A); B 2003-04; K 1997-98 (Eng A). 1000 runs (2); most – 1203 (2009). HS 240 v Essex (Chelmsford) 2007. LO HS 135 v Durham (Nottingham) 2006 (CGT). IT20 HS 13. T20 HS 58*.

SHAFAYAT, Bilal Mustapha (Greenwood Dale; Nottingham Bluecoat SFC), b Nottingham 10 Jul 1984. 5'7". RHB, RMF. Nottinghamshire 2001-04, 2007 to date. National Bank of Pakistan 2004-05. Northamptonshire 2005-06. Pakistan Customs 2007-08 to 2008-09. Captained Eng U19 tour of Australia 2002-03. F-c Tour (Eng A): 1 2003-04. 1000 runs (1): 1058 (2005). HS 161 Nh v Derbys (Derby) 2005. Nt HS 118 v Sussex (Hove) 2008. BB 2-25 Nh v P (Northampton) 2006. Nt BB 1-22 v OU (Nottingham) 2003. CC BB 1-24 v Essex (Chelmsford) 2007. LO HS 104 v Northants (Northampton) 2007 (FPT). LO BB 4-33 Nh v Worcs (Worcester) 2005 (NL). T20 HS 40. T20 BB 2-13.

SHRECK, Charles Edward (Truro S), b Truro, Cornwall 6 Jan 1978. 6'7". RHB, RFM. Debut (Nottinghamshire) 2003; cap 2006. Wellington 2005-06 to 2008-09. MCC 2008. Cornwall 1997-2002. HS 19 v Essex (Chelmsford) 2003. 50 wkts (2); most – 61 (2006, 2008). BB 8-31 (12-129 match) v Middx (Nottingham) 2006. Hat-trick v Middx (Lord's) 2006. LO HS 9* Wellington v CD (Palmerston N) 2005-06. LO BB 5-19 Cornwall v Worcs (Truro) 2002 (CGT). Took 5-35 v Worcs (Nottingham) 2002 (NL) – on 1st XI debut. T20 HS 6*. T20 BB 4-22.

SIDEBOTTOM, Ryan Jay (King James's GS, Almondbury), b Huddersfield, Yorks 15 Jan 1978. Son of A.Sidebottom (Yorks, OFS and England 1973-91). 6'3". LHB, LFM. Yorkshire 1997-2003; cap 2000. Nottinghamshire debut/cap 2004; benefit 2010. **ECB central contract 2009-10. Tests**: 22 (2001 to 2009-10); HS 31 vSL (Kandy) 2007-08; BB 7-47 v NZ (Napier) 2007-08. Hat-trick v NZ (Hamilton) 2007-08. **LOI**: 24 (2001-02 to 2009-10); HS 24 v A (Southampton) 2009; BB 3-19 v SL (Dambulla) 2007-08. F-c Tours: SA 2009-10; WI 2000-01 (Eng A), 2008-09; NZ 2007-08; SL 2007-08. HS 54 Y v Glamorgan (Cardiff) 1998. Nt HS 46 v Lancs (Nottingham) 2009. 50 wkts (2); most – 50 (2005, 2006). BB 7-97 Y v Derbys (Leeds) 2003. Nt BB 5-22 v Kent (Nottingham) 2006. LO HS 32 v Middx (Nottingham) 2005 (NL). LO BB 6-40 Y v Glamorgan (Cardiff) 1998 (SL). IT20 HS 5*. IT20 BB 3-16. T20 HS 17*. T20 BB 3-16.

SWANN, Graeme Peter (Sponne S, Towcester), b Northampton 24 Mar 1979. Son of R.Swann (Northumberland 1969-72; Bedfordshire 1988-95); younger brother of A.J.Swann (Northamptonshire and Lancashire 1996-2004). 6'0". RHB, OB. Northamptonshire 1998-2004; cap 1999. Nottinghamshire debut/cap 2005. MCC 2005. Bedfordshire 1996. **ECB central contract 2009-10. Tests**: 16 (2008-09 to 2009-10); HS 85 v SA (Centurion) 2009-10. BB 5-54 (9-164 match) v SA (Durban) 2009-10. **LOI**: 29 (1999-00 to 2009-10); HS 34 v SL (Dambulla) 2007-08; BB 5-28 v A (Chester-le-St) 2009. F-c Tours: SA 1998-99 (Eng A), 1999-00, 2009-10); WI 2000-01 (Eng A part), 2008-09; I 2008-09; SL 2004-05 (Eng A); Z 1998-99 (Eng A); B 2009-10. HS 183 Nh v Glos (Bristol) 2002 – including 114 before lunch on third day. Nt HS 97 v Essex (Chelmsford) 2007. 50 wkts (1): 57 (1999). BB 7-33 Nh v Derbys (Northampton) 2003. Nt BB 7-100 v Glamorgan (Swansea) 2007. LO HS 83 Nh v Leics (Northampton) 2001 (NL). LO BB 5-17 v Glos (Nottingham) 2007 (P40). IT20 HS 15*. IT20 BB 3-14. T20 HS 90*. T20 BB 3-14.

WAGH, Mark Anant (King Edward's S, Birmingham; Keble C, Oxford), b Birmingham, Warwks 20 Oct 1976. 6'2". RHB, OB. Oxford U 1996-98; blue 1996-97-98; captain 1997. Warwickshire 1997-2006; cap 2000. British U 1996-1998. Mashonaland A 1998-99. Nottinghamshire debut/cap 2007. Zimbabwe CA (List A) 1998-99. 1000 runs (6); most – 1310 (2007). HS 315 Wa v Middx (Lord's) 2001. Nt HS 152 v Northants (Northampton) 2007. BB 7-222 Wa v Lancs (Birmingham) 2003. Nt BB 2-6 v Somerset (Taunton) 2007. LO HS 102* Wa v Kent (Birmingham) 2004 (NL). LO BB 4-35 Wa v Glamorgan (Birmingham) 2004 (NL). T20 HS 56. T20 BB 2-16.

‡**WHITE, Graeme** Geoffrey (Stowe S), b Milton Keynes, Bucks 18 Apr 1987. 5'11". RHB, SLA. Northamptonshire 2006-09. HS 65 and CC BB 1-18 Nh v Glamorgan (Colwyn Bay) 2007. BB 2-35 Nh v CU (Cambridge) 2007. LO HS 14 Nh v Middx (Southgate) 2007 (P40). LO BB 3-30 Nh v Middx (Uxbridge) 2009 (P40). T20 HS 8. T20 BB 1-10.

WOOD, Matthew James (Exmouth Community C; Exeter U), b Exeter, Devon 30 Sep 1980. 5'11". RHB, OB. Somerset 2001-07; cap 2005. Nottinghamshire debut 2008. MCC 2007. Devon 1998-2004. 1000 (1): 1058 (2005). HS 297 Sm v Yorks (Taunton) 2005. Nt HS 98 v Sussex (Hove) 2008. LO HS 129 Sm v Yorks (Taunton) 2005 (NL). T20 HS 94.

BROWN, Jason Fred (St Margaret Ward HS & SFC), b Newcastle-under-Lyme, Staffs 10 Oct 1974. 6'0". RHB, OB. Northamptonshire 1996-2008; cap 2000; benefit 2008. Nottinghamshire 2009 (one f-c match). Staffordshire 1994-95. F-c Tours: WI 2000-01 (part) (Eng A); SL 2000-01 (no f-c). HS 38 Nh v Hants (Northampton) 2003. 50 wkts (3); most – 66 (2003). BB 7-69 Nh v Durham (Chester-le-St) 2003. LO HS 16 Nh v Lancs (Manchester) 2002 (NL). LO BB 5-19 Nh v Cambs (Northampton) 2004 (CGT). T20 HS 13*. T20 BB 5-27.

EALHAM, Mark Alan (Stour Valley SS, Chartham), b Willesborough, Ashford, Kent 27 Aug 1969. Son of A.G.E.Ealham (Kent 1966-82). 5'9". RHB, RMF. Kent 1989-2003; cap 1992; benefit 2003. Nottinghamshire 2004-09; cap 2004. Walter Lawrence Trophy (fastest f-c hundred of 2006 – 45 balls v MCC at Lord's). **Tests:** 8 (1996 to 1998); HS 53* v A (Birmingham) 1997; BB 4-21 v I (Nottingham) 1996. **LOI:** 64 (1996 to 2001); HS 45 v WI (Bridgetown) 1997-98; BB 5-15 v Z (Kimberley) 1999-00 – Eng record (then). F-c Tours: A 1996-97 (Eng A); SA 1999-00 (part); SL 1997-98; Z 1992-93 (K); K 1997-98. 1000 runs (1): 1055 (1997). HS 153* K v Northants (Canterbury) 2001. Nt HS 139 v Leics (Leicester) 2004. 50 wkts (1): 56 (2005). BB 8-36 (10-74 match) K v Warwks (Birmingham) 1996. Nt BB 7-59 (10-76 match) v Yorks (Nottingham) 2008. LO HS 112 K v Derbys (Maidstone) 1995 (off 44 balls – SL record). LO BB 6-53 K v Hampshire (Basingstoke) 1993 (SL). T20 HS 91 v Yorks (Nottingham) 2004 – Nt record. T20 BB 3-20.

FOOTITT, M.H.A. – see DERBYSHIRE.

JEFFERSON, W.I. – see LEICESTERSHIRE.

NQ**VOGES, Adam** Charles (Edith Cowan U, Perth), b Perth, Australia 4 Oct 1979. 6'0". RHB, SLC. W Australia 2002-03 to date. Hampshire (l-o) 2007. Nottinghamshire debut/cap 2008. **LOI** (A): 11 (2006-07 to 2009-10); HS 72 v Scotland (Edinburgh) 2009. BB 1-22 v I (Vadodara) 2009-10. F-c Tours (Aus A): I 2008-09; P 2007-08. HS 180 WA v Tas (Hobart) 2007-08. Nt HS 139 v Sussex (Horsham) 2009. BB 4-92 WA v S Aus (Adelaide) 2006-07. Nt BB 3-21 v Durham (Nottingham) 2008. LO HS 104* WA v S Aus (Adelaide) 2008-09. LO BB 3-25 v Sussex (Hove) 2009 (P40). IT20 HS 26. IT20 BB 2-5. T20 HS 82*. T20 BB 2-4.

NOTTINGHAMSHIRE 2009

RESULTS SUMMARY

	Place	Won	Lost	Tied	Drew	NR
County Championship (1st Division)	2nd	4	2		10	
All First-Class Matches		4	2		11	
FP Trophy (Group A)	QF	5	4			
Pro40 League (1st Division)	9th		6			2
Twenty20 Cup (North Division)	4th	4	6			

LV COUNTY CHAMPIONSHIP AVERAGES

BATTING AND FIELDING

Cap		M	I	NO	HS	Runs	Avge	100	50	Ct/St
2004	D.J.Hussey	3	5	–	189	407	81.40	2	1	5
2008	A.C.Voges	8	10	1	139	697	77.44	1	6	8
1999	C.M.W.Read	16	22	6	125	1203	75.18	4	6	46/4
1999	P.J.Franks	4	4	–	64	167	41.75	–	2	1
2009	A.D.Brown	16	24	3	148	849	40.42	1	6	18
2004	M.A.Ealham	14	20	7	70*	493	37.92	–	2	6
2007	M.A.Wagh	15	24	2	147	814	37.00	3	2	4
	A.D.Hales	6	10	–	78	358	35.80	–	3	2
2008	S.R.Patel	15	23	–	95	712	30.95	–	4	7
2007	A.R.Adams	11	13	1	84	300	25.00	–	1	13
	M.J.Wood	6	9	1	86	200	25.00	–	1	–
	L.J.Fletcher	8	8	3	92	121	24.20	–	1	–
	B.M.Shafayat	13	21	–	69	485	23.09	–	2	13
	S.A.Newman	7	11	–	87	249	22.63	–	2	3
2004	R.J.Sidebottom	7	9	3	46	100	16.66	–	–	1
2008	D.J.Pattinson	8	8	–	59	102	12.75	–	1	1
	W.I.Jefferson	3	5	–	21	48	9.60	–	–	5
2006	C.E.Shreck	11	12	7	12*	28	5.60	–	–	1

Also batted: S.C.J.Broad (1 match) 60 (2 ct); A.Carter (1) 4; A.Patel (1) 0, 37 (2 ct); G.P.Swann (2 – cap 2005) 26, 0 (1 ct).

BOWLING

	O	M	R	W	Avge	Best	5wI	10wM
R.J.Sidebottom	260.2	70	760	31	24.51	5-59	2	–
L.J.Fletcher	245.3	58	800	29	27.58	4-38	–	–
A.R.Adams	409	103	1224	43	28.46	4-39	–	–
M.A.Ealham	387	117	983	28	35.10	5-31	1	–
S.R.Patel	473.2	83	1531	32	47.84	6-84	2	–
C.E.Shreck	363.2	77	1281	21	61.00	4-63	–	–
D.J.Pattinson	219.5	40	872	10	87.20	4-53	–	–
Also bowled:								
S.C.J.Broad	48	12	106	7	15.14	5-79	1	–
G.P.Swann	55	14	127	6	21.16	3-52	–	–
P.J.Franks	116	33	323	9	35.88	3-52	–	–

A.D.Brown 23.1-2-83-1; A.Carter 24.5-96-1; A.D.Hales 40.6-140-3; D.J.Hussey 5-2-18-0; S.A.Newman 6-1-25-0; C.M.W.Read 1-0-2-0; B.M.Shafayat 8-1-32-1; A.C.Voges 33.3-2-100-3.

The First-Class Averages (pp228–244) give the records of Nottinghamshire players in all first-class county matches (Nottinghamshire's other opponents being Oxford UCCE), with the exception of S.C.J.Broad, S.A.Newman and G.P.Swann, whose first-class figures for Nottinghamshire are as above, and:

S.R.Patel 16-25-0-95-794-31.76-0-4-9ct. 484.2-86-1558-33-47.21-6/84-2-0.

NOTTINGHAMSHIRE RECORDS

FIRST-CLASS CRICKET

Highest Total	For 791		v	Essex	Chelmsford	2007
	V 781-7d		by	Northants	Northampton	1995
Lowest Total	For 13		v	Yorkshire	Nottingham	1901
	V 16		by	Derbyshire	Nottingham	1879
	16		by	Surrey	The Oval	1880
Highest Innings	For 312*	W.W.Keeton	v	Middlesex	The Oval	1939
	V 345	C.G.Macartney	for	Australians	Nottingham	1921

Highest Partnership for each Wicket

1st	406*	D.J.Bicknell/G.E.Welton	v	Warwicks	Birmingham	2000
2nd	398	A.Shrewsbury/W.Gunn	v	Sussex	Nottingham	1890
3rd	367	W.Gunn/J.R.Gunn	v	Leics	Nottingham	1903
4th	361	A.O.Jones/J.R.Gunn	v	Essex	Leyton	1905
5th	359	D.J.Hussey/C.M.W.Read	v	Essex	Nottingham	2007
6th	372*	K.P.Pietersen/J.E.Morris	v	Derbyshire	Derby	2001
7th	301	C.C.Lewis/B.N.French	v	Durham	Chester-le-St	1993
8th	220	G.F.H.Heane/R.Winrow	v	Somerset	Nottingham	1935
9th	170	J.C.Adams/K.P.Evans	v	Somerset	Taunton	1994
10th	152	E.B.Alletson/W.Riley	v	Sussex	Hove	1911
	152	U.Afzaal/A.J.Harris	v	Worcs	Nottingham	2000

Best Bowling	For 10-66	K.Smales	v	Glos	Stroud	1956
(Innings)	V 10-10	H.Verity	for	Yorkshire	Leeds	1932
Best Bowling	For 17-89	F.C.L.Matthews	v	Northants	Nottingham	1923
(Match)	V 17-89	W.G.Grace	for	Glos	Cheltenham	1877

Most Runs – Season	2620	W.W.Whysall	(av 53.46)	1929
Most Runs – Career	31592	G.Gunn	(av 35.69)	1902-32
Most 100s – Season	9	W.W.Whysall		1928
	9	M.J.Harris		1971
	9	B.C.Broad		1990
Most 100s – Career	65	J.Hardstaff jr		1930-55
Most Wkts – Season	181	B.Dooland	(av 14.96)	1954
Most Wkts – Career	1653	T.G.Wass	(av 20.34)	1896-1920
Most Career W-K Dismissals	957	T.W.Oates	(733 ct; 224 st)	1897-1925
Most Career Catches in the Field	466	A.O.Jones		1892-1914

LIMITED-OVERS CRICKET

Highest Total	FPT	346-9	v	Ireland	Nottingham	2009
	P40	329-6	v	Derbyshire	Nottingham	1993
	T20	213-6	v	Northants	Nottingham	2006
Lowest Total	FPT	123	v	Yorkshire	Scarborough	1969
	P40	57	v	Glos	Nottingham	2009
	T20	91	v	Lancashire	Manchester	2006
Highest Innings	FPT	149*	D.W.Randall	v	Devon	Torquay	1988
	P40	167*	P.Johnson	v	Kent	Nottingham	1993
	T20	91	M.A.Ealham	v	Yorkshire	Nottingham	2004
Best Bowling	FPT	6-10	K.P.Evans	v	Northumb	Jesmond	1994
	P40	6-12	R.J.Hadlee	v	Lancashire	Nottingham	1980
	T20	5-26	R.J.Logan	v	Lancashire	Nottingham	2003

SOMERSET

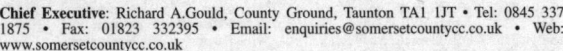

Formation of Present Club: 18 August 1875
Inaugural First-Class Match: 1882
Colours: Black, White and Maroon
Badge: Somerset Dragon
County Champions: (0); best – 2nd (Div 1) 2001
Gillette/NatWest/C&G/FP Trophy Winners: (3) 1979, 1983, 2001
Benson and Hedges Cup Winners: (2) 1981, 1982
Pro 40/National League (Div 1) Winners: (0); best – 4th 2001
Sunday League Winners: (1) 1979
Twenty20 Cup Winners: (1) 2005

Chief Executive: Richard A.Gould, County Ground, Taunton TA1 1JT • Tel: 0845 337 1875 • Fax: 01823 332395 • Email: enquiries@somersetcountycc.co.uk • Web: www.somersetcountycc.co.uk

Director of Cricket: Brian C.Rose. **Head Coach:** Andy Hurry. **Captain:** M.E.Trescothick. **Vice-Captain:** tba. **Overseas Player:** M.Kartik. **2010 Beneficiary:** Children's Hospice South West. **Scorer:** Gerald A.Stickley. ‡ New registration. NQ Not qualified for England.

‡**BURKE, James** Edward, b Plymouth, Devon 25 Jan 1991. RHB, RMF. Somerset 2nd XI debut 2008. Devon 2008-09. England U19s 2008-09. Awaiting 1st XI debut.

‡**BUTTLER, Joseph** Charles (*'Jos'*) (King's C, Taunton), b Taunton 8 Sep 1990. 6'0". RHB, WK. Debut (Somerset) 2009. Somerset 2nd XI debut 2007. England U19s 2009 to 2009-10. HS 30 v Lancs (Taunton) 2009. T20 HS 6*.

‡**COMPTON, Nicholas** Richard Denis (Harrow S; Durham U), b Durban, South Africa 26 Jun 1983. 6'1". Son of R.Compton (Natal 1978-79 to 1980-81). Grandson of D.C.S.Compton (Middlesex, England, Holkar, Europeans, Commonwealth and Cavaliers 1936-64); great-nephew of L.H.Compton (Middlesex 1938-56). RHB, OB. Middlesex 2004-09; cap 2006. MCC 2007. F-c Tour (Eng A): B 2006-07. 1000 runs (1): 1315 (2006). HS 190 M v Durham (Lord's) 2006. BB 1-94 M v Sussex (Southgate) 2007. LO HS 131 M v Kent (Canterbury) 2009 (FPT). LO BB 1-0 M v Scotland (Lord's) 2009 (FPT). T20 HS 50*.

NQ**DE BRUYN, Zander** (Helpmekaar HS; Randburg HS; Rand Afrikaans U, Jo'burg), b Johannesburg, South Africa 5 Jul 1975. 6'0". RHB, RMF. Transvaal B 1995-96 to 1996-97. Gauteng 1996-97 to 2001-02. Easterns 2002-03 to 2005-06. Titans 2004-05 to 2005-06. Worcestershire 2005. Warriors 2006-07 to 2008-09. Somerset debut 2008 (Kolpak registration); cap 2008. Lions 2009-10. **Tests** (SA): 3 (2004-05); HS 83 v I (Kanpur) 2004-05 – on debut; BB 2-32 v I (Calcutta) 2004-05. F-c Tours (SA): I 2004-05; SL 2005-06 (SA A). 1000 runs (0+1): 1048 (2003-04). HS 266* Easterns v GW (Kimberley) 2003-04. UK HS 161 Wo v Somerset (Worcester) 2005. Sm HS 120 v Durham (Chester-le-St) 2008. BB 7-67 Warriors v Titans (Pt Elizabeth) 2007-08. Sm BB 3-47 v Lancs (Manchester) 2009. LO HS 113* Surrey CB v Hunts (Cheam) 2001. LO BB 5-44 Easterns v WP (Cape Town) 2003-04. T20 HS 83*. T20 BB 4-18.

‡**DIBBLE, Adam** John, b Exeter, Devon 9 Mar 1991. RHB, RMF. Somerset 2nd XI debut 2006, aged 15 years 103 days. Awaiting 1st XI debut.

‡**HAGGETT, Calum** John (Millfield S), b Taunton 30 Oct 1990. LHB, RM. Somerset 2nd XI debut 2005 aged 14y 240d. England U19s 2009-10. Awaiting 1st XI debut.

HILDRETH, James Charles (Millfield S), b Milton Keynes, Bucks 9 Sep 1984. 5'10", RHB, RMF. Debut (Somerset) 2003; cap 2007. 1000 runs (1): 1270 (2007). HS 303* v Warwks (Taunton) 2009. BB 2-39 v Hampshire (Taunton) 2004. LO HS 151 v Scotland (Taunton) 2009 (FPT). LO BB 2-26 v Worcs (Worcester) 2008 (FPT). T20 HS 71. T20 BB 3-24.

‡**JONES, Chris** Robert, b Harold Wood, Essex 5 Nov 1990. RHB. Somerset 2nd XI debut 2006. Dorset 2007-09. Awaiting 1st XI debut.

‡[NQ]**KARTIK, Murali** (educated in New Delhi), b Madras, India 11 Sep 1976. 6'0". LHB, SLA. Railways 1996-97 to date. Central Zone 1997-98 to date. Lancashire 2005-06. Middlesex 2007-09; cap 2007. **Tests** (I): 8 (1999-00 to 2004-05); HS 43 v B (Dhaka) 2000-01; BB 4-44 v A (Bombay) 2004-05. **LOI** (I): 37 (2001-02 to 2007-08); HS 32* v A (Perth) 2003-04; BB 6-27 v A (Bombay) 2007-08. F-c Tours (Ind A): E 2003; A 2003-04 (Ind); SA 2001-02; WI 1999-00, 2002-03; P 1997-98; SL 2002; B 2000-01 (Ind). HS 96 Railways v Rest of India (Delhi) 2005-06. CC HS 62* M v Essex (Chelmsford) 2009. 50 wkts (1): 51 (2007). BB 9-70 Rest of India v Bombay (Bombay) 2000-01. CC BB 6-21 M v Glamorgan (Lord's) 2007. LO HS 44 Railways v Rajasthan (Indore) 2008-09. LO BB 6-27 (*see LOI*). IT20 HS – . IT20 BB – . T20 HS 17. T20 BB 5-13 M v Essex (Lord's) 2007 – M record.

KIESWETTER, Craig (Diocesan C; Millfield S), b Johannesburg, South Africa 18 Nov 1987. 6'1". RHB, WK. Debut (Somerset) 2007; cap 2009. Represented South Africa in U19 World Cup 2006. Qualified for England Feb 2010. 1000 runs (1): 1242 (2009). HS 153 v Lancs (Taunton) 2009. LO HS 143 England XI v Bangladesh CB (Fatullah) 2009-10. T20 HS 84.

LETT, Robin Jonathan Hugh (Millfield S; Oxford Brookes U), b Westminster, London 23 Dec 1986. Grandson of P.H.Jaques (Leicestershire 1949). 6'2". RHB, RM. Debut (Somerset) 2006 – summer contract; no 1st XI appearances in 2008-09. Oxford UCCE 2007-09. HS 57 OU v Glamorgan (Oxford) 2007. Sm HS 50 v Glamorgan (Taunton) 2006 – on debut.

MUNDAY, Michael Kenneth (Truro S, Cornwall; Corpus Christi C, Oxford), b Nottingham 22 Oct 1984. 5'7½". RHB, LB. Oxford U 2003-06; blue 2003-04-05-06. Somerset debut 2005. Cornwall 2001-08. HS 21 v Lancashire (Manchester) 2008. BB 8-55 (10-65 match) v Notts (Taunton) 2007. LO HS – and BB 1-39 Cornwall v Sussex (Truro) 2001 (CGT).

PHILLIPS, Ben James (Langley Park S and SFC, Beckenham), b Lewisham, London 30 Sep 1974. 6'6". RHB, RFM. Kent 1996-98. Northamptonshire 2002-06. Joined Somerset staff 2007 but injury prevented his appearing for 1st XI. HS 100* K v Lancs (Manchester) 1997. Sm HS 84 v Worcs (Taunton) 2009. BB 6-29 Nh v CU (Cambridge) 2006. CC BB 5-47 K v Sussex (Horsham) 1997. Sm BB 4-46 v Lancs (Taunton) 2009. LO HS 44* Nh v Kent (Canterbury) 2004 (NL). LO BB 4-25 K v Northants (Canterbury) 2000 (NL). T20 HS 41*. T20 BB 4-18.

‡[NQ]**POLLARD, Kieron** Adrian, b Tacarigua, Trinidad 12 May 1987. RHB, RMF. Trinidad & Tobago 2006-07 to date, scoring 126 (inc 7 sixes) v Barbados on debut. Signed by Somerset for T20 only in 2010. **LOI** (WI): 20 (2006-07 to 2009-10); HS 62 v A (Brisbane) 2009-10; BB 3-45 v A (Melbourne) 2009-10. HS 174 T&T v Barbados (Pointe-a-Pierre) 2008-09. BB 2-29 T&T v Jamaica (Nain) 2006-07. LO HS 87 T&T v Guyana (Port-of-Spain) 2007-07. LO BB 4-32 T&T v Jamaica (Kingston) 2006-07. IT20 HS 38. IT20 BB 2-29. T20 HS 83. T20 BB 3-17.

STIFF, David Alexander (Batley GS; Wakefield C), b Dewsbury, Yorks 20 Oct 1984. RHB, RFM. Kent 2004-06. Somerset debut 2009. Yorkshire 2nd XI 2001-03. Signed for Leicestershire in 2007 – no 1st XI appearances. HS 49 v Yorks (Taunton) 2009. BB 5-91 v Hampshire (Taunton) 2009. LO HS and BB 1-27 Y CB v Glos CB (Bristol) 2001 (CGT).

NQSUPPIAH, Arul Vivasvan (Exeter U), b Kuala Lumpur, Malaysia 30 Aug 1983. Son of R.Suppiah (Kuala Lumpur). Brother of R.V.Suppiah (Malaysia 1997-98 to 2006; f-c 2004). 6'0". RHB, SLA. Debut (Somerset) 2002; cap 2009. Kolpak registration. Malaysia 2000-01 to 2005 (*not f-c*). Devon 2003-05. 1000 runs (1): 1201 (2009). HS 151 v Notts (Taunton) 2009. BB 3-46 v WI A (Taunton) 2002. CC BB 3-58 v Hampshire (Taunton) 2009. LO HS 79 v Derbys (Derby) 2005 (NL). LO BB 4-39 v Surrey (Oval) 2006 (CGT). T20 HS 32*. T20 BB 3-25.

NQTHOMAS, Alfonso Clive (Ravensmead SS; Parow HS), b Cape Town, South Africa 9 Feb 1977. RHB, RFM. W Province 1998-99. North West 2000-01 to 2002-03. Northerns 2003-04 to 2005-06. Titans 2004-05 to 2007-08. Warwickshire 2007. Dolphins 2007-08 to date (no f-c apps). Somerset debut 2008; cap 2008. F-c Tour (SA A): Z 2004. HS 119* North West v Northerns (Pretoria) 2002-03. UK HS 70 v Hampshire (Taunton) 2009. BB 7-54 Titans v Cape Cobras (Cape Town) 2005-06. UK BB 5-46 v Yorks (Taunton) 2008. LO HS 28* v Scotland (Edinburgh) 2009 (FPT). LO BB 4-18 v Glos (Bristol) 2009 (P40). IT20 HS – . IT20 BB 3-25. T20 HS 30*. T20 BB 4-27.

TREGO, Peter David (Wyvern CS, W-s-M), b Weston-super-Mare 12 Jun 1981. 6'0". RHB, RMF. Somerset 2000-02, 2006 to date; cap 2007; 2nd XI debut 1997 when aged 16 years 20 days. Kent 2003. Middlesex 2005. Herefordshire 2005. HS 140 v WI A (Taunton) 2002. CC HS 135 v Derbys (Taunton) 2006. BB 6-59 M v Notts (Nottingham) 2005. Sm BB 4-49 v Leics (Leicester) 2007. LO HS 78 v Middx (Lord's) 2007 (FPT). LO BB 5-44 v Kent (Canterbury) 2007 (P40). T20 HS 79. T20 BB 2-17.

TRESCOTHICK, Marcus Edward (Sir Bernard Lovell S), b Keynsham 25 Dec 1975. 6'2". LHB, RM, occ WK. Debut (Somerset) 1993; cap 1999; joint captain 2002; benefit 2008; captain 2010. PCA 2000, 2009. *Wisden* 2000. MBE 2005. **Tests**: 76 (2000 to 2006, 2 as captain); HS 219 v SA (Oval) 2003; BB 1-34 v P (Karachi) 2000-01. **LOI**: 123 (2000 to 2006, 10 as captain); HS 137 v P (Lord's) 2001; BB 2-7 v Z (Manchester) 2000. F-c Tours: A 2002-03; SA 2004-05; WI 2003-04; NZ 1999-00 (Eng A), 2001-02; I 2001-02, 2005-06 (*part*); P 2000-01, 2005-06; SL 2000-01, 2003-04; B 1999-00 (Eng A), 2003-04. 1000 runs (3); most – 1817 (2009). HS 284 v Northants (Northampton) 2007. BB 4-36 (inc hat-trick) v Young A (Taunton) 1995. CC BB 4-82 v Yorks (Leeds) 1998. Hat-trick 1995. LO HS 184 v Glos (Taunton) 2008 (P40) – Sm record. LO BB 4-50 v Northants (Northampton) 2000 (NL). T20 HS 107.

TURNER, Mark Leif (Thornhill CS), b Sunderland, Co Durham 23 Oct 1984. 5'11". RHB, RMF. Durham 2005-06. Somerset debut 2007. HS 57 v Derbys (Taunton) 2007. BB 4-30 v LU (Taunton) 2007. CC BB 3-53 v Lancs (Manchester) 2008. LO HS 15* v Essex (Taunton) 2009 (P40). LO BB 3-27 v Glos (Bristol) 2009 (P40). T20 HS 7. T20 BB 2-20.

WALLER, Maximilian Thomas Charles (Millfield S; Bournemouth U), b Salisbury, Wiltshire 3 March 1988. 6'0". RHB, LB. Debut (Somerset) 2009. Somerset 2nd XI debut 2006. Dorset 2007-08. HS 28 v Hampshire (Southampton) 2009. BB 2-27 v Sussex (Hove) 2009. LO HS 2* v Kent (Canterbury) 2009 (FPT). LO BB 2-34 v Sussex (Taunton) 2009 (P40). T20 HS 1. T20 BB 3-17.

‡**NQWHITE, Cameron** Leon, b Bairnsdale, Victoria, Australia 18 Aug 1983. 6'1½". RHB, LBG. Victoria 2000-01 to date; captain 2004-05 to date. Somerset 2006-07; captain 2006 (*part*); cap 2007. Rejoins for T20 only. **Tests** (A): 4 (2008-09); HS 46 v I (Nagpur) 2008-09; BB 2-71 v I (Chandigarh) 2008-09. **LOI** (A): 57 (2005-06 to 2009-10); HS 105 v E (Southampton) 2009; BB 3-5 v B (Darwin) 2008. F-c Tours (A): I 2008-09; P 2005-06 (Aus A), 2007-08 (Aus A). 1000 runs (1); most – 1190 (2006). HS 260* v Derbys (Derby) 2006 – world record score in the fourth innings of a f-c match. BB 6-66 Vic v WA (Perth) 2002-03. Sm BB 5-148 v Surrey (Guildford) 2006. LO HS 126* Vic v NSW (Canberra) 2006-07. LO BB 4-15 Vic v Tas (Melbourne) 2004-05. IT20 HS 64*. IT20 BB 1-11. T20 HS 141* v Worcs (Worcester) 2006 – Sm record and 3rd highest in all T20. T20 BB 4-10.

^{NQ}**WILLOUGHBY, Charl** Myles (Wynberg BHS; Stellenbosch U), b Cape Town, South Africa 3 Dec 1974. 6'2". LHB, LMF. Boland 1994-95 to 1999-00. W Province 2000-01 to 2003-04. MCC 2001, 2004. WP-Boland 2004-05. Leicestershire 2005 (Kolpak registration). Cape Cobras 2005-06 to 2006-07. Somerset debut 2006 (Kolpak); cap 2007. Berkshire 2000. **Tests** (SA): 2 (2003); HS – ; BB 1-47 v B (Chittagong) 2002-03 – on debut. **LOI** (SA): 3 (1999-00 to 2003); HS 0; BB 2-39 v P (Sharjah) 1999-00 – on debut. F-c Tours (SA): E 2003; WI 2000 (SA A); Z 1998-99 (SA Acad), 2004 (SA A); B 2003. HS 47 v Worcs (Taunton) 2006. 50 wkts (4+2); most – 66 (2006). BB 7-44 v Glos (Taunton) 2006. LO HS 15 v Kent (Canterbury) 2009 (FPT). LO BB 6-16 Le v Somerset (Leicester) 2005 (CGT) – Le record. T20 HS 11. T20 BB 4-9.

RELEASED/RETIRED
(Having made a County First-Class or List A appearance in 2009)

^{NQ}**BANKS, Omari** Ahmed Clement (Albena Lake Hodge CS), b Road Bay, Antigua 17 Jul 1982. 6'4". RHB, OB. Leeward Islands 2000-01 to date. Leicestershire 2001 (1 match – v Pakistanis). Carib Beer XI 2002-03 to 2003-04. Somerset 2009. **Tests** (WI): 10 (2002-03 to 2005); HS 50* v SL (Gros Islet, St Lucia) 2003; BB 4-87 v B (Kingston) 2004. **LOI** (WI): 5 (2002-03 to 2005); HS 33 and BB 2-24 v SL (Colombo) 2005. F-c Tours (WI): E 2004, 2006 (WI A); SL 2005; Z 2003-04. HS 108 Leeward Is v Jamaica (Basseterre) 2008-09. Sm HS 53 v Sussex (Taunton) 2009. BB 7-41 (13-154 match) Leeward Is v Windward Is (Georgetown) 2009-10. Sm BB 4-120 v Hampshire (Southampton) 2009. LO HS 77* Rest of Leeward Is v Canada (Kingston) 2003-04. LO BB 4-23 Rest of Leeward Is v N Windward Is (Kingston) 2001-02. T20 HS 50*. T20 BB 1-14.

CADDICK, Andrew Richard (Papanui HS), b Christchurch, NZ 21 Nov 1968. Son of English emigrants – qualified for England 1992. 6'5". RHB, RFM. Somerset 1991-2009; cap 1992; benefit 1999, 2009. Represented NZ in 1987-88 Youth World Cup. *Wisden* 2000. **Tests**: 62 (1993 to 2002-03); HS 49* v A (Birmingham) 2001; BB 7-46 v SA (Durban) 1999-00. **LOI**: 54 (1993 to 2002-03); HS 36 v A (Oval) 2001; BB 4-19 v SA (Johannesburg) 1999-00. F-c Tours: A 1992-93 (Eng A), 2002-03; SA 1999-00; WI 1993-94, 1997-98; NZ 1996-97, 2000-01; P 2000-01; SL 2000-01; Z 1996-97. HS 92 v Worcs (Worcester) 1995. 50 wkts (12) inc 100 (1): 105 (1998). BB 9-32 (12-120 match) v Lancs (Taunton) 1993. LO HS 39 v Hampshire (Taunton) 1996 (SL). LO BB 6-30 v Glos (Taunton) 1992 (NWT). T20 HS 0. T20 BB 2-12.

DURSTON, Wesley John (Millfield S; University C, Worcester), b Taunton 6 Oct 1980. 5'10". RHB, OB. Somerset 2002-09. HS 146* v Derbys (Derby) 2005. BB 3-23 v SL A (Taunton) 2004. CC BB 2-31 v Surrey (Bath) 2006. LO HS 62* v Yorks (Taunton) 2006 (P40). LO BB 3-44 v Surrey (Taunton) 2006 (P40). T20 HS 57. T20 BB 3-25.

GAZZARD, Carl Matthew (Mounts Bay CS, Penzance; Richard Huish C), b Penzance, Cornwall 15 Apr 1982. 6'0". RHB, WK. Somerset 2002-08. Cornwall 1998-2007. HS 74 v Worcs (Worcester) 2005. LO HS 157 v Derbys (Derby) 2004 (NL). T20 HS 39.

^{NQ}**LANGER, Justin** Lee (Aquinas C; U of WA), b Perth, Australia 21 Nov 1970. Nephew of R.S.Langer (W Australia 1973-74 to 1981-82). 5'8". LHB, RM. W Australia 1991-92 to 2007-08. Middlesex 1998-2000; cap 1998; captain 2000. Somerset 2006-09; cap 2007; captain 2007-09. *Wisden* 2004. **Tests** (A): 105 (1992-93 to 2006-07); HS 250 v E (Melbourne) 2002-03. **LOI**: 8 (1993-94 to 1997); HS 36 v I (Sharjah) 1993-94. F-c Tours (A): E 1995 (Young A), 1997, 2001, 2005; SA 1996-97, 2001-02, 2005-06; WI 1994-95, 1998-99, 2002-03; NZ 1992-93, 1999-00, 2004-05; I 2000-01, 2004-05; P 1994-95, 1998-99, 2002-03 (*in UAE*); SL 1999, 2002-03 (*v P*), 2003-04; Z 1999-00. 1000 runs (5+6); most – 1472 (2000). HS 342 v Surrey (Guildford) 2006 – Somerset record f-c score. Scored 315 v Middx (Taunton) 2007 in his next CC innings. BB 2-17 Aus A v SA A (Brisbane) 1997-98. UK BB 1-10 M v Northants (Northampton) 1998. LO HS 146 WA v S Aus (Perth) 1999-00. LO BB 3-51 M v Surrey (Guildford) 1998 (SL). T20 HS 97.

N.J.Edwards and P.S.Jones left the staff, without making a County First-Class or List A appearance in 2009.

SOMERSET 2009

RESULTS SUMMARY

	Place	Won	Lost	Tied	Drew	NR
County Championship (1st Division)	3rd	3	1		12	
All First-Class Matches		3	1		12	
FP Trophy (Group B)	QF	7	1			1
Pro40 League (1st Division)	2nd	5	2			1
Twenty20 Cup (Midlands/West/Wales Division)	Finalist	8	3			1

LV COUNTY CHAMPIONSHIP AVERAGES
BATTING AND FIELDING

Cap		M	I	NO	HS	Runs	Avge	100	50	Ct/St
1999	M.E.Trescothick	16	26	2	146	1817	75.70	8	9	21
2009	C.Kieswetter	16	24	3	153	1242	59.14	4	7	48
2009	A.V.Suppiah	16	26	1	151	1201	48.04	3	6	18
2007	J.C.Hildreth	15	23	2	303*	934	44.47	2	4	10
2007	J.L.Langer	15	21	2	122*	831	43.73	2	4	17
2007	P.D.Trego	16	23	5	103*	610	33.88	1	3	5
	B.J.Phillips	7	8	2	84	190	31.66	–	1	4
	O.A.C.Banks	6	7	2	53	156	31.20	–	1	1
2008	Z.de Bruyn	16	25	3	106	686	31.18	1	6	3
2008	A.C.Thomas	14	15	3	70	338	28.16	–	3	2
	D.A.Stiff	10	14	5	49	193	21.44	–	–	–
	M.T.C.Waller	4	6	1	28	67	13.40	–	–	1
2007	C.M.Willoughby	16	13	4	23	40	4.44	–	–	4

Also batted: J.C.Buttler (1 match) 30; A.R.Caddick (5 – cap 1992) 1, 3, 11* (1 ct); W.J.Durston (1) 0, 54*; M.K.Munday (1) 1; M.L.Turner (1) did not bat (1 ct).

BOWLING

	O	M	R	W	Avge	Best	5wI	10wM
C.M.Willoughby	555.4	161	1622	54	30.03	5- 56	3	–
D.A.Stiff	268.2	33	1120	31	36.12	5- 91	1	–
A.C.Thomas	401.1	77	1317	35	37.62	5- 53	1	–
B.J.Phillips	158.1	37	456	12	38.00	4- 46	–	–
A.V.Suppiah	212.5	47	682	15	45.46	3- 58	–	–
P.D.Trego	256.5	57	889	19	46.78	3- 53	–	–
A.R.Caddick	131.1	24	525	10	52.50	3- 53	–	–
Also bowled:								
M.T.C.Waller	82.4	11	320	5	64.00	2- 27	–	–
O.A.C.Banks	111.1	15	456	7	65.14	4-120	–	–
Z.de Bruyn	136	23	541	7	77.28	3- 47	–	–

W.J.Durston 2-0-13-0; M.K.Munday 25.1-0-114-4; M.E.Trescothick 5-2-10-0; M.L.Turner 30-4-111-2.

Somerset played no fixtures outside the County Championship in 2009. The First-Class Averages (pp 228–244) give the records of their players in all first-class county matches.

SOMERSET RECORDS

FIRST-CLASS CRICKET

Highest Total	For 850-7d		v	Middlesex	Taunton	2007
	V 811		by	Surrey	The Oval	1899
Lowest Total	For 25		v	Glos	Bristol	1947
	V 22		by	Glos	Bristol	1920
Highest Innings	For 342	J.L.Langer	v	Surrey	Guildford	2006
	V 424	A.C.MacLaren	for	Lancashire	Taunton	1895

Highest Partnership for each Wicket

1st	346	L.C.H.Palairet/H.T.Hewett	v	Yorkshire	Taunton	1892
2nd	290	J.C.W.MacBryan/M.D.Lyon	v	Derbyshire	Burton upon T	1924
3rd	319	P.M.Roebuck/M.D.Crowe	v	Leics	Taunton	1984
4th	310	P.W.Denning/I.T.Botham	v	Glos	Taunton	1980
5th	320	J.D.Francis/I.D.Blackwell	v	Durham UCCE	Taunton	2005
6th	265	W.E.Alley/K.E.Palmer	v	Northants	Northampton	1961
7th	279	R.J.Harden/G.D.Rose	v	Sussex	Taunton	1997
8th	172	I.V.A.Richards/I.T.Botham	v	Leics	Leicester	1983
	172	A.R.K.Pierson/P.S.Jones	v	N Zealanders	Taunton	1999
9th	183	C.H.M.Greetham/H.W.Stephenson	v	Leics	Weston-s-Mare	1963
	183	C.J.Tavaré/N.A.Mallender	v	Sussex	Hove	1990
10th	163	I.D.Blackwell/N.A.M.McLean	v	Derbyshire	Taunton	2003

Best Bowling	For 10- 49	E.J.Tyler	v	Surrey	Taunton	1895
(Innings)	V 10- 35	A.Drake	for	Yorkshire	Weston-s-Mare	1914
Best Bowling	For 16- 83	J.C.White	v	Worcs	Bath	1919
(Match)	V 17-137	W.Brearley	for	Lancashire	Manchester	1905

Most Runs – Season	2761	W.E.Alley	(av 58.74)		1961
Most Runs – Career	21142	H.Gimblett	(av 36.96)		1935-54
Most 100s – Season	11	S.J.Cook			1991
Most 100s – Career	49	H.Gimblett			1935-54
Most Wkts – Season	169	A.W.Wellard	(av 19.24)		1938
Most Wkts – Career	2165	J.C.White	(av 18.03)		1909-37
Most Career W-K Dismissals	1007	H.W.Stephenson	(698 ct; 309 st)		1948-64
Most Career Catches in the Field	381	J.C.White			1909-37

LIMITED-OVERS CRICKET

Highest Total	FPT	413-4	v	Devon	Torquay	1990
	P40	377-9	v	Sussex	Hove	2003
	T20	250-3	v	Glos	Taunton	2006
Lowest Total	FPT	58	v	Middlesex	Southgate	2000
	P40	58	v	Essex	Chelmsford	1977
	T20	109	v	Sussex	Birmingham	2009
		106	v	Trinidad & T	Bangalore	2009-10
Highest Innings	FPT	162*	C.J.Tavaré	v	Devon	Torquay	1990
	P40	184	M.E.Trescothick	v	Glos	Taunton	2008
	T20	141*	C.L.White	v	Worcs	Worcester	2006
Best Bowling	FPT	8-66	S.R.G.Francis	v	Derbyshire	Derby	2004
	P40	6-24	I.V.A.Richards	v	Lancashire	Manchester	1983
	T20	4-15	A.W.Laraman	v	Worcs	Taunton	2004

SURREY

Formation of Present Club: 22 August 1845
Inaugural First-Class Match: 1864
Colours: Chocolate
Badge: Prince of Wales' Feathers
County Champions (since 1890): (18) 1890, 1891, 1892, 1894, 1895, 1899, 1914, 1952, 1953, 1954, 1955, 1956, 1957, 1958, 1971, 1999, 2000, 2002
Joint Champions: (1) 1950
Gillette/NatWest/C&G/FP Trophy Winners: (1) 1982
Benson and Hedges Cup Winners: (3) 1974, 1997, 2001
Pro 40/National League (Div 1) Winners: (1) 2003
Sunday League Winners: (1) 1996
Twenty20 Cup Winners: (1) 2003

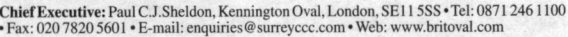

Chief Executive: Paul C.J.Sheldon, Kennington Oval, London, SE11 5SS • Tel: 0871 246 1100
• Fax: 020 7820 5601 • E-mail: enquiries@surreyccc.com • Web: www.britoval.com

Cricket Manager: Chris Adams. Assistant Coach: I.D.K.Salisbury. Captain: R.J.Hamilton-Brown. Vice-Captain: tba. Overseas Player: P.P.Chawla. 2010 Beneficiary: Surrey Cricket Foundation. Head Groundsman: W.H. (Bill) Gordon. Scorer: Keith R.Booth. ‡ New registration. NQ Not qualified for England.

AFZAAL, Usman (Manvers Pierrepont CS; S Notts C), b Rawalpindi, Pakistan 9 Jun 1977. 6'0". LHB, SLA. Nottinghamshire 1995-2003; cap 2000. MCC 2002. Northamptonshire 2004-07; cap 2005. Surrey debut 2008, scoring 134* v Lancs; cap 2009. Tests: 3 (2001); HS 54 and BB 1-49 v A (Oval) 2001. F-c Tours: SA 1996-97 (Nt); WI 2000-01 (Eng A); NZ 2001-02. 1000 runs (1); most – 1365 (2004). HS 204* v Northants (Northampton) 2009. BB 4-101 Nt v Glos (Nottingham) 1998. Sy BB 3-51 v Leics (Leicester) 2009. LO HS 132 Nh v Yorks (Leeds) 2007 (FPT). Sy BB 4-49 v Derbys (Chesterfield) 2008 (P40). T20 HS 98* v Middx (Lord's) 2009 – Sy record. T20 BB 2-15.

‡BATTY, Gareth Jon (Bingley GS), b Bradford, Yorks 13 Oct 1977. Younger brother of J.D.Batty (Yorkshire and Somerset 1989-96). 5'11". RHB, OB. Yorkshire 1997. Surrey 1999-2001. Worcestershire 2002-09. Tests: 7 (2003-04 to 2005); HS 38 v SL (Kandy) 2003-04; BB 3-55 v SL (Galle) 2003-04. Took wicket with his third ball in Test cricket. LOI: 10 (2002-03 to 2008-09); HS 17 v WI (Bridgetown) 2008-09; BB 2-40 v WI (Gros Islet, St Lucia) 2003-04. F-c Tours: WI 2003-04, 2005-06; NZ 2008-09 (Eng A); SL 2002-03 (ECB Acad); SL 2003-04; B 2003-04. HS 133 Wo v Surrey (Oval) 2004. Sy HS 25* and Sy BB 2-45 v Sri Lanka A (Oval) 1990. 50 wkts (2); most – 60 (2003). BB 7-52 (10-113 match) v Northants (Northampton) 2004. LO HS 83* Sy v Yorks (Oval) 2001 (NL). LO BB 5-35 Wo v Hampshire (Southampton) 2009 (FPT). IT20 HS 4. IT20 BB – . T20 HS 87. T20 BB 3-21.

BROWN, Michael James (Queen Elizabeth GS, Blackburn; Collingwood C, Durham U), b Burnley, Lancs 9 Feb 1980. 6'0" Elder brother of D.O.Brown (see GLOUCESTERSHIRE). RHB, OB. Middlesex 1999-2003. Durham UCCE 2001-02. British U 2001-02. Hampshire 2004-08; cap 2007. Surrey debut 2009. 1000 runs (1): 1078 (2007). HS 133 Ha v LU (Southampton) 2006. CC HS 126* Ha v Durham (Chester-le-St) 2007. Sy HS 120 v Derbys (Croydon) 2009. LO HS 96* Ha v Worcs (Southampton) 2008 (FPT). T20 HS 77.

BURNS, Rory Joseph (City of London Freemen's S), b Epsom 26 Aug 1990. LHB, WK. Surrey 2nd XI debut 2009. Awaiting 1st XI debut.

‡^{NQ}**CHAWLA, Piyush** Pramod, b Aligarh, Uttar Pradesh, India 24 Dec 1988. LHB, LB. Central Zone 2005-06 to date. Uttar Pradesh 2005-06 to date. Sussex 2009; cap 2009. **Tests** (I): 2 (2005-06 to 2007-08); HS 4 and BB 2-66 v SA (Kanpur) 2007-08. **LOI** (I): 21 (2007 to 2008); HS 13* v E (Manchester) 2007; BB 4-23 v Hong Kong (Karachi) 2008. F-c Tours (I A): A 2006; Z 2007. HS 102* Sx v Worcs (Worcester) 2009. BB 6-46 (10-58 match) India A v Zimbabwe Select (Bulawayo) 2007. UK BB 6-52 (11-170 match) Sx v Somerset (Hove) 2009. LO HS 93 Central Zone v East Zone (Cuttack) 2008-09. LO BB 6-46 Uttar Pradesh v Railways (Indore) 2009-10. T20 HS 33. T20 BB 3-23.

‡**DAVIES, Steven** Michael (King Charles I S, Kidderminster), b Bromsgrove, Worcs 17 Jun 1986. 5'10". LHB, WK. Worcestershire 2005-09. Worcs 2nd XI debut 2001 when 15 years 8 days. MCC 2006-07. **LOI**: 1 (2009-10); HS 5 v A (Centurion) 2009-10. F-c Tour (Eng A): B 2006-07. 1000 runs (2); most – 1052 (2006). HS 192 Wo v Glos (Bristol) 2006. LO HS 119 Wo v Glos (Worcester) 2008 (P40). IT20 HS 27. T20 HS 73.

DERNBACH, Jade Winston (St John the Baptist S), b Johannesburg, South Africa 3 Mar 1986. 6'1½". RHB, RMF. Italian passport. UK resident since 1998. Debut (Surrey) 2003, when aged 17. HS 19 v Northants (Northampton) 2009. BB 6-47 v Leics (Leicester) 2009. LO HS 21 v Warwks (Birmingham) 2005 (NL). LO BB 5-31 v Derbys (Chesterfield) 2008 (P40). T20 HS 9. T20 BB 3-32.

EVANS, Laurie John (Whitgift S; The John Fisher S; St Mary's C, Durham U), b Lambeth, London 12 Oct 1987. 6'0". RHB, RFM. Durham UCCE 2007. MCC 2007. Surrey debut 2009. Surrey 2nd XI debut 2005. HS 133* DU v Lancs (Durham) 2007. Sy HS 9 v Glos (Oval) 2009. LO HS 36* v Derbys (Croydon) 2009 (P40). T20 HS 7.

‡**HAMILTON-BROWN, Rory** James (Millfield S), b St John's Wood, London 3 Sep 1987. 6'0". RHB, OB. Surrey 2005; rejoins as captain 2010. No f-c appearances 2006-07. Sussex 2008-09. HS 171* and BB 2-49 Sx v Yorks (Hove) 2009. Sy HS 9 v Bangladesh A (Oval) 2005. LO HS 49 Sx v Notts (Hove) 2009 (P40). LO BB 3-28 v Leics (Leicester) 2007 (P40). T20 HS 69*. T20 BB 4-15.

HARINATH, Arun (Whitgift S; Loughborough U), b Sutton 26 Mar 1987. LHB, OB. Loughborough UCCE 2007-09. MCC 2008. Surrey debut 2009. Surrey 2nd XI debut 2003. Buckinghamshire 2007-08. HS 69 LU v Worcs (Worcester) 2007. Sy HS 57 v Glamorgan (Oval) 2009. BB – . LO HS 21* v Warwks (Oval) 2009 (P40).

JORDAN, Christopher James (Comber Mere S, Barbados; Dulwich C), b Christ Church, Barbados 4 Oct 1988. 6'0". RHB, RFM. Debut (Surrey) 2007. HS 57 v Notts (Nottingham) 2008. BB 4-84 v Essex (Guildford) 2009. LO HS 38 v Yorkshire (Guildford) 2008 (P40). LO BB 3-28 v Yorks (Scarborough) 2007 (P40). T20 HS 31. T20 BB 2-34.

KING, Simon James (Warlingham S; John Fisher S), b Warlingham 4 Sep 1987. RHB, OB. Debut (Surrey) 2009. Surrey 2nd XI debut 2005. HS 8 v Derbys (Croydon) 2009. BB 3-61 v Middx (Lord's) 2009 – on debut. LO HS 5* v Kent (Beckenham) 2009.

LINLEY, Timothy Edward (St Mary's RC CS, Menston; Notre Dame SFC; Oxford Brookes U), b Leeds, Yorkshire 23 Mar 1982. 6'2". RHB, RFM. Oxford UCCE 2003-05. British U 2004. Sussex 2006 (1 match). Surrey debut 2009. HS 42 OU v Derbys (Oxford) 2005. Sy HS 36 v Kent (Canterbury) 2009. BB 4-77 v Essex (Guildford) 2009. LO HS 20* v Warwks (Oval) 2009 (P40). LO BB 2-38 v Glamorgan (Oval) 2009 (P40). T20 HS 8. T20 BB – .

MEAKER, Stuart Christopher (Cranleigh S), b Durban, South Africa 21 Jan 1989. Moved to UK in 2001. 6'1". RHB, RFM. Debut (Surrey) 2008. England U19s 2007-08. Surrey 2nd XI debut 2007. HS 72 v Essex (Colchester) 2009. BB 3-86 v Notts (Oval) 2008. LO HS 10* and BB 2-21 v Kent (Canterbury) 2009 (P40).

NQNEL, Andre (Dr E.G.Jansen S, Boksburg), b Germiston, Transvaal, South Africa 15 Jul 1977. 6'4". RHB, RFM. Easterns 1996-97 to 2003-04. Northamptonshire 2003; cap 2003. Titans 2004-05. Essex 2005 (one match), 2007-08. Lions 2008-09 to date. Gauteng 2008-09. Surrey debut 2009 (Kolpak registration). **Tests** (SA): 36 (2001-02 to 2008); HS 34 v WI (Port Elizabeth) 2007-08; BB 6-32 (10-88 match) v WI (Bridgetown) 2004-05. **LOI** (SA): 79 (2000-01 to 2008); HS 30* v NZ (Port Elizabeth) 2007-08; BB 5-45 v B (Providence, Guyana) 2006-07. F-c Tours (SA): E 2008; A 2005-06; WI 2000-01, 2004-05; NZ 2003-04; P 2003-04, 2007-08; SL 2006; Z 2001-02, 2007 (SA A); Ireland/Scotland 1999 (SA Acad). HS 56 SA v Bangladesh A (Worcester) 2008. CC HS 42 Nh v Glamorgan (Cardiff) 2003. Sy HS 32 v Middx (Oval) 2009. BB 6-25 Easterns v Gauteng (Johannesburg) 2001-02. UK BB 6-36 v Northants (Northampton) 2009. LO HS 58 Lions v Cape Cobras (Paarl) 2008-09. LO BB 6-27 Easterns v GW (Benoni) 2000-01. IT20 HS 0*. IT20 BB 2-19. T20 HS 19. T20 BB 2-13.

RAMPRAKASH, Mark Ravin (Gayton HS; Harrow Weald SFC), b Bushey, Herts 5 Sep 1969. 5'9". RHB, OB. Middlesex 1987-2000; cap 1990; captain 1997-99. Surrey debut 2001 – scoring 146 v Kent (Oval); cap 2002; joint Testimonial 2008. YC 1991. *Wisden* 2006. PCA 2006. **Tests**: 52 (1991 to 2001-02); HS 154 v WI (Bridgetown) 1997-98; BB 1-2 v WI (Georgetown) 1997-98. **LOI**: 18 (1991 to 2001-02); HS 51 v WI (Port-of-Spain) 1997-98; BB 3-28 v Z (Harare) 2001-02. F-c Tours: A 1994-95 (*part*), 1998-99; SA 1995-96; WI 1991-92 (Eng A), 1993-94, 1997-98; NZ 1991-92, 2001-02; I 1994-95 (Eng A), 2001-02; P 1990-91 (Eng A); SL 1990-91 (Eng A). 1000 runs (19, inc 2000 (3): 2258 (1995), 2278 (2006), 2026 (2007)). Averaged 103.54 in f-c matches 2006, the second-highest average by any batsman scoring 1000 runs in a season (105.28 in CC), setting world records by scoring 2000 runs in only 20 innings, posting scores of at least 150 in five successive matches and reaching double figures in each of his 24 innings. In 2007 he became the first to score 2000 f-c runs in a season and average over 100 (101.30) twice. Ten hundreds in a season (2): 1995, 2007. HS 301* v Northants (Oval) 2006. BB 3-32 M v Glamorgan (Lord's) 1998. Sy BB 2-35 v Northants (Northampton) 2004. LO HS 147* M v Worcs (Lord's) 1990 (SL) – M record. LO BB 5-38 M v Leics (Lord's) 1993 (SL). T20 HS 85*.

SCHOFIELD, Christopher Paul (Wardle HS), b Birch Hill, Rochdale, Lancs 6 Oct 1978. 6'2". LHB, LBG. Lancashire 1998-2004; cap 2002. Surrey debut 2006. **Tests**: 2 (2000); HS 57 v Z (Nottingham) 2000. BB – . F-c Tours (Eng A): WI 2000-01; NZ 1999-00; B 1999-00. HS 144 v Essex (Colchester) 2009. BB 6-120 Eng A v Bangladesh (Chittagong) 1999-00. Sy BB 5-40 v Northants (Northampton) 2009. LO HS 75* v Hants (Southampton) 2007 (FPT). LO BB 5-31 La v Derbys (Manchester) 2001 (NL). IT20 HS 9*. IT20 BB 2-15. T20 HS 27. T20 BB 4-12.

SPRIEGEL, Matthew Neil William (Whitgift S; Loughborough U), b Epsom 4 Mar 1987. 6'3". LHB, OB. Loughborough UCCE 2007-08; captain 2007-08. Surrey debut 2008. Surrey 2nd XI debut 2004. HS 100 v Glamorgan (Oval) 2009. BB 2-28 v Hampshire (Oval) 2008. LO HS 81* v Leics (Leicester) 2009 (P40). LO BB 2-23 v Kent (Canterbury) 2009 (P40). T20 HS 25. T20 BB 4-33.

‡TREMLETT, Christopher Timothy (Thornden S, Chandler's Ford; Taunton's C, Southampton), b Southampton, Hampshire 2 Sep 1981. Son of T.M.Tremlett (Hampshire 1976-91); grandson of M.F.Tremlett (Somerset, CD and England 1947-60). 6'7". RHB, RMF. Hampshire 2000-09, taking wicket of M.H.Richardson (NZ A) with his first ball; cap 2004. **Tests**: 3 (2007); HS 25* v I (Oval) 2007; BB 3-12 v I (Nottingham) 2007. **LOI**: 9 (2005 to 2008); HS 19* v I (Birmingham) 2007; BB 4-32 v B (Nottingham) 2005 – on debut (hat-trick ball hit stump without dislodging bails). F-c Tour (ECB Acad): SL 2002-03. HS 64 H v Glos (Southampton) 2005. BB 6-44 H v Sussex (Hove) 2005. Hat-trick: H v Notts (Nottingham) 2005. LO HS 38* H v Cheshire (Alderley Edge) 2004 (CGT). LO BB 4-25 H v Essex (Southend) 2002 (NL). IT20 HS – . IT20 BB 2-45.T20 HS 13. T20 BB 4-25.

^{NQ}**WALTERS, Stewart** Jonathan (Guildford GS, Perth, WA), b Mornington, Victoria, Australia 25 Jun 1983. 6'1". RHB, RM. Debut (Surrey) 2006. HS 188 v Leics (Oval) 2009. BB 1-4 v Durham (Chester-le-St) 2007. LO HS 91 v Northants (Oval) 2008 (P40). LO BB 1-12 v Yorks (Scarborough) 2007 (P40). T20 HS 34. T20 BB 1-9.

^{NQ}**WATERS, Seren** Robert (Cranleigh S), b Nairobi, Kenya 11 Apr 1990. 6'0". RHB, LBG. British passport. Kenya 2008-09 to 2009-10. Surrey 2nd XI debut 2008. Awaiting 1st XI debut. **LOI** (K): 12 (2008-09 to 2009); HS 74 v SA (Kimberley) 2008-09. HS 157* Kenya v Canada (King City) 2009. LO HS 74 (*see LOI*).

^{NQ}**WILSON, Gary** Craig (Methodist C, Belfast; Manchester Met), b Dundonald, N Ireland 5 Feb 1986. RHB, WK. 5'10". Ireland 2005 to 2009-10. MCC YC 2005. Surrey 2nd XI debut 2006. Awaiting Surrey f-c debut. **LOI** (Ire): 16 (2007 to 2009); HS 51 v Scotland (Dublin) 2008. HS 53 Ireland v Afghanistan (Dambulla) 2009-10. LO HS 61 Ireland v Uganda (Krugersdorp) 2008-09. IT20 HS 29. T20 HS 29.

RELEASED/RETIRED
(Having made a County First-Class or List A appearance in 2009)

BATTY, J.N. – *see GLOUCESTERSHIRE.*

BENNING, J.G.E. – *see LEICESTERSHIRE.*

BUTCHER, Mark Alan (Trinity S; Archbishop Tenison's S, Croydon), b Croydon 23 Aug 1972. Son of A.R.Butcher (Surrey, Glamorgan and England 1972-92, 1998); brother of G.P.Butcher (Glamorgan and Surrey 1994-2001); nephew of I.P.Butcher (Leics and Glos 1980-90) and M.S.Butcher (Surrey 1982). 5'11". LHB, RM/OB. Surrey 1992-2009; cap 1996; captain 2005-09; benefit 2005. TCCB XI 1995-96. **Tests**: 71 (1997 to 2004-05, 1 as captain); HS 173* v A (Leeds) 2001; BB 4-42 v A (Birmingham) 2001. F-c Tours: A 1996-97 (Eng A), 1998-99, 2002-03; SA 1999-00, 2004-05; WI 1997-98, 2003-04; NZ 2001-02; I 2001-02; SL 2003-04; B 2003-04. 1000 runs (8); most – 1604 (1996). HS 259 v Leics (Leicester) 1999. BB 5-86 v Lancs (Manchester) 2000. LO HS 139 v Kent (Canterbury) 2008 (FPT). LO BB 3-23 v Sussex (Oval) 1992 (SL). T20 HS 60.

^{NQ}**COLLINS, Pedro** Tyrone (St James S), b Boscobelle, Barbados 12 Aug 1976. Half-brother of F.H.Edwards (Barbados & West Indies 2001-02 to date). 6'2". RHB, LFM. Barbados 1996-97 to date. Busta Cup XI 2001-02. Surrey 2008-09 (Kolpak registration). **Tests** (WI): 32 (1998-99 to 2006); HS 24 v I (Kingston) 2001-02; BB 6-53 v B (Kingston) 2004. **LOI** (WI): 30 (1999-00 to 2004-05); HS 10* v NZ (Wellington) 1999-00; BB 5-43 v A (Adelaide) 2004-05. F-c Tours (WI): E 2004; SA 1997-98 (WI A), 2007-08; NZ 1999-00; I 1998-99 (WI A), 2002-03; P (Sharjah) 2001-02; SL 2001-02; Z 2001; B 1998-99 (WI A), 1999-00, 2002-03; Kenya 2001. HS 25 Barbados v T&T (Pointe-a-Pierre) 2003-04. Sy HS 23 v Kent (Canterbury) 2009. 50 wkts (0+1): 54 (2003-04). BB 6-24 Barbados v Windward Is (Portsmouth, Dominica) 2006-07. Sy BB 5-75 v Derbys (Derby) 2009. LO HS 55* Barbados v Guyana (Georgetown) 2001-02. LO BB 7-11 Barbados v WI U-19 (Blairmont, Berbice) 2007-08. T20 HS 1*. T20 BB 3-13.

^{NQ}**ELLIOTT, Grant** David (St Stithians) b Johannesburg, South Africa 21 Mar 1979. 6'1". RHB, RFM. Debut Transvaal B 1996-97. SA Academy 1998. Griqualand West 1999-00 to 2000-01. Gauteng 2001-02 to 2002-03. Wellington 2005-06 to date. Surrey 2009 (one f-c match). Qualified for NZ in 2007. **Tests** (NZ): 5 (2007-08 to 2009-10); HS 25 v P (Dunedin) 2009-10. BB 2-8 v P (Wellington) 2009-10. **LOI** (NZ): 28 (2008 to 2009-10); HS 115 v A (Sydney) 2008-09; BB 4-31 v E (Johannesburg) 2009-10. F-c Tours (NZ): E 2008; A 2008-09; B 2008-09. HS 196* Wellington v Auckland (Wellington) 2007-08. Sy HS 22 v Middx (Oval) 2009. BB 4-56 Gauteng v Easterns (Johannesburg) 2002-03. LO HS 115 (*see LOI*). LO BB 5-34 Wellington v Otago (Wellington) 2007-08. IT20 HS 23*. IT20 BB 1-11. T20 HS 57. T20 BB 2-13.

HARRIS, R.J. – *see YORKSHIRE.*

NO**HERATH**, Herath Mudiyanselage **Rangana** Keerthi Bandara, b Kurunegala, Sri Lanka 19 Mar 1978. LHB, SLA. Kurunegala Youth 1996-97 to 1997-98. Moors Sports Club 1998-99 to date. Colombo District 2000-01 to 2001-02. North Central Province 2003-04 to 2004-05. Wayamba 2008-09. Surrey 2009. **Tests** (SL): 21 (1999-00 to 2009-10); HS 33* v P (Faisalabad) 2004-05; BB 5-99 v P (Colombo, PSS) 2009. **LOI** (SL): 6 (2003-04 to 2004); HS 0*; BB 3-28 v SA (Dambulla) 2004. F-c Tours (SL): E 1999 (SL A), 2007 (SL A); SA 2003-04 (SL A), 2008-09 (SL A); WI 2007-08; NZ 2004-05; I 2003-04 (SL A), 2009-10; P 1999-00, 2004-05; Z 1999-00, 2004, 2007-08 (SL A); B 2005-06 (SL A), 2008-09. HS 71* Moors SC v Nondescripts (Colombo) 2002-03. Sy HS 52* v Glos (Bristol) 2009. 50 wkts (0+2); most – 72 (2000-01). BB 8-43 (11-72 match) Moors SC v Police SC (Colombo) 2003-04. Sy BB 4-151 v Northants (Oval) 2009. LO HS 88* SL A v SA A (Benoni) 2008-09. LO BB 4-19 SL A v Z Select (Bulawayo) 2007-08. T20 HS 9. T20 BB 3-14.

LOGAN, Richard James (Wolverhampton GS), b Stone, Staffs 28 Jan 1980. 6'1". RHB, RMF. Northamptonshire 1999-2000, 2007-08. Nottinghamshire 2001-04. Hampshire 2005-06. Surrey 2009. HS 37* Nt v Hampshire (Nottingham) 2001. Sy HS 6 and Sy BB 2-101 v Glamorgan (Oval) 2009. BB 6-93 Nt v Derbys (Nottingham) 2001. LO HS 28* H v Northants (Northampton) 2005 (NL). LO BB 5-24 Nt v Suffolk (Mildenhall) 2001 (CGT). T20 HS 11*. T20 BB 5-26 v Lancs (Nottingham) 2003 – Nt record.

MURTAGH, Christopher Paul (John Fisher S; Loughborough U), b Lambeth, S London 14 Oct 1984. Younger brother of T.J.Murtagh (see *MIDDLESEX*); nephew of A.J.Murtagh (Hampshire and E Province 1973-77). 5'10". RHB, OB. Loughborough UCCE 2005-07. Surrey 2008-09. Surrey 2nd XI debut 2002. HS 107 LU v Yorkshire (Leeds) 2007. Sy HS 15 v Essex (Guildford) 2009. LO HS 74 v Leics (Oval) 2008 (P40). T20 HS 28.

NO**MURTAZA HUSSAIN** (Abbasia HS), b Bahawalpur, Pakistan 20 Dec 1974. British passport. 5'11". RHB, OB. Bahawalpur 1990-91 to 2001-02. Pakistan Automobiles Corp 1992-93 to 1993-94. United Bank 1994-95. PNSC 1995-96 to 1996-97. KRL 1997-98 to 1999-00. Islamabad 1998-99. Pakistan Customs 2004-05 to 2008-09. Surrey 2007-09. HS 117 Pakistan Customs v Attock Group (Karachi) 2006-07. Sy HS 56 v Yorkshire (Oval) 2008. 50 wkts (0+5), inc 100 wkts (1): 105 (1995-96). BB 9-54 Bahawalpur v Islamabad (Bahawalpur) 1995-96. Sy BB 4-70 v Middx (Oval) 2009. LO HS 85 KRL v Rawalpindi (Rawalpindi) 1998-99. LO BB 5-18 Bahawalpur v Lahore City (Bahawalpur) 1992-93.

NEWMAN, S.A. – *see MIDDLESEX.*

TUDOR, Alex Jeremy (St Mark's S, Hammersmith; City of Westminster C), b West Brompton, London 23 Oct 1977. 6'5". RHB, RF. Surrey 1995-2004, 2008; cap 1999. Essex 2005-08. YC 1999. **Tests**: 10 (1998-99 to 2002-03); HS 99* v NZ (Birmingham) 1999 – record score by an England 'night-watchman'; BB 5-44 v A (Nottingham) 2001. **LOI**: 3 (2002); HS 6; BB 2-30 v I (Oval) 2002. F-c Tours: A 1998-99, 2002-03; SA 1999-00; WI 2000-01 (Eng A); P 2000-01. HS 144 Ex v Derbys (Chelmsford) 2006. Sy HS 116 v Essex (Oval) 2001. BB 7-48 v Lancs (Oval) 2000. LO HS 56 v Lancs (Croydon) 2004 (NL). LO BB 4-26 v Hampshire (Oval) 2000 (NL).

J.Ormond left the staff, without making a County First-Class or List A appearance in 2009.

SURREY 2009
RESULTS SUMMARY

	Place	Won	Lost	Tied	Drew	NR
County Championship (2nd Division)	7th	1	4		11	
All First-Class Matches		1	4		11	
FP Trophy (Group C)	4th	3	5			
Pro40 League (2nd Division)	9th	2	6			
Twenty20 Cup (South Division)	5th	2	8			

LV COUNTY CHAMPIONSHIP AVERAGES
BATTING AND FIELDING

Cap		M	I	NO	HS	Runs	Avge	100	50	Ct/St
2002	M.R.Ramprakash	11	14	2	274	1350	90.00	5	4	5
2009	U.Afzaal	16	28	6	204*	1269	57.68	3	7	3
1996	M.A.Butcher	5	8	2	65	251	41.83	–	2	10
	M.J.Brown	16	28	1	120	992	36.74	2	4	7
2001	J.N.Batty	16	26	–	120	937	36.03	2	1	46/4
	C.P.Schofield	14	21	3	144	644	35.77	1	3	7
	S.J.Walters	11	18	–	188	573	31.83	2	1	15
	C.J.Jordan	8	10	3	42	213	30.42	–	–	4
	A.Harinath	3	6	–	57	165	27.50	–	1	–
2005	S.A.Newman	5	8	–	124	217	27.12	1	–	2
	S.C.Meaker	5	9	1	72	214	26.75	–	2	–
	M.N.W.Spriegel	6	11	–	100	294	26.72	1	2	7
1999	A.J.Tudor	4	6	2	33	83	20.75	–	–	1
	H.M.R.K.B.Herath	3	5	1	52*	80	20.00	–	1	–
	T.E.Linley	5	6	1	36	98	19.60	–	–	1
	Murtaza Hussain	7	8	1	34	111	15.85	–	–	–
	A.Nel	9	10	2	32	117	14.62	–	–	3
	J.W.Dernbach	14	19	6	19	138	10.61	–	–	1
	P.T.Collins	5	8	3	23	49	9.80	–	–	1
	L.J.Evans	2	4	–	9	23	5.75	–	–	–

Also batted: J.E.Anyon (1 match) 0*, 1*; J.G.E.Benning (2) 0, 5, 36; G.D.Elliott (1) 1, 22 (2 ct); R.J.Harris (2) 4, 94 (1 ct); S.J.King (2) 0, 8; R.J.Logan 0, 6; C.P.Murtagh (2) 15, 14* (2 ct).

BOWLING

	O	M	R	W	Avge	Best	5wI	10wM
A.Nel	260.4	69	754	27	27.92	6- 36	1	–
P.T.Collins	137.2	25	504	16	31.50	5- 75	1	–
J.W.Dernbach	395.2	67	1436	37	38.81	6- 47	2	–
Murtaza Hussain	271	47	825	19	43.42	4- 70	–	–
S.C.Meaker	110.4	11	498	10	49.80	3-114	–	–
C.J.Jordan	208.2	36	764	13	58.76	4- 84	–	–
C.P.Schofield	363.5	35	1357	22	61.68	5- 40	1	–
Also bowled:								
U.Afzaal	87.5	6	348	7	49.71	3- 51		
H.M.R.K.B.Herath	108.2	8	431	8	53.87	4-151		
T.E.Linley	131	23	442	8	55.25	4- 77		

J.E.Anyon 7-0-59-0; J.G.E.Benning 15-2-52-2; M.J.Brown 3-0-20-0; G.D.Elliott 2-0-15-0; R.J.Harris 33.5-6-135-3; S.J.King 39.3-2-156-4; R.J.Logan 30-6-101-2; S.A.Newman 3-0-10-0; M.N.W.Spriegel 44.4-2-205-2; A.J.Tudor 100-18-417-4; S.J.Walters 19-2-75-0.

Surrey played no first-class fixtures outside the County Championship in 2009. The First-Class Averages (pp 228–244) give the records of Surrey players in all first-class county matches, with the exception of J.E.Anyon, J.G.E.Benning, A.Harinath and S.A.Newman, whose first-class figures for Surrey are as above.

SURREY RECORDS

FIRST-CLASS CRICKET

Highest Total	For 811		v	Somerset	The Oval	1899
	V 863		by	Lancashire	The Oval	1990
Lowest Total	For 14		v	Essex	Chelmsford	1983
	V 16		by	MCC	Lord's	1872
Highest Innings	For 357*	R.Abel	v	Somerset	The Oval	1899
	V 366	N.H.Fairbrother	for	Lancashire	The Oval	1990

Highest Partnership for each Wicket

1st	428	J.B.Hobbs/A.Sandham	v	Oxford U	The Oval	1926
2nd	371	J.B.Hobbs/E.G.Hayes	v	Hampshire	The Oval	1909
3rd	413	D.J.Bicknell/D.M.Ward	v	Kent	Canterbury	1990
4th	448	R.Abel/T.W.Hayward	v	Yorkshire	The Oval	1899
5th	318	M.R.Ramprakash/Azhar Mahmood	v	Middlesex	The Oval	2005
6th	298	A.Sandham/H.S.Harrison	v	Sussex	The Oval	1913
7th	262	C.J.Richards/K.T.Medlycott	v	Kent	The Oval	1987
8th	205	I.A.Greig/M.P.Bicknell	v	Lancashire	The Oval	1990
9th	168	E.R.T.Holmes/E.W.J.Brooks	v	Hampshire	The Oval	1936
10th	173	A.Ducat/A.Sandham	v	Essex	Leyton	1921

Best Bowling	For	10-43	T.Rushby	v	Somerset	Taunton	1921
(Innings)	V	10-28	W.P.Howell	for	Australians	The Oval	1899
Best Bowling	For	16-83	G.A.R.Lock	v	Kent	Blackheath	1956
(Match)	V	15-57	W.P.Howell	for	Australians	The Oval	1899

Most Runs – Season	3246	T.W.Hayward	(av 72.13)	1906
Most Runs – Career	43554	J.B.Hobbs	(av 49.72)	1905-34
Most 100s – Season	13	T.W.Hayward		1906
	13	J.B.Hobbs		1925
Most 100s – Career	144	J.B.Hobbs		1905-34
Most Wkts – Season	252	T.Richardson	(av 13.94)	1895
Most Wkts – Career	1775	T.Richardson	(av 17.87)	1892-1904
Most Career W-K Dismissals	1221	H.Strudwick	(1035 ct; 186 st)	1902-27
Most Career Catches in the Field	605	M.J.Stewart		1954-72

LIMITED-OVERS CRICKET

Highest Total	FPT	496-4		v	Glos	The Oval	2007
	P40	375-4		v	Yorkshire	Scarborough	1994
	T20	224-5		v	Glos	Bristol	2006
Lowest Total	FPT	74		v	Kent	The Oval	1967
	P40	64		v	Worcs	Worcester	1978
	T20	94		v	Essex	Chelmsford	2008
Highest Innings	FPT	268	A.D.Brown	v	Glamorgan	The Oval	2002
	P40	203	A.D.Brown	v	Hampshire	Guildford	1997
	T20	98*	U.Afzaal	v	Middlesex	Lord's	2009
Best Bowling	FPT	7-33	R.D.Jackman	v	Yorkshire	Harrogate	1970
	P40	7-30	M.P.Bicknell	v	Glamorgan	The Oval	1999
	T20	6-24	T.J.Murtagh	v	Middlesex	Lord's	2005

SUSSEX

Formation of Present Club: 1 March 1839
Substantial Reorganisation: August 1857
Inaugural First-Class Match: 1864
Colours: Dark Blue, Light Blue and Gold
Badge: County Arms of Six Martlets
County Champions: (3) 2003, 2006, 2007
Gillette/NatWest/C&G/FP Trophy Winners: (5) 1963, 1964, 1978, 1986, 2006
Benson and Hedges Cup Winners: (0); best – Semi-Finalist 1982, 1999
Pro 40/National League (Div 1) Winners: (2) 2008, 2009
Sunday League Winners: (1) 1982
Twenty20 Cup Winners: (1) 2009

Chief Executive: David Brooks, County Ground, Eaton Road, Hove BN3 3AN • Tel: 0844 264 0202 • Fax: 01273 771549 • Email: info@sussexcricket.co.uk • Web: www.sussexcricket.co.uk

Professional Cricket Manager: Mark A.Robinson. **Club Coach:** Mark J.G.Davis. **Captain:** M.H.Yardy. **Vice-Captain:** None. **Overseas Player:** Yasir Arafat. **2010 Beneficiary:** Mushtaq Ahmed (testimonial). **Head Groundsman:** Andy Mackay. **Scorer:** M.J. (Mike) Charman. ‡ New registration. NO Not qualified for England.

AGA, Ragheb Gul (Hillcrest S; Brighton U), b Nairobi, Kenya 10 Jul 1984. RHB, RMF. Kenya 2003-04 to date. Sussex debut 2008. **LOI** (Kenya): 2 (2004); HS 1 and BB 2-17 K v P (Birmingham) 2004. F-c Tours (K): WI 2003-04; Z 2005-06; UAE 2004-05. HS 43 K v Namibia (Nairobi) 2004-05. Sx HS 26 v Kent (Hove) 2008. BB 4-63 v Hampshire (Canterbury) 2008. LO HS 16 Kenya v India A (Nairobi) 2004. LO BB 4-14 Kenya v Zimbabwe A (Harare) 2005-06. T20 HS 28. T20 BB 2-12.

‡ANYON, James Edward (Garstang HS; Preston U; Loughborough U), b Lancaster, Lancs 5 May 1983. 6'1". LHB, RFM. Loughborough U 2003-04. Warwickshire 2005-09. Surrey 2009 (on loan). Cumberland 2003. HS 37* Wa v Durham (Chester-le-St) 2007. BB 6-82 Wa v Glamorgan (Cardiff) 2008. LO HS 12 Wa v Worcs (Birmingham) 2006 (CGT). LO BB 3-6 Wa v Notts (Nottingham) 2008 (FPT). T20 HS 8*. T20 BB 3-6.

BEER, William Andrew Thomas (Reigate GS; Collyer's C, Horsham), b Crawley 8 Oct 1988. RHB, LB. Debut (Sussex) 2008. Sussex 2nd XI debut 2006. HS 6* and BB 1-18 v MCC (Lord's) 2008 – on debut. No f-c appearances in 2009. LO HS 14 v Glos (Bristol) 2009 (FPT). LO BB 2-17 v Durham (Hove) 2009 (P40). T20 HS 17*. T20 BB 2-27.

BROWN, Ben Christopher (Ardingly C), b Crawley 23 Nov 1988. RHB, WK. Debut (Sussex) 2007 – awaiting CC debut. No f-c appearances in 2008 or 2009. HS 46 v Sri Lanka A (Hove) 2007 – on debut. LO HS 18* v Yorks (Hove) 2009 (FPT). T20 HS 7.

NOCOLLYMORE, Corey Dalanelo (Alexandra SS), b St Peter, Barbados 21 Dec 1977. 6'0". RHB, RFM. Barbados 1998-99 to 2008-09. Warwickshire 2003. Sussex debut 2008. **Tests** (WI): 30 (1998-99 to 2007); HS 16* v Z (Bulawayo) 2003-04 and v E (Chester-le-St) 2007; BB 7-57 v SL (Kingston) 2003. **LOI** (WI): 84 (1999 to 2006-07); HS 13* v I (Toronto) 1999; BB 5-51 v SL (Colombo) 2001-02. F-c tours (WI): E 2000, 2004, 2007; A 2005-06; SA 2003-04; P 2006-07; Z 2002, 2003-04; K 2000-01. HS 23 v Notts (Horsham) 2009. BB 7-57 (*see Tests*). Sx BB 4-47 v Notts (Nottingham) 2008. LO HS 13* (*see LOI*). LO BB 5-27 Barbados v Leeward Is (Weymouth) 2005-06. T20 HS 4. T20 BB 1-21.

GATTING, Joe Stephen, b Brighton 25 Nov 1987. Son of S.P.Gatting (Middlesex 2nd XI, football for Arsenal, Brighton & Hove Albion, Charlton Athletic, nephew of M.W.Gatting (Middlesex and England 1975-98). RHB, OB. Debut (Sussex) 2009, scoring 152 v CU (Cambridge). Sussex 2nd XI debut 2005. HS 152 (*see above*). CC HS 70 v Notts (Nottingham) 2009. LO HS 99* v Yorks (Scarborough) 2009 (P40). T20 HS 25.

^{NQ}**GOODWIN, Murray** William (Newton Moore HS, Bunbury, WA), b Salisbury, Rhodesia 11 Dec 1972. Younger brother of D.G.Goodwin (Zimbabwe 1986-87 to 1989-90). 5'9". Migrated to Australia in Nov 1986 and gained Australian citizenship in Sep 1997. Kolpak registration 2005 to date. RHB, LB. W Australia 1994-95 to 1996-97, 2000-01 to 2005-06. Mashonaland 1997-98 to 1998-99. Sussex debut/cap 2001. Warriors 2006-07. Holland 1997. **Tests** (Z): 19 (1997-98 to 2000); HS 166* v P (Bulawayo) 1997-98. **LOI** (Z): 71 (1997-98 to 2000); HS 112* v WI (Chester-le-St) 2000; BB 1-12 v SL (Sharjah) 1998-99. F-c Tours (Z): E 2000, SA 1999-00; WI 1999-00; NZ 1997-98; P 1998-99; SL 1997-98. 1000 runs (7+1); most – 1654 (2001). HS 344* (Sx record) v Somerset (Taunton) 2009, sharing record Sx 4th wkt partnership of 363 with C.D.Hopkinson. BB 2-23 Z v Lahore City (Lahore) 1998-99. Sx BB – . LO HS 167 WA v NSW (Perth) 2000-01. LO BB 1-9 Mashonaland v Eng A (Harare) 1998-99. T20 HS 102*.

HODD, Andrew John (Bexhill C), b Chichester 12 Jan 1984. 5'9". RHB, WK. Sussex 2003 (1 match), 2006 to date. Surrey 2005 (1 match). HS 123 v Yorks (Hove) 2007. LO HS 42 v Notts (Hove) 2007 (P40). T20 HS 16.

HOPKINSON, Carl Daniel (Brighton C), b Brighton 14 Sep 1981. 5'11". RHB, RM. Debut (Sussex) 2002; cap 2008. HS 139 v Somerset (Taunton) 2009, sharing Sx record 4th wkt partnership with M.W.Goodwin. BB 1-20 v LU (Hove) 2004. CC BB 1-35 v Warwks (Hove) 2002. LO HS 123* v Notts (Hove) 2007 (P40). LO BB 3-19 v Scot (Edinburgh) 2003 (NL). T20 HS 26*.

JOYCE, Edmund Christopher (Presentation C, Bray, Co Wicklow; Trinity C, Dublin), b Dublin, Ireland 22 Sep 1978. 5'11". Brother of four Ireland cricketers: Augustine (2000), Dominick (2004-06), Cecilia (2001-07) and Isobel, her twin (1999-2007). LHB, RM. Ireland 1997-98. Middlesex 1999-2008; cap 2002. Sussex debut/cap 2009. Qualified for England 2005. MCC 2006, 2008. **LOI**: 17 (2006 to 2006-07); HS 107 v A (Sydney) 2006-07. F-c Tour (Eng A): WI 2005-06. 1000 runs (5); most – 1668 (2005). HS 211 Mx v Warwks (Birmingham) 2006. Sx HS 183 v Notts (Horsham) 2009. BB Mx 2-34 v CU (Cambridge) 2004. CC BB 1-4 Mx v Glamorgan (Cardiff) 2005. Sx BB 1-9 v Hampshire (Southampton) 2009. LO HS 146 v Glos (Hove) 2009 (FPT). LO BB 2-10 Mx v Notts (Nottingham) 2003 (NL). IT20 HS 1. T20 HS 47.

KIRTLEY, Robert James (Clifton C), b Eastbourne 10 Jan 1975. 6'0". RHB, RFM. Debut (Sussex) 1995; cap 1998; benefit 2006. TCCB XI 1996. Mashonaland 1996-97. MCC 2002. **Tests**: 4 (2003 to 2003-04); HS 12 v SL (Colombo) 2003-04; BB 6-34 v SA (Nottingham) 2003 – on debut. **LOI**: 11 (2001-02 to 2003-04); HS 1 (*twice*); BB 2-33 v Z (Harare) 2001-02 on debut, and v B (Dhaka) 2003-04. F-c Tours (Eng A): NZ 1999-00; SL 2003-04 (Eng); B 1999-00. HS 59 v Durham (Eastbourne) 1998. 50 wkts (7); most – 75 (2001). BB 7-21 v Hampshire (Southampton) 1999. LO HS 30* v Middx (Lord's) 2003 (CGT). LO BB 6-50 v Durham (Hove) 2009 (FPT). IT20 HS 2*. IT20 BB – . T20 HS 2*. T20 BB 4-22.

LIDDLE, Christopher John (Nunthorpe CS), b Middlesbrough, Yorks 1 Feb 1984. 6'5". RHB, LFM. Leicestershire 2005-06. Sussex debut 2007. Missed entire 2009 season with a stress fracture of the right ankle. HS 53 v Worcs (Hove) 2007. BB 3-42 Le v Somerset (Leicester) 2006. Sx BB 2-43 v Sri Lanka A (Hove) 2007. LO HS 11 v Essex (Arundel) 2007 (FPT). LO BB 3-60 v Notts (Hove) 2007 (P40). T20 HS 10*. T20 BB 4-15.

MARTIN-JENKINS, Robin Simon Christopher (Radley C; Durham U), b Guildford, Surrey 28 Oct 1975. Son of C.D.A.Martin-Jenkins (Cricket Broadcaster and Writer). 6'5". RHB, RMF. Debut (Sussex) 1995; cap 2000; benefit 2008. British U 1996. 1000 runs (1): 1008 (2002). HS 205* v Somerset (Taunton) 2002. BB 7-51 v Leics (Horsham) 2002. LO HS 68* v Northants (Hove) 2003 (NL). LO BB 4-22 v Kent (Canterbury) 2002 (BHC). T20 HS 56*. T20 BB 4-20.

NASH, Christopher David (Collyer's SFC; Loughborough U), b Cuckfield 19 May 1983. 5'11". RHB, OB. Debut (Sussex) 2002 – no f-c appearances 2003-04; cap 2008. Loughborough UCCE 2003-04. British U 2004. 1000 runs (1): 1321 (2009). HS 157 v Somerset (Taunton) 2009. BB 3-7 v Surrey (Oval) 2008. LO HS 82 v Warwks (Hove) 2006 (P40). LO BB 4-40 v Yorks (Hove) 2009 (FPT). T20 HS 56*.

‡**PANESAR,** Mudhsuden Singh ('*Monty*') (Stopsley HS; Bedford Modern S; Loughborough U), b Luton, Beds 25 Apr 1982. 6'0". LHB, SLA. Northamptonshire 2001-09; cap 2006. British U 2002-05. Loughborough UCCE 2004. MCC 2006. Lions 2009-10. Bedfordshire 1998-99. *Wisden* 2007. **Tests**: 39 (2005-06 to 2009); HS 26 v SL (Nottingham) 2006; BB 6-37 v NZ (Manchester) 2008. **LOI**: 26 (2006-07 to 2007-08); HS 13 v WI (Nottingham) 2007; BB 3-25 v B (Bridgetown) 2006-07. F-c Tours: A 2006-07; WI 2008-09; NZ 2007-08; I 2005-06, 2008-09; SL 2002-03 (ECB Acad), 2007-08. HS 39* Nh v Worcs (Northampton) 2005. 50 wkts (3); most – 71 (2006). BB 7-181 Nh v Essex (Chelmsford) 2005. LO HS 17* Nh v Leics (Northampton) 2008 (FPT). LO BB 5-20 ECB Acad v SL Acad XI (Colombo) 2002-03. IT20 HS 1. IT20 BB 2-40. T20 HS 3*. T20 BB 2-22.

PRIOR, Matthew James (Brighton C), b Johannesburg, South Africa 26 Feb 1982. 5'11". RHB, WK. Debut (Sussex) 2001; cap 2003. MCC 2005. **ECB central contract 2009-10. Tests**: 27 (2007 to 2009-10); HS 131* v WI (Port-of-Spain) 2008-09 (scored 126* v WI on debut – first instance while keeping wicket for England). **LOI**: 52 (2004-05 to 2009-10); HS 87 v WI (Birmingham) 2009. F-c Tours: SA 2009-10; WI 2008-09; I 2003-04 (Eng A), 2008-09; SL 2004-05 (Eng A), 2007-08; B 2006-07 (Eng A), 2009-10. 1000 runs (3); most – 1158 (2004). HS 201* v LU (Hove) 2004. CC HS 153* v Essex (Colchester) 2003. LO HS 144 v Warwks (Hove) 2005 (NL). IT20 HS 32. T20 HS 73.

RAYNER, Oliver Philip (St Bede's S, Sussex), b Fallingbostel, W Germany, 1 Nov 1985. 6'5". RHB, OB. Debut (Sussex) 2006, scoring 101 v SL (Hove) – first hundred on debut for Sussex since 1920. HS 101 (*see above*). CC HS 60 v Hampshire (Arundel) 2009. BB 5-49 v Hampshire (Arundel) 2008. LO HS 61 v Lancs (Hove) 2006 (P40). LO BB 2-31 v Durham (Chester-le-St) 2008 (P40). T20 HS 24. T20 BB 1-19.

SMITH, Dwayne Romel, b St Michael, Barbados, 12 Apr 1983. RHB, RM. Barbados 2001-02 to date. Sussex 2009 (Kolpak registration), joined in 2008 but no f-c appearances. **Tests** (WI): 10 (2003-04 to 2005-06); HS 105* v SA (Cape Town) 2003-04 – on debut; BB 3-71 v NZ (Auckland) 2005-06. **LOI** (WI): 76 (2003-04 to 2009-10); HS 68 v SL (Dambulla) 2005; BB 5-45 v NZ (Auckland) 2005-06. F-c Tours (WI): E 2004; A 2005-06; SA 2003-04; NZ 2005-06; SL 2005. HS 155 Barbados v CCC (Crab Hill) 2008-09. Sx HS 80 and Sx BB 4-58 v Notts (Nottingham) 2009. BB 4-22 Barbados v T&T (Pointe-à-Pierre) 2006-07. LO HS 96 Barbados v Windward Is (Georgetown) 2005-06. LO BB 6-29 v Notts (Hove) 2009 (P40). IT20 HS 29. IT20 BB 3-24. T20 HS 72*. T20 BB 4-9.

THORNELY, Michael Alistair (Brighton C), b Camden, London 19 Oct 1987. 6'1". RHB, RM. Debut (Sussex) 2007. HS 19 v Yorks (Leeds) 2009. BB – . LO HS – 2007 (P40).

‡**WELLS,** Luke William Peter (St Bede's S), b Eastbourne 29 Dec 1990. Son of A.P.Wells (Border, Kent, Sussex and England 1981-2000) and nephew of C.M.Wells (Border, Derbyshire, Sussex and WP 1979-96). 6'4". LHB, OB. Sussex 2nd XI debut 2008. England U19s 2009. Awaiting 1st XI debut.

WRIGHT, Luke James (Belvoir HS; Ratcliffe C; Loughborough U), b Grantham, Lincs 7 Mar 1985. 5'11". Younger brother of A.S.Wright (Leicestershire 2001-02). RHB, RM. Leicestershire 2003 (one f-c match). Sussex debut 2004; cap 2007. **LOI**: 28 (2007 to 2009-10); HS 52 v NZ (Birmingham) 2008; BB 2-34 v NZ (Bristol) 2008. F-c Tour (Eng A): NZ 2008-09. HS 155* v MCC (Lord's) 2008. CC HS 118* v Durham (Chester-le-St) 2009. BB 5-66 v Worcs (Hove) 2009. LO HS 125 v Glos (Hove) 2007 (P40). LO BB 4-12 v Middx (Hove) 2004 (NL). IT20 HS 71. IT20 BB 1-32. T20 HS 103 v Kent (Canterbury) 2007 – Sx record. T20 BB 3-17.

YARDY, Michael Howard (William Parker S, Hastings), b Pembury, Kent 27 Nov 1980. 6'0". LHB, LM/SLA. Debut (Sussex) 2000; cap 2005; captain 2009 to date. **LOI**: 6 (2006 to 2007); HS 19 v WI (Birmingham) 2007; BB 3-24 v P (Nottingham) 2006 – on debut. F-c Tours (Eng A): WI 2005-06; I 2007-08 (captain); B 2006-07 (captain). 1000 runs (2); most – 1520 (2005). HS 257 (record Sussex score v touring team) and BB 5-83 v B (Hove) 2005. CC HS 179 v Middx (Lord's) 2005. CC BB 3-15 v Yorks (Leeds) 2009. LO HS 98* v Surrey (Oval) 2006 (CGT). LO BB 6-27 v Warwks (Birmingham) 2005 (NL). IT20 HS 24*. IT20 BB 1-20. T20 HS 68*. T20 BB 3-21.

[NO]**YASIR ARAFAT** Satti (Gordon C, Rawalpindi), b Rawalpindi, Pakistan 12 Mar 1982. 5'9½". RHB, RMF. Rawalpindi 1997-98 to 2006-07. Pakistan Reserves 1999-00. KRL 2000-01 to date. National Bank 2005-06. Sussex 2006, 2009 to date; cap 2006. Kent 2007-08; cap 2007. Federal Areas 2007-08 to 2008-09. Scotland (not f-c) 2004-05. Otago (not f-c) 2009-10. **Tests** (P): 3 (2007-08 to 2008-09); HS 50* v SL (Karachi) 2008-09; BB 5-161 v I (Bangalore) 2007-08 – on debut. **LOI** (P): 11 (1999-00 to 2009); HS 27 v SA (Chandigarh) 2006-07; BB 1-28 v SL (Karachi) 1999-00. F-c Tours (P): I 2007-08; SL 2001 (Pak A), 2004-05 (Pak A). HS 122 K v Sussex (Canterbury) 2007. Sx HS 37 v Hampshire (Arundel) 2009. 50 wkts (0+4); most – 91 (2001-02). BB 9-35 KRL v SSGC (Rawalpindi) 2008-09. UK BB 6-86 K v Hampshire (Canterbury) 2008. Sx BB 3-83 v Worcs (Hove) 2009. LO HS 110* Otago v Auckland (Oamaru) 2009-10. LO BB 6-24 Pakistan A v England A (Colombo) 2004-05. IT20 HS 17. IT20 BB 3-32. T20 HS 49. T20 BB 4-17.

RELEASED/RETIRED
(Having made a County First-Class or List A appearance in 2009)

CHAWLA, P.P. – *see SURREY.*

HAMILTON-BROWN, R.J. – *see SURREY.*

LEWRY, Jason David (Durrington HS, Worthing), b Worthing 2 Apr 1971. 6'2". LHB, LFM. Sussex 1994-2009; cap 1996; benefit 2002. F-c Tour: Z 1998-99 (Eng A). HS 72 v Surrey (Oval) 2004. 50 wkts (5); most – 62 (1998). BB 8-106 v Leics (Hove) 2003. 2 hat-tricks (1998, 2001). LO HS 16* v Yorks (Arundel) 2004 (NL). LO BB 4-29 v Somerset (Bath) 1995 (SL). T20 HS 8*. T20 BB 3-34.

SANDRI, Pepler Sacto Emiliano, b Cape Town, South Africa 14 Jan 1983. Italian passport. RHB, RMF. Boland 2003-04 to 2008-09. Cape Cobras 2006-07 to 2008-09. Sussex 2009 (1 f-c match). HS 26* Boland v WP (Paarl) 2007-08. Sx HS 0* and BB– v Notts (Horsham) 2009. BB 5-32 (9-56 match) Boland v EP (Paarl) 2005-06. LO HS 14* Boland v SW Districts (Oudtshoorn) 2007-08. LO BB 2-18 Boland v Gauteng (Paarl) 2008-09.

SMITH, T.M.J. – *see MIDDLESEX.*

[NO]**WRIGHT, Damien** Geoffrey (Terrigal HS, NSW), b Casino, NSW, Australia 25 Jul 1975. 6'1". RHB, RFM. Tasmania 1997-98 to 2006-07. Scotland 2001 (CGT). Northamptonshire 2003, 2005. Glamorgan 2007. Victoria 2008-09 to date. Sussex 2009. HS 111 Tas v Vic (Hobart) 2004-05. UK HS 85 Nh v Worcs (Worcester) 2005. Sx HS 42 v Hampshire (Southampton) 2009. 50 wkts (1): 53 (2005). BB 8-60 Nh v Yorks (Leeds) 2005. Sx BB 3-64 v Durham (Hove) 2009. LO HS 55 Scotland v Middx CB (Southgate) 2001 (CGT). LO BB 5-37 Nh v Notts (Northampton) 2005. T20 HS 38*. T20 BB 3-17.

SUSSEX 2009

RESULTS SUMMARY

	Place	Won	Lost	Tied	Drew	NR
County Championship (1st Division)	8th	2	6		8	
All First-Class Matches		2	6		9	
FP Trophy (Group C)	Final	6	4			1
Pro40 League (1st Division)	**1st**	6	2			
Twenty20 Cup (South Division)	Winners	10	3			

LV COUNTY CHAMPIONSHIP AVERAGES

BATTING AND FIELDING

Cap		M	I	NO	HS	Runs	Avge	100	50	Ct/St
2008	C.D.Nash	14	25	3	157	1298	59.00	4	6	3
2007	L.J.Wright	8	13	2	118*	527	47.90	2	3	1
2003	M.J.Prior	5	8	–	140	362	45.25	1	2	12
	E.C.Joyce	14	23	1	183	936	42.54	3	3	12
2005	M.H.Yardy	16	28	3	152	1046	41.84	2	5	13
2008	C.D.Hopkinson	9	13	1	139	443	36.91	2	–	2
	R.J.Hamilton-Brown	4	7	1	171*	205	34.16	1	–	5
2001	M.W.Goodwin	16	27	3	344*	800	33.33	1	2	6
	J.S.Gatting	3	5	–	70	158	31.60	–	1	2
	P.P.Chawla	6	10	3	102*	206	29.42	1	–	2
	D.G.Wright	3	4	1	42	88	29.33	–	–	–
	A.J.Hodd	15	22	3	101	489	25.73	1	2	23/3
	Yasir Arafat	5	5	–	37	108	21.60	–	–	–
	D.R.Smith	9	14	–	80	261	18.64	–	2	1
2000	R.S.C.Martin-Jenkins	12	16	2	67	259	18.50	–	1	5
	O.P.Rayner	10	11	1	60	173	17.30	–	1	14
1996	J.D.Lewry	6	10	4	25	51	8.50	–	–	–
	C.D.Collymore	14	17	5	23	89	7.41	–	–	2

Also batted: R.G.Aga (2 matches) 1*, 2, 24; R.J.Kirtley (2 – cap 1998) 33, 2*, 10 (2 ct); P.S.E.Sandri (1) 0*; T.M.J.Smith (1) 10, 1; M.A.Thornely (1) 8, 19 (1 ct).

BOWLING

	O	M	R	W	Avge	Best	5wI	10wM
P.P.Chawla	341.5	72	981	36	27.25	6- 52	4	1
D.R.Smith	301	84	814	25	32.56	4- 58	–	–
C.D.Collymore	396	102	1104	33	33.45	4- 66	–	–
L.J.Wright	210.1	35	710	21	33.80	5- 66	2	–
R.S.C.Martin-Jenkins	275.4	74	781	23	33.95	5- 43	1	–
O.P.Rayner	294.3	48	870	20	43.50	4-186	–	–
Yasir Arafat	151	24	621	12	51.75	3- 83	–	–
J.D.Lewry	159.1	39	535	10	53.50	2- 53	–	–

Also bowled:

R.J.Kirtley	50.5	6	177	5	35.40	2- 59	–	–
D.G.Wright	83.5	33	187	5	37.40	3- 64	–	–
C.D.Nash	114.4	22	394	7	56.28	1- 3	–	–

R.G.Aga 37-2-147-1; M.W.Goodwin 2-0-13-0; R.J.Hamilton-Brown 37-6-109-3; A.J.Hodd 1.4-0-7-0; E.C.Joyce 2-0-9-1; P.S.E.Sandri 14-2-80-0; T.M.J.Smith 12.4-1-70-0; M.H.Yardy 69-4-320-4.

The First-Class Averages (pp 228–244) give the records of Sussex players in all first-class county matches (Sussex's other opponents being Cambridge UCCE), with the exception of M.J.Prior, whose full first-class figures for Sussex are as above, and:
   L.J.Wright 9-14-2-118*-633-52.75-3-3-1ct. 213.1-35-717-21-34.14-5/66-2-0.

SUSSEX RECORDS

FIRST-CLASS CRICKET

Highest Total	For 742-5d		v	Somerset	Taunton	2009
	V 726		by	Notts	Nottingham	1895
Lowest Total	For 19		v	Surrey	Godalming	1830
	19		v	Notts	Hove	1873
	V 18		by	Kent	Gravesend	1867
Highest Innings	For 344*	M.W.Goodwin	v	Somerset	Taunton	2009
	V 322	E.Paynter	for	Lancashire	Hove	1937

Highest Partnership for each Wicket

1st	490	E.H.Bowley/J.G.Langridge	v	Middlesex	Hove	1933
2nd	385	E.H.Bowley/M.W.Tate	v	Northants	Hove	1921
3rd	385*	M.H.Yardy/M.W.Goodwin	v	Warwicks	Hove	2006
4th	363	M.W.Goodwin/C.D.Hopkinson	v	Somerset	Taunton	2009
5th	297	J.H.Parks/H.W.Parks	v	Hampshire	Portsmouth	1937
6th	255	K.S.Duleepsinhji/M.W.Tate	v	Northants	Hove	1930
7th	344	K.S.Ranjitsinhji/N.Newham	v	Essex	Leyton	1902
8th	291	R.S.C.Martin-Jenkins/M.J.G.Davis	v	Somerset	Taunton	2002
9th	178	H.W.Parks/A.F.Wensley	v	Derbyshire	Horsham	1930
10th	156	G.R.Cox/H.R.Butt	v	Cambridge U	Cambridge	1908

Best Bowling	For	10- 48	C.H.G.Bland	v	Kent	Tonbridge	1899
(Innings)	V	9- 11	A.P.Freeman	for	Kent	Hove	1922
Best Bowling	For	17-106	G.R.Cox	v	Warwicks	Horsham	1926
(Match)	V	17- 67	A.P.Freeman	for	Kent	Hove	1922

Most Runs – Season	2850	J.G.Langridge	(av 64.77)		1949
Most Runs – Career	34150	J.G.Langridge	(av 37.69)		1928-55
Most 100s – Season	12	J.G.Langridge			1949
Most 100s – Career	76	J.G.Langridge			1928-55
Most Wkts – Season	198	M.W.Tate	(av 13.47)		1925
Most Wkts – Career	2211	M.W.Tate	(av 17.41)		1912-37
Most Career W-K Dismissals	1176	H.R.Butt	(911 ct; 265 st)		1890-1912
Most Career Catches in the Field	779	J.G.Langridge			1928-55

LIMITED-OVERS CRICKET

Highest Total	FPT	384-9		v	Ireland	Belfast	1996
	P40	323-5		v	Leics	Horsham	2004
	T20	205-5		v	Hampshire	Hove	2007
Lowest Total	FPT	49		v	Derbyshire	Chesterfield	1969
	P40	59		v	Glamorgan	Hove	1996
	T20	67		v	Hampshire	Hove	2004
Highest Innings	FPT	158*	M.W.Goodwin	v	Essex	Chelmsford	2006
	P40	163	C.J.Adams	v	Middlesex	Arundel	1999
	T20	103	L.J.Wright	v	Kent	Canterbury	2007
Best Bowling	FPT	6- 9	A.I.C.Dodemaide	v	Ireland	Downpatrick	1990
	P40	7-41	A.N.Jones	v	Notts	Nottingham	1986
	T20	5-11	Mushtaq Ahmed	v	Essex	Hove	2005

WARWICKSHIRE

Formation of Present Club: 8 April 1882
Substantial Reorganisation: 19 January 1884
Inaugural First-Class Match: 1894
Colours: Dark Blue, Gold and Silver
Badge: Bear and Ragged Staff
County Champions: (6) 1911, 1951, 1972, 1994, 1995, 2004
Gillette/NatWest/C&G/FP Trophy Winners: (5) 1966, 1968, 1989, 1993, 1995
Benson and Hedges Cup Winners: (2) 1994, 2002
Pro 40/National League (Div 1) Winners: (0); best – 3rd 2001, 2002
Sunday League Winners: (3) 1980, 1994, 1997
Twenty20 Cup Winners: (0); best – Finalist 2003

Chief Executive: Colin Povey, County Ground, Edgbaston, Birmingham, B5 7QU • Tel: 0121 446 4422 • Fax: 0121 446 4544 • Email: info@edgbaston.com • Web: www.edgbaston.com

Director of Coaching/First XI Coach: Ashley F.Giles. **Captain:** I.J.Westwood. **Vice-Captain:** tba. **Overseas Player:** Imran Tahir. **2010 Beneficiary:** none. **Head Groundsman:** Steve Rouse. **Scorer:** David E.Wainwright. ‡ New registration. NQ Not qualified for England.

ALLIN, Thomas William (Cardiff U), b Devon 27 Nov 1987. Son of A.W.Allin (Glamorgan 1976) and brother of M.L.Allin (Devon 2003). RHB, RMF. Devon 2007-08. Cardiff UCCE (not f-c) 2008-09. Warwickshire 2nd XI debut 2008. Awaiting 1st XI debut.

AMBROSE, Timothy Raymond (Merewether HS, NSW; TAFE C), b Newcastle, NSW, Australia 1 Dec 1982. ECB qualified – British/EU passport. 5"7". RHB, WK. Sussex 2001-05; cap 2003. Warwickshire debut 2006; cap 2007. **Tests:** 11 (2007-08 to 2008-09); HS 102 v NZ (Wellington) 2007-08. **LOI:** 5 (2008); HS 6 v NZ (Oval) 2008. F-c Tours: WI 2008-09; NZ 2007-08. HS 251* v Worcs (Worcester) 2007. LO HS 135 v Durham (Birmingham) 2007 (FPT). IT 20 HS – . T20 HS 77.

BARKER, Keith Hubert Douglas (Moorhead HS; Fulwood C, Preston), b Manchester 21 Oct 1986. 6'3". Son of K.H.Barker (British Guiana 1960-61 to 1963-64). Played football for Blackburn Rovers and Rochdale. LHB, LM. Debut (Warwickshire) 2009. Warwickshire 2nd XI debut 2008. HS 23 v DU (Durham) 2009. CC HS 0. BB 1-51 v England (Birmingham) 2009. LO HS 30* v Scotland (Edinburgh) 2009 (FPT). LO BB 3-23 v Lancs (Manchester) 2009 (P40). T20 HS 9. T20 BB 4-19.

BELL, Ian Ronald (Princethorpe C), b Walsgrave-on-Stowe 11 Apr 1982. 5'9". RHB, RM. Debut (Warwickshire) 1999; cap 2001. MCC 2004. YC 2004. MBE 2005. **ECB central contract 2009-10. Tests:** 53 (2004 to 2009-10); HS 199 v SA (Lord's) 2008; BB 1-33 v P (Faisalabad) 2005-06. **LOI:** 79 (2004-05 to 2008-09); HS 126* v I (Southampton) 2007; BB 3-9 v Z (Bulawayo) 2004-05 – taking a wicket with his third ball in LOI. F-c Tours: A 2006-07; SA 2009-10; WI 2000-01 (Eng A – *part*), 2008-09; NZ 2007-08; I 2005-06, 2008-09; P 2005-06; SL 2002-03 (ECB Acad), 2004-05, 2007-08; B 2009-10. 1000 runs (3); most – 1714 (2004). Scored 480 runs (avge 80.00) in April 2005 – record f-c UK aggregate before May. HS 262* v Sussex (Horsham) 2004. BB 4-4 v Middx (Lord's) 2004. LO HS 137 v Yorks (Birmingham) 2005 (NL) – Wa record. LO BB 5-41 v Essex (Chelmsford) 2003 (NL). IT20 HS 60*. T20 HS 66*. T20 BB 1-12.

185

^{NQ}BOTHA, Anthony Greyvensteyn (Maritzburg C; Maritzburg Technikon), b Pretoria, South Africa 17 Nov 1976. 6'0". LHB, SLA. Natal/KwaZulu Natal 1995-96 to 1998-99. EP/Easterns 1999-00 to 2002-03. Derbyshire 2004-07; cap 2004. Moved to Warwickshire in mid-season – debut 2007. HS 156* De v Yorks (Derby) 2005. Wa HS 64 v Notts (Nottingham) 2009. 50 wkts (1): 55 (2007). BB 8-53 Natal B v Northerns B (Pretoria) 1997-98. CC BB 6-101 De v Somerset (Derby) 2007. Wa BB 4-77 v Worcs (Birmingham) 2008. LO HS 60* Easterns v EP (Benoni) 2001-02. LO BB 5-43 v Leics (Leicester) 2008. T20 HS 35*. T20 BB 4-14.

CARTER, Neil Miller (Hottentots Holland HS; Cape Technicon), b Cape Town, South Africa 29 Jan 1975. British passport. 6'2". LHB, LFM. Boland 1999-00 to 2000-01. Warwickshire debut 2001; cap 2005. HS 103 v Sussex (Hove) 2002 – completed maiden hundred off 67 balls. BB 6-63 Boland v GW (Kimberley) 2000-01 and 6-63 v Sussex (Birmingham) 2006. LO HS 135 v Scotland (Birmingham) 2006 (CGT). LO BB 5-31 v Durham (Birmingham) 2002 (NL). T20 HS 58. T20 BB 5-19 v Worcs (Birmingham) 2005 – Wa record.

‡CHOPRA, Varun (Ilford County HS), b Barking, Essex 21 Jun 1987. 6'1". RHB, LB. Essex 2006-09. HS 155 v Glos (Bristol) 2008. Scored 106 v Glos (Chelmsford) 2006 – on CC debut. BB – . LO HS 102 v Middx (Chelmsford) 2007 (FPT). T20 HS 51.

CLARKE, Rikki (Broadwater SS; Godalming S), b Orsett, Essex 29 Sep 1981. 6'4". RHB, RFM. Surrey 2002-07, scoring 107* v CU (Cambridge) on debut; cap 2005. MCC 2006. Derbyshire cap/captain 2008. Warwickshire debut 2008. YC 2002. **Tests**: 2 (2003-04); HS 55 and BB 2-7 v B (Chittagong) 2003-04. **LOI**: 20 (2003 to 2006); HS 39 v P (Lord's) 2006; BB 2-28 v B (Dhaka) 2003-04. F-c Tours: WI 2003-04, 2005-06; SL 2002-03 (ECB Acad), 2004-05; B 2003-04. 1000 runs (1): 1027 (2006). HS 214 Sy v Somerset (Guildford) 2006. Wa HS 112 v Hampshire (Birmingham) 2009. BB 4-21 Sy v Leics (Leicester) 2003. Wa BB 2-15 v Notts (Nottingham) 2009. LO HS 98* Sy v Derbys (Derby) 2002 (NL). LO BB 4-49 Sy v Warwks (Birmingham) 2005 (NL). T20 HS 79*. T20 BB 3-11.

‡^{NQ}IMRAN TAHIR, Mohammad (Government Pakistan Angels HS and MAO College, Lahore), b Lahore, Pakistan 4 Jun 1979. 5'11". RHB, LB. Lahore City 1996-97 to 1997-98. WAPDA 1998-99. REDCO 1999-00. Lahore Whites 2000-01. Sui Northern Gas Pipelines 2001-02 to 2003-04. Sialkot 2002-03. Middlesex 2003. Lahore Blues 2004-05. PIA 2004-05 to 2006-07. Lahore Ravi 2005-06. Yorkshire (1 match) 2007. Titans 2007-08 to date. Hampshire 2008-09; cap 2009. Easterns 2008-09 to date. Staffordshire 2004-05. Qualified for SA on 1 Apr 2009. F-c Tour (Pak A): SL 2004-05. HS 77* H v Somerset (Southampton) 2009. 50 wkts (1+1); most – 74 (2004-05). BB 8-76 REDCO v Karachi Blues (Lahore) 1999-00. UK BB 7-66 (12-189 match) H v Lancs (Manchester) 2008 – on debut. LO HS 41* Staffs v Lancs (Stone) 2004 (CGT). LO BB 5-27 H v Sussex (Southampton) 2008 (P40). T20 HS 13. T20 BB 3-13.

‡JAVID, Ateeq, b Birmingham 15 Oct 1991. RHB, RM. Debut (Warwickshire) 2009. Warwickshire 2nd XI debut 2008. England U19s 2009 to 2009-10. HS 21 v Durham (Chester-le-St) 2009. BB – .

JOHNSON, Richard Matthew, b Solihull 1 Sep 1988. RHB, WK. Debut (Warwickshire) 2008. Herefordshire 2006. Warwickshire 2nd XI debut 2007. HS 72 v CU (Cambridge) 2008 – on debut. Awaiting CC debut. LO HS 20 v Northants (Birmingham) 2008 (FPT). T20 HS 0.

MacLEOD, Calum Scott (Hillpark S), b Glasgow, Scotland 15 Nov 1988. 6'1". RHB, RMF. Scotland 2007-09. Warwickshire debut 2008. **LOI** (Scot): 4 (2008 to 2008-09); HS 10* v E (Edinburgh) 2008; BB 2-46 v Canada (Benoni) 2008. HS 26 v DU (Durham) 2009. BB 4-66 Scotland v Canada (Aberdeen) 2009. Wa BB 3-36 v CU (Cambridge) 2008. Awaiting CC debut. LO HS 10* (*see LOI*). LO BB 2-38 Scotland v Namibia (Pretoria) 2008-09. IT20 HS 0. IT20 BB – .

MADDY, Darren Lee (Wreake Valley C), b Leicester 23 May 1974. 5'9". RHB, RM/OB. Leicestershire 1994-2006; cap 1996; benefit 2006. Warwickshire debut/cap 2007; captain 2007-08. **Tests**: 3 (1999 to 1999-00); HS 24 v SA (Durban) 1999-00; BB – . **LOI**: 8 (1998 to 1999-00); HS 53 v Z (Harare) 1999-00. F-c Tours (Eng A): SA 1996-97 (Le), 1998-99, 1999-00 (Eng); SL 1997-98; Z 1998-99; K 1997-98. 1000 runs (4); most – 1187 (2002). HS 229* Le v LU (Leicester) 2003. CC HS 162 Le v Durham (Darlington) 1998. Wa HS 148* v Kent (Canterbury) 2007. BB 5-37 Le v Hampshire (Southampton) 2002. Wa BB 5-63 v Durham (Chester-le-St) 2007. LO HS 167* Le v Scot (Edinburgh) 2006 (CGT). LO BB 4-16 Le v Somerset (Taunton) 2000 (NL). IT20 HS 50. IT20 BB 2-6. T20 HS 111 Le v Yorks (Leeds) 2004 – Le record. T20 BB 2-6.

MILLER, Andrew Stephen (St Cecilia's RC HS; Preston C), b Preston, Lancs 27 Sep 1987. 6'4". RHB, RMF. Debut (Warwickshire) 2008. Lancashire 2nd XI 2004-05. Warwickshire 2nd XI debut 2006. England U19s 2004-05 to 2007. HS 4* v Bangladesh A (Birmingham) 2008. BB 4-76 v Lancs (Manchester) 2009.

‡**NEWPORT, Nathan** Alexander, b Worcester 10 May 1989. Son of P.J.Newport (Boland, NT, Worcestershire and England 1982-99). RHB, RM. Debut (Warwickshire) 2009, but did not bat or bowl.

ORD, James Edward (Loughborough U), b Birmingham 9 Nov 1987. RHB, OB. Loughborough UCCE 2009. Warwickshire 2nd XI debut 2006. HS 9 LU v Hampshire (Southampton) 2009 – only f-c game. Awaiting Wa f-c debut. LO HS 27 v Northants (Northampton) 2009 (P40).

PIOLET, Steffan Andrew (Warden Park S; Central Sussex C), b Redhill, Surrey 8 Aug 1988. 6'1". RHB, RM. Debut (Warwickshire) 2009. Sussex 2nd XI 2006-08. Warwickshire 2nd XI debut 2008. HS 26* and BB 6-17 (10-43 match) v DU (Durham) 2009 – on only f-c appearance. LO HS 4 and LO BB 3-34 v Northants (Northampton) 2009 (P40). T20 HS 3. T20 BB 2-17.

NQ**RANKIN, William Boyd** (Strabane GS; Harper Adams UC), b Londonderry, Co Derry, N Ireland 5 Jul 1984. 6'8". LHB, RMF. Brother of R.J.Rankin (Ireland U19 2003-04). Debut (Ireland) 2006-07. Derbyshire 2007. Warwickshire debut 2008. Middlesex summer contract 2004-05. **LOI** (Ireland): 20 (2006-07 to 2009) HS 7* v SL (St George's) 2006-07; BB 3-32 v P (Kingston) 2006-07. F-c Tour (Ire): SA/Kenya 2008-09. HS 12* v Glamorgan (Birmingham) 2008. BB 5-39 Ire v Namibia (Windhoek) 2008-09. CC BB 5-85 v Durham (Chester-le-St) 2009. LO HS 9 v Kent (Canterbury) 2009 (FPT). LO BB 3-32 (*see LOI*). IT20 HS 5*. IT20 BB 2-27. T20 HS 5*. T20 BB 2-27.

TAHIR, Naqaash Sarosh (Moseley S; Spring Hill C), b Birmingham 14 Nov 1983. 5'10", RHB, RFM. Debut (Warwickshire) 2004. HS 49 v Worcs (Worcester) 2004. BB 7-107 v Lancs (Blackpool) 2006. LO HS 13* v Leics (Oakham) 2008 (FPT). LO BB 2-47 v Notts (Nottingham) 2008 (FPT).

TROTT, Ian Jonathan Leonard (Rondebosch BHC; Stellenbosch U), b Cape Town, South Africa 22 Apr 1981. 6'0". Stepbrother of K.C.Jackson (WP and Boland 1988-89 to 2001-02). RHB, RM. Boland 2000-01. W Province 2001-02. EU/British passport. Warwickshire debut 2003 scoring 134 v Sussex (Birmingham); cap 2005. Otago 2005-06. **Tests**: 5 (2009 to 2009-10); HS 119 v A (Oval) 2009 – on debut; BB – . **LOI**: 4 (2009 to 2009-10); HS 87 v SA (Centurion) 2009-10. F-c Tours: SA 2009-10; NZ 2008-09 (Eng A); I 2007-08 (Eng A); B 2009-10. 1000 runs (5); most – 1400 (2009). HS 210 v Sussex (Birmingham) 2005. BB 7-39 v Kent (Canterbury) 2003. LO HS 125* v Northants (Birmingham) 2007 (FPT). LO BB 4-55 v Hampshire (Lord's) 2005 (CGT). IT20 HS 51. T20 HS 86*. T20 BB 2-19.

TROUGHTON, Jamie Oliver (*'Jim'*) (Trinity S; Leamington Spa; Birmingham U), b Camden, London 2 Mar 1979. Great-grandson of H.T.Crichton (Warwicks 1908). 5'11". LHB, SLA. Debut (Warwickshire) 2001; cap 2002. **LOI**: 6 (2003); HS 20 v P (Lord's) 2003. F-c Tour (ECB Acad): SL 2002-03. 1000 runs (1): 1067 (2002). HS 223 v Hampshire (Birmingham) 2009. BB 3-1 v CU (Cambridge) 2004. CC BB 2-26 v Lancs (Birmingham) 2006. LO HS·115* and BB 4-23 Wa CB v Cumb (Millom) 2001 (CGT). T20 HS 62. T20 BB 2-10.

WESTWOOD, Ian James (Wheelers Lane S; Solihull SFC), b Birmingham 13 Jul 1982. 5'7½". LHB, OB. Debut (Warwickshire) 2001; cap 2008; captain 2009 to date. HS 178 v WI A (Birmingham) 2006. CC HS 176 v Glamorgan (Cardiff) 2008. BB 2-39 v Hampshire (Southampton) 2009. LO HS 65 v Northants (Northampton) 2008 (FPT). BB 1-28 Wa CB v Cambs (March) 2001 (CGT). T20 HS 49*. T20 BB 3-29.

WOAKES, Christopher Roger (Barr Beacon Language S, Walsall), b Birmingham 2 March 1989. 6'2". RHB, RMF. Debut (Warwickshire) 2006; cap 2009. MCC 2009. Herefordshire 2006-07. HS 131* v Hampshire (Southampton) 2009. BB 6-43 EL v West Indians (Derby) 2009. Wa BB 6-68 (10-162 match) v Glamorgan (Birmingham) 2008. LO HS 31* v Glamorgan (Cardiff) 2008 (P40). LO BB 4-38 EL v Pakistan A (Dubai) 2009-10. T20 HS 11*. T20 BB 4-21.

RELEASED/RETIRED
(Having made a County First-Class or List A appearance in 2009)

ANYON, J.E. – *see* SUSSEX.

CHOUDRY, Shaaiq Hussain (Fir Vale S; Bradford U), b Sheffield, Yorkshire 3 Nov 1985. 5'10". RHB, SLA. MCC 2007. Warwickshire 2009. Bradford/Leeds UCCE 2006-08 (not f-c). Warwickshire 2nd XI debut 2007. HS 75 v DU (Durham) 3009. BB – . Awaiting CC debut.

FROST, Tony (James Brinkley HS; Stoke-on-Trent C), b Stoke-on-Trent, Staffs 17 Nov 1975. 5'11". RHB, WK. Warwickshire 1997-2006, 2008-09; cap 1999. 1000 runs (1): 1003 (2008). HS 242* v Essex (Chelmsford) 2008. BB 1-12 v Hampshire (Southampton) 2009. LO HS 56 v Ireland (Belfast) (FPT). T20 HS 53.

[NQ]**PATEL, Jeetan** Shashi, b Wellington, New Zealand 7 May 1980. RHB, OB. Wellington 1999-00 to date. **Tests** (NZ): 10 (2006-07 to 2009-10); HS 27* v SA (Cape Town) 2006-07; BB 5-110 v WI (Napier) 2008-09. **LOI** (NZ): 39 (2005 to 2009-10); HS 34 v SL (Kingston) 2006-07; BB 3-11 v SA (Mumbai, BS) 2005-06. F-c Tours (NZ): E 2008; SA 2005-06; SL 2009; B 2008-09. HS 120 v Yorks (Birmingham) 2009. BB 6-32 Wellington v Otago (Queenstown) 2004-05. Wa BB 3-112 v Durham (Birmingham) 2009. LO HS 34 (*see LOI*). LO BB 4-16 NZ A v Aus A (Hyderabad) 2008-09. IT20 HS 5. IT20 BB 3-20. T20 HS 12. T20 BB 3-15.

POONIA, Navdeep Singh (Moseley Park S; Wolverhampton U), b Govan, Glasgow, Scotland 11 May 1986. 6'3". RHB, RM. Warwickshire 2006-09. Scotland 2006 to date (no f-c appearances). **LOI** (Scot): 21 (2006 to 2009-10); HS 67 v Canada (Mombasa) 2006-07. HS 111 v CU (Cambridge) 2008. CC HS 50 v Worcs (Birmingham) 2008. LO HS 79 Scotland v Oman (Johannesburg) 2008-09. IT20 HS 38*. T20 HS 38*.

[NQ]**SREESANTH, Shanthakumaran**, b Kerala, India 6 Feb 1983. RHB, RFM. Kerala 2002-03 to date. South Zone 2003-04 to date. Warwickshire 2009. **Tests** (I): 17 (2005-06 to 2009-10); HS 35 v E (Oval) 2007; BB 5-40 v SA (Johannesburg) 2006-07. **LOI** (I): 49 (2005-06 to 2009-10); HS 10* v P (Jaipur) 2007-08; BB 6-55 v E (Indore) 2005-06. F-c Tours (I): E 2007; SA 2006-07; WI 2006; B 2009-10. HS 35 (*see Tests*). Wa HS 30* v Notts (Nottingham) 2009. Wa BB 5-93 v Yorks (Scarborough) 2009. LO HS 33 Kerala v Karnataka (Margao) 2004-05. LO BB 6-55 (*see LOI*). IT20 HS 19*. IT20 BB 2-12. T20 HS 19*. T20 BB 3-29.

WARWICKSHIRE 2009

RESULTS SUMMARY

	Place	Won	Lost	Tied	Drew	NR
County Championship (1st Division)	5th	3	3		10	
All First-Class Matches		4	3		11	
FP Trophy (Group C)	3rd	3	3	1		1
Pro40 League (2nd Division)	**1st**	5		1		2
Twenty20 Cup (Midlands/Wales/West Division)	QF	7	4			

LV COUNTY CHAMPIONSHIP AVERAGES

BATTING AND FIELDING

Cap		M	I	NO	HS	Runs	Avge	100	50	Ct/St
2005	I.J.L.Trott	14	20	5	184*	1207	80.46	4	5	10
2001	I.R.Bell	13	21	3	172	986	54.77	4	4	10
	J.S.Patel	3	4	1	120	131	43.66	1	–	1
2002	J.O.Troughton	16	21	–	223	823	39.19	2	3	10
	R.Clarke	13	17	1	112	619	38.68	1	5	22
2007	T.R.Ambrose	16	21	1	153	686	34.30	2	4	37/2
2009	C.R.Woakes	16	21	7	131*	480	34.28	1	–	3
2008	I.J.Westwood	14	23	3	133	605	30.25	1	4	10
	A.G.Botha	14	19	2	64	444	26.11	–	2	5
2005	N.M.Carter	9	13	–	67	318	24.46	–	2	–
1999	T.Frost	13	20	1	94	463	24.36	–	2	7
	N.S.Tahir	10	12	3	24	145	16.11	–	–	1
	S.Sreesanth	5	7	2	30*	74	14.80	–	–	3
	W.B.Rankin	12	14	4	7	18	2.25	–	–	7

Also played: J.E.Anyon (2 matches) 15*, 14*; K.H.D.Barker (1) 0; A.Javid (1) 8, 21 (1 ct); D.L.Maddy (2 – cap 2007) 17, 36, 8 (2 ct); A.S.Miller (2) 0, 0; N.A.Newport (1) did not bat.

BOWLING

	O	M	R	W	Avge	Best	5wI	10wM
N.S.Tahir	232.5	55	711	30	23.70	5- 67	1	–
S.Sreesanth	109.3	21	418	13	32.15	5- 93	1	–
W.B.Rankin	316.1	54	1164	35	33.25	5- 85	1	–
C.R.Woakes	415.5	91	1354	37	36.59	5- 40	1	–
A.G.Botha	316.3	61	941	23	40.91	5- 51	1	–
N.M.Carter	190	30	704	16	44.00	5- 37	1	–
Also bowled:								
A.S.Miller	61	12	184	7	26.28	4- 76	–	–
R.Clarke	146.1	21	567	9	63.00	2- 15	–	–
J.S.Patel	94	4	399	6	66.50	3-112	–	–

J.E.Anyon 44.2-7-199-2; K.H.D.Barker 14-1-54-0; I.R.Bell 10-1-43-0; T.Frost 5.1-1-12-1; D.L.Maddy 31.1-8-100-1; I.J.L.Trott 77.2-9-281-4; I.J.Westwood 19-2-49-2.

The First-Class Averages (pp 228–244) give the records of Warwickshire players in all first-class county matches (Warwickshire's other opponents being Durham UCCE and England), with the exception of I.R.Bell, whose first-class figures for Warwickshire are as above, and:

    T.R.Ambrose 17-23-2-153-697-33.19-2-4-38ct/2st. Did not bowl.

    J.E.Anyon 3-3-2-15*-38-38.00-0-0-0ct. 65.2-13-252-4-63.00-2/38-0-0.

    I.J.L.Trott 15-22-6-184*-1240-77.50-4-5-11ct. 94.2-10-346-5-69.20-2/26-0-0.

    C.R.Woakes 17-22-7-131*-493-32.86-1-1-4ct. 445.5-96-1436-38-37.78-5/40-1-0.

WARWICKSHIRE RECORDS

FIRST-CLASS CRICKET

Highest Total	For 810-4d			v	Durham	Birmingham	1994
	V 887			by	Yorkshire	Birmingham	1896
Lowest Total	For 16			v	Kent	Tonbridge	1913
	V 15			by	Hampshire	Birmingham	1922
Highest Innings	For 501*	B.C.Lara		v	Durham	Birmingham	1994
	V 322	I.V.A.Richards	for		Somerset	Taunton	1985

Highest Partnership for each Wicket

1st	377*	N.F.Horner/K.Ibadulla	v	Surrey	The Oval	1960
2nd	465*	J.A.Jameson/R.B.Kanhai	v	Glos	Birmingham	1974
3rd	327	S.P.Kinneir/W.G.Quaife	v	Lancashire	Birmingham	1901
4th	470	A.I.Kallicharran/G.W.Humpage	v	Lancashire	Southport	1982
5th	335	J.O.Troughton/T.R.Ambrose	v	Hampshire	Birmingham	2009
6th	226	T.R.Ambrose/H.H.Streak	v	Worcs	Worcester	2007
7th	289*	I.R.Bell/T.Frost	v	Sussex	Horsham	2004
8th	228	A.J.W.Croom/R.E.S.Wyatt	v	Worcs	Dudley	1925
9th	233	I.J.L.Trott/J.S.Patel	v	Yorkshire	Birmingham	2009
10th	214	N.V.Knight/A.Richardson	v	Hampshire	Birmingham	2002

Best Bowling	For 10-41	J.D.Bannister	v	Comb Servs	Birmingham	1959
(Innings)	V 10-36	H.Verity	for	Yorkshire	Leeds	1931
Best Bowling	For 15-76	S.Hargreave	v	Surrey	The Oval	1903
(Match)	V 17-92	A.P.Freeman	for	Kent	Folkestone	1932

Most Runs – Season	2417	M.J.K.Smith	(av 60.42)	1959
Most Runs – Career	35146	D.L.Amiss	(av 41.64)	1960-87
Most 100s – Season	9	A.I.Kallicharran		1984
	9	B.C.Lara		1994
Most 100s – Career	78	D.L.Amiss		1960-87
Most Wkts – Season	180	W.E.Hollies	(av 15.13)	1946
Most Wkts – Career	2201	W.E.Hollies	(av 20.45)	1932-57
Most Career W-K Dismissals	800	E.J.Smith	(662 ct; 138 st)	1904-30
Most Career Catches in the Field	422	M.J.K.Smith		1956-75

LIMITED-OVERS CRICKET

Highest Total	FPT	392-5		v	Oxfordshire	Birmingham	1984
	P40	310-5		v	Lancs	Birmingham	2004
	T20	205-2		v	Northants	Birmingham	2005
		205-7		for	Glamorgan	Swansea	2005
Lowest Total	FPT	98		v	Leics	Leicester	1998
	P40	59		v	Yorkshire	Leeds	2001
	T20	114		v	Sussex	Hove	2009
Highest Innings	FPT	206	A.I.Kallicharran	v	Oxfordshire	Birmingham	1984
	P40	137	I.R.Bell	v	Yorkshire	Birmingham	2005
	T20	89	N.V.Knight	v	Worcs	Worcester	2003
Best Bowling	FPT	6-32	K.Ibadulla	v	Hampshire	Birmingham	1965
		6-32	A.I.Kallicharran	v	Oxfordshire	Birmingham	1984
	P40	6-15	A.A.Donald	v	Yorkshire	Birmingham	1995
	T20	5-19	N.M.Carter	v	Worcs	Birmingham	2005

WORCESTERSHIRE

Formation of Present Club: 11 March 1865
Inaugural First-Class Match: 1899
Colours: Dark Green and Black
Badge: Shield Argent a Fess between three Pears Sable
County Championships: (5) 1964, 1965, 1974, 1988, 1989
Gillette/NatWest/C&G/FP Trophy Winners: (1) 1994
Benson and Hedges Cup Winners: (1) 1991
Pro 40/National League (Div 1) Winners: (1) 2007
Sunday League Winners: (3) 1971, 1987, 1988
Twenty20 Cup Winners: (0); best – Quarter-Finalist 2004, 2007

Chief Executive: Mark S.Newton, County Ground, New Road, Worcester, WR2 4QQ • Tel: 01905 748474 • Fax: 01905 748005 • Email: admin@wccc.co.uk • Web: www.wccc.co.uk

Director of Cricket: Steve J.Rhodes. **Captain:** V.S.Solanki. **Vice-Captain:** D.K.H.Mitchell. **Overseas Player:** P.A.Jaques. **2010 Beneficiary:** none. **Head Groundsman:** Tim Packwood. **Scorer:** Neil D.Smith. ‡ New registration. ^{NQ} Not qualified for England.

Worcestershire revised their capping policy in 2002 and now award players with their County Colours when they make their Championship debut.

ALI, Moeen Munir (Moseley S), b Birmingham, Warwks 18 Jun 1987. Brother of Kadeer Ali (*see GLOUCESTERSHIRE*) and cousin of Kabir Ali (*see HAMPSHIRE*). 6'0". LHB, OB. Warwickshire 2005-06, having joined staff when aged 15. Worcestershire debut 2007. HS 153 v Yorks (Leeds) 2009. BB 4-29 v Hampshire (Worcester) 2009. LO HS 125 v Hampshire (Southampton) 2009 (FPT). LO BB 3-32 v Yorks (Worcester) 2009 (P40). T20 HS 46. T20 BB 2-15.

ANDREW, Gareth Mark (Ansford Community S; Richard Huish C), b Yeovil, Somerset 27 Dec 1983. 6'0". LHB, RMF. Somerset 2003-05; 2nd XI debut 1999 when aged 15 years 247 days. Worcestershire debut 2008. HS 92* v Notts (Worcester) 2009. BB 5-58 v Middx (Kidderminster) 2008. LO HS 33 Sm v Leics (Leicester) 2006 (P40). LO BB 5-31 v Yorks (Worcester) 2009 (P40). T20 HS 14. T20 BB 4-22.

‡^{NQ}**CAMERON, James** Gair, b Harare, Zimbabwe 31 Jan 1986. LHB, RM. British passport holder. Zimbabwe U19s 2003-04. Awaiting f-c debut.

‡**COX, Oliver** Ben (Bromsgrove S), b Wordsley, Stourbridge 2 Feb 1992. 5'10". RHB, WK. Debut (Worcestershire) 2009, scoring 61 v Somerset (Taunton), his only f-c innings. Worcs 2nd XI debut 2009.

IMRAN ARIF (Govt HS, Saidpur Kotli; Bradford C), b Kotli, Azad Kashmir, Pakistan 15 Jan 1984. UK passport 2009. 5'11". RHB, RFM. Debut (Worcestershire) 2008. Sussex 2nd XI 2007. HS 35 v Sussex (Hove) 2009. BB 5-50 v Glamorgan (Worcester) 2008 – on debut. LO HS 16* v Durham (Worcester) 2008. LO BB 1-17 v Notts (Nottingham) 2009 (P40).

^{NQ}**JAQUES, Philip** Anthony (Fig Tree HS, Wollongong; Australian C of PE, Homebush), b Wollongong, NSW, Australia 3 May 1979. 6'1". LHB, SLC. British passport (English parents). NSW 2000-01 to date. Northamptonshire 2003; cap 2003. Yorkshire 2004-05; cap 2005. Worcestershire 2006-07, rejoins in 2010. **Tests** (A): 11 (2005-06 to 2008); HS 150 v SL (Hobart) 2007-08. **LOI** (A): 6 (2005-06 to 2006-07); HS 94 v SA (Melbourne) 2005-06. F-c Tours (A): WI 2008; P 2005-06 (Aus A), 2007-08 (Aus A); B 2005-06. 1000 runs (4+2); most – 1409 (2003). HS 244 v Essex (Chelmsford) 2006. BB – . LO HS 171* NSW v Q (Sydney) 2009-10. T20 HS 92.

JONES, Richard Alan (Grange HS and King Edward VI C, Stourbridge; Loughborough U), b Wordsley, Stourbridge 6 Nov 1986. 6'2". RHB, RMF. Debut (Worcestershire) 2007. HS 53* v Durham (Worcester) 2009. BB 6-100 v Warwks (Birmingham) 2009. LO HS 6 v Somerset (Taunton) 2008 (FPT). LO BB – .

‡**KAPIL, Aneesh** (Tettenhall C), b Wolverhampton 3 Aug 1993. 5'8". RHB, RMF. Worcestershire 2nd XI debut 2008. Summer contract. Awaiting 1st XI debut.

^{NQ}**KERVEZEE, Alexei** Nicolaas (Duneside HS, Namibia; Grenoobi HS, SA; Segbroek C, Holland), b Walvis Bay, Namibia 11 Sep 1989. 5'8". RHB, OB. Netherlands 2005 to date. Worcestershire debut 2008. Worcestershire 2nd XI debut 2007. **LOI** (Ne): 26 (2006 to 2009-10); HS 75 v Canada (Amstelveen) 2009; BB – . HS 98 Netherlands v Canada (King City, Ontario) 2007. Wo HS 66 v Durham (Chester-le-St) 2009. BB 1-14 Netherlands v Namibia (Windhoek) 2007-08. LO HS 121* Netherlands v Denmark (Potchefstroom) 2008-09. LO BB – . IT20 HS 39. T20 HS 39.

MANUEL, Jack Kenneth (Wilnecote HS, Tamworth), b Sutton Coldfield, Warwks 13 Feb 1991. 6'1". LHB, OB. Worcestershire 2nd XI debut 2008. England U19s 2009 to 2009-10. Awaiting 1st XI debut.

MASON, Matthew Sean (Mazenod C, Lesmurdie, WA), b Claremont, Perth, Australia 20 Mar 1974. British passport. 6'5". RHB, RFM. W Australia 1996-97 to 1997-98. Worcestershire debut 2002. HS 63 v Warwks (Worcester) 2004. 50 wkts (3); most – 53 (2003, 2005). BB 8-45 (10-117) v Glos (Worcester) 2006. LO HS 25 v Durham (Worcester) 2004 (NL). LO BB 4-34 v Surrey (Guildford) 2003 (NL). T20 HS 8*. T20 BB 3-42.

MITCHELL, Daryl Keith Henry (Prince Henry's HS; University C, Worcester), b Badsey, near Evesham 25 Nov 1983. 5'10". RHB, RM. Debut (Worcestershire) 2005. 1000 runs (1): 1162 (2009). HS 298 v Somerset (Taunton) 2009. BB 4-49 v Yorks (Leeds) 2009. LO HS 92 v Somerset (Taunton) 2008 (FPT). LO BB 4-42 v Lancs (Worcester) 2006 (CGT). T20 HS 35. T20 BB 4-11 v Glos (Bristol) 2008 – Wo record.

‡**RICHARDSON, Alan** (Alleyne's HS, Stone; Stafford CFE; Durham U), b Newcastle-under-Lyme, Staffs 6 May 1975. 6'2". RHB, RMF. Derbyshire 1995 (one match). Warwick-shire 1999-2004; cap 2002. Middlesex 2005-09; cap 2005, taking 7-113 v Notts (Lord's) on debut. Staffordshire 1996-98. Minor Counties 1998. HS 91 Wa v Hampshire (Birmingham) 2002 – adding Wa record 214 for 10th wicket with N.V.Knight. 50 wkts (1): 57 (2005). BB 8-46 Wa v Sussex (Birmingham) 2002. LO HS 21* M v Lancs (Lord's) 2005 (NL). LO BB 5-35 Wa v Staffs (Stone) 2002 (CGT). T20 HS 6*. T20 BB 3-13.

‡**RUSSELL, Christopher** James (Medina HS), b Newport, I-o-W 16 Feb 1989. 6'1". RHB, RMF. Worcestershire 2nd XI debut 2008. Awaiting 1st XI debut.

‡NOSHAKIB AL HASAN, b Magura, Jessore, Bangladesh 24 Mar 1987. LHB, SLA. Debut Bangladesh CB President's XI 2004-05. Khulna Division 2004-05 to date. **Tests** (B): 17 (2007 to 2009-10); HS 100 v NZ (Hámilton) 2009-10; BB 7-36 (9-115 match) v NZ (Chittagong) 2008-09. **LOI** (B): 82 (2006 to 2009-10); HS 134* v Canada (St John's) 2006-07; BB 4-33 v NZ (Christchurch) 2009-10. F-c Tours (B): E 2008 (Ba A); SA 2008-09; WI 2009; NZ 2007-08, 2009-10; SL 2007; Z 2004-05 (Ba A), 2006 (Ba A). HS 129 Khulna v Dhaka (Khulna) 2008-09. BB 7-36 (*see Tests*). LO HS 134* (*see LOI*). LO BB 4-30 Bangladesh A v Zimbabwe A (Bulawayo) 2006. IT20 HS 26. IT20 BB 4-34.

‡SHANTRY, Jack David (Priory SS; Shrewsbury SFC; Liverpool U), b Shrewsbury, Shropshire 29 Jan 1988. Son of B.K.Shantry (Gloucestershire 1978-79) and brother of A.J.Shantry (*see GLAMORGAN*). 6'4". LHB, LM. Debut (Worcestershire) 2009. Shropshire 2007-09. HS 6 v Durham (Worcester) 2009. BB 2-53 v Notts (Worcester) 2009. LO HS 7* v Somerset (Worcester) 2009 (P40). LO BB 2-43 v Hampshire (Worcester) 2009 (P40).

SMITH, Benjamin Francis (Kibworth HS), b Corby, Northants 3 Apr 1972. 5'9". RHB, RM. Leicestershire 1990-2001; cap 1995. MCC 1999-00. Central Districts 2000-01 to 2001-02. Worcestershire debut 2002; captain 2003 to 2004 (*part*). F-c Tours (Le): SA 1996-97; B 1999-00 (MCC). 1000 runs (8); most – 1546 (2005). HS 204 Le v Surrey (Oval) 1998. Wo HS 203 v Somerset (Taunton) 2006, sharing Wo 4th wkt record partnership of 330 with G.A.Hick. BB 1-5 Le v Essex (Ilford) 1991. Wo BB 1 39 v Surrey (Oval) 2006. LO HS 115 Le v Somerset (Weston-s-M) 1995 (SL). LO BB 1-2 v Worcs CB (Worcester) 2003 (CGT). T20 HS 105.

‡NOSMITH, Steven Peter Devereux, b Sydney, NSW, Australia 2 Jun 1989. RHB, LBG. NSW 2007-08 to date. Joins Worcestershire for T20 only in 2010. **LOI** (A): 1 (2009-10); BB 2-78 v WI (Melbourne) 2009-10. HS 177 and BB 3-99 NSW v Tas (Hobart) 2009-10. LO HS 92 NSW v S Aus (Wollongong) 2009-10. LO BB 3-43 NSW v Tas (Launceston) 2009-10. IT20 HS 8. IT20 BB 2-34. T20 HS 35*. T20 BB 4-13.

SOLANKI, Vikram Singh (Regis S, Wolverhampton), b Udaipur, India 1 Apr 1976. 6'0". RHB, OB, occ WK. Debut (Worcestershire) 1995; cap 1998; captain 2005 to date; benefit 2007. Rajasthan 2006-07. **LOI**: 51 (1999-00 to 2006); HS 106 v SA (Oval) 2003; BB 1-17 v SL (Leeds) 2006. F-c Tours (Eng A): SA 1998-99, 1999-00 (Eng – *part*); WI 2000-01, 2005-06 (Captain); NZ 1999-00; SL 2004-05; Z 1999-97 (Wo), 1998-99; B 1999-00. 1000 runs (5); most – 1339 (1999). HS 270 v Glos (Cheltenham) 2008, sharing Wo 2nd wkt record partnership of 316 with S.C.Moore. BB 5-40 v Middx (Lord's) 2004. LO HS 164* v Worcs CB (Worcester) 2003 (CGT). LO BB 4-14 v Somerset (Taunton) 2006 (P40). IT20 HS 43. T20 HS 100. T20 BB 1-9.

WHEELDON, David Anthony (Painsley RC HS; Moorlands SFC; Worcester U), b Stoke-on-Trent, Staffordshire 12 Apr 1989. 5'8". LHB, LB. Debut (Worcestershire) 2009. Worcestershire 2nd XI debut 2006. Staffordshire 2006-09. HS 87 v Somerset (Taunton) 2009.

WHELAN, Christopher David (St Margaret's HS), b Liverpool, Lancs 8 May 1986. 6'2". RHB, RMF. Middlesex 2005-07. Worcestershire debut 2008. HS 58 v Middx (Kidderminster) 2008. BB 5-95 v Lancs (Worcester) 2009. LO HS 11 v Yorks (Worcester) 2009 (P40). LO BB 4-27 v Hampshire (Worcester) 2009 (FPT). T20 HS 2*. T20 BB 2-24.

RELEASED/RETIRED
(Having made a County First-Class or List A appearance in 2009)

AHMED, Mehraj, b Birmingham, Warwks 5 Jan 1989. RHB, RFM. Worcestershire 2008-09. Worcestershire 2nd XI debut 2006. HS 0* and CC BB – v Sussex (Hove) 2009. BB 1-28 v LU (Kidderminster) 2008. LO BB 1-34 v Glamorgan (Worcester) 2008.

ALI, K. – *see HAMPSHIRE.*

BATTY, G.J. – *see SURREY.*

DAVIES, S.M. – *see SURREY.*

FISHER, Ian Douglas (Beckfoot GS, Bingley; Thomas Danby C, Leeds), b Bradford, Yorks 31 Mar 1976. 5'10½". LHB, SLA. Yorkshire 1995-96 (Y in Zim) to 2001. Gloucestershire 2002-08; cap 2004. Worcestershire 2009, one non-CC f-c game. F-c Tour: Z 1995-96 (Y). HS 103* Gs v Essex (Gloucester) 2002. BB 5-30 (10-123 match) Gs v Durham (Bristol) 2003. LO HS 37* Gs v Glamorgan (Colwyn Bay) 2007 (FPT). LO BB 3-18 Gs v Northants (Northampton) 2004 (NL) and v Sussex (Worcester) 2009 (P40). T20 HS 14. T20 BB 4-22.

JONES, S.P. – *see HAMPSHIRE.*

KNAPPETT, Joshua Philip Thomas (East Barnet S; Oxford Brookes U), b Westminster, London 15 Apr 1985. 6'0". RHB, occ RM, WK. Oxford UCCE 2004-06. British U 2005-06. Worcestershire 2007-09. No 1st XI appearances in 2008. HS 100* OU v Durham (Oxford) 2006. Wo HS 18 v Sussex (Hove) 2007 – on Wo debut.

MOORE, S.C. – *see LANCASHIRE.*

^NQ^**NOFFKE, Ashley** Allan (Immanuel Lutheran C; Sunshine Coast U), b Nambour, Queensland, Australia 30 Apr 1977. 6'3". RHB, RFM. Debut (Aus CA in Zim) 1998-99. Queensland 1999-00 to 2008-09. Middlesex 2002-03; cap 2003. Durham 2005. Gloucestershire debut/cap 2007 – taking 6-68 (9-113 match) v Notts (Bristol). Worcestershire 2009. W Australia 2009-10. **LOI** (A): 1 (2007-08), taking 1-46 v I (Brisbane). F-c Tours (A): E 2001 (*part*); WI 2002-03; I 2008-09 (Aus A); P 2007-08 (Aus A); Z 1998-99 (Aus CA). HS 114* Q v S Aus (Brisbane) 2003-04. UK HS 89 and Wo BB 4-92 v Sussex (Worcester) 2009. BB 8-24 (12-108 match) M v Derbys (Derby) 2002. LO HS 58 M v Sussex (Lord's) 2002 (BHC). LO BB 4-32 Q v Tasmania (Hobart) 2001-02. IT20 HS 0. IT20 BB 3-18. T20 HS 34. T20 BB 3-18.

O.M.Ali and J.N.K.Shannon left the staff, without making a First-Class County or List A appearance in 2009.

WORCESTERSHIRE 2009

RESULTS SUMMARY

	Place	Won	Lost	Tied	Drew NR
County Championship (1st Division)	9th		10		6
All First-Class Matches			10		7
FP Trophy (Group A)	3rd	4	3		1
Pro40 League (1st Division)	3rd	5	2		1
Twenty20 Cup (Midlands/Wales/West Division)	4th	5	5		

LV COUNTY CHAMPIONSHIP AVERAGES

BATTING AND FIELDING

Cap†		M	I	NO	HS	Runs	Avge	100	50	Ct/St
2005	S.M.Davies	14	26	2	126	952	39.66	2	4	39/2
2008	G.M.Andrew	9	16	5	92*	391	35.54	–	3	–
1998	V.S.Solanki	15	28	1	206*	953	35.29	1	4	13
2005	D.K.H.Mitchell	16	30	–	298	1022	34.06	1	5	17
2008	M.M.Ali	16	30	2	153	803	28.67	2	3	4
2009	A.A.Noffke	6	9	–	89	258	28.66	–	2	–
2009	D.A.Wheeldon	4	5	–	87	138	27.60	–	1	3
2003	S.C.Moore	14	27	–	107	738	27.33	1	5	5
2009	A.N.Kervezee	8	14	–	66	381	27.21	–	2	2
2002	B.F.Smith	13	26	2	80*	565	23.54	–	3	9
2007	R.A.Jones	7	11	2	53*	209	23.22	–	1	4
2008	C.D.Whelan	11	17	3	47	205	14.64	–	–	1
2002	Kabir Ali	4	7	1	30*	81	13.50	–	–	2
2008	Imran Arif	8	13	7	35	81	13.50	–	–	4
2002	M.S.Mason	14	23	6	28	207	12.17	–	–	6
2002	G.J.Batty	10	16	–	46	175	10.93	–	–	8
2009	J.D.Shantry	4	5	1	6	12	3.00	–	–	2

Also batted: (1 match each): M.Ahmed (cap 2009) 0*, 0*; O.B.Cox (cap 2009) 61 (4 ct, 1 st); J.P.T.Knappett (cap 2007) 4*, 1 (5 ct).

BOWLING

	O	M	R	W	Avge	Best	5wI	10wM
M.S.Mason	418.4	125	1186	43	27.58	7- 39	2	–
R.A.Jones	174	25	745	22	33.86	6-100	1	–
Kabir Ali	97	10	416	11	37.81	6- 68	1	–
G.M.Andrew	249.3	37	964	22	43.81	5-117	1	–
A.A.Noffke	158	38	452	10	45.20	4- 92	–	–
C.D.Whelan	223	20	1040	22	47.27	5- 95	1	–
Imran Arif	172.5	18	855	15	57.00	5- 93	1	–
Also bowled:								
D.K.H.Mitchell	90	13	252	9	28.00	4- 49	–	–
J.D.Shantry	127.1	31	382	8	47.75	2- 53	–	–
M.M.Ali	94.1	15	461	7	65.85	4- 29	–	–
G.J.Batty	218.1	33	707	9	78.55	2- 71	–	–

M.Ahmed 9-0-73-0; V.S.Solanki 12-2-36-0.

The First-Class Averages (pp 228–244) give the records of Worcestershire players in all first-class county matches (Worcestershire's other opponents being Oxford UCCE), with the exception of Kabir Ali, S.M.Davies and S.C.Moore, whose first-class figures for Worcestershire are as above, and:

V.S.Solanki 16-29-1-206*-980-35.00-1-4-13ct. 12-2-36-0.

† Worcestershire revised their capping policy in 2002 and now award players with their County Colours when they make their Championship debut.

WORCESTERSHIRE RECORDS

FIRST-CLASS CRICKET

Highest Total	For 701-6d		v	Surrey	Worcester	2007
	V 701-4d		by	Leics	Worcester	1906
Lowest Total	For 24		v	Yorkshire	Huddersfield	1903
	V 30		by	Hampshire	Worcester	1903
Highest Innings	For 405*	G.A.Hick	v	Somerset	Taunton	1988
	V 331*	J.D.B.Robertson	for	Middlesex	Worcester	1949

Highest Partnership for each Wicket

1st	309	H.K.Foster/F.L.Bowley	v	Derbyshire	Derby	1901
2nd	316	S.C.Moore/V.S.Solanki	v	Glos	Cheltenham	2008
3rd	438*	G.A.Hick/T.M.Moody	v	Hampshire	Southampton	1997
4th	330	B.F.Smith/G.A.Hick	v	Somerset	Taunton	2006
5th	393	E.G.Arnold/W.B.Burns	v	Warwicks	Birmingham	1909
6th	265	G.A.Hick/S.J.Rhodes	v	Somerset	Taunton	1988
7th	256	D.A.Leatherdale/S.J.Rhodes	v	Notts	Nottingham	2002
8th	184	S.J.Rhodes/S.R.Lampitt	v	Derbyshire	Kidderminster	1991
9th	181	J.A.Cuffe/R.D.Burrows	v	Glos	Worcester	1907
10th	119	W.B.Burns/G.A.Wilson	v	Somerset	Worcester	1906

Best Bowling	For 9- 23	C.F.Root	v	Lancashire	Worcester	1931
(Innings)	V 10- 51	J.Mercer	for	Glamorgan	Worcester	1936
Best Bowling	For 15- 87	A.J.Conway	v	Glos	Moreton-in-M	1914
(Match)	V 17-212	J.C.Clay	for	Glamorgan	Swansea	1937

Most Runs – Season	2654	H.H.I.H.Gibbons (av 52.03)		1934
Most Runs – Career	34490	D.Kenyon (av 34.18)		1946-67
Most 100s – Season	10	G.M.Turner		1970
	10	G.A.Hick		1988
Most 100s – Career	106	G.A.Hick		1984-2008
Most Wkts – Season	207	C.F.Root (av 17.52)		1925
Most Wkts – Career	2143	R.T.D.Perks (av 23.73)		1930-55
Most Career W-K Dismissals	1095	S.J.Rhodes (991 ct; 104 st)		1985-2004
Most Career Catches in the Field	528	G.A.Hick		1984-2008

LIMITED-OVERS CRICKET

Highest Total	FPT	404-3	v	Devon	Worcester	1987
	P40	316-5	v	Glos	Worcester	2008
	T20	227-6	v	Northants	Kidderminster	2007
Lowest Total	FPT	58	v	Ireland	Worcester	2009
	P40	86	v	Yorkshire	Leeds	1969
	T20	86	v	Northants	Worcester	2006
Highest Innings	FPT	180*	T.M.Moody	v	Surrey	The Oval	1994
	P40	160	T.M.Moody	v	Kent	Worcester	1991
	T20	116*	G.A.Hick	v	Northants	Luton	2004
Best Bowling	FPT	7-19	N.V.Radford	v	Beds	Bedford	1991
	P40	6-16	Shoaib Akhtar	v	Glos	Worcester	2005
	T20	4-11	D.K.H.Mitchell	v	Glos	Bristol	2008

YORKSHIRE

Formation of Present Club: 8 January 1863
Substantial Reorganisation: 10 December 1891
Inaugural First-Class Match: 1864
Colours: Dark Blue, Light Blue and Gold
Badge: White Rose
County Championships (since 1890): (30) 1893, 1896, 1898, 1900, 1901, 1902, 1905, 1908, 1912, 1919, 1922, 1923, 1924, 1925, 1931, 1932, 1933, 1935, 1937, 1938, 1939, 1946, 1959, 1960, 1962, 1963, 1966, 1967, 1968, 2001
Joint Champions: (1) 1949
Gillette/NatWest/C&G/FP Trophy Winners: (3) 1965, 1969, 2002
Benson and Hedges Cup Winners: (1) 1987
Pro 40/National League (Div 1) Winners: (0); best – 2nd 2000
Sunday League Winners: (1) 1983
Twenty20 Cup Winners: (0); best – Quarter-Finalist 2007

Chief Executive: Stewart M.Regan, Headingley Cricket Ground, Leeds, LS6 3BU • Tel: 0113 278 7394 • Fax: 0113 278 4099 • Email: cricket@yorkshireccc.org.uk • Web: www.yorkshireccc.org.uk

Director of Cricket: Martyn D.Moxon. **Captain:** A.W.Gale. **Vice-Captain:** J.A.Rudolph. **Overseas Players:** R.J.Harris and D.R.Tuffey. **2010 Beneficiary:** none. **Head Groundsman:** Andy Fogarty. **Scorer:** John T.Potter. ‡ New registration. NQ Not qualified for England.

AZEEM Muhammad **RAFIQ** (Holgate S Sports C; Barnsley C), b Karachi, Pakistan 27 Feb 1991. 5'11". RHB, OB. Debut (Yorkshire) 2009. Yorkshire 2nd XI debut 2007. England U19s 2008-09 to 2009-10. HS 100 v Worcs (Worcester) 2009. BB 3-34 v Sussex (Leeds) 2009 – on debut. LO HS – . LO BB 1-36 v Sussex (Scarborough) 2009 (P40). T20 HS 11*. T20 BB 2-21.

BAIRSTOW, Jonathan Marc (St Peter's S, York; Leeds Met U), b Bradford 26 Sep 1989. Son of D.L.Bairstow (Yorkshire, GW, England 1970-90) and brother of A.D.Bairstow (Derbyshire 1995). 6'0". RHB, WK. Debut (Yorkshire) 2009. Winner of Young Wisden Schools Cricketer of the Year 2008. Yorkshire 2nd XI debut 2007. HS 84* v Notts (Scarborough) 2009. LO HS 20 v Somerset (Taunton) 2009 (P40).

BALLANCE, Gary Simon (Peterhouse S, Marondera, Zimbabwe; Harrow S; Leeds Met U), b Harare, Zimbabwe 22 Nov 1989. Nephew of G.S.Ballance (Rhodesia B 1978-79) and D.L.Houghton (Rhodesia/Zimbabwe 1978-79 to 1997-98). 6'0". LHB, LB. Debut (Yorkshire) 2008. Derbyshire (List A) 2006-07. HS 5 v Kent (Canterbury) 2008 – on debut. LO HS 73 De v Hampshire (Southampton) 2006 (P40).

BRESNAN, Timothy Thomas (Castleford HS and TC; Pontefract New C), b Pontefract 28 Feb 1985. 6'0". RHB, RFM. Debut (Yorkshire) 2003; cap 2006. MCC 2006, 2009. **Tests:** 2 (2009); HS 9 v WI (Lord's) 2009; BB 3-45 v WI (Chester-le-St) 2009. **LOI:** 18 (2006 to 2009-10); HS 80 v SA (Centurion) 2009-10; BB 2-10 v Ire (Belfast) 2009. F-c Tours: B 2006-07 (Eng A), 2009-10. HS 126* Eng A v Indians (Chelmsford) 2007. Y HS 116 v Surrey (Oval) 2007, sharing in Y record 9th wicket partnership of 246 with J.N.Gillespie. BB 5-42 v Worcs (Worcester) 2005. LO HS 80 (*see LOI*). BB 4-25 v Somerset (Leeds) 2005 (NL). IT20 6*. IT20 BB 2-30. T20 HS 42. T20 BB 3-21.

BROPHY, Gerard Louis (Christian Brothers C, Boksburg; Witwatersrand TC), b Welkom, Orange Free State, South Africa 26 Nov 1975. 5'11". British/EU passport. Qualified for England 2006. RHB, WK. Transvaal/Gauteng 1996-97 to 1998-99. Free State 1999-00 to 2000-01. Northamptonshire 2002-05. Yorkshire debut 2006; cap 2008. F-c Tour (SA Acad): Z 1998. HS 185 SA Academy v Zim President's XI (Harare) 1998-99. UK HS 181 Nh v Sussex (Hove) 2004. Y HS 100* v Hampshire (Southampton) 2007. LO HS 68* v Sussex (Leeds) 2009 (FPT). T20 HS 57*.

GALE, Andrew William (Whitcliffe Mount S; Heckmondwike GS), b Dewsbury 28 Nov 1983. 6'2". LHB, LB. Debut (Yorkshire) 2004, 2006 to date; cap 2008; captain 2010. HS 150 v Surrey (Oval) 2008. BB 1-33 v LU (Leeds) 2007. LO HS 89 v Leics (Leeds) 2008. T20 HS 91.

‡^{NQ}**GIBBS, Herschelle** Herman, b Green Point, Cape Town, South Africa 23 Feb 1974. RHB/RM. Western Province 1990-91 to 2004-05. Cape Cobras 2005-06 to date. Glamorgan 2009 (T20 contract in 2008). Joins Yorkshire on a T20 only contract. **Tests** (SA): 90 (1996-97 to 2007-08); HS 228 v P (Cape Town) 2002-03. BB – . **LOI** (SA): 248 (1996-97 to 2009-10); HS 175 v A (Johannesburg) 2005-06 in total of 438-9 – highest ever l-o run chase. F-c Tours (SA): E 1995 (SA A), 2003; A 1997-98, 2001-02, 2005-06; WI 2000-01, 2004-05; NZ 1998-99, 2003-04; I 1996-97, 1999-00; P 2003-04, 2007-08; SL 2004, 2006; Z 2001-02; B 2003. HS (see Tests). CC HS 96 Gm v Glos (Bristol) 2009. BB 2-14 SA A v Somerset (Taunton) 1996. LO HS 175 (see LOI). LO BB 1-16 SA A v Essex (Chelmsford) 1996. IT20 HS 90*. T20 HS 98.

HANNON-DALBY, Oliver James (Brooksbank S, Leeds Met U), b Halifax 20 Jun 1989. 6'7". LHB, RMF. Debut (Yorkshire) 2008. No 1st XI appearances in 2009. Yorkshire 2nd XI debut 2006. HS 1 and BB 1-58 v Surrey (Oval) 2008 – on debut.

‡^{NQ}**HARRIS, Ryan** James, b Nowra, NSW, Australia 11 Oct 1979. 5'10". British passport. RHB, RFM. South Australia 2001-02 to 2007-08. Sussex (one f-c match only) 2008. Queensland 2008-09 to date. Surrey 2009. **LOI** (A): 8 (2008-09 to 2009-10); HS 21 v WI (Sydney) 2009-10; BB 5-19 v P (Perth) 2009-10. HS 94 Sy v Northants (Northampton) 2009. BB 7-108 S Aus v Tas (Adelaide) 2007-08. UK BB 4-36 Sx v MCC (Lord's) 2008. LO HS 39 S Aus v Vic (Traralgon) 2007-08. LO BB 5-19 (see LOI). IT20 HS – . IT20 BB 2-27. T20 HS 31. T20 BB 3-23.

HODGSON, Lee John (De Brus SS), b Middlesbrough 29 Jun 1986. 5'11". RHB, RFM. Surrey 2008 (1 match). Yorkshire debut 2009. HS 63 Sy v Notts (Oval) 2008 – on debut. Y HS 32 v CU (Cambridge) 2009. LO HS 9 v Essex (Leeds) 2009 (P40). BB 2-44 v Glos (Leeds) 2009 (P40).

LEE, James Edward (Immanuel Community C), b Sheffield 23 Dec 1988. 6'1". LHB, RMF. Debut (Yorkshire) 2006. HS 21* v Lancs (Manchester) 2006. BB 2-63 v Somerset (Taunton) 2009. LO HS – . LO BB 3-43 v Glos (Leeds) 2009 (P40).

LYTH, Adam (Caedmon S, Whitby; Whitby Community C), b Whitby 25 Sep 1987. 5'8". LHB, RM. Debut (Yorkshire) 2007. HS 132 v Notts (Nottingham) 2008. BB 1-12 v LU (Leeds) 2007. CC BB 1-20 v Somerset (Scarborough) 2008. LO HS 109* v Sussex (Scarborough) 2009 (P40). T20 HS 10.

McGRATH, Anthony (Yorkshire Martyrs Collegiate S), b Bradford 6 Oct 1975. 6'2". RHB, RM. Debut (Yorkshire) 1995; cap 1999; captain 2003, 2009; benefit 2009. MCC 1999-00. **Tests**: 4 (2003); HS 81 v Z (Chester-le-St) 2003; BB 3-16 v Z (Lord's) 2003 – on debut. **LOI**: 14 (2003 to 2004); HS 52 v SA (Manchester) 2003; BB 1-13 v WI (Nottingham) 2004. F-c Tours (Eng A): A 1996-97; P 1995-96; Z 1995-96 (Y); B 1999-00 (MCC). 1000 runs (2); most – 1425 (2005). HS 211 v Warwks (Birmingham) 2009. BB 5-39 v Derbys (Derby) 2004. LO HS 148 v Somerset (Taunton) 2006 (P40). LO BB 4-41 v Surrey (Leeds) 2003 (NL). T20 HS 72*. T20 BB 3-27.

PATTERSON, Steven Andrew (Malet Lambert CS; St Mary's SFC, Hull; Leeds U), b Hull 3 Oct 1983. 6'4". RHB, RMF. Debut (Yorkshire) 2005. Bradford/Leeds UCCE 2003 (not f-c). HS 46 v Lancs (Manchester) 2006. BB 4-41 v CU (Cambridge) 2009. CC BB 3-19 v Somerset (Taunton) 2008. LO HS 25* v Worcs (Leeds) 2006 (P40). LO BB 3-11 Yorks CB v Northants CB (Northampton) 2002. T20 HS 0. T20 BB 1-42.

PYRAH, Richard Michael (Ossett S; Wakefield C), b Dewsbury 1 Nov 1982. 6'0". RHB, RM. Debut (Yorkshire) 2004. HS 106 v LU (Leeds) 2007. CC HS 78 v Worcs (Worcester) 2005. BB 2-53 v Notts (Nottingham) 2009. LO HS 67 v Glos (Bristol) 2009 (FPT). LO BB 5-50 Yorks CB v Somerset (Scarborough) 2002 (CGT). T20 HS 33*. T20 BB 4-20 v Durham (Leeds) 2008 – Y record.

RASHID, Adil Usman (Belle Vue S, Bradford), b Bradford 17 Feb 1988. 5'8". RHB, LBG. Debut (Yorkshire) 2006; cap 2008. MCC 2007-09. NC 2007. Match double (114, 48, 8-157 and 2-45) for England U19 v India U19 (Taunton) 2006. **LOI**: 5 (2009 to 2009-10); HS 31* v A (Oval) 2009; BB 1-16 v Ireland (Belfast) 2009. F-c Tours: WI 2008-09; I 2008-09; B 2006-07 (Eng A). HS 157* v Lancs (Leeds) 2009. BB 7-107 v Hampshire (Southampton) 2008. LO HS 41* v Derbys (Leeds) 2008 (FPT). BB 3-37 v Derbys (Derby) 2008 (P40). IT20 HS 9*. IT20 BB 1-11. T20 HS 28*. T20 BB 4-24.

[NQ]**RUDOLPH, Jacobus** Andries (*'Jacques'*) (Afrikaanse Hoer Seunskool), b Springs, Transvaal, South Africa 4 May 1981. Elder brother of G.J.Rudolph (Limpopo and Namibia 2006-07 to date). 5'11". LHB, LBG. Northerns 1999-00 to 2003-04. Titans 2004-05, 2008-09 to date. Eagles 2005-06 to 2007-08. Yorkshire debut 2007 (Kolpak registration) scoring 122 v Surrey (Oval); cap 2007. **Tests** (SA): 35 (2003 to 2006); HS 222* v B (Chittagong) 2003 – on debut; BB 1-1 v E (Leeds) 2003. **LOI** (SA): 45 (2003 to 2005-06); HS 81 v B (Dhaka) 2003. F-c Tours (SA): E 2003; A 2001-02, 2005-06; WI 2004-05; NZ 2003-04; I 2004-05; SL 2004, 2005-06, 2006; B 2003. 1000 runs (3); most – 1366 (2009). HS 222* (*see Tests*). UK HS 220 v Warwks (Scarborough) 2007. BB 5-80 Eagles v Cape Cobras (Cape Town) 2007-08. UK BB 1-1 (*see Tests*). Y BB 1-13 v Somerset (Scarborough) 2008. LO HS 134* South Africa A v Kenya (Laudium) 2001-02. LO BB 4-41 South Africa A v New Zealand A (Colombo) 2005-06. IT20 HS 6*. T20 HS 71. T20 BB 3-16.

SAYERS, Joseph John (St Mary's RC CS, Menston; Worcester C, Oxford) b Leeds 5 Nov 1983. 6'0". LHB, OB. Oxford U 2002-04; blue 2002-03-04. Yorkshire debut 2004; cap 2007. HS 187 v Kent (Tunbridge Wells) 2007. BB 3-20 v Warwks (Scarborough) 2009. LO HS 62 v Glos (Leeds) 2003 (NL). LO BB 1-31 v Warwks (Birmingham) 2005 (NL). T20 HS 12.

SHAHZAD, Ajmal (Woodhouse Grove S; Bradford U), b Huddersfield 27 Jul 1985. 6'0". RHB, RMF. Debut (Yorkshire) 2006 (first British-born Asian to play for Yorkshire). F-c Tour: B 2009-10. HS 88 v Sussex (Hove) 2009. BB 4-22 v Sussex (Leeds) 2007. LO HS 43* v Sussex (Leeds) 2009 (FPT). LO BB 5-51 v Sri Lanka A (Leeds) 2007. IT20 HS – . IT20 BB 2-38. T20 HS 17*. T20 BB 2-22.

‡[NQ]**TUFFEY, Daryl** Raymond, b Milton, Otago, New Zealand 11 Jun 1978. RHB, RFM. Northern Districts 1996-97 to 2006-07. Auckland 2008-09 to date. **Tests** (NZ): 25 (1999-00 to 2009-10); HS 80* v P (Napier) 2009-10; BB 6-54 (9-116 match) v E (Auckland) 2001-02. **LOI** (NZ): 85 (2000-01 to 2009-10); HS 20* v SL (Colombo, SSC) 2001; BB 4-24 v P (Napier) 2000-01. F-c Tours (NZ): E 2000 (NZ A), 2004; A 2001-02; SA 2000-01; WI 2002; I 2003-04; P 2002; SL 2003, 2009; Z 2000-01. HS 89* ND v Wellington (Wellington) 1999-00. BB 7-12 (11-56 match) ND v Wellington (Hamilton) 2000-01. LO HS 38* New Zealanders v Border (Alice) 2000-01. LO BB 5-21 NZ A v Worcs (Worcester) 2000. IT20 HS 5*. IT20 BB 2-16. T20 HS 17*. T20 BB 3-19.

WAINWRIGHT, David John (Hemsworth HS and SFC; Loughborough U); b Pontefract 21 Mar 1985. 5'9". LHB, SLA. Debut (Yorkshire) 2004. Loughborough UCCE 2005-06. British U 2006. HS 104* (batting at No 10) v Sussex (Hove) 2008. BB 5-134 v Sussex (Hove) 2009. LO HS 26 v Surrey (Scarborough) 2007 (P40). LO BB 3-26 EL v Pakistan A (Dubai) 2009-10. T20 HS 3*. T20 BB 3-6.

RELEASED/RETIRED
(Having made a County First-Class or List A appearance in 2009)

GUY, Simon Mark (Wickersley CS), b Rotherham 17 Nov 1978. 5'7". RHB, WK. Yorkshire 2000-07. No f-c appearances in 2008-09. HS 52* v Durham (Leeds) 2006. LO HS 40 v Leics (Leeds) 2005 (NL). T20 HS 13.

HOGGARD, M.J. – *see LEICESTERSHIRE.*

^NQ^KRUIS, Gideon ('Deon') Jacobus (St Albans C, Pretoria; Pretoria U), b Pretoria, South Africa 9 May 1974. 6'3". RHB, RFM. N Transvaal 1993-94 to 1996-97. Griqualand West 1997-98 to 2003-04. Eagles 2004-05. Yorkshire 2005-09; cap 2006. Kolpak registration. HS 59 GW v B (Kimberley) 2000-01. Y HS 50* and BB 5-47 v Surrey (Leeds) 2008. 50 wkts (1): 64 (2005). BB 7-58 GW v Northerns (Pretoria) 1997-98. LO HS 31* v Surrey (Oval) 2006 (P40). LO BB 4-17 v Derbys (Leeds) 2007 (P40). T20 HS 22. T20 BB 2-15.

^NQ^NAVED-UL-HASAN, Rana (Government HS, Sheikhupura), b Sheikhupura, Pakistan 28 Feb 1978. 5'11". RHB, RMF. Debut Pakistan A v England A (Multan) 1995-96. Lahore 1999-00. Pakistan Customs 2000-01. Sheikhupura 2000-01 to 2001-02. Allied Bank 2001-02. WAPDA 2002-03 to date. Sialkot 2003-04 to 2005-06. Sussex 2005-07; cap 2005. Punjab 2006-07. Yorkshire 2008-09. Herefordshire 2002. **Tests** (P): 9 (2004-05 to 2006-07); HS 42* v E (Lahore) 2005-06; BB 3-30 v E (Faisalabad) 2005-06. **LOI** (P): 74 (2002-03 to 2009-10); HS 33 v SL (Colombo, RPS) 2009 and v A (Adelaide) 2009-10; BB 6-27 v I (Jamshedpur) 2004-05. F-c Tours (P): A 2004-05; SA 2006-07; WI 2004-05; I 2004-05. HS 139 Sx v Middx (Lord's) 2005. Y HS 32 v Warwks (Birmingham) 2009. 50 wkts (2+3); most – 91 (2000-01). BB 7-49 Sheikhupura v Sialkot (Muridke) 2001-02. CC BB 7-62 (11-148 match) Sx v Yorks (Leeds) 2006. Y BB 4-86 v Kent (Scarborough) 2008. LO HS 74 Y v Derbys (Derby) 2008. LO BB 6-27 (*see LOI*). IT20 HS 17*. IT20 BB 3-19. T20 HS 95. T20 BB 4-23.

VAUGHAN, Michael Paul (Silverdale CS, Sheffield), b Salford, Lancs 29 Oct 1974. 6'2". RHB, OB. Yorkshire 1993-2009; cap 1995; benefit 2005. MCC 2009. *Wisden* 2002. PCA 2002. OBE 2005. **Tests**: 82 (1999-00 to 2008, 51 as captain); HS 197 and BB 2-71 v I (Nottingham) 2002. Scored Eng record 1,481 runs (avge 61.70) with six hundreds in 2002. **LOI**: 86 (2000-01 to 2006-07, 60 as captain); HS 90* v Z (Bulawayo) 2004-05; BB 4-22 v SL (Manchester) 2002. F-c Tours (C=captain): A 1996-97 (Eng A), 2002-03; SA 1998-99C (Eng A), 1999-00, 2004-05C; WI 2003-04C; NZ 2001-02, 2007-08C; I 1994-95 (Eng A), 2001-02; P 2000-01, 2005-06C; SL 2000-01, 2003-04C, 2007-08C; Z 1995-96 (Y), 1998-99C (Eng A); B 2003-04C. 1000 runs (4); most – 1244 (1995). HS 197 (*see Tests*). Y HS 183 v Glamorgan (Cardiff) 1996. BB 4-39 v OU (Oxford) 1994. CC BB 4-47 v Somerset (Leeds) 2001. LO HS 125* v Somerset (Taunton) 2001 (BHC). LO BB 4-22 (*see LOI*). IT20 HS 27. T20 HS 34. T20 BB 1-21.

C.R.Taylor left the staff, without making a County First-Class or List A appearance in 2009.

YORKSHIRE 2009

RESULTS SUMMARY

	Place	Won	Lost	Tied	Drew	NR
County Championship (1st Division)	7th	2	2		12	
All First-Class Matches		2	2		13	
FP Trophy (Group C)	3rd	4	4			
Pro40 League (1st Division)	7th	2	5			1
Twenty20 Cup (North Division)	5th	4	6			

LV COUNTY CHAMPIONSHIP AVERAGES

BATTING AND FIELDING

Cap		M	I	NO	HS	Runs	Avge	100	50	Ct/St
2008	A.U.Rashid	7	9	4	157*	387	77.40	2	1	4
2007	J.A.Rudolph	16	27	1	198	1334	51.30	4	6	13
	J.M.Bairstow	12	19	6	84*	592	45.53	–	6	21
	D.J.Wainwright	9	12	4	102*	356	44.50	1	1	–
2008	G.L.Brophy	13	21	5	99	709	44.31	–	6	35/2
2007	J.J.Sayers	16	27	1	173	1103	42.42	2	5	15
	A.Shahzad	13	17	6	88	445	40.45	–	2	4
2008	A.W.Gale	16	25	1	121	828	34.50	2	4	6
1999	A.McGrath	16	26	1	211	825	33.00	2	2	10
	A.Lyth	4	7	–	71	220	31.42	–	2	1
2006	T.T.Bresnan	10	14	2	97	372	31.00	–	1	5
	Azeem Rafiq	4	5	–	100	117	23.40	1	–	1
1995	M.P.Vaughan	5	7	–	43	147	21.00	–	–	–
	R.M.Pyrah	3	4	1	50*	59	19.66	–	1	3
2006	G.J.Kruis	9	9	2	37	131	18.71	–	–	1
	Naved-ul-Hasan	4	6	–	32	93	15.50	–	–	–
2000	M.J.Hoggard	15	16	3	56*	195	15.00	–	1	5

Also batted: J.E.Lee (1 match) 2 (1 ct); S.A.Patterson (3) 3, 4*, 8.

BOWLING

	O	M	R	W	Avge	Best	5wI	10wM
D.J.Wainwright	244.2	50	797	26	30.65	5-134	1	–
A.U.Rashid	242.4	37	818	26	31.46	5- 41	2	–
M.J.Hoggard	466.1	100	1467	43	34.11	5- 56	2	–
A.Shahzad	409.5	81	1376	40	34.40	4- 72	–	–
G.J.Kruis	252.1	56	816	22	37.09	3- 51	–	–
T.T.Bresnan	352.4	91	909	24	37.87	4-116	–	–
Naved-ul-Hasan	124	23	412	10	41.20	3-102	–	–
Azeem Rafiq	124.3	9	487	10	48.70	3- 34	–	–

Also bowled: G.L.Brophy 1-1-0-0; A.W.Gale 1-0-11-0; J.E.Lee 19-1-113-2; A.Lyth 19-9-38-1; A.McGrath 106-24-279-3; S.A.Patterson 96-18-368-3; R.M.Pyrah 60-7-213-4; J.A.Rudolph 25-0-111-0; J.J.Sayers 10.5-0-32-3.

The First-Class Averages (pp 228–244) give the records of Yorkshire players in all first-class county matches (Yorkshire's other opponents being Cambridge UCCE), with the exception of T.T.Bresnan, A.U.Rashid and M.P.Vaughan, whose first-class figures for Yorkshire are as above.

YORKSHIRE RECORDS

FIRST-CLASS CRICKET

Highest Total	For 887		v	Warwicks	Birmingham	1896
	V 681-7d		by	Leics	Bradford	1996
Lowest Total	For 23		v	Hampshire	Middlesbrough	1965
	V 13		by	Notts	Nottingham	1901
Highest Innings	For 341	G.H.Hirst	v	Leics	Leicester	1905
	V 318*	W.G.Grace	for	Glos	Cheltenham	1876

Highest Partnership for each Wicket

1st	555	P.Holmes/H.Sutcliffe	v	Essex	Leyton	1932
2nd	346	W.Barber/M.Leyland	v	Middlesex	Sheffield	1932
3rd	346	J.J.Sayers/A.McGrath	v	Warwicks	Birmingham	2009
4th	358	D.S.Lehmann/M.J.Lumb	v	Durham	Leeds	2006
5th	340	E.Wainwright/G.H.Hirst	v	Surrey	The Oval	1899
6th	276	M.Leyland/E.Robinson	v	Glamorgan	Swansea	1926
7th	254	W.Rhodes/D.C.F.Burton	v	Hampshire	Dewsbury	1919
8th	292	R.Peel/Lord Hawke	v	Warwicks	Birmingham	1896
9th	246	T.T.Bresnan/J.N.Gillespie	v	Surrey	The Oval	2007
10th	149	G.Boycott/G.B.Stevenson	v	Warwicks	Birmingham	1982

Best Bowling	For	10-10	H.Verity	v	Notts	Leeds	1932
(Innings)	V	10-37	C.V.Grimmett	for	Australians	Sheffield	1930
Best Bowling	For	17-91	H.Verity	v	Essex	Leyton	1933
(Match)	V	17-91	H.Dean	for	Lancashire	Liverpool	1913

Most Runs – Season	2883	H.Sutcliffe	(av 80.08)		1932
Most Runs – Career	38558	H.Sutcliffe	(av 50.20)		1919-45
Most 100s – Season	12	H.Sutcliffe			1932
Most 100s – Career	112	H.Sutcliffe			1919-45
Most Wkts – Season	240	W.Rhodes	(av 12.72)		1900
Most Wkts – Career	3597	W.Rhodes	(av 16.02)		1898-1930
Most Career W-K Dismissals	1186	D.Hunter	(863 ct; 323 st)		1888-1909
Most Career Catches in the Field	665	J.Tunnicliffe			1891-1907

LIMITED-OVERS CRICKET

Highest Total	FPT	411-6		v	Devon	Exmouth	2004
	P40	352-6		v	Notts	Scarborough	2001
	T20	211-6		v	Leics	Leeds	2004
Lowest Total	FPT	76		v	Surrey	Harrogate	1970
	P40	54		v	Essex	Leeds	2003
	T20	90-9		v	Durham	Chester-le-St	2009
Highest Innings	FPT	160	M.J.Wood	v	Devon	Exmouth	2004
	P40	191	D.S.Lehmann	v	Notts	Scarborough	2001
	T20	109	I.J.Harvey	v	Derbyshire	Leeds	2005
Best Bowling	FPT	7-27	D.Gough	v	Ireland	Leeds	1997
	P40	7-15	R.A.Hutton	v	Worcs	Leeds	1969
	T20	4-20	R.M.Pyrah	v	Durham	Leeds	2008

FIRST-CLASS UMPIRES 2010

† New appointment. See page 89 for key to abbreviations.

BAILEY, Robert John (Biddulph HS), b Biddulph, Staffs 28 Oct 1963. RHB, OB. Northamptonshire 1982-99; cap 1985; benefit 1993; captain 1996-97. Derbyshire 2000-01; cap 2000. Staffordshire 1980. YC 1984. **Tests:** 4 (1988 to 1989-90); HS 43 v WI (Oval) 1988. **LOI:** 4 (1984-85 to 1989-90); HS 43* v SL (Oval) 1988. Tours: SA 1991-92 (Nh); WI 1989-90; Z 1994-95 (Nh). 1000 runs (13); most – 1987 (1990). HS 224* Nh v Glamorgan (Swansea) 1986. BB 5-54 Nh v Notts (Northampton) 1993. F-c career: 374 matches; 21844 runs @ 40.52, 47 hundreds; 121 wickets @ 42.51; 272 ct. Appointed 2006.

BAINTON, Neil Laurence, b Romford, Essex 2 October 1970. No f-c appearances. Appointed 2006.

BODENHAM, Martin John Dale, b Brighton, Sussex 23 Apr 1950. No f-c appearances. Former football referee who officiated at the 1997 League Cup final and four internationals. Appointed 2009.

COOK, Nicholas Grant Billson (Lutterworth GS), b Leicester 17 Jun 1956. 6'0". RHB, SLA. Leicestershire 1978-85; cap 1982. Northamptonshire 1986-94; cap 1987; benefit 1995. **Tests:** 15 (1983 to 1989); HS 31 v A (Oval) 1989; BB 6-65 (11-83 match) v P (Karachi) 1983-84. **LOI:** 3 (1983-84 to 1989-90); HS – ; BB 2-18 v P (Peshawar) 1987-88. F-c Tours: NZ 1979-80 (DHR), 1983-84; P 1983-84, 1987-88; SL 1985-86 (Eng B); Z 1980-81 (Le), 1984-85 (Le). HS 75 Le v Somerset (Taunton) 1980. 50 wkts (8); most – 90 (1982). BB 7-34 (10-97 match) Nh v Essex (Chelmsford) 1992. F-c career: 356 matches; 3137 runs @ 11.66; 879 wickets @ 29.01; 197 ct. Appointed 2009.

COWLEY, Nigel Geoffrey (Dutchy Manor SS, Mere), b Shaftesbury, Dorset 1 Mar 1953. RHB, OB. Dorset 1972. Hampshire 1974-89; cap 1978; benefit 1988. Glamorgan 1990. 1000 runs (1): 1042 (1984). HS 109* H v Somerset (Taunton) 1977. BB 6-48 H v Leics (Southampton) 1982. F-c career: 271 matches; 7309 runs @ 23.35, 2 hundreds; 437 wickets @ 34.04. Appointed 2000.

DUDLESTON, Barry (Stockport S), b Bebington, Cheshire 16 Jul 1945. RHB, SLA. Leicestershire 1966-80; cap 1969; benefit 1980. Gloucestershire 1981-83. Rhodesia 1976-77 to 1979-80. 1000 runs (8); most – 1374 (1970). HS 202 Le v Derbys (Leicester) 1979. BB 4-6 Le v Surrey (Leicester) 1972. F-c career: 295 matches; 14747 runs @ 32.48, 32 hundreds; 47 wickets @ 29.04. Appointed 1984. Umpired 2 Tests (1991 to 1992) and 4 LOI (1992 to 2001).

EVANS, Jeffery Howard, b Llanelli, Carms 7 Aug 1954. No f-c appearances. Appointed 2001. Umpired in Indian Cricket League 2007-08.

GARRATT, Steven Arthur, b Nottingham 5 Jul 1953. No f-c appearances. Reserve List 2003-07 standing in 20 f-c matches. Appointed 2008.

GOUGH, Michael Andrew (English Martyrs RCS; Hartlepool SFC), b Hartlepool, Co Durham 18 Dec 1979. Son of M.P.Gough (Durham 1974-77). 6'5". RHB, OB. Durham 1998-2003. F-c Tours (Eng A): NZ 1999-00; B 1999-00. HS Du v CU (Cambridge) 1998. CC HS 103 Du v Essex (Colchester) 2002. BB 5-56 Du v Middlesex (Chester-le-St) 2001. F-c career: 67 matches; 2952 runs @ 25.44, 2 hundreds; 30 wickets @ 45.00; 57 catches. Reserve List 2006-08. Appointed 2009.

GOULD, Ian James (Westgate SS, Slough), b Taplow, Bucks 19 Aug 1957. LHB, WK. Middlesex 1975 to 1980-81, 1996; cap 1977. Auckland 1979-80. Sussex 1981-90; cap 1981; captain 1987; benefit 1990. MCC YC. **LOI:** 18 (1982-83 to 1983); HS 42 v A (Sydney) 1982-83. Tours: A 1982-83; P 1980-81 (Int); Z 1980-81 (M). HS 128 M v Worcs (Worcester) 1978. BB 3-10 Sx v Surrey (Oval) 1989. Middlesex coach 1991-2000. Reappeared in one match (v OU) 1996. F-c career: 298 matches; 8756 runs @ 26.05, 4 hundreds; 7 wickets @ 52.14; 603 dismissals (536 ct, 67 st). Appointed 2002. Umpired 11 Tests (2008-09 to 2009-10) and 44 LOI (2006 to 2009-10).

HARTLEY, Peter John (Greenhead GS; Bradford C), b Keighley, Yorks 18 Apr 1960. RHB, RMF. Warwickshire 1982. Yorkshire 1985-97; cap 1987; benefit 1996. Hampshire 1998-2000; cap 1998. Tours (Y): SA 1991-92; WI 1986-87; Z 1995-96. HS 127* Y v Lancs (Manchester) 1988. 50 wkts (7); most – 81 (1995). BB 9-41 (inc hat-trick, 4 wkts in 5 balls and 5 in 9; 11-68 match) Y v Derbys (Chesterfield) 1995. Hat-trick 1995. F-c career: 232 matches; 4321 runs @ 19.91, 2 hundreds; 683 wickets @ 30.21. Appointed 2003. Umpired 6 LOI (2007 to 2009). **ICC International Panel 2006 to date.**

HOLDER, Vanburn Alonza (Richmond SM), b Deans Village, St Michael, Barbados 8 Oct 1945. RHB, RFM. Barbados 1966-67 to 1977-78. Worcestershire 1968-80; cap 1970; benefit 1979. Shropshire 1981. Tests (WI): 40 (1969 to 1978-79); HS 42 v NZ (P-o-S) 1971-72; BB 6-28 v A (P-o-S) 1977-78. **LOI** (WI): 12 (1973 to 1977-78); HS 30 v A (Castries) 1977-78; BB 5-50 v E (Birmingham) 1976. Tours (WI): E 1969, 1973, 1976; A 1975-76; I 1974-75, 1978-79; P 1973-74 (RW), 1974-75; SL 1974-75, 1978-79. HS 122 Barbados v Trinidad (Bridgetown) 1973-74. BB 7-40 Wo v Glamorgan (Cardiff) 1974. F-c career: 311 matches; 3559 runs @ 13.03, 1 hundred; 947 wickets @ 24.48. Appointed 1992.

ILLINGWORTH, Richard Keith (Salts GS), b Bradford, Yorks 23 Aug 1963. RHB, SLA. Worcestershire 1982-2000; cap 1986; benefit 1997. Natal 1988-89. Derbyshire 2001. Wiltshire 2005. **Tests:** 9 (1991 to 1995-96); HS 28 v SA (Pt Elizabeth) 1995-96; BB 4-96 v WI (Nottingham) 1995. Took wicket of P.V.Simmons with his first ball in Tests – v WI (Nottingham) 1991. **LOI:** 25 (1991 to 1995-96); HS 14 v P (Melbourne) 1991-92; BB 3-33 v Z (Albury) 1991-92. Tours: SA 1995-96; NZ 1991-92; P 1990-91 (Eng A); SL 1990-91 (Eng A); Z 1989-90 (Eng A), 1990-91 (Wo), 1993-94 (Wo), 1996-97 (Wo). HS 120* Wo v Warwks (Worcester) 1987 – as night-watchman. Scored 106 for England A v Z (Harare) 1989-90 – also as night-watchman. 50 wkts (5); most – 75 (1990). BB 7-50 Wo v OU (Oxford) 1985. F-c career: 376 matches; 7027 runs @ 22.45, 4 hundreds; 831 wickets @ 31.54; 161 ct. Appointed 2006. **ICC International Panel (Third Umpire) 2009.**

JESTY, Trevor Edward (Privet County SS, Gosport), b Gosport, Hants 2 Jun 1948. RHB, RM. Hampshire 1966-84; cap 1971; benefit 1982. Surrey 1985-87; cap 1985; captain 1985. Lancashire 1987-88 to 1991; cap 1989. Border 1973-74. GW 1974-75 to 1980-81. Canterbury 1979-80. *Wisden* 1982. **LOI:** 10 (1982-83); HS 52* v NZ (Adelaide) 1982-83; BB 1-23 v A (Sydney) 1982-83. Tours: WI 1987-88 (La), 1982-83 (Int); Z 1988-89 (La). 1000 runs (10); most – 1645 (1982). HS 248 H v CU (Cambridge) 1984. Scored 122* La v OU (Oxford) 1991 in his final f-c innings. 50 wkts (2); most – 52 (1981). BB 7-75 H v Worcs (Southampton) 1976. F-c career: 490 matches; 21916 runs @ 32.71, 35 hundreds; 585 wickets @ 27.47. Appointed 1994. Umpired in Indian Cricket League 2007-08.

KETTLEBOROUGH, Richard Allan (Worksop C), b Sheffield, Yorks 15 Mar 1973. LHB, RM. Yorkshire 1994-97. Middlesex 1998-99. Tour: Z 1995-96 (Y). HS 108 Y v Essex (Leeds) 1996. BB 2-26 Y v Notts (Scarborough) 1996. F-c career: 33 matches; 1258 runs @ 25.16, 1 hundred; 3 wickets @ 81.00; 20 ct. Appointed 2006. Umpired 5 LOI (2009 to 2009-10). **ICC International Panel 2009.**

LLONG, Nigel James (Ashford North S), b Ashford, Kent 11 Feb 1969. LHB, OB. Kent 1990-98; cap 1993. Tour: Z 1992-93 (K). HS 130 K v Hants (Canterbury) 1996. BB 5-21 K v Middx (Canterbury) 1996. F-c career: 68 matches; 3024 runs @ 31.17, 6 hundreds; 35 wickets @ 35.97. Appointed 2002. Umpired 8 Tests (2007-08 to 2009-10) and 32 LOI (2006 to 2009). **ICC International Panel 2004 to date.**

LLOYDS, Jeremy William (Blundell's S), b Penang, Malaya 17 Nov 1954. LHB, OB. Somerset 1979-84; cap 1982. Gloucestershire 1985-91; cap 1985. Orange Free State 1983-84 to 1987-88. Tour (Glos): SL 1986-87. 1000 runs (3); most – 1295 (1986). HS 132* Sm v Northants (Northampton) 1982. BB 7-88 Sm v Essex (Chelmsford) 1982. F-c career: 267 matches; 10679 runs @ 31.04, 10 hundreds; 333 wickets @ 38.86; 229 ct. Appointed 1998. Umpired 5 Tests (2003-04 to 2004-05) and 18 LOI (2000 to 2005-06). **ICC International Panel 2003-06.**

MALLENDER, Neil Alan (Beverley GS), b Kirk Sandall, Yorks 13 Aug 1961. RHB, RFM. Northamptonshire 1980-86 and 1995-96; cap 1984. Somerset 1987-94; cap 1987; benefit 1994. Otago 1983-84 to 1992-93; captain 1990-91 to 1992-93. **Tests:** 2 (1992) HS 4 v P (Oval) 1992; BB 5-50 v P (Leeds) 1992 – on debut. Tour: Z 1994-95 (Nh). HS 100* Otago v CD (Palmerston N) 1991-92. UK HS 87* Sm v Sussex (Hove) 1990. 50 wkts (6); most – 56 (1983). BB 7-27 Otago v Auckland (Auckland) 1984-85. UK BB 7-41 Nh v Derbys (Northampton) 1982. F-c career: 345 matches; 4709 runs @ 17.18, 1 hundred; 937 wickets @ 26.31; 111 ct. Appointed 1999. Umpired 3 Tests (2003-04) and 22 LOI (2001 to 2003-04), including 2002-03 World Cup. **ICC Elite Panel 2004**.

MILLNS, David James (Garibaldi CS; N Notts C; Nottingham Trent U), b Clipstone, Notts 27 Feb 1965. 6'3". LHB, RF. Nottinghamshire 1988-89, 2000-01; cap 2000. Leicestershire 1990-99; cap 1991; benefit 1999. Tasmania 1994-95. Boland 1996-97. F-c Tours: A 1992-93 (Eng A); SA 1996-97 (Le). HS Le v Northants (Northampton) 1997. 50 wkts (4); most – 76 (1994). BB 9-37 (12-91 match) Le v Derbys (Derby) 1991. F-c career: 171 matches; 3082 runs @ 22.01, 3 hundreds; 553 wickets @ 27.35; 76 catches. Reserve List 2007-08. Appointed 2009.

ROBINSON, Robert Timothy (Dunstable GS; High Pavement SFC; Sheffield U), b Sutton in Ashfield 21 Nov 1958. RHB, RM. Nottinghamshire 1978-99; cap 1983; captain 1988-95; benefit 1992. *Wisden* 1985. **Tests:** 29 (1984-85 to 1989) HS 175 v A (Leeds) 1985. **LOI:** 26 (1984-85 to 1988); HS 83 v P (Sharjah) 1986-87. Tours: A 1987-88; SA 1989-90 (Eng XI), 1996-97 (Nt); NZ 1987-88; WI 1985-86; I/SL 1984-85; P 1987-88. 1000 runs (14) inc 2000 (1): 2032 (1984). HS 220* v Yorks (Nottingham) 1990. BB 1-22. F-c career: 425 matches; 27571 runs @ 42.15, 63 hundreds; 4 wickets @ 72.25; 257 ct. Appointed 2007.

SHARP, George (Elwick Road SS, Hartlepool), b West Hartlepool, Co Durham 12 Mar 1950. RHB, WK, occ LM. Northamptonshire 1968-85; cap 1973; benefit 1982. HS 98 Nh v Yorks (Northampton) 1983. BB 1-47. F-c career: 306 matches; 6254 runs @ 19.85; 1 wicket @ 70.00; 655 dismissals (565 ct, 90 st). Appointed 1992. Umpired 15 Tests (1996 to 2001-02) and 31 LOI (1995-96 to 2001-02). **ICC International Panel 1996 to 2001-02.**

STEELE, John Frederick (Endon SS), b Brown Edge, Staffs 23 Jul 1946. RHB, SLA. Brother of D.S. (Northants, Derbys and England 1963-84). Leicestershire 1970-83; cap 1971; benefit 1983. Glamorgan 1984-86; cap 1984. Natal 1973-74 to 1977-78. Staffordshire 1965-69. Tour: SA 1974-75 (DHR). 1000 runs (6); most – 1347 (1972). HS 195 Le v Derbys (Leicester) 1971. BB 7-29 Natal B v GW (Umzinto) 1973-74 and 7-29 Le v Glos (Leicester) 1980. F-c career: 379 matches; 15054 runs @ 28.95, 21 hundreds; 584 wickets @ 27.04; 413 ct. Appointed 1997.

WILLEY, Peter (Seaham SS), b Sedgefield, Co Durham 6 Dec 1949. RHB, OB. Northamptonshire 1966-83; cap 1971; benefit 1981. Leicestershire 1984-91; cap 1984; captain 1987. E Province 1982-83 to 1984-85. Northumberland 1992. **Tests:** 26 (1976 to 1986); HS 102* v WI (St John's) 1980-81; BB 2-73 v WI (Lord's) 1980. **LOI:** 26 (1977 to 1985-86); HS 64 v A (Sydney) 1979-80; BB 3-33 v A (Melbourne) 1979. Tours: A 1979-80; SA 1972-73 (DHR), 1981-82 (SAB); WI 1980-81, 1985-86; I 1979-80; SL 1977-78 (DHR). 1000 runs (10); most – 1783 (1982). HS 227 Nh v Somerset (Northampton) 1976. 50 wkts (3); most – 52 (1979). BB 7-37 Nh v OU (Oxford) 1975. F-c career: 559 matches; 24361 runs @ 30.56, 44 hundreds; 756 wickets @ 30.95. Appointed 1993. Umpired 25 Tests (1995-96 to 2003-04) and 34 LOI (1996 to 2003), including 1999 and 2002-03 World Cups. **ICC International Panel 1996 to 2001-02 and 2003-04.**

RESERVE FIRST-CLASS LIST: Paul Baldwin, Keith Coburn, Ismail Dawood, Mark A.Eggleston, Stephen C.Gale, Andrew Hicks, Graham D.Lloyd, Steven J.Malone, Martin Saggers, Steve J.O'Shaughnessy.

Test Match statistics to 20 February 2010; LOI statistics to 27 February 2010.

UNIVERSITY FIRST-CLASS REGISTER 2009

CAMBRIDGE († Blue 2009)

Full Names	Birthdate	Birthplace	College	Bat/Bowl	F-C Debut
†ANSARI, Akbar Shahzaman	03.07.88	Ascot, Berkshire	Trinity H	RHB/LB	2008
†ASHOK, Anand	28.11.88	Hyderabad, India	Queens'	RHB/RM	2009
†ASHTON, Philip Peter	02.08.88	Cambridge	Queens'	RHB/LB	2009
BAKER, Fergus Braan	18.05.87	Leicester	Downing	LHB/SLA	2007
BALLARD, Edward Christopher	15.08.89	Harlow, Essex	(Anglia RU)	RHB/LB	2008
BOTT, Mark Daniel	13.05.86	Nottingham	(Anglia RU)	RHB/LB	2006
†BRATHWAITE, Ruel Marlon Ricardo	06.09.85	Barbados	Queens'	RHB/RFM	2009
†BROWN, Francis Andrew	21.03.90	Nottingham	Jesus	RHB/SLA	2009
CHANDRA, Utkarsh Saurabh	24.03.83	Lucknow, India	(Anglia RU)	RHB/RM	2009
†COOK, Matthew Philip	01.09.88	Ashton under Lyne	Girton	RHB/RFM	2009
†GRAMMER, Christopher Mark	01.10.84	Brighton	Homerton	LHB/SLA	2009
GRAY, Stephen Kevin	06.07.88	Barking, Essex	(Anglia RU)	RHB/WK	2008
JOSLIN, Andrew James Philip	18.12.89	Leytonstone	(Anglia RU)	RHB/RM	2009
LEE, Nicholas Trevor	16.10.83	Dartford	(Anglia RU)	RHB/LB	2004
LOTAY, Jivan Daulat Singh	25.07.90	High Wycombe	(Anglia RU)	LHB/OB	2009
†MacLENNAN, Scott Keith	30.11.87	Glasgow, Scotland	St John's	RHB/RM	2007
MOHAMMAD AMIN	19.10.84	Gujranwala, Pakistan	(Anglia RU)	RHB/RMF	2005
†PEARSON, Edward George	15.05.88	Cambridge	Robinson	RHB/OB	2009
†PROBERT, Thomas John William	25.09.86	Pembury	Peterhouse	LHB/RM	2009
ROSENBERG, Marc Christopher	10.02.82	Johannesburg, SA	Hughes	RHB/RM	2004
†SEN, Ananya	22.06.87	Illinois, USA	St. Edmund's	RHB/WK	2009
TURNBULL, Peter Thomas	20.05.89	Pontypridd	(Anglia RU)	RHB/RMF	2009
WOOLLEY, Robert James Joseph	06.08.90	Tameside	(Anglia RU)	RHB/RM	2009

DURHAM

Full Names	Birthdate	Birthplace	College	Bat/Bowl	F-C Debut
ATKINSON, James John	24.08.90	Hong Kong	St Mary's	RHB/WK	2009
BUTTLEMAN, Joseph Edward Lewis	23.08.87	Basildon, Essex	St Hild & St Bede	RHB/RFM	2005
DIXEY, Paul Garrod	02.11.87	Canterbury	Hatfield	RHB/WK	2005
FOSTER, Patrick John	20.03.87	Nairobi, Kenya	St Hild & St Bede	RHB/RFM	2007
GALE, Daniel James	15.06.89	Tadworth, Surrey	St Aidan's	RHB/SLA	2009
GLOVER, John Charles	29.08.89	Cardiff, Wales	St Aidan's	RHB/RMF	2009
HARPER, George Michael	05.12.88	Minnesota, USA	St Hild & St Bede	RHB/LFM	2009
JOHNSTON, Paul Robert Archibald	13.12.88	Hartlepool, Co. Durham	John Snow	LHB	2008
MORGAN, Charles Felix Derrington	09.07.89	Leicester	Van Mildert	RHB/WK	2008
PAGET, Christopher David	02.11.87	Stafford	Van Mildert	RHB/OB	2004
SMITH, Gregory Philip	16.11.88	Leicester	St Hild & St Bede	RHB/LB	2009
WESTLEY, Thomas	13.03.89	Cambridge	St Cuthbert's	RHB/OB	2007
WILLIAMS, Robert Edward Morgan	19.01.87	Pembury, Kent	St Mary's	RHB/RMF	2007

LOUGHBOROUGH

Full Names	Birthdate	Birthplace		Bat/Bowl	F-C Debut
BAER, Michael	31.03.87	St Asaph, N Wales		RHB/RM	2008
BAKER, Gavin Charles	03.10.88	Edgware		RHB/RMF	2009
BORRINGTON, Paul Michael	24.05.88	Nottingham		RHB/OB	2005
EVANS, Alasdair Campbell	12.01.89	Kent		RHB/RMF	2009
EVANS, Rhodri Francis	06.12.89	Swansea		LHB/RM	2009
GROVES, Peter R	30.06.88	Bromley		RHB/RMF	2009
HARINATH, Arun	26.03.87	Sutton		LHB/OB	2007
HAYES, Phillip Lee	17.05.86	Bolton		LHB/LB	2009
JONES, Henry David	08.03.89	Kingston, Surrey		RHB/RFM	2008
LYNCH, Ashleigh Aaron	28.04.90	Burton-upon-Trent		RHB/RM	2009
MALAN, Charl Christiaan	23.02.89	London		RHB/OB	2009
MURPHY, David	24.06.89	Welwyn Garden City		RHB/WK	2009
ORD, James Edward	09.11.87	Birmingham		RHB/OB	2009

OXFORD († Blue 2009)

Full Names	Birthdate	Birthplace	College	Bat/Bowl	F-C Debut
ABEL, Edward	30.01.81	Salisbury, Wiltshire	Brookes U	LHB/SLA	2008
ALI, Morteza	01.01.87	Ghazni, Afghanistan	(Brookes U)	RHB/RM	2009
†BALL, Alexander Henry	03.10.86	Westminster, London	St Catherine's	RHB/OB	2007
BRADSHAW, Duncan Phillip	19.02.86	Harare, Zimbabwe	(Brookes U)	RHB/RFM	2006
†BRYAN, Thomas Edward	31.10.88	Colchester, Essex	Worcester	RHB/RM	2009
†BUCHANAN, Nicholas John Scouler	11.06.89	Basingstoke	Hertford	RHB/RM	2009
COUGHTRIE, Richard George	01.09.88	North Shields	(Brookes U)	RHB/WK	2009
†HILL, Charles Michael McLean	27.11.85	Wimbledon	Trinity	LHB/SLC	2007
KHALID, Mohammed Faisal	05.12.85	Banbury	(Brookes U)	RHB/RM	2009
†KING, Daniel Alexander	26.02.83	Canberra, Australia	Merton	LHB/WK	2009
†KLOPPER, Willem Abraham	29.05.85	Bloemfontein, SA	Green	RHB/LB	2009
†KRUGER, Neil	15.08.81	Cape Town, SA	Green	RHB/RM	2008
LETT, Robin Jonathan Hugh	23.12.86	Westminster	(Brookes U)	RHB/RM	2006
LEWIS, Mark Fenn	13.10.87	Coventry	(Brookes U)	RHB/RM	2009
†McKERCHAR, Brendan Thomas	23.01.83	Edinburgh	Keble	RHB/RM	2008
MARTIN, Jak	07.09.88	Kingston-upon-Thames	(Brookes U)	LHB/RM	2009
MILLIGAN, Marc Jon	01.08.87	Pretoria, SA	(Brookes U)	RHB/RFM	2009
†PASCOE, Daniel Charles	14.05.83	Canberra, Australia	Lincoln	RHB/SLA	2009
RYAN, Luke Charles	05.08.88	Welwyn Garden City	(Brookes U)	RHB/SLA	2007
†SHARMA, Rajiv	10.06.84	Auckland, NZ	Mansfield	RHB/RMF	2009
SMITH, David Thomas	13.09.89	Canterbury	(Brookes U)	RHB/RM	2009
†STRACHAN, Jonathan Peter	09.08.87	Cape Town, SA	Queen's	RHB/RMF	2008
SWAINLAND, Christopher James	05.11.86	Harold Wood	(Brookes U)	RHB/WK	2009
WATSON, Matthew John Corbett	04.04.87	Barnet	(Brookes U)	RHB/LB	2009
YOUNG, Edward George Christopher	21.05.89	Chertsey	(Brookes U)	RHB/SLA	2009

2009 TOURING TEAMS FIRST-CLASS REGISTER

WEST INDIES

Full Names	Birthdate	Birthplace	Team	Type	F-C Debut
BAKER, Lionel Sionne	06.09.84	Montserrat	Leeward Is	RHB/RMF	2002-03
BENN, Sulieman Jamaal	22.07.81	St James	Barbados	LHB/SLA	1999-00
BERNARD, David Eddison	19.07.81	Kingston	Jamaica	RHB/RMF	2000-01
CHANDERPAUL, Shivnarine	16.08.74	Unity Village	Guyana	LHB/LB	1991-92
DEONARINE, Narsingh	16.08.83	Albion, Berbice	Guyana	LHB/OB	1999-00
EDWARDS, Fidel Henderson	06.02.82	St Peter	Barbados	RHB/RF	2001-02
GAYLE, Christopher Henry	21.09.79	Kingston	Jamaica	LHB/OB	1998-99
NASH, Brendan Paul	14.12.77	Attadale, W Aus	Jamaica	LHB/LM	2000-01
PASCAL, Nelon Troy	25.04.87	St David's, Grenada	Windward Is	RHB/RF	2007-08
RAMDIN, Denesh	13.03.85	Freeport, Couva	Trinidad	RHB/WK	2003-04
RICHARDS, Dale Maurice	16.07.76	St Andrew	Barbados	RHB/RM	1999-00
RICHARDSON, Andrew Peter	06.09.81	Kingston	Jamaica	LHB/RFM	2002-03
SAMMY, Darren Julius Garvey	20.12.83	Micoud, St Lucia	Windward Is	RHB/RM	2002-03
SARWAN, Ramnaresh Ronnie	23.06.80	Wakenaam Is	Guyana	RHB/LB	1995-96
SIMMONS, Lendl Mark Platter	25.01.85	Port-of-Spain	Trinidad	RHB/RMF	2001-02
SMITH, Devon Sheldon	21.10.81	Sauters, Grenada	Windward Is	LHB/OB	1998-99
TAYLOR, Jerome Everton	22.06.84	St Elizabeth	Jamaica	RHB/RF	2002-03

AUSTRALIA

Full Names	Birthdate	Birthplace	Team	Type	F-C Debut
CLARK, Stuart Rupert	28.09.75	Sydney	NSW	RHB/RFM	1997-98
CLARKE, Michael John	02.04.81	Liverpool	NSW	RHB/SLA	1999-00
HADDIN, Bradley James	23.10.77	Cowra	NSW	RHB/WK	1999-00
HAURITZ, Nathan Michael	18.10.81	Wondai	NSW	RHB/OB	2000-01
HILFENHAUS, Benjamin William	15.03.83	Ulverstone	Tasmania	RHB/RFM	2005-06
HUGHES, Phillip Joel	30.11.88	Macksville	NSW	LHB	2007-08
HUSSEY, Michael Edward Killeen	27.05.75	Morley	W Australia	LHB/RM	1994-95
JOHNSON, Mitchell Guy	02.11.81	Townsville	Queensland	LHB/LF	2001-02
KATICH, Simon Mathew	21.08.75	Middle Swan	NSW	LHB/SLC	1996-97
LEE, Brett	08.11.76	Wollongong	NSW	RHB/RF	1994-95
McDONALD, Andrew Barry	15.06.81	Wodonga	Victoria	RHB/RFM	2001-02
MANOU, Graham Allan	23.04.79	Modbury	S Australia	RHB/WK	1998-99
NORTH, Marcus James	28.07.79	Melbourne	W Australia	LHB/OB	1998-99
PONTING, Ricky Thomas	19.12.74	Launceston	Tasmania	RHB/RM	1992-93
SIDDLE, Peter Matthew	25.11.84	Traralgon	Victoria	RHB/RFM	2005-06
WATSON, Shane Robert	17.06.81	Ipswich	Queensland	RHB/RFM	2000-01

THE 2009 FIRST-CLASS SEASON STATISTICAL HIGHLIGHTS

FIRST TO INDIVIDUAL TARGETS

1000 RUNS	M.E.Trescothick	Somerset	31 July
2000 RUNS	–	Most 1817 – M.E.Trescothick (Somerset)	
50 WICKETS	G.Onions	Durham, England, Eng Lions	19 June
100 WICKETS	–	Most 75 – Danish Kaneria (Essex)	

TEAM HIGHLIGHTS

HIGHEST INNINGS TOTALS († *County record*)

742-5d†	Sussex v Somerset	Taunton
702-8d	Glamorgan v Surrey	The Oval
674-6d	Australia v England (*1st Test*)	Cardiff
672-4d	Somerset v Warwickshire	Taunton
654-8d	Hampshire v Nottinghamshire	Nottingham
652-7d	Kent v Middlesex	Uxbridge
648-5d†	Durham v Nottinghamshire	Chester-le-Street
634-8d	Durham v Worcestershire	Worcester
630-8d	Warwickshire v Hampshire	Birmingham
620-7d	Kent v Surrey	The Oval
620-9d	Sussex v Worcestershire	Worcester
608-4d	Surrey v Leicestershire	The Oval
600-8d	Yorkshire v Warwickshire	Birmingham
600-8d	Northamptonshire v Leicestershire	Northampton

HIGHEST FOURTH INNINGS TOTALS

479-6	Somerset (set 476) v Yorkshire	Taunton

The second highest successful run chase in County Championship history.

406	Australia (set 522) v England (*2nd Test*)	Lord's

LOWEST INNINGS TOTALS

69	Somerset v Durham	Taunton
83	Nottinghamshire v Durham	Nottingham
83	Sussex v Yorkshire	Hove
90	Northamptonshire v Kent	Northampton
91	Middlesex v Leicestershire	Leicester
96	Hampshire v Durham	Chester-le-Street

MATCH AGGREGATES OF 1500 RUNS

1606-31	Yorkshire (438, 363-5) v Somerset (326, 479-6)	Taunton

BATSMEN'S MATCH (Qualification: 1200 runs, average 70 per wicket)

136.00 (1224-9)	Leics (593-5d and 23-0) v Surrey (608-4d)	The Oval
114.82 (1263-11)	Susssex (742-5d) v Somerset (521-6)	Taunton
85.33 (1280-15)	Warwicks (500 & 108-1) v Somerset (672-4)	Taunton

LARGE MARGINS OF VICTORY

Inns & 196 runs	Northamptonshire v Leicestershire	Northampton
Inns & 110 runs	Durham v Hampshire	Chester-le-Street
Inns & 102 runs	Durham v Nottinghamshire	Nottingham
286 runs	Lancashire v Durham UCCE	Durham

NARROW MARGINS OF VICTORY

23 runs	Glamorgan (224 & 135) beat Middlesex (169 & 167)	Swansea
2 wickets	Northants (246 & 245-8) beat Derbyshire (255 & 233)	Chesterfield

VICTORY AFTER FOLLOWING ON

Essex (370 and 155) lost to Kent (205 and 512-9d) by 192 runs   Chelmsford
A record margin of victory in first-class cricket after being asked to follow on.

FOUR HUNDREDS IN AN INNINGS

Australia (674-6) v England (*1st Test*)	Cardiff
Durham (648-5d) v Nottinghamshire	Chester-le-Street
Glamorgan (702-8d) v Surrey	The Oval
Kent (620-7d) v Surrey	The Oval

SIX FIFTIES IN AN INNINGS

Warwickshire (428) v Sussex	Hove
Somerset (523-8) v Worcestershire	Taunton

SIXTY EXTRAS IN AN INNINGS

B	LB	W	NB		
62	13	11	12	26	Durham (543) v Somerset	Taunton
61	20	5	8	28	England (569-6d) v West Indies	Chester-le-Street

BATTING HIGHLIGHTS

TRIPLE HUNDREDS († *County record*)

M.W.Goodwin		344*†	Sussex v Somerset	Taunton
J.C.Hildreth		303*	Somerset v Warwickshire	Taunton

DOUBLE HUNDREDS

U.Afzaal		204*	Surrey v Northamptonshire	Northampton
R.S.Bopara		201	Essex v Surrey	Colchester
M.A.Carberry		204	Hampshire v Warwickshire	Southampton
S.Chanderpaul		201*	Durham v Worcestershire	Worcester
M.J.Di Venuto	(2)	254*	Durham v Sussex	Chester-le-Street
		219	Durham v Nottinghamshire	Chester-le-Street
R.W.T.Key		270*	Kent v Glamorgan	Cardiff
M.J.Lumb		219	Hampshire v Nottinghamshire	Nottingham
A.McGrath		211	Yorkshire v Warwickshire	Birmingham
D.K.H.Mitchell		298	Worcestershire v Somerset	Taunton
M.R.Ramprakash		274	Surrey v Leicestershire	The Oval
C.J.L.Rogers	(2)	208	Derbyshire v Kent	Derby
		222	Derbyshire v Essex	Derby
V.S.Solanki		206*	Worcestershire v Yorkshire	Leeds
D.I.Stevens		208	Kent v Middlesex	Uxbridge
J.W.A.Taylor		207*	Leicestershire v Surrey	The Oval
J.O.Troughton		223	Warwickshire v Hampshire	Birmingham

HUNDRED IN EACH INNINGS OF A MATCH

N.J.Dexter	146	118	Middlesex v Kent	Uxbridge
M.E.Trescothick	108	107*	Somerset v Warwickshire	Birmingham

FASTEST HUNDRED AGAINST GENUINE BOWLING

P.D.Trego (103*)		54 balls	Somerset v Yorkshire	Taunton

200 RUNS FROM BOUNDARIES IN AN INNINGS

Runs	*6s*	*4s*			
222	1	54	D.K.H.Mitchell (298)	Worcs v Somerset	Taunton
208	6	43	M.W.Goodwin (344*)	Sussex v Somerset	Taunton

HUNDRED ON FIRST-CLASS DEBUT

J.S.Gatting		152	Sussex v Cambridge UCCE	Cambridge

HUNDRED ON FIRST-CLASS DEBUT IN BRITAIN

P.P.Chawla	102*	Sussex v Worcestershire	Worcester
P.J.Hughes	118	Middlesex v Glamorgan	Lord's
W.L.Madsen	170*	Derbyshire v Gloucestershire	Cheltenham

CARRYING BAT THROUGH COMPLETED INNINGS

S.A.Northeast	128*	Kent (265) v Gloucestershire	Bristol

LONGEST INNINGS (Qualification 600 mins and/or 400 balls)

Mins	*Balls*			
537	441	J.J.Sayers (173)	Yorkshire v Warwickshire	Birmingham
554	426	U.Afzaal (204*)	Surrey v Northamptonshire	Northampton

NOTABLE PARTNERSHIPS († *County record*)

Qualifications: 1st-4th wkts: 250 runs; 5th-6th: 225; 7th: 200; 8th: 175; 9th: 150; 10th: 100.

First Wicket

315	G.P.Rees/M.J.Cosgrove	Glamorgan v Surrey	The Oval
314	M.J.Di Venuto/K.J.Coetzer	Durham v Nottinghamshire	Chester-le-Street
261	M.A.Carberry/J.H.K.Adams	Hampshire v Warwickshire	Southampton

Third Wicket

404	M.R.Ramprakash/S.J.Walters	Surrey v Leicestershire	The Oval
346†	J.J.Sayers/A.McGrath	Yorkshire v Warwickshire	Birmingham
317	V.S.Solanki/M.M.Ali	Worcestershire v Yorkshire	Leeds
314	H.H.Dippenaar/H.D.Ackerman	Leicestershire v Surrey	Leicester
309	G.O.Jones/M.van Jaarsveld	Kent v Glamorgan	Canterbury

Fourth Wicket

363†	M.W.Goodwin/C.D.Hopkinson	Sussex v Somerset	Taunton

Fifth Wicket

335†	J.O.Troughton/T.R.Ambrose	Warwickshire v Hampshire	Birmingham
318*	J.C.Hildreth/C.Kieswetter	Somerset v Warwickshire	Taunton
228	D.I.Stevens/J.M.Kemp	Kent v Middlesex	Uxbridge

Sixth Wicket

268	R.A.White/A.J.Hall	Northamptonshire v Leics	Northampton
240†	J.Allenby/M.A.Wallace	Glamorgan v Surrey	The Oval
230*	J.W.A.Taylor/J.Du Toit	Leicestershire v Surrey	The Oval

Eighth Wicket

222*	I.J.L.Trott/C.R.Woakes	Warwickshire v Hampshire	Southampton

| 195† | J.W.A.Taylor/J.K.H.Naik | Leicestershire v Derbyshire | Leicester |
| 192 | A.U.Rashid/A.Shahzad | Yorkshire v Hampshire | Basingstoke |

Ninth Wicket

233†	I.J.L.Trott/J.S.Patel	Warwickshire v Yorkshire	Birmingham
197	R.D.B.Croft/A.J.Shantry	Glamorgan v Leicestershire	Colwyn Bay
150	Azeem Rafiq/M.J.Hoggard	Yorkshire v Worcestershire	Worcester

BOWLING HIGHLIGHTS
EIGHT OR MORE WICKETS IN AN INNINGS

| Danish Kaneria | 8-116 | Essex v Leicestershire | Chelmsford |
| J.C.Tredwell | 8- 66 | Kent v Glamorgan | Canterbury |

TEN OR MORE WICKETS IN A MATCH

J.M.Anderson		11-109	Lancashire v Sussex	Hove
P.P.Chawla		11-160	Sussex v Somerset	Hove
D.A.Cosker		11-126	Glamorgan v Essex	Cardiff
Danish Kaneria	(2)	12-203	Essex v Leicestershire	Chelmsford
		10-219	Essex v Glamorgan	Cardiff
D.S.Lucas		12- 73	Northamptonshire v Glos	Cheltenham
S.I.Mahmood		10-140	Lancashire v Worcestershire	Worcester
S.A.Piolet		10- 43	Warwicks v Durham UCCE	Durham
L.E.Plunkett		11-119	Durham v Worcestershire	Chester-le-Street
J.C.Tredwell	(2)	11-120	Kent v Glamorgan	Canterbury
		10-100	Kent v Northamptonshire	Northampton
S.D.Udal		10- 95	Middlesex v Glamorgan	Swansea

OUTSTANDING INNINGS ANALYSIS

| I.D.Blackwell | 8.1-5-7-5 | Durham v Somerset | Chester-le-Street |

HAT-TRICKS

| J.E.C.Franklin† | | Gloucestershire v Derbyshire | Cheltenham |

† Two wickets at the end of the first innings and one at the beginning of the second. He also became the second player for Glos, after M.J.Procter, to take a hat-trick and score a century in the same match.

| M.J.Hoggard | | Yorkshire v Sussex | Hove |
| Danish Kaneria | | Essex v Derbyshire | Derby |

200 RUNS CONCEDED IN AN INNINGS

| Murtaza Hussain | 54.2-4-208-2 | Surrey v Kent | The Oval |
| S.R.Patel | 60-7-206-1 | Nottinghamshire v Durham | Chester-le-Street |

60 OVERS BOWLED IN AN INNINGS

C.W.Henderson	67-16-152-6	Leicestershire v Glamorgan	Colwyn Bay
C.W.Henderson	64-11-178-2	Leicestershire v Surrey	The Oval
S.R.Patel	60-7-206-1	Nottinghamshire v Durham	Chester-le-Street

WICKET-KEEPING HIGHLIGHTS
SIX OR MORE WICKET-KEEPING DISMISSALS IN AN INNINGS

G.L.Brophy	6ct	Yorkshire v Durham	Chester-le-Street
S.M.Davies	6ct	Worcestershire v Notts	Worcester
J.S.Foster	6ct	Essex v Glamorgan	Cardiff
C.Kieswetter	6ct	Somerset v Lancashire	Taunton
T.J.New	6ct	Leicestershire v Derbyshire	Derby

NINE OR MORE WICKET-KEEPING DISMISSALS IN A MATCH

J.S.Foster	9ct	Essex v Gloucestershire	Bristol

NO BYES CONCEDED IN AN INNINGS OF 600 OR MORE

652-7d	J.A.Simpson	Middlesex v Kent	Uxbridge

FIELDING HIGHLIGHTS
SEVEN OR MORE CATCHES IN THE FIELD IN A MATCH

S.D.Robson	7ct	Middlesex v Glamorgan	Swansea

COUNTY CHAMPIONSHIP 2009
LV FINAL TABLES

DIVISION 1

	P	W	L	D	Bonus Points Bat	Bonus Points Bowl	Deduct Points	Total Points
1 DURHAM (1)	16	8	–	8	49	48	1	240
2 Nottinghamshire (2)	16	4	2	10	56	41	–	193
3 Somerset (4)	16	3	1	12	50	43	1	182
4 Lancashire (5)	16	4	2	10	35	44	–	175
5 Warwickshire (–)	16	3	3	10	54	38	–	174
6 Hampshire (3)	16	3	3	10	50	40	1	169
7 Yorkshire (7)	16	2	2	12	46	44	–	166
8 Sussex (6)	16	2	6	8	45	39	1	143
9 Worcestershire (–)	16	–	10	6	30	40	–	94

DIVISION 2

	P	W	L	D	Bonus Points Bat	Bonus Points Bowl	Deduct Points	Total Points
1 Kent (–)	16	8	3	5	43	44	–	219
2 Essex (2)	16	6	3	7	40	43	1	194
3 Northamptonshire (4)	16	6	4	6	40	45	–	193
4 Gloucestershire (9)	16	6	6	4	39	46	–	185
5 Glamorgan (8)	16	2	2	12	56	43	–	175
6 Derbyshire (6)	16	2	3	11	55	45	–	172
7 Surrey (–)	16	1	4	11	54	36	–	148
8 Middlesex (3)	16	2	7	7	43	41	–	140
9 Leicestershire (7)	16	2	3	11	31	35	–	138

SCORING OF CHAMPIONSHIP POINTS 2009

(a) For a win, 14 points, plus any points scored in the first innings.

(b) In a tie, each side to score seven points, plus any points scored in the first innings.

(c) In a drawn match, each side to score four points, plus any points scored in the first innings (see also paragraph (f) below).

(d) If the scores are equal in a drawn match, the side batting in the fourth innings to score seven points plus any points scored in the first innings, and the opposing side to score four points plus any points scored in the first innings.

(e) **First Innings Points** (awarded only for performances **in the first 120 overs** of each first innings and retained whatever the result of the match):
    (i) A maximum of five batting points to be available as under:
        200 to 249 runs – 1 point; 250 to 299 runs – 2 points; 300 to 349 runs – 3 points; 350 to 399 runs – 4 points; 400 runs or over – 5 points.
    (ii) A maximum of three bowling points to be available as under:
        3 to 5 wickets taken – 1 point; 6 to 8 wickets taken – 2 points; 9 to 10 wickets taken – 3 points.

(f) If a match is abandoned without a ball being bowled, each side to score four points.

(g) The side which has the highest aggregate of points gained at the end of the season shall be the Champion County of their respective Division. Should any sides in the Championship table be equal on points, the following tie-breakers will be applied in the order stated: most wins, fewest losses, team achieving most points in contests between teams level on points, most wickets taken, most runs scored. At the end of the season, the top two teams from the Second Division will be promoted and the bottom two teams from the First Division will be relegated.

COUNTY CHAMPIONS

The English County Championship was not officially constituted until December 1889. Prior to that date there was no generally accepted method of awarding the title; although the 'least matches lost' method existed, it was not consistently applied. Rules governing playing qualifications were agreed in 1873 and the first unofficial points system 15 years later.

Research has produced a list of champions dating back to 1826, but at least seven different versions exist for the period from 1864 to 1889 (see *The Wisden Book of Cricket Records*). Only from 1890 can any authorised list of county champions commence.

That first official Championship was contested between eight counties: Gloucestershire, Kent, Lancashire, Middlesex, Nottinghamshire, Surrey, Sussex and Yorkshire. The remaining counties were admitted in the following seasons: 1891 – Somerset, 1895 – Derbyshire, Essex, Hampshire, Leicestershire and Warwickshire, 1899 – Worcestershire, 1905 – Northamptonshire, 1921 – Glamorgan, and 1992 – Durham.

The Championship pennant was introduced by the 1951 champions, Warwickshire, and the Lord's Taverners' Trophy was first presented in 1973. The first sponsors, Schweppes (1977 to 1983), were succeeded by Britannic Assurance (1984 to 1998), PPP Healthcare (1999-2000), CricInfo (2001), Frizzell (2002 to 2005) and Liverpool Victoria (2006 to 2009). Based on their previous season's positions, the 18 counties were separated into two divisions in 2000. From 2000 to 2005 the bottom three Division 1 teams were relegated and the top three Division 2 sides promoted. This was reduced to two teams from the end of the 2006 season.

1890	Surrey	1932	Yorkshire	1974	Worcestershire
1891	Surrey	1933	Yorkshire	1975	Leicestershire
1892	Surrey	1934	Lancashire	1976	Middlesex
1893	Yorkshire	1935	Yorkshire	1977	{ Kent
1894	Surrey	1936	Derbyshire		{ Middlesex
1895	Surrey	1937	Yorkshire	1978	Kent
1896	Yorkshire	1938	Yorkshire	1979	Essex
1897	Lancashire	1939	Yorkshire	1980	Middlesex
1898	Yorkshire	1946	Yorkshire	1981	Nottinghamshire
1899	Surrey	1947	Middlesex	1982	Middlesex
1900	Yorkshire	1948	Glamorgan	1983	Essex
1901	Yorkshire	1949	{ Middlesex	1984	Essex
1902	Yorkshire		{ Yorkshire	1985	Middlesex
1903	Middlesex	1950	{ Lancashire	1986	Essex
1904	Lancashire		{ Surrey	1987	Nottinghamshire
1905	Yorkshire	1951	Warwickshire	1988	Worcestershire
1906	Kent	1952	Surrey	1989	Worcestershire
1907	Nottinghamshire	1953	Surrey	1990	Middlesex
1908	Yorkshire	1954	Surrey	1991	Essex
1909	Kent	1955	Surrey	1992	Essex
1910	Kent	1956	Surrey	1993	Middlesex
1911	Warwickshire	1957	Surrey	1994	Warwickshire
1912	Yorkshire	1958	Surrey	1995	Warwickshire
1913	Kent	1959	Yorkshire	1996	Leicestershire
1914	Surrey	1960	Yorkshire	1997	Glamorgan
1919	Yorkshire	1961	Hampshire	1998	Leicestershire
1920	Middlesex	1962	Yorkshire	1999	Surrey
1921	Middlesex	1963	Yorkshire	2000	Surrey
1922	Yorkshire	1964	Worcestershire	2001	Yorkshire
1923	Yorkshire	1965	Worcestershire	2002	Surrey
1924	Yorkshire	1966	Yorkshire	2003	Sussex
1925	Yorkshire	1967	Yorkshire	2004	Warwickshire
1926	Lancashire	1968	Yorkshire	2005	Nottinghamshire
1927	Lancashire	1969	Glamorgan	2006	Sussex
1928	Lancashire	1970	Kent	2007	Sussex
1929	Nottinghamshire	1971	Surrey	2008	Durham
1930	Lancashire	1972	Warwickshire	2009	Durham
1931	Yorkshire	1973	Hampshire		

COUNTY CHAMPIONSHIP RESULTS 2009

DIVISION 1

	DURHAM	HANTS	LANCS	NOTTS	SOM'T	SUSSEX	WARWKS	WORCS	YORKS
DURHAM	–	C-le-St D I/110	C-le-St D 138	C-le-St D I/52	C-le-St Drawn	C-le-St D 9w	C-le-St D 8w	C-le-St D 5w	C-le-St Drawn
HANTS	So'ton Drawn	–	So'ton Drawn	So'ton N 191	So'ton Drawn	So'ton Drawn	So'ton Drawn	So'ton H 7w	B'stoke Y I/22
LANCS	Man Drawn	L'pool H 10w	–	Man Drawn	Man Drawn	Man Drawn	Man L 10w	Man L 7w	Man Drawn
NOTTS	N'ham D I/102	N'ham Drawn	N'ham Drawn	–	N'ham N 6w	N'ham N 35	N'ham Drawn	N'ham N I/5	N'ham Drawn
SOM'T	Taunton Drawn	Taunton Drawn	Taunton Drawn	Taunton Drawn	–	Taunton Drawn	Taunton Drawn	Taunton Drawn	Taunton Sm 4w
SUSSEX	Hove Drawn	Arundel Drawn	Hove L 8w	Horsham Drawn	Hove Sm 35	–	Hove Wa I/2	Hove Sx 8w	Hove Y 156
WARWKS	B'ham D 10w	B'ham Drawn	B'ham Drawn	B'ham Drawn	B'ham Drawn	B'ham Drawn	–	B'ham Wa I/18	B'ham Drawn
WORCS	Worcs Drawn	Worcs H 10w	Worcs L 6w	Worcs Drawn	Worcs Drawn	Worcs Sx 10w	Worcs Wa 9w	–	Worcs Drawn
YORKS	Leeds Drawn	Leeds Drawn	Leeds Drawn	Scar Drawn	Leeds Sm 4w	Leeds Drawn	Scar Drawn	Leeds Drawn	–

DIVISION 2

	DERBYS	ESSEX	GLAM	GLOS	KENT	LEICS	MIDDX	N'HANTS	SURREY
DERBYS	–	Derby E 5w	Derby Drawn	Ch'field Drawn	Derby Drawn	Derby Drawn	Derby Drawn	Ch'field N 2w	Derby D 5w
ESSEX	Chelms Drawn	–	Chelms Drawn	Southend Gs 10w	Chelms K 192	Chelms Drawn	Chelms Drawn	Chelms E 4w	Colchester E 9w
GLAM	Cardiff Drawn	Cardiff Drawn	–	Cardiff Drawn	Cardiff K I/45	Col B Gm I/72	Swansea Gm 22	Cardiff Drawn	Cardiff Drawn
GLOS	Chelt'm D 185	Bristol E 7w	Bristol Drawn	–	Bristol Gs I/23	Bristol Gs 10w	Bristol Gs 9w	Bristol N 9w	Bristol Gs I/1
KENT	Cant K 3w	Tun W E 122	Cant K 76	Beck'm K 76	–	Cant Drawn	Cant M 47	Cant Drawn	Cant K 6w
LEICS	Leics Drawn	Leics Drawn	Leics Drawn	Leics L 44	Leics Drawn	–	Leics L 8w	Leics Drawn	Leics Drawn
MIDDX	Uxbridge Drawn	Lord's E 5w	Lord's Drawn	Lord's M 180	Lord's K 10w	S'gate Drawn	–	Lord's N 35	Lord's Drawn
N'HANTS	No'ton Drawn	No'ton N 8w	No'ton Drawn	No'ton Gs 44	No'ton K 238	No'ton N I/196	No'ton N 6w	–	No'ton S I/95
SURREY	Croydon Drawn	Guildford Drawn	Oval Drawn	Oval Drawn	Oval Drawn	Oval Drawn	Oval Drawn	Oval Drawn	–

COUNTY CHAMPIONSHIP RESULTS 2010

KEEP YOUR OWN RECORD (see page 216)

DIVISION 1

	DURHAM	ESSEX	HANTS	KENT	LANCS	NOTTS	SOM'T	WARWKS	YORKS
DURHAM	–	C-le-St	C-le-St	C-le-St	C-le-St	C-le-St	C-le-St	C-le-St	C-le-St
ESSEX	Chelms	–	Chelms	Chelms	Chelms	Chelms	Colchester	Southend	Chelms
HANTS	B'stoke	So'ton	–	So'ton	So'ton	So'ton	So'ton	So'ton	So'ton
KENT	Cant	Cant	Cant	–	Cant	Tun W	Cant	Cant	Cant
LANCS	Man	Man	L'pool	Man	–	Man	Man	Man	Man
NOTTS	N'ham	N'ham	N'ham	N'ham	N'ham	–	N'ham	N'ham	N'ham
SOM'T	Taunton	Taunton	Taunton	Taunton	Taunton	Taunton	–	Taunton	Taunton
WARWKS	B'ham	B'ham	B'ham	B'ham	B'ham	B'ham	B'ham	–	Birm
YORKS	Leeds	Scar	Scar	Leeds	Leeds	Leeds	Leeds	Leeds	–

DIVISION 2

	DERBYS	GLAM	GLOS	LEICS	MIDDX	N'HANTS	SURREY	SUSSEX	WORCS
DERBYS	–	Derby	Derby	Derby	Derby	C'field	C'field	Derby	Derby
GLAM	Cardiff	–	Cardiff	Swansea	Cardiff	Cardiff	Cardiff	Cardiff	Col B
GLOS	Bristol	Chelt'm	–	Bristol	Bristol	Bristol	Bristol	Bristol	Chelt'm
LEICS	Leics	Leics	Leics	–	Leics	Leics	Leics	Leics	Leics
MIDDX	Lord's	Lord's	Lord's	Lord's	–	Lord's	Lord's	Uxbridge	Lord's
N'HANTS	No'ton	No'ton	No'ton	No'ton	No'ton	–	No'ton	No'ton	No'ton
SURREY	Oval	Oval	Oval	Oval	Oval	Oval	–	Guildford	Croydon
SUSSEX	Horsham	Hove	Arundel	Hove	Hove	Hove	Hove	–	Hove
WORCS	Worcs	Worcs	Worcs	Worcs	Worcs	Worcs	Worcs	Worcs	–

FRIENDS PROVIDENT TROPHY 2009

After following virtually the same knockout format since its inauguration as the Gillette Cup in 1963, this competition was drastically revamped for the 2006 season. The Minor Counties were omitted and the 18 first-class counties, joined by Ireland and Scotland, were divided into two leagues or conferences. The winner of each league contested the final at Lord's. A semi-final stage was added for the 2007 competition when Friends Provident took over the sponsorship. Quarter-finals were restored in 2008 when the 20 teams were divided into four divisions.

GROUP A

	P	W	L	T	NR	A	Pts	Net RR
Hampshire	8	5	2	–	–	1	11	0.34
Nottinghamshire	8	5	3	–	–	–	10	0.42
Worcestershire	8	4	3	–	1	–	9	0.29
Leicestershire	8	2	4	–	1	1	6	–0.64
Ireland	8	1	5	–	–	2	4	–0.75

GROUP B

	P	W	L	T	NR	A	Pts	Net RR
Somerset	8	7	–	–	1	–	15	2.00
Middlesex	8	4	4	–	–	–	8	0.14
Warwickshire	8	3	3	1	1	–	8	0.47
Kent	8	3	4	1	–	–	7	–0.41
Scotland	8	1	7	–	–	–	2	–1.78

GROUP C

	P	W	L	T	NR	A	Pts	Net RR
Gloucestershire	8	5	2	–	1	–	11	0.45
Sussex	8	4	3	–	1	–	9	0.12
Yorkshire	8	4	4	–	–	–	8	–0.15
Surrey	8	3	5	–	–	–	6	0.30
Durham	8	3	5	–	–	–	6	–0.63

GROUP D

	P	W	L	T	NR	A	Pts	Net RR
Lancashire	8	6	2	–	–	–	12	0.64
Essex	8	5	2	–	1	–	11	0.41
Derbyshire	8	3	4	–	–	1	7	–0.30
Glamorgan	8	2	5	–	–	1	5	–0.78
Northamptonshire	8	1	4	–	1	2	5	–0.16

QUARTER-FINALS

At Rose Bowl, Southampton, on 23 May. Toss: Hampshire. HAMPSHIRE won by 44 runs. Hampshire 310-4 (50; M.J.Lumb 100, J.H.K.Adams 76, L.A.Dawson 51*). Middlesex 266 (49.2; N.J.Dexter 79, B.V.Taylor 3-44). Award: M.J.Lumb.

At Old Trafford, Manchester, on 23 May. Toss: Essex. LANCASHIRE won by 67 runs. Lancashire 262-6 (50; F.du Plessis 113*). Essex 195 (44; G.Keedy 4-45). Award: F.du Plessis.

At County Ground, Taunton, on 23 May. Toss: Somerset. SUSSEX won by six wickets. Somerset 285-8 (50; C.Kieswetter 106, Z.de Bruyn 96, Yasir Arafat 3-52). Sussex 288-4 (49.1; M.W.Goodwin 93, E.C.Joyce 74, M.H.Yardy 57*). Award: M.W.Goodwin.

At County Ground, Bristol, on 16 June. Toss: Nottinghamshire. GLOUCESTERSHIRE won by six wickets. Nottinghamshire 189 (44.2; C.M.W.Read 57, J.Lewis 4-34, S.P.Kirby 3-33). Gloucestershire 190-4 (37.3; C.M.Spearman 50*). Award: S.P.Kirby.

At Old Trafford, Manchester, on 5 July. Toss: Lancashire. HAMPSHIRE won by 64 runs. Hampshire 271 (48.4; J.H.K.Adams 78, M.J.Lumb 76, G.Chapple 3-46, G.Keedy 3-49, S.I.Mahmood 3-56). Lancashire 207 (45.4; V.V.S.Laxman 54, Imran Tahir 3-38). Award: J.H.K.Adams.

At County Ground, Hove, on 5 July. Toss: Gloucestershire. SUSSEX won by 34 runs. Sussex 326-7 (50; E.C.Joyce 146, M.W.Goodwin 60). Gloucestershire 292 (47.4; A.P.R.Gidman 116, H.J.H.Marshall 57, M.H.Yardy 4-54). Award: E.C.Joyce.

STATISTICAL HIGHLIGHTS in 2009

Highest total	403-3		Somerset v Scotland	Taunton	11 May
Lowest total	58		Worcs v Ireland	Worcester	20 May
Highest innings	176	S.A.Newman	Surrey v Yorkshire	Oval	20 May
Fastest hundred	71 balls	F.du Plessis	Lancs v Essex	Manchester	23 May
Highest partnership	277	N.R.D.Compton/E.J.G.Morgan	Middx v Kent	Canterbury	11 May
Best bowling	6-13	S.R.Patel	Notts v Ireland	Dublin	16 May
Most WK dismissals	7 (5ct, 2st)	T.R.Ambrose	Warwks v Middx	Birmingham	12 May
Most runs in tournament			E.C.Joyce 546 in 10 inns, ave 60.66, HS 146		
Most wickets in tournament			20 C.P.Schofield (Surrey), ave 15.35, BB 5-32		
			20 D.G.Cork (Hampshire), ave 17.60, BB 4-18		
			20 A.C.Thomas (Somerset), ave 18.05, BB 4-22		
Most dismissals in tournament			16 (11ct, 5st) J.S.Foster (Essex)		
Most catches in tournament			9 C.C.Benham (Hampshire)		

WHAT IS A KOLPAK REGISTRATION?

The Kolpak ruling was made by the European Court of Justice on 8 May 2003 in favour of Maros Kolpak, a Slovak handball player. The Court's decision was based upon the dictum that no resident of the European Union should be prevented from working in another part of the EU.

Specifically the case meant that, in professional sports, if a sporting club chose a player who resided in the EU, then there could be no law preventing this. For example, a German basketball team could not be prevented from hiring a Greek player since both nations are members of the EU. Moreover, since Kolpak was not from the EU at the time the case was decided, but from a country that had an associate trading relationship, the decision meant that any player from any nation which had such a relationship with the EU, provided that they held a valid UK work permit, must be treated for the purposes of employment as if they were a citizen of an EU country.

Counties could already employ any number of EU residents under the Bosman ruling. However, there are no other strong cricketing countries within the EU, and so Kolpak, not Bosman, has had the significant impact on county cricket. The largest group of countries with an associate agreement with the EU is the ACP countries, which include South Africa, Zimbabwe, and many of the islands which supply the West Indies cricket team.

There is no residential requirement. The ECB had initially stated that a player must not have represented their own country for over twelve months in order to qualify for Kolpak status but after Jacques Rudolph signed for Yorkshire, they admitted that they were powerless to enforce this rule.

In an effort to combat the influx of Kolpak players, the ECB has linked the central payments made to counties, to the amount of English qualified players who represent the county.

Kolpak players are not qualified for England; the main requirement for that qualification is that the player must be a British or an Irish citizen and, if born outside England or Wales, he must complete a four-year residence period.

2009 FRIENDS PROVIDENT TROPHY FINAL

HAMPSHIRE v SUSSEX

At Lord's, London, on 25 July.
Result: **HAMPSHIRE** won by six wickets.
Toss: Sussex. Award: D.G.Cork.

SUSSEX		Runs	Balls	4/6	Fall
E.C.Joyce	b Cork	15	21	2	1- 30
C.D.Nash	lbw b Cork	21	32	3	3- 39
† M.J.Prior	c Pothas b Cork	0	2	–	2- 30
M.W.Goodwin	run out (Tremlett)	1	13	–	4- 43
* M.H.Yardy	not out	92	127	7	
L.J.Wright	b Tremlett	7	26	–	5- 77
D.R.Smith	c Carberry b Tahir	20	20	–/1	6-111
R.J.Hamilton-Brown	c Mascarenhas b Tahir	32	39	4	7-171
Yasir Arafat	c Pothas b Mascarenhas	9	9	–	8-186
R.S.C.Martin-Jenkins	c Benham b Cork	4	8	–	9-203
R.J.Kirtley	not out	3	4	–	
Extras	(LB 9, W 4, NB 2)	15			
Total	(9 wkts; 50 overs)	**219**			

HAMPSHIRE		Runs	Balls	4/6	Fall
M.J.Lumb	c Prior b Wright	38	58	4	2-110
J.H.K.Adams	lbw b Wright	55	65	6	1- 93
M.A.Carberry	c and b Arafat	30	23	3	3-137
S.M.Ervine	c Nash b Wright	15	20	1/1	4-154
C.C.Benham	not out	37	48	4/1	
† N.Pothas	not out	35	31	5/1	
L.A.Dawson					
* A.D.Mascarenhas					
D.G.Cork					
C.T.Tremlett					
Imran Tahir					
Extras	(LB 2, W 5, NB 4)	11			
Total	(4 wkts; 40.3 overs)	**221**			

HAMPSHIRE	O	M	R	W	SUSSEX	O	M	R	W
Cork	10	1	41	4	Kirtley	5	0	26	0
Mascarenhas	9	0	27	1	Yasir Arafat	10	0	54	1
Imran Tahir	10	0	50	2	Martin-Jenkins	4	0	21	0
Tremlett	10	0	40	1	Wright	9	1	50	3
Ervine	6	0	31	0	Nash	3	0	15	0
Dawson	5	0	21	0	Hamilton-Brown	3.3	0	27	0
					Yardy	6	1	26	0

Umpires: N.J.Llong and N.A.Mallender

FRIENDS PROVIDENT TROPHY

PRINCIPAL RECORDS 1963-2009
(Including Gillette Cup, NatWest Trophy and C&G Trophy Matches)

Highest Total		496-4	Surrey v Glos	The Oval	2007
Highest Total in a Final		322-5	Warwicks v Sussex	Lord's	1993
Highest Total Batting Second		429	Glamorgan v Surrey	The Oval	2002
Highest Total to Win Batting Second		359-8	Hampshire v Surrey	The Oval	2005
Lowest Total		39	Ireland v Sussex	Hove	1985
Lowest Total in a Final		57	Essex v Lancashire	Lord's	1996
Lowest Total to Win Batting First		98	Worcs v Durham	Chester-le-St	1968

Highest Score	268	A.D.Brown	Surrey v Glamorgan	The Oval	2002
	206	A.I.Kallicharan	Warwicks v Oxon	Birmingham	1984
Fastest Hundred	36 balls	G.D.Rose	Somerset v Devon	Torquay	1990
Most Hundreds	8	R.A.Smith	Hampshire		1985-03
	8	N.V.Knight	Essex/Warwickshire		1992-06
	8	G.A.Hick	Worcestershire		1986-08
Most Runs	3040	(av 51.52)	G.A.Hick	Worcestershire	1986-08

Highest Partnership for each Wicket

1st	311	A.J.Wright/N.J.Trainor	Glos v Scotland	Bristol	1997
2nd	286	I.S.Anderson/A.Hill	Derbys v Cornwall	Derby	1986
3rd	309*	T.S.Curtis/T.M.Moody	Worcs v Surrey	The Oval	1994
4th	234*	D.Lloyd/C.H.Lloyd	Lancashire v Glos	Manchester	1978
5th	202*	I.J.L.Trott/T.R.Ambrose	Warwicks v Northants	Birmingham	2007
6th	226	N.J.Llong/M.V.Fleming	Kent v Cheshire	Bowdon	1999
7th	170	D.R.Brown/A.F.Giles	Warwicks v Essex	Birmingham	2003
8th	174	R.W.T.Key/J.C.Tredwell	Kent v Surrey	The Oval	2007
9th	155	C.M.W.Read/A.J.Harris	Notts v Durham	Nottingham	2006
10th	81	S.Turner/R.E.East	Essex v Yorkshire	Leeds	1982

Best Bowling	8-21	M.A.Holding	Derbys v Sussex	Hove	1988
Most Wickets	97	(av 19.76)	D. Gough	Yorks/Essex	1990-08

Most Wicket-Keeping Dismissals in an Innings

8 (8ct)		D.J.Pipe	Worcs v Herts	Hertford	2001

Most Match Wins: 111 – Lancashire.   **Most Cup/Trophy Wins:** 7 – Lancashire.

GILLETTE CUP WINNERS

1963	Sussex	1970	Lancashire	1977	Middlesex
1964	Sussex	1971	Lancashire	1978	Sussex
1965	Yorkshire	1972	Lancashire	1979	Somerset
1966	Warwickshire	1973	Gloucestershire	1980	Middlesex
1967	Kent	1974	Kent		
1968	Warwickshire	1975	Lancashire		
1969	Yorkshire	1976	Northamptonshire		

NATWEST TROPHY WINNERS

1981	Derbyshire	1988	Middlesex	1995	Warwickshire
1982	Surrey	1989	Warwickshire	1996	Lancashire
1983	Somerset	1990	Lancashire	1997	Essex
1984	Middlesex	1991	Hampshire	1998	Lancashire
1985	Essex	1992	Northamptonshire	1999	Gloucestershire
1986	Sussex	1993	Warwickshire	2000	Gloucestershire
1987	Nottinghamshire	1994	Worcestershire		

CHELTENHAM & GLOUCESTER TROPHY WINNERS

2001	Somerset	2003	Gloucestershire	2005	Hampshire
2002	Yorkshire	2004	Gloucestershire	2006	Sussex

FRIENDS PROVIDENT TROPHY WINNERS

2007	Durham	2008	Essex	2009	Hampshire

PRO40 LEAGUE 2009

This competition was drastically revamped in 2006, with each county playing its divisional opponents once instead of twice and with Scotland omitted. The bottom two First Division teams were relegated and replaced by the top two teams from the Second Division. In 2009, with the competition due to be discontinued, there was no promotion or relegation at the end of the season.

FIRST DIVISION	P	W	L	T	NR	Pts	Net RR
1 SUSSEX (1)	8	6	2	–	–	12	+1.25
2 Somerset (6)	8	5	2	–	1	11	+1.14
3 Worcestershire (7)	8	5	2	–	1	11	–0.33
4 Essex (–)	8	5	3	–	–	10	+0.33
5 Hampshire (2)	8	4	4	–	–	8	+0.23
6 Durham (3)	8	4	4	–	–	8	–0.35
7 Yorkshire (–)	8	2	5	–	1	5	–0.18
8 Gloucestershire (5)	8	2	5	–	1	5	–0.36
9 Nottinghamshire (4)	8	–	6	–	2	2	–2.41

SECOND DIVISION	P	W	L	T	NR	Pts	Net RR
1 WARWICKSHIRE (6)	8	5	–	1	2	13	+1.28
2 Middlesex (–)	8	5	1	–	2	12	+0.99
3 Kent (4)	8	4	3	–	1	9	–0.63
4 Northamptonshire (9)	8	3	2	1	2	9	+0.60
5 Lancashire (–)	8	3	3	–	2	8	–0.19
6 Glamorgan (3)	8	2	4	–	2	6	–0.36
7 Derbyshire (8)	8	2	4	–	2	6	–0.57
8 Leicestershire (7)	8	2	5	–	1	5	–0.23
9 Surrey (5)	8	2	6	–	–	4	–0.77

Final positions for that division in 2008 are shown in brackets. Win = 2 points. Tie (T)/No Result (NR) = 1 point.

Positions of counties finishing equal on points are decided by most wins or, if equal, the team that achieved the most points in the matches played between them; if still equal, the team with the higher net run rate (ie deducting from the average runs per over scored by that team in matches where a result was achieved, the average runs per over scored against that team). If still equal, the team with the higher number of wickets taken per balls bowled in completed matches will take precedence. If still equal, lots will be drawn.

STATISTICAL HIGHLIGHTS IN 2009

Highest total	286-3	Worcestershire v Notts	Nottingham
	286-6	Derbyshire v Surrey	Croydon
Lowest total	57	Nottinghamshire v Glos	Nottingham
Most runs	458 (ave 91.60)	N.R.D.Compton (Middlesex)	
Highest innings	150* A.D.Hales	Nottinghamshire v Worcs	Nottingham
Most sixes	10 D.J.Hussey	Nottinghamshire v Somerset	Nottingham
Highest partnership	204 M.J.Wood/D.J.Hussey	Nottinghamshire v Somerset	Nottingham
Most wickets	14 (ave 14.00)	B.J.Phillips (Somerset)	
	14 (ave 21.35)	R.J.Kirtley (Sussex)	
	14 (ave 23.64)	G.M.Andrew (Worcestershire)	
Best bowling	6-29 D.R.Smith	Sussex v Nottinghamshire	Hove
Most economical	8-4-10-3 A.J.Ireland	Gloucestershire v Notts	Nottingham
Most expensive	8-0-72-3 A.G.Botha	Warwickshire v Kent	Canterbury

222

PRO40/NATIONAL/SUNDAY LEAGUE CHAMPIONS

1969	Lancashire	1983	Yorkshire	1997	Warwickshire
1970	Lancashire	1984	Essex	1998	Lancashire
1971	Worcestershire	1985	Essex	1999	Lancashire
1972	Kent	1986	Hampshire	2000	Gloucestershire
1973	Kent	1987	Worcestershire	2001	Kent
1974	Leicestershire	1988	Worcestershire	2002	Glamorgan
1975	Hampshire	1989	Lancashire	2003	Surrey
1976	Kent	1990	Derbyshire	2004	Glamorgan
1977	Leicestershire	1991	Nottinghamshire	2005	Essex
1978	Hampshire	1992	Middlesex	2006	Essex
1979	Somerset	1993	Glamorgan	2007	Worcestershire
1980	Warwickshire	1994	Warwickshire	2008	Sussex
1981	Essex	1995	Kent	2009	Sussex
1982	Sussex	1996	Surrey		

PRINCIPAL PRO40 RECORDS 1969-2009

Highest Total		377-9	Somerset v Sussex	Hove	2003
Highest Total Batting Second		323-5	Sussex v Leics	Horsham	2004
Lowest Total		23	Middlesex v Yorks	Leeds	1974
Largest Victory (Runs)		220	Somerset v Glamorgan	Neath	1990
Highest Scores	203	A.D.Brown	Surrey v Hampshire	Guildford	1997
	191	D.S.Lehmann	Yorks v Notts	Scarborough	2001
	184	M.E.Trescothick	Somerset v Glos	Taunton	2008
	176	G.A.Gooch	Essex v Glamorgan	Southend	1983
	175*	I.T.Botham	Somerset v Northants	Wellingborough	1986
Fastest Hundred	44 balls	M.A.Ealham	Kent v Derbyshire	Maidstone	1995
Most Sixes (Inns)	13	I.T.Botham	Somerset v Northants	Wellingborough	1986
Highest Partnership for each Wicket					
1st	239	G.A.Gooch/B.R.Hardie	Essex v Notts	Nottingham	1985
2nd	302	M.E.Trescothick/C.Kieswetter	Somerset v Glos	Taunton	2008
3rd	228*	M.W.Goodwin/C.J.Adams	Sussex v Middlesex	Hove	2003
4th	219	C.G.Greenidge/C.L.Smith	Hampshire v Surrey	Southampton	1987
5th	221*	R.R.Sarwan/M.A.Hardinges	Glos v Lancashire	Manchester	2005
6th	167	C.L.Cairns/C.M.W.Read	Notts v Sussex	Nottingham	2003
7th	164	J.N.Snape/M.A.Hardinges	Glos v Notts	Nottingham	2001
8th	116*	N.D.Burns/P.A.J.DeFreitas	Leics v Northants	Leicester	2001
9th	105	D.G.Moir/R.W.Taylor	Derbyshire v Kent	Derby	1984
10th	82	G.Chapple/P.J.Martin	Lancashire v Worcs	Manchester	1996
Best Bowling	8-26	K.D.Boyce	Essex v Lancashire	Manchester	1971
	7-15	R.A.Hutton	Yorkshire v Worcs	Leeds	1969
	7-16	S.D.Thomas	Glamorgan v Surrey	Swansea	1998
	7-30	M.P.Bicknell	Surrey v Glamorgan	The Oval	1999
	7-39	A.Hodgson	Northants v Somerset	Northampton	1976
	7-41	A.N.Jones	Sussex v Notts	Nottingham	1986
Four Wkts in Four Balls		A.Ward	Derbyshire v Sussex	Derby	1970
		V.C.Drakes	Notts v Derbys	Nottingham	1999
Most Economical Analysis					
8-8-0-0		B.A.Langford	Somerset v Essex	Yeovil	1969
Most Expensive Analysis					
9-0-99-1		M.R.Strong	Northants v Glos	Cheltenham	2001
Most Wicket-Keeping Dismissals in an Innings					
7 (6ct, 1st)		R.W.Taylor	Derbyshire v Lancs	Manchester	1975
Most Catches in an Innings by a Fielder					
5		J.M.Rice	Hampshire v Warwicks	Southampton	1978
5		D.J.G.Sales	Northants v Essex	Northampton	2007

TWENTY20 CUP 2009

MIDLANDS/WALES/WEST	P	W	L	T	NR	Pts	Net RR
NORTHAMPTONSHIRE (2)	10	7	2	–	1	15	+0.58
WARWICKSHIRE (1)	10	7	3	–	–	14	+0.24
SOMERSET (4)	10	6	3	–	1	13	+0.42
Worcestershire (5)	10	5	5	–	–	10	+0.58
Gloucestershire (6)	10	2	8	–	–	4	–0.66
Glamorgan (3)	10	2	8	–	–	4	–1.03

NORTH	P	W	L	T	NR	Pts	Net RR
LANCASHIRE (2)	10	8	1	–	1	17	+1.11
DURHAM (1)	10	5	4	–	1	11	+0.16
Leicestershire (6)	10	5	5	–	–	10	–0.04
Nottinghamshire (4)	10	4	6	–	–	8	–0.01
Yorkshire (3)	10	4	6	–	–	8	–0.48
Derbyshire (5)	10	3	7	–	–	6	–0.61

SOUTH	P	W	L	T	NR	Pts	Net RR
KENT (3)	10	7	2	–	1	15	+0.64
SUSSEX (5)	10	7	3	–	–	14	+0.32
HAMPSHIRE (4)	10	6	4	–	–	12	+0.85
Essex (2)	10	5	4	–	1	11	+0.15
Surrey (6)	10	2	8	–	–	4	–0.66
Middlesex (1)	10	2	8	–	–	4	–1.19

(Last year's positions in brackets)

QUARTER-FINALS: SUSSEX beat Warwickshire by 38 runs at Hove.
KENT beat Durham by 56 runs at Canterbury.
SOMERSET beat Lancashire 5-1 in a bowl-out at Manchester.
NORTHANTS beat Hampshire by 13 runs at Northampton.

SEMI-FINALS: SUSSEX beat Northamptonshire by seven wickets at Birmingham.
SOMERSET beat Kent by seven wickets at Birmingham.

LEADING AGGREGATES AND RECORDS 2009

BATTING (350 runs)		M	I	NO	HS	Runs	Avge	100	50	R/100b	Sixes
I.J.L.Trott	(Warwicks)	11	11	3	86*	525	65.62	–	5	133.6	11
M.J.Lumb	(Hampshire)	11	11	1	124*	442	44.20	1	3	160.7	13
J.Allenby	(Leics)	10	10	1	110	432	48.00	1	3	139.8	20
Z.de Bruyn	(Somerset)	12	10	3	83*	391	55.85	–	3	112.7	8
A.W.Gale	(Yorkshire)	10	10	1	91	383	42.55	–	3	133.9	6
D.I.Stevens	(Kent)	11	11	5	77	356	59.33	–	4	144.1	15

BOWLING (15 wkts)		O	M	R	W	Avge	BB	4w	R/Over
A.C.Thomas	(Somerset)	40.2	–	310	18	17.22	3-31	–	7.69
R.J.Kirtley	(Sussex)	27.0	2	185	17	10.88	3- 9	–	6.85
M.E.Claydon	(Durham)	37.5	–	254	17	14.94	5-26	1	6.71
K.H.D.Barker	(Warwicks)	35.0	–	283	16	17.69	4-19	1	8.09
Azhar Mahmood	(Kent)	45.1	–	328	16	20.50	3-16	–	7.26
Yasir Arafat	(Sussex)	34.3	3	210	15	14.00	2-13	–	6.09
J.S.Patel	(Warwicks)	37.4	–	270	15	18.00	3-15	–	7.17

Highest total	222-4		Worcestershire v Glamorgan	Worcester
Highest innings	124*	M.J.Lumb	Hampshire v Essex	Southampton
Most sixes	8	J.Allenby	Leicestershire v Notts	Leicester
Best bowling	5-16	R.E.Watkins	Glamorgan v Gloucestershire	Cardiff
Most economical	4-1-10-1	S.J.Cook	Kent v Durham	Canterbury
Most expensive	4-0-56-0	T.Henderson	Middlesex v Kent	Lord's

2009 TWENTY20 CUP FINAL

SOMERSET v SUSSEX

At Edgbaston, Birmingham, on 15 August.
Result: **SUSSEX** won by 63 runs.
Toss: Somerset. Award: D.R.Smith.

SUSSEX		Runs	Balls	4/6	Fall
M.W.Goodwin	c Kieswetter b Willoughby	7	5	1	1- 16
L.J.Wright	run out (Kieswetter)	20	20	2	2- 48
R.J.Hamilton-Brown	lbw b Waller	25	22	4	3- 67
D.R.Smith	st Kieswetter b Waller	59	26	7/3	5-122
E.C.Joyce	b Trego	4	6	–	4- 80
* M.H.Yardy	b Suppiah	4	6	–	6-126
C.D.Nash	b Thomas	28	22	3	7-172
Yasir Arafat	not out	20	13	3	
† A.J.Hodd					
W.A.T.Beer					
R.J.Kirtley					
Extras	(B 1, LB 1, W 3)	5			
Total	(7 wkts; 20 overs)	**172**			

SOMERSET		Runs	Balls	4/6	Fall
M.E.Trescothick	c Hamilton-Brown b Kirtley	33	15	3/3	1- 43
* J.L.Langer	b Arafat	15	14	2	2- 51
Z.de Bruyn	c Yardy b Wright	22	32	1	6-108
J.C.Hildreth	c Hamilton-Brown b Beer	1	7	–	3- 57
† C.Kieswetter	st Hodd b Beer	1	8	–	4- 63
P.D.Trego	c Smith b Hamilton-Brown	27	14	2/2	5-104
A.V.Suppiah	c Goodwin b Kirtley	2	5	–	8-109
B.J.Phillips	c Hamilton-Brown b Kirtley	1	4	–	7-109
A.C.Thomas	c Yardy b Arafat	0	4	–	10-109
M.T.C.Waller	run out (Hodd)	0	0	–	9-109
C.M.Willoughby	not out	0	1	–	
Extras	(LB 5, W 2)	7			
Total	(17.2 overs)	**109**			

SOMERSET	O	M	R	W	SUSSEX	O	M	R	W
Thomas	4	0	37	1	Wright	3	0	25	1
Willoughby	4	0	27	1	Yasir Arafat	2.2	0	14	2
Phillips	3	0	36	0	Kirtley	2	1	9	3
Trego	4	0	26	1	Smith	1	0	3	0
Waller	3	0	33	2	Yardy	4	0	17	0
Suppiah	2	0	11	1	Beer	4	0	29	2
					Hamilton-Brown	1	0	7	1

Umpires: R.K.Illingworth and R.A.Kettleborough

TWENTY20 CUP WINNERS

2003	Surrey	2006	Leicestershire	2008	Middlesex
2004	Leicestershire	2007	Kent	2009	Sussex
2005	Somerset				

TWENTY20 CUP RECORDS 2003-09

Highest Total	250-3		Somerset v Glos	Taunton	2006
Lowest Total	67		Sussex v Hampshire	Hove	2004
Highest Scores	152*	G.R.Napier	Essex v Sussex	Chelmsford	2008
	141*	C.L.White	Somerset v Worcs	Worcester	2006
	124*	M.J.Lumb	Hampshire v Essex	Southampton	2009
	116*	G.A.Hick	Worcs v Northants	Luton	2004
	116*	I.J.Thomas	Glamorgan v Somerset	Taunton	2004
	116*	C.L.White	Somerset v Glos	Taunton	2006
Most Sixes (Innings)	16	G.R.Napier	Essex v Sussex	Chelmsford	2008

Highest Partnership for each Wicket

1st	175	V.S.Solanki/G.A.Hick	Worcs v Northants	Kidderminster	2007
2nd	186	J.L.Langer/C.L.White	Somerset v Glos	Taunton	2006
3rd	121	S.R.Patel/D.J.Hussey	Notts v Northants	Nottingham	2006
	121	H.D.Ackerman/P.A.Nixon	Leics v Derbys	Derby	2007
	121	J.A.Rudolph/A.McGrath	Yorkshire v Leics	Leicester	2009
4th	139	M.R.Ramprakash/R.Clarke	Surrey v Glos	Bristol	2006
5th	117	M.van Jaarsveld/M.J.Walker	Kent v Leics	Leicester	2006
6th	98*	R.W.T.Key/M.J.Walker	Kent v Middlesex	Beckenham	2008
7th	67	O.A.C.Banks/B.J.Phillips	Somerset v Northants	Northampton	2008
8th	68	M.W.Alleyne/J.Lewis	Glos v Glamorgan	Cardiff	2005
9th	59*	G.Chapple/P.J.Martin	Lancs v Leics	Leicester	2003
10th	59	H.H.Streak/J.E.Anyon	Warwicks v Worcs	Birmingham	2005

Best Analyses

6-21	A.J.Hall	Northants v Worcs	Northampton	2008
6-24	T.J.Murtagh	Surrey v Middlesex	Lord's	2005
5-11	Mushtaq Ahmed	Sussex v Essex	Hove	2005
5-13	M.Kartik	Middlesex v Leics	Lord's	2007
5-14	A.D.Mascarenhas	Hampshire v Sussex	Hove	2004
5-16	R.E.Watkins	Glamorgan v Glos	Cardiff	2009
5-19	N.M.Carter	Warwicks v Worcs	Birmingham	2008

Hat-Tricks

A.D.Mascarenhas	Hampshire v Sussex	Hove	2004
D.G.Cork	Lancs v Notts	Manchester	2004
J.E.Anyon	Warwicks v Somerset	Birmingham	2005
J.N.Snape	Leics v Yorkshire	Leicester	2007
R.McLaren	Kent v Glos	Birmingham	2007
N.D.Doshi	Derbys v Durham	Chester-le-St	2008
J.Allenby	Leics v Lancs	Manchester	2008
D.P.Nannes	Middlesex v Essex	Chelmsford	2008
I.D.Fisher	Worcestershire v Glos	Worcester	2009

Most Economical Innings Analyses (Qualification: 4 overs)

4-1-6-2	J.Louw	Northants v Warwicks	Birmingham	2004
4-0-6-1	M.W.Alleyne	Glos v Worcs	Worcester	2005
4-1-7-1	R.S.C.Martin-Jenkins	Sussex v Hampshire	Hove	2004
4-1-7-4	N.Killeen	Durham v Leics	Leicester	2004
4-0-7-0	R.J.Sidebottom	Notts v Surrey	Nottingham	2006

Most Maiden Overs in an Innings

4-2-9-1	M.Morkel	Kent v Surrey	Beckenham	2007

Most Expensive Innings Analyses

4-0-67-1	R.J.Kirtley	Sussex v Essex	Chelmsford	2008
4-0-65-2	M.J.Hoggard	Yorkshire v Lancs	Leeds	2005
4-0-63-1	R.J.Kirtley	Sussex v Surrey	Hove	2004
4-0-61-0	A.P.Davis	Glamorgan v Glos	Bristol	2006

Most Wicket-Keeping Dismissals in an Innings

5 (5 ct)	M.J.Prior	Sussex v Middlesex	Richmond	2006
5 (4 ct, 1 st)	G.L.Brophy	Yorkshire v Durham	Chester-le-Street	2008

Most Catches in an Innings by a Fielder

4	D.Pretorius	Warwickshire v Glamorgan	Swansea	2005
4	W.R.Smith	Nottinghamshire v Surrey	Nottingham	2006
4	D.J.G.Sales	Northamptonshire v Worcs	Northampton	2008
4	G.D.Elliot	Surrey v Kent	The Oval	2009

YOUNG CRICKETER OF THE YEAR

This annual award, made by The Cricket Writers' Club, is currently restricted to players qualified for England, Andrew Symonds meeting that requirement at the time of his award, and under the age of 23 on 1st May. In 1986 their ballot resulted in a dead heat. Up to 11 March 2010 their selections have gained a tally of 2,077 international Test match caps (shown in brackets).

1950	R.Tattersall (16)	1981	M.W.Gatting (79)
1951	P.B.H.May (66)	1982	N.G.Cowans (19)
1952	F.S.Trueman (67)	1983	N.A.Foster (29)
1953	M.C.Cowdrey (114)	1984	R.J.Bailey (4)
1954	P.J.Loader (13)	1985	D.V.Lawrence (5)
1955	K.F.Barrington (82)	1986 {	A.A.Metcalfe
1956	B.Taylor		J.J.Whitaker (1)
1957	M.J.Stewart (8)	1987	R.J.Blakey (2)
1958	A.C.D.Ingleby-Mackenzie	1988	M.P.Maynard (4)
1959	G.Pullar (28)	1989	N.Hussain (96)
1960	D.A.Allen (39)	1990	M.A.Atherton (115)
1961	P.H.Parfitt (37)	1991	M.R.Ramprakash (52)
1962	P.J.Sharpe (12)	1992	I.D.K.Salisbury (15)
1963	G.Boycott (108)	1993	M.N.Lathwell (2)
1964	J.M.Brearley (39)	1994	J.P.Crawley (37)
1965	A.P.E.Knott (95)	1995	A.Symonds (26 – Australia)
1966	D.L.Underwood (86)	1996	C.E.W.Silverwood (6)
1967	A.W.Greig (58)	1997	B.C.Hollioake (2)
1968	R.M.H.Cottam (4)	1998	A.Flintoff (79)
1969	A.Ward (5)	1999	A.J.Tudor (10)
1970	C.M.Old (46)	2000	P.J.Franks
1971	J.Whitehouse	2001	O.A.Shah (6)
1972	D.R.Owen-Thomas	2002	R.Clarke (2)
1973	M.Hendrick (30)	2003	J.M.Anderson (46)
1974	P.H.Edmonds (51)	2004	I.R.Bell (53)
1975	A.Kennedy	2005	A.N.Cook (52)
1976	G.Miller (34)	2006	S.C.J.Broad (26)
1977	I.T.Botham (102)	2007	A.U.Rashid
1978	D.I.Gower (117)	2008	R.S.Bopara (10)
1979	P.W.G.Parker (1)	2009	J.W.A.Taylor
1980	G.R.Dilley (41)		

THE PROFESSIONAL CRICKETERS' ASSOCIATION
PLAYER OF THE YEAR

Founded in 1967, the Professional Cricketers' Association introduced this award, decided by their membership, in 1970. The NatWest-sponsored award is presented at the PCA's Annual Awards Dinner at Old Billingsgate. Only John Lever and Andrew Flintoff have won the award in successive years.

1970 {	M.J.Procter	1983	K.S.McEwan	1997	S.P.James
	J.D.Bond	1984	R.J.Hadlee	1998	M.B.Loye
1971	L.R.Gibbs	1985	N.V.Radford	1999	S.G.Law
1972	A.M.E.Roberts	1986	C.A.Walsh	2000	M.E.Trescothick
1973	P.G.Lee	1987	R.J.Hadlee	2001	D.P.Fulton
1974	B.Stead	1988	G.A.Hick	2002	M.P.Vaughan
1975	Zaheer Abbas	1989	S.J.Cook	2003	Mushtaq Ahmed
1976	P.G.Lee	1990	G.A.Gooch	2004	A.Flintoff
1977	M.J.Procter	1991	Waqar Younis	2005	A.Flintoff
1978	J.K.Lever	1992	C.A.Walsh	2006	M.R.Ramprakash
1979	J.K.Lever	1993	S.L.Watkin	2007	O.D.Gibson
1980	R.D.Jackman	1994	B.C.Lara	2008	M.van Jaarsveld
1981	R.J.Hadlee	1995	D.G.Cork	2009	M.E.Trescothick
1982	M.D.Marshall	1996	P.V.Simmons		

These averages involve the 482 players who appeared in the 171 first-class matches played by 27 teams in England and Wales during the 2009 season.

'Cap' denotes the season in which the player was awarded a 1st XI cap by the county he represented in 2009. If he played for more than one county in 2009, the county(ies) who awarded him his cap is (are) underlined. Durham abolished both their capping and 'awards' system after the 2005 season. Gloucestershire now cap players on first-class debut. Worcestershire now award county colours when players make their Championship debut.

Team abbreviations: A – Australia(ns); CU – Cambridge University/Cambridge UCCE; De – Derbyshire; Du – Durham; DU – Durham UCCE; E – England (XI); EL – England Lions; Ex – Essex; Gm – Glamorgan; Gs – Gloucestershire; H – Hampshire; K – Kent; La – Lancashire; Le – Leicestershire; LU – Loughborough UCCE; M – Middlesex; MCC – Marylebone Cricket Club; Nh – Northamptonshire; Nt – Nottinghamshire; OU – Oxford University/Oxford UCCE; Sm – Somerset; Sy – Surrey; Sx – Sussex; Wa – Warwickshire; WI – West Indies/Indians; Wo – Worcestershire; Y – Yorkshire.

† Left-handed batsman. Cap: a dash (–) denotes a non-county player. A blank denotes uncapped by his current county.

BATTING AND FIELDING

	Cap	M	I	NO	HS	Runs	Avge	100	50	Ct/St
† E.Abel (OU)	–	1	1	–	26	26	26.00	–	–	1
H.D.Ackerman (Le)	2005	12	21	1	180	827	41.35	1	5	5
A.R.Adams (Nt)	2007	11	13	1	84	300	25.00	–	1	13
† J.H.K.Adams (H)	2006	17	30	4	147	1351	51.96	3	10	17
S.J.Adshead (Gs)	2004	7	10	1	156*	367	40.77	2	–	22/1
† U.Afzaal (Sy)	2009	16	28	6	204*	1269	40.77	3	7	3
R.G.Aga (Sx)		3	3	1	24	27	13.50	–	–	–
J.S.Ahmed (Ex)		1	1	–	5	5	5.00	–	–	–
M.Ahmed (Wo)		1	2	2	0*	0	–	–	–	–
Kabir Ali (MCC/Wo)	2002	5	8	2	30	81	13.50	–	–	3
Kadeer Ali (Gs)	2005	16	28	4	90	834	34.75	–	4	10
M.Ali (OU)	–	1	1	–			–	–	–	–
† M.M.Ali (Wo)	2007	17	30	4	153	803	28.67	2	3	4
J.Allenby (Gm/Le)		12	18	2	137	662	41.37	1	6	10
T.R.Ambrose (EL/Wa)	2007	18	24	2	153	814	37.00	3	4	43/2
H.M.Amla (Ex)		3	5	1	181	410	102.50	2	1	1
† J.M.Anderson (E/La)	2003	9	11	3	29	123	15.37	–	–	4
† G.M.Andrew (Wo)	2008	10	16	5	92*	391	35.54	–	3	–
A.S.Ansari (CU)	–	3	3	1	132	140	70.00	1	–	1
† J.E.Anyon (Sy/Wa)		4	5	4	15*	39	39.00	–	–	–
C.P.Ashling (Gm)		1	1	–	12	12	12.00	–	–	–
A.Ashok (CU)	–	1	2	1	112	131	131.00	1	–	1
P.P.Ashton (CU)	–	1	1	–	4	4	4.00	–	–	1
J.J.Atkinson (DU)	–	2	4	–	16	21	5.25	–	–	2
Azeem Rafiq (Y)		4	5	–	100	117	23.40	1	–	1
Azhar Mahmood (K)	2008	4	6	–	35	78	13.00	–	–	–
† M.Baer (LU)	–	3	2	2	4*	4	–	–	–	–
J.M.Bairstow (Y)		12	19	6	84*	592	45.53	–	6	21
F.B.Baker (CU)	–	1					–	–	–	–
G.C.Baker (LU)	–	2	3	1	66	143	71.50	–	2	1
L.S.Baker (WI)		4	5	3	17	32	16.00	–	–	–
D.J.Balcombe (H)		3	3	–	10	10	3.33	–	–	–
A.H.Ball (OU)	–	2	4	–	5	7	1.75	–	–	3

F-C	Cap	M	I	NO	HS	Runs	Avge	100	50	Ct/St
E.C.Ballard (CU)	–	2	2	–	33	33	16.50	–	–	–
† V.Banerjee (Gs)	2006	7	12	3	16	71	7.88	–	–	2
O.A.C.Banks (Sm)		6	7	2	53	156	31.20	–	1	1
† K.H.D.Barker (Wa)		3	4	–	23	28	7.00	–	–	–
G.J.Batty (Wo)	2002	11	16	–	46	175	10.93	–	–	9
J.N.Batty (Sy)	2001	16	26	–	120	937	36.03	2	1	46/4
I.R.Bell (E/EL/MCC/Wa)	2001	19	30	3	172	1185	43.88	4	6	15
C.C.Benham (H)		6	9	2	111	316	45.14	2	1	7
D.M.Benkenstein (Du)	2005	18	24	–	181	1168	48.66	5	4	10
S.J.Benn (WI)		4	7	1	35	86	14.33	–	–	1
J.G.E.Benning (Le/Sy)		7	12	2	72	282	28.20	–	1	2
G.K.Berg (M)		13	23	2	98	668	31.80	–	7	9
D.E.Bernard (WI)		2	3	1	58	80	40.00	–	1	1
† I.D.Blackwell (Du)		18	24	3	158	949	45.19	2	6	4
A.J.Blake (K)		4	5	–	47	125	25.00	–	–	1
† N.Boje (Nh)	2008	15	25	5	98	801	40.05	–	8	7
R.S.Bopara (E/Ex)	2005	9	15	2	201	772	59.38	4	1	7
P.M.Borrington (LU)		3	3	–	105	174	58.00	1	–	–
S.G.Borthwick (Du)		1	1	–	26*	26	–	–	–	–
† A.G.Botha (Wa)		14	19	2	64	444	26.11	–	2	5
M.D.Bott (CU)		1	1	–	10	10	10.00	–	–	2
† M.A.G.Boyce (Le)		15	29	2	98	738	27.33	–	5	5
D.P.Bradshaw (OU)		3	3	–	38	64	21.33	–	–	–
† W.D.Bragg (Gm)		9	12	–	92	367	30.58	–	2	4
R.M.R.Brathwaite (CU)	–	4	2	–	2	2	1.00	–	–	–
G.R.Breese (Du)	2005	2	2	–	48	62	31.00	–	–	3
T.T.Bresnan (E/EL/MCC/Y)	2006	14	17	2	97	386	25.73	–	1	7
D.R.Briggs (H)		3	3	–	36	37	12.33	–	–	1
† S.C.J.Broad (E/Nt)		9	13	3	61	382	38.20	–	3	3
J.A.Brooks (Nh)		3	3	3	10*	20	–	–	–	1
G.L.Brophy (Y)	2008	14	22	5	99	748	44.00	–	6	37/2
A.D.Brown (Nt)		16	24	3	148	849	40.42	1	6	18
F.A.Brown (CU)	–	2	2	–	30	31	15.50	–	–	1
J.F.Brown (Nt)		1	–							
† K.R.Brown (La)		2	4	–	19	40	10.00	–	–	5
M.J.Brown (Sy)		16	28	1	120	992	36.74	2	4	7
T.E.Bryan (OU)	–	1	2	–	16	17	8.50	–	–	–
N.J.S.Buchanan (OU)	–	1	2	1	7	8	8.00	–	–	–
N.L.Buck (Le)		4	5	2	24*	29	9.66	–	–	1
T.G.Burrows (H)		6	7	1	32	78	13.00	–	–	14/1
D.A.Burton (M)		2	4	2	2*	3	1.50	–	–	–
† M.A.Butcher (Sy)	1996	5	8	2	65	251	41.83	–	2	10
J.E.L.Buttleman (DU)	–	3	6	–	33	67	11.16	–	–	1
J.C.Buttler (Sm)		1	1	–	30	30	30.00	–	–	1
A.R.Caddick (Sm)	1992	5	3	1	11*	15	7.50	–	–	1
† M.A.Carberry (H)	2006	12	21	3	204	1251	69.50	4	8	6
A.Carter (Nt)		2	1	–	4	4	4.00	–	–	–
† N.M.Carter (Wa)	2005	9	13	–	67	318	24.46	–	2	–
M.A.Chambers (Ex)		7	8	5	19	57	19.00	–	–	1
† S.Chanderpaul (Du/WI)		9	13	5	201*	683	85.37	3	2	3
U.S.Chandra (CU)		1	–							
G.Chapple (La)	1994	11	14	2	89	390	32.50	–	3	3

F-C	Cap	M	I	NO	HS	Runs	Avge	100	50	Ct/St
† P.P.Chawla (Sx)		6	10	3	102*	206	29.42	1	–	2
M.J.Chilton (La)	2002	16	23	6	114	891	52.41	2	6	15
V.Chopra (Ex)		12	21	–	88	537	25.57	–	5	6
S.H.Choudhry (Wa)		1	1	–	75	75	75.00	–	1	–
J.L.Clare (De)		5	5	–	6	13	2.60	–	–	1
S.R.Clark (A)	–	4	4	1	32	48	16.00	–	–	–
M.J.Clarke (A)	–	6	10	1	136	532	59.11	2	3	9
R.Clarke (Wa)		14	18	1	112	631	37.11	1	5	25
† M.E.Claydon (Du)		12	12	1	38	110	10.00	–	–	3
S.J.Cliff (Le)		1	1	–	26	26	26.00	–	–	–
J.J.Cobb (Le)		14	26	–	95	510	19.61	–	4	4
† K.J.Coetzer (Du)		6	9	1	107	284	35.50	1	–	7
M.T.Coles (K)		2	2	–	16	30	15.00	–	–	–
P.D.Collingwood (E)	–	8	13	2	79*	413	37.54	–	5	7
P.T.Collins (Sy)		5	8	3	23	49	9.80	–	–	1
C.D.Collymore (Sx)		14	17	5	23	89	7.41	–	–	2
N.R.D.Compton (M)	2006	14	28	2	178	860	33.07	2	3	8
† A.N.Cook (E/Ex)	2005	17	30	3	160	1168	43.25	2	6	20
M.P.Cook (CU)	–	1	1	–	3	3	3.00	–	–	–
S.J.Cook (K)	2007	13	13	4	60*	220	24.44	–	1	–
D.G.Cork (H)	2009	12	15	2	52	290	22.30	–	1	18
† M.J.Cosgrove (Gm)		10	15	2	175	780	60.00	3	5	4
D.A.Cosker (Gm)	2000	8	11	3	46*	107	13.37	–	–	5
R.G.Coughtrie (OU)	–	2	2	–	27	31	15.50	–	–	2
O.B.Cox (Wo)	2009	1	1	–	61	61	61.00	–	1	4/1
J.P.Crawley (H)	2002	8	14	3	81*	308	28.00	–	2	8
R.D.B.Croft (Gm)	1992	17	21	4	121	574	33.76	1	1	4
S.J.Croft (La)		9	14	2	79	360	30.00	–	2	6
S.P.Crook (Nh)		2	3	–	55	84	28.00	–	1	2
C.D.Crowe (Le)		4	7	2	41*	114	22.80	–	–	–
L.M.Daggett (Nh)		5	4	–	2	3	0.75	–	–	1
J.W.M.Dalrymple (Gm)		17	23	3	128	1009	50.45	3	5	17
Danish Kaneria (Ex)	2004	11	15	2	37	158	12.15	–	–	5
A.M.Davies (Du)	2005	9	8	4	16*	37	9.25	–	–	2
† S.M.Davies (EL/Wo)	2005	15	28	3	126	1023	40.92	2	5	40/2
L.A.Dawson (H)		15	23	4	69	571	30.05	–	4	13
R.K.J.Dawson (Gs)	2008	7	10	–	50	254	25.40	–	1	12
Z.de Bruyn (Sm)	2008	16	25	3	106	686	31.18	1	6	3
J.L.Denly (EL/K)	2008	11	17	1	123	680	42.50	3	2	7
† N.Deonarine (WI)	–	2	2	–	15	15	7.50	–	–	1
J.W.Dernbach (Sy)		14	19	6	19	138	10.61	–	–	1
N.J.Dexter (M)		10	19	2	146	709	41.70	2	2	15
H.H.Dippenaar (Le)	2008	17	31	5	143	1121	43.11	2	8	6
† M.J.Di Venuto (Du)		17	27	6	254*	1654	78.76	6	6	23
P.G.Dixey (DU)	–	3	6	–	103	142	23.66	1	–	8/2
F.du Plessis (La)	13	20	3	86*	531	31.23	–	5	8	
W.J.Durston (Sm)		1	1	–	54*	54	54.00	–	1	–
J.du Toit (Le)		2	3	1	100*	142	71.00	1	–	1
M.A.Ealham (Nt)	2004	14	20	7	70*	493	37.92	–	2	6
F.H.Edwards (WI)	–	2	4	1	11	27	9.00	–	–	–
P.D.Edwards (K)		5	4	2	5	5	2.50	–	–	1
G.D.Elliott (Sy)		1	2	–	22	23	11.50	–	–	2

F-C	Cap	M	I	NO	HS	Runs	Avge	100	50	Ct/St
† S.M.Ervine (H)	2005	15	22	2	114	832	41.60	3	3	6
A.C.Evans (LU)	–	2	–							
D.Evans (M)		1	–							
L.J.Evans (Sy)		2	4	–	9	23	5.75	–	–	–
† R.F.Evans (LU)	–	2	2	–	12	12	6.00	–	–	1
R.S.Ferley (K)		3	1	–	17	17	17.00	–	–	1
S.T.Finn (M)	2009	14	22	4	24*	107	5.94	–	–	4
† I.D.Fisher (Wo)		1	–							
L.J.Fletcher (Nt)		8	8	3	92	121	24.20	–	1	–
A.Flintoff (E/La)	1998	7	12	1	74	288	26.18	–	2	5
G.W.Flower (Ex)	2005	1	1	–	9	9	9.00	–	–	–
M.H.A.Footitt (Nt)		1	1	–	9*	9	–	–	–	–
J.S.Foster (Ex/MCC)	2001	17	27	2	103*	980	39.20	1	6	61/4
P.J.Foster (DU)	–	3	6	–	24	48	8.00	–	–	5
J.E.C.Franklin (Gs)	2004	14	22	4	109	904	50.22	3	4	6
† P.J.Franks (Nt)	1999	5	6	–	64	201	33.50	–	2	1
T.Frost (Wa)	1999	15	23	1	105	598	27.18	1	2	8
† A.W.Gale (Y)	2008	17	26	1	121	921	36.84	2	5	6
D.J.Gale (DU)	–	3	6	6	11*	22	–	–	–	2
J.E.R.Gallian (Ex)	2008	7	13	1	125	245	20.41	1	–	5
J.S.Gatting (Sx)		4	6	–	152	310	51.66	1	1	2
† C.H.Gayle (WI)	–	2	4	–	54	101	25.25	–	1	1
H.H.Gibbs (Gm)		5	7	–	96	259	37.00	–	2	7
A.P.R.Gidman (Gs)	2004	15	23	–	176	1028	44.69	4	4	9
J.C.Glover (DU)	–	3	6	–	14	27	6.50	–	–	–
† B.A.Godleman (M)		5	9	–	48	160	17.77	–	–	3
M.W.Goodwin (Sx)	2001	16	27	3	344*	800	33.33	1	2	6
† C.M.Grammer (CU)	–	4	6	1	64	113	22.60	–	1	2
S.K.Gray (CU)	–	3	3	1	19	28	14.00	–	–	7/1
† D.A.Griffiths (H)		10	13	4	20*	45	5.00	–	–	–
T.D.Groenewald (De)		9	11	1	50	194	19.40	–	1	2
P.R.Groves (LU)	–	3	2	1	52	59	59.00	–	1	–
H.F.Gurney (Le)		10	11	6	24*	54	10.80	–	–	2
B.J.Haddin (A)	–	5	8	1	121	310	44.28	1	1	17
A.D.Hales (Nt)		7	12	1	78	447	40.63	–	4	3
A.J.Hall (Nh)	2009	16	25	2	159	1161	50.47	2	6	16
R.J.Hamilton-Brown (Sx)		5	8	2	171*	311	51.83	2	–	5
† A.Harinath (LU/Sy)		6	9	–	57	219	24.33	–	1	–
† B.W.Harmison (Du)		1	1	–	0	0	0.00	–	–	1
S.J.Harmison (Du/E/EL)	1999	17	15	5	25*	79	7.90	–	–	2
G.M.Harper (DU)	–	1	2	–	0	0	0.00	–	–	–
A.J.Harris (Le)		16	19	3	22*	143	8.93	–	–	1
J.A.R.Harris (Gm)		14	16	3	76*	256	19.69	–	1	1
R.J.Harris (Sy)		2	2	–	94	98	49.00	–	1	1
D.S.Harrison (Gm)	2006	8	7	2	51	98	19.60	–	1	2
P.W.Harrison (Nh)		2	3	–	32	53	17.66	–	–	–
N.M.Hauritz (A)	–	5	5	2	24	68	22.66	–	–	1
P.L.Hayes (LU)	–	2	1	–	38	38	38.00	–	–	–
† M.Hayward (De)		5	5	2	6	14	4.66	–	–	1
C.W.Henderson (Le)	2004	10	13	2	79*	241	21.90	–	1	1
† H.M.R.K.B.Herath (Sy)		3	5	1	52*	80	20.00	–	1	–
J.C.Hildreth (Sm)	2007	15	23	2	303*	934	44.47	2	4	10

231

F-C	Cap	M	I	NO	HS	Runs	Avge	100	50	Ct/St
B.W.Hilfenhaus (A)	–	5	6	4	20	40	20.00	–	–	–
† C.M.M.Hill (OU)	–	1	2	–	29	48	24.00	–	–	–
† W.W.Hinds (De)	2009	16	26	2	148	841	35.04	2	2	7
J.B.Hockley (K)		5	8	2	72	240	40.00	–	2	5
A.J.Hodd (Sx)		16	23	3	101	499	24.95	1	2	25/3
L.J.Hodgson (Y)		1	1	–	32	32	32.00	–	–	–
G.P.Hodnett (Gs)	2005	1	1	–	31	31	31.00	–	–	–
† K.W.Hogg (La)		14	15	2	69	333	25.61	–	2	2
M.J.Hoggard (Y)	2000	16	17	4	56*	195	15.00	–	1	5
C.D.Hopkinson (Sx)	2008	9	13	1	139	443	36.91	2	–	2
P.J.Horton (La)	2007	17	30	2	173	881	31.46	2	4	16
D.M.Housego (M)		3	6	–	34	86	14.33	–	–	2
† B.H.N.Howgego (Nh)		6	11	1	47	219	21.90	–	–	3
† P.J.Hughes (A/M)		7	12	1	195	724	65.81	3	3	6
I.D.Hunter (De)		7	7	3	47	129	32.25	–	–	2
G.M.Hussain (Gs)	2009	1	2	–	8	16	8.00	–	–	1
D.J.Hussey (Nt)	2004	3	5	–	189	407	81.40	2	1	5
M.E.K.Hussey (A)		7	12	2	150	572	57.20	2	4	7
Imran Arif (Wo)	2008	9	13	7	35	81	13.50	–	–	4
Imran Tahir (H)	2009	12	15	4	77*	206	18.72	–	1	4
A.J.Ireland (Gs)	2007	7	7	2	16	21	4.20	–	–	3
A.Javid (Wa)		3	6	–	21	55	9.16	–	–	3
W.I.Jefferson (Nt)		4	6	–	133	181	30.16	1	–	7
† M.G.Johnson (A)		7	8	–	63	166	20.75	–	1	1
R.M.Johnson (Wa)		1	2	–	22	33	16.50	–	–	7
† P.R.A.Johnston (DU)		3	6	–	73	99	16.50	–	1	2
G.O.Jones (K)	2003	17	26	–	156	1345	51.73	5	6	41/3
H.D.Jones (LU)		3	2	–	2	2	1.00	–	–	1
P.S.Jones (De/K)		12	13	3	54*	225	22.50	–	2	5
R.A.Jones (Wo)	2007	7	11	2	53*	209	23.22	–	1	3
C.J.Jordan (Sy)		8	10	3	42	213	30.42	–	–	4
R.H.Joseph (K)		4	5	2	9*	11	3.66	–	–	–
A.J.P.Joslin (CU)		1	2	–	33	62	31.00	–	–	1
† E.C.Joyce (Sx)		15	24	1	183	945	41.08	3	3	12
† M.Kartik (M)	2007	10	19	5	62*	336	24.00	–	2	11
† S.M.Katich (A)		7	11	–	122	498	45.27	1	2	10
† G.Keedy (La)	2000	17	16	7	18	63	7.00	–	–	–
J.M.Kemp (K)	2006	14	21	3	183	780	43.33	2	3	30
A.N.Kervezee (Wo)	2009	8	14	–	66	381	27.21	–	2	2
R.W.T.Key (EL/K/MCC)	2001	17	28	4	270*	1209	50.37	4	3	15
M.F.Khalid (OU)		1	–	–				–	–	–
A.Khan (K)		11	12	3	62*	153	17.00	–	1	2
C.Kieswetter (Sm)	2009	16	24	3	153	1242	59.14	4	7	48
D.King (OU)		1	2	–	1	2	1.00	–	–	2
S.J.King (Sy)		2	2	–	8	8	4.00	–	–	–
S.P.Kirby (Gs)	2005	16	22	8	27	157	11.21	–	–	2
R.J.Kirtley (Sx)	1998	3	3	1	33	45	22.50	–	–	2
† F.A.Klokker (De)		2	4	1	32*	53	17.66	–	–	3
W.A.Klopper (OU)		1	2	–	18	24	12.00	–	–	–
J.P.T.Knappett (Wo)	2007	2	2	1	4*	5	5.00	–	–	5
G.J-P.Kruger (Gm)		13	13	7	28*	91	15.16	–	–	2
N.Kruger (OU)	–	1	2	–	98	124	62.00	–	1	2

232

F-C	Cap	M	I	NO	HS	Runs	Avge	100	50	Ct/St
G.J.Kruis (Y)	2006	9	9	2	37	131	18.71	–	–	1
† J.L.Langer (Sm)	2007	15	21	2	122*	831	43.73	2	4	17
S.G.Law (De)		2	4	–	29	39	9.75	–	–	2
M.A.K.Lawson (De)		6	5	2	24*	75	25.00	–	–	3
V.V.S.Laxman (La)	2009	11	16	3	135	857	65.92	4	4	15
B.Lee (A)		1	1	–	6	6	6.00	–	–	–
J.E.Lee (Y)		1	1	–	2	2	2.00	–	–	1
N.T.Lee (CU)	–	3	4	3	79*	169	169.00	–	2	1
R.J.H.Lett (OU)	–	3	4	1	76*	138	46.00	–	1	1
J.Lewis (Gs)	1998	15	22	6	61*	358	22.37	–	2	5
M.F.Lewis (OU)	–	1	1	1	74*	74	–	–	1	–
† J.D.Lewry (Sx)	1996	6	10	4	25	51	8.50	–	–	1
T.E.Linley (Sy)		5	6	1	36	98	19.60	–	–	1
R.J.Logan (Sy)		1	2	–	6	6	3.00	–	–	–
† A.B.London (M)		4	8	1	68	190	27.14	–	2	1
† J.D.S.Lotay (CU)	–	3	3	–	23	44	14.66	–	–	1
M.B.Loye (La)	2003	14	22	4	151*	996	55.33	2	6	4
D.S.Lucas (Nh)	2009	16	24	7	55*	312	18.35	–	1	5
† M.J.Lumb (H)	2008	16	24	1	219	1006	50.73	2	5	10
† T.Lungley (De/La)	2007	6	6	2	33	99	24.75	–	–	4
A.A.Lynch (LU)	–	3	3	–	61	96	32.00	–	1	2
† A.Lyth (Y)		5	8	–	71	240	30.00	–	2	1
A.B.McDonald (A)	–	1	2	–	75	107	53.50	–	1	–
A.McGrath (Y)	1999	17	27	1	211	871	33.50	2	2	11
B.T.McKerchar (OU)	–	1	2	–	0	0	0.00	–	–	–
† R.McLaren (K)	2007	7	8	1	44	127	18.14	–	–	1
S.K.MacLennan (CU)	–	1	1	–	3	3	3.00	–	–	–
C.S.MacLeod (Wa)		1	1	–	26	26	26.00	–	–	3
D.L.Maddy (Wa)	2007	2	3	–	36	61	20.33	–	–	2
W.L.Madsen (De)		9	16	2	170*	809	57.78	3	3	8
S.I.Mahmood (EL/La/MCC)	2007	14	14	1	30*	100	7.69	–	–	6
C.C.Malan (LU)	–	3	3	–	24	32	10.66	–	–	–
† D.J.Malan (M)		15	28	3	88	930	37.20	–	8	19
G.A.Manou (A)	–	2	4	2	59*	80	40.00	–	1	8
H.J.H.Marshall (Gs)	2006	16	26	2	158	844	35.16	1	5	13
† J.Martin (OU)	–	3	4	–	38	95	23.75	–	–	1
R.S.C.Martin-Jenkins (Sx)	2000	13	17	2	67	299	19.93	–	1	5
A.D.Mascarenhas (H)	1998	10	11	2	108	254	28.22	1	–	4
M.S.Mason (Wo)	2002	14	23	6	28	207	12.17	–	–	6
D.D.Masters (Ex)	2008	15	16	1	67	341	22.73	–	2	7
† J.K.Maunders (Ex)		11	18	–	150	621	34.50	1	3	12
T.L.Maynard (Gm)		6	7	1	51*	115	19.16	–	1	6
S.C.Meaker (Sy)		5	9	1	72	214	26.75	–	2	–
J.C.Mickleburgh (Ex)		6	12	–	62	285	23.75	–	2	3
J.D.Middlebrook (Ex)	2003	8	11	3	46	196	24.50	–	–	2
A.S.Miller (Wa)		3	3	1	1*	1	0.50	–	–	–
M.J.Milligan (OU)	–	2	1	–	2	2	2.00	–	–	–
D.K.H.Mitchell (Wo)	2005	17	31	1	298	1162	38.73	2	5	18
Mohammad Amin (CU)	–	2	1	1	2*	2	–	–	–	–
S.C.Moore (EL/MCC/Wo)	2003	17	32	1	120	952	30.70	2	5	6
C.F.D.Morgan (DU)	–	2	4	–	38	45	11.25	–	–	–
† E.J.G.Morgan (EL/M)	2008	11	20	2	114*	445	24.72	1	1	13

233

F-C	Cap	M	I	NO	HS	Runs	Avge	100	50	Ct/St
G.J.Muchall (Du)	2005	13	19	2	106*	515	30.29	1	2	14
M.K.Munday (Sm)		1	1	–	1	1	1.00	–	–	–
D.Murphy (LU/Nh)		5	6	1	69*	101	20.20	–	1	11/1
C.P.Murtagh (Sy)		2	2	1	15	29	29.00	–	–	2
† T.J.Murtagh (M)	2008	13	20	6	51*	249	17.78	–	1	2
Murtaza Hussain (Sy)		7	8	1	34	111	15.85	–	–	–
† P.Mustard (Du)		18	22	7	94*	627	41.80	–	5	69/1
J.K.H.Naik (Le)		6	10	3	109*	200	28.57	1	–	1
G.R.Napier (Ex)	2003	10	16	6	64*	348	34.80	–	2	3
† B.P.Nash (WI)	–	5	8	1	81	227	32.42	–	2	1
C.D.Nash (Sx)	2008	15	26	3	157	1321	57.43	4	6	3
D.C.Nash (M)	2000	5	8	–	43	152	19.00	–	–	16
Naved-ul-Hasan (Y)		4	6	–	32	93	15.50	–	–	–
J.Needham (De)		5	7	3	20	55	13.75	–	–	3
A.Nel (Sy)		9	10	2	32	117	14.62	–	–	3
† M.A.G.Nelson (Nh)		4	7	–	38	131	18.71	–	–	3
† T.J.New (Le)		18	30	4	85*	813	31.26	–	6	29/1
O.J.Newby (La)		13	11	1	15	64	6.40	–	–	2
† S.A.Newman (Nt/Sy)	2005	12	19	–	124	466	24.52	1	2	5
N.A.Newport (Wa)		1	–							–
† P.A.Nixon (Le)	1994	9	17	2	173*	531	35.40	1	2	10
A.A.Noffke (Wo)		6	9	–	89	258	28.66	–	2	–
† M.J.North (A/H)		8	12	2	191*	613	61.30	3	1	4
S.A.Northeast (K)		11	19	2	128*	667	39.23	1	3	10
I.E.O'Brien (Le)		7	9	1	31	110	13.75	–	–	1
K.J.O'Brien (Nt)		1	2	–	13	18	9.00	–	–	1
† N.J.O'Brien (Nh)		9	16	–	128	434	27.12	1	1	34/1
G.Onions (Du/E/EL)		14	14	6	17*	52	6.50	–	–	5
J.E.Ord (LU)		1	2	–	9	10	5.00	–	–	–
M.P.O'Shea (Gm)		1	2	–	50	75	37.50	–	1	–
C.D.Paget (DU)	–	3	6	–	18	27	4.50	–	–	3
A.P.Palladino (Ex)		4	2	–	5	5	2.50	–	–	–
† M.S.Panesar (E/Nh)	2006	15	22	6	38	193	12.06	–	–	–
G.T.Park (De)		16	27	2	178*	1059	42.36	2	8	14
† W.D.Parnell (K)		5	6	1	90	183	36.60	–	2	–
S.D.Parry (La)		2	2	–	2	3	1.50	–	–	1
T.W.Parsons (H)		1	1	–	0	0	0.00	–	–	–
N.T.Pascal (WI)	–	2	3	1	1*	2	1.00	–	–	–
D.C.Pascoe (OU)	–	1	2	–	37	67	33.50	–	–	–
† A.Patel (Nt)		2	4	1	69*	110	36.66	–	1	2
J.S.Patel (Wa)		3	4	1	120	131	43.66	1	–	1
S.R.Patel (EL/Nt)	2008	17	26	–	95	821	31.57	–	4	11
S.A.Patterson (Y)		4	4	2	30*	45	22.50	–	–	–
D.J.Pattinson (Nt)	2008	8	8	–	59	102	12.75	–	1	1
E.G.Pearson (CU)	–	1	1	–	0	0	0.00	–	–	–
S.D.Peters (Nh)	2007	14	25	1	175	1050	43.75	3	5	12
M.L.Pettini (Ex)	2006	15	28	6	101*	870	39.54	1	4	10
B.J.Phillips (Sm)		7	8	2	84	190	31.66	–	1	4
† T.J.Phillips (Ex)	2006	4	5	–	69	122	24.40	–	1	2
K.P.Pietersen (E)	–	5	8	–	69	209	26.12	–	1	1
S.A.Piolet (Wa)		1	2	1	26*	31	31.00	–	–	–
D.J.Pipe (Du)	2007	14	18	5	64*	493	37.92	–	3	36/2

234

F-C	Cap	M	I	NO	HS	Runs	Avge	100	50	Ct/St
L.E.Plunkett (Du/EL)		15	14	3	94*	425	38.63	–	3	13
R.T.Ponting (A)	–	6	10	–	150	401	40.10	1	2	12
N.S.Poonia (Wa)		1	2	–	6	6	3.00	–	–	–
† W.T.S.Porterfield (Gs)	2008	9	16	1	81	341	22.73	–	2	17
N.Pothas (H)	2003	11	15	4	122*	816	74.18	1	6	24
M.J.Powell (Gm)	2000	17	25	2	108	934	40.60	2	7	8
† A.G.Prince (La)		6	12	2	135*	526	52.60	1	3	9
M.J.Prior (E/Sx)	2003	13	21	2	140	788	41.47	1	6	30/1
† T.J.W.Probert (CU)	–	1	1	1	0*	0	–	–	–	1
R.M.Pyrah (Y)		3	4	1	50*	59	19.66	–	1	3
D.Ramdin (WI)	–	4	7	–	61	165	23.57	–	2	7
M.R.Ramprakash (Sy)	2002	11	17	2	274	1350	90.00	5	4	5
† W.B.Rankin (Wa)		13	13	4	7	19	2.11	–	–	4
A.U.Rashid (EL/MCC/Y)	2008	10	12	4	157*	545	68.12	2	3	6
O.P.Rayner (Sx)		11	11	1	60	173	17.30	–	1	15
C.M.W.Read (Nt)	1999	16	22	6	125	1203	75.18	4	6	46/4
† D.J.Redfern (De)		14	23	1	95	668	30.36	–	5	8
† G.P.Rees (Gm)	2009	17	25	2	154	1061	46.13	3	4	15
H.Riazuddin (H)		1	1	–	3	3	3.00	–	–	–
D.M.Richards (WI)	–	2	2	–	15	23	11.50	–	–	1
A.Richardson (M)	2005	6	7	4	18*	40	13.33	–	–	5
† A.P.Richardson (WI)	–	2	1	–	4	4	4.00	–	–	–
S.D.Robson (M)		7	13	–	110	441	33.92	1	2	12
C.J.L.Rogers (De)	2008	13	21	1	222	1461	73.05	6	4	21
M.C.Rosenberg (CU)	–	1	1	–	0	0	0.00	–	–	–
† J.A.Rudolph (Y)	2007	17	29	1	198	1366	48.78	4	6	14
L.C.Ryan (OU)	–	3	2	–	21	21	10.50	–	–	3
† J.L.Sadler (De)		3	4	3	27*	71	71.00	–	–	3
M.J.Saggers (K)	2001	4	4	2	5*	5	2.50	–	–	–
D.J.G.Sammy (WI)	–	3	4	–	22	30	7.50	–	–	4
P.S.E.Sandri (Sx)		1	1	1	0*	0	–	–	–	–
R.R.Sarwan (WI)	–	4	7	–	100	184	26.28	1	–	1
I.D.Saxelby (Gs)	2008	9	13	3	60*	168	16.80	–	1	5
† J.J.Sayers (Y)	2007	17	29	2	173	1150	42.59	2	5	16
† C.P.Schofield (Sy)		14	21	3	144	644	35.77	1	3	7
B.J.M.Scott (M)	2007	8	14	1	44	167	12.84	–	–	18/2
A.Sen (CU)		3	3	–	17	34	11.33	–	–	4
B.M.Shafayat (Nt)		14	23	1	90*	590	26.81	–	3	13
O.A.Shah (M)	2000	8	16	2	159	591	42.21	2	2	5
A.Shahzad (Y)		14	18	6	88	451	37.58	–	2	4
† A.J.Shantry (Gm)		13	17	3	100	314	22.42	1	–	–
† J.D.Shantry (Wo)	2009	4	5	1	6	12	3.00	–	–	2
R.Sharma (OU)	–	4	6	2	58*	179	44.75	–	1	1
C.E.Shreck (Nt)	2006	11	12	7	12*	28	5.60	–	–	1
P.M.Siddle (A)	–	6	7	2	35	102	20.40	–	–	5
† R.J.Sidebottom (Nt)	2004	7	9	3	46	100	16.66	–	–	1
C.E.W.Silverwood (M)	2006	5	8	1	46	113	16.14	–	–	2
L.M.P.Simmons (WI)	–	5	8	1	102*	228	32.57	1	1	3
J.A.Simpson (M)		3	6	–	87	170	28.33	–	1	5
B.F.Smith (Wo)	2002	14	27	3	80*	626	26.08	–	4	9
D.R.Smith (Sx)		9	14	–	80	261	18.64	–	2	1
† D.S.Smith (WI)	–	5	8	–	46	151	18.87	–	–	6

F-C	Cap	M	I	NO	HS	Runs	Avge	100	50	Ct/St
D.T.Smith (OU)	–	1	1	–	6	6	6.00	–	–	1
G.M.Smith (De)	2009	16	27	4	126	977	42.47	1	6	5
G.P.Smith (DU/Le)		7	14	1	51	231	17.76	–	1	3
† T.C.Smith (La)		9	15	3	104*	390	32.50	1	2	7
T.M.J.Smith (Sx)		1	2	–	10	11	5.50	–	–	–
W.R.Smith (Du)		17	25	3	150	834	37.90	2	5	6
S.D.Snell (Gs)	2005	9	14	1	85	215	16.53	–	1	28/2
V.S.Solanki (EL/Wo)	1998	17	31	1	206*	1016	33.86	1	4	14
C.M.Spearman (Gs)	2002	6	9	–	57	206	22.88	–	1	9
† M.N.W.Spriegel (Sy)		6	11	–	100	294	26.72	1	2	7
S.Sreesanth (Wa)		5	7	2	30*	74	14.80	–	–	3
T.P.Stayt (Gs)	2007	1	1	–	36	36	36.00	–	–	–
D.I.Stevens (K)	2005	17	24	3	208	1050	50.00	4	2	11
D.A.Stiff (Sm)		10	14	5	49	193	21.44	–	–	–
† M.D.Stoneman (Du)		13	21	1	64	466	23.30	1	10	14
J.P.Strachan (OU)	–	2	3	1	13*	13	6.50	–	–	–
† A.J.Strauss (E/M)	2001	11	19	1	161	917	50.94	2	5	12
† S.D.Stubbings (De)	2001	7	11	1	83	296	29.60	–	1	4
A.V.Suppiah (Sm)	2009	16	26	1	151	1201	48.04	3	6	18
L.D.Sutton (La)	2007	17	23	7	53*	438	27.37	–	1	56/3
C.J.Swainland (OU)	–	1	1	–	2	2	2.00	–	–	–
G.P.Swann (E/Nt)	2005	10	12	2	63*	352	35.20	–	3	6
N.S.Tahir (Wa)		12	14	4	24	152	15.20	–	–	2
† B.V.Taylor (H)	2006	1	–					–	–	–
C.G.Taylor (Gs)	2001	15	22	1	111	705	33.57	1	5	11
J.E.Taylor (WI)	–	3	6	–	15	35	5.83	–	–	1
J.W.A.Taylor (Le)	2009	17	28	7	207*	1207	57.47	3	6	9
R.N.ten Doeschate (Ex)	2006	14	22	4	159*	823	45.72	2	2	5
A.C.Thomas (Sm)	2008	14	15	3	70	338	28.16	–	3	2
C.E.J.Thompson (Le)		1	2	–	16	16	8.00	–	–	–
† M.A.Thornely (Sx)		1	2	–	19	27	13.50	–	–	1
C.D.Thorp (Du)		13	12	–	42	207	17.25	–	–	15
† J.A.Tomlinson (H)	2008	12	14	7	23	92	13.14	–	–	3
† J.C.Tredwell (K)	2007	17	21	5	86*	484	30.25	–	4	12
P.D.Trego (Sm)	2007	16	23	5	103*	610	33.88	1	5	5
C.T.Tremlett (H)	2004	7	8	–	36	75	9.37	–	–	2
† M.E.Trescothick (Sm)	1999	16	26	4	146	1817	75.70	8	9	21
I.J.L.Trott (E/EL/Wa)	2005	17	25	6	184*	1400	73.68	5	5	13
† J.O.Troughton (Wa)	2002	17	23	–	223	828	36.00	2	3	10
A.J.Tudor (Sy)	1999	4	6	2	33	83	20.75	–	–	1
P.T.Turnbull (CU)	–	1	1	1	0*	0	–	–	–	1
M.L.Turner (Sm)		1								1
S.D.Udal (M)	2008	14	24	4	55	398	19.90	–	1	4
J.J.van der Wath (Nh)	2009	13	19	1	85	452	25.11	–	3	4
M.van Jaarsveld (K)	2005	16	25	3	182	1509	68.59	7	7	30
M.P.Vaughan (MCC/Y)	1995	6	8	–	43	159	19.87	–	–	–
J.M.Vince (H)		9	13	1	75	301	25.08	–	1	3
A.C.Voges (Nt)	2008	8	10	1	139	697	77.44	1	6	8
G.G.Wagg (De)	2007	14	14	1	71	273	21.00	–	1	4
M.A.Wagh (Nt)	2007	15	24	2	147	814	37.00	3	2	4
† D.J.Wainwright (Y)		10	13	4	102*	378	42.00	1	1	–
A.G.Wakely (Nh)		12	20	1	113*	457	24.05	1	2	10

F-C	Cap	M	I	NO	HS	Runs	Avge	100	50	Ct/St
† G.W.Walker (Le)		3	4	–	13	21	5.25	–	–	–
† M.J.Walker (Ex)		17	31	3	150	1004	35.85	2	3	13
† M.A.Wallace (Gm)	2003	17	22	–	139	645	29.31	2	–	31/6
M.T.C.Waller (Sm)		4	6	1	28	67	13.40	–	–	1
S.J.Walters (Sy)		11	18	–	188	573	31.83	2	1	15
M.J.C.Watson (OU)	–	3	2	1	22	43	43.00	–	–	–
S.R.Watson (A)	–	4	7	–	84	374	53.42	–	5	2
M.H.Wessels (Nh)		15	25	–	109	887	35.48	1	7	27/1
M.S.Westfield (Ex)		2	1	–	1	1	1.00	–	–	–
T.Westley (DU/Ex/MCC)		10	17	3	132	547	39.07	1	2	6
† I.J.Westwood (Wa)	2008	15	25	3	133	612	27.81	1	4	10
A.J.Wheater (Ex)		2	2	–	36	36	18.00	–	–	6
† D.A.Wheeldon (Wo)	2009	5	6	–	87	160	26.66	–	1	3
C.D.Whelan (Wo)	2008	12	17	3	47	205	14.64	–	–	5
G.G.White (Nh)		2	4	2	29*	32	16.00	–	–	–
R.A.White (Nh)	2008	17	31	4	193	992	36.74	1	7	11
W.A.White (Le)		12	19	2	68	340	20.00	–	1	5
D.H.Wigley (Nh)		12	15	8	16	74	10.57	–	–	5
D.J.Willey (Nh)		10	17	1	60	331	20.68	–	1	3
R.E.M.Williams (DU)	–	3	6	1	31	85	17.00	–	–	2
† C.M.Willoughby (Sm)	2007	16	13	4	23	40	4.44	–	–	4
C.R.Woakes (EL/MCC/Wa)	2009	19	23	8	131*	495	33.00	1	1	5
M.J.Wood (Nt)		7	11	1	86	270	27.00	–	1	–
† R.J.Woodman (Gs)	2008	6	10	1	32	144	16.00	–	–	3
R.J.J.Woolley (CU)	–	3	2	–	17	18	9.00	–	–	4
B.J.Wright (Gm)		9	14	–	81	279	19.92	–	1	3
C.J.C.Wright (Ex)		14	16	7	24*	130	14.44	–	–	2
D.G.Wright (Sx)		3	4	1	42	88	29.33	–	–	–
L.J.Wright (EL/Sx)	2007	10	15	2	118*	637	49.00	3	3	1
A.F.C.Wyatt (Le)		3	3	1	3	4	2.00	–	–	1
† R.J.Hardy (Sx)	2005	17	29	3	152	1096	42.15	2	6	13
Yasir Arafat (Sx)		5	5	–	37	108	21.60	–	–	–
E.G.C.Young (OU)	–	3	3	1	31	40	20.00	–	–	1

BOWLING

See BATTING AND FIELDING section for details of matches, caps and teams

	Cat	O	M	R	W	Avge	Best	5wI	10wM
A.R.Adams (Nt)	RMF	409	103	1224	43	28.46	4- 39	–	–
J.H.K.Adams (H)	LM	18	0	88	1	88.00	1- 49	–	–
U.Afzaal (Sy)	SLA	87.5	6	348	7	49.71	3- 51	–	–
R.G.Aga (Sx)	RMF	44	6	155	3	51.66	2- 8	–	–
J.S.Ahmed (Ex)	RMF	11	1	55	2	27.50	2- 55	–	–
M.Ahmed (Wo)	RFM	9	0	73	0			–	–
Kabir Ali (Wo)	RMF	117	12	485	11	44.09	6- 68	1	–
Kadeer Ali (Gl)	RM/LB	4	0	15	0			–	–
M.M.Ali (Wo)	OB	94.1	15	461	7	65.85	4- 29	–	–
J.Allenby (Gm/Le)	RM	190.4	52	471	17	27.70	3- 70	–	–
J.M.Anderson (E/La)	RFM	290.3	72	886	39	22.71	6- 56	5	1
G.M.Andrew (Wo)	RMF	257.3	38	991	23	43.08	5-117	1	–
A.S.Ansari (CU)	LB	32.2	3	118	3	39.33	1- 14	–	–
J.E.Anyon (Sy/Wa)	RFM	72.2	13	311	4	77.75	2- 38	–	–

237

F-C	Cat	O	M	R	W	Avge	Best	5wI	10wM
C.P.Ashling (Gm)	RFM	28	3	116	3	38.66	2- 66	–	–
A.Ashok (CU)	RM	7	3	15	1	15.00	1- 15	–	–
Azeem Rafiq (Y)	OB	124.3	9	487	10	48.70	3- 34	–	–
Azhar Mahmood (K)	RFM	130.3	38	382	21	18.19	5- 39	1	–
M.Baer (LU)	SLA	64	2	220	3	73.33	2- 19	–	–
F.B.Baker (CU)	SLA	18	0	96	1	96.00	1- 96	–	–
G.C.Baker (LU)	RMF	27.2	5	134	2	67.00	1- 31	–	–
L.S.Baker (WI)	RMF	106	20	337	7	48.14	2- 31	–	–
D.J.Balcombe (H)	RFM	78	13	288	9	32.00	3- 76	–	–
V.Banerjee (Gs)	SLA	200.3	38	667	21	31.76	4- 58	–	–
O.A.C.Banks (Sm)	OB	111.1	15	456	7	65.14	4-120	–	–
K.H.D.Barker (Wa)	LM	53	8	175	1	175.00	1- 51	–	–
G.J.Batty (Wo)	OB	227.1	37	724	10	72.40	2- 71	–	–
I.R.Bell (E/EL/MCC/Wa)	RM	10	1	43	0			–	–
D.M.Benkenstein (Du)	RM/OB	50	13	173	8	21.62	3- 20	–	–
S.J.Benn (WI)	SLA	120	23	353	10	35.30	4- 31	–	–
J.G.E.Benning (Le/Sy)	RM	127	22	436	9	48.44	3- 43	–	–
G.K.Berg (M)	RMF	249.1	46	886	23	38.52	5- 55	2	–
D.E.Bernard (WI)	RMF	46	9	134	3	44.66	2- 86	–	–
I.D.Blackwell (Sm)	SLA	456.5	135	1064	47	22.63	7- 85	3	–
A.J.Blake (K)	RMF	4	0	15	0			–	–
N.Boje (Nh)	SLA	311	81	891	30	29.70	4- 59	–	–
R.S.Bopara (E/Ex)	RM	18.2	4	82	0			–	–
S.G.Borthwick (Du)	LBG	27	2	95	3	31.66	3- 95	–	–
A.G.Botha (Wa)	SLA	316.3	61	941	23	40.91	5- 51	1	–
D.P.Bradshaw (OU)	RFM	38	6	128	1	128.00	1- 32	–	–
W.D.Bragg (Gm)	(WK)	5	0	23	0			–	–
R.M.R.Brathwaite (CU)	RFM	142.4	31	428	13	32.92	5- 54	1	–
G.R.Breese (Du)	OB	37.1	15	76	6	12.66	4- 10	–	–
T.T.Bresnan (E/EL/MCC/Y)	RFM	443.4	111	1168	32	36.50	4-116	–	–
D.R.Briggs (H)	SLA	85.4	13	295	8	36.87	3- 62	–	–
S.C.J.Broad (E/Nt)	RFM	268.3	47	887	34	26.08	6- 91	3	–
J.A.Brooks (Nh)	RMF	81	9	325	9	36.11	4- 76	–	–
G.L.Brophy (Y)	(WK)	1	1	0	0			–	–
A.D.Brown (Nt)	LB	23.1	2	83	1	83.00	1- 16	–	–
F.A.Brown (CU)	SLA	45	10	136	4	34.00	3- 26	–	–
J.F.Brown (Nh)	OB	1	0	4	0			–	–
K.R.Brown (La)	RMF	8	0	37	2	18.50	2- 30	–	–
M.J.Brown (S)	OB	3	0	20	0			–	–
T.E.Bryan (OU)	RM	1	0	6	0			–	–
N.J.S.Buchanan (OU)	RM	11	1	39	1	39.00	1- 30	–	–
N.L.Buck (Le)	RMF	88	17	276	3	92.00	1- 35	–	–
D.A.Burton (M)	RMF	53.2	3	249	8	31.12	5- 68	1	–
J.E.L.Buttleman (DU)	RFM	45.1	8	142	4	35.50	1- 7	–	–
A.R.Caddick (Sm)	RFM	131.1	24	525	10	52.50	3- 53	–	–
M.A.Carberry (H)	OB	43.1	3	242	2	121.00	1- 64	–	–
A.Carter (Nt)	RM	53	15	164	3	54.66	1- 27	–	–
N.M.Carter (Wa)	LFM	190	30	704	16	44.00	5- 37	1	–
M.A.Chambers (Ex)	RFM	141.4	19	526	15	35.06	4- 62	–	–
U.S.Chandra (CU)	RM	19	0	112	1	112.00	1-112	–	–
G.Chapple (La)	RFM	335.4	87	884	35	25.25	6- 19	2	–
P.P.Chawla (Sx)	LB	341.5	72	981	36	27.25	6- 52	4	1

F-C	Cat	O	M	R	W	Avge	Best	5wI	10wM
M.J.Chilton (La)	RM	5.2	3	3	2	1.50	2- 3	–	–
V.Chopra (Ex)	RM	15.1	3	39	0				
S.H.Choudhry (Wa)	SLA	1	0	11	0				
J.L.Clare (De)	RMF	119	27	407	10	40.70	3- 64	–	–
S.R.Clark (A)	RMF	94	19	301	10	30.10	3- 18	–	–
M.J.Clarke (A)	SLA	23	2	90	1	90.00	1- 12	–	–
R.Clarke (Wa)	RFM	164.1	23	640	11	58.18	2- 15	–	–
M.E.Claydon (Du)	RMF	234	51	777	25	31.08	4- 90	–	–
S.J.Cliff (Le)	RM	23	2	92	2	46.00	2- 92	–	–
J.J.Cobb (Le)	LB	19	1	71	1	71.00	1- 8	–	–
M.T.Coles (K)	RMF	17.4	0	130	2	65.00	2-130	–	–
P.D.Collingwood (E)	RMF	18	1	76	1	76.00	1- 38	–	–
P.T.Collins (Sy)	LFM	137.2	25	504	16	31.50	5- 75	1	–
C.D.Collymore (Sx)	RFM	396	102	1104	33	33.45	4- 66	–	–
N.R.D.Compton (Mx)	OB	2	0	5	0				
A.N.Cook (E/Ex)	OB	10	0	51	2	25.50	1- 3	–	–
M.P.Cook (CU)	RFM	3	0	9	0				
S.J.Cook (K)	RMF	374.1	88	1047	34	30.79	5- 22	3	–
D.G.Cork (H)	RFM	287	69	767	27	28.40	5- 14	1	–
M.J.Cosgrove (Gm)	RM	58	8	202	6	33.66	3- 30	–	–
D.A.Cosker (Gm)	SLA	312.1	83	769	26	29.57	6- 91	2	1
R.D.B.Croft (Gm)	OB	737	154	1727	58	29.77	5- 65	1	–
S.J.Croft (La)	RMF	30	4	193	4	38.75	2- 42	–	–
S.P.Crook (Nh)	RFM	48	8	193	6	32.16	5- 71	1	–
C.D.Crowe (Le)	OB	103	19	346	3	115.33	3- 84	–	–
L.M.Daggett (Nh)	RFM	88	15	311	8	38.87	3- 39	–	–
J.W.M.Dalrymple (Gm)	OB	231.5	29	726	22	33.00	3- 11	–	–
Danish Kaneria (Ex)	LBG	597.5	124	1777	75	23.69	8-116	6	2
A.M.Davies (Du)	RMF	217.1	60	562	19	29.57	4- 87	–	–
L.A.Dawson (H)	SLA	97	11	421	10	42.10	2- 3	–	–
R.K.J.Dawson (Gs)	OB	158.4	13	610	12	50.83	4- 76	–	–
Z.de Bruyn (Sm)	RM	136	23	541	7	77.28	3- 47	–	–
J.L.Denly (EL/K)	LB	29	7	93	0				
N.Deonarine (WI)	OB	24.2	3	75	3	25.00	3- 32	–	–
J.W.Dernbach (Sy)	RMF	395.2	67	1436	37	38.81	6- 47	2	–
N.J.Dexter (M)	RM	88	25	266	6	44.33	2- 37	–	–
H.H.Dippenaar (Le)	OB	9.5	0	44	1	4.00	1- 6	–	–
F.du Plessis (La)	LB	54.1	1	199	4	49.75	2- 14	–	–
W.J.Durston (Sm)	OB	2	0	13	0				
J.du Toit (Le)	RM	19	1	89	0				
M.A.Ealham (Nt)	RMF	387	117	983	28	35.10	5- 31	1	–
F.H.Edwards (WI)	RF	54.4	5	217	7	31.00	6- 92	1	–
P.D.Edwards (K)	RMF	95	18	325	7	46.42	3- 72	–	–
G.D.Elliott (Sy)	RMF	2	0	15	0				
S.M.Ervine (H)	RM	233.3	55	793	13	61.00	3- 22	–	–
A.C.Evans (LU)	RMF	25	2	127	3	42.33	2- 41	–	–
D.Evans (M)	RFM	42	3	190	3	63.33	2- 69	–	–
R.F.Evans (LU)	RM	20	3	117	1	117.00	1- 86	–	–
R.S.Ferley (Sx)	SLA	75	15	189	7	27.00	3- 73	–	–
S.T.Finn (M)	RFM	418.3	64	1624	53	30.64	5- 57	1	–
I.D.Fisher (Wo)	SLA	3	0	15	0				
L.J.Fletcher (Nt)	RMF	245.3	62	800	29	27.58	4- 38	–	–

F-C	Cat	O	M	R	W	Avge	Best	5wI	10wM
A.Flintoff (E/La)	RF	193.2	39	586	19	30.84	5- 92	1	–
G.W.Flower (Ex)	SLA	21	1	69	2	34.50	1- 10	–	–
M.H.A.Footitt (Nt)	LFM	16	5	58	3	19.33	3- 58	–	–
P.J.Foster (DU)	RFM	90	23	268	8	33.50	3- 36	–	–
J.E.C.Franklin (Gs)	LFM	292.4	63	904	31	29.16	5- 30	1	–
P.J.Franks (Nt)	RMF	141	37	428	11	38.90	3- 52	–	–
T.Frost (Wa)	(WK)	5.1	1	12	1	12.00	1- 12	–	–
A.W.Gale (Y)	LB	1	0	11	0				
D.J.Gale (DU)	SLA	36.5	3	113	1	113.00	1- 67	–	–
C.H.Gayle (WI)	OB	17	2	42	1	42.00	1- 31	–	–
A.P.R.Gidman (Gs)	RM	59.1	13	162	4	40.50	3- 23	–	–
J.C.Glover (DU)	RMF	76	16	233	7	33.28	5- 38	1	–
M.W.Goodwin (Sx)	LB	2	0	13	0				
C.M.Grammer (CU)	SLA	22.4	4	74	3	24.66	2- 35	–	–
D.A.Griffiths (H)	RFM	283.2	52	1039	32	32.46	4- 48	–	–
T.D.Groenewald (De)	RFM	273.2	49	921	34	27.08	6- 50	2	–
P.R.Groves (LU)	RMF	50	13	207	8	25.87	5- 72	1	–
H.F.Gurney (Le)	LF	228.5	42	829	16	51.81	5- 82	1	–
A.D.Hales (Nt)	RM	40	6	140	3	46.66	2- 63	–	–
A.J.Hall (Nh)	RFM	310.2	76	911	40	22.77	5- 29	1	–
R.J.Hamilton-Brown (Sx)	OB	37	6	109	3	36.33	2- 49	–	–
A.Harinath (LU/Sy)	OB	4	0	18	0				
B.W.Harmison (Du)	RMF	6	1	19	0				
S.J.Harmison (Du/E/EL)	RF	513.2	131	1503	63	23.85	6- 20	4	–
G.M.Harper (DU)	LFM	14.5	3	49	4	12.25	4- 49	–	–
A.J.Harris (Le)	RM	395.1	79	1439	35	41.11	5- 26	1	–
J.A.R.Harris (Gm)	RFM	439.2	86	1498	43	34.83	4- 69	–	–
R.J.Harris (Sy)	RM	33.5	6	135	3	45.00	2- 66	–	–
D.S.Harrison (Gm)	RMF	207.1	32	770	20	38.50	4- 60	–	–
N.M.Hauritz (A)	OB	154.4	26	492	12	41.00	3- 63	–	–
M.Hayward (De)	RF	123.2	19	472	11	42.90	4- 99	–	–
C.W.Henderson (Le)	SLA	394.5	70	1044	23	45.39	6-152	1	–
H.M.R.K.B.Herath (Sy)	SLA	108.2	8	431	8	53.87	4-151	–	–
B.W.Hilfenhaus (A)	RFM	180.5	40	604	22	27.45	4- 60	–	–
C.M.M.Hill (OU)	SLC	4	1	4	0				
W.W.Hinds (De)	RM	60	6	181	4	45.25	2- 19	–	–
A.J.Hodd (Sx)	(WK)	1.4	0	7	0				
L.J.Hodgson (Y)	RFM	10	3	30	0				
G.P.Hodnett (Gs)	LB	6	0	41	1	41.00	1- 41	–	–
K.W.Hogg (La)	RFM	338.2	91	1000	34	29.41	4- 22	–	–
M.J.Hoggard (Y)	RMF	479.1	107	1486	46	32.30	5- 56	2	–
P.J.Horton (La)	RM	2	1	10	0				
D.M.Housego (M)	LB	1.1	0	17	0				
P.J.Hughes (A/M)	OB	3	0	9	0				
I.D.Hunter (De)	RMF	181.4	33	593	21	28.23	5- 46	2	–
G.M.Hussain (Gs)	RM	22	1	107	2	53.50	2- 73	–	–
D.J.Hussey (Nt)	OB	5	2	18	0				
Imran Arif (Wo)	RFM	184.5	21	899	17	52.88	5- 93	1	–
Imran Tahir (H)	LBG	487.4	81	1711	52	32.90	7-140	4	–
A.J.Ireland (Gs)	RMF	167	34	664	21	31.61	6- 31	1	–
A.Javid (Wa)	RM	13	0	78	0				
M.G.Johnson (A)	LF	215.2	19	924	24	38.50	5- 69	1	–

F-C	Cat	O	M	R	W	Avge	Best	5wI	10wM
P.R.A.Johnston (DU)		1	0	1	0			–	–
H.D.Jones (LU)	RFM	51	12	230	5	46.00	4- 57	–	–
P.S.Jones (De/K)	RMF	398	84	1210	34	35.58	5- 35	1	–
R.A.Jones (Wo)	RMF	174	25	745	22	33.86	6-100	1	–
C.J.Jordan (Sy)	RFM	208.2	36	764	13	58.76	4- 84	–	–
R.H.Joseph (K)	RFM	97.2	9	373	12	31.08	6- 55	1	–
E.C.Joyce (Sx)	RM	2	0	9	1	9.00	1- 9	–	–
M.Kartik (M)	SLA	317.1	103	755	33	22.87	5- 65	1	–
S.M.Katich (A)	SLC	15	2	38	0			–	–
G.Keedy (La)	SLA	543.5	107	1540	45	34.22	6- 30	3	–
J.M.Kemp (K)	RFM	165.5	35	568	8	71.00	3- 12	–	–
R.W.T.Key (EL/K/MCC)	RM/OB	22	5	59	1	59.00	1- 14	–	–
M.F.Khalid (OU)	RM	12	1	57	0			–	–
A.Khan (K)	RFM	339.1	65	1146	36	31.83	5-113	1	–
S.J.King (Gs)	OB	39.3	2	156	4	39.00	3- 61	–	–
S.P.Kirby (Gs)	RFM	472.4	107	1420	64	22.18	5- 44	1	–
R.J.Kirtley (Sx)	RFM	56.5	9	185	6	30.83	2- 59	–	–
W.A.Klopper (OU)	LB	29	5	76	0			–	–
G.J-P.Kruger (Gm)	RMF	353.4	59	1283	33	38.87	6- 93	1	–
G.J.Kruis (Y)	RFM	252.1	56	816	22	37.09	3- 51	–	–
M.A.K.Lawson (De)	LB	105	15	333	4	83.25	2- 20	–	–
V.V.S.Laxman (La)	OB	13	4	26	1	26.00	1- 13	–	–
B.Lee (A)	RF	35	7	114	7	16.28	6- 76	1	–
J.E.Lee (Y)	RMF	19	1	113	2	56.50	2- 63	–	–
R.J.H.Lett (OU)	RMF	17	1	67	1	67.00	1- 39	–	–
J.Lewis (Gs)	RMF	426.3	110	1146	57	20.10	5- 73	1	–
J.D.Lewry (Sx)	LFM	159.1	39	535	10	53.50	2- 53	–	–
T.E.Linley (Sy)	RFM	131	23	442	8	55.25	4- 77	–	–
R.J.Logan (Sy)	RMF	30	6	101	2	50.50	2-101	–	–
A.B.London (M)	OB	8	0	39	0			–	–
J.D.S.Lotay (CU)	OB	45.1	8	187	5	37.40	3-147	–	–
D.S.Lucas (Nh)	LMF	414.3	86	1299	60	21.65	7- 24	3	–
T.Lungley (De/La)	RM	132.5	16	531	13	40.84	3- 56	–	–
A.A.Lynch (LU)	RM	1	0	8	0			–	–
A.Lyth (Y)	RM	19	9	38	1	38.00	1- 38	–	–
A.B.McDonald (A)	RFM	16	5	38	4	9.50	4- 15	–	–
A.McGrath (Y)	RM	109	26	280	5	56.00	2- 1	–	–
R.McLaren (K)	RMF	164.5	38	608	19	32.00	4- 51	–	–
C.S.MacLeod (Wa)	RMF	10	2	26	1	26.00	1- 10	–	–
D.L.Maddy (Wa)	RM/OB	31.1	8	100	1	100.00	1- 48	–	–
W.L.Madsen (De)	OB	18	2	67	0			–	–
S.I.Mahmood (EL/La/MCC)	RF	379.3	67	1394	41	34.00	6- 30	2	1
C.C.Malan (LU)	OB	57	11	150	3	50.00	1- 35	–	–
D.J.Malan (M)	LB	96.4	10	358	7	51.14	2- 21	–	–
H.J.H.Marshall (Gs)	RM	104	24	360	16	22.50	4- 24	–	–
R.S.C.Martin-Jenkins (Sx)	RFM	277.4	74	793	23	34.47	5- 43	1	–
A.D.Mascarenhas (H)	RMF	241	70	618	13	47.53	2- 46	–	–
M.S.Mason (Wo)	RFM	418.4	125	1186	43	27.58	7- 39	2	–
D.D.Masters (Ex)	RMF	557.2	184	1212	45	26.93	5- 65	1	–
S.C.Meaker (Sy)	RMF	110.4	11	498	10	49.80	3-114	–	–
J.C.Mickleburgh (Ex)	RMF	7.5	1	28	0			–	–
J.D.Middlebrook (Ex)	OB	138	29	449	14	32.07	3- 80	–	–

F-C	Cat	O	M	R	W	Avge	Best	5wI	10wM
A.S.Miller (Wa)	RFM	83	18	249	8	31.12	4- 76	–	–
M.J.Milligan (OU)	RFM	23	5	75	1	75.00	1- 17	–	–
D.K.H.Mitchell (Wo)	RM	90	13	252	9	28.00	4- 49	–	–
Mohammad Amin (CU)	RMF	30.3	2	152	4	38.00	3- 63	–	–
M.K.Munday (Sm)	LB	25.1	0	114	4	28.50	2- 46	–	–
T.J.Murtagh (M)	RFM	443	81	1521	60	25.35	7- 82	3	–
Murtaza Hussain (Sy)	OB	271	47	825	19	43.42	4- 70	–	–
J.K.H.Naik (Le)	OB	120.5	22	367	9	40.77	2- 32	–	–
G.R.Napier (Ex)	RM	271.3	55	1005	29	34.65	4- 32	–	–
B.P.Nash (WI)	LM	7	4	9	0			–	–
C.D.Nash (Sx)	OB	114.4	22	394	7	56.28	1- 3	–	–
Naved-ul-Hasan (Y)	RMF	124	23	412	10	41.20	3-102	–	–
J.Needham (De)	OB	101.4	11	353	7	50.42	3- 47	–	–
A.Nel (Sy)	RFM	260.4	69	754	27	27.92	6- 36	1	–
T.J.New (Le)	RM	8	1	36	0			–	–
O.J.Newby (La)	RMF	297.1	43	1107	31	35.70	4- 21	–	–
S.A.Newman (Nt/Sy)	RM	9	1	35	0			–	–
P.A.Nixon (Le)	RM	1.1	0	9	0			–	–
A.A.Noffke (Wo)	RFM	158	38	452	10	45.20	4- 92	–	–
M.J.North (A/H)	OB	84.3	15	249	5	49.80	4- 98	–	–
S.A.Northeast (K)	OB	1	0	2	0			–	–
I.E.O'Brien (Le)	RMF	181.2	38	547	21	26.04	6- 39	2	–
K.J.O'Brien (Nt)	RMF	14	4	33	2	16.50	1- 9	–	–
G.Onions (Du/E/EL)	RFM	428.4	88	1377	69	19.95	7- 38	5	–
C.D.Paget (DU)	OB	37.4	1	168	4	42.00	2- 26	–	–
A.P.Palladino (Ex)	RMF	99	26	302	9	33.55	4- 68	–	–
M.S.Panesar (E/Nh)	SLA	454.5	97	1195	22	54.31	3- 10	–	–
G.T.Park (De)	RM	90.3	8	311	7	44.42	3- 25	–	–
W.D.Parnell (K)	LFM	166.3	35	529	17	31.11	4- 78	–	–
S.D.Parry (La)	SLA	68	10	210	4	52.50	2- 51	–	–
T.W.Parsons (RFM)	RFM	18	4	63	3	21.00	3- 39	–	–
N.T.Pascal (WI)	RF	40.5	2	184	5	36.80	4- 68	–	–
D.C.Pascoe (OU)	SLA	27.5	3	79	2	39.50	2- 79	–	–
A.Patel (Nt)	SLC	14.5	3	46	1	46.00	1- 34	–	–
J.S.Patel (Wa)	OB	94	4	399	6	66.50	3-112	–	–
S.R.Patel (EL/Nt)	SLA	484.2	86	1558	33	47.21	6- 84	2	–
S.A.Patterson (Y)	RMF	110.1	22	409	7	58.42	4- 41	–	–
D.J.Pattinson (Nt)	RFM	219.5	40	872	10	87.20	4-115	–	–
M.L.Pettini (Ex)	RM	6.5	0	62	0			–	–
B.J.Phillips (Sm)	RFM	158.1	37	456	12	38.00	4- 46	–	–
T.J.Phillips (Ex)	SLA	127	26	357	8	44.62	3- 61	–	–
S.A.Piolet (Wa)	RM	27	13	43	10	4.30	6- 17	1	1
D.J.Pipe (De)	(WK)	1	0	5	0			–	–
L.E.Plunkett (Du/EL)	RFM	409.3	75	1401	60	23.35	6- 63	3	1
T.J.W.Probert (CU)	RM	28	15	43	2	21.50	2- 20	–	–
R.M.Pyrah (Y)	RM	60	7	213	4	53.25	2- 53	–	–
W.B.Rankin (Wa)	RFM	340.1	54	1279	37	34.56	5- 85	1	–
A.U.Rashid (EL/MCC/Y)	LB	306.4	41	1118	31	36.06	5- 41	2	–
O.P.Rayner (Sx)	OB	294.3	48	870	20	43.50	4-186	–	–
C.M.W.Read (Nt)	(WK)	1	0	2	0			–	–
D.J.Redfern (De)	OB	32	3	117	2	58.50	1- 26	–	–
H.Riazuddin (H)	RFM	22	4	72	2	36.00	1- 25	–	–

F-C	Cat	O	M	R	W	Avge	Best	5wI	10wM
A.Richardson (M)	RMF	222.2	53	618	11	56.18	3-52	–	–
A.P.Richardson (WI)	RFM	53.3	17	160	6	26.66	3-46	–	–
S.D.Robson (M)	LBG	2	0	5	0				
M.C.Rosenberg (CU)	RM	16	4	56	2	28.00	2-56	–	–
J.A.Rudolph (Y)	LBG	25	0	111	0				
L.C.Ryan (OU)	SLA	47	6	176	4	44.00	3-89	–	–
M.J.Saggers (K)	RMF	108.5	34	264	10	26.40	3-45	–	–
D.J.Sammy (WI)	RM	59.5	16	183	3	61.00	1-32	–	–
P.S.E.Sandri (Sx)	RMF	14	2	80	0				
R.R.Sarwan (WI)	LB	1	0	7	0				
I.D.Saxelby (Gs)	RMF	185.2	30	620	20	31.00	3-31	–	–
J.J.Sayers (Y)	OB	10.5	0	32	3	10.66	3-20	–	–
C.P.Schofield (Sy)	LBG	363.5	35	1357	22	61.68	5-40	1	–
B.M.Shafayat (Nt)	RMF	11	1	63	1	63.00	1-32	–	–
O.A.Shah (M)	OB	1	0	1	0				
A.Shahzad (Y)	RMF	422.5	86	1405	41	34.26	4-72	–	–
A.J.Shantry (Gm)	LFM	278	47	898	29	30.96	5-62	1	–
R.Sharma (OU)	RMF	71.3	16	210	7	30.00	5-81	1	–
C.E.Shreck (Nt)	RFM	363.2	77	1281	21	61.00	4-63	–	–
P.M.Siddle (A)	RFM	175.1	25	680	23	29.56	5-21	1	–
R.J.Sidebottom (Nt)	LFM	260.2	70	760	31	24.51	5-59	2	–
C.E.W.Silverwood (M)	RFM	115	21	355	4	88.75	1-23	–	–
L.M.P.Simmons (WI)	RMF	31	3	134	3	44.66	1-10	–	–
D.R.Smith (Sx)	RM	301	84	814	25	32.56	4-58	–	–
G.M.Smith (De)	OB/RM	330.2	64	1098	32	34.31	5-65	1	–
T.C.Smith (La)	RMF	199.4	45	623	15	41.53	6-46	1	–
T.M.J.Smith (Sx)	SLA	12.4	1	70	0				
W.R.Smith (Du)	OB	10	2	31	0				
V.S.Solanki (EL/Wo)	RM	17	2	68	1	68.00	1-32	–	–
M.N.W.Spriegel (Sy)	OB	44.4	2	205	2	102.50	1-22	–	–
S.Sreesanth (Wa)	RFM	109.3	21	418	13	32.15	5-93	1	–
T.P.Stayt (Gs)	RMF	34	7	77	2	38.50	1-19	–	–
D.I.Stevens (K)	RM	68	13	256	2	128.00	1-42	–	–
D.A.Stiff (Sm)	RFM	268.2	33	1120	31	36.12	5-91	1	–
J.P.Strachan (OU)	RMF	42	9	136	3	45.33	2-48	–	–
A.J.Strauss (E/M)	LM	2	1	10	0				
A.V.Suppiah (Sm)	SLA	212.5	47	682	15	45.46	3-58	–	–
G.P.Swann (E/Nt)	OB	269.2	55	824	27	30.51	4-38	–	–
N.S.Tahir (Wa)	RFM	274.2	62	843	38	22.18	5-67	1	–
B.V.Taylor (H)	RMF	21	4	52	1	52.00	1-52	–	–
C.G.Taylor (Gs)	OB	86.2	22	242	6	40.33	1- 6	–	–
J.E.Taylor (WI)	RF	67	6	239	5	47.80	3-54	–	–
J.W.A.Taylor (Le)	LB	19	1	82	0				
R.N.ten Doeschate (Ex)	RMF	246	32	970	22	44.09	5-62	1	–
A.C.Thomas (Sm)	RFM	401.1	77	1317	35	37.62	5-53	1	–
C.E.J.Thompson (Le)	RMF	15.2	2	45	1	45.00	1-45	–	–
C.D.Thorp (Du)	RMF	320.5	94	846	34	24.88	5-49	2	–
J.A.Tomlinson (H)	LFM	318.1	58	1193	30	39.76	3-53	–	–
J.C.Tredwell (K)	OB	681.5	178	1838	69	26.63	8-66	4	2
P.D.Trego (Sm)	RMF	256.5	57	889	19	46.78	3-53	–	–
C.T.Tremlett (H)	RMF	173	34	564	14	40.28	4-49	–	–
M.E.Trescothick (Sm)	RM	5	2	10	0				

F-C	Cat	O	M	R	W	Avge	Best	5wI	10wM
I.J.L.Trott (E/EL/Wa)	RM	98.2	11	355	5	71.00	2- 26	–	–
A.J.Tudor (Sy)	RFM	100	18	417	4	104.25	2-109	–	–
P.T.Turnbull (CU)	RMF	31	6	103	1	103.00	1- 43	–	–
M.L.Turner (Sm)	RMF	30	4	111	2	55.50	2- 82	–	–
S.D.Udal (M)	OB	368.5	67	1007	37	27.21	6- 36	2	1
J.J.van der Wath (Nh)	RFM	364.3	75	1237	50	24.74	5- 71	1	–
M.van Jaarsveld (K)	OB	71.1	10	241	4	60.25	2- 15	–	–
J.M.Vince (H)	RM	10	0	37	0				
A.C.Voges (Nt)	SLA	33.3	2	100	3	33.33	1- 2	–	–
G.G.Wagg (De)	LM	521.3	85	1773	47	37.72	6- 35	3	–
D.J.Wainwright (Y)	SLA	250.2	50	824	26	31.69	5-134	1	–
A.G.Wakely (Nh)	OB	11	0	64	0				
G.W.Walker (Le)	SLA	50	8	159	2	79.50	1- 75	–	–
M.J.Walker (Ex)	RM	3.2	0	22	0				
M.T.C.Waller (Sm)	LB	82.4	11	320	5	64.00	2- 27	–	–
S.J.Walters (Sy)	RM	19	2	75	0				
M.J.C.Watson (OU)	LB	34	5	143	4	35.75	4- 78	–	–
S.R.Watson (A)	RMF	23	3	103	3	34.33	2- 20	–	–
M.H.Wessels (Nh)	(WK)	1	1	0	0				
M.S.Westfield (Ex)	RFM	35.1	13	82	4	20.50	3- 25	–	–
T.Westley (DU/Ex/MCC)	OB	29	2	104	2	52.00	2- 33	–	–
I.J.Westwood (Wa)	OB	19	2	49	2	24.50	2- 39	–	–
C.D.Whelan (Wo)	RMF	232	24	1067	22	48.50	5- 95	1	–
G.G.White (Nh)	SLA	28	2	110	2	55.00	1- 48	–	–
W.A.White (Le)	RMF	197.3	23	852	19	44.84	3- 91	–	–
D.H.Wigley (Nh)	RFM	314.1	60	1230	32	38.43	6- 72	2	–
D.J.Willey (Nh)	LFM	68.4	5	295	6	49.16	2- 21	–	–
R.E.M.Williams (DU)	RMF	61.1	17	192	6	32.00	3- 51	–	–
C.M.Willoughby (Sm)	LMF	555.4	161	1622	54	30.03	5- 56	3	–
C.R.Woakes (EL/MCC/Wa)	RMF	489.5	105	1576	47	33.53	6- 43	2	–
R.J.Woodman (Gs)	LMF	5	3	8	1	8.00	1- 4	–	–
R.J.J.Woolley (CU)	RM	75.5	14	295	5	59.00	3- 71	–	–
B.J.Wright (Gm)	RM	8	0	41	0				
C.J.C.Wright (Ex)	RFM	437.1	67	1538	40	38.45	4- 43	–	–
D.G.Wright (Sx)	RFM	83.5	33	187	5	37.40	3- 64	–	–
L.J.Wright (EL/Sx)	RM	224.1	38	764	22	34.72	5- 66	2	–
A.C.F.Wyatt (Le)	RMF	61	17	159	7	22.71	3- 42	–	–
M.H.Yardy (Sx)	LM/SLA	69	4	320	4	80.00	3- 15	–	–
Yasir Arafat (Sx)	RMF	151	24	621	12	51.75	3- 83	–	–
E.G.C.Young (OU)	SLA	44	8	151	2	75.50	2- 74	–	–

FIRST-CLASS CAREER RECORDS

Compiled by **Philip Bailey**

The following career records are for all players who appeared in first-class cricket during the 2009 season, and are complete to the end of that season. Some players who did not appear in 2009 but may do so in 2010 are included.

BATTING AND FIELDING

'1000' denotes instances of scoring 1000 runs in a season. Where these have been achieved outside the British Isles they are shown after a plus sign.

	M	I	NO	HS	Runs	Avge	100	50	1000	Ct/St
Abel, E.	4	5	1	27*	94	23.50	–	–	–	4
Ackerman, H.D.	220	369	34	309*	14625	43.65	40	75	3+1	183
Adams, A.R.	101	133	11	124	2918	23.91	3	12	–	68
Adams, J.H.K.	88	157	15	262*	5072	35.71	7	28	2	74
Adshead, S.J.	73	118	18	156*	3179	31.79	3	17	–	192/15
Afzaal, U.	222	384	45	204*	13373	39.44	31	70	7	100
Aga, R.G.	16	25	4	43	236	11.23	–	–	–	6
Ahmed, J.S.	7	6	4	16*	49	24.50	–	–	–	3
Ahmed, M.	2	2	2	0*	0	–	–	–	–	2
Ali, Kabir	113	156	23	84*	2319	17.43	–	7	–	30
Ali, Kadeer	93	168	9	161	4666	29.34	6	24	–	49
Ali, M.M.	33	54	4	153	1427	28.54	2	9	–	9
Allenby, J.	47	71	11	138*	2242	37.36	3	15	–	44
Ambrose, T.R.	109	165	15	251*	5266	35.10	9	30	–	246/16
Amla, H.M.	113	187	17	249	8074	47.49	24	40	0+2	91
Anderson, J.M.	97	112	49	37*	667	10.58	–	–	–	40
Andrew, G.M.	33	45	9	92*	753	20.91	–	3	–	10
Ansari, A.S.	7	10	3	193	448	64.00	2	1	–	3
Anyon, J.E.	47	59	25	37*	364	10.70	–	–	–	15
Ashling, C.P.	1	1	–	12	12	12.00	–	–	–	–
Ashok, A.	1	2	1	112	131	131.00	1	–	–	–
Ashton, P.P.	1	1	–	4	4	4.00	–	–	–	–
Atkinson, J.J.	2	4	–	16	21	5.25	–	–	–	1
Azeem Rafiq	4	5	–	100	117	23.40	1	–	–	1
Azhar Mahmood	155	240	29	204*	6635	31.44	9	33	–	126
Baer, M.	4	3	2	8	12	12.00	–	–	–	–
Bairstow, J.M.	12	19	6	84*	592	45.53	–	6	–	21
Baker, F.B.	5	5	–	18	41	8.20	–	–	–	1
Baker, G.C.	2	3	1	66	143	71.50	–	2	–	1
Baker, L.S.	20	27	9	26	180	10.00	–	–	–	5
Balcombe, D.J.	21	30	6	73	366	15.25	–	1	–	6
Ball, A.H.	5	9	2	44*	155	22.14	–	–	–	6
Ballance, G.S.	1	2	–	5	6	3.00	–	–	–	–
Ballard, E.C.	4	6	–	33	34	5.66	–	–	–	1
Bandara, C.M.	129	183	39	79	2903	20.15	–	13	–	88
Banerjee, V.	33	48	17	29	278	8.96	–	–	–	8
Banks, O.A.C.	72	111	18	108	2398	25.78	2	14	–	40
Barker, K.H.D.	3	4	–	23	28	7.00	–	–	–	–
Batty, G.J.	135	204	36	133	4302	25.60	2	22	–	91
Batty, J.N.	191	294	34	168*	8788	33.80	20	38	1	500/64
Beer, W.A.T.	2	1	1	6*	6	6.00	–	–	–	–
Bell, I.R.	157	267	25	262*	10475	43.28	27	56	3	111
Benham, C.C.	41	67	3	111	1825	28.51	2	10	–	40

245

F-C	M	I	NO	HS	Runs	Avge	100	50	1000	Ct/St
Benkenstein, D.M.	209	315	37	259	12901	46.40	33	67	4	139
Benn, S.J.	53	80	12	79	1358	19.97	–	6	–	36
Benning, J.G.E.	41	65	6	128	1883	31.91	4	8	–	16
Berg, G.K.	16	28	2	98	786	30.23	–	7	–	10
Bernard, D.E.	74	126	10	120	3264	28.13	3	17	–	61
Blackwell, I.D.	165	245	19	247*	9103	40.27	23	47	3	59
Blake, A.J.	5	5	–	47	125	25.00	–	–	–	1
Boje, N.	203	303	54	226*	8504	34.15	8	51	–	120
Bopara, R.S.	89	146	20	229	5448	43.23	15	20	1	60
Borrington, P.M.	19	29	4	105	863	34.52	2	4	–	12
Borthwick, S.G.	1	1	1	26*	26	–	–	–	–	–
Botha, A.G.	127	195	27	156*	4063	24.18	4	19	–	95
Bott, M.D.	7	11	1	27	84	8.40	–	–	–	9
Boyce, M.A.G.	34	58	3	106	1427	25.94	1	9	–	7
Bradshaw, D.P.	10	14	3	127*	413	37.54	1	1	–	2
Bragg, W.D.	11	16	–	92	418	26.12	–	2	–	4
Brathwaite, R.M.R.	12	12	3	76*	142	15.77	–	1	–	–
Breese, G.R.	114	182	20	165*	4332	26.74	4	27	–	95
Bresnan, T.T.	87	116	21	126*	2563	26.97	3	11	–	38
Briggs, D.R.	3	3	–	36	37	12.33	–	–	–	1
Broad, S.C.J.	61	77	18	91*	1569	26.59	–	11	–	17
Brooks, J.A.	3	3	3	10*	20	–	–	–	–	1
Brophy, G.L.	106	167	21	185	4646	31.82	6	25	–	266/21
Brown, A.D.	263	412	46	295*	15806	43.18	45	68	8	264/1
Brown, B.C.	1	1	–	46	46	46.00	–	–	–	–
Brown, D.O.	23	39	4	83	975	27.85	–	7	–	12
Brown, F.A.	2	2	–	30	31	15.50	–	–	–	1
Brown, J.F.	130	147	59	38	655	7.44	–	–	–	26
Brown, K.R.	7	12	1	40	156	14.18	–	–	–	7
Brown, M.J.	92	164	16	133	5131	34.66	9	28	1	71
Bryan, T.E.	1	2	–	16	17	8.50	–	–	–	–
Buchanan, N.J.S.	1	2	1	7	8	8.00	–	–	–	–
Buck, N.L.	4	5	2	24*	29	9.66	–	–	–	1
Burrows, T.G.	12	16	3	42	247	19.00	–	–	–	36/1
Burton, D.A.	4	6	3	52*	56	18.66	–	1	–	–
Butcher, M.A.	280	478	39	259	17870	40.70	38	95	8	263
Buttleman, J.E.L.	7	12	1	56*	156	14.18	–	1	–	2
Buttler, J.C.	1	1	–	30	30	30.00	–	–	–	–
Caddick, A.R.	275	356	70	92	4259	14.89	–	9	–	88
Carberry, M.A.	95	168	17	204	6383	42.27	17	32	2	40
Carter, A.	2	1	–	4	4	4.00	–	–	–	–
Carter, N.M.	96	128	21	103	2255	21.07	1	9	–	24
Chambers, M.A.	11	14	11	8*	30	10.00	–	–	–	2
Chanderpaul, S.	245	395	71	303*	17569	54.22	51	88	1+1	141
Chandra, U.S.	1									–
Chapple, G.	238	324	59	155	6701	25.28	6	31	–	79
Chawla, P.P.	52	75	7	102*	1764	25.94	1	12	–	22
Chilton, M.J.	166	268	23	131	8159	33.30	20	32	1	126
Chopra, V.	48	81	5	155	2252	29.63	2	16	–	40
Choudhry, S.H.	2	3	2	75	136	136.00	–	2	–	–
Clare, J.L.	20	26	5	129*	610	29.04	1	5	–	6
Clark, S.R.	102	130	37	62	1314	14.12	–	1	–	27
Clarke, M.J.	109	185	18	201*	7489	44.84	25	30	–	104
Clarke, R.	103	160	14	214	5350	36.64	11	25	1	138
Claydon, M.E.	18	17	2	40	206	13.73	–	–	–	3
Cliff, S.J.	6	7	2	26	71	14.20	–	–	–	1

F-C	M	I	NO	HS	Runs	Avge	100	50	1000	Ct/St
Cobb, J.J.	23	38	3	148*	952	27.20	1	6	–	9
Coetzer, K.J.	33	57	7	153*	1676	33.52	4	4	–	23
Coles, M.T.	2	2	–	16	30	15.00	–	–	–	–
Collingwood, P.D.	177	308	25	206	10354	36.58	23	52	2	194
Collins, P.T.	125	158	43	25	767	6.66	–	–	–	29
Collymore, C.D.	120	170	77	23	741	7.96	–	–	–	42
Compton, N.R.D.	54	97	9	190	2988	33.95	8	12	1	28
Cook, A.N.	113	202	16	195	8298	44.61	21	47	4	111
Cook, M.P.	1	1	–	3	3	3.00	–	–	–	–
Cook, S.J.	117	146	22	93*	2107	16.99	–	6	–	31
Cork, D.G.	299	433	57	200*	9417	25.04	8	51	–	223
Cosgrove, M.J.	67	120	7	233	4751	42.04	12	31	–	45
Cosker, D.A.	161	206	61	52	1891	13.04	–	1	–	103
Coughtrie, R.G.	2	2	–	27	31	15.50	–	–	–	2
Cox, O.B.	1	1	–	61	61	61.00	–	1	–	4/1
Crawley, J.P.	351	584	60	311*	24361	46.49	54	133	10	222/1
Croft, R.D.B.	382	562	100	143	12365	26.76	8	52	–	175
Croft, S.J.	43	64	6	122	1626	28.03	1	9	–	35
Crook, S.P.	35	47	7	97	1261	31.52	–	9	–	12
Cross, G.D.	8	13	1	72	309	25.75	–	3	–	27/8
Crowe, C.D.	42	56	12	44*	695	15.79	–	–	–	18
Daggett, L.M.	27	33	13	33	135	6.75	–	–	–	2
Dalrymple, J.W.M.	108	170	16	244	5459	35.44	9	30	1	63
Danish Kaneria	163	202	77	65	1297	10.37	–	1	–	56
Davies, A.M.	77	102	39	62	701	11.12	–	1	–	17
Davies, S.M.	77	130	15	192	4281	37.22	6	19	2	237/14
Dawson, L.A.	21	31	5	100*	764	29.38	1	4	–	13
Dawson, R.K.J.	103	153	17	87	2927	21.52	–	12	–	63
de Bruyn, Z.	145	246	27	266*	8726	39.84	20	46	0+1	89
Denly, J.L.	52	88	5	149	3058	36.84	9	14	1	23
Deonarine, N.	76	130	17	198	4237	37.49	6	28	0+1	48
Dernbach, J.W.	34	42	14	19	250	8.92	–	–	–	3
Dexter, N.J.	39	60	10	146	2048	40.96	5	10	–	34
Dippenaar, H.H.	175	296	28	250*	11124	41.50	31	48	1+1	177
Di Venuto, M.J.	298	528	38	254*	22751	46.43	53	134	9	349
Dixey, P.G.	12	21	4	103	312	15.60	1	–	–	27/3
du Plessis, F.	61	101	9	176	3262	35.45	4	24	–	52
Durston, W.J.	34	57	12	146*	1726	38.35	1	13	–	34
du Toit, J.	15	23	2	103	700	33.33	2	3	–	8
Ealham, M.A.	281	422	67	153*	11349	31.96	13	67	1	158
Edwards, F.H.	63	97	34	40	394	6.25	–	–	–	11
Edwards, N.J.	49	82	–	212	2898	35.34	3	15	–	35
Edwards, P.D.	10	12	7	43	101	20.20	–	–	–	2
Elliott, G.D.	49	76	4	196*	2193	30.45	5	12	–	31
Ervine, S.M.	98	154	15	126	4494	32.33	8	25	–	88
Evans, A.C.	3	1	–	2	2	2.00	–	–	–	–
Evans, D.	15	18	4	12*	52	3.71	–	–	–	3
Evans, L.	1	2	1	1	1	1.00	–	–	–	–
Evans, L.J.	6	12	1	133*	388	35.27	1	–	–	4
Evans, R.F.	2	2	–	12	12	6.00	–	–	–	1
Ferley, R.S.	33	39	10	78*	630	21.72	–	2	–	10
Finn, S.T.	31	42	11	26*	198	6.38	–	–	–	9
Fisher, I.D.	80	119	19	103*	2201	22.01	1	7	–	27
Fletcher, L.J.	9	8	3	92	121	24.20	–	1	–	–
Flintoff, A.	183	290	23	167	9027	33.80	15	53	–	185
Flower, G.W.	185	313	23	243*	10775	37.15	23	58	–	171

247

F-C	M	I	NO	HS	Runs	Avge	100	50	1000	Ct/St
Footitt, M.H.A.	9	7	5	19*	49	24.50	–	–	–	1
Foster, J.S.	157	234	29	212	7342	35.81	13	37	1	435/38
Foster, P.J.	9	14	–	24	97	6.92	–	–	–	6
Franklin, J.E.C.	114	169	25	219	4875	33.85	9	22	–	41
Franks, P.J.	159	227	43	123*	4878	26.51	3	24	–	55
Frost, T.	120	175	28	242*	4779	32.51	6	22	1	259/18
Gale, A.W.	47	73	1	150	2340	32.50	6	10	–	24
Gale, D.J.	5	8	7	11*	22	22.00	–	–	–	3
Gallian, J.E.R.	259	443	36	312	15266	37.50	38	72	6	231
Gatting, J.S.	4	6	–	152	310	51.66	1	1	–	2
Gayle, C.H.	156	277	20	317	11256	43.79	26	57	0+1	137
Gibbs, H.H.	193	331	13	228	13425	42.21	31	60	–	176
Gidman, A.P.R.	113	196	20	176	6623	37.63	15	37	4	63
Gidman, W.R.S.	1	2	–	8	8	4.00	–	–	–	–
Gilchrist, A.C.	190	280	46	204*	10334	44.16	30	43	–	756/55
Glover, J.C.	6	9	1	14	37	4.62	–	–	–	–
Goddard, L.J.	10	14	4	91	324	32.40	–	2	–	22
Godleman, B.A.	36	59	3	113*	1807	32.26	2	10	–	30
Goodwin, M.W.	250	435	35	344*	19180	47.95	59	79	7+1	139
Grammer, C.M.	4	6	1	64	113	22.60	–	1	–	2
Gray, S.K.	5	7	2	26*	59	11.80	–	–	–	9/1
Griffiths, D.A.	17	23	8	31*	107	7.13	–	–	–	1
Groenewald, T.D.	26	32	5	78	562	20.81	–	3	–	13
Groves, P.R.	3	2	1	52	59	59.00	–	1	–	–
Gurney, H.F.	11	13	7	24*	55	9.16	–	–	–	4
Haddin, B.J.	112	185	19	169	6767	40.76	12	35	–	342/26
Hales, A.D.	8	12	1	78	447	40.63	–	4	–	3
Hall, A.J.	152	218	28	163	6771	35.63	7	44	1	126
Hamilton-Brown, R.J.	8	13	2	171*	433	39.36	2	1	–	6
Harinath, A.	10	15	–	69	380	25.33	–	3	–	4
Harmison, B.W.	31	52	5	110	1202	25.57	3	5	–	23
Harmison, S.J.	189	246	68	49*	1776	9.97	–	–	–	27
Harper, G.M.	1	2	–	0	0	0.00	–	–	–	–
Harris, A.J.	143	190	46	41*	1226	8.51	–	–	–	36
Harris, J.A.R.	28	39	7	87*	619	19.34	–	2	–	5
Harris, R.J.	37	63	7	94	1063	18.98	–	5	–	17
Harrison, D.S.	90	123	18	88	1764	16.80	–	7	–	28
Harrison, P.W.	13	20	4	54	351	21.93	–	1	–	16
Hauritz, N.M.	50	64	14	94	800	16.00	–	2	–	26
Hayes, P.L.	2	1	–	38	38	38.00	–	–	–	–
Hayward, M.	133	169	57	55*	1074	11.30	–	1	–	36
Henderson, C.W.	223	305	69	81	4510	19.11	–	15	–	76
Herath, H.M.R.K.B.	171	242	56	71*	3034	16.31	–	10	–	79
Hildreth, J.C.	94	156	13	303*	5670	39.65	12	30	1	71
Hilfenhaus, B.W.	45	60	21	34	375	9.61	–	–	–	12
Hill, C.M.M.	3	5	–	29	90	18.00	–	–	–	1
Hinds, W.W.	163	277	13	213	9146	34.64	20	46	–	74
Hockley, J.B.	24	38	4	74	663	19.50	–	3	–	14
Hodd, A.J.	38	54	10	123	1367	31.06	3	7	–	64/10
Hodge, B.J.	220	384	38	302*	16808	48.57	50	63	2+3	125
Hodgson, L.J.	2	3	–	63	98	32.66	–	1	–	2
Hodnett, G.P.	20	33	1	168	1051	32.84	2	7	–	14
Hogg, K.W.	55	65	7	71	1348	23.24	–	9	–	13
Hoggard, M.J.	195	246	71	89*	1653	9.44	–	4	–	55
Hopkinson, C.D.	64	103	5	139	2705	27.60	3	15	–	39
Horton, P.J.	59	99	10	173	3685	41.40	8	20	2	49/1

F-C	M	I	NO	HS	Runs	Avge	100	50	1000	Ct/St
Housego, D.M.	5	10	–	36	152	15.20	–	–	–	2
Howgego, B.H.N.	7	13	2	47	235	21.36	–	–	–	3
Hughes, P.J.	28	50	5	198	2786	61.91	10	15	–	22
Hunter, I.D.	63	81	21	65	1064	17.73	–	2	–	18
Hussain, G.M.	1	2	–	8	16	8.00	–	–	–	1
Hussey, D.J.	132	203	21	275	10048	55.20	35	44	4+1	159
Hussey, M.E.K.	225	401	40	331*	19242	53.30	51	87	4	242
Imran Arif	15	16	8	35	94	11.75	–	–	–	5
Imran Tahir	95	115	26	77*	1177	13.22	–	1	–	43
Ireland, A.J.	28	41	14	16*	114	4.22	–	–	–	9
James, N.A.	1	1	–	34	34	34.00	–	–	–	1
Jaques, P.A.	129	229	9	244	11707	53.21	35	54	4+2	97
Javid, A.	3	6	–	21	55	9.16	–	–	–	3
Jefferson, W.I.	91	159	12	222	5292	36.00	12	20	1	88
Johnson, M.G.	54	72	19	123*	1479	27.90	1	8	–	13
Johnson, R.M.	2	3	–	72	105	35.00	–	1	–	8
Johnston, P.R.A.	5	10	1	73	164	18.22	–	1	–	6
Jones, G.O.	126	187	20	156	5696	34.10	12	30	1	382/25
Jones, H.D.	5	4	1	6*	8	2.66	–	–	–	1
Jones, P.S.	134	157	39	114	2228	18.88	2	7	–	29
Jones, R.A.	12	17	3	53*	249	17.78	–	1	–	4
Jones, S.P.	88	108	35	46	899	12.31	–	–	–	17
Jordan, C.J.	21	25	7	57	433	24.05	–	1	–	7
Joseph, R.H.	44	56	20	36*	384	10.66	–	–	–	9
Joslin, A.J.P.	1	2	–	33	62	31.00	–	–	–	1
Joyce, E.C.	142	234	18	211	9606	44.47	22	53	5	109
Kartik, M.	142	179	28	96	2953	19.55	–	14	–	102
Katich, S.M.	207	354	45	306	16787	54.32	47	87	3+4	191
Keedy, G.	187	210	104	64	1201	11.33	–	2	–	46
Kemp, J.M.	123	198	24	188	6225	35.77	14	29	–	170
Kervezee, A.N.	19	30	2	98	805	28.75	–	4	–	6
Key, R.W.T.	210	362	26	270*	14225	42.33	41	55	6	126
Khalid, M.F.	1	–	–	0	0	–	–	–	–	–
Khan, A.	75	84	27	78	1023	17.94	–	4	–	12
Kieswetter, C.	47	66	10	153	2254	40.25	4	12	1	142/2
Killeen, N.	102	145	31	48	1302	11.42	–	–	–	26
King, D.A.	1	2	–	1	2	1.00	–	–	–	2
King, S.J.	2	2	–	8	8	4.00	–	–	–	1
Kirby, S.P.	118	161	52	57	932	8.55	–	–	–	22
Kirtley, R.J.	170	231	76	59	2040	13.16	–	1	–	60
Klokker, F.A.	9	16	3	103*	424	32.61	2	–	–	19
Klopper, W.A.	1	2	–	18	24	12.00	–	–	–	–
Knappett, J.P.T.	13	20	3	100*	523	30.76	1	3	–	26/3
Kruger, G.J.P.	111	135	40	58	1075	11.31	–	2	–	25
Kruger, N.	2	4	–	172	333	83.25	1	1	–	2
Kruis, G.J.	130	180	58	59	1849	15.15	–	3	–	45
Langer, J.L.	360	622	57	342	28382	50.23	86	110	5+6	324
Law, S.G.	367	601	65	263	27080	50.52	79	128	9+2	408
Lawson, M.A.K.	23	28	8	44	280	14.00	–	–	–	10
Laxman, V.V.S.	233	378	45	353	17384	52.20	51	79	0+4	248/1
Lee, B.	116	139	25	97	2120	18.59	–	8	–	35
Lee, J.E.	2	3	1	21*	24	12.00	–	–	–	1
Lee, N.T.	10	16	4	79*	379	31.58	–	2	–	2
Lett, R.J.H.	12	17	2	76*	401	26.73	–	5	–	4
Lewis, J.	195	272	59	62	3215	15.09	–	1	–	46
Lewis, M.F.	1	1	1	74*	74	–	–	1	–	–

F-C	M	I	NO	HS	Runs	Avge	100	50	1000	Ct/St
Lewry, J.D.	187	247	66	72	1834	10.13	–	2	–	52
Linley, T.E.	13	14	1	42	173	13.30	–	–	–	2
Logan, R.J.	55	75	16	37*	533	9.03	–	–	–	16
London, A.B.	4	8	1	68	190	27.14	–	2	–	1
Lotay, J.D.S.	3	3	–	23	44	14.66	–	–	–	1
Loye, M.B.	246	392	37	322*	14516	40.89	41	60	6	119
Lucas, D.S.	64	81	23	55*	1075	18.53	–	1	–	13
Lumb, M.J.	129	217	15	219	6885	34.08	11	44	2	88
Lungley, T.	48	67	15	50	800	15.38	–	1	–	19
Lynch, A.A.	3	3	–	61	96	32.00	–	1	–	2
Lyth, A.	20	30	–	132	916	30.53	1	7	–	12
McDonald, A.B.	51	81	19	150*	2318	37.38	2	17	–	41
McGrath, A.	215	360	26	211	12346	36.96	29	57	2	155
McKenzie, N.D.	184	312	36	226	11823	42.83	29	59	–	155
McKerchar, B.T.	2	4	–	16	23	5.75	–	–	–	–
McLaren, J.H.	78	112	18	140	2577	27.41	2	13	–	39
MacLennan, S.K.	3	5	1	43	63	15.75	–	–	–	–
MacLeod, C.S.	4	3	1	26	38	19.00	–	–	–	4
Maddy, D.L.	244	395	27	229*	12308	33.44	26	58	4	253
Madsen, W.L.	33	57	6	170*	2117	41.50	4	12	–	40
Mahmood, S.I.	81	102	16	94	1134	13.18	–	3	–	20
Malan, C.C.	3	3	–	24	32	10.66	–	–	–	–
Malan, D.J.	29	51	5	132*	1644	35.73	1	13	–	24
Manou, G.A.	89	153	18	190	3340	24.74	5	16	–	283/20
Marshall, H.J.H.	133	226	15	168	7391	35.02	16	35	1	69
Martin, J.	3	4	–	38	95	23.75	–	–	–	1
Martin-Jenkins, R.S.C.	175	263	38	205*	6819	30.30	3	36	1	51
Mascarenhas, A.D.	181	271	30	131	6185	25.66	8	22	–	72
Mason, M.S.	90	115	29	63	1183	13.75	–	3	–	21
Masters, D.D.	118	143	26	119	1683	14.38	1	4	–	37
Maunders, J.K.	83	147	3	180	4382	30.43	7	22	–	50
Maynard, T.L.	13	17	1	51*	232	14.50	–	1	–	11
Meaker, S.C.	7	11	1	72	236	23.60	–	2	–	–
Mendis, B.A.W.	30	40	3	37	429	11.59	–	–	–	10
Mickleburgh, J.C.	9	16	–	72	435	27.18	–	4	–	6
Middlebrook, J.D.	143	202	28	127	4405	25.31	4	16	–	72
Miller, A.S.	4	4	2	4*	5	2.50	–	–	–	–
Milligan, M.J.	2	1	–	2	2	2.00	–	–	–	–
Mitchell, D.K.H.	48	86	13	298	2822	38.65	5	14	1	43
Mohammad Amin	11	10	3	25*	52	7.42	–	–	–	2
Moore, S.C.	103	187	16	246	6862	40.12	15	33	3	49
Morgan, C.F.D.	3	5	–	38	45	9.00	–	–	–	1
Morgan, E.J.G.	48	81	11	209*	2558	36.54	6	11	1	43/1
Morteza Ali	1	–	–	0	0	–	–	–	–	–
Muchall, G.J.	105	185	9	219	5056	28.72	8	25	–	74
Mullaney, S.J.	4	5	1	165*	257	64.25	1	–	–	3
Munday, M.K.	28	25	10	21	107	7.13	–	–	–	11
Murphy, D.	5	6	1	69*	101	20.20	–	1	–	11/1
Murtagh, C.P.	14	20	3	107	316	18.58	1	–	–	9
Murtagh, T.J.	82	114	32	74*	1851	22.57	–	7	–	25
Murtaza Hussain	148	211	40	117	3571	20.88	1	12	–	70
Mustard, P.	101	156	14	130	3956	27.85	2	22	–	346/13
Naik, J.K.H.	13	17	6	109*	260	23.63	1	–	–	6
Nannes, D.P.	22	24	8	31*	108	6.75	–	–	–	6
Napier, G.R.	99	136	29	125	3283	30.68	3	20	–	38
Nash, B.P.	54	91	7	176	2568	30.57	6	10	–	25

F-C	M	I	NO	HS	Runs	Avge	100	50	1000	Ct/St
Nash, C.D.	62	105	9	157	3683	38.36	6	23	1	20
Nash, D.C.	140	203	43	114	5684	35.52	11	27	–	297/23
Naved-ul-Hasan	115	162	18	139	3263	22.65	4	9	–	55
Needham, J.	19	31	12	48	384	20.21	–	–	–	10
Nel, A.	122	139	41	56	1389	14.17	–	2	–	48
Nelson, M.A.G.	7	11	–	42	195	17.72	–	–	–	4
New, T.J.	68	114	14	125	3180	31.80	2	23	–	95/6
Newby, O.J.	43	37	8	38*	238	8.20	–	–	–	8
Newman, S.A.	100	170	3	219	6771	40.54	14	40	4	75
Newport, N.A.	1	–	–	–	–	–	–	–	–	–
Nixon, P.A.	335	499	110	173*	13486	34.66	20	65	1	885/67
Noffke, A.A.	111	154	23	114*	3508	26.77	2	16	–	41
North, M.J.	136	239	24	239*	9652	44.89	26	52	0+1	103
Northeast, S.A.	12	21	2	128*	672	35.36	1	3	–	10
O'Brien, I.E.	80	97	24	44	649	8.89	–	–	–	15
O'Brien, K.J.	13	17	1	171*	517	32.31	1	3	–	10
O'Brien, N.J.	78	117	14	176	3618	35.12	9	14	–	225/25
Onions, G.	69	88	27	41	747	12.24	–	–	–	17
Ord, J.E.	1	2	–	9	10	5.00	–	–	–	–
O'Shea, M.P.	6	9	–	50	137	15.22	–	1	–	1
Paget, C.D.	12	18	3	46	120	8.00	–	–	–	6
Palladino, A.P.	40	45	16	41	333	11.48	–	–	–	18
Panesar, M.S.	109	141	48	39*	789	8.48	–	–	–	25
Park, G.T.	34	57	8	178*	1904	38.85	3	12	1	35
Parnell, W.D.	16	21	3	90	347	19.27	–	2	–	2
Parry, S.D.	3	2	–	2	3	1.50	–	–	–	1
Parsons, T.W.	6	6	1	12	24	4.80	–	–	–	–
Pascal, N.T.	17	26	10	19	67	4.18	–	–	–	8
Pascoe, D.C.	1	2	–	37	67	33.50	–	–	–	–
Patel, A.	3	6	2	69*	153	38.25	–	1	–	2
Patel, J.S.	81	95	33	120	1224	19.74	1	3	–	27
Patel, S.R.	60	90	6	176	3680	43.80	9	20	–	32
Patterson, S.A.	15	16	5	46	166	15.09	–	–	–	3
Pattinson, D.J.	29	34	3	59	326	10.51	–	1	–	3
Pearson, E.G.	1	1	–	0	0	0.00	–	–	–	–
Peters, S.D.	178	304	25	178	9365	33.56	21	46	3	137
Peterson, R.J.	91	143	18	130	3164	25.31	5	10	–	40
Pettini, M.L.	78	131	17	208*	4064	35.64	5	24	1	60
Phillips, B.J.	97	135	23	100*	2402	21.44	1	13	–	26
Phillips, T.J.	51	69	8	89	1196	19.60	–	4	–	32
Pietersen, K.P.	140	233	16	254*	11026	50.81	38	44	3	112
Piolet, S.A.	1	2	1	26*	31	31.00	–	–	–	–
Pipe, D.J.	82	121	22	133*	2870	28.98	4	12	–	226/21
Plunkett, L.E.	85	118	24	94*	2067	21.98	–	9	–	50
Pollard, K.A.	20	33	1	174	1199	37.46	3	5	–	32
Ponting, R.T.	236	400	53	257	20192	58.19	72	86	–	248
Poonia, N.S.	14	22	–	111	557	25.31	1	2	–	5
Porterfield, W.T.S.	34	58	2	166	1807	32.26	2	11	–	38
Pothas, N.	201	310	59	165	10604	42.24	24	54	–	559/45
Powell, D.B.L.	96	138	29	69	1477	12.73	–	4	–	31
Powell, M.J.	193	323	30	299	11511	39.28	25	58	5	121
Poynton, T.	3	5	–	14	17	3.40	–	–	–	7/2
Prince, A.G.	166	265	37	254	10204	44.75	25	48	0+1	109
Prior, M.J.	154	243	25	201*	8785	40.29	20	50	3	354/24
Probert, T.J.W.	1	1	1	0*	0	–	–	–	–	1
Pyrah, R.M.	15	21	2	106	497	26.15	1	3	–	9

251

F-C	M	I	NO	HS	Runs	Avge	100	50	1000	Ct/St
Ramdin, D.	71	118	14	166	2807	26.99	5	13	–	188/19
Ramprakash, M.R.	426	701	89	301*	33244	54.32	108	139	19	244
Rankin, W.B.	25	26	10	12*	65	4.06	–	–	–	9
Rashid, A.U.	53	73	13	157*	2205	36.75	4	13	–	23
Rayner, O.P.	31	35	7	101	526	18.78	1	1	–	32
Read, C.M.W.	222	328	56	240	9755	35.86	16	52	2	647/36
Redfern, D.J.	23	36	3	95	1007	30.51	–	7	–	14
Rees, G.P.	46	76	4	154	2662	36.97	8	13	2	44
Riazuddin, H.	2	2	–	4	7	3.50	–	–	–	–
Richards, D.M.	41	73	1	159	2708	37.61	4	17	–	40
Richardson, A.	108	109	42	91	761	11.35	–	1	–	33
Richardson, A.P.	44	61	8	31*	384	8.93	–	–	–	13
Robson, S.D.	7	13	–	110	441	33.92	1	2	–	12
Rogers, C.J.L.	149	263	17	319	12865	52.29	39	61	3+2	150
Rosenberg, M.C.	14	19	2	86	385	22.64	–	2	–	3
Rudolph, J.A.	160	272	18	222*	11371	44.76	33	52	3	145
Ryan, L.C.	6	5	–	21	44	8.80	–	–	–	4
Sadler, J.L.	63	107	15	145	3002	32.63	3	16	1	43
Saggers, M.J.	119	147	43	64	1165	11.20	–	2	–	27
Sammy, D.J.G.	58	97	7	121	2285	25.38	1	16	–	75
Sandri, P.S.E.	29	41	20	26*	217	10.33	–	–	–	4
Sangakkara, K.C.	170	271	20	287	11692	46.58	28	56	0+1	317/33
Sarwan, R.R.	183	307	22	291	11396	39.98	30	60	–	131
Saxelby, I.D.	12	16	4	60*	188	15.66	–	1	–	6
Sayers, J.J.	76	125	10	187	3965	34.47	10	17	1	48
Schofield, C.P.	92	130	18	144	3303	29.49	1	24	–	52
Scott, B.J.M.	70	107	20	164*	2397	27.55	3	13	–	181/21
Sen, A.	3	3	–	17	34	11.33	–	–	–	4
Shafayat, B.M.	112	190	7	161	5551	30.33	8	31	1	101/8
Shah, O.A.	209	356	33	203	13717	42.46	37	69	8	160
Shahid Afridi	109	180	4	164	5598	31.80	12	30	–	75
Shahzad, A.	22	27	9	88	553	30.72	–	2	–	4
Shakib Al Hasan	38	70	7	129	2164	34.34	3	11	–	24
Shantry, A.J.	28	36	12	100	422	17.58	1	–	–	6
Shantry, J.D.	4	5	1	6	12	3.00	–	–	–	2
Sharma, R.	4	6	2	58*	179	44.75	–	1	–	1
Shreck, C.E.	80	90	53	19	144	3.89	–	–	–	27
Siddle, P.M.	27	36	9	38	374	13.85	–	–	–	12
Sidebottom, R.J.	137	175	52	54	1511	12.28	–	1	–	46
Silverwood, C.E.W.	183	242	48	80	3075	15.85	–	9	–	43
Simmons, L.M.P.	62	108	9	282	3372	34.06	7	15	–	75/4
Simpson, J.A.	3	6	–	87	170	28.33	–	1	–	5
Smith, B.F.	326	515	56	204	18495	40.29	40	98	8	205
Smith, D.R.	80	132	9	155	3656	29.72	7	14	–	77
Smith, D.S.	119	211	8	212	7254	35.73	15	34	0+1	101
Smith, D.T.	1	1	–	6	6	6.00	–	–	–	1
Smith, G.M.	55	95	9	126	2587	30.08	2	18	–	15
Smith, G.P.	13	24	1	54	446	19.39	–	2	–	5
Smith, S.P.D.	5	9	1	68	240	30.00	–	1	–	4
Smith, T.C.	42	53	13	104*	1050	26.25	1	3	–	36
Smith, T.M.J.	2	3	–	10	13	4.33	–	–	–	–
Smith, W.R.	70	112	9	201*	3433	33.00	8	11	–	33
Snell, S.D.	31	50	6	127	1357	30.84	1	11	–	78/3
Solanki, V.S.	252	418	25	270	14322	36.44	26	75	5	258
Spearman, C.M.	201	360	16	341	13021	37.85	30	56	3	197
Spriegel, M.N.W.	21	36	2	100	812	23.88	1	3	–	13

F-C	M	I	NO	HS	Runs	Avge	100	50	1000	Ct/St
Sreesanth, S.	50	69	21	35	477	9.93	–	–	–	11
Stayt, T.P.	4	4	1	36	45	15.00	–	–	–	2
Stevens, D.I.	155	250	17	208	7857	33.72	17	40	2	122
Stiff, D.A.	18	20	8	49	250	20.83	–	–	–	1
Stirling, P.R.	5	8	–	100	201	25.12	1	–	–	3
Stoneman, M.D.	34	58	2	101	1264	22.57	1	5	–	23
Strachan, J.P.	3	4	1	13*	18	6.00	–	–	–	1
Strauss, A.J.	181	321	16	177	13090	42.91	35	56	4	148
Stubbings, S.D.	139	251	14	151	7557	31.88	12	38	3	64
Suppiah, A.V.	44	73	2	151	2525	35.56	4	14	1	29
Sutton, L.D.	147	233	37	151*	6250	31.88	9	19	–	371/17
Swainland, C.J.	1	1	–	2	2	2.00	–	–	–	–
Swann, G.P.	187	258	21	183	6440	27.17	4	34	–	134
Tahir, N.S.	49	53	16	49	589	15.91	–	–	–	5
Tait, S.W.	50	70	29	68	509	12.41	–	2	–	15
Taylor, B.V.	54	68	26	40	431	10.26	–	–	–	6
Taylor, C.G.	129	223	16	196	7141	34.49	17	31	2	85
Taylor, J.E.	63	95	17	106	1077	13.80	1	1	–	15
Taylor, J.W.A.	21	33	7	207*	1271	48.88	3	7	1	13
ten Doeschate, R.N.	69	97	12	259*	4132	48.61	15	12	–	35
Thomas, A.C.	97	138	29	119*	2830	25.96	2	11	–	30
Thompson, C.E.J.	1	2	–	16	16	8.00	–	–	–	–
Thornely, M.A.	5	9	1	19	55	6.87	–	–	–	7
Thorp, C.D.	50	66	7	75	833	14.11	–	2	–	30
Tomlinson, J.A.	50	64	30	35*	332	9.76	–	–	–	13
Tredwell, J.C.	88	124	17	123*	2478	23.15	2	12	–	84
Trego, P.D.	83	120	18	140	3659	35.87	7	22	–	25
Tremlett, C.T.	92	122	31	64	1638	18.00	–	–	6	27
Trescothick, M.E.	255	438	23	284	16645	40.10	39	85	3	314
Trott, I.J.L.	135	225	29	210	8773	44.76	20	44	5	131
Troughton, J.O.	110	166	14	223	5913	38.90	16	30	1	53
Tudor, A.J.	129	169	34	144	2960	21.92	2	9	–	36
Tuffey, D.R.	79	93	22	89*	1012	14.25	–	4	–	33
Turnbull, P.T.	1	1	1	0*	0		–	–	–	1
Turner, M.L.	9	8	2	57	89	14.83	–	1	–	3
Udal, S.D.	288	411	78	117*	7715	23.16	1	33	–	121
van der Wath, J.J.	94	139	23	113*	2828	24.37	2	17	–	29
van Jaarsveld, M.	222	373	34	262*	15587	45.97	48	75	5+1	328
Vaughan, M.P.	268	468	27	197	16295	36.95	42	68	4	117
Vince, J.M.	9	13	1	75	301	25.08	–	1	–	3
Voges, A.C.	73	122	15	180	4176	39.02	8	22	–	95
Wagg, G.G.	64	87	11	108	1942	25.55	1	10	–	22
Wagh, M.A.	187	308	26	315	11234	39.83	28	55	6	80
Wainwright, D.J.	24	31	8	104*	817	35.52	2	2	–	9
Wakely, A.G.	21	36	2	113*	744	21.88	1	5	–	15
Walker, G.W.	7	9	2	37*	95	13.57	–	–	–	2
Walker, M.J.	200	332	35	275*	10772	36.26	27	43	4	134
Wallace, M.A.	151	241	16	139	6222	27.65	8	28	–	375/33
Waller, M.T.C.	4	6	1	28	67	13.40	–	–	–	1
Walters, S.J.	28	44	1	188	1094	25.44	2	3	–	30
Waters, H.T.	23	37	18	34	145	7.63	–	–	–	6
Watson, M.J.C.	3	2	1	22	43	43.00	–	–	–	–
Watson, S.R.	75	129	15	203*	5190	45.52	13	27	–	56
Wessels, M.H.	66	108	7	109	3037	30.06	4	20	–	127/11
Westfield, M.S.	7	8	3	32	46	9.20	–	–	–	1
Westley, T.	25	43	8	132	1077	30.77	1	5	–	14

F-C	M	I	NO	HS	Runs	Avge	100	50	1000	Ct/St
Westwood, I.J.	66	112	12	178	3423	34.23	7	18	–	34
Wheater, A.J.	4	3	–	36	58	19.33	–	–	–	9
Wheeldon, D.A.	5	6	–	87	160	26.66	–	1	–	3
Whelan, C.D.	21	25	6	58	297	15.63	–	1	–	3
White, C.L.	103	172	21	260*	6351	42.05	15	28	2	97
White, G.G.	8	10	2	65	140	17.50	–	1	–	1
White, R.A.	87	150	15	277	4682	34.68	7	24	1	55
White, W.A.	23	35	5	68	486	16.20	–	1	–	10
Whiteley, R.A.	1	2	–	27	45	22.50	–	–	–	–
Wigley, D.H.	50	62	22	70	532	13.30	–	2	–	22
Willey, D.J.	10	17	1	60	331	20.68	–	1	–	3
Williams, R.E.M.	9	15	5	31	119	11.90	–	–	–	4
Willoughby, C.M.	193	215	96	47	716	6.01	–	–	–	41
Wilson, G.C.	7	10	1	38	127	14.11	–	–	–	13
Woakes, C.R.	32	38	12	131*	769	29.57	1	2	–	16
Wood, M.J.	97	164	8	297	5184	33.23	9	32	1	30
Woodman, R.J.	10	16	2	46*	213	15.21	–	–	–	3
Woolley, R.J.J.	3	2	–	17	18	9.00	–	–	–	4
Wright, B.J.	21	33	2	108	680	21.93	1	3	–	18
Wright, C.J.C.	43	53	13	76	755	18.87	–	3	–	11
Wright, D.G.	97	146	22	111	3059	24.66	1	16	–	45
Wright, L.J.	57	81	14	155*	2402	35.85	7	12	–	26
Wyatt, A.C.F.	3	3	1	3	4	2.00	–	–	–	1
Yardy, M.H.	120	204	19	257	7261	39.24	14	37	2	87
Yasir Arafat	157	237	35	122	5476	27.10	4	29	–	44
Young, E.G.C.	3	3	1	31	40	20.00	–	–	–	1

BOWLING

'50wS' denotes instances of taking 50 or more wickets in a season. Where these have been achieved outside the British Isles they are shown after a plus sign.

	Runs	Wkts	Avge	Best	5wI	10wM	50wS
Ackerman, H.D.	57	0					
Adams, A.R.	9582	395	24.25	6- 25	13	2	–
Adams, J.H.K.	657	11	59.72	2- 16	–	–	–
Afzaal, U.	4861	90	54.01	4-101	–	–	–
Aga, R.G.	823	25	32.92	4- 63	–	–	–
Ahmed, J.S.	542	13	41.69	3- 42	–	–	–
Ahmed, M.	143	2	71.50	1- 28	–	–	–
Ali, Kabir	11520	429	26.85	8- 50	21	4	5
Ali, Kadeer	304	3	101.33	1- 4	–	–	–
Ali, M.M.	1033	10	103.30	4- 29	–	–	–
Allenby, J.	1892	58	32.62	5-125	1	–	–
Ambrose, T.R.	1	0					
Amla, H.M.	221	1	221.00	1- 10	–	–	–
Anderson, J.M.	9910	345	28.72	7- 43	18	2	2
Andrew, G.M.	2998	78	38.43	5- 58	2	–	–
Ansari, A.S.	429	12	35.75	4- 50	–	–	–
Anyon, J.E.	4509	112	40.25	6- 82	2	–	–
Ashling, C.P.	116	3	38.66	2- 66	–	–	–
Ashok, A.	15	1	15.00	1- 15	–	–	–
Azeem Rafiq	487	10	48.70	3- 34	–	–	–
Azhar Mahmood	13430	536	25.05	8- 61	22	3	0+1
Baer, M.	330	3	110.00	2- 19	–	–	–
Baker, F.B.	441	5	88.20	2- 75	–	–	–
Baker, G.C.	134	2	67.00	1- 31	–	–	–

F-C	Runs	Wkts	Avge	Best	5wI	10wM	50wS
Baker, L.S.	1655	43	38.48	6- 84	1	–	–
Balcombe, D.J.	2020	45	44.88	5-112	1	–	–
Bandara, C.M.	9169	359	25.54	8- 49	11	2	–
Banerjee, V.	3391	70	48.44	4- 38	–	–	–
Banks, O.A.C.	6977	179	38.97	7- 70	6	1	–
Barker, K.H.D.	175	1	175.00	1- 51	–	–	–
Batty, G.J.	12380	368	33.64	7- 52	15	1	2
Batty, J.N.	61	1	61.00	1- 21	–	–	–
Beer, W.A.T.	81	1	81.00	1- 18	–	–	–
Bell, I.R.	1564	47	33.27	4- 4	–	–	–
Benham, C.C.	37	0					
Benkenstein, D.M.	3232	93	34.75	4- 16	–	–	–
Benn, S.J.	5427	172	31.55	5- 51	5	–	–
Benning, J.G.E.	1374	21	65.42	3- 43	–	–	–
Berg, G.K.	1057	28	37.75	5- 55	2	–	–
Bernard, D.E.	3842	128	30.01	5- 44	2	–	–
Blackwell, I.D.	11140	286	38.95	7- 85	10	–	–
Blake, A.J.	32	0					
Boje, N.	17960	562	31.95	8- 93	22	2	–
Bopara, R.S.	4094	90	45.48	5- 75	1	–	–
Borrington, P.M.	5	0					
Borthwick, S.G.	95	3	31.66	3- 95	–	–	–
Botha, A.G.	10321	298	34.63	8- 53	9	1	1
Boyce, M.A.G.	61	0					
Bradshaw, D.P.	304	2	152.00	1- 28	–	–	–
Bragg, W.D.	23	0					
Brathwaite, R.M.R.	1176	26	45.23	5- 54	1	–	–
Breese, G.R.	8364	280	29.87	7- 60	12	3	–
Bresnan, T.T.	7176	222	32.32	5- 42	3	–	–
Briggs, D.R.	295	8	36.87	3- 62	–	–	–
Broad, S.C.J.	6005	201	29.87	6- 91	10	–	–
Brooks, J.A.	325	9	36.11	4- 76	–	–	–
Brophy, G.L.	1	0					
Brown, A.D.	718	6	119.66	3- 25	–	–	–
Brown, D.O.	1251	28	44.67	5- 38	1	–	–
Brown, F.A.	136	4	34.00	3- 26	–	–	–
Brown, J.F.	14039	414	33.91	7- 69	22	5	3
Brown, K.R.	44	2	22.00	2- 30	–	–	–
Brown, M.J.	20	0					
Bryan, T.E.	6	0					
Buchanan, N.J.S.	39	1	39.00	1- 30	–	–	–
Buck, N.L.	276	3	92.00	1- 35	–	–	–
Burton, D.A.	475	9	52.77	5- 68	1	–	–
Butcher, M.A.	4237	125	33.89	5- 86	1	–	–
Buttleman, J.E.L.	309	10	30.90	2- 32	–	–	–
Caddick, A.R.	31387	1180	26.59	9- 32	78	17	12
Carberry, M.A.	763	9	84.77	2- 85	–	–	–
Carter, A.	164	3	54.66	1- 27	–	–	–
Carter, N.M.	9129	246	37.10	6- 63	9	–	–
Chambers, M.A.	861	24	35.87	4- 62	–	–	–
Chanderpaul, S.	2453	56	43.80	4- 48	–	–	–
Chandra, U.S.	112	1	112.00	1-112	–	–	–
Chapple, G.	20097	728	27.60	7- 53	29	2	4
Chawla, P.P.	5683	211	26.93	6- 46	14	2	–
Chilton, M.J.	667	12	55.58	2- 3	–	–	–
Chopra, V.	78	0					

255

F-C	Runs	Wkts	Avge	Best	5wI	10wM	50wS
Choudhry, S.H.	54	0					
Clare, J.L.	1481	51	29.03	7- 74	2	–	–
Clark, S.R.	10047	369	27.22	8- 58	13	1	–
Clarke, M.J.	1443	30	48.10	6- 9	1	–	–
Clarke, R.	5855	136	43.05	4- 21	–	–	–
Claydon, M.E.	1353	35	38.65	4- 90	–	–	–
Cliff, S.J.	459	13	35.30	4- 42	–	–	–
Cobb, J.J.	205	5	41.00	2- 11	–	–	–
Coetzer, K.J.	22	0					
Coles, M.T.	130	2	65.00	2-130	–	–	–
Collingwood, P.D.	4818	120	40.15	5- 52	1	–	–
Collins, P.T.	11068	416	26.60	6- 24	11	–	0+1
Collymore, C.D.	9584	349	27.46	7- 57	10	2	–
Compton, N.R.D.	128	1	128.00	1- 94	–	–	–
Cook, A.N.	169	5	33.80	3- 13	–	–	–
Cook, M.P.	9	0					
Cook, S.J.	9394	293	32.06	8- 63	12	–	–
Cork, D.G.	24595	922	26.67	9- 43	33	5	7
Cosgrove, M.J.	1174	29	40.48	3- 3	–	–	–
Cosker, D.A.	14666	392	37.41	6- 91	6	1	–
Crawley, J.P.	283	2	141.50	1- 7	–	–	–
Croft, R.D.B.	39190	1107	35.40	8- 66	49	9	10
Croft, S.J.	1324	30	44.13	4- 51	–	–	–
Crook, S.P.	2842	59	48.16	5- 71	1	–	–
Crowe, C.D.	2271	60	37.85	4- 47	–	–	–
Daggett, L.M.	2270	61	37.21	8- 94	2	–	–
Dalrymple, J.W.M.	6502	149	43.63	5- 49	1	–	–
Danish Kaneria	21157	805	26.28	8- 59	57	9	3+1
Davies, A.M.	5444	251	21.68	8- 24	12	2	1
Dawson, L.A.	634	16	39.62	2- 3	–	–	–
Dawson, R.K.J.	8770	199	44.07	6- 82	5	–	–
de Bruyn, Z.	6616	167	39.61	7- 67	3	–	–
Denly, J.L.	447	10	44.70	2- 13	–	–	–
Deonarine, N.	2596	77	33.71	5- 94	1	–	–
Dernbach, J.W.	3115	78	39.93	6- 47	3	–	–
Dexter, N.J.	789	15	52.60	2- 37	–	–	–
Dippenaar, H.H.	61	1	61.00	1- 6	–	–	–
Di Venuto, M.J.	484	5	96.80	1- 0	–	–	–
du Plessis, F.	1029	30	34.30	4- 39	–	–	–
Durston, W.J.	1420	24	59.16	3- 23	–	–	–
du Toit, J.	335	5	67.00	3- 31	–	–	–
Ealham, M.A.	17962	643	27.93	8- 36	24	2	1
Edwards, F.H.	6634	187	35.47	7- 87	10	1	–
Edwards, N.J.	194	2	97.00	1- 16	–	–	–
Edwards, P.D.	820	12	68.33	3- 72	–	–	–
Elliott, G.D.	2393	63	37.98	4- 56	–	–	–
Ervine, S.M.	6563	157	41.80	6- 82	5	–	–
Evans, A.C.	210	4	52.50	2- 41	–	–	–
Evans, D.	1313	38	34.55	6- 35	2	–	–
Evans, L.	115	4	28.75	2- 39	–	–	–
Evans, R.F.	117	1	117.00	1- 86	–	–	–
Ferley, R.S.	2876	64	44.93	6-136	1	–	–
Finn, S.T.	3002	94	31.93	5- 57	1	–	1
Fisher, I.D.	6728	157	42.85	5- 30	7	1	–
Fletcher, L.J.	870	30	29.00	4- 38	–	–	–
Flintoff, A.	11059	350	31.59	5- 24	4	–	–

F-C	Runs	Wkts	Avge	Best	5wI	10wM	50wS
Flower, G.W.	5573	165	33.77	7- 31	3	–	–
Footitt, M.H.A.	729	23	31.69	5- 45	2	–	–
Foster, J.S.	128	1	128.00	1-122	–	–	–
Foster, P.J.	773	24	32.20	4- 26	–	–	–
Franklin, J.E.C.	9573	359	26.66	7- 30	12	1	–
Franks, P.J.	13556	418	32.43	7- 56	11	–	2
Frost, T.	30	1	30.00	1- 12	–	–	–
Gale, A.W.	47	1	47.00	1- 33	–	–	–
Gale, D.J.	148	1	148.00	1- 67	–	–	–
Gallian, J.E.R.	4164	96	43.37	6-115	1	–	–
Gayle, C.H.	4949	128	38.66	5- 34	2	–	–
Gibbs, H.H.	78	3	26.00	2- 14	–	–	–
Gidman, A.P.R.	3994	87	45.90	4- 47	–	–	–
Gidman, W.R.S.	86	4	21.50	3- 37	–	–	–
Glover, J.C.	421	13	32.38	5- 38	1	–	–
Godleman, B.A.	35	0					
Goodwin, M.W.	376	7	53.71	2- 23	–	–	–
Grammer, C.M.	74	3	24.66	2- 35	–	–	–
Griffiths, D.A.	1657	46	36.02	4- 46	–	–	–
Groenewald, T.D.	2050	60	34.16	6- 50	3	–	–
Groves, P.R.	207	8	25.87	5- 72	1	–	–
Gurney, H.F.	1002	18	55.66	5- 82	1	–	–
Hales, A.D.	140	3	46.66	2- 63	–	–	–
Hall, A.J.	11439	446	25.64	6- 77	15	1	–
Hamilton-Brown, R.J.	194	6	32.33	2- 49	–	–	–
Harinath, A.	18	0					
Harmison, B.W.	742	19	39.05	4- 27	–	–	–
Harmison, S.J.	19032	679	28.02	7- 12	26	1	6
Harper, G.M.	49	4	12.25	4- 49	–	–	–
Harris, A.J.	14348	442	32.46	7- 54	17	3	2
Harris, J.A.R.	2671	87	30.70	7- 66	2	1	–
Harris, R.J.	3524	107	32.93	7-108	2	–	–
Harrison, D.S.	8120	220	36.90	5- 48	6	–	1
Hauritz, N.M.	4587	100	45.87	4- 86	–	–	–
Hayward, M.	12735	442	28.81	6- 31	9	2	1
Henderson, C.W.	23234	735	31.61	7- 57	27	1	–
Herath, H.M.R.K.B.	14814	615	24.08	8- 43	34	5	0+2
Hildreth, J.C.	316	4	79.00	2- 39	–	–	–
Hilfenhaus, B.W.	5456	182	29.97	7- 58	6	1	0+1
Hill, C.M.M.	202	2	101.00	1- 77	–	–	–
Hinds, W.W.	1736	48	36.16	3- 9	–	–	–
Hockley, J.B.	233	3	77.66	1- 21	–	–	–
Hodd, A.J.	7	0					
Hodge, B.J.	3038	74	41.05	4- 17	–	–	–
Hodgson, L.J.	88	0					
Hodnett, G.P.	183	3	61.00	2- 91	–	–	–
Hogg, K.W.	3756	104	36.11	5- 48	1	–	–
Hoggard, M.J.	18288	668	27.37	7- 49	22	1	2
Hopkinson, C.D.	262	2	131.00	1- 20	–	–	–
Horton, P.J.	10	0					
Housego, D.M.	17	0					
Hughes, P.J.	9	0					
Hunter, I.D.	5835	150	38.90	5- 46	3	–	–
Hussain, G.M.	107	2	53.50	2- 73	–	–	–
Hussey, D.J.	1281	20	64.05	4-105	–	–	–
Hussey, M.E.K.	872	21	41.52	3- 34	–	–	–

F-C	Runs	Wkts	Avge	Best	5wI	10wM	50wS
Imran Arif	1474	39	37.79	5- 50	2	–	–
Imran Tahir	9891	382	25.89	8- 76	24	5	1+1
Ireland, A.J.	2487	77	32.29	7- 36	2	1	–
James, N.A.	6	1	6.00	1- 6	–	–	–
Jaques, P.A.	87	0					
Javid, A.	78	0					
Jefferson, W.I.	60	1	60.00	1- 16	–	–	–
Johnson, M.G.	6094	200	30.47	8- 61	5	2	–
Johnston, P.R.A.	1	0					
Jones, G.O.	18	0					
Jones, H.D.	344	6	57.33	4- 57	–	–	–
Jones, P.S.	13163	353	37.28	6- 25	10	1	2
Jones, R.A.	1180	30	39.33	6-100	1	–	–
Jones, S.P.	7947	260	30.56	6- 45	15	1	–
Jordan, C.J.	1824	45	40.53	4- 84	–	–	–
Joseph, R.H.	4073	128	31.82	6- 32	5	–	1
Joyce, E.C.	1025	11	93.18	2- 34	–	–	–
Kartik, M.	12430	475	26.16	9- 70	25	3	1
Katich, S.M.	3405	92	37.01	7-130	3	–	–
Keedy, G.	17810	554	32.14	7- 95	27	5	3
Kemp, J.M.	5564	194	28.68	6- 56	5	–	–
Kervezee, A.N.	59	2	29.50	1- 14	–	–	–
Key, R.W.T.	153	1	153.00	1- 14	–	–	–
Khalid, M.F.	57	0					
Khan, A.	7893	248	31.82	6- 52	7	–	2
Killeen, N.	8215	262	31.35	7- 70	9	–	1
King, S.J.	156	4	39.00	3- 61	–	–	–
Kirby, S.P.	12038	428	28.12	8- 80	15	4	2
Kirtley, R.J.	16607	614	27.04	7- 21	29	4	7
Klokker, F.A.	99	0					
Klopper, W.A.	76	0					
Kruger, G.J.P.	11042	356	31.01	8-112	14	2	–
Kruis, G.J.	12804	406	31.53	7- 58	19	1	1
Langer, J.L.	210	5	42.00	2- 17	–	–	–
Law, S.G.	4236	83	51.03	5- 39	1	–	–
Lawson, M.A.K.	2115	46	45.97	6- 88	4	–	–
Laxman, V.V.S.	754	22	34.27	3- 11	–	–	–
Lee, B.	13747	487	28.22	7-114	20	2	–
Lee, J.E.	149	2	74.50	2- 63	–	–	–
Lee, N.T.	24	1	24.00	1- 24	–	–	–
Lett, R.J.H.	67	1	67.00	1- 39	–	–	–
Lewis, J.	17827	678	26.29	8- 95	33	5	7
Lewry, J.D.	16834	621	27.10	8-106	31	4	5
Liddle, C.J.	962	17	56.58	3- 42	–	–	–
Linley, T.E.	978	22	44.45	4- 77	–	–	–
Logan, R.J.	5347	135	39.60	6- 93	4	–	–
London, A.B.	39	0					
Lotay, J.D.S.	187	5	37.40	3-147	–	–	–
Loye, M.B.	61	1	61.00	1- 8	–	–	–
Lucas, D.S.	5576	175	31.86	7- 24	7	1	1
Lumb, M.J.	242	6	40.33	2- 10	–	–	–
Lungley, T.	4154	130	31.95	5- 20	3	–	1
Lynch, A.A.	8	0					
Lyth, A.	155	3	51.66	1- 12	–	–	–
McDonald, A.B.	3332	115	28.97	6- 34	3	–	–
McGrath, A.	4008	114	35.15	5- 39	1	–	–

F-C	Runs	Wkts	Avge	Best	5wI	10wM	50wS
McKenzie, N.D.	369	7	52.71	2- 13	–	–	–
McLaren, R.	6201	249	24.90	8- 38	10	1	1+1
MacLeod, C.S.	214	11	19.45	4- 66	–	–	–
Maddy, D.L.	6685	206	32.45	5- 37	5	–	–
Madsen, W.L.	304	6	50.66	3- 45	–	–	–
Mahmood, S.I.	7491	231	32.42	6- 30	6	1	–
Malan, C.C.	150	3	50.00	1- 35	–	–	–
Malan, D.J.	714	14	51.00	2- 21	–	–	–
Manou, G.A.	8	0					
Marshall, H.J.H.	1083	27	40.11	4- 24	–	–	–
Martin-Jenkins, R.S.C.	11660	354	32.93	7- 51	7	–	–
Mascarenhas, A.D.	11818	418	28.27	6- 25	16	–	1
Mason, M.S.	7561	280	27.00	8- 45	10	1	3
Masters, D.D.	9669	323	29.93	6- 24	11	–	–
Maunders, J.K.	928	24	38.66	4- 15	–	–	–
Maynard, T.L.	18	0					
Meaker, S.C.	637	14	45.50	3- 86	–	–	–
Mendis, B.A.W.	2916	163	17.88	7- 37	9	2	0+1
Mickleburgh, J.C.	39	0					
Middlebrook, J.D.	12310	319	38.58	6- 82	8	1	1
Miller, A.S.	294	11	26.72	4- 76	–	–	–
Milligan, M.J.	75	1	75.00	1- 17	–	–	–
Mitchell, D.K.H.	532	16	33.25	4- 49	–	–	–
Mohammad Amin	1195	15	79.66	3- 63	–	–	–
Moore, S.C.	321	5	64.20	1- 13	–	–	–
Morgan, E.J.G.	46	2	23.00	2- 24	–	–	–
Muchall, G.J.	615	15	41.00	3- 26	–	–	–
Mullaney, S.J.	84	1	84.00	1- 3	–	–	–
Munday, M.K.	2296	80	28.70	8- 55	4	2	–
Murtagh, C.P.	8	0					
Murtagh, T.J.	7117	242	29.40	7- 82	10	1	2
Murtaza Hussain	14305	573	24.96	9- 54	36	7	0+5
Naik, J.K.H.	881	16	55.06	3- 70	–	–	–
Nannes, D.P.	2205	89	24.77	7- 50	2	1	–
Napier, G.R.	7854	207	37.94	6-103	3	–	–
Nash, B.P.	380	10	38.00	2- 7	–	–	–
Nash, C.D.	1041	19	54.78	3- 7	–	–	–
Nash, D.C.	105	2	52.50	1- 8	–	–	–
Naved-ul-Hasan	12027	494	24.34	7- 49	27	4	2+3
Needham, J.	1268	35	36.22	6- 49	1	–	–
Nel, A.	11257	414	27.19	6- 25	13	1	–
Nelson, M.A.G.	124	2	62.00	2- 62	–	–	–
New, T.J.	211	5	42.20	2- 18	–	–	–
Newby, O.J.	3505	105	33.38	5- 69	1	–	–
Newman, S.A.	57	0					
Nixon, P.A.	150	0					
Noffke, A.A.	10692	374	28.58	8- 24	18	1	0+1
North, M.J.	4433	103	43.03	6- 69	1	–	–
Northeast, S.A.	2	0					
O'Brien, I.E.	7204	278	25.91	8- 55	12	1	–
O'Brien, K.J.	238	11	21.63	4- 38	–	–	–
O'Brien, N.J.	4	1	4.00	1- 4	–	–	–
Onions, G.	6557	222	29.53	8-101	9	–	2
Paget, C.D.	617	10	61.70	3- 63	–	–	–
Palladino, A.P.	3056	79	38.68	6- 41	2	–	–
Panesar, M.S.	11640	352	33.06	7-181	19	3	3

F-C	Runs	Wkts	Avge	Best	5wI	10wM	50wS
Park, G.T.	631	9	70.11	3- 25	–	–	–
Parnell, W.D.	1427	44	32.43	4- 7	–	–	–
Parry, S.D.	256	9	28.44	5- 23	1	–	–
Parsons, T.W.	375	11	34.09	3- 39	–	–	–
Pascal, N.T.	1499	47	31.89	5- 57	1	–	–
Pascoe, D.C.	79	2	39.50	2- 79	–	–	–
Patel, A.	76	1	76.00	1- 34	–	–	–
Patel, J.S.	7159	171	41.86	6- 32	5	–	–
Patel, S.R.	2761	67	41.20	6- 84	2	–	–
Patterson, S.A.	983	22	44.68	4- 41	–	–	–
Pattinson, D.J.	2793	78	35.80	6- 30	5	–	–
Peters, S.D.	31	1	31.00	1- 19	–	–	–
Peterson, R.J.	8272	240	34.46	6- 67	11	1	–
Pettini, M.L.	191	0					
Phillips, B.J.	6460	209	30.90	6- 29	4	–	–
Phillips, T.J.	4294	90	47.71	5- 41	1	–	–
Pietersen, K.P.	3229	61	52.93	4- 31	–	–	–
Piolet, S.A.	43	10	4.30	6- 17	1	1	–
Pipe, D.J.	5	0					
Plunkett, L.E.	8021	266	30.15	6- 63	8	1	3
Pollard, K.A.	313	6	52.16	2- 29	–	–	–
Ponting, R.T.	768	14	54.85	2- 10	–	–	–
Porterfield, W.T.S.	57	1	57.00	1- 57	–	–	–
Pothas, N.	63	1	63.00	1- 16	–	–	–
Powell, D.B.L.	8829	267	33.06	6- 49	6	–	–
Powell, M.J.	132	2	66.00	2- 39	–	–	–
Prince, A.G.	166	4	41.50	2- 11	–	–	–
Probert, T.J.W.	43	2	21.50	2- 20	–	–	–
Pyrah, R.M.	491	9	54.55	2- 53	–	–	–
Ramprakash, M.R.	2196	34	64.58	3- 32	–	–	–
Rankin, W.B.	2273	79	28.77	5- 39	2	–	–
Rashid, A.U.	5809	171	33.97	7-107	10	–	1
Rayner, O.P.	2674	71	37.66	5- 49	3	–	–
Read, C.M.W.	90	0					
Redfern, D.J.	241	5	48.20	1- 7	–	–	–
Riazuddin, H.	171	3	57.00	1- 21	–	–	–
Richardson, A.	9357	314	29.79	8- 46	9	1	1
Richardson, A.P.	3301	133	24.81	5- 32	4	–	–
Robson, S.D.	5	0					
Rogers, C.J.L.	126	1	126.00	1- 16	–	–	–
Rosenberg, M.C.	170	4	42.50	2- 56	–	–	–
Rudolph, J.A.	2440	58	42.06	5- 80	3	–	–
Ryan, L.C.	459	8	57.37	3- 89	–	–	–
Sadler, J.L.	250	3	83.33	1- 5	–	–	–
Saggers, M.J.	10513	415	25.33	7- 79	18	–	4
Sammy, D.J.G.	3611	140	25.79	7- 66	9	–	–
Sandri, P.S.E.	2126	72	29.52	5- 32	1	–	–
Sangakkara, K.C.	108	1	108.00	1- 13	–	–	–
Sarwan, R.R.	2208	54	40.88	6- 62	1	–	–
Saxelby, I.D.	838	22	38.09	3- 31	–	–	–
Sayers, J.J.	86	3	28.66	3- 20	–	–	–
Schofield, C.P.	7793	218	35.74	6-120	6	–	–
Scott, B.J.M.	1	0					
Shafayat, B.M.	642	8	80.25	2- 25	–	–	–
Shah, O.A.	1356	22	61.63	3- 33	–	–	–
Shahid Afridi	6954	257	27.05	6-101	8	–	–

F-C	Runs	Wkts	Avge	Best	5wI	10wM	50wS
Shahzad, A.	1857	53	35.03	4- 22	–	–	–
Shakib Al Hasan.	3035	102	29.75	7- 36	7	–	–
Shantry, A.J.	1882	80	23.52	5- 49	4	1	–
Shantry, J.D.	382	8	47.75	2- 53	–	–	–
Sharma, R.	210	7	30.00	5- 81	1	–	–
Shreck, C.E.	8813	289	30.49	8- 31	18	2	2
Siddle, P.M.	2662	98	27.16	6- 57	6	–	–
Sidebottom, R.J.	11378	443	25.68	7- 47	19	2	2
Silverwood, C.E.W.	15749	574	27.43	7- 93	25	1	3
Simmons, L.M.P.	313	10	31.30	3- 6	–	–	–
Smith, B.F.	488	4	122.00	1- 5	–	–	–
Smith, D.R.	3907	121	32.28	4- 22	–	–	–
Smith, D.S.	211	2	105.50	1- 2	–	–	–
Smith, G.M.	2722	71	38.33	5- 65	1	–	–
Smith, G.P.	64	1	64.00	1- 64	–	–	–
Smith, S.P.D.	338	5	67.60	2- 85	–	–	–
Smith, T.C.	2879	84	34.27	6- 46	1	–	–
Smith, T.M.J.	149	1	149.00	1- 52	–	–	–
Smith, W.R.	525	8	65.62	3- 34	–	–	–
Snell, S.D.	15	0					
Solanki, V.S.	4024	85	47.34	5- 40	4	1	–
Spearman, C.M.	55	1	55.00	1- 37	–	–	–
Spriegel, M.N.W.	560	12	46.66	2- 28	–	–	–
Sreesanth, S.	5025	156	32.21	5- 40	4	–	–
Stayt, T.P.	295	6	49.16	3- 51	–	–	–
Stevens, D.I.	2639	66	39.98	4- 36	–	–	–
Stiff, D.A.	1699	41	41.43	5- 91	1	–	–
Stirling, P.R.	12	0					
Strachan, J.P.	234	4	58.50	2- 48	–	–	–
Strauss, A.J.	89	2	44.50	1- 16	–	–	–
Stubbings, S.D.	121	0					
Suppiah, A.V.	1632	29	56.27	3- 46	–	–	–
Swann, G.P.	15978	486	32.87	7- 33	17	3	1
Tahir, N.S.	3577	123	29.08	7-107	2	–	–
Tait, S.W.	5661	198	28.59	7- 29	7	1	0+1
Taylor, B.V.	4535	136	33.34	6- 32	4	–	–
Taylor, C.G.	1280	24	53.33	4- 52	–	–	–
Taylor, J.E.	5378	202	26.62	8- 59	11	2	–
Taylor, J.W.A.	82	0					
ten Doeschate, R.N.	4368	124	35.22	6- 20	5	–	–
Thomas, A.C.	8453	304	27.80	7- 54	14	1	–
Thompson, C.E.J.	45	1	45.00	1- 45	–	–	–
Thornely, M.A.	25	0					
Thorp, C.D.	3716	143	25.98	7- 88	7	1	1
Tomlinson, J.A.	5111	144	35.49	8- 46	6	1	1
Tredwell, J.C.	8202	223	36.78	8- 66	7	3	1
Trego, P.D.	5527	144	38.38	6- 59	1	–	–
Tremlett, C.T.	8283	289	28.66	6- 44	7	–	–
Trescothick, M.E.	1551	36	43.08	4- 36	–	–	–
Trott, I.J.L.	2314	51	45.37	7- 39	1	–	–
Troughton, J.O.	1416	22	64.36	3- 1	–	–	–
Tudor, A.J.	11023	351	31.40	7- 48	14	–	–
Tuffey, D.R.	6805	267	25.48	7- 12	10	1	–
Turnbull, P.T.	103	1	103.00	1- 43	–	–	–
Turner, M.L.	853	17	50.17	4- 30	–	–	–
Udal, S.D.	25778	795	32.42	8- 50	36	5	7

F-C	Runs	Wkts	Avge	Best	5wI	10wM	50wS
van der Wath, J.J.	7937	310	25.60	7- 60	15	1	1
van Jaarsveld, M.	1516	42	36.09	5- 33	1	–	–
Vaughan, M.P.	5245	114	46.00	4- 39	–	–	–
Vince, J.M.	37	0					
Voges, A.C.	1228	34	36.11	4- 92	–	–	–
Wagg, G.G.	6778	206	32.90	6- 35	8	1	2
Wagh, M.A.	4611	100	46.11	7-222	2	–	–
Wainwright, D.J.	1836	56	32.78	5-134	1	–	–
Wakely, A.G.	195	3	65.00	2- 62	–	–	–
Walker, G.W.	349	3	116.33	1- 75	–	–	–
Walker, M.J.	1143	22	51.95	2- 21	–	–	–
Waller, M.T.C.	320	5	64.00	2- 27	–	–	–
Walters, S.J.	224	3	74.66	1- 4	–	–	–
Waters, H.T.	1479	39	37.92	5- 86	1	–	–
Watson, M.J.C.	143	4	35.75	4- 78	–	–	–
Watson, S.R.	3977	135	29.45	7- 69	3	1	–
Wessels, M.H.	13	0					
Westfield, M.S.	416	11	37.81	4- 72	–	–	–
Westley, T.	186	4	46.50	2- 33	–	–	–
Westwood, I.J.	222	6	37.00	2- 39	–	–	–
Whelan, C.D.	1681	43	39.09	5- 95	1	–	–
White, C.L.	6773	170	39.84	6- 66	2	1	–
White, G.G.	394	5	78.80	2- 35	–	–	–
White, R.A.	800	14	57.14	2- 30	–	–	–
White, W.A.	2052	50	41.04	5- 87	1	–	–
Whiteley, R.A.	38	0					
Wigley, D.H.	4932	136	36.26	6- 72	4	–	–
Willey, D.J.	295	6	49.16	2- 21	–	–	–
Williams, R.E.M.	755	23	32.82	5- 70	2	–	–
Willoughby, C.M.	18064	716	25.22	7- 44	30	3	4+2
Woakes, C.R.	2690	96	28.02	6- 43	5	1	–
Wood, M.J.	68	0					
Woodman, R.J.	341	7	48.71	4- 65	–	–	–
Woolley, R.J.J.	295	5	59.00	3- 71	–	–	–
Wright, B.J.	130	2	65.00	1- 14	–	–	–
Wright, C.J.C.	3954	92	42.97	6- 22	1	–	–
Wright, D.G.	9120	300	30.40	8- 60	9	–	1
Wright, L.J.	3351	78	42.96	5- 66	2	–	–
Wyatt, A.C.F.	159	7	22.71	3- 42	–	–	–
Yardy, M.H.	2003	26	77.03	5- 83	1	–	–
Yasir Arafat	15098	628	24.04	9- 35	36	5	0+4
Young, E.G.C.	151	2	75.50	2- 74	–	–	–

LEADING CURRENT FIRST-CLASS PLAYERS

These are the leading career batting/bowling averages and wicket-keeping/fielding aggregates among players currently registered for first-class county cricket at the time of going to press. All figures are to the end of the 2009 English season.

BATTING (Qualification: 100 innings)

	Runs	Avge		Runs	Avge
D.J.Hussey	10048	55.20	R.S.Bopara	5448	43.23
M.R.Ramprakash	33244	54.32	A.D.Brown	15806	43.18
P.A.Jaques	11707	53.21	A.J.Strauss	13090	42.91
C.J.L.Rogers	12865	52.29	N.D.McKenzie	11823	42.83
K.P.Pietersen	11026	50.81	O.A.Shah	13717	42.46
B.J.Hodge	16808	48.57	R.W.T.Key	14225	42.33
M.W.Goodwin	19180	47.95	M.A.Carberry	6383	42.27
H.M.Amla	8074	47.49	N.Pothas	10604	42.24
K.C.Sangakkara	11692	46.58	H.H.Gibbs	13425	42.21
M.J.Di Venuto	22751	46.43	C.L.White	6351	42.05
D.M.Benkenstein	12901	46.40	M.J.Cosgrove	4751	42.04
M.van Jaarsveld	15587	45.97	M.B.Loye	14516	40.89
J.A.Rudolph	11371	44.76	S.A.Newman	6771	40.54
I.J.L.Trott	8773	44.76	B.F.Smith	18495	40.29
A.G.Prince	10204	44.75	M.J.Prior	8785	40.29
A.N.Cook	8298	44.61	I.D.Blackwell	9103	40.27
E.C.Joyce	9606	44.47	S.C.Moore	6862	40.12
A.C.Gilchrist	10334	44.16	M.E.Trescothick	16645	40.10
I.R.Bell	10475	43.28	Z.de Bruyn	8726	39.84

WICKET-KEEPING (Qualification: 300 dismissals)

	Total	Ct	St		Total	Ct	St
P.A.Nixon	952	885	67	M.A.Wallace	408	375	33
A.C.Gilchrist	811	756	55	G.O.Jones	407	382	25
C.M.W.Read	683	647	36	L.D.Sutton	388	371	17
N.Pothas	604	559	45	M.J.Prior	378	354	24
J.N.Batty	564	500	64	P.Mustard	359	346	13
J.S.Foster	473	435	38	K.C.Sangakkara	350	317	33

BOWLING (Qualification: 100 wickets)

	Wkts	Avge		Wkts	Avge
B.A.W.Mendis	163	17.88	I.E.O'Brien	278	25.91
A.M.Davies	251	21.68	C.D.Thorp	143	25.98
Yasir Arafat	628	24.04	M.Kartik	475	26.16
A.R.Adams	395	24.25	Danish Kaneria	805	26.28
Naved-ul-Hasan	494	24.34	J.Lewis	678	26.29
Azhar Mahmood	536	25.05	J.E.C.Franklin	359	26.66
C.M.Willoughby	716	25.22	D.G.Cork	922	26.67
D.R.Tuffey	267	25.48	Kabir Ali	429	26.85
C.M.Bandara	359	25.54	P.P.Chawla	211	26.93
A.J.Hall	446	25.64	M.S.Mason	280	27.00
R.J.Sidebottom	443	25.68	R.J.Kirtley	614	27.04
Imran Tahir	382	25.89	Shahid Afridi	257	27.05

FIELDING (Qualification 250 catches in the field)

M.J.Di Venuto	349	A.D.Brown	262
M.van Jaarsveld	328	V.S.Solanki	258
M.E.Trescothick	314	D.L.Maddy	253

LIMITED-OVERS CAREER RECORDS

Compiled by **Philip Bailey**

The following career records, to the end of the 2009 season, include all players currently registered with first-class counties. These records are restricted to performances in limited-overs matches of 'List A' status as defined by the Association of Cricket Statisticians and Historians now incorporated by ICC into their Classification of Cricket. The following matches qualify for List A status and are included in the figures that follow: Limited-Overs Internationals; Other International matches (e.g. Commonwealth Games, 'A' team internationals); Premier domestic limited-overs tournaments in Test status countries; Official tourist matches against the main first-class teams.

The following matches do NOT qualify for inclusion: World Cup warm-up games; Tourist matches against first-class teams outside the major domestic competitions (e.g. Universities, Minor Counties etc.); Festival, pre-season friendly games and Twenty20 Cup matches.

	M	Runs	Avge	HS	100	50	Wkts	Avge	Best	Econ
Adams, A.R.	146	1425	18.03	90*	–	1	178	29.65	5- 7	4.74
Adams, J.H.K.	36	1058	34.12	90	–	8	1	105.00	1-34	7.97
Afzaal, U.	186	5367	35.54	132	6	33	59	26.49	4-49	5.87
Aga, R.G.	12	72	7.20	16	–	–	14	30.00	4-14	6.36
Ali, Kabir	156	1091	15.15	92	–	3	226	25.27	5-36	5.15
Ali, Kadeer	62	1750	29.66	114	3	11	1	68.00	1- 4	5.44
Ali, M.M.	51	1124	24.97	125	2	7	12	38.33	3-32	5.54
Allenby, J.	51	1007	25.82	91*	–	5	46	27.41	5-43	5.09
Ambrose, T.R.	103	2221	28.47	135	3	8	–	–	–	108/18
Amla, H.M.	61	1861	33.83	140	4	10	0	–	–	10.50
Anderson, J.M.	162	226	8.07	15	–	–	216	28.56	4-23	4.81
Andrew, G.M.	72	391	12.61	33	–	–	75	32.92	5-31	6.15
Anyon, J.E.	37	22	4.40	12	–	–	38	32.23	3- 6	5.51
Ashling, C.P.	3	7	7.00	6*	–	–	4	26.75	2-33	5.35
Azeem Rafiq	2	0	–	0	–	–	1	36.00	1-36	7.20
Azhar Mahmood	281	3789	21.05	101*	2	15	304	31.56	6-18	4.61
Bairstow, J.M.	8	26	5.20	20	–	–	–	–	–	4/–
Balcombe, D.J.	9	4	1.33	2*	–	–	10	37.80	2-39	5.90
Ball, J.T.	1	0	0.00	0	–	–	1	33.00	1-33	5.50
Ballance, G.S.	5	162	32.40	73	–	1	–	–	–	–
Bandara, C.M.	109	776	15.21	64	–	1	151	23.70	5-22	4.69
Banerjee, V.	10	11	3.66	6	–	–	14	27.57	3-47	4.70
Barker, K.H.D.	12	85	42.50	30*	–	–	12	29.50	3-23	5.28
Batty, G.J.	185	1969	16.97	83*	–	5	160	34.07	5-35	4.50
Batty, J.N.	181	2743	22.48	158*	1	13	–	–	–	191/33
Beer, W.A.T.	14	34	8.50	14	–	–	8	52.50	2-17	4.66
Bell, I.R.	185	5808	36.75	137	5	42	33	34.48	5-41	5.29
Benham, C.C.	55	1564	35.54	158	4	7	–	–	–	–
Benkenstein, D.M.	267	6471	35.55	107*	1	39	83	30.61	4-16	5.03
Benning, J.G.E.	83	2670	33.79	189*	3	17	35	36.28	4-43	6.49
Berg, G.K.	21	228	16.28	65	–	1	22	26.50	4-50	5.60
Blackwell, I.D.	231	5337	27.51	134*	3	33	184	34.90	5-26	4.78
Blake, A.J.	10	157	26.16	80	–	1	1	61.00	1-25	5.08
Boje, N.	271	3815	26.13	129	2	16	262	31.38	5-21	4.31
Bopara, R.S.	138	3406	33.72	201*	4	18	81	28.96	4-52	5.48
Borrington, P.M.	1	25	25.00	25	–	–	–	–	–	–
Borthwick, S.G.	6	5	–	3*	–	–	4	44.50	2-11	8.90
Botha, A.G.	137	1608	22.64	60*	–	4	137	29.16	5-43	4.85
Boyce, M.A.G.	24	544	28.63	80	–	3	–	–	–	–
Bragg, W.D.	7	231	38.50	78	–	1	–	–	–	1/–

264

L-O	M	Runs	Avge	HS	100	50	Wkts	Avge	Best	Econ
Breese, G.R.	138	1569	19.86	68*	–	3	146	27.99	5-41	4.59
Bresnan, T.T.	141	1251	18.39	61	–	2	141	34.17	4-25	4.98
Briggs, D.R.	4	4	4.00	4	–	–	2	78.00	2-36	4.72
Broad, S.C.J.	68	362	15.08	45*	–	–	101	28.16	5-23	5.13
Brooks, J.A.	3	10	10.00	10	–	–	0	–	–	5.50
Brophy, G.L.	101	1677	25.80	68*	–	10	–	–	–	102/19
Brown, A.D.	390	11052	31.22	268	19	50	14	40.07	3-39	6.47
Brown, B.C.	9	31	10.33	18*	–	–	–	–	–	5/1
Brown, D.O.	28	361	22.56	63*	–	1	12	43.41	3-29	6.20
Brown, K.R.	5	72	14.40	41	–	–	–	–	–	–
Brown, M.J.	30	922	34.14	96*	–	7	–	–	–	–
Buck, N.L.	4	21	21.00	21	–	–	4	37.75	2-38	6.04
Burton, D.A.	3	2	2.00	2	–	–	2	47.00	1-26	6.26
Buttler, J.C.	1	0	–	0	–	–	–	–	–	1/–
Carberry, M.A.	105	2555	28.70	121*	1	20	3	33.66	2-11	4.80
Carter, A.	6	20	4.00	12	–	–	7	24.14	3-32	5.45
Carter, N.M.	149	2388	21.32	135	2	10	204	24.98	5-31	4.75
Chambers, M.A.	3	1	–	1*	–	–	3	31.00	1-26	6.20
Chapple, G.	267	1987	17.74	81*	–	9	299	28.69	6-18	4.49
Chawla, P.P.	66	637	21.96	93	–	4	98	27.11	4-23	4.99
Chilton, M.J.	176	4356	30.89	115	5	20	41	24.19	5-26	5.50
Chopra, V.	34	1179	38.03	102	2	10	0	–	–	6.00
Clare, J.L.	19	143	11.00	34	–	–	15	44.26	3-39	5.57
Clark, S.R.	134	196	8.16	26*	–	–	182	26.74	6-27	4.30
Clarke, R.	138	2525	25.50	98*	–	12	80	38.81	4-49	5.60
Claydon, M.E.	22	66	6.60	19	–	–	22	35.63	3-31	4.77
Cliff, S.J.	7	10	5.00	4	–	–	6	51.33	4-26	5.81
Cobb, J.J.	10	117	16.71	43	–	–	1	12.00	1-12	12.00
Coetzer, K.J.	55	1385	29.46	127	1	8	0	–	–	5.21
Coles, M.T.	4	10	5.00	5	–	–	4	31.75	3-50	7.47
Collingwood, P.D.	334	8457	33.03	120*	6	50	209	34.11	6-31	4.86
Collymore, C.D.	131	151	6.04	13*	–	–	139	31.46	5-27	4.27
Compton, N.R.D.	56	1525	40.13	131	4	6	1	53.00	1- 0	5.21
Cook, A.N.	62	1980	35.35	125	4	9	0	–	–	3.33
Cook, S.J.	170	1234	16.90	67*	–	2	214	27.77	6-37	4.71
Cork, D.G.	297	4056	21.34	93	–	19	367	27.14	6-21	4.25
Cosgrove, M.J.	81	2577	33.90	121	2	20	12	65.91	2-21	6.33
Cosker, D.A.	190	595	10.43	50*	–	1	194	33.02	5-54	4.74
Croft, R.D.B.	399	6400	23.35	143	4	31	408	32.20	6-20	4.33
Croft, S.J.	63	1227	28.53	70	–	7	36	29.58	4-24	5.14
Cross, G.D.	35	491	18.88	76	–	1	2	13.00	2-26	21/9
Crowe, C.D.	40	187	15.58	23*	–	–	33	32.45	4-30	4.81
Daggett, L.M.	31	69	34.50	14*	–	–	34	32.02	4-51	5.03
Dalrymple, J.W.M.	154	3110	27.28	107	2	18	110	36.11	4-14	5.05
Danish Kaneria	138	274	8.30	33*	–	–	211	22.89	5-21	4.26
Davies, A.M.	72	166	7.54	31*	–	–	68	29.94	4-13	4.16
Davies, S.M.	84	2257	35.82	119	4	12	–	–	–	69/24
Dawson, L.A.	28	470	26.11	69*	–	2	24	30.41	4-45	5.30
Dawson, R.K.J.	119	594	10.06	41	–	–	118	30.90	4-13	4.88
de Bruyn, Z.	158	4062	35.63	113*	3	26	107	31.79	5-44	5.21
Denly, J.L.	60	1736	33.38	115	3	9	0	–	–	7.50
Dent, C.D.J.	1	–	–	–	–	–	–	–	–	2/–
Dernbach, J.W.	49	111	8.53	21	–	–	83	24.59	5-31	6.12
Dexter, N.J.	40	955	32.93	135*	2	4	17	37.17	3-17	5.19
Di Venuto, M.J.	295	8948	33.01	173*	15	45	5	36.20	1-10	5.43
Dixey, P.G.	4	32	32.00	16	–	–	–	–	–	4/–

L-O	M	Runs	Avge	HS	100	50	Wkts	Avge	Best	Econ
du Toit, J.	24	403	20.15	144	1	–	2	33.00	2-30	6.00
Edwards, N.J.	5	113	22.60	65	–	1	–	–	–	1
Edwards, P.D.	7	3	3.00	2*	–	–	7	34.42	3-57	7.08
Ervine, S.M.	159	3676	31.41	167*	6	15	152	33.94	5-50	5.54
Evans, D.	6	1	–	1*	–	–	9	32.33	3-36	5.32
Evans, L.	3	0	0.00	0	–	–	4	23.75	2-53	6.78
Evans, L.J.	1	36	–	36*	–	–	–	–	–	–
Ferley, R.S.	54	285	14.25	42	–	–	66	30.04	4-33	4.92
Finn, S.T.	27	33	6.60	13	–	–	28	33.17	3-23	5.46
Fletcher, L.J.	15	63	12.60	40*	–	–	14	36.21	2-35	4.67
Flintoff, A.	282	6641	29.78	143	6	34	289	22.61	5-19	4.16
Flower, G.W.	351	10186	34.29	148*	11	68	183	35.12	4-32	4.45
Footitt, M.H.A.	1	0	–	0	–	–	0	–	–	6.00
Foster, J.S.	151	2257	27.19	83*	–	10	–	–	–	183/49
Franklin, J.E.C.	154	2283	27.17	87*	–	11	160	32.84	5-42	4.80
Franks, P.J.	156	1757	21.96	84*	–	5	165	29.09	6-27	4.92
Gale, A.W.	72	1650	29.46	89	–	10	–	–	–	–
Gatting, J.S.	13	325	29.54	99*	–	2	0	–	–	3.75
Gibbs, H.H.	367	11284	34.93	175	25	59	2	28.50	1-16	5.18
Gidman, A.P.R.	142	2968	24.94	116	3	15	57	41.57	5-42	5.15
Gidman, W.R.S.	16	105	13.12	21	–	–	13	28.38	2-21	4.44
Gilchrist, A.C.	355	11288	34.94	172	18	63	0	–	–	526/65
Goddard, L.J.	9	100	25.00	36	–	–	–	–	–	16/–
Godleman, B.A.	14	321	24.69	82	–	1	–	–	–	–
Goodman, J.E.	3	38	38.00	26*	–	–	–	–	–	–
Goodwin, M.W.	329	9982	35.90	167	13	62	7	43.71	1- 9	5.23
Griffiths, D.A.	4	3	–	3*	–	–	5	34.20	4-29	5.89
Groenewald, T.D.	37	285	12.95	36	–	–	31	36.70	3-25	5.62
Gurney, H.F.	10	0	0.00	0	–	–	3	109.00	1-16	5.68
Hales, A.D.	14	427	35.58	150*	2	1	–	–	–	–
Hall, A.J.	261	5035	29.97	129*	6	27	296	27.08	5-18	4.55
Hamilton-Brown, R.J.	37	542	19.35	49	–	–	24	34.04	3-28	5.63
Harinath, A.	1	21	–	21*	–	–	–	–	–	–
Harmison, B.W.	36	627	21.62	67	–	2	18	32.66	3-43	5.81
Harmison, S.J.	140	259	8.09	25*	–	–	182	30.74	5-33	4.96
Harris, A.J.	149	224	7.00	34	–	–	194	28.77	5-35	5.06
Harris, J.A.R.	18	97	8.08	21	–	–	23	27.34	4-48	4.95
Harris, R.J.	54	339	14.73	39	–	–	59	35.64	5-58	4.91
Harrison, D.S.	81	423	12.81	37*	–	–	95	28.94	5-26	4.84
Harrison, P.W.	9	165	20.62	61	–	1	–	–	–	5/–
Henderson, C.W.	235	1093	15.61	45	–	–	292	25.53	6-29	4.28
Hildreth, J.C.	109	2674	29.38	151	3	9	6	30.83	2-26	7.40
Hockley, J.B.	69	1586	26.00	121	1	8	3	22.33	2-32	5.58
Hodd, A.J.	27	327	20.43	42	–	–	–	–	–	22/2
Hodge, B.J.	223	7633	40.81	164	21	35	38	35.36	5-28	5.29
Hodgson, L.J.	6	9	9.00	9	–	–	2	80.00	2-44	6.15
Hogg, K.W.	115	835	15.75	66*	–	1	113	29.75	4-20	4.62
Hoggard, M.J.	130	67	3.72	7*	–	–	179	25.33	5-28	4.44
Hopkinson, C.D.	92	1400	22.95	123*	1	6	15	37.33	3-19	5.93
Horton, P.J.	42	993	26.83	111*	2	3	–	–	–	–
Howgego, B.H.N.	1	7	7.00	7	–	–	–	–	–	–
Hughes, C.F.	6	65	13.00	31	–	–	2	68.00	1-17	5.23
Hunter, I.D.	87	325	8.33	39	–	–	96	32.42	4-29	4.95
Hussain, G.M.	1	0	–	0	–	–	2	8.50	2-17	3.40
Hussey, D.J.	162	5224	40.49	130	8	34	28	43.10	3-26	5.32
Imran Arif	10	17	–	16*	–	–	8	46.87	2-51	6.32

L-O	M	Runs	Avge	HS	100	50	Wkts	Avge	Best	Econ
Imran Tahir	64	185	13.21	41*	–	–	95	22.85	5-27	4.35
Ireland, A.J.	57	82	6.30	17	–	–	76	28.46	4-16	5.14
James, N.A.	11	112	18.66	30	–	–	7	25.14	2-34	4.29
Jaques, P.A.	122	4737	42.67	158*	12	26	0	–	–	6.33
Jefferson, W.I.	93	2969	34.92	132	4	17	2	4.50	2- 9	2.25
Jewell, T.M.	2	1	1.00	1	–	–	0	–	–	9.33
Johnson, R.M.	2	26	13.00	20	–	–	–	–	–	2/–
Jones, G.O.	149	2569	24.46	86	–	11	–	–	–	171/27
Jones, P.S.	180	639	12.52	42	–	–	241	29.51	6-56	5.25
Jones, R.A.	4	8	4.00	6	–	–	0	–	–	8.23
Jones, S.P.	34	76	15.20	26	–	–	31	39.96	5-32	5.11
Jordan, C.J.	18	74	7.40	38	–	–	22	29.77	3-28	5.59
Joseph, R.H.	33	43	21.50	15	–	–	39	28.56	5-13	5.11
Joyce, E.C.	184	5698	36.76	146	7	37	6	51.50	2-10	7.02
Kartik, M.	166	612	11.12	44	–	–	208	29.62	6-27	4.33
Keedy, G.	68	129	9.92	33	–	–	78	27.25	5-30	4.60
Kervezee, A.N.	34	946	33.78	121*	1	5	–	–	–	9.40
Key, R.W.T.	184	5115	31.00	120*	5	32	–	–	–	–
Khan, A.	56	276	12.00	65*	–	1	61	32.34	4-26	5.20
Kieswetter, C.	45	1500	39.47	138*	3	6	–	–	–	45/11
Killeen, N.	224	694	9.50	32	–	–	301	24.28	6-31	4.15
Kirby, S.P.	66	76	4.22	15	–	–	80	32.13	5-36	5.58
Kirtley, R.J.	249	440	10.00	30*	–	–	371	23.33	6-50	4.75
Lancefield, T.J.	1	20	20.00	20	–	–	–	–	–	–
Lee, J.E.	4	0	0.00	0	–	–	7	16.57	3-43	6.56
Lee, W.W.	2	0	0.00	0	–	–	4	27.50	3-39	8.14
Lewis, J.	199	822	11.10	54	–	1	261	26.57	5-19	4.51
Liddle, C.J.	14	13	4.33	11	–	–	10	53.20	3-60	6.33
Linley, T.E.	8	37	–	20*	–	–	4	63.25	2-38	5.27
London, A.B.	2	0	–	0	–	–	0	–	–	5.00
Loye, M.B.	291	8661	34.36	127	10	56	–	–	–	–
Lucas, D.S.	60	185	10.27	32*	–	–	72	29.73	4-27	5.59
Lumb, M.J.	157	4477	31.97	108	2	35	0	–	–	14.00
Lungley, T.	76	384	11.29	45	–	–	82	30.75	4-28	5.21
Lyth, A.	29	535	25.47	109*	1	1	0	–	–	4.66
McDonald, A.B.	60	1045	31.66	67	–	5	51	36.41	3-41	4.87
McGrath, A.	276	7058	32.37	148	7	40	75	32.97	4-41	5.01
McGuire, B.T.	1	0	0.00	0	–	–	–	–	–	–
McKenzie, N.D.	207	5627	35.84	131*	7	38	4	62.00	2-19	5.83
MacLeod, C.S.	11	22	4.40	10*	–	–	8	42.25	2-38	5.63
Maddy, D.L.	323	8263	30.71	167*	11	50	188	29.20	4-16	5.07
Madsen, W.L.	14	223	22.30	55*	–	1	5	14.80	2-18	4.35
Mahmood, S.I.	121	409	8.52	29	–	–	170	26.47	5-16	5.11
Malan, D.J.	29	477	18.34	60	–	2	10	34.40	2- 4	5.84
Marshall, H.J.H.	223	5350	28.15	122	6	35	4	60.75	2-21	6.17
Martin-Jenkins, R.S.C.	223	1922	14.89	68*	–	3	231	29.95	4-22	4.28
Mascarenhas, A.D.	244	4107	25.35	79	–	27	281	26.24	5-27	4.25
Mason, M.S.	80	171	7.43	25	–	–	91	28.65	4-34	4.30
Masters, D.	1	0	–	0	–	–	1	49.00	1-49	6.39
Masters, D.D.	120	449	12.82	39	–	–	111	33.06	5-17	4.44
Maunders, J.K.	36	748	24.93	109*	1	2	4	25.75	2-16	4.44
Maynard, T.L.	30	824	30.51	108	1	6	–	–	–	–
Meaker, S.C.	11	14	–	10*	–	–	9	41.33	2-21	6.41
Mendis, B.A.W.	52	400	20.00	71*	–	2	105	14.01	6-13	3.79
Middlebrook, J.D.	146	1256	18.74	47	–	–	112	34.80	4-27	4.62
Mitchell, D.K.H.	42	747	31.12	92	–	6	24	38.12	4-42	6.02

L-O	M	Runs	Avge	HS	100	50	Wkts	Avge	Best	Econ
Moore, S.C.	95	2199	26.81	105*	2	12	1	53.00	1- 1	7.75
Morgan, E.J.G.	107	3048	35.03	161	4	18	0	–	–	7.00
Muchall, G.J.	86	1835	28.23	101*	1	9	1	137.00	1-15	5.07
Munday, M.K.	1	0	–	0	–	–	1	39.00	1-39	7.80
Murtagh, T.J.	104	554	12.31	35*	–	–	148	26.64	4-14	5.14
Mustard, P.	117	2831	29.18	108	2	19	–	–	–	120/25
Naik, J.K.H.	13	59	11.80	18	–	–	14	29.64	3-21	4.96
Nannes, D.P.	21	18	3.60	5*	–	–	28	30.89	4-38	4.70
Napier, G.R.	185	2251	18.00	79	–	11	205	24.79	6-29	5.08
Nash, C.D.	39	835	23.19	82	–	3	13	26.15	4-40	5.36
Needham, J.	34	213	16.38	42	–	–	17	55.94	2-36	5.32
Nel, A.	204	473	12.44	58	–	1	281	25.61	6-27	4.30
New, T.J.	44	941	26.13	68	–	4	–	–	–	15/4
Newby, O.J.	17	36	7.20	12*	–	–	15	42.13	4-41	5.88
Newman, S.A.	82	2280	29.61	177	3	13	–	–	–	–
Newton, R.I.	1	9	9.00	9	–	–	–	–	–	–
Nixon, P.A.	401	7134	26.13	101	1	33	0	–	–	417/99
Northeast, S.A.	7	144	24.00	69	–	1	–	–	–	–
O'Brien, I.E.	56	89	22.25	19*	–	–	69	32.55	5-35	4.95
O'Brien, K.J.	74	1728	30.31	142	2	8	38	44.50	4-31	5.44
O'Brien, N.J.	106	2023	27.33	95	–	14	–	–	–	86/30
Onions, G.	49	106	7.06	19	–	–	55	31.18	3-39	5.14
Ord, J.E.	2	27	27.00	27	–	–	–	–	–	–
Palladino, A.P.	21	43	4.77	16	–	–	22	30.63	3-32	5.18
Panesar, M.S.	54	126	10.50	17*	–	–	51	35.68	5-20	4.48
Park, G.T.	29	495	24.75	64	–	1	6	57.16	2-40	9/–
Parry, S.D.	9	44	11.00	31	–	–	13	19.38	2-12	3.81
Patel, A.	4	92	23.00	41	–	–	2	17.00	2-34	6.80
Patel, S.R.	102	2092	29.46	114	1	10	86	26.50	6-13	5.13
Patterson, S.A.	26	83	83.00	25*	–	–	23	41.00	3-11	5.02
Pattinson, D.J.	32	57	6.33	13*	–	–	40	26.15	4-29	5.05
Payne, D.A.	3	4	–	3*	–	–	6	12.33	3-10	5.69
Peters, S.D.	151	2832	21.78	107	2	16	–	–	–	–
Peterson, R.J.	126	1893	24.58	101	1	11	130	28.57	7-24	4.42
Pettini, M.L.	100	2187	25.72	144	4	14	–	–	–	–
Phillips, B.J.	112	871	18.14	44*	–	–	128	28.90	4-25	4.78
Phillips, T.J.	42	260	17.33	41	–	–	46	21.86	5-34	4.92
Pietersen, K.P.	200	6562	44.04	147	12	41	39	49.23	3-14	5.29
Piolet, S.A.	11	6	3.00	4	–	–	13	22.92	3-34	5.24
Plunkett, L.E.	95	859	20.45	72	–	2	115	32.19	4-15	5.34
Pollard, K.A.	30	644	28.00	87	–	5	34	19.73	4-32	5.26
Porterfield, W.T.S.	80	2625	35.00	112*	4	15	–	–	–	–
Pothas, N.	229	4456	36.52	114*	3	24	–	–	–	204/52
Powell, D.B.L.	96	236	7.15	48*	–	–	138	27.41	5-23	4.75
Powell, M.J.	204	4665	26.96	114*	1	25	1	26.00	1-26	6.50
Poynton, T.	6	52	26.00	24	–	–	–	–	–	5/1
Prince, A.G.	196	4146	30.26	89*	–	22	0	–	–	5.67
Prior, M.J.	187	4275	26.71	144	4	23	–	–	–	160/26
Procter, L.A.	1	2	2.00	2	–	–	–	–	–	–
Pyrah, R.M.	69	742	20.05	67	–	1	80	24.68	5-50	5.63
Ramprakash, M.R.	398	12947	40.08	147*	17	83	46	29.43	5-38	4.68
Rankin, W.B.	41	34	6.80	9	–	–	50	27.04	3-32	4.98
Rashid, A.U.	37	288	15.15	41*	–	–	29	38.20	3-37	5.18
Rayner, O.P.	15	151	21.57	61	–	1	10	50.60	2-31	6.24
Read, C.M.W.	250	4071	26.96	135	2	13	–	–	–	248/57
Redfern, D.J.	23	410	21.57	57*	–	2	5	37.60	2-10	4.99

L-O	M	Runs	Avge	HS	100	50	Wkts	Avge	Best	Econ
Rees, G.P.	16	490	32.66	123*	1	3	–	–	–	–
Riazuddin, H.	12	2	–	2*	–	–	8	50.25	2-47	4.51
Richardson, A.	62	104	10.40	21*	–	–	58	36.56	5-35	4.68
Robson, S.D.	4	69	34.50	48	–	–	–	–	–	–
Rogers, C.J.L.	109	3495	35.66	117*	3	26	2	13.00	2-22	6.50
Root, J.E.	1	63	63.00	63	–	1	–	–	–	–
Roy, J.J.	3	12	4.00	6	–	–	0	–	–	12.00
Rudolph, J.A.	169	5922	44.19	134*	8	39	10	34.10	4-40	5.42
Sadler, J.L.	88	1821	26.77	113*	1	6	1	33.00	1-33	4.12
Sangakkara, K.C.	326	10284	37.94	156*	14	65	–	–	–	316/82
Saxelby, I.D.	6	25	8.33	7*	–	–	8	21.37	4-31	5.63
Sayers, J.J.	20	415	23.05	62	–	4	1	71.00	1-31	7.88
Schofield, C.P.	129	1667	23.47	75*	–	7	133	26.51	5-31	5.16
Scott, B.J.M.	95	759	19.97	73*	–	4	–	–	–	78/30
Shafayat, B.M.	105	2016	22.40	104	1	7	24	30.41	4-33	5.54
Shah, O.A.	307	8734	34.38	134	12	55	26	31.26	4-11	5.76
Shahid Afridi	371	8363	25.34	114	6	48	361	33.53	6-38	4.62
Shahzad, A.	15	126	14.00	43*	–	–	18	28.77	5-51	4.58
Shakib Al Hasan	87	2271	31.98	134*	3	15	89	32.02	4-30	4.07
Shantry, A.J.	12	48	16.00	19*	–	–	13	25.00	5-37	4.77
Shantry, J.D.	5	7	–	7*	–	–	5	42.40	2-43	6.23
Shreck, C.E.	50	45	6.42	9*	–	–	63	31.31	5-19	5.19
Sidebottom, R.J.	165	478	11.11	32	–	–	168	31.53	6-40	4.32
Simpson, J.A.	6	108	21.60	32	–	–	–	–	–	3/1
Smith, B.F.	394	9869	30.55	115	3	61	2	60.50	1- 2	5.71
Smith, D.R.	124	2130	21.95	96	–	13	83	33.38	6-29	4.75
Smith, G.M.	51	1155	25.10	88	–	5	42	31.16	4-53	5.76
Smith, G.P.	3	72	24.00	58	–	1	–	–	–	–
Smith, S.P.D.	9	152	25.33	48	–	–	6	35.66	2-25	4.86
Smith, T.C.	37	567	28.35	87*	–	5	44	25.63	3- 8	4.69
Smith, T.M.J.	10	87	29.00	65	–	1	7	52.00	2-45	5.96
Smith, W.R.	65	1439	25.24	103	1	10	2	25.50	1- 6	5.77
Snell, S.D.	13	61	6.10	19	–	–	–	–	–	19/-
Solanki, V.S.	350	9339	31.76	164*	13	53	27	34.59	4-14	5.34
Spriegel, M.N.W.	25	526	37.57	81*	–	4	15	45.06	2-23	4.97
Stevens, D.I.	202	5003	29.25	133	4	32	48	32.91	5-32	4.92
Stiff, D.A.	1	0	–	0	–	–	1	27.00	1-27	5.40
Stirling, P.R.	20	426	22.42	84	–	4	–	–	–	–
Stokes, B.A.	3	22	11.00	11*	–	–	2	18.00	2-22	6.00
Stoneman, M.D.	1	21	21.00	21	–	–	–	–	–	–
Strauss, A.J.	213	5988	31.18	163	7	38	0	–	–	3.00
Suppiah, A.V.	59	1174	27.95	79	–	6	34	32.14	4-39	5.72
Sutton, L.D.	149	1911	19.30	83	–	6	–	–	–	168/21
Swann, G.P.	208	2834	19.27	83	–	14	224	26.75	5-17	4.41
Tahir, N.S.	14	19	9.50	13*	–	–	5	78.00	2-47	4.81
Tait, S.W.	77	98	7.53	22*	–	–	144	22.40	8-43	5.00
Taylor, C.G.	157	2998	24.77	93	–	18	12	40.83	2- 5	5.12
Taylor, J.W.A.	19	636	48.92	101	1	3	0	–	–	6.00
ten Doeschate, R.N.	113	2848	45.20	134*	3	17	111	25.59	5-50	5.41
Thomas, A.C.	110	461	14.87	28*	–	–	141	28.38	4-18	4.92
Thompson, C.E.J.	3	56	56.00	39*	–	–	1	51.00	1-22	8.50
Thornely, M.A.	1	0	–	0	–	–	–	–	–	–
Thorp, C.D.	38	286	16.82	52	–	1	47	27.36	6-17	4.37
Tomlinson, J.A.	22	18	2.25	6	–	–	20	35.75	4-47	4.83
Toor, K.S.	2	8	8.00	5	–	–	1	32.00	1-25	8.00
Tredwell, J.C.	136	1229	18.62	88	–	4	130	32.89	6-27	4.73

L-O	M	Runs	Avge	HS	100	50	Wkts	Avge	Best	Econ
Trego, P.D.	87	1030	18.39	78	–	4	91	31.09	5-44	5.63
Tremlett, C.T.	112	415	9.43	38*	–	–	156	26.16	4-25	4.71
Trescothick, M.E.	320	10770	38.19	184	27	51	57	28.84	4-50	4.90
Trott, I.J.L.	149	4705	43.16	125*	9	29	52	24.69	4-55	5.67
Troughton, J.O.	123	2805	28.91	115*	2	16	25	25.76	4-23	5.25
Tuffey, D.R.	195	633	11.72	38*	–	–	228	31.39	5-21	4.63
Turner, M.L.	15	38	19.00	15*	–	–	19	28.10	3-27	5.75
Udal, S.D.	400	2884	16.38	79*	–	9	452	29.90	5-43	4.42
van Jaarsveld, M.	250	7973	40.88	132*	14	48	30	40.93	3-13	5.30
Vince, J.M.	6	257	51.40	93	–	2	–	–	–	–
Wagg, G.G.	71	764	15.28	45	–	–	77	32.10	4-35	5.49
Wagh, M.A.	111	2715	27.70	102*	1	21	25	34.48	4-35	4.71
Wainwright, D.J.	31	117	23.40	26	–	–	22	37.13	3-33	4.61
Wakely, A.G.	12	103	11.44	32	–	–	2	7.00	2-14	4.66
Walker, M.J.	271	5921	28.33	117	3	35	30	25.30	4-24	5.03
Wallace, M.A.	142	1689	19.41	85	–	3	–	–	–	138/36
Waller, M.T.C.	7	3	–	2*	–	–	7	31.28	2-34	5.47
Walters, S.J.	35	729	26.03	91	–	4	3	59.66	1-12	6.50
Waters, H.T.	15	24	4.80	8	–	–	11	56.54	3-47	5.98
Westfield, M.S.	8	31	31.00	17	–	–	5	48.60	2-32	5.92
Westley, T.	4	37	12.33	36	–	–	–	–	–	–
Westwood, I.J.	48	762	21.77	65	–	3	2	83.50	1-28	4.77
Whelan, C.D.	22	40	4.44	11	–	–	23	29.30	4-27	5.91
White, C.L.	140	3306	33.39	126*	4	18	92	35.60	4-15	5.32
White, G.G.	8	23	5.75	14	–	–	10	24.60	3-30	4.83
White, R.A.	76	1534	22.23	111	2	7	2	27.50	2-18	6.11
White, W.A.	29	219	18.25	46*	–	–	23	43.65	4-36	6.06
Whiteley, R.A.	4	41	13.66	24	–	–	0	–	–	2/–
Wigley, D.H.	24	34	2.83	10	–	–	16	54.37	4-37	6.35
Willey, D.J.	12	75	10.71	21	–	–	3	42.00	2-44	7.00
Willoughby, C.M.	206	147	5.44	15	–	–	254	27.38	6-16	4.16
Wilson, G.C.	56	976	20.76	61	–	7	–	–	–	42/11
Woakes, C.R.	20	99	16.50	31*	–	–	12	44.58	2-28	5.03
Wood, M.J.	91	2229	27.18	129	2	15	–	–	–	–
Woodman, R.J.	5	14	14.00	14	–	–	1	163.00	1-38	6.52
Wright, B.J.	38	749	23.40	65	–	4	1	126.00	1-19	5.72
Wright, C.J.C.	48	118	9.07	23	–	–	38	44.10	3- 3	5.47
Wright, L.J.	112	1570	21.80	125	1	4	84	37.07	4-12	5.21
Wyatt, A.C.F.	2	0	–	0	–	–	2	31.00	1-31	5.63
Yardy, M.H.	146	2556	22.82	98*	–	16	87	37.37	6-27	4.92
Yasir Arafat	196	2158	20.75	87	–	7	317	24.06	6-24	4.82

FIRST-CLASS CRICKET RECORDS

To the end of the 2009 season

TEAM RECORDS

HIGHEST INNINGS TOTALS

1107	Victoria v New South Wales	Melbourne	1926-27
1059	Victoria v Tasmania	Melbourne	1922-23
952-6d	Sri Lanka v India	Colombo	1997-98
951-7d	Sind v Baluchistan	Karachi	1973-74
944-6d	Hyderabad v Andhra	Secunderabad	1993-94
918	New South Wales v South Australia	Sydney	1900-01
912-8d	Holkar v Mysore	Indore	1945-46
910-6d	Railways v Dera Ismail Khan	Lahore	1964-65
903-7d	England v Australia	The Oval	1938
900-6d	Queensland v Victoria	Brisbane	2005-06
887	Yorkshire v Warwickshire	Birmingham	1896
863	Lancashire v Surrey	The Oval	1990
860-6d	Tamil Nadu v Goa	Panjim	1988-89
850-7d	Somerset v Middlesex	Taunton	2007

Excluding penalty runs in India, there have been 34 innings totals of 800 runs or more in first-class cricket. Tamil Nadu's total of 860-6d was boosted to 912 by 52 penalty runs.

HIGHEST SECOND INNINGS TOTAL

770	New South Wales v South Australia	Adelaide	1920-21

HIGHEST FOURTH INNINGS TOTAL

654-5	England (set 696 to win) v South Africa	Durban	1938-39

HIGHEST MATCH AGGREGATE

2376-37	Maharashtra v Bombay	Poona	1948-49

RECORD MARGIN OF VICTORY

Innings and 851 runs: Railways v Dera Ismail Khan   Lahore   1964-65

MOST RUNS IN A DAY

721	Australians v Essex	Southend	1948

MOST HUNDREDS IN AN INNINGS

6	Holkar v Mysore	Indore	1945-46

LOWEST INNINGS TOTALS

12	†Oxford University v MCC and Ground	Oxford	1877
12	Northamptonshire v Gloucestershire	Gloucester	1907
13	Auckland v Canterbury	Auckland	1877-78
13	Nottinghamshire v Yorkshire	Nottingham	1901
14	Surrey v Essex	Chelmsford	1983
15	MCC v Surrey	Lord's	1839
15	†Victoria v MCC	Melbourne	1903-04
15	†Northamptonshire v Yorkshire	Northampton	1908
15	Hampshire v Warwickshire	Birmingham	1922

† *Batted one man short*

There have been 27 instances of a team being dismissed for under 20.

LOWEST MATCH AGGREGATE BY ONE TEAM

34 (16 and 18) Border v Natal   East London   1959-60

LOWEST COMPLETED MATCH AGGREGATE BY BOTH TEAMS

105   MCC v Australians   Lord's   1878

FEWEST RUNS IN AN UNINTERRUPTED DAY'S PLAY

95   Australia (80) v Pakistan (15-2)   Karachi   1956-57

TIED MATCHES

Before 1949 a match was considered to be tied if the scores were level after the fourth innings, even if the side batting last had wickets in hand when play ended. Law 22 was amended in 1948 and since then a match has been tied only when the scores are level after the fourth innings has been completed. There have been 56 tied first-class matches, five of which would not have qualified under the current law. The most recent are:

Warwickshire (446-7d & forfeit) v Essex (66-0d & 380)	Birmingham	2003
Worcestershire (262 & 247) v Zimbabweans (334 & 175)	Worcester	2003

BATTING RECORDS
HIGHEST INDIVIDUAL INNINGS

501*	B.C.Lara	Warwickshire v Durham	Birmingham	1994
499	Hanif Mohammed	Karachi v Bahawalpur	Karachi	1958-59
452*	D.G.Bradman	New South Wales v Queensland	Sydney	1929-30
443*	B.B.Nimbalkar	Maharashtra v Kathiawar	Poona	1948-49
437	W.H.Ponsford	Victoria v Queensland	Melbourne	1927-28
429	W.H.Ponsford	Victoria v Tasmania	Melbourne	1922-23
428	Aftab Baloch	Sind v Baluchistan	Karachi	1973-74
424	A.C.MacLaren	Lancashire v Somerset	Taunton	1895
405*	G.A.Hick	Worcestershire v Somerset	Taunton	1988
400*	B.C.Lara	West Indies v England	St John's	2003-04
394	Naved Latif	Sargodha v Gujranwala	Gujranwala	2000-01
385	B.Sutcliffe	Otago v Canterbury	Christchurch	1952-53
383	C.W.Gregory	New South Wales v Queensland	Brisbane	1906-07
380	M.L.Hayden	Australia v Zimbabwe	Perth	2003-04
377	S.V.Manjrekar	Bombay v Hyderabad	Bombay	1990-91
375	B.C.Lara	West Indies v England	St John's	1993-94
374	D.P.M.D.Jayawardena	Sri Lanka v South Africa	Colombo	2006
369	D.G.Bradman	South Australia v Tasmania	Adelaide	1935-36
366	N.H.Fairbrother	Lancashire v Surrey	The Oval	1990
366	M.V.Sridhar	Hyderabad v Andhra	Secunderabad	1993-94
365*	C.Hill	South Australia v NSW	Adelaide	1900-01
365*	G.St A.Sobers	West Indies v Pakistan	Kingston	1957-58
364	L.Hutton	England v Australia	The Oval	1938
359*	V.M.Merchant	Bombay v Maharashtra	Bombay	1943-44
359	R.B.Simpson	New South Wales v Queensland	Brisbane	1963-64
357*	R.Abel	Surrey v Somerset	The Oval	1899
357	D.G.Bradman	South Australia v Victoria	Melbourne	1935-36
356	B.A.Richards	South Australia v W Australia	Perth	1970-71
355*	G.R.Marsh	W Australia v S Australia	Perth	1989-90
355	B.Sutcliffe	Otago v Auckland	Dunedin	1949-50
353	V.V.S.Laxman	Hyderabad v Karnataka	Bangalore	1999-00
352	W.H.Ponsford	Victoria v New South Wales	Melbourne	1926-27
350	Rashid Israr	Habib Bank v National Bank	Lahore	1976-77

There have been 172 triple hundreds in first-class cricket, W.V.Raman (313) and Arjan Kripal Singh (302*) for Tamil Nadu v Goa at Panjim in 1988-89 providing the only instance of two batsmen scoring 300 in the same innings.

MOST HUNDREDS IN SUCCESSIVE INNINGS

6	C.B.Fry	Sussex and Rest of England		1901
6	D.G.Bradman	South Australia and D.G.Bradman's XI		1938-39
6	M.J.Procter	Rhodesia		1970-71

TWO DOUBLE HUNDREDS IN A MATCH

| 244 | 202* A.E.Fagg | Kent v Essex | Colchester | 1938 |

TRIPLE HUNDRED AND HUNDRED IN A MATCH

| 333 | 123 G.A.Gooch | England v India | Lord's | 1990 |

DOUBLE HUNDRED AND HUNDRED IN A MATCH MOST TIMES

| 4 | Zaheer Abbas | Gloucestershire | 1976-81 |

TWO HUNDREDS IN A MATCH MOST TIMES

8	Zaheer Abbas	Gloucestershire and PIA	1976-82
8	R.T.Ponting	Tasmania, Australia and Australians	1992-2006
7	W.R.Hammond	Gloucestershire, England and MCC	1927-45

MOST HUNDREDS IN A SEASON

| 18 | D.C.S.Compton | 1947 | 16 | J.B.Hobbs | 1925 |

100 HUNDREDS IN A CAREER

| | Total | | 100th Hundred | |
	Hundreds	Inns	Season	Inns
J.B.Hobbs	197	1315	1923	821
E.H.Hendren	170	1300	1928-29	740
W.R.Hammond	167	1005	1935	679
C.P.Mead	153	1340	1927	892
G.Boycott	151	1014	1977	645
H.Sutcliffe	149	1088	1932	700
F.E.Woolley	145	1532	1929	1031
G.A.Hick	136	871	1998	574
L.Hutton	129	814	1951	619
G.A.Gooch	128	990	1992-93	820
W.G.Grace	126	1493	1895	1113
D.C.S.Compton	123	839	1952	552
T.W.Graveney	122	1223	1964	940
D.G.Bradman	117	338	1947-48	295
I.V.A.Richards	114	796	1988-89	658
M.R.Ramprakash	108	701	2008	676
Zaheer Abbas	108	768	1982-83	658
A.Sandham	107	1000	1935	871
M.C.Cowdrey	107	1130	1973	1035
T.W.Hayward	104	1138	1913	1076
G.M.Turner	103	792	1982	779
J.H.Edrich	103	979	1977	945
L.E.G.Ames	102	951	1950	915
G.E.Tyldesley	102	961	1934	919
D.L.Amiss	102	1139	1986	1081

MOST 400s: 2 – B.C.Lara, W.H.Ponsford
MOST 300s or more: 6 – D.G.Bradman; 4 – W.R.Hammond, W.H.Ponsford
MOST 200s or more: 37 – D.G.Bradman; 36 – W.R.Hammond; 22 – E.H.Hendren

MOST RUNS IN A MONTH

1294 (avge 92.42) L.Hutton Yorkshire June 1949

MOST RUNS IN A SEASON

Runs			I	NO	HS	Avge	100	Season
3816	D.C.S.Compton	Middlesex	50	8	246	90.85	18	1947
3539	W.J.Edrich	Middlesex	52	8	267*	80.43	12	1947
3518	T.W.Hayward	Surrey	61	8	219	66.37	13	1906

The feat of scoring 3000 runs in a season has been achieved 28 times, the most recent instance being by W.E.Alley (3019) in 1961. The highest aggregate in a season since 1969 is 2755 by S.J.Cook in 1991.

1000 RUNS IN A SEASON MOST TIMES

28 W.G.Grace (Gloucestershire), F.E.Woolley (Kent)

HIGHEST BATTING AVERAGE IN A SEASON

(Qualification: 12 innings)

Avge			I	NO	HS	Runs	100	Season
115.66	D.G.Bradman	Australians	26	5	278	2429	13	1938
104.66	D.R.Martyn	Australians	14	5	176*	942	5	2001
103.54	M.R.Ramprakash	Surrey	24	2	301*	2278	8	2006
102.53	G.Boycott	Yorkshire	20	5	175*	1538	6	1979
102.00	W.A.Johnston	Australians	17	16	28*	102	–	1953
101.70	G.A.Gooch	Essex	30	3	333	2746	12	1990
101.30	M.R.Ramprakash	Surrey	25	5	266*	2026	10	2007
100.12	G.Boycott	Yorkshire	30	5	233	2503	13	1971

FASTEST HUNDRED AGAINST AUTHENTIC BOWLING

35 min P.G.H.Fender Surrey v Northamptonshire Northampton 1920

FASTEST DOUBLE HUNDRED

113 min R.J.Shastri Bombay v Baroda Bombay 1984-85

FASTEST TRIPLE HUNDRED

181 min D.C.S.Compton MCC v NE Transvaal Benoni 1948-49

MOST SIXES IN AN INNINGS

16 A.Symonds Gloucestershire v Glamorgan Abergavenny 1995

MOST SIXES IN A MATCH

20 A.Symonds Gloucestershire v Glamorgan Abergavenny 1995

MOST SIXES IN A SEASON

80 I.T.Botham Somerset and England 1985

MOST FOURS IN AN INNINGS

72 B.C.Lara Warwickshire v Durham Birmingham 1994

MOST RUNS OFF ONE OVER

| 36 | G.St A.Sobers | Nottinghamshire v Glamorgan | Swansea | 1968 |
| 36 | R.J.Shastri | Bombay v Baroda | Bombay | 1984-85 |

Both batsmen hit for six all six balls of overs bowled by M.A.Nash and Tilak Raj respectively.

MOST RUNS IN A DAY

390* B.C.Lara Warwickshire v Durham Birmingham 1994

There have been 19 instances of a batsman scoring 300 or more runs in a day.

LONGEST INNINGS
1015 min R.Nayyar (271)   Himachal Pradesh v Jammu & Kashmir Chamba   1999-00

HIGHEST PARTNERSHIPS FOR EACH WICKET

First Wicket

561	Waheed Mirza/Mansoor Akhtar	Karachi W v Quetta	Karachi	1976-77
555	P.Holmes/H.Sutcliffe	Yorkshire v Essex	Leyton	1932
554	J.T.Brown/J.Tunnicliffe	Yorkshire v Derbys	Chesterfield	1898

Second Wicket

576	S.T.Jayasuriya/R.S.Mahanama	Sri Lanka v India	Colombo	1997-98
475	Zahir Alam/L.S.Rajput	Assam v Tripura	Gauhati	1991-92
465*	J.A.Jameson/R.B.Kanhai	Warwickshire v Glos	Birmingham	1974

Third Wicket

624	K.C.Sangakkara/D.P.M.D.Jayawardena	Sri Lanka v South Africa	Colombo	2006
467	A.H.Jones/M.D.Crowe	N Zealand v Sri Lanka	Wellington	1990-91
459	C.J.L.Rogers/M.J.North	W Australia v Victoria	Perth	2006-07
456	Khalid Irtiza/Aslam Ali	United Bank v Multan	Karachi	1975-76
451	Mudassar Nazar/Javed Miandad	Pakistan v India	Hyderabad	1982-83
445	P.E.Whitelaw/W.N.Carson	Auckland v Otago	Dunedin	1936-37
438*	G.A.Hick/T.M.Moody	Worcestershire v Hants	Southampton	1997

Fourth Wicket

577	V.S.Hazare/Gul Mahomed	Baroda v Holkar	Baroda	1946-47
574*	C.L.Walcott/F.M.M.Worrell	Barbados v Trinidad	Port-of-Spain	1945-46
502*	F.M.M.Worrell/J.D.C.Goddard	Barbados v Trinidad	Bridgetown	1943-44
470	A.I.Kallicharran/G.W.Humpage	Warwickshire v Lancs	Southport	1982

Fifth Wicket

520*	C.A.Pujara/R.A.Jadeja	Saurashtra v Orissa	Rajkot	2008-09
464*	M.E.Waugh/S.R.Waugh	NSW v W Australia	Perth	1990-91
420	Mohd. Ashraful/Marshall Ayub	Dhaka v Chittagong	Chittagong	2006-07
410*	A.S.Chopra/S.Badrinath	India A v South Africa A	Delhi	2007-08
405	S.G.Barnes/D.G.Bradman	Australia v England	Sydney	1946-47
401	M.B.Loye/D.Ripley	Northants v Glamorgan	Northampton	1998

Sixth Wicket

487*	G.A.Headley/C.C.Passailaigue	Jamaica v Tennyson's	Kingston	1931-32
428	W.W.Armstrong/M.A.Noble	Australians v Sussex	Hove	1902
411	R.M.Poore/E.G.Wynyard	Hampshire v Somerset	Taunton	1899

Seventh Wicket

460	Bhupinder Singh jr/P.Dharmani	Punjab v Delhi	Delhi	1994-95
347	D.St E.Atkinson/C.C.Depeiza	W Indies v Australia	Bridgetown	1954-55
344	K.S.Ranjitsinhji/W.Newham	Sussex v Essex	Leyton	1902

Eighth Wicket

433	V.T.Trumper/A.Sims	Australians v C'bury	Christchurch	1913-14
313-	Wasim Akram/Saqlain Mushtaq	Pakistan v Zimbabwe	Sheikhupura	1996-97
292	R.Peel/Lord Hawke	Yorkshire v Warwicks	Birmingham	1896

Ninth Wicket

283	J.Chapman/A.Warren	Derbys v Warwicks	Blackwell	1910
268	J.B.Commins/N.Boje	SA 'A' v Mashonaland	Harare	1994-95
251	J.W.H.T.Douglas/S.N.Hare	Essex v Derbyshire	Leyton	1921

Tenth Wicket

307	A.F.Kippax/J.E.H.Hooker	NSW v Victoria	Melbourne	1928-29
249	C.T.Sarwate/S.N.Banerjee	Indians v Surrey	The Oval	1946
239	Aqil Arshad/Ali Raza	Lahore Whites v Hyderabad	Lahore	2004-05
235	F.E.Woolley/A.Fielder	Kent v Worcs	Stourbridge	1909

35,000 RUNS IN A CAREER

	Career	I	NO	HS	Runs	Avge	100
J.B.Hobbs	1905-34	1315	106	316*	61237	50.65	197
F.E.Woolley	1906-38	1532	85	305*	58969	40.75	145
E.H.Hendren	1907-38	1300	166	301*	57611	50.80	170
C.P.Mead	1905-36	1340	185	280*	55061	47.67	153
W.G.Grace	1865-1908	1493	105	344	54896	39.55	126
W.R.Hammond	1920-51	1005	104	336*	50551	56.10	167
H.Sutcliffe	1919-45	1088	123	313	50138	51.95	149
G.Boycott	1962-86	1014	162	261*	48426	56.83	151
T.W.Graveney	1948-71/72	1223	159	258	47793	44.91	122
G.A.Gooch	1973-2000	990	75	333	44846	49.01	128
T.W.Hayward	1893-1914	1138	96	315*	43551	41.79	104
D.L.Amiss	1960-87	1139	126	262*	43423	42.86	102
M.C.Cowdrey	1950-76	1130	134	307	42719	42.89	107
A.Sandham	1911-37/38	1000	79	325	41284	44.82	107
G.A.Hick	1983/84-2008	871	84	405*	41112	52.23	136
L.Hutton	1934-60	814	91	364	40140	55.51	129
M.J.K.Smith	1951-75	1091	139	204	39832	41.84	69
W.Rhodes	1898-1930	1528	237	267*	39802	30.83	58
J.H.Edrich	1956-78	979	104	310*	39790	45.47	103
R.E.S.Wyatt	1923-57	1141	157	232	39405	40.04	85
D.C.S.Compton	1936-64	839	88	300	38942	51.85	123
G.E.Tyldesley	1909-36	961	106	256*	38874	45.46	102
J.T.Tyldesley	1895-1923	994	62	295*	37897	40.60	86
K.W.R.Fletcher	1962-88	1167	170	228*	37665	37.77	63
C.G.Greenidge	1970-92	889	75	273*	37354	45.88	92
J.W.Hearne	1909-36	1025	116	285*	37252	40.98	96
L.E.G.Ames	1926-51	951	95	295	37248	43.51	102
D.Kenyon	1946-67	1159	59	259	37002	33.63	74
W.J.Edrich	1934-58	964	92	267*	36965	42.39	86
J.M.Parks	1949-76	1227	172	205*	36673	34.76	51
M.W.Gatting	1975-98	861	123	258	36549	49.52	94
D.Denton	1894-1920	1163	70	221	36479	33.37	69
G.H.Hirst	1891-1929	1215	151	341	36323	34.13	60
I.V.A.Richards	1971/72-93	796	63	322	36212	49.40	114
A.Jones	1957-83	1168	72	204*	36049	32.89	56
W.G.Quaife	1894-1928	1203	185	255*	36012	35.37	72
R.E.Marshall	1945/46-72	1053	59	228*	35725	35.94	68
G.Gunn	1902-32	1061	82	220	35208	35.96	62

BOWLING RECORDS

ALL TEN WICKETS IN AN INNINGS

This feat has been achieved 80 times in first-class matches (excluding 12-a-side fixtures).

Three Times: A.P.Freeman (1929, 1930, 1931)
Twice: V.E.Walker (1859, 1865); H.Verity (1931, 1932); J.C.Laker (1956)

Instances since 1945:

W.E.Hollies	Warwickshire v Notts	Birmingham	1946
J.M.Sims	East v West	Kingston on Thames	1948
J.K.R.Graveney	Gloucestershire v Derbyshire	Chesterfield	1949
T.E.Bailey	Essex v Lancashire	Clacton	1949
R.Berry	Lancashire v Worcestershire	Blackpool	1953
S.P.Gupte	President's XI v Combined XI	Bombay	1954-55
J.C.Laker	Surrey v Australians	The Oval	1956

K.Smales	Nottinghamshire v Glos	Stroud	1956
G.A.R.Lock	Surrey v Kent	Blackheath	1956
J.C.Laker	England v Australia	Manchester	1956
P.M.Chatterjee	Bengal v Assam	Jorhat	1956-57
J.D.Bannister	Warwicks v Combined Services	Birmingham (M & B)	1959
A.J.G.Pearson	Cambridge U v Leicestershire	Loughborough	1961
N.I.Thomson	Sussex v Warwickshire	Worthing	1964
P.J.Allan	Queensland v Victoria	Melbourne	1965-66
I.J.Brayshaw	Western Australia v Victoria	Perth	1967-68
Shahid Mahmood	Karachi Whites v Khairpur	Karachi	1969-70
E.E.Hemmings	International XI v W Indians	Kingston	1982-83
P.Sunderam	Rajasthan v Vidarbha	Jodhpur	1985-86
S.T.Jefferies	Western Province v OFS	Cape Town	1987-88
Imran Adil	Bahawalpur v Faisalabad	Faisalabad	1989-90
G.P.Wickremasinghe	Sinhalese v Kalutara	Colombo	1991-92
R.L.Johnson	Middlesex v Derbyshire	Derby	1994
Naeem Akhtar	Rawalpindi B v Peshawar	Peshawar	1995-96
A.Kumble	India v Pakistan	Delhi	1998-99
D.S.Mohanty	East Zone v South Zone	Agartala	2000-01
O.D.Gibson	Durham v Hampshire	Chester-le-Street	2007
M.W.Olivier	Warriors v Eagles	Bloemfontein	2007-08

MOST WICKETS IN A MATCH

| 19 | J.C.Laker | England v Australia | Manchester | 1956 |

MOST WICKETS IN A SEASON

Wkts		Season	Matches	Overs	Mdns	Runs	Avge
304	A.P.Freeman	1928	37	1976.1	423	5489	18.05
298	A.P.Freeman	1933	33	2039	651	4549	15.26

The feat of taking 250 wickets in a season has been achieved on 12 occasions, the last instance being by A.P.Freeman in 1933. 200 or more wickets in a season have been taken on 59 occasions, the last being by G.A.R.Lock (212 wickets, average 12.02) in 1957.

The highest aggregates of wickets taken in a season since the reduction of County Championship matches in 1969 are as follows:

Wkts		Season	Matches	Overs	Mdns	Runs	Avge
134	M.D.Marshall	1982	22	822	225	2108	15.73
131	L.R.Gibbs	1971	23	1024.1	295	2475	18.89
125	F.D.Stephenson	1988	22	819.1	196	2289	18.31
121	R.D.Jackman	1980	23	746.2	220	1864	15.40

Since 1969 there have been 50 instances of bowlers taking 100 wickets in a season.

MOST HAT-TRICKS IN A CAREER

7	D.V.P.Wright
6	T.W.J.Goddard, C.W.L.Parker
5	S.Haigh, V.W.C.Jupp, A.E.G.Rhodes, F.A.Tarrant

2000 WICKETS IN A CAREER

	Career	Runs	Wkts	Avge	100w
W.Rhodes	1898-1930	69993	4187	16.71	23
A.P.Freeman	1914-36	69577	3776	18.42	17
C.W.L.Parker	1903-35	63817	3278	19.46	16
J.T.Hearne	1888-1923	54352	3061	17.75	15
T.W.J.Goddard	1922-52	59116	2979	19.84	16
W.G.Grace	1865-1908	51545	2876	17.92	10
A.S.Kennedy	1907-36	61034	2874	21.23	15
D.Shackleton	1948-69	53303	2857	18.65	20
G.A.R.Lock	1946-70/71	54709	2844	19.23	14
F.J.Titmus	1949-82	63313	2830	22.37	16

	Career	Runs	Wkts	Avge	100w
M.W.Tate	1912-37	50571	**2784**	18.16	13+1
G.H.Hirst	1891-1929	51282	**2739**	18.72	15
C.Blythe	1899-1914	42136	**2506**	16.81	14
D.L.Underwood	1963-87	49993	**2465**	20.28	10
W.E.Astill	1906-39	57783	**2431**	23.76	9
J.C.White	1909-37	43759	**2356**	18.57	14
W.E.Hollies	1932-57	48656	**2323**	20.94	14
F.S.Trueman	1949-69	42154	**2304**	18.29	12
J.B.Statham	1950-68	36999	**2260**	16.37	13
R.T.D.Perks	1930-55	53771	**2233**	24.07	16
J.Briggs	1879-1900	35431	**2221**	15.95	12
D.J.Shepherd	1950-72	47302	**2218**	21.32	12
E.G.Dennett	1903-26	42571	**2147**	19.82	12
T.Richardson	1892-1905	38794	**2104**	18.43	10
T.E.Bailey	1945-67	48170	**2082**	23.13	9
R.Illingworth	1951-83	42023	**2072**	20.28	10
F.E.Woolley	1906-38	41066	**2068**	19.85	8
N.Gifford	1960-88	48731	**2068**	23.56	4
G.Geary	1912-38	41339	**2063**	20.03	11
D.V.P.Wright	1932-57	49307	**2056**	23.98	10
J.A.Newman	1906-30	51111	**2032**	25.15	9
A.Shaw	1864-97	24580	**2026+1**	12.12	9
S.Haigh	1895-1913	32091	**2012**	15.94	11

ALL-ROUND RECORDS
THE 'DOUBLE'

3000 runs and 100 wickets: J.H.Parks (1937)
2000 runs and 200 wickets: G.H.Hirst (1906)
2000 runs and 100 wickets: F.E.Woolley (4), J.W.Hearne (3), W.G.Grace (2), G.H.Hirst (2), W.Rhodes (2), T.E.Bailey, D.E.Davies, G.L.Jessop, V.W.C.Jupp, J.Langridge, F.A.Tarrant, C.L.Townsend, L.F.Townsend
1000 runs and 200 wickets: M.W.Tate (3), A.E.Trott (2), A.S.Kennedy

Most Doubles: 16 – W.Rhodes; 14 – G.H.Hirst; 10 – V.W.C.Jupp

Double in Debut Season: D.B.Close (1949) – aged 18, the youngest to achieve this feat.
 The feat of scoring 1000 runs and taking 100 wickets in a season has been achieved on 305 occasions, R.J.Hadlee (1984) and F.D.Stephenson (1988) being the only players to complete the 'double' since the reduction of County Championship matches in 1969.

WICKET-KEEPING RECORDS
EIGHT DISMISSALS IN AN INNINGS

9	(8ct, 1st)	Tahir Rashid	Habib Bank v PACO	Gujranwala	1992-93
9	(7ct, 2st)	W.R.James	Matabeleland v Mashonaland CD	Bulawayo	1995-96
8	(8ct)	A.T.W.Grout	Queensland v W Australia	Brisbane	1959-60
8	(8ct)	D.E.East	Essex v Somerset	Taunton	1985
8	(8ct)	S.A.Marsh	Kent v Middlesex	Lord's	1991
8	(6ct, 2st)	T.J.Zoehrer	Australians v Surrey	The Oval	1993
8	(7ct, 1st)	D.S.Berry	Victoria v South Australia	Melbourne	1996-97
8	(7ct, 1st)	Y.S.S.Mendis	Bloomfield v Kurunegala Youth	Colombo	2000-01
8	(7ct, 1st)	S.Nath	Assam v Tripura (on debut)	Gauhati	2001-02
8	(8ct)	J.N.Batty	Surrey v Kent	The Oval	2004
8	(8ct)	Golam Mabud	Sylhet v Dhaka	Dhaka	2005-06

TWELVE DISMISSALS IN A MATCH

13	(11ct, 2st)	W.R.James	Matabeleland v Mashonaland CD	Bulawayo	1995-96
12	(8ct, 4st)	E.Pooley	Surrey v Sussex	The Oval	1868
12	(9ct, 3st)	D.Tallon	Queensland v NSW	Sydney	1938-39
12	(9ct, 3st)	H.B.Taber	NSW v South Australia	Adelaide	1968-69

MOST DISMISSALS IN A SEASON

128 (79ct, 49st) L.E.G.Ames   1929

1000 DISMISSALS IN A CAREER

	Career	Dismissals	Ct	St
R.W.Taylor	1960-88	1649	1473	176
J.T.Murray	1952-75	1527	1270	257
H.Strudwick	1902-27	1497	1242	255
A.P.E.Knott	1964-85	1344	1211	133
R.C.Russell	1981-2004	1320	1192	128
F.H.Huish	1895-1914	1310	933	377
B.Taylor	1949-73	1294	1083	211
S.J.Rhodes	1981-2004	1263	1139	124
D.Hunter	1889-1909	1253	906	347
H.R.Butt	1890-1912	1228	953	275
J.H.Board	1891-1914/15	1207	852	355
H.Elliott	1920-47	1206	904	302
J.M.Parks	1949-76	1181	1088	93
R.Booth	1951-70	1126	948	178
L.E.G.Ames	1926-51	1121	703	418
D.L.Bairstow	1970-90	1099	961	138
G.Duckworth	1923-47	1096	753	343
H.W.Stephenson	1948-64	1082	748	334
J.G.Binks	1955-75	1071	895	176
T.G.Evans	1939-67	1066	816	250
A.Long	1960-80	1046	922	124
G.O.Dawkes	1937-61	1043	895	148
R.W.Tolchard	1965-83	1037	912	125
W.L.Cornford	1921-47	1017	675	342

FIELDING RECORDS

MOST CATCHES IN AN INNINGS

7	M.J.Stewart	Surrey v Northamptonshire	Northampton	1957
7	A.S.Brown	Gloucestershire v Nottinghamshire	Nottingham	1966

MOST CATCHES IN A MATCH

10	W.R.Hammond	Gloucestershire v Surrey	Cheltenham	1928

MOST CATCHES IN A SEASON

78	W.R.Hammond	1928	77	M.J.Stewart	1957

750 CATCHES IN A CAREER

1018	F.E.Woolley	1906-38	784	J.G.Langridge	1928-55
887	W.G.Grace	1865-1908	764	W.Rhodes	1898-1930
830	G.A.R.Lock	1946-70/71	758	C.A.Milton	1948-74
819	W.R.Hammond	1920-51	754	E.H.Hendren	1907-38
813	D.B.Close	1949-86			

ENGLAND LIMITED-OVERS INTERNATIONALS 2009

WEST INDIES v ENGLAND

TWENTY20 INTERNATIONAL
Queen's Park Oval, Port-of-Spain, Trinidad, 15 March. Toss: West Indies. **WEST INDIES** won by six wickets. England 121 (19.1; S.J.Benn 3-24). West Indies 123-4 (18; R.R.Sarwan 59). Award: R.R.Sarwan.

LIMITED-OVERS INTERNATIONALS
Providence Stadium, Guyana, 20 March. Toss: England. **ENGLAND** won by 1 run (D/L Method). England 270-7 (50; P.D.Collingwood 69, O.A.Shah 62). West Indies 244-7 (46.2; L.M.P.Simmons 62, R.R.Sarwan 57, S.C.J.Broad 3-41). Award: P.D.Collingwood.

Providence Stadium, Guyana, 22 March. Toss: West Indies. **WEST INDIES** won by 21 runs. West Indies 264-8 (50; S.Chanderpaul 112*, R.R.Sarwan 74, J.M.Anderson 3-37, P.D.Collingwood 3-49). England 243 (48.2; A.J.Strauss 105). Award: S.Chanderpaul.

Kensington Oval, Bridgetown, Barbados, 27 March. Toss: West Indies. **WEST INDIES** won by eight wickets (D/L Method). England 117 (41.3/44; D.J.Bravo 4-19, F.H.Edwards 3-28). West Indies 117-2 (14.4; C.H.Gayle 80). Award: D.J.Bravo.

Kensington Oval, Bridgetown, Barbados, 29 March. Toss: England. **ENGLAND** won by nine wickets (D/L Method). West Indies 239-9 (50; D.J.Bravo 69, A.D.Mascarenhas 3-26, S.C.J.Broad 3-62). England 136-1 (18.3/20; A.J.Strauss 79*). Award: A.J.Strauss.

Beausejour Stadium, Gros Islet, St Lucia, 3 April. Toss: West Indies. **ENGLAND** won by 26 runs. England 172-5 (29/29). West Indies 146 (28/29; A.Flintoff 5-19). Award: A.Flintoff. Series award: A.J.Strauss.

ENGLAND v WEST INDIES

NATWEST LIMITED-OVERS INTERNATIONAL SERIES
Headingley, Leeds, 21 May. MATCH ABANDONED without a ball bowled. No toss.

County Ground, Bristol, 24 May. Toss: England. **ENGLAND** won by six wickets. West Indies 160 (38.3; D.J.Bravo 50, S.C.J.Broad 4-46, P.D.Collingwood 3-16). England 161-4 (36). Award: P.D.Collingwood. England debut: E.J.G.Morgan (having already made 23 LOI apps for Ireland).

Edgbaston, Birmingham, 26 May. Toss: West Indies. **ENGLAND** won by 58 runs. England 328-7 (50; M.J.Prior 87, O.A.Shah 75, A.J.Strauss 52, J.E.Taylor 3-59). West Indies 270 (49.4; S.Chanderpaul 68, J.M.Anderson 3-58). Award: M.J.Prior. Series award: S.C.J.Broad.

ICC WORLD TWENTY20 2009

See pages 283-284 for details of these matches.

ENGLAND v AUSTRALIA

TWENTY20 INTERNATIONALS
Old Trafford, Manchester, 30 August. Toss: England. **NO RESULT**. Australia 145-4 (20; C.L.White 55). England 4-2 (1.1). England debut: J.L.Denly.

Old Trafford, Manchester, 1 September. MATCH ABANDONED without a ball bowled. No toss.

NATWEST LIMITED-OVERS INTERNATIONAL SERIES
The Oval, London, 4 September. Toss: England. **AUSTRALIA** won by 4 runs. Australia 260-5 (50; C.J.Ferguson 71*, C.L.White 53). England 256-8 (50). Award: C.J.Ferguson.

Lord's, London, 6 September. Toss: England. **AUSTRALIA** won by 39 runs. Australia 249 (50; C.J.Ferguson 55). England 210 (46.1; P.D.Collingwood 56). Award: M.G.Johnson (43* and 2-50).

Rose Bowl, Southampton, 9 September. Toss: England. **AUSTRALIA** won by six wickets. England 228-9 (50; A.J.Strauss 63). Australia 230-4 (48.3; C.L.White 105, M.J.Clarke 52). Award: C.L.White.

Lord's, London, 12 September. Toss: England. **AUSTRALIA** won by seven wickets. England 220 (46.3; A.J.Strauss 63, B.Lee 5-49). Australia 221-3 (43.4; M.J.Clarke 62*, T.D.Paine 51). Award: B.Lee.

Trent Bridge, Nottingham, 15 September. Toss: England. **AUSTRALIA** won by four wickets. England 299 (50; E.J.G.Morgan 58). Australia 302-6 (48.2; R.T.Ponting 126, M.J.Clarke 52). Award: R.T.Ponting.

Trent Bridge, Nottingham, 17 September. Toss: Australia. **AUSTRALIA** won by 111 runs. Australia 296-8 (50; T.D.Paine 111, M.E.K.Hussey 65, J.M.Anderson 4-55). England 185 (41). Award: T.D.Paine.

Riverside, Chester-le-Street, 20 September. Toss: England. **ENGLAND** won by four wickets. Australia 176 (45.5; R.T.Ponting 53, G.P.Swann 5-28). England 177-6 (40; J.L.Denly 53). Award: G.P.Swann. Series Award: C.L.White. England debut: G. Onions.

ICC CHAMPIONS TROPHY
The Wanderers, Johannesburg, 25 September. Toss: England. **ENGLAND** won by six wickets. Sri Lanka 212 (47.3; S.H.T.Kandamby 53, A.D.Mathews 52). England 213-4 (45; E.J.G.Morgan 62*). Award: P.D.Collingwood (46 and 0-24).

Centurion Park (Verwoerdburg), Pretoria, 27 September. Toss: England. **ENGLAND** won by 22 runs. England 323-8 (50; O.A.Shah 98, P.D.Collingwood 82, E.J.G.Morgan 67). South Africa 301-9 (50; G.C.Smith 141). Award: O.A.Shah.

The Wanderers, Johannesburg, 29 September. Toss: New Zealand. **NEW ZEALAND** won by four wickets. England 146 (43.1; G.D.Elliott 4-31). New Zealand 147-6 (M.J.Guptill 53, S.C.J.Broad 4-39). Award: G.D.Elliott.

Semi-final, Centurion Park (Verwoerdburg), Pretoria, 2 October. Toss: England. **AUSTRALIA** won by nine wickets. England 257 (47.4; T.T.Bresnan 80). Australia 258-1 (41.5; S.R.Watson 136*, R.T.Ponting 111*). Award: S.R.Watson. England debut: S.M.Davies.

Australia beat New Zealand by six wickets in the final.

SOUTH AFRICA v ENGLAND
TWENTY20 INTERNATIONALS
New Wanderers, Johannesburg, 13 November. Toss: South Africa. **ENGLAND** won by 1 run (D/L Method). England 202-6 (20; E.J.G.Morgan 85*, P.D.Collingwood 57, R.McLaren 3-33). South Africa 127-3 (13/20; L.L.Bosman 58). Award: E.J.G.Morgan.
Record total for England in T20 internationals, and highest individual innings.

Centurion Park (Verwoerdburg), Pretoria, 15 November. Toss: South Africa. **SOUTH AFRICA** won by 84 runs. South Africa 241-6 (20; L.L.Bosman 94, G.C.Smith 88). England 157-8 (20; I.J.L.Trott 51). Award: L.L.Bosman.

LIMITED-OVERS INTERNATIONALS
New Wanderers, Johannesburg, 20 November. **MATCH ABANDONED** without a ball bowled. No toss.

Centurion Park (Verwoerdburg), Pretoria, 22 November. Toss: England. **ENGLAND** won by seven wickets. South Africa 250-9 (50; A.N.Petersen 64, H.M.Amla 57, J.M.Anderson 3-60). England 252-3 (46; P.D.Collingwood 105*, I.J.L.Trott 87). Award: P.D.Collingwood.
In this match, P.D.Collingwood set a new England record of 171 LOI appearances, beating A.J.Stewart's total of 170.

Newlands, Cape Town, 27 November. Toss: South Africa. **SOUTH AFRICA** won by 112 runs. South Africa 354-6 (50; A.B.de Villiers 121, H.M.Amla 86, G.C.Smith 54, A.N.Petersen 51*, S.C.J.Broad 4-71). England 242 (41.3; P.D.Collingwood 86, W.D.Parnell 5-48, M.Morkel 3-39). Award: A.B.de Villiers.

St George's Park, Port Elizabeth, 29 November. Toss: South Africa. **ENGLAND** won by seven wickets. South Africa 119 (36.5; A.N.Petersen 51, J.M.Anderson 5-23). England 121-3 (31.2; I.J.L.Trott 52*). Award: J.M.Anderson.

Kingsmead, Durban, 4 December. MATCH ABANDONED without a ball bowled. No toss.

England's Results in 2009

	P	W	L	NR	A
Limited Overs	24	10	11	–	3
Twenty20	10	3	5	1	1
Overall	34	13	16	1	4

ICC WORLD TWENTY20 2009

GROUP A	P	W	L	T	Pts	Net RR
India	2	2	–	–	4	+1.23
Ireland	2	1	1	–	2	–0.16
Bangladesh	2	–	2	–	0	–1.00

GROUP B	P	W	L	T	Pts	Net RR
England	2	1	1	–	2	+1.18
Pakistan	2	1	1	–	2	+0.85
Netherlands	2	1	1	–	2	–2.03

Lord's, London, 5 June. Toss: Netherlands. **NETHERLANDS** won by four wickets. England 162-5 (20; L.J.Wright 71). Netherlands 163-6 (20; J.M.Anderson 3-23). Award: T.N.de Grooth (49).

The Oval, London, 7 June. Toss: Pakistan. **ENGLAND** won by 48 runs. England 185-5 (20; K.P.Pietersen 58). Pakistan 137-7 (20; S.C.J.Broad 3-17). Award: L.J.Wright (34, 1-24, 2ct).

GROUP C	P	W	L	T	Pts	Net RR
Sri Lanka	2	2	–	–	4	+0.63
West Indies	2	1	1	–	2	+0.72
Australia	2	–	2	–	0	–1.33

GROUP D	P	W	L	T	Pts	Net RR
South Africa	2	2	–	–	4	+3.28
New Zealand	2	1	1	–	2	+0.31
Scotland	2	–	2	–	0	–5.28

SUPER EIGHTS

GROUP E	P	W	L	T	Pts	Net RR
South Africa	3	3	–	–	6	+0.79
West Indies	3	2	1	–	4	+0.06
England	3	1	2	–	2	–0.41
India	3	–	3	–	0	–0.47

Trent Bridge, Nottingham, 11 June. Toss: England. **SOUTH AFRICA** won by seven wickets. England 111 (19.5; W.D.Parnell 3-14). South Africa 114-3 (18.2; J.H.Kallis 57*). Award: J.H.Kallis.

Lord's, London, 12 June. Toss: India. **WEST INDIES** won by seven wickets. India 153-7 (20; Yuvraj Singh 67, D.J.Bravo 4-38, F.H.Edwards 3-24). West Indies 156-3 (18.4; D.J.Bravo 66*). Award: D.J.Bravo.

The Oval, London, 13 June. Toss: West Indies. **SOUTH AFRICA** won by 20 runs. South Africa 183-7 (20; H.H.Gibbs 55, J.E.Taylor 3-30). West Indies 163-9 (20; L.M.P.Simmons 77, W.D.Parnell 4-13). Award: W.D.Parnell.

Lord's, London, 14 June. Toss: India. **ENGLAND** won by 3 runs. England 153-7 (20; Harbhajan Singh 3-30). India 150-5 (20). Award: R.J.Sidebottom (2-31).

The Oval, London, 15 June. Toss: England. **WEST INDIES** won by five wickets (D/L Method). England 161-6 (20; R.S.Bopara 55). West Indies 82-5 (8.2/9). Award: R.R.Sarwan.

Trent Bridge, Nottingham, 16 June. Toss: South Africa. **SOUTH AFRICA** won by 12 runs. South Africa 130-5 (20; A.B.de Villiers 63). India 118-8 (20; J.Botha 3-16). Award: A.B.de Villiers.

GROUP F

	P	W	L	T	Pts	Net RR
Sri Lanka	3	3	–	–	6	+1.27
Pakistan	3	2	1	–	4	+1.19
New Zealand	3	1	2	–	2	–0.23
Ireland	3	–	3	–	0	–2.18

Trent Bridge, Nottingham, 11 June. Toss: Ireland. **NEW ZEALAND** won by 83 runs. New Zealand 198-5 (20; A.J.Redmond 63). Ireland 115 (16.4; N.L.McCullum 3-15). Award: A.J.Redmond.

Lord's, London, 12 June. Toss: Sri Lanka. **SRI LANKA** won by 19 runs. Sri Lanka 150-7 (20). Pakistan 131-9 (20; Younus Khan 50, S.L.Malinga 3-17). Award: T.M.Dilshan (46).

The Oval, London, 13 June. Toss: New Zealand. **PAKISTAN** won by six wickets. New Zealand 99 (18.3; Umar Gul 5-6). Pakistan 100-4 (13.1). Award: Umar Gul.

Lord's, London, 14 June. Toss: Sri Lanka. **SRI LANKA** won by 9 runs. Sri Lanka 144-9 (20; D.P.M.D.Jayawardena 78, A.R.Cusack 4-18). Ireland 135-7 (20). Award: D.P.M.D.Jayawardena.

The Oval, London, 15 June. Toss: Pakistan. **PAKISTAN** won by 39 runs. Pakistan 159-5 (20; Kamran Akmal 57). Ireland 120-9 (20; Saeed Ajmal 4-19). Award: Kamran Akmal.

Trent Bridge, Nottingham, 16 June. Toss: Sri Lanka. **SRI LANKA** won by 48 runs. Sri Lanka 158-5 (20). New Zealand 110 (17; B.A.W.Mendis 3-9). Award: B.A.W.Mendis.

SEMI-FINALS

Trent Bridge, Nottingham, 18 June. Toss: Pakistan. **PAKISTAN** won by 7 runs. Pakistan 149-4 (20; Shahid Afridi 51). South Africa 142-5 (20; J.H.Kallis 64). Award: Shahid Afridi.

The Oval, London, 19 June. Toss: West Indies. **SRI LANKA** won by 57 runs. Sri Lanka 158-5 (20; T.M.Dilshan 96*). West Indies 101 (17.4; C.H.Gayle 63*, A.D.Mathews 3-16, M.Muralitharan 3-29). Award: T.M.Dilshan.

FINAL

Lord's, London, 21 June. Toss: **PAKISTAN** won by eight wickets. Sri Lanka 138-6 (20; K.C.Sangakkara 64*, Abdul Razzaq 3-20). Pakistan 139-2 (18.4; Shahid Afridi 54*). Award: Shahid Afridi.

RECORDS

Match

Highest score	211-5 (20)		South Africa v Scotland	Group D	Oval
Lowest score	81 (15.4)		Scotland v South Africa	Group D	Oval
Highest innings	96*	T.M.Dilshan	Sri Lanka v West Indies	Semi-final	Oval
Fastest fifty	23 balls	C.H.Gayle	West Indies v Australia	Group C	Oval
	23 balls	A.J.Redmond	New Zealand v Ireland	Group F	Nottingham
Highest partnership	133	C.H.Gayle/A.D.S.Fletcher	West Indies v Australia	Group C	Oval
Best analysis	5-6	Umar Gul	Pakistan v New Zealand	Group B	Oval
Most dismissals	4 (4st)	Kamran Akmal	Pakistan v Netherlands	Group B	Lord's
	4 (3ct, 1st)	N.J.O'Brien	Ireland v Sri Lanka	Group F	Lord's

Tournament

Man of the series		T.M.Dilshan	317 runs @ 52.83
Most runs	317	T.M.Dilshan	Sri Lanka (ave 52.83, strike rate 144.7)
Highest strike rate	177.2	A.J.Redmond	New Zealand (101 runs in 57 balls) Qual: 100 runs plus.
Most wickets	13	Umar Gul	Pakistan (ave 12.15, economy 6.44)
Most economical	5.32	Shahid Afridi	Pakistan (149 runs in 28 overs) Qual: 15 overs
Most dismissals	9 (5ct, 4st)	K.C.Sangakkara	Sri Lanka
Most catches	6	A.D.S.Fletcher	West Indies

These records, complete to 27 February 2010 (the conclusion of the India v South Africa series), include all players registered for county cricket for the 2010 season at the time of going to press, plus those who have appeared in LOI matches for ICC full member countries since 1 October 2008.

ENGLAND – BATTING AND FIELDING

	M	I	NO	HS	Runs	Avge	100	50	Ct/St
K.Ali	14	9	3	39*	93	15.50	–	–	1
T.R.Ambrose	5	5	1	6	10	2.50	–	–	3
J.M.Anderson	120	50	25	15	147	5.88	–	–	30
G.J.Batty	10	8	2	17	30	5.00	–	–	4
I.R.Bell	79	76	6	126*	2483	35.47	1	15	23
I.D.Blackwell	34	29	2	82	403	14.92	–	1	8
R.S.Bopara	50	46	8	60	1037	27.28	–	4	17
T.T.Bresnan	18	14	6	80	253	31.62	–	1	3
S.C.J.Broad	57	37	14	45*	338	14.69	–	–	13
A.D.Brown	16	16	–	118	354	22.12	1	1	6
G.Chapple	1	1	–	14	14	14.00	–	–	–
R.Clarke	20	13	–	39	144	11.07	–	–	11
P.D.Collingwood	173	157	33	120*	4478	36.11	5	24	99
A.N.Cook	23	23	–	102	702	30.52	1	3	7
D.G.Cork	32	21	3	31*	180	10.00	–	–	6
R.D.B.Croft	50	36	12	32	345	14.37	–	–	11
J.W.M.Dalrymple	27	26	1	67	487	19.48	–	2	12
S.M.Davies	1	1	–	5	5	5.00	–	–	1
J.L.Denly	9	9	–	67	268	29.77	–	2	5
A.Flintoff	141	122	16	123	3394	32.01	3	18	47
J.S.Foster	11	6	3	13	41	13.66	–	–	13/7
P.J.Franks	1	1	–	4	4	4.00	–	–	1
S.J.Harmison	58	25	14	18*	91	8.27	–	–	10
M.J.Hoggard	26	6	2	7	17	4.25	–	–	5
G.O.Jones	49	41	8	80	815	24.69	–	4	68/4
S.P.Jones	8	1	–	1	1	1.00	–	–	–
E.C.Joyce	17	17	–	107	471	27.70	1	3	6
R.W.T.Key	5	5	–	19	54	10.80	–	–	1
R.J.Kirtley	11	2	–	1	2	1.00	–	–	5
J.Lewis	13	8	2	17	50	8.33	–	–	1
M.B.Loye	7	7	–	45	142	20.28	–	–	–
A.McGrath	14	12	2	52	166	16.60	–	1	4
D.L.Maddy	8	6	–	53	113	18.83	–	1	1
S.I.Mahmood	26	15	4	22*	85	7.72	–	–	1
A.D.Mascarenhas	20	13	2	52	245	22.27	–	1	4
E.J.G.Morgan †	15	15	5	67	363	36.30	–	3	6
P.Mustard	10	10	–	83	233	23.30	–	1	9/2
P.A.Nixon	19	18	4	49	297	21.21	–	–	20/3
G.Onions	4	1	–	1	1	1.00	–	–	–
M.S.Panesar	26	8	3	13	26	5.20	–	–	3
S.R.Patel	11	5	–	31	116	23.20	–	–	4
K.P.Pietersen	95	85	15	116	3179	45.41	7	20	32
L.E.Plunkett	27	24	10	56	295	21.07	–	1	7
M.J.Prior	52	48	7	87	994	24.24	–	2	57/4
A.U.Rashid	5	4	1	31*	60	20.00	–	–	2
C.M.W.Read	36	24	7	30*	300	17.64	–	–	41/2
O.A.Shah	71	66	6	107*	1834	30.56	1	12	21
R.J.Sidebottom	24	18	8	24	133	13.30	–	–	5

	M	I	NO	HS	Runs	Avge	100	50	Ct/St
V.S.Solanki	51	46	5	106	1097	26.75	2	5	16
A.J.Strauss	99	98	8	152	2886	32.06	3	18	38
G.P.Swann	29	20	3	34	227	13.35	–	–	13
C.T.Tremlett	9	6	2	19*	38	9.50	–	–	2
M.E.Trescothick	123	122	6	137	4335	37.37	12	21	49
I.J.L.Trott	4	4	1	87	148	49.33	–	2	2
J.O.Troughton	6	5	1	20	36	9.00	–	–	1
S.D.Udal	11	7	4	11*	35	11.66	–	–	1
L.J.Wright	28	20	1	52	428	22.52	–	2	10
M.H.Yardy	6	5	1	19	49	12.25	–	–	1

ENGLAND – BOWLING

	O	M	R	W	Avge	Best	4wI	R/Over
K.Ali	112.1	4	682	20	34.10	4-45	1	6.08
J.M.Anderson	974	80	4820	161	29.93	5-23	9	4.94
G.J.Batty	73.2	1	366	5	73.20	2-40	–	4.99
I.R.Bell	14.4	0	88	6	14.66	3- 9	–	6.00
I.D.Blackwell	205	8	877	24	36.54	3-26	–	4.27
R.S.Bopara	55.1	2	293	6	48.83	2-43	–	5.31
T.T.Bresnan	135.5	7	715	17	42.05	2-10	–	5.26
S.C.J.Broad	475.2	32	2441	94	25.96	5-23	6	5.13
A.D.Brown	1	0	5	0	–	–	–	5.00
G.Chapple	4	0	14	0	–	–	–	3.50
R.Clarke	78.1	3	415	11	37.72	2-28	–	5.30
P.D.Collingwood	759.2	11	3824	101	37.86	6-31	4	5.03
D.G.Cork	295.2	18	1368	41	33.36	3-27	–	4.63
R.D.B.Croft	411	25	1743	45	38.73	3-51	–	4.24
J.W.M.Dalrymple	140	2	666	14	47.57	2- 5	–	4.75
A.Flintoff	937.2	67	4121	169	24.38	5-19	8	4.39
P.J.Franks	9	0	48	0	–	–	–	5.33
S.J.Harmison	483.1	29	2481	76	32.64	5-33	3	5.13
M.J.Hoggard	217.4	13	1152	32	36.00	5-49	1	5.29
S.P.Jones	58	9	275	7	39.28	2-43	–	4.74
R.J.Kirtley	91.3	4	481	9	53.44	2-33	–	5.25
J.Lewis	119.2	13	500	18	27.77	4-36	1	4.18
A.McGrath	38	2	175	4	43.75	1-13	–	4.60
S.I.Mahmood	199.3	7	1169	30	38.96	4-50	1	5.85
A.D.Mascarenhas	137	6	634	13	48.76	3-23	–	4.62
G.Onions	34	1	185	4	46.25	2-58	–	5.44
M.S.Panesar	218	10	980	24	40.83	3-25	–	4.49
S.R.Patel	56.4	2	319	11	29.00	5-41	1	5.62
K.P.Pietersen	35.4	0	201	5	40.20	2-22	–	5.63
L.E.Plunkett	215.1	7	1260	37	34.05	3-24	–	5.85
A.U.Rashid	34	0	191	3	63.66	1-16	–	5.61
O.A.Shah	32.1	1	184	7	26.28	3-15	–	5.72
R.J.Sidebottom	205.1	12	993	28	35.46	3-19	–	4.83
V.S.Solanki	18.3	0	105	1	105.00	1-17	–	5.67
A.J.Strauss	1	0	3	0	–	–	–	3.00
G.P.Swann	194	9	913	31	29.45	5-28	2	4.70
C.T.Tremlett	79.5	2	419	8	46.55	4-32	1	5.24
M.E.Trescothick	38.4	0	219	4	54.75	2- 7	–	5.66
I.J.L.Trott	8	0	29	0	–	–	–	3.62
S.D.Udal	102	4	400	9	44.44	2-37	–	3.92
L.J.Wright	89	1	468	11	42.54	2-34	–	5.25
M.H.Yardy	42	3	135	4	33.75	3-24	–	3.21

† *E.J.G.Morgan made 23 appearances for Ireland (see below).*

AUSTRALIA – BATTING AND FIELDING

	M	I	NO	HS	Runs	Avge	100	50	Ct/St
D.E.Bollinger	15	2	1	0*	0	–	–	–	2
N.W.Bracken	116	35	18	21*	199	11.70	–	–	26
S.R.Clark	39	12	7	16*	69	13.80	–	–	10
M.J.Clarke	171	155	32	130	5256	42.73	4	40	69
M.J.Cosgrove	3	3	–	74	112	37.33	–	1	–
M.J.Di Venuto	9	9	–	89	241	26.77	–	2	1
C.J.Ferguson	25	22	9	71*	599	46.07	–	5	6
B.Geeves	2	2	2	10*	10	–	–	–	1
A.C.Gilchrist	287	279	11	172	9619	35.89	16	55	417/55
B.J.Haddin	61	56	6	109	1604	32.08	1	9	81/7
R.J.Harris	8	6	3	21	36	12.00	–	–	1
N.M.Hauritz	47	25	16	53*	276	30.66	–	1	22
M.C.Henriques	2	2	–	12	18	9.00	–	–	–
B.W.Hilfenhaus	15	7	4	16	29	9.66	–	–	7
B.J.Hodge	25	21	2	123	575	30.26	1	3	16
J.R.Hopes	72	53	7	63*	1151	25.02	–	3	21
D.J.Hussey	23	21	–	111	598	28.47	1	4	12
M.E.K.Hussey	135	110	37	109*	3938	53.94	2	28	76
P.A.Jaques	6	6	–	94	125	20.83	–	1	3
M.G.Johnson	77	42	14	73*	424	15.14	–	1	20
B.Laughlin	5	1	1	1*	1	–	–	–	2
B.Lee	186	92	37	57	897	16.30	–	2	44
C.J.McKay	9	1	–	10	10	10.00	–	–	1
G.A.Manou	4	1	–	7	7	7.00	–	–	5
S.E.Marsh	26	26	1	112	949	37.96	1	6	4
D.P.Nannes	1	1	–	1	1	1.00	–	–	–
M.J.North	2	2	–	5	6	3.00	–	–	1
T.D.Paine	17	17	1	111	487	30.43	1	3	22/4
R.T.Ponting	340	331	37	164	12731	43.30	29	76	144
P.M.Siddle	15	3	1	8*	12	6.00	–	–	1
S.P.D.Smith	1	–	–	–	–	–	–	–	2
A.Symonds	198	161	33	156	5088	40.61	6	30	82
S.W.Tait	22	4	2	11	24	12.00	–	–	2
A.C.Voges	11	10	3	72	260	37.14	–	1	2
D.A.Warner	7	7	–	69	106	15.14	–	1	1
S.R.Watson	103	85	22	136*	2572	40.82	4	14	28
C.L.White	57	45	8	105	1287	29.20	2	7	28

AUSTRALIA – BOWLING

	O	M	R	W	Avge	Best	4wI	R/Over
D.E.Bollinger	124.2	15	491	29	16.93	5-35	3	3.94
N.W.Bracken	959.5	90	4240	174	24.36	5-47	7	4.41
S.R.Clark	304.5	18	1477	53	27.86	4-54	2	4.84
M.J.Clarke	366.2	7	1853	52	35.63	5-35	2	5.05
M.J.Cosgrove	5	0	13	1	13.00	1- 1	–	2.60
B.Geeves	15	0	78	3	26.00	2-11	–	5.20
R.J.Harris	65.5	7	274	21	13.04	5-19	2	4.16
N.M.Hauritz	366	12	1689	53	31.86	4-29	2	4.61
M.C.Henriques	15	0	84	1	84.00	1-51	–	5.60
B.W.Hilfenhaus	126.2	11	717	18	39.83	2-42	–	5.67
B.J.Hodge	11	0	51	1	51.00	1- 1	–	4.63
J.R.Hopes	438	30	1928	56	34.42	3-30	–	4.40
D.J.Hussey	42.5	0	230	3	76.66	1- 6	–	5.36
M.E.K.Hussey	37	1	205	2	102.50	1-22	–	5.54
M.G.Johnson	619.4	37	3072	116	26.48	5-26	5	4.95

AUSTRALIA – BOWLING (continued)

	O	M	R	W	Avge	Best	4wI	R/Over
B.Laughlin	37.2	1	219	4	54.75	1-28	–	5.86
B.Lee	1579.4	120	7456	324	23.01	5-22	20	4.71
C.J.McKay	77.4	9	346	20	17.30	4-35	1	4.45
D.P.Nannes	7	1	20	1	20.00	1-20	–	2.85
M.J.North	3	0	16	0	–	–	–	5.33
R.T.Ponting	25	0	104	3	34.66	1-12	–	4.16
P.M.Siddle	110	8	499	14	35.64	3-55	–	4.53
S.P.D.Smith	9.5	0	78	2	39.00	2-78	–	7.93
A.Symonds	989.1	30	4955	133	37.25	5-18	3	5.00
S.W.Tait	180	4	961	38	25.28	4-39	1	5.33
A.C.Voges	25	0	159	1	159.00	1-22	–	6.36
S.R.Watson	626.1	19	3035	107	28.36	4-36	3	4.84
C.L.White	54.1	2	345	12	28.75	3- 5	–	6.36

SOUTH AFRICA – BATTING AND FIELDING

	M	I	NO	HS	Runs	Avge	100	50	Ct/St
H.M.Amla	24	23	3	140	969	47.26	1	7	11
D.M.Benkenstein	23	20	3	69	305	17.94	–	1	3
N.Boje	115	71	18	129	1414	26.67	2	4	33
L.L.Bosman	14	12	–	88	301	25.08	–	2	3
J.Botha	52	28	10	46	307	17.05	–	–	23
M.V.Boucher	291	217	56	147*	4658	28.93	1	26	399/22
A.B.de Villiers	96	92	13	146	3333	42.18	6	20	58
J.P.Duminy	55	48	11	111*	1293	34.94	1	6	22
H.H.Gibbs	248	240	16	175	8094	36.13	21	37	108
A.J.Hall	88	56	13	81	905	21.04	–	3	29
C.W.Henderson	4	–	–	–	–	–	–	–	–
J.H.Kallis	298	284	52	139	10613	45.74	17	75	108
C.K.Langeveldt	65	18	8	12	63	6.30	–	–	10
J.Louw	3	1	–	23	23	23.00	–	–	–
N.D.McKenzie	64	55	10	131*	1688	37.51	2	10	21
R.McLaren	5	4	1	6*	11	3.66	–	–	2
J.A.Morkel	47	34	8	97	621	23.88	–	2	12
M.Morkel	24	9	3	25	88	14.66	–	–	6
A.Nel	79	22	12	30*	127	12.70	–	–	21
M.Ntini	173	47	24	42*	199	8.65	–	–	30
J.L.Ontong	26	15	1	32	167	11.92	–	–	13
W.D.Parnell	11	4	1	49	78	26.00	–	–	1
A.N.Petersen	12	10	1	80	360	40.00	–	4	1
R.J.Peterson	35	15	4	36	147	13.36	–	–	7
A.G.Prince	52	41	12	89*	1018	35.10	–	3	26
J.A.Rudolph	45	39	6	81	1174	35.57	–	7	11
G.C.Smith	149	147	9	141	5613	40.67	8	41	77
D.W.Steyn	38	12	4	35	84	10.50	–	–	7
L.L.Tsotsobe	4	–	–	–	–	–	–	–	3
R.E.van der Merwe	12	6	2	12	29	7.25	–	–	4
M.van Jaarsveld	11	7	1	45	124	20.66	–	–	4
V.B.van Jaarsveld	2	2	–	5	9	4.50	–	–	1
C.M.Willoughby	3	2	–	0	0	0.00	–	–	–
M.Zondeki	13	3	2	3*	4	4.00	–	–	3

SOUTH AFRICA – BOWLING

	O	M	R	W	Avge	Best	4wI	R/Over
D.M.Benkenstein	10.5	1	44	4	11.00	3- 5	–	4.06
N.Boje	756.5	22	3415	96	35.57	5-21	3	4.51
J.Botha	416	10	1911	48	39.81	4-19	1	4.59
A.B.de Villiers	2	0	12	0	–	–	–	11.00
J.P.Duminy	113.1	2	562	16	35.12	3-31	–	4.96
A.J.Hall	556.5	30	2515	95	26.47	5-18	4	4.51
C.W.Henderson	36.1	2	132	7	18.85	4-17	1	3.64
J.H.Kallis	1661.4	74	8035	251	32.01	5-30	4	4.83
C.K.Langeveldt	519.3	28	2591	88	29.44	5-39	3	4.98
J.Louw	26	1	148	2	74.00	1-45	–	5.69
N.D.McKenzie	7.4	0	27	0	–	–	–	3.52
R.McLaren	34	3	163	4	40.75	3-51	–	4.79
J.A.Morkel	302.4	12	1629	48	33.93	4-29	2	5.38
M.Morkel	207.4	9	1041	34	30.61	4-36	1	5.01
A.Nel	633.3	58	2935	106	27.68	5-45	4	4.63
M.Ntini	1447.5	123	6559	266	24.65	6-22	12	4.53
J.L.Ontong	89.4	3	396	9	44.00	3-30	–	4.41
W.D.Parnell	98.3	7	626	25	25.04	5-48	3	6.35
A.N.Petersen	1	0	7	0	–	–	–	7.00
R.J.Peterson	208.4	4	992	17	58.35	2-26	–	4.75
A.G.Prince	2	0	3	0	–	–	–	1.50
J.A.Rudolph	4	0	26	0	–	–	–	6.50
G.C.Smith	171	0	951	18	52.83	3-30	–	5.56
D.W.Steyn	310.2	22	1663	54	30.79	4-16	3	5.35
L.L.Tsotsobe	33.3	3	172	9	19.11	4-50	1	5.13
R.E.van der Merwe	107.3	1	534	16	33.37	3-27	–	4.96
M.van Jaarsveld	5.1	1	18	2	9.00	1- 0	–	3.48
C.M.Willoughby	28	2	148	2	74.00	2-39	–	5.28
M.Zondeki	93	8	504	11	45.81	2-40	–	5.41

WEST INDIES – BATTING AND FIELDING

	M	I	NO	HS	Runs	Avge	100	50	Ct/St
L.S.Baker	10	4	2	11*	13	6.50	–	–	1
C.S.Baugh	30	22	7	29	223	14.86	–	–	19/4
S.J.Benn	11	8	1	31	70	10.00	–	–	1
D.E.Bernard	14	9	–	38	123	13.66	–	–	4
T.L.Best	12	8	3	24	52	10.40	–	–	3
D.J.Bravo	99	79	16	112*	1511	23.98	1	4	43
D.M.Bravo	4	2	–	21	40	20.00	–	–	1
S.Chanderpaul	252	236	38	150	8250	41.66	10	55	69
S.Chattergoon	18	17	2	54*	370	24.66	–	2	6
C.D.Collymore	84	35	17	13*	104	5.77	–	–	12
R.T.Crandon	1	1	–	5	5	5.00	–	–	–
N.Deonarine	10	9	–	53	198	22.00	–	1	4
T.M.Dowlin	11	11	2	100*	228	25.33	1	1	2
F.H.Edwards	50	22	14	13	73	9.12	–	–	4
S.E.Findlay	9	8	1	59*	146	20.85	–	1	5
A.D.S.Fletcher	10	10	–	54	198	19.80	–	2	3
C.H.Gayle	210	205	15	153*	7484	39.38	19	39	90
R.N.Lewis	28	21	5	49	291	18.18	–	–	7
X.M.Marshall	24	24	3	157*	375	17.85	1	–	9
N.O.Miller	25	16	7	51	198	22.00	–	1	6
R.S.Morton	56	51	6	110*	1519	33.75	2	10	20
B.P.Nash	9	7	3	39*	104	26.00	–	–	1
N.T.Pascal	1	1	–	0	0	0.00	–	–	–

	M	I	NO	HS	Runs	Avge	100	50	Ct/St
K.A.Pollard	20	17	–	62	317	18.64	–	1	9
D.B.L.Powell	55	25	3	48*	118	5.36	–	–	13
K.O.A.Powell	2	2	–	5	5	2.50	–	–	1
D.Ramdin	72	55	14	74*	805	19.63	–	2	100/5
R.Rampaul	41	15	2	26*	136	10.46	–	–	5
F.L.Reifer	8	8	–	40	117	14.62	–	–	3
D.M.Richards	4	3	–	20	22	7.33	–	–	2
K.A.J.Roach	9	6	2	10	17	4.25	–	–	1
D.J.G.Sammy	32	24	6	51	398	22.11	–	1	14
R.R.Sarwan	152	142	28	115*	4907	43.04	3	33	39
L.M.P.Simmons	19	18	2	70	308	19.25	–	2	4
D.R.Smith	76	60	4	68	921	16.44	–	3	26
D.S.Smith	32	30	2	91	681	24.32	–	3	10
J.E.Taylor	62	27	7	43*	198	9.90	–	–	16
D.C.Thomas	2	1	1	29*	29	–	–	–	3
G.C.Tonge	5	4	2	5	10	5.00	–	–	–
C.A.K.Walton	2	2	–	0	0	0.00	–	–	6/1

WEST INDIES – BOWLING

	O	M	R	W	Avge	Best	4wI	R/Over
L.S.Baker	71	6	355	11	32.27	3-47	–	5.00
S.J.Benn	89	2	429	6	71.50	2-23	–	4.82
D.E.Bernard	72	1	385	10	38.50	2-59	–	5.34
T.L.Best	90.5	3	477	13	36.69	4-35	1	5.25
D.J.Bravo	638.4	25	3382	114	29.66	4-19	3	5.29
S.Chanderpaul	123.2	0	636	14	45.42	3-18	–	5.15
S.Chattergoon	13.2	0	48	1	48.00	1- 1	–	3.60
C.D.Collymore	679	45	2924	83	35.22	5-51	2	4.30
N.Deonarine	33.3	0	212	5	42.40	2-18	–	6.32
F.H.Edwards	356.2	23	1812	60	30.20	6-22	2	5.08
C.H.Gayle	1093.5	36	5204	152	34.23	5-46	4	4.75
R.N.Lewis	191.4	2	983	22	44.68	3-43	–	5.12
X.M.Marshall	1.3	0	6	0	–	–	–	4.00
N.O.Miller	179.1	0	838	18	46.55	3-19	–	4.67
R.S.Morton	1	0	2	0	–	–	–	2.00
B.P.Nash	49	3	224	5	44.80	3-56	–	4.57
N.T.Pascal	4	0	29	0	–	–	–	7.25
K.A.Pollard	98.2	2	539	19	28.36	3-45	–	5.48
D.B.L.Powell	475	35	2239	71	31.53	4-27	2	4.71
R.Rampaul	256.4	15	1329	39	34.07	4-37	3	5.17
K.A.J.Roach	77.4	4	425	18	23.61	5-44	2	5.47
D.J.G.Sammy	226.2	8	1049	21	49.95	2- 2	–	4.63
R.R.Sarwan	96.5	3	586	16	36.62	3-31	–	6.05
L.M.P.Simmons	1	0	9	0	–	–	–	9.00
D.R.Smith	415.2	18	2042	56	36.46	5-45	4	4.91
J.E.Taylor	511.4	31	2442	92	26.54	5-48	4	4.77
D.C.Thomas	1.1	0	11	2	5.50	2-11	–	9.42
G.C.Tonge	50	6	224	5	44.80	4-25	1	4.48

NEW ZEALAND – BATTING AND FIELDING

	M	I	NO	HS	Runs	Avge	100	50	Ct/St
S.E.Bond	77	35	20	31*	239	15.93	–	–	8
N.T.Broom	19	19	3	71	290	18.12	–	1	2
I.G.Butler	26	13	5	25	84	10.50	–	–	8
C.D.Cumming	13	13	1	45*	161	13.41	–	–	6

	M	I	NO	HS	Runs	Avge	100	50	Ct/St
B.J.Diamanti	1	1	1	26*	26	–	–	–	1
G.D.Elliott	28	20	6	115	610	43.57	1	3	5
D.R.Flynn	16	13	2	35	167	15.18	–	–	4
J.E.C.Franklin	72	50	19	45*	612	19.74	–	–	20
P.G.Fulton	49	46	5	112	1334	32.53	1	8	18
M.R.Gillespie	32	14	8	28	93	15.50	–	–	6
M.J.Guptill	25	24	3	122*	863	41.09	1	7	11
G.J.Hopkins	14	7	–	25	56	8.00	–	–	16
J.M.How	31	28	1	139	930	34.44	1	7	13
P.J.Ingram	3	3	–	69	122	40.66	–	1	1
B.B.McCullum	166	140	22	166	3415	28.94	2	16	186/13
N.L.McCullum	2	2	–	0	0	0.00	–	–	4
P.D.McGlashan	4	2	1	56*	63	63.00	–	1	7
A.J.McKay	3	1	1	3*	3	–	–	–	1
H.J.H.Marshall	66	62	9	101*	1454	27.43	1	12	18
K.D.Mills	110	62	24	54	589	15.50	–	1	29
I.E.O'Brien	10	2	2	3*	3	–	–	–	1
J.D.P.Oram	138	101	13	101*	2189	24.87	1	12	41
J.S.Patel	39	13	7	34	88	14.66	–	–	12
A.J.Redmond	5	5	–	52	136	27.20	–	1	2
J.D.Ryder	21	19	1	105	637	35.38	1	3	5
M.S.Sinclair	54	50	4	118*	1304	28.34	2	8	17
T.G.Southee	26	13	3	32	101	10.10	–	–	4
S.B.Styris	160	138	21	141	3743	31.99	4	23	63
L.R.P.L.Taylor	76	70	11	128*	2080	35.25	3	13	52
E.P.Thompson	1	–	–	–	–	–	–	–	–
D.R.Tuffey	85	44	21	20*	170	7.39	–	–	20
D.L.Vettori	251	156	49	83	1785	16.68	–	3	68

NEW ZEALAND – BOWLING

	O	M	R	W	Avge	Best	4wI	R/Over
S.E.Bond	672.4	84	2881	138	20.87	6-19	10	4.28
I.G.Butler	184.5	6	1038	28	37.07	4-44	1	5.61
C.D.Cumming	3	0	17	0	–	–	–	5.66
B.J.Diamanti	2	0	25	0	–	–	–	12.50
G.D.Elliott	76.2	5	376	17	22.11	4-31	1	4.92
D.R.Flynn	1	0	6	0	–	–	–	6.00
J.E.C.Franklin	508.2	32	2572	66	38.96	5-42	1	5.05
M.R.Gillespie	253.3	30	1369	37	37.00	4-58	1	5.40
M.J.Guptill	8.5	0	40	2	20.00	2- 7	–	4.52
N.L.McCullum	10	1	56	0	–	–	–	5.60
A.J.McKay	26	3	105	5	21.00	2-17	–	4.03
K.D.Mills	914	83	4286	162	26.45	5-25	7	4.68
I.E.O'Brien	75.3	3	488	14	34.85	3-68	–	6.46
J.D.P.Oram	977.5	83	4264	139	30.67	5-26	4	4.36
J.S.Patel	300.4	9	1513	42	36.02	3-11	–	5.03
J.D.Ryder	42.4	0	282	8	35.25	3-29	–	6.60
T.G.Southee	216	11	1122	33	34.00	4-38	1	5.19
S.B.Styris	889.3	38	4231	125	33.84	6-25	5	4.75
L.R.P.L.Taylor	5	0	32	0	–	–	–	6.40
E.P.Thompson	4	0	42	0	–	–	–	10.50
D.R.Tuffey	655	68	3130	98	31.93	4-24	2	4.77
D.L.Vettori	1981.3	83	8220	262	31.37	5- 7	9	4.14

INDIA – BATTING AND FIELDING

	M	I	NO	HS	Runs	Avge	100	50	Ct/St
L.Balaji	30	16	6	21*	120	12.00	–	–	11
P.P.Chawla	21	10	5	13*	28	5.60	–	–	9
M.S.Dhoni	162	143	37	183*	5420	51.13	7	35	154/52
R.S.Dravid	339	313	40	153	10765	39.43	12	82	196/14
G.Gambhir	96	92	8	150*	3148	37.47	7	19	30
Harbhajan Singh	209	110	28	49	1061	12.93	–	–	59
R.A.Jadeja	22	13	3	60*	336	33.60	–	2	7
K.D.Karthik	41	33	7	79	769	29.57	–	4	27/4
M.Kartik	37	14	5	32*	126	14.00	–	–	10
Z.Khan	171	90	35	34*	719	13.07	–	–	35
V.Kohli	23	20	4	107	847	52.93	2	6	12
P.Kumar	36	18	6	54*	201	16.75	–	1	8
A.Mishra	7	–	–	–	–	–	–	–	1
A.Mithun	1	1	–	24	24	24.00	–	–	–
A.M.Nayar	3	1	1	0*	0	–	–	–	–
A.Nehra	99	36	20	24	124	7.75	–	–	14
P.P.Ojha	9	4	3	16*	27	27.00	–	–	5
M.M.Patel	43	17	9	15	54	6.75	–	–	6
I.K.Pathan	107	78	18	83	1368	22.80	–	5	18
Y.K.Pathan	33	23	8	59*	306	20.40	–	2	7
S.K.Raina	90	73	15	116*	2214	38.17	3	15	41
V.Sehwag	221	215	8	146	7091	34.25	12	35	82
I.Sharma	41	11	5	13	36	6.00	–	–	10
R.G.Sharma	42	39	10	70*	743	25.62	–	4	18
R.P.Singh	55	20	10	23	104	10.40	–	–	12
S.Sreesanth	49	20	10	10*	40	4.00	–	–	7
S.R.Tendulkar	442	431	41	200*	17598	45.12	46	93	134
S.Tyagi	4	1	1	1*	1	–	–	–	1
M.Vijay	1	1	–	25	25	25.00	–	–	1
Yuvraj Singh	250	230	32	139	7345	37.09	12	43	72

INDIA – BOWLING

	O	M	R	W	Avge	Best	4wI	R/Over
L.Balaji	241.1	11	1344	34	39.52	4-48	1	5.57
P.P.Chawla	183.4	6	911	28	32.53	4-23	2	4.96
M.S.Dhoni	2	0	14	1	14.00	1-14	–	7.00
R.S.Dravid	31	1	170	4	42.50	2-43	–	5.48
G.Gambhir	1	0	13	0	–	–	–	13.00
Harbhajan Singh	1821.5	77	7840	239	32.80	5-31	5	4.30
R.A.Jadeja	158.3	8	778	17	45.76	4-32	1	4.90
M.Kartik	317.5	19	1612	37	43.56	6-27	1	5.07
Z.Khan	1429.3	103	7035	235	29.93	5-42	8	4.92
V.Kohli	6.4	0	44	0	–	–	–	6.60
P.Kumar	279.2	21	1438	41	35.07	4-31	3	5.14
A.Mishra	48.1	2	233	7	33.28	3-40	–	4.83
A.Mithun	8	0	63	0	–	–	–	7.87
A.M.Nayar	3	0	17	0	–	–	–	5.66
A.Nehra	796.5	47	4078	130	31.36	6-23	5	5.11
P.P.Ojha	80	5	336	12	28.00	4-38	1	4.20
M.M.Patel	317.1	28	1550	47	32.97	4-49	1	4.88
I.K.Pathan	865.4	48	4547	152	29.91	5-27	5	5.25
Y.K.Pathan	140.2	1	794	21	37.80	3-56	–	5.65
S.K.Raina	57.2	0	309	6	51.50	1-13	–	5.38
V.Sehwag	690.1	12	3648	88	41.45	3-25	–	5.28
I.Sharma	313	11	1819	56	32.48	4-38	3	5.81

	O	M	R	W	Avge	Best	4wI	R/Over
R.G.Sharma	33.5	2	160	2	80.00	2-27	–	4.72
R.P.Singh	405.3	31	2201	65	33.86	4-35	2	5.42
S.Sreesanth	385.2	15	2326	68	34.20	6-55	2	6.03
S.R.Tendulkar	1336.4	24	6817	154	44.26	5-32	6	5.10
S.Tyagi	27.3	4	144	3	48.00	1-15	–	5.23
Yuvraj Singh	655.2	15	3314	82	40.41	4- 6	2	5.05

PAKISTAN – BATTING AND FIELDING

	M	I	NO	HS	Runs	Avge	100	50	Ct/St
Abdul Razzaq	237	204	49	112	4590	29.61	2	22	33
Abdur Rauf	4	–	–	–	–	–	–	–	2
Ahmed Shehzad	4	4	–	43	106	26.50	–	–	–
Azhar Mahmood	143	110	26	67	1521	18.10	–	3	37
Danish Kaneria	18	10	8	6*	12	6.00	–	–	2
Fawad Alam	17	15	7	63*	327	40.87	–	2	5
Iftikhar Anjum	62	34	19	32	234	15.60	–	–	10
Imran Nazir	79	79	2	160	1895	24.61	2	9	26
Kamran Akmal	115	100	13	124	2288	26.29	5	4	116/20
Khalid Latif	5	5	–	64	147	29.40	–	1	1
Khurram Manzoor	7	7	–	83	236	33.71	–	3	3
Misbah-ul-Haq	56	50	11	79*	1523	39.05	–	9	32
Mohammad Aamer	13	10	4	73*	159	26.50	–	1	6
Mohammad Asif	36	15	7	6	34	4.25	–	–	5
Mohammad Yousuf	282	267	40	141*	9624	42.39	15	64	57
Nasir Jamshed	12	12	2	74	353	35.30	–	4	4
Naved-ul-Hasan	74	51	18	33	524	15.87	–	–	16
Saeed Ajmal	26	16	9	33	92	13.14	–	–	5
Salman Butt	76	76	4	136	2651	36.81	8	13	19
Sarfraz Ahmed	9	3	–	19	32	10.66	–	–	7/3
Shahid Afridi	293	275	18	109	5957	23.17	4	30	99
Shoaib Akhtar	144	70	32	43	373	9.81	–	–	17
Shoaib Malik	190	170	21	143	5141	34.50	7	31	68
Sohail Khan	4	1	–	4	4	4.00	–	–	–
Sohail Tanvir	31	18	5	59	182	14.00	–	1	8
Umar Akmal	15	15	3	102*	498	41.50	1	4	4
Umar Gul	69	31	9	33	195	8.86	–	–	9
Yasir Arafat	11	8	3	27	74	14.80	–	–	2
Younus Khan	202	196	19	144	57765	32.57	6	37	107

PAKISTAN – BOWLING

	O	M	R	W	Avge	Best	4wI	R/Over
Abdul Razzaq	1683.5	93	7905	254	31.12	6-35	11	4.69
Abdur Rauf	35.4	1	212	8	26.50	3-24	–	5.94
Azhar Mahmood	1040.2	58	4813	123	39.13	6-18	5	4.62
Danish Kaneria	142.2	11	683	15	45.53	3-31	–	4.79
Fawad Alam	60.2	0	332	4	83.00	1- 8	–	5.50
Iftikhar Anjum	493.2	41	2430	77	31.55	5-30	3	4.92
Imran Nazir	8.1	0	48	1	48.00	1- 3	–	5.87
Misbah-ul-Haq	4	0	30	0	–	–	–	7.50
Mohammad Aamer	111.4	8	487	23	21.17	4-28	1	4.36
Mohammad Asif	304.3	29	1409	44	32.02	3-28	–	4.62
Mohammad Yousuf	0.2	0	1	1	1.00	1- 0	–	3.00
Naved-ul-Hasan	577.4	25	3221	110	29.28	6-27	7	5.57
Saeed Ajmal	229	5	941	30	31.36	4-33	1	4.10
Salman Butt	11.3	0	90	0	–	–	–	7.82

PAKISTAN – BOWLING (continued)

	O	M	R	W	Avge	Best	4wI	R/Over
Shahid Afridi	2062.3	54	9518	275	34.61	6-38	5	4.61
Shoaib Akhtar	1133	91	5321	223	23.86	6-16	10	4.69
Shoaib Malik	1056	31	4822	132	36.53	4-19	1	4.56
Sohail Khan	33.1	1	163	5	32.60	3-30	–	4.91
Sohail Tanvir	257	15	1272	44	28.90	5-48	3	4.94
Umar Gul	552.4	41	2801	103	27.19	5-17	3	5.06
Yasir Arafat	99	2	373	4	93.25	1-28	–	5.40
Younus Khan	37.2	1	224	2	112.00	1- 3	–	6.00

SRI LANKA – BATTING AND FIELDING

	M	I	NO	HS	Runs	Avge	100	50	Ct/St
C.M.Bandara	31	17	4	31	160	12.30	–	–	9
T.M.Dilshan	174	151	27	160	4180	33.70	6	16	75/1
C.R.D.Fernando	134	53	30	20	231	10.04	–	–	25
S.T.Jayasuriya	444	432	18	189	13428	32.43	28	68	123
D.P.M.D.Jayawardena	317	298	30	128	8702	32.47	12	52	165
H.K.S.R.Kaluhalamulla	9	5	–	56	82	16.40	–	–	4
S.H.T.Kandamby	31	29	5	93*	776	32.33	–	5	5
C.K.Kapugedera	68	60	2	95	1224	21.85	–	6	21
K.M.D.N.Kulasekara	67	44	22	57*	393	17.86	–	1	16
R.A.S.Lakmal	6	1	1	0*	0	–	–	–	2
M.F.Maharoof	91	62	15	69*	973	20.70	–	2	19
S.L.Malinga	64	31	12	15	124	6.52	–	–	11
A.D.Mathews	18	16	2	52*	375	26.78	–	3	6
B.A.W.Mendis	38	20	9	15*	89	9.14	–	–	13
J.Mubarak	38	36	6	72	696	23.20	–	4	12
M.Muralitharan	334	157	60	33*	660	6.80	–	–	128
N.L.T.Perera	6	4	2	36*	84	42.00	–	–	1
K.T.G.D.Prasad	5	3	–	8	17	5.66	–	–	–
M.Pushpakumara	3	1	1	7*	7	–	–	–	–
T.T.Samaraweera	33	28	5	105*	625	27.17	2	–	9
K.C.Sangakkara	267	250	27	138*	8152	36.55	10	55	254/66
L.P.C.Silva	56	49	5	107*	1328	30.18	1	11	17
W.U.Tharanga	92	88	2	120	2818	32.76	8	13	16
H.D.R.L.Thirimanne	2	1	–	22	22	22.00	–	–	1
T.Thushara	36	26	6	54*	385	19.25	–	1	3
M.L.Udawatte	9	9	–	73	257	28.55	–	2	–
U.W.M.B.C.A.Welegedara	8	3	2	2*	4	4.00	–	–	2

SRI LANKA – BOWLING

	O	M	R	W	Avge	Best	4wI	R/Over
C.M.Bandara	245	3	1232	36	34.22	4-31	2	5.02
T.M.Dilshan	453.1	13	2160	49	44.08	4-29	2	4.76
C.R.D.Fernando	974	48	5080	169	30.05	6-27	4	5.21
S.T.Jayasuriya	2473	45	11825	322	36.72	6-29	12	4.78
D.P.M.D.Jayawardena	97	1	558	7	79.71	2-56	–	5.75
H.K.S.R.Kaluhalamulla	73	2	334	10	33.40	3-51	–	4.57
S.H.T.Kandamby	18	1	113	0	–	–	–	6.27
C.K.Kapugedera	38	0	192	2	96.00	1-24	–	5.05
K.M.D.N.Kulasekara	516.4	49	2365	86	27.50	4-40	1	4.57
R.A.S.Lakmal	45	2	298	4	74.50	2-55	–	6.62
M.F.Maharoof	631.2	45	2997	116	25.83	6-14	5	4.74
S.L.Malinga	519	34	2631	90	29.23	4-28	5	5.06
A.D.Mathews	109	6	524	17	30.82	6-20	1	4.80
B.A.W.Mendis	299.3	16	1286	72	17.86	6-13	6	4.29

	O	M	R	W	Avge	Best	4wI	R/Over
J.Mubarak	18.3	0	76	2	38.00	1-10	–	4.10
M.Muralitharan	3000.1	195	11742	512	22.93	7-30	24	3.91
N.L.T.Perera	38.2	1	206	6	34.33	2-27	–	5.37
K.T.G.D.Prasad	36	2	217	5	43.40	2-29	–	6.02
M.Pushpakumara	5	0	21	0	–	–	–	4.20
T.T.Samaraweera	115	2	538	10	53.80	3-34	–	4.67
L.P.C.Silva	4	1	21	1	21.00	1-21	–	5.25
T.Thushara	260.3	15	1286	46	27.95	5-47	1	4.93
U.W.M.B.C.A.Welegedara	60.4	3	360	13	27.69	5-66	1	5.93

ZIMBABWE – BATTING AND FIELDING

	M	I	NO	HS	Runs	Avge	100	50	Ct/St
R.W.Chakabva	1	1	–	41	41	41.00	–	–	2
C.J.Chibhabha	49	49	–	73	1034	21.10	–	7	22
E.Chigumbura	103	96	9	79	2093	24.05	–	12	34
C.K.Coventry	26	24	1	194*	629	27.34	1	2	14/1
A.G.Cremer	19	11	4	31*	95	13.57	–	–	6
K.M.Dabengwa	32	29	7	45	433	19.68	–	–	10
S.M.Ervine	42	34	7	100	698	25.85	1	2	5
G.W.Flower	219	212	18	142*	6536	33.69	6	40	86
T.N.Garwe	1	–	–	–	–	–	–	–	1
M.W.Goodwin	71	70	3	112*	1818	27.13	2	8	20
A.J.Ireland	26	13	5	8*	30	3.75	–	–	2
K.M.Jarvis	9	5	2	13	19	6.33	–	–	1
T.Maruma	5	4	–	32	41	10.25	–	–	1
H.Masakadza	85	85	4	178*	2330	28.76	3	14	35
S.Matsikenyeri	105	102	8	90	2177	23.15	–	13	35
C.B.Mpofu	37	22	12	4	23	2.30	–	–	5
T.Mupariwa	35	28	9	33	165	8.68	–	–	8
F.Mutizwa	9	8	1	79	263	37.57	–	3	5/2
R.W.Price	69	38	11	46	274	10.14	–	–	13
E.C.Rainsford	36	21	12	9*	40	4.44	–	–	7
V.Sibanda	79	78	2	116	1677	22.06	1	11	26
T.Taibu	112	99	18	107*	2238	27.62	2	11	99/15
B.R.M.Taylor	92	91	9	118*	2519	30.71	1	17	48/18
P.Utseya	101	80	27	68*	708	13.35	–	2	32
M.A.Vermeulen	43	43	4	92	868	22.25	–	6	18
M.N.Waller	14	13	1	63	189	15.75	–	1	4
S.C.Williams	41	40	7	75	983	29.78	–	10	14
C.Zhuwawo	1	1	–	16	16	16.00	–	–	–

ZIMBABWE – BOWLING

	O	M	R	W	Avge	Best	4wI	R/Over
C.J.Chibhabha	132	2	941	20	47.05	2-28	–	7.12
E.Chigumbura	459.1	21	2697	73	36.94	4-28	1	5.87
A.G.Cremer	157.5	9	709	32	22.15	6-46	3	4.49
K.M.Dabengwa	156.5	2	790	21	37.61	3-15	–	5.03
S.M.Ervine	274.5	10	1561	41	38.07	3-29	–	5.67
G.W.Flower	903.2	11	4187	104	40.25	4-32	2	4.63
T.N.Garwwe	6	0	50	1	50.00	1-50	–	8.33
M.W.Goodwin	41.2	1	210	4	52.50	1-12	–	5.08
A.J.Ireland	221	13	1115	38	29.34	3-41	–	5.04
K.M.Jarvis	68.5	1	422	10	42.20	3-36	–	6.13
T.Maruma	24.5	1	150	2	75.00	2-50	–	6.04
H.Masakadza	146.1	3	820	23	35.65	3-39	–	5.61

ZIMBABWE – BOWLING (continued)

	O	M	R	W	Avge	Best	4wI	R/Over
S.Matsikenyeri	151.2	2	770	16	48.12	2-25	–	5.08
C.B.Mpofu	293.5	21	1524	40	38.10	6-52	2	5.18
T.Mupariwa	295.3	22	1446	55	26.29	4-39	3	4.89
R.W.Price	596.3	52	2317	69	33.57	4-22	1	3.88
E.C.Rainsford	292.5	27	1286	35	36.74	3-16	–	4.39
V.Sibanda	23	1	148	2	74.00	1-12	–	6.43
T.Taibu	14	1	61	2	30.50	2-42	–	4.35
B.R.M.Taylor	35	0	224	8	28.00	3-54	–	6.40
P.Utseya	849.3	49	3467	75	46.22	4-46	1	4.08
M.A.Vermeulen	0.5	0	5	1	5.00	1- 5	–	6.00
M.N.Waller	16	0	109	0	–	–	–	6.81
S.C.Williams	111.3	2	574	9	63.77	3-23	–	5.14
C.Zhuwawo	3	0	15	0	–	–	–	5.00

BANGLADESH – BATTING AND FIELDING

	M	I	NO	HS	Runs	Avge	100	50	Ct/St
Abdur Razzak	93	60	25	33	489	13.97	–	–	23
Aftab Ahmed	82	82	6	92	1902	25.02	–	14	28
Dolar Mahmud	7	4	–	41	61	15.25	–	–	–
Enamul Haque[2]	10	5	1	5	12	3.00	–	–	8
Imrul Kayes	10	10	–	101	314	31.40	1	1	2
Junaid Siddique	29	28	5	85	488	17.42	–	2	12
Mahbubul Alam	5	2	–	59	81	40.50	–	1	1
Mahmudullah	44	36	11	64*	793	31.72	–	4	12
Mashrafe Mortaza	103	81	14	51*	1466	15.61	–	1	33
Mehrab Hossain[2]	18	16	–	54	276	17.25	–	1	7
Mohammad Ashraful	159	152	13	109	3298	23.72	3	20	32
Mushfiqur Rahim	66	58	10	98	1100	22.91	–	5	43/13
Naeem Islam	31	26	12	73*	433	30.92	–	1	13
Nazmul Hossain	32	19	11	6*	35	4.37	–	–	5
Raqibul Hasan	41	40	5	89	1027	29.34	–	6	12
Rubel Hossain	13	5	3	1*	1	0.50	–	–	2
Shafiul Islam	5	3	2	11	14	7.00	–	–	–
Shahadat Hossain	46	25	15	16*	79	7.90	–	–	5
Shakib Al Hasan	82	78	14	134*	2224	34.75	4	13	18
Syed Rasel	49	24	9	15	79	5.26	–	–	8
Tamim Iqbal	73	73	–	154	2073	28.39	2	13	21

BANGLADESH – BOWLING

	O	M	R	W	Avge	Best	4wI	R/Over
Abdur Razzak	809.3	38	3614	133	27.17	5-29	5	4.46
Aftab Ahmed	123.1	0	656	12	54.66	5-31	1	5.32
Dolar Mahmud	35	0	258	8	32.25	4-28	1	7.37
Enamul Haque[2]	96	3	422	14	30.14	3-16	–	4.39
Junaid Siddique	2	0	13	0	–	–	–	6.50
Mahbubul Alam	37	2	280	7	40.00	2-42	–	7.56
Mahmudullah	233.1	5	1228	24	51.16	3-52	–	5.26
Mashrafe Mortaza	880	79	4025	135	29.81	6-26	6	4.57
Mehrab Hossain[2]	42.1	0	214	4	53.50	2-30	–	5.07
Mohammad Ashraful	90	4	526	15	35.06	3-26	–	5.84
Naeem Islam	182	4	887	24	36.95	3-32	–	4.87
Nazmul Hossain	231.5	20	1194	36	33.16	4-40	1	5.15
Rubel Hossain	94	5	565	15	37.66	4-33	1	6.01
Shafiul Islam	40	2	265	9	29.44	4-68	1	6.62
Shahadat Hossain	321.2	18	1824	42	43.42	3-34	–	5.67

BANGLADESH – BOWLING (continued)

	O	M	R	W	Avge	Best	4wI	R/Over
Shakib Al Hasan	684.2	47	2801	90	31.12	4-33	1	4.09
Syed Rasel	420.5	41	1912	60	31.86	4-22	1	4.54
Tamim Iqbal	1	0	13	0	–	–	–	13.00

ASSOCIATES – BATTING AND FIELDING

	M	I	NO	HS	Runs	Avge	100	50	Ct/St
R.G.Aga (Kenya)	2	2	–	1	1	0.50	–	–	–
K.J.Coetzer (Scotland)	4	4	–	44	81	20.25	–	–	2
A.N.Kervezee (Netherlands)	26	23	2	75	522	24.85	–	2	11
C.S.MacLeod (Scotland)	4	3	1	10*	12	6.00	–	–	–
E.J.G.Morgan (Ireland)	23	23	2	115	744	35.42	1	5	9
D.P.Nannes (Netherlands)	1	1	–	1	1	1.00	–	–	–
K.J.O'Brien (Ireland)	35	31	3	142	884	31.57	1	4	18
N.J.O'Brien (Ireland)	33	33	3	72	815	27.16	–	7	24/6
W.T.S.Porterfield (Ireland)	37	37	3	112*	1150	33.82	4	4	20
W.B.Rankin (Ireland)	20	6	4	7*	16	8.00	–	–	4
P.R.Stirling (Ireland)	6	6	1	84	128	25.60	–	1	2
R.N.ten Doeschate (Netherlands)	26	25	8	109*	1144	67.29	3	7	11
S.R.Waters (Kenya)	12	12	–	74	261	21.75	–	1	3
G.C.Wilson (Ireland)	16	16	1	51*	290	19.33	–	2	10/4

ASSOCIATES – BOWLING

	O	M	R	W	Avge	Best	4wI	R/Over
R.G.Aga	13	0	87	2	43.50	2-17	–	6.69
A.N.Kervezee	1	0	8	0	–	–	–	8.00
C.S.MacLeod	23	0	139	3	46.33	2-46	–	6.04
D.P.Nannes	7	1	20	1	20.00	1-20	–	2.85
K.J.O'Brien	143	7	757	18	42.05	3-30	–	5.29
R.N.ten Doeschate	201.2	16	967	46	21.02	4-31	3	4.80
A.N.Kervezee	1	0	8	0	–	–	–	8.00
W.B.Rankin	139.2	11	693	28	24.75	3-32	–	4.97

LIMITED-OVERS INTERNATIONALS RESULTS

1970-71 to 27 February 2010

This chart excludes all matches involving multinational teams.

Opponents		Matches	Won											Tied	NR
			E	A	SA	WI	NZ	I	P	SL	Z	B	Ass		
England	Australia	101	38	59	–	–	–	–	–	–	–	–	–	2	2
	South Africa	44	18	–	23	–	–	–	–	–	–	–	–	1	2
	West Indies	82	37	–	–	41	–	–	–	–	–	–	–	–	4
	New Zealand	70	29	–	–	–	35	–	–	–	–	–	–	2	4
	India	70	30	–	–	–	–	38	–	–	–	–	–	–	2
	Pakistan	63	35	–	–	–	–	–	26	–	–	–	–	–	2
	Sri Lanka	44	23	–	–	–	–	–	–	21	–	–	–	–	2
	Zimbabwe	30	21	–	–	–	–	–	–	–	8	–	–	–	1
	Bangladesh	8	8	–	–	–	–	–	–	–	–	0	–	–	–
	Associates	13	12	–	–	–	–	–	–	–	–	–	0	–	1
Australia	South Africa	77	–	39	35	–	–	–	–	–	–	–	–	3	–
	West Indies	125	–	63	–	57	–	–	–	–	–	–	–	2	3
	New Zealand	118	–	81	–	–	32	–	–	–	–	–	–	–	5
	India	103	–	61	–	–	–	34	–	–	–	–	–	–	8
	Pakistan	85	–	52	–	–	–	–	29	–	–	–	–	1	3
	Sri Lanka	68	–	46	–	–	–	–	–	20	–	–	–	–	2
	Zimbabwe	27	–	25	–	–	–	–	–	–	1	–	–	–	1
	Bangladesh	16	–	15	–	–	–	–	–	–	–	1	–	–	–
	Associates	13	–	13	–	–	–	–	–	–	–	–	0	–	–
S Africa	West Indies	45	–	–	32	12	–	–	–	–	–	–	–	–	1
	N Zealand	51	–	–	30	–	17	–	–	–	–	–	–	–	4
	India	60	–	–	36	–	–	22	–	–	–	–	–	–	2
	Pakistan	52	–	–	35	–	–	–	16	–	–	–	–	–	1
	Sri Lanka	46	–	–	22	–	–	–	–	22	–	–	–	1	1
	Zimbabwe	29	–	–	26	–	–	–	–	–	2	–	–	–	1
	Bangladesh	13	–	–	12	–	–	–	–	–	–	1	–	–	–
	Associates	17	–	–	17	–	–	–	–	–	–	–	0	–	–
W Indies	New Zealand	51	–	–	–	24	20	–	–	–	–	–	–	–	7
	India	95	–	–	–	54	–	38	–	–	–	–	–	1	2
	Pakistan	114	–	–	–	64	–	–	48	–	–	–	–	2	–
	Sri Lanka	46	–	–	–	26	–	–	–	18	–	–	–	–	2
	Zimbabwe	36	–	–	–	27	–	–	–	–	8	–	–	–	1
	Bangladesh	16	–	–	–	11	–	–	–	–	–	3	–	–	2
	Associates	15	–	–	–	13	–	–	–	–	–	–	1	–	1
N Zealand	India	81	–	–	–	–	36	40	–	–	–	–	–	–	5
	Pakistan	82	–	–	–	–	32	–	48	–	–	–	–	1	1
	Sri Lanka	70	–	–	–	–	35	–	–	31	–	–	–	1	3
	Zimbabwe	28	–	–	–	–	19	–	–	–	7	–	–	1	1
	Bangladesh	17	–	–	–	–	16	–	–	–	–	1	–	–	–
	Associates	11	–	–	–	–	11	–	–	–	–	–	0	–	–
India	Pakistan	118	–	–	–	–	–	45	69	–	–	–	–	–	4
	Sri Lanka	121	–	–	–	–	–	64	–	46	–	–	–	–	11
	Zimbabwe	49	–	–	–	–	–	39	–	–	8	–	–	2	–
	Bangladesh	21	–	–	–	–	–	19	–	–	–	2	–	–	–
	Associates	22	–	–	–	–	–	20	–	–	–	–	2	–	–
Pakistan	Sri Lanka	119	–	–	–	–	–	–	70	45	–	–	–	1	3
	Zimbabwe	40	–	–	–	–	–	–	36	–	2	–	–	1	1
	Bangladesh	25	–	–	–	–	–	–	24	–	–	1	–	–	–
	Associates	17	–	–	–	–	–	–	16	–	–	–	1	–	–
Sri Lanka	Zimbabwe	43	–	–	–	–	–	–	–	36	6	–	–	–	1
	Bangladesh	26	–	–	–	–	–	–	–	26	–	2	–	–	–
	Associates	13	–	–	–	–	–	–	–	12	–	–	1	–	–
Zimbabwe	Bangladesh	47	–	–	–	–	–	–	–	–	22	25	–	–	–
	Associates	38	–	–	–	–	–	–	–	–	30	–	5	1	2
Bangladesh	Associates	27	–	–	–	–	–	–	–	–	–	19	8	–	–
Associates	Associates	93	–	–	–	–	–	–	–	–	–	–	88	–	5
		2953	**251**	**454**	**268**	**329**	**253**	**359**	**382**	**277**	**94**	**55**	**106**	**23**	**102**

MERIT TABLE OF ALL L-O INTERNATIONALS
1970-71 to 27 February 2010

	Matches	Won	Lost	Tied	No Result	% Won (exc NR)
Australia	733	454	247	8	24	64.03
South Africa	434	268	149	5	12	63.50
West Indies	625	329	268	5	23	54.65
Pakistan	715	382	312	6	15	54.57
India	740	359	344	3	34	50.84
England	525	251	251	5	18	49.50
Sri Lanka	598	277	295	3	23	48.17
New Zealand	579	253	291	5	30	46.08
Zimbabwe	367	94	259	5	9	26.25
Bangladesh	218	55	161	–	2	25.46
Associate Members (v Full*)	186	18	163	1	4	9.89

* Results of games between two Associate Members are excluded from this list; Associate Members have participated in 279 LOIs, 93 LOIs being between Associate Members.

TEAM RECORDS
HIGHEST TOTALS

443-9	(50 overs)	Sri Lanka v Holland	Amstelveen	2006
438-9	(49.5 overs)	South Africa v Australia	Johannesburg	2005-06
434-4	(50 overs)	Australia v South Africa	Johannesburg	2005-06
418-5	(50 overs)	South Africa v Zimbabwe	Potchefstroom	2006-07
414-7	(50 overs)	India v Sri Lanka	Rajkot	2009-10
413-5	(50 overs)	India v Bermuda	Port-of-Spain	2006-07
411-8	(50 overs)	Sri Lanka v India	Rajkot	2009-10
402-2	(50 overs)	New Zealand v Ireland	Aberdeen	2008
401-3	(50 overs)	India v South Africa	Gwalior	2009-10
398-5	(50 overs)	Sri Lanka v Kenya	Kandy	1995-96
397-5	(44 overs)	New Zealand v Zimbabwe	Bulawayo	2005
392-4	(50 overs)	India v New Zealand	Christchurch	2008-09
392-6	(50 overs)	South Africa v Pakistan	Pretoria	2006-07
391-4	(50 overs)	England v Bangladesh	Nottingham	2005
387-5	(50 overs)	India v England	Rajkot	2008-09
377-6	(50 overs)	Australia v South Africa	Basseterre	2006-07
376-2	(50 overs)	India v New Zealand	Hyderabad, India	1999-00
374-4	(50 overs)	India v Hong Kong	Karachi	2008
373-6	(50 overs)	India v Sri Lanka	Taunton	1999
371-9	(50 overs)	Pakistan v Sri Lanka	Nairobi	1996-97
368-5	(50 overs)	Australia v Sri Lanka	Sydney	2005-06
365-2	(50 overs)	South Africa v India	Ahmedabad	2009-10
363-3	(50 overs)	South Africa v Zimbabwe	Bulawayo	2001-02
363-5	(50 overs)	New Zealand v Canada	Gros Islet	2006-07
363-5	(50 overs)	India v Sri Lanka	Colombo (RPS)	2008-09
363-7	(55 overs)	England v Pakistan	Nottingham	1992
360-4	(50 overs)	West Indies v Sri Lanka	Karachi	1987-88
359-2	(50 overs)	Australia v India	Johannesburg	2002-03
359-5	(50 overs)	Australia v India	Sydney	2003-04
358-4	(50 overs)	South Africa v Bangladesh	Benoni	2008-09
358-5	(50 overs)	Australia v Netherlands	Basseterre	2006-07
357-9	(50 overs)	Sri Lanka v Bangladesh	Lahore	2008
356-4	(50 overs)	South Africa v West Indies	St George's	2006-07
356-9	(50 overs)	India v Pakistan	Vishakhapatnam	2004-05
354-3	(50 overs)	South Africa v Kenya	Cape Town	2001-02
354-6	(50 overs)	South Africa v England	Cape Town	2009-10
354-7	(50 overs)	India v Australia	Nagpur	2009-10
353-3	(40 overs)	South Africa v Holland	Basseterre	2006-07
353-5	(50 overs)	India v New Zealand	Hyderabad, India	2003-04
353-6	(50 overs)	Pakistan v England	Karachi	2005-06
351-3	(50 overs)	India v Kenya	Paarl	2001-02

299

351-4	(50 overs)	Pakistan v South Africa	Durban	2006-07
351-7	(50 overs)	Zimbabwe v Kenya	Mombasa	2008-09
350-4	(50 overs)	Australia v India	Hyderabad, India	2009-10
350-6	(50 overs)	India v Sri Lanka	Nagpur	2005-06
350-9	(49.3 overs)	New Zealand v Australia	Hamilton	2006-07

The highest for Bangladesh is 320-8 (v Zimbabwe, Bulawayo, 2009).

HIGHEST TOTALS BATTING SECOND

WINNING:	438-9	(49.5 overs)	South Africa v Australia	Johannesburg	2005-06
LOSING:	411-8	(50.0 overs)	Sri Lanka v India	Rajkot	2009-10

HIGHEST MATCH AGGREGATES

872-13	(99.5 overs)	South Africa v Australia	Johannesburg	2005-06
825-15	(100 overs)	India v Sri Lanka	Rajkot	2009-10

LARGEST RUNS MARGINS OF VICTORY

290 runs	New Zealand beat Ireland	Aberdeen	2008
257 runs	India beat Bermuda	Port-of-Spain	2006-07
256 runs	Australia beat Namibia	Potchefstroom	2002-03
256 runs	India beat Hong Kong	Karachi	2008
245 runs	Sri Lanka beat India	Sharjah	2000-01
243 runs	Sri Lanka beat Bermuda	Port-of-Spain	2006-07
234 runs	Sri Lanka beat Pakistan	Lahore	2008-09
233 runs	Pakistan beat Bangladesh	Dhaka	1999-00
232 runs	Australia beat Sri Lanka	Adelaide	1984-85
229 runs	Australia beat Holland	Basseterre	2006-07
224 runs	Australia beat Pakistan	Nairobi	2002
221 runs	South Africa beat Holland	Basseterre	2006-07
217 runs	Pakistan beat Sri Lanka	Sharjah	2001-02
215 runs	Australia beat New Zealand	St George's	2006-07
212 runs	South Africa beat Zimbabwe	Centurion	2009-10
210 runs	New Zealand beat USA	The Oval	2004
209 runs	South Africa beat West Indies	Cape Town	2003-04
208 runs	South Africa beat Kenya	Cape Town	2001-02
208 runs	Australia beat India	Sydney	2003-04
206 runs	New Zealand beat Australia	Adelaide	1985-86
206 runs	Sri Lanka beat Holland	Colombo (RPS)	2002-03
203 runs	Australia beat Scotland	Basseterre	2006-07
202 runs	England beat India	Lord's	1975
202 runs	South Africa beat Kenya	Nairobi	1996-97
202 runs	Zimbabwe beat Kenya	Dhaka	1998-99
200 runs	India beat Bangladesh	Dhaka	2002-03

LOWEST TOTALS (Excluding reduced innings)

35	(18.0 overs)	Zimbabwe v Sri Lanka	Harare	2003-04
36	(18.4 overs)	Canada v Sri Lanka	Paarl	2002-03
38	(15.4 overs)	Zimbabwe v Sri Lanka	Colombo (SSC)	2001-02
43	(19.5 overs)	Pakistan v West Indies	Cape Town	1992-93
44	(24.5 overs)	Zimbabwe v Bangladesh	Chittagong	2009-10
45	(40.3 overs)	Canada v England	Manchester	1979
45	(14.0 overs)	Namibia v Australia	Potchefstroom	2002-03
54	(26.3 overs)	India v Sri Lanka	Sharjah	2000-01
54	(23.2 overs)	West Indies v South Africa	Cape Town	2003-04
55	(28.3 overs)	Sri Lanka v West Indies	Sharjah	1986-87
63	(25.5 overs)	India v Australia	Sydney	1980-81
64	(35.5 overs)	New Zealand v Pakistan	Sharjah	1985-86
65	(24.0 overs)	USA v Australia	Southampton	2004
65	(24.3 overs)	Zimbabwe v India	Harare	2005
67	(31.0 overs)	Zimbabwe v Sri Lanka	Harare	2008-09
68	(31.3 overs)	Scotland v West Indies	Leicester	1999

69	(28.0 overs)	South Africa v Australia	Sydney	1993-94
69	(22.5 overs)	Zimbabwe v Kenya	Harare	2005-06
70	(25.2 overs)	Australia v England	Birmingham	1977
70	(26.3 overs)	Australia v New Zealand	Adelaide	1985-86

The lowest for England is 86 (v A, Manchester, 2001), and for Bangladesh 74 (v A, Darwin, 2008).

LOWEST MATCH AGGREGATES

73-11	(23.2 overs)	Canada (36) v Sri Lanka (37-1)	Paarl	2002-03
75-11	(27.2 overs)	Zimbabwe (35) v Sri Lanka (40-1)	Harare	2003-04
78-11	(20.0 overs)	Zimbabwe (38) v Sri Lanka (40-1)	Colombo (SSC)	2001-02

BATTING RECORDS

HIGHEST INDIVIDUAL INNINGS

200*	S.R.Tendulkar	India v South Africa	Gwalior	2009-10
194*	C.K.Coventry	Zimbabwe v Bangladesh	Bulawayo	2009
194	Saeed Anwar	Pakistan v India	Madras	1996-97
189*	I.V.A.Richards	West Indies v England	Manchester	1984
189	S.T.Jayasuriya	Sri Lanka v India	Sharjah	2000-01
188*	G.Kirsten	South Africa v UAE	Rawalpindi	1995-96
186*	S.R.Tendulkar	India v New Zealand	Hyderabad	1999-00
183*	M.S.Dhoni	India v Sri Lanka	Jaipur	2005-06
183	S.C.Ganguly	India v Sri Lanka	Taunton	1999
181*	M.L.Hayden	Australia v New Zealand	Hamilton	2006-07
181	I.V.A.Richards	West Indies v Sri Lanka	Karachi	1987-88
178*	H.Masakadza	Zimbabwe v Kenya	Harare	2009-10
175*	Kapil Dev	India v Zimbabwe	Tunbridge Wells	1983
175	H.H.Gibbs	South Africa v Australia	Johannesburg	2005-06
175	S.R.Tendulkar	India v Australia	Hyderabad, India	2009-10
173	M.E.Waugh	Australia v West Indies	Melbourne	2000-01
172*	C.B.Wishart	Zimbabwe v Namibia	Harare	2002-03
172	A.C.Gilchrist	Australia v Zimbabwe	Hobart	2003-04
172	L.Vincent	New Zealand v Zimbabwe	Bulawayo	2005
171*	G.M.Turner	New Zealand v East Africa	Birmingham	1975
169*	D.J.Callaghan	South Africa v New Zealand	Pretoria	1994-95
169	B.C.Lara	West Indies v Sri Lanka	Sharjah	1995-96
167*	R.A.Smith	England v Australia	Birmingham	1993
166	B.B.McCullum	New Zealand v Ireland	Aberdeen	2008
164	R.T.Ponting	Australia v South Africa	Johannesburg	2005-06
163*	S.R.Tendulkar	India v New Zealand	Christchurch	2008-09
161	A.C.Hudson	South Africa v Holland	Rawalpindi	1995-96
161	J.A.H.Marshall	New Zealand v Ireland	Aberdeen	2008
160	Imran Nazir	Pakistan v Zimbabwe	Kingston	2006-07
160	T.M.Dilshan	Sri Lanka v India	Rajkot	2009-10
159*	D.Mongia	India v Zimbabwe	Gauhati	2001-02
158	D.I.Gower	England v New Zealand	Brisbane	1982-83
158	M.L.Hayden	Australia v West Indies	North Sound	2006-07
157*	X.M.Marshall	West Indies v Canada	King City (NW)	2008
157	S.T.Jayasuriya	Sri Lanka v Holland	Amstelveen	2006
156	B.C.Lara	West Indies v Pakistan	Adelaide	2004-05
156	A.Symonds	Australia v New Zealand	Wellington	2005-06
156	H.Masakadza	Zimbabwe v Kenya	Harare	2009-10
154	A.C.Gilchrist	Australia v Sri Lanka	Melbourne	1998-99
154	Tamim Iqbal	Bangladesh v Zimbabwe	Bulawayo	2009
153*	I.V.A.Richards	West Indies v Australia	Melbourne	1979-80
153*	M.Azharuddin	India v Zimbabwe	Cuttack	1997-98
153*	S.C.Ganguly	India v New Zealand	Gwalior	1999-00
153*	C.H.Gayle	West Indies v Zimbabwe	Bulawayo	2003-04
153	B.C.Lara	West Indies v Pakistan	Sharjah	1993-94
153	R.Dravid	India v New Zealand	Hyderabad	1999-00

153	H.H.Gibbs	South Africa v Bangladesh	Potchefstroom	2002-03
152*	D.L.Haynes	West Indies v India	Georgetown	1988-89
152*	C.H.Gayle	West Indies v South Africa	Johannesburg	2003-04
152	C.H.Gayle	West Indies v Kenya	Nairobi	2001-02
152	S.R.Tendulkar	India v Namibia	Pietermaritzburg	2002-03
152	A.J.Strauss	England v Bangladesh	Nottingham	2005
152	S.T.Jayasuriya	Sri Lanka v England	Leeds	2006
151*	S.T.Jayasuriya	Sri Lanka v India	Bombay	1996-97
151	A.Symonds	Australia v Sri Lanka	Sydney	2005-06
150*	G.Gambhir	India v Sri Lanka	Kolkata	2009-10
150	S.Chanderpaul	West Indies v South Africa	East London	1998-99
150	G.Gambhir	India v Sri Lanka	Colombo (RPS)	2008-09

HUNDRED ON DEBUT

D.L.Amiss	103	England v Australia	Manchester	1972
D.L.Haynes	148	West Indies v Australia	St John's	1977-78
A.Flower	115*	Zimbabwe v Sri Lanka	New Plymouth	1991-92
Salim Elahi	102*	Pakistan v Sri Lanka	Gujranwala	1995-96
M.J.Guptill	122*	New Zealand v West Indies	Auckland	2008-09

Shahid Afridi scored 102 for P v SL, Nairobi, 1996-97, in his second match having not batted in his first.

Fastest 100	37 balls	Shahid Afridi (102)	P v SL	Nairobi	1996-97
Fastest 50	17 balls	S.T.Jayasuriya (76)	SL v P	Singapore	1995-96

CARRYING BAT THROUGH INNINGS (SIDE ALL OUT)

G.W.Flower	84*	Zimbabwe (205) v England	Sydney	1994-95
Saeed Anwar	103*	Pakistan (219) v Zimbabwe	Harare	1994-95
N.V.Knight	125*	England (246) v Pakistan	Nottingham	1996
R.D.Jacobs	49*	West Indies (110) v Australia	Manchester	1999
D.R.Martyn	116*	Australia (191) v New Zealand	Auckland	1999-00
H.H.Gibbs	59*	South Africa (101†) v Pakistan	Sharjah	1999-00
A.J.Stewart	100*	England (192) v West Indies	Nottingham	2000
Javed Omar	33*	Bangladesh (103) v Zimbabwe	Harare	2000-01

† One batsman retired hurt.

5000 RUNS IN A CAREER

		LOI	I	NO	HS	Runs	Avge	100	50
S.R.Tendulkar	I	442	431	41	200*	17598	45.12	46	93
S.T.Jayasuriya	SL/Asia	444	432	18	189	13428	32.43	28	68
R.T.Ponting	A/ICC	340	331	37	164	12731	43.30	29	76
Inzamam-ul-Haq	P/Asia	378	350	53	137*	11739	39.52	10	83
S.C.Ganguly	I/Asia	311	300	23	183	11363	41.02	22	72
R.Dravid	I/Asia/ICC	339	313	40	153	10765	39.43	12	82
J.H.Kallis	SA/Afr/ICC	298	284	52	139	10613	45.74	17	75
B.C.Lara	WI/ICC	299	289	32	169	10405	40.48	19	63
Mohammad Yousuf	P/Asia	282	267	40	141*	9624	42.39	15	64
A.C.Gilchrist	A/ICC	287	279	11	172	9619	35.89	16	55
M.Azharuddin	I	334	308	54	153*	9378	36.92	7	58
P.A.de Silva	SL	308	296	30	145	9284	34.90	11	64
Saeed Anwar	P	247	244	19	194	8824	39.21	20	43
D.P.M.D.Jayawardena	SL/Asia	317	298	30	128	8702	32.47	12	57
D.L.Haynes	WI	238	237	28	152*	8648	41.37	17	57
M.S.Atapattu	SL	268	259	32	132*	8529	37.57	11	59
M.E.Waugh	A	244	236	20	173	8500	39.35	18	50
S.Chanderpaul	WI	252	236	38	150	8250	41.66	10	55
K.C.Sangakkara	SL/Asia/ICC	267	250	27	138*	8152	36.55	10	55
H.H.Gibbs	SA	248	240	16	175	8094	36.13	21	37
S.P.Fleming	NZ/ICC	280	269	21	134*	8037	32.40	8	49
S.R.Waugh	A	325	288	58	120*	7569	32.90	3	45
C.H.Gayle	WI/ICC	210	205	15	153*	7484	39.38	19	39

		LOI	I	NO	HS	Runs	Avge	100	50
A.Ranatunga	SL	269	255	47	131*	7456	35.84	4	49
Javed Miandad	P	233	218	41	119*	7381	41.70	8	50
Yuvraj Singh	I/Asia	250	230	32	139	7345	37.09	12	43
Salim Malik	P	283	256	38	102	7170	32.88	5	47
V.Sehwag	I/Asia/ICC	221	215	8	146	7091	34.25	12	35
N.J.Astle	NZ	223	217	14	145*	7090	34.92	16	41
M.G.Bevan	A	232	196	67	108*	6912	53.58	6	46
G.Kirsten	SA	185	185	19	188*	6798	40.95	13	45
A.Flower	Z	213	208	16	145	6786	35.34	4	55
I.V.A.Richards	WI	187	167	24	189*	6721	47.00	11	45
Ijaz Ahmed	P	250	232	29	139*	6564	32.33	10	37
G.W.Flower	Z	219	212	18	142*	6536	33.69	6	40
A.R.Border	A	273	252	39	127*	6524	30.62	3	39
R.B.Richardson	WI	224	217	30	122	6248	33.41	5	44
M.L.Hayden	A/ICC	161	155	15	181*	6133	43.80	10	36
D.M.Jones	A	164	161	25	145	6068	44.61	7	46
D.C.Boon	A	181	177	16	122	5964	37.04	5	37
Shahid Afridi	P/Asia/ICC	293	275	18	109	5957	23.17	4	30
J.N.Rhodes	SA	245	220	51	121	5935	35.11	2	33
Ramiz Raja	P	198	197	15	119*	5841	32.09	9	31
Younus Khan	P	202	196	19	144	5765	32.57	6	37
C.L.Hooper	WI	227	206	43	113*	5761	35.34	7	29
G.C.Smith	SA/Afr	149	147	9	141	5613	40.67	8	41
W.J.Cronje	SA	188	175	31	112	5565	38.64	2	39
M.S.Dhoni	I/Asia	162	143	37	183*	5420	51.13	7	35
A.Jadeja	I	196	179	36	119	5359	37.47	6	30
D.R.Martyn	A	208	182	51	144*	5346	40.80	5	37
M.J.Clarke	A	171	155	32	130	5256	42.73	4	40
A.D.R.Campbell	Z	188	184	14	131*	5185	30.50	7	30
R.S.Mahanama	SL	213	198	23	119*	5162	29.49	4	35
Shoaib Malik	P	190	170	21	143	5141	34.50	7	31
C.G.Greenidge	WI	128	127	13	133*	5134	45.03	11	31
A.Symonds	A	198	161	33	156	5088	39.75	6	30

The most for England is 4677 in 162 innings by A.J.Stewart, and for Bangladesh 3298 (152) by Mohammad Ashraful.

15 HUNDREDS

		Inns	100	E	A	SA	WI	NZ	I	P	SL	Z	B	Ass
S.R.Tendulkar	I	431	46	1	9	4	4	5	–	5	8	5	–	5
R.T.Ponting	A	331*	29	5	–	2	2	6	5	1	4	1	1	1
S.T.Jayasuriya	SL	444	28	4	2	–	1	5	7	3	–	1	4	1
S.C.Ganguly	I	311	22	1	1	3	–	3	–	2	4	3	1	4
H.H.Gibbs	SA	240	21	2	3	–	5	2	2	2	1	2	1	1
Saeed Anwar	P	244	20	–	1	–	2	4	4	–	7	2	–	–
C.H.Gayle	WI	205	19	2	3	3	–	1	3	4	2	0	1	–
B.C.Lara	WI	289	19	1	5	2	–	2	5	2	1	1	1	
M.E.Waugh	A	236	18	1	–	3	3	3	1	1	3	1	–	2
D.L.Haynes	WI	237	17	2	6	–	2	2	4	1	–	–		
J.H.Kallis	SA	284	17	1	1	–	4	3	2	1	3	1	–	1
N.J.Astle	NZ	217	16	2	1	1	1	–	5	2	–	3		1
A.C.Gilchrist	A	279*	16	2	–	2	–	2	1	1	6	1	–	–
Mohammad Yousuf	P	267	15	–	1	2	2	1	3	–	2	4	–	2

* = Includes hundred scored against multi-national side. The most for England is 12 by M.E.Trescothick (in 122 innings), for Zimbabwe 7 by A.D.R.Campbell (184), and for Bangladesh 4 by Shahriar Nafis (60) and Shakib Al Hasan (78).

HIGHEST PARTNERSHIP FOR EACH WICKET

1st	286	W.U.Tharanga/S.T.Jayasuriya	Sri Lanka v England	Leeds	2006
2nd	331	S.R.Tendulkar/R.Dravid	India v New Zealand	Hyderabad (Ind)	1999-00
3rd	237*	R.Dravid/S.R.Tendulkar	India v Kenya	Bristol	1999
4th	275*	M.Azharuddin/A.Jadeja	India v Zimbabwe	Cuttack	1997-98
5th	223	M.Azharuddin/A.Jadeja	India v Sri Lanka	Colombo (RPS)	1997-98
6th	218	D.P.M.D.Jayawardena/M.S.Dhoni	Asia XI v Africa XI	Chennai	2007
7th	130	A.Flower/H.H.Streak	Zimbabwe v England	Harare	2001-02
8th	138*	J.M.Kemp/A.J.Hall	South Africa v India	Cape Town	2006-07
9th	126*	Kapil Dev/S.M.H.Kirmani	India v Zimbabwe	Tunbridge Wells	1983
10th	106*	I.V.A.Richards/M.A.Holding	West Indies v England	Manchester	1984

BOWLING RECORDS
SIX WICKETS IN AN INNINGS

8-19	W.P.U.C.J Vaas	Sri Lanka v Zimbabwe	Colombo (SSC)	2001-02
7-15	G.D.McGrath	Australia v Namibia	Potchefstroom	2002-03
7-20	A.J.Bichel	Australia v England	Port Elizabeth	2002-03
7-30	M.Muralitharan	Sri Lanka v India	Sharjah	2000-01
7-36	Waqar Younis	Pakistan v England	Leeds	2001
7-37	Aqib Javed	Pakistan v India	Sharjah	1991-92
7-51	W.W.Davis	West Indies v Australia	Leeds	1983
6-12	A.Kumble	India v West Indies	Calcutta	1993-94
6-13	B.A.W.Mendis	Sri Lanka v India	Karachi	2008
6-14	G.J.Gilmour	Australia v England	Leeds	1975
6-14	Imran Khan	Pakistan v India	Sharjah	1984-85
6-14	M.F.Maharoof	Sri Lanka v West Indies	Bombay	2006-07
6-15	C.E.H.Croft	West Indies v England	Kingstown	1980-81
6-16	Shoaib Akhtar	Pakistan v New Zealand	Karachi	2001-02
6-18	Azhar Mahmood	Pakistan v West Indies	Sharjah	1999-00
6-19	H.K.Olonga	Zimbabwe v England	Cape Town	1999-00
6-19	S.E.Bond	New Zealand v Zimbabwe	Harare	2005
6-20	B.C.Strang	Zimbabwe v Bangladesh	Nairobi	1997-98
6-20	A.D.Mathews	Sri Lanka v India	Colombo (RPS)	2009-10
6-22	F.H.Edwards	West Indies v Zimbabwe	Harare	2003-04
6-22	M.Ntini	South Africa v Australia	Cape Town	2005-06
6-23	A.A.Donald	South Africa v Kenya	Nairobi	1996-97
6-23	A.Nehra	India v England	Durban	2002-03
6-23	S.E.Bond	New Zealand v Australia	Port Elizabeth	2002-03
6-25	S.B.Styris	New Zealand v West Indies	Port-of-Spain	2002
6-25	W.P.U.C.J Vaas	Sri Lanka v Bangladesh	Pietermaritzburg	2002-03
6-26	Waqar Younis	Pakistan v Sri Lanka	Sharjah	1989-90
6-26	Mashrafe Mortaza	Bangladesh v Kenya	Nairobi	2006
6-27	Naved-ul-Hasan	Pakistan v India	Jamshedpur	2004-05
6-27	M.Kartik	India v Australia	Bombay	2007-08
6-27	C.R.D.Fernando	Sri Lanka v England	Colombo (RPS)	2007-08
6-28	H.K.Olonga	Zimbabwe v Kenya	Bulawayo	2002-03
6-29	B.P.Patterson	West Indies v India	Nagpur	1987-88
6-29	S.T.Jayasuriya	Sri Lanka v England	Moratuwa	1992-93
6-29	B.A.W.Mendis	Sri Lanka v Zimbabwe	Harare	2008-09
6-30	Waqar Younis	Pakistan v New Zealand	Auckland	1993-94
6-31	P.D.Collingwood	England v Bangladesh	Nottingham	2005
6-35	S.M.Pollock	South Africa v West Indies	East London	1998-99
6-35	Abdul Razzaq	Pakistan v Bangladesh	Dhaka	2001-02
6-38	Shahid Afridi	Pakistan v Australia	Dubai	2009
6-39	K.H.MacLeay	Australia v India	Nottingham	1983
6-41	I.V.A.Richards	West Indies v India	Delhi	1989-90
6-42	A.B.Agarkar	India v Australia	Melbourne	2003-04
6-44	Waqar Younis	Pakistan v New Zealand	Sharjah	1996-97
6-46	A.G.Cremer	Zimbabwe v Kenya	Harare	2009-10
6-49	L.Klusener	South Africa v Sri Lanka	Lahore	1997-98
6-50	A.H.Gray	West Indies v Australia	Port-of-Spain	1990-91
6-52	C.B.Mpofu	Zimbabwe v Kenya	Nairobi (Gym)	2008-09
6-55	S.Sreesanth	India v England	Indore	2005-06
6-59	Waqar Younis	Pakistan v Australia	Nottingham	2001
6-59	A.Nehra	India v Sri Lanka	Colombo (RPS)	2005

150 WICKETS IN A CAREER

		LOI	Balls	R	W	Avge	Best	5w	R/Over
M.Muralitharan	SL/Asia/ICC	334	18001	11742	512	22.93	7-30	10	3.91
Wasim Akram	P	356	18186	11812	502	23.52	5-15	6	3.89
Waqar Younis	P	262	12698	9919	416	23.84	7-36	13	4.68
W.P.U.C.J.Vaas	SL/Asia	322	15775	11014	400	27.53	8-19	4	4.18
S.M.Pollock	SA/Afr/ICC	303	15712	9631	393	24.50	6-35	5	3.67
G.D.McGrath	A/ICC	250	12970	8391	381	22.02	7-15	7	3.88
A.Kumble	I/Asia	271	14496	10412	337	30.89	6-12	2	4.30
B.Lee	A	186	9478	7456	324	23.01	5-22	9	4.71
S.T.Jayasuriya	SL	444	14838	11825	322	36.72	6-29	4	4.78
J.Srinath	I	229	11935	8847	315	28.08	5-23	3	4.44
S.K.Warne	A/ICC	194	10642	7541	293	25.73	5-33	1	4.25
Saqlain Mushtaq	P	169	8770	6275	288	21.78	5-20	6	4.29
A.B.Agarkar	I	191	9484	8021	288	27.85	6-42	2	5.07
Shahid Afridi	P/Asia/ICC	293	12375	9518	275	34.61	5-11	3	4.61
A.A.Donald	SA	164	8561	5926	272	21.78	6-23	2	4.15
M.Ntini	SA/ICC	173	8687	6559	266	24.65	6-22	4	4.53
D.L.Vettori	NZ/ICC	251	11889	8220	262	31.37	5- 7	2	4.14
Abdul Razzaq	P/Asia	237	10103	7905	254	31.12	6-35	3	4.69
Kapil Dev	I	225	11202	6945	253	27.45	5-43	1	3.72
J.H.Kallis	SA/Afr/ICC	298	9970	8035	251	32.01	5-30	2	4.83
H.H.Streak	Z/Afr	189	9468	7129	239	29.82	5-32	1	4.51
Harbhajan Singh	I/Asia	209	10931	7840	239	32.80	5-31	3	4.30
D.Gough	E/ICC	159	8470	6209	235	26.42	5-44	2	4.39
Z.Khan	I/Asia	171	8577	7035	235	29.93	5-42	1	4.92
C.A.Walsh	WI	205	10822	6918	227	30.47	5- 1	1	3.83
C.E.L.Ambrose	WI	176	9353	5429	225	24.12	5-17	4	3.48
Shoaib Akhtar	P/Asia/ICC	144	6798	5321	223	23.86	6-16	4	4.69
C.Z.Harris	NZ	248	10667	7613	203	37.50	5-42	1	4.28
C.J.McDermott	A	138	7460	5018	203	24.71	5-44	1	4.03
C.L.Cairns	NZ/ICC	215	8168	6594	201	32.80	5-42	1	4.84
B.K.V.Prasad	I	161	8129	6332	196	32.30	5-27	1	4.67
S.R.Waugh	A	325	8883	6761	195	34.67	4-33	–	4.56
C.L.Hooper	WI	227	9573	6958	193	36.05	4-34	–	4.36
L.Klusener	SA	171	7336	5751	192	29.95	6-49	6	4.70
Aqib Javed	P	163	8012	5721	182	31.43	7-37	4	4.28
Imran Khan	P	175	7461	4844	182	26.61	6-14	1	3.89
N.W.Bracken	A	116	5759	4240	174	24.36	5-47	2	4.41
A.Flintoff	E/ICC	141	5624	4121	169	24.38	5-19	2	4.39
C.R.D.Fernando	SL/Asia	134	5844	5080	169	30.05	6-27	1	5.21
K.D.Mills	NZ	110	5484	4286	162	26.45	5-25	1	4.68
Mushtaq Ahmed	P	144	7543	5361	161	33.29	5-36	1	4.26
J.M.Anderson	E	120	5844	4820	161	29.93	5-23	1	4.94
R.J.Hadlee	NZ	115	6182	3407	158	21.56	5-25	5	3.31
M.Prabhakar	I	130	6360	4534	157	28.87	5-33	2	4.27
M.D.Marshall	WI	136	7175	4233	157	26.96	4-18	–	3.54
G.B.Hogg	A	123	5564	4188	156	26.84	5-32	2	4.51
S.R.Tendulkar	I	442	8020	6817	154	44.26	5-32	2	5.10
I.K.Pathan	I	107	5194	4547	152	29.91	5-27	1	5.25
C.H.Gayle	WI/ICC	210	6563	5204	152	34.23	5-46	1	4.75
U.D.U.Chandana	SL	147	6142	4818	151	31.90	5-61	1	4.70

The most for Bangladesh is 135 by Mashrafe Mortaza (103 LOI).

HAT-TRICKS

Jalaluddin	Pakistan v Australia	Hyderabad	1982-83
B.A.Reid	Australia v New Zealand	Sydney	1985-86
C.Sharma	India v New Zealand	Nagpur	1987-88
Wasim Akram	Pakistan v West Indies	Sharjah	1989-90
Wasim Akram	Pakistan v Australia	Sharjah	1989-90
Kapil Dev	India v Sri Lanka	Calcutta	1990-91
Aqib Javed	Pakistan v India	Sharjah	1991-92
D.K.Morrison	New Zealand v India	Napier	1993-94

Waqar Younis	Pakistan v New Zealand	East London	1994-95
Saqlain Mushtaq	Pakistan v Zimbabwe	Peshawar	1996-97
E.A.Brandes	Zimbabwe v England	Harare	1996-97
A.M.Stuart	Australia v Pakistan	Melbourne	1996-97
Saqlain Mushtaq	Pakistan v Zimbabwe	The Oval	1999
W.P.U.C.J Vaas	Sri Lanka v Zimbabwe	Colombo (SSC)	2001-02
Mohammad Sami	Pakistan v West Indies	Sharjah	2001-02
W.P.U.C.J Vaas[1]	Sri Lanka v Bangladesh	Pietermaritzburg	2002-03
B.Lee	Australia v Kenya	Durban	2002-03
J.M.Anderson	England v Pakistan	The Oval	2003
S.J.Harmison	England v India	Nottingham	2004
C.K.Langeveldt	South Africa v West Indies	Bridgetown	2004-05
Shahadat Hossain	Bangladesh v Zimbabwe	Harare	2006
J.E.Taylor	West Indies v Australia	Bombay	2006-07
S.E.Bond	New Zealand v Australia	Hobart	2006-07
S.L.Malinga[2]	Sri Lanka v South Africa	Providence	2006-07
A.Flintoff	England v West Indies	St Lucia	2008-09

[1] The first three balls of the match. Took four wickets in opening over (W W W 4 wide W 0).
[2] Four wickets in four balls.

WICKET-KEEPING RECORDS

SIX DISMISSALS IN AN INNINGS

6	(6ct)	A.C.Gilchrist	Australia v South Africa	Cape Town	1999-00
6	(6ct)	A.J.Stewart	England v Zimbabwe	Manchester	2000
6	(5ct/1st)	R.D.Jacobs	West Indies v Sri Lanka	Colombo (RPS)	2001-02
6	(5ct/1st)	A.C.Gilchrist	Australia v England	Sydney	2002-03
6	(6ct)	A.C.Gilchrist	Australia v Namibia	Potchefstroom	2002-03
6	(6ct)	A.C.Gilchrist	Australia v Sri Lanka	Colombo (RPS)	2003-04
6	(6ct)	M.V.Boucher	South Africa v Pakistan	Cape Town	2006-07
6	(5ct/1st)	M.S.Dhoni	India v England	Leeds	2007
6	(6ct)	A.C.Gilchrist	Australia v India	Baroda	2007-08
6	(5ct/1st)	A.C.Gilchrist	Australia v India	Sydney	2007-08
6	(6ct)	M.J.Prior	England v South Africa	Nottingham	2008

100 DISMISSALS IN A CAREER

Total			LOI	Ct	St
472‡	A.C.Gilchrist	Australia/ICC	287	417	55
421	M.V.Boucher	South Africa/Africa	291	399	22
301†‡	K.C.Sangakkara	Sri Lanka/Asia/ICC	267	236	65
287‡	Moin Khan	Pakistan	219	214	73
233	I.A.Healy	Australia	168	194	39
220‡	Rashid Latif	Pakistan	166	182	38
206‡	R.S.Kaluwitharana	Sri Lanka	187	131	75
206	M.S.Dhoni	India/Asia	162	154	52
204‡	P.J.L.Dujon	West Indies	169	183	21
195†‡	B.B.McCullum	New Zealand	166	182	13
187	R.D.Jacobs	West Indies	147	159	28
165	D.J.Richardson	South Africa	122	148	17
165†‡	A.Flower	Zimbabwe	213	133	32
163†‡	A.J.Stewart	England	170	148	15
154‡	N.R.Mongia	India	140	110	44
136†‡	A.C.Parore	New Zealand	179	111	25
136	Kamran Akmal	Pakistan	115	116	20
126	Khaled Masud	Bangladesh	126	91	35
124	R.W.Marsh	Australia	92	120	4
112	T.Taibu	Zimbabwe/Africa	112	97	15
105	D.Ramdin	West Indies	72	100	5
103	Salim Yousuf	Pakistan	86	81	22

† Excluding catches taken in the field. ‡ Excluding matches when not wicket-keeper.

FIELDING RECORDS
FIVE CATCHES IN AN INNINGS

5	J.N.Rhodes	South Africa v West Indies	Bombay	1993-94

100 CATCHES IN A CAREER

Total			LOI
165	D.P.M.D.Jayawardena	Sri Lanka/Asia	317
156	M.Azharuddin	India	334
144	R.T.Ponting	Australia/ICC	340
134	S.R.Tendulkar	India	442
133	S.P.Fleming	New Zealand/ICC	280
128	M.Muralitharan	Sri Lanka/Asia/ICC	334
127	A.R.Border	Australia	273
124	R.Dravid	India/Asia/ICC	339
123	S.T.Jayasuriya	Sri Lanka/Asia	444
120	C.L.Hooper	West Indies	227
120	B.C.Lara	West Indies/ICC	299
113	Inzamam-ul-Haq	Pakistan/Asia	378
111	S.R.Waugh	Australia	325
109	R.S.Mahanama	Sri Lanka	213
108	H.H.Gibbs	South Africa	248
108	J.H.Kallis	South Africa/Africa/ICC	298
108	S.M.Pollock	South Africa/Africa/ICC	303
108	M.E.Waugh	Australia	244
105	J.N.Rhodes	South Africa	245
102	Younus Khan	Pakistan	202
100	S.C.Ganguly	India/Asia	311
100	I.V.A.Richards	West Indies	187

The most for England is 99 by P.D.Collingwood (173), for Zimbabwe 86 by G.W.Flower (219), and for Bangladesh 32 by Mashrafe Mortaza (101) and Mohammad Ashraful (157).

ALL-ROUND RECORDS
50 RUNS AND 5 WICKETS IN A MATCH

I.V.A.Richards	119	5-41	West Indies v New Zealand	Dunedin	1986-87
K.Srikkanth	70	5-27	India v New Zealand	Vishakhapatnam	1988-89
M.E.Waugh	57	5-24	Australia v West Indies	Melbourne	1992-93
L.Klusener	54	6-49	South Africa v Sri Lanka	Lahore	1997-98
Abdul Razzaq	70*	5-48	Pakistan v India	Hobart	1999-00
G.A.Hick	80	5-33	England v Zimbabwe	Harare	1999-00
Shahid Afridi	61	5-40	Pakistan v England	Lahore	2000-01
S.C.Ganguly	71*	5-34	India v Zimbabwe	Kanpur	2000-01
S.B.Styris	63*	6-25	New Zealand v West Indies	Port-of-Spain	2002
R.C.Irani	53	5-26	England v India	The Oval	2002
C.H.Gayle	60	5-46	West Indies v Australia	St George's	2002-03
P.D.Collingwood	112*	6-31	England v Bangladesh	Nottingham	2005
S.Dhaniram	79	5-32	Canada v Bermuda	King City (NW)	2008

APPEARANCE RECORDS
250 MATCHES

444	S.T.Jayasuriya	Sri Lanka/Asia		291	M.V.Boucher	South Africa/Africa
442	S.R.Tendulkar	India		287	A.C.Gilchrist	Australia/ICC
378	Inzamam-ul-Haq	Pakistan/Asia		283	Salim Malik	Pakistan
356	Wasim Akram	Pakistan		282	Mohammad Yousuf	Pakistan/Asia
340	R.T.Ponting	Australia/ICC		280	S.P.Fleming	New Zealand/ICC
339	R.Dravid	India/Asia/ICC		273	A.R.Border	Australia
334	M.Azharuddin	India		271	A.Kumble	India/Asia
334	M.Muralitharan	Sri Lanka/Asia/ICC		269	A.Ranatunga	Sri Lanka
325	S.R.Waugh	Australia		268	M.S.Atapattu	Sri Lanka
322	W.P.U.C.J.Vaas	Sri Lanka/Asia		267	K.C.Sangakkara	Sri Lanka/Asia/ICC
317	D.P.M.D.Jayawardena	Sri Lanka/Asia		262	Waqar Younis	Pakistan
311	S.C.Ganguly	India/Asia		252	S.Chanderpaul	West Indies
308	P.A.de Silva	Sri Lanka		251	D.L.Vettori	New Zealand/ICC
303	S.M.Pollock	South Africa/Africa/ICC		250	Ijaz Ahmed	Pakistan
299	B.C.Lara	West Indies		250	C.Z.Harris	New Zealand
298	J.H.Kallis	South Africa/Africa/ICC		250	G.D.McGrath	Australia/ICC
293	Shahid Afridi	Pakistan/Asia/ICC		250	Yuvraj Singh	India/Asia

The most for England is 173 by P.D.Collingwood, for Zimbabwe 219 by G.W.Flower, and for Bangladesh 157 by Mohammad Ashraful.

The most consecutive appearances is 172 by A.Flower for Zimbabwe (Feb 1992-Apr 2001).

100 MATCHES AS CAPTAIN

			W	L	T	NR	% Won (exc NR)
218	S.P.Fleming	New Zealand	98	106	1	13	47.80
209	R.T.Ponting	Australia/ICC	154	42	2	11	77.77
193	A.Ranatunga	Sri Lanka	89	95	1	8	48.10
178	A.R.Border	Australia	107	67	1	3	61.14
174	M.Azharuddin	India	90	76	2	6	53.57
147	S.C.Ganguly	India/Asia	76	66	—	5	53.52
139	Imran Khan	Pakistan	75	59	1	4	55.55
138	W.J.Cronje	South Africa	99	35	1	3	73.33
127	G.C.Smith	South Africa/Africa	74	46	1	6	61.15
125	B.C.Lara	West Indies	59	59	—	7	50.42
118	S.T.Jayasuriya	Sri Lanka	66	47	2	3	57.39
109	Wasim Akram	Pakistan	66	41	2	—	60.55
106	S.R.Waugh	Australia	67	35	3	1	63.80
105	I.V.A.Richards	West Indies	67	36	—	2	65.04

The most for England is 60 by M.P.Vaughan, for Zimbabwe 86 by A.D.R.Campbell, and for Bangladesh 69 by Habibul Bashar.

100 LOI UMPIRING APPEARANCES

202	R.E.Koertzen	South Africa	09.12.1992	to	08.11.2009
181	S.A.Bucknor	West Indies	18.03.1989	to	29.03.2009
172	D.R.Shepherd	England	09.06.1983	to	12.07.2005
161	D.J.Harper	Australia	14.01.1994	to	29.09.2009
147	S.J.A.Taufel	Australia	13.01.1999	to	26.01.2010
141	B.F.Bowden	New Zealand	23.03.1995	to	19.02.2010
139	D.B.Hair	Australia	14.12.1991	to	24.08.2008
127	Alim Dar	Pakistan	16.02.2000	to	16.02.2010
111	R.B.Tiffin	Zimbabwe	25.10.1992	to	14.08.2009
107	D.L.Orchard	South Africa	02.12.1994	to	07.12.2003
100	R.S.Dunne	New Zealand	06.02.1989	to	26.02.2002
100	E.A.R.de Silva	Sri Lanka	22.08.1999	to	31.01.2010

MATCH RESULTS

Matches completed by 1 March 2010

	Opponents	Matches	Won											Tied	NR
			E	A	SA	WI	NZ	I	P	SL	Z	B	Ass		
England	Australia	4	1	2	–	–	–	–	–	–	–	–	–	–	1
	South Africa	4	1	–	3	–	–	–	–	–	–	–	–	–	–
	West Indies	4	1	–	–	3	–	–	–	–	–	–	–	–	–
	New Zealand	4	3	–	–	–	1	–	–	–	–	–	–	–	–
	India	2	1	–	–	–	–	1	–	–	–	–	–	–	–
	Pakistan	4	2	–	–	–	–	–	2	–	–	–	–	–	–
	Sri Lanka	1	0	–	–	–	–	–	–	1	–	–	–	–	–
	Zimbabwe	1	1	–	–	–	–	–	–	–	0	–	–	–	–
	Bangladesh	0	0	–	–	–	–	–	–	–	–	0	–	–	–
	Associates	1	0	–	–	–	–	–	–	–	–	–	1	–	–
Australia	South Africa	6	–	3	3	–	–	–	–	–	–	–	–	–	–
	West Indies	4	–	2	–	2	–	–	–	–	–	–	–	–	–
	New Zealand	5	–	4	–	–	0	–	–	–	–	–	–	1	–
	India	3	–	1	–	–	–	2	–	–	–	–	–	–	–
	Pakistan	3	–	1	–	–	–	–	2	–	–	–	–	–	–
	Sri Lanka	2	–	1	–	–	–	–	–	1	–	–	–	–	–
	Zimbabwe	1	–	0	–	–	–	–	–	–	1	–	–	–	–
	Bangladesh	1	–	1	–	–	–	–	–	–	–	0	–	–	–
	Associates	0	–	0	–	–	–	–	–	–	–	–	0	–	–
S Africa	West Indies	4	–	–	3	1	–	–	–	–	–	–	–	–	–
	N Zealand	4	–	–	3	–	1	–	–	–	–	–	–	–	–
	India	3	–	–	1	–	–	2	–	–	–	–	–	–	–
	Pakistan	2	–	–	1	–	–	–	1	–	–	–	–	–	–
	Sri Lanka	0	–	–	0	–	–	–	–	0	–	–	–	–	–
	Zimbabwe	0	–	–	0	–	–	–	–	–	0	–	–	–	–
	Bangladesh	2	–	–	2	–	–	–	–	–	–	0	–	–	–
	Associates	1	–	–	1	–	–	–	–	–	–	–	0	–	–
W Indies	New Zealand	3	–	–	–	0	1	–	–	–	–	–	–	2	–
	India	1	–	–	–	1	–	0	–	–	–	–	–	–	–
	Pakistan	0	–	–	–	0	–	–	0	–	–	–	–	–	–
	Sri Lanka	2	–	–	–	0	–	–	–	2	–	–	–	–	–
	Zimbabwe	1	–	–	–	0	–	–	–	–	1	–	–	–	–
	Bangladesh	2	–	–	–	1	–	–	–	–	–	1	–	–	–
	Associates	0	–	–	–	0	–	–	–	–	–	–	0	–	–
N Zealand	India	3	–	–	–	–	3	0	–	–	–	–	–	–	–
	Pakistan	4	–	–	–	–	0	–	4	–	–	–	–	–	–
	Sri Lanka	6	–	–	–	–	3	–	–	3	–	–	–	–	–
	Zimbabwe	0	–	–	–	–	0	–	–	–	0	–	–	–	–
	Bangladesh	1	–	–	–	–	1	–	–	–	–	0	–	–	–
	Associates	3	–	–	–	–	3	–	–	–	–	–	0	–	–
India	Pakistan	2	–	–	–	–	–	1	0	–	–	–	–	1	–
	Sri Lanka	3	–	–	–	–	–	2	–	1	–	–	–	–	–
	Zimbabwe	0	–	–	–	–	–	0	–	–	0	–	–	–	–
	Bangladesh	1	–	–	–	–	–	1	–	–	–	0	–	–	–
	Associates	2	–	–	–	–	–	1	–	–	–	–	0	–	1
Pakistan	Sri Lanka	6	–	–	–	–	–	–	4	2	–	–	–	–	–
	Zimbabwe	1	–	–	–	–	–	–	1	–	0	–	–	–	–
	Bangladesh	3	–	–	–	–	–	–	3	–	–	0	–	–	–
	Associates	5	–	–	–	–	–	–	5	–	–	–	0	–	–
Sri Lanka	Zimbabwe	1	–	–	–	–	–	–	–	1	0	–	–	–	–
	Bangladesh	1	–	–	–	–	–	–	–	1	–	0	–	–	–
	Associates	3	–	–	–	–	–	–	–	3	–	–	0	–	–
Zimbabwe	Bangladesh	1	–	–	–	–	–	–	–	–	0	1	–	–	–
	Associates	2	–	–	–	–	–	–	–	–	1	–	0	1	–
Bangladesh	Associates	2	–	–	–	–	–	–	–	–	–	1	1	–	–
Associates	Associates	25	–	–	–	–	–	–	–	–	–	–	24	–	1
		150	10	15	17	8	13	10	22	15	3	3	26	5	3

MATCH RESULTS SUMMARY

	Matches	Won	Lost	Tied	NR	Win %
Pakistan	30	22	7	1	0	73.33
Afghanistan	6	4	2	0	0	66.66
Netherlands	10	6	3	0	1	66.66
South Africa	26	17	9	0	0	65.38
Sri Lanka	25	15	10	0	0	60.00
Australia	29	15	12	1	1	53.57
India	20	10	8	1	1	52.63
Ireland	15	7	7	0	1	50.00
England	25	10	14	0	1	41.66
New Zealand	33	13	17	3	0	39.39
West Indies	21	8	11	2	0	38.09
Zimbabwe	8	3	4	1	0	37.50
Kenya	12	4	8	0	0	33.33
Canada	11	3	7	1	0	27.27
Bangladesh	14	3	11	0	0	21.42
Scotland	12	2	9	0	1	18.18
Bermuda	3	0	3	0	0	0.00

INTERNATIONAL TWENTY20 RECORDS

(To 1 March 2010)

TEAM RECORDS

HIGHEST INNINGS TOTALS

† Batting Second

260-6	Sri Lanka v Kenya	Johannesburg	2007-08
241-6	South Africa v England	Centurion	2009-10
221-5	Australia v England	Sydney	2006-07
218-4	India v England	Durban	2007-08
215-5	Sri Lanka v India	Nagpur	2009-10
214-5	Australia v New Zealand	Auckland	2004-05
214-6	New Zealand v Australia	Christchurch	2009-10
214-4†	Australia v New Zealand	Christchurch	2009-10
211-5	South Africa v Scotland	The Oval	2009
211-4†	India v Sri Lanka	Mohali	2009-10
209-3	Australia v South Africa	Brisbane	2005-06
208-2†	South Africa v West Indies	Johannesburg	2007-08
208-8	West Indies v England	The Oval	2007
206-7	Sri Lanka v India	Mohali	2009-10
205-6	West Indies v South Africa	Johannesburg	2007-08
203-5	Pakistan v Bangladesh	Karachi	2007-08
202-6	England v South Africa	Johannesburg	2009-10
201-4	South Africa v Australia	Johannesburg	2005-06
200-6†	England v India	Durban	2007-08

The highest total for Zimbabwe is 184-5 (v Canada, King City, 2008-09) and for Bangladesh 166 (v Zimbabwe, Khulna, 2006-07).

LOWEST COMPLETED INNINGS TOTALS

† Batting Second

67	(17.2)	Kenya v Ireland	Belfast	2008
70		Bermuda v Canada	Belfast	2008
73	(16.5)	Kenya v New Zealand	Durban	2007-08
74	(17.3)	India v Australia	Melbourne	2007-08
75†	(19.2)	Canada v Zimbabwe	King City (NW)	2008-09

78	(17.3)	Bangladesh v New Zealand	Hamilton	2009-10
79†	(14.3)	Australia v England	Southampton	2005
79-7†		West Indies v Zimbabwe	Port-of-Spain	2009-10
81†	(15.4)	Scotland v South Africa	The Oval	2009
83†	(15.5)	Bangladesh v Sri Lanka	Johannesburg	2007-08
86†	(15.3)	Netherlands v Ireland	Dubai	2009-10
88†	(19.3)	Kenya v Sri Lanka	Johannesburg	2007-08
91	(19.4)	Canada v Kenya	Belfast	2008
92	(19.4)	Kenya v Pakistan	Nairobi	2007-08
93†	(17.3)	Netherlands v Pakistan	Lord's	2009
97	(18.4)	Netherlands v Canada	Belfast	2008
99-7		Bermuda v Scotland	Belfast	2008
99	(18.3)	New Zealand v Pakistan	The Oval	2009
99	(18.3)	Scotland v Ireland	Dubai	2009-10

BATTING RECORDS

500 RUNS IN A CAREER

Runs			M	I	NO	HS	Avge	50	R/100B
987	B.B.McCullum	NZ	33	33	6	116*	36.55	7	133.1
663	K.P.Pietersen	E	22	22	2	79	33.15	3	143.1
642	G.C.Smith	SA	20	20	2	89*	35.66	4	131.0
607	T.M.Dilshan	SL	23	22	3	96*	31.94	5	129.4
606	S.T.Jayasuriya	SL	23	23	1	88	27.54	4	136.7
603	Shoaib Malik	P	30	29	6	57	26.21	2	114.8
572	K.C.Sangakkara	SL	20	19	2	78	33.64	5	126.8
552	G.Gambhir	I	19	18	–	75	30.66	6	126.0
509	Misbah-ul-Haq	P	23	19	8	87*	46.27	3	120.9

HIGHEST INDIVIDUAL INNINGS

Score	Balls				
117	57	C.H.Gayle	WI v SA	Johannesburg	2007-08
116*	56	B.B.McCullum	NZ v A	Christchurch	2009-10
98*	55	R.T.Ponting	A v NZ	Auckland	2004-05
96*	57	T.M.Dilshan	SL v WI	The Oval	2009
96	56	D.R.Martyn	A v SA	Brisbane	2005-06
94	45	L.L.Bosman	SA v E	Centurion	2009-10
90*	55	H.H.Gibbs	SA v WI	Johannesburg	2007-08
89*	58	G.C.Smith	SA v A	Johannesburg	2005-06
89*	56	J.M.Kemp	SA v NZ	Durban	2007-08
89	43	D.A.Warner	A v SA	Melbourne	2008-09
88*	44	D.J.Hussey	A v SA	Johannesburg	2008-09
88*	61	H.Patel	C v Ire	Colombo (SSC)	2009-10
88	44	S.T.Jayasuriya	SL v K	Johannesburg	2007-08
88	50	C.H.Gayle	WI v A	The Oval	2009
88	44	G.C.Smith	SA v E	Centurion	2009-10
87*	53	Misbah-ul-Haq	P v B	Karachi	2007-08
85*	46	A.Symonds	A v NZ	Perth	2007-08
85*	45	E.J.G.Morgan	E v SA	Johannesburg	2009-10
81	50	Nazimuddin	B v P	Nairobi	2007-08
81	47	S.T.Jayasuriya	SL v WI	Nottingham	2009

HIGHEST PARTNERSHIP FOR EACH WICKET

1st	170	G.C.Smith/L.L.Bosman	SA v E	Centurion	2009-10
2nd	111	G.C.Smith/H.H.Gibbs	SA v A	Johannesburg	2005-06
3rd	120*	H.H.Gibbs/J.M.Kemp	SA v WI	Johannesburg	2007-08
4th	112*	K.P.Pietersen/E.J.G.Morgan	E v P	Dubai	2009-10
5th	119*	Shoaib Malik/Misbah-ul-Haq	P v A	Johannesburg	2007-08
6th	77*	R.T.Ponting/M.E.K.Hussey	A v NZ	Auckland	2004-05
7th	91	P.D.Collingwood/M.H.Yardy	E v WI	The Oval	2007
8th	61	S.K.Raina/Harbhajan Singh	I v NZ	Christchurch	2008-09
9th	44	S.L.Malinga/C.R.D.Fernando	SL v NZ	Auckland	2006-07
10th	28	J.D.P.Oram/J.S.Patel	NZ v A	Perth	2007-08

BOWLING RECORDS

20 WICKETS IN A CAREER

Wkts			Matches	Overs	Mdns	Runs	Avge	Best	R/Over
43	Umar Gul	P	26	93.2	1	551	12.81	5- 6	5.90
37	Shahid Afridi	P	27	104	3	604	16.32	4-11	5.80
31	D.L.Vettori	NZ	21	83	1	450	14.51	4-20	5.42
25	B.A.W.Mendis	SL	12	46	1	244	9.76	4-15	5.30
25	S.C.J.Broad	E	20	73	0	565	22.60	3-17	7.73
24	S..Malinga	SL	20	66.4	0	500	20.83	3-17	7.50
23	D.W.Steyn	SA	14	51	0	359	15.60	4- 9	7.03
20	Saeed Ajmal	P	14	53.5	0	307	15.35	4-19	5.70
20	S.E.Bond	NZ	15	58.3	2	398	19.90	3-18	6.80

BEST FIGURES IN AN INNINGS

5- 6	Umar Gul	P v NZ	The Oval	2009
5-20	N.Odhiambo	K v Sc	Nairobi (Gym)	2009-10
5-20	D.J.G.Sammy	WI v Z	Port-of-Spain	2009-10
4- 6	S.J.Benn	WI v Z	Port-of-Spain	2009-10
4- 7	M.R.Gillespie	NZ v K	Durban	2007-08
4- 8	Umar Gul	P v A	Dubai	2009
4- 9	D.W.Steyn	SA v WI	Port Elizabeth	2007-08
4-11	Shahid Afridi	P v Ne	Lord's	2009
4-13	R.P.Singh	I v SA	Durban	2007-08
4-13	Umar Gul	P v SL	King City (NW)	2008-09
4-13	W.D.Parnell	SA v WI	The Oval	2009
4-15	B.A.W.Mendis	SL v Z	King City (NW)	2008-09

HAT-TRICKS

B.Lee	Australia v Bangladesh	Melbourne	2007-08
J.D.P.Oram	New Zealand v Sri Lanka	Colombo (RPS)	2009

WICKET-KEEPING RECORDS

15 DISMISSALS IN A CAREER

Dis			Matches	Ct	St
32	Kamran Akmal	Pakistan	28	13	19
18	B.B.McCullum	New Zealand	33	14	4
17	A.C.Gilchrist	Australia	13	17	0
16	N.E.O'Brien	Ireland	14	8	8
16	D.Ramdin	West Indies	19	14	2
16	K.C.Sangakkara	Sri Lanka	20	9	7

MOST DISMISSALS IN AN INNINGS

4 (4 ct)	A.C.Gilchrist	Australia v Zimbabwe	Cape Town	2007-08
4 (4 ct)	M.J.Prior	England v South Africa	Cape Town	2007-08
4 (4 ct)	A.C.Gilchrist	Australia v New Zealand	Perth	2007-08
4 (4 st)	Kamran Akmal	Pakistan v Netherlands	Lord's	2009
4 (3 ct, 1 st)	N.J.O'Brien	Ireland v Sri Lanka	Lord's	2009

MOST STUMPINGS IN AN INNINGS

4	Kamran Akmal	Pakistan v Netherlands	Lord's	2009

FIELDING RECORDS
10 CATCHES IN A CAREER

Total			Matches	Total			Matches
19	L.R.P.L.Taylor	New Zealand	27	11	Younus Khan	Pakistan	22
17	A.B.de Villiers	South Africa	23	10	S.C.J.Broad	England	20
12	Shoaib Malik	Pakistan	30	10	M.E.K.Hussey	Australia	18
11	J.P.Duminy	South Africa	18	10	G.C.Smith	South Africa	20
11	J.A.Morkel	South Africa	24				

MOST CATCHES IN AN INNINGS

3	K.P.Pietersen	England v Australia	Southampton	2005
3	B.Lee	Australia v Sri Lanka	Cape Town	2007-08
3	L.R.P.L.Taylor	New Zealand v Australia	Perth	2007-08
3	S.J.Benn	West Indies v Australia	The Oval	2009
3	L.M.P.Simmons	West Indies v India	Lord's	2009
3	A.B.de Villiers	South Africa v India	Nottingham	2009
3	L.R.P.L.Taylor	New Zealand v Sri Lanka	Colombo (RPS)	2009
3	D.F.Watts	Scotland v Ireland	Dubai	2009-10
3	S.C.J.Broad	England v Pakistan	Dubai	2009-10
3	E.J.G.Morgan	England v Pakistan	Dubai	2009-10

APPEARANCE RECORDS
25 APPEARANCES

33	B.B.McCullum	New Zealand		27	Shahid Afridi	Pakistan
30	Shoaib Malik	Pakistan		27	L.R.P.L.Taylor	New Zealand
28	Kamran Akmal	Pakistan		26	Umar Gul	Pakistan

20 MATCHES AS CAPTAIN

IT20			W	L	T	NR	%age wins
21	D.L.Vettori	New Zealand	9	10	2	–	42.85
20	G.C.Smith	South Africa	14	6	–	–	70.00

UNIVERSITY MATCH RESULTS

Played: 164. Wins: Cambridge 57; Oxford 53. Drawn: 54. Abandoned: 1

In 2001, for the very first time, Cambridge hosted the University Match, cricket's oldest surviving first-class fixture, after the ECB's re-organisation of university cricket around six centres of excellence had removed it from Lord's. Dating from 1827 it has, wartime interruptions apart, been played annually since 1838. With the exception of five matches played in the area of Oxford (1829, 1843, 1846, 1848 and 1850), all the previous fixtures had been staged at Lord's. Since 2001 it has been played over four days rather than three.

In 2003, Oxford (with Brookes), Cambridge (with Anglia) and Durham were joined by Loughborough in playing three first-class matches against counties. The other two centres – Cardiff (with UWIC and Glamorgan), and Leeds (with Bradford and Leeds Metropolitan) – also play three counties apiece but without first-class status. That status is under severe threat beyond the 2010 season.

1827	Drawn	1877	Oxford	1923	Oxford	1971	Drawn
1829	Oxford	1878	Cambridge	1924	Cambridge	1972	Cambridge
1836	Oxford	1879	Cambridge	1925	Drawn	1973	Drawn
1838	Oxford	1880	Cambridge	1926	Cambridge	1974	Drawn
1839	Cambridge	1881	Oxford	1927	Cambridge	1975	Drawn
1840	Cambridge	1882	Cambridge	1928	Drawn	1976	Oxford
1841	Cambridge	1883	Cambridge	1929	Drawn	1977	Drawn
1842	Cambridge	1884	Oxford	1930	Cambridge	1978	Drawn
1843	Cambridge	1885	Cambridge	1931	Oxford	1979	Cambridge
1844	Drawn	1886	Oxford	1932	Drawn	1980	Drawn
1845	Cambridge	1887	Oxford	1933	Drawn	1981	Drawn
1846	Oxford	1888	Drawn	1934	Drawn	1982	Cambridge
1847	Cambridge	1889	Cambridge	1935	Cambridge	1983	Drawn
1848	Oxford	1890	Cambridge	1936	Cambridge	1984	Oxford
1849	Cambridge	1891	Cambridge	1937	Oxford	1985	Drawn
1850	Oxford	1892	Oxford	1938	Drawn	1986	Cambridge
1851	Cambridge	1893	Cambridge	1939	Oxford	1987	Drawn
1852	Oxford	1894	Oxford	1946	Oxford	1988	Abandoned
1853	Oxford	1895	Cambridge	1947	Drawn	1989	Drawn
1854	Oxford	1896	Oxford	1948	Oxford	1990	Drawn
1855	Oxford	1897	Cambridge	1949	Cambridge	1991	Drawn
1856	Cambridge	1898	Oxford	1950	Drawn	1992	Cambridge
1857	Oxford	1899	Drawn	1951	Oxford	1993	Oxford
1858	Oxford	1900	Drawn	1952	Drawn	1994	Drawn
1859	Cambridge	1901	Drawn	1953	Cambridge	1995	Oxford
1860	Cambridge	1902	Cambridge	1954	Drawn	1996	Drawn
1861	Cambridge	1903	Oxford	1955	Drawn	1997	Drawn
1862	Cambridge	1904	Drawn	1956	Drawn	1998	Cambridge
1863	Oxford	1905	Cambridge	1957	Cambridge	1999	Drawn
1864	Oxford	1906	Cambridge	1958	Cambridge	2000	Drawn
1865	Oxford	1907	Cambridge	1959	Oxford	2001	Oxford
1866	Oxford	1908	Oxford	1960	Drawn	2002	Drawn
1867	Cambridge	1909	Drawn	1961	Drawn	2003	Oxford
1868	Cambridge	1910	Oxford	1962	Drawn	2004	Oxford
1869	Cambridge	1911	Oxford	1963	Drawn	2005	Oxford
1870	Cambridge	1912	Cambridge	1964	Drawn	2006	Oxford
1871	Oxford	1913	Oxford	1965	Drawn	2007	Drawn
1872	Cambridge	1914	Oxford	1966	Oxford	2008	Drawn
1873	Oxford	1919	Oxford	1967	Drawn	2009	Cambridge
1874	Oxford	1920	Drawn	1968	Drawn		
1875	Oxford	1921	Cambridge	1969	Drawn		
1876	Cambridge	1922	Cambridge	1970	Drawn		

CAMBRIDGE UNIVERSITY RECORDS

ALL FIRST-CLASS MATCHES

Highest Total	For 703-9d		v	Sussex	Hove	1890
	V 730-3		by	W Indians	Cambridge	1950
Lowest Total	For 30		v	Yorkshire	Cambridge	1928
	V 32		by	Oxford U	Lord's	1878
Highest Innings	For 254*	K.S.Duleepsinhji	v	Middlesex	Cambridge	1927
	V 304*	E.de C.Weekes	for	W Indians	Cambridge	1950
Highest Partnership						
(2nd wicket)	429*	J.G.Dewes/G.H.G.Doggart	v	Essex	Cambridge	1949
Best Innings Bowling	10-69	S.M.J.Woods	v	Thornton's XI	Cambridge	1890
Best Match Bowling	15-88	S.M.J.Woods	v	Thornton's XI	Cambridge	1890
Most Runs – Season	1581	D.S.Sheppard		(av 79.05)		1952
Most Runs – Career	4310	J.M.Brearley		(av 38.48)		1961-68
Most 100s – Season	7	D.S.Sheppard				1952
Most 100s – Career	14	D.S.Sheppard				1950-52
Most Wkts – Season	80	O.S.Wheatley		(av 17.63)		1958
Most Wkts – Career	208	G.Goonesena		(av 21.82)		1954-57

UNIVERSITY MATCH RECORDS

Highest Total	604		Oxford	2002
Lowest Total	39		Lord's	1858
Highest Innings	211	G.Goonesena	Lord's	1957
Best Innings Bowling	8-44	G.E.Jeffery	Lord's	1873
Best Match Bowling	13-73	A.G.Steel	Lord's	1878

Hat Tricks: F.C.Cobden (1870), A.G.Steel (1879), P.H.Morton (1880), J.F.Ireland (1911), R.G.H.Lowe (1926).

OXFORD UNIVERSITY RECORDS

ALL FIRST-CLASS MATCHES

Highest Total	For 651		v	Sussex	Hove	1895
	V 679-7d		by	Australians	Oxford	1938
Lowest Total	For 12		v	MCC	Oxford	1877
	V 24		by	MCC	Oxford	1846
Highest Innings	For 281	K.J.Key	v	Middlesex	Chiswick Park	1887
	V 338	W.W.Read	for	Surrey	The Oval	1888
Highest Partnership						
(3rd wicket)	408	S.Oberoi/D.R.Fox	v	Cambridge U	Cambridge	2005
Best Innings Bowling	10-38	S.E.Butler	v	Cambridge U	Lord's	1871
Best Match Bowling	15-65	B.J.T.Bosanquet	v	Sussex	Oxford	1900
Most Runs – Season	1307	Nawab of Pataudi sr		(av 93.35)		1931
Most Runs – Career	3319	N.S.Mitchell-Innes		(av 47.41)		1934-37
Most 100s – Season	6	Nawab of Pataudi sr				1931
	6	M.P.Donnelly				1946
Most 100s – Career	9	A.M.Crawley				1927-30
	9	Nawab of Pataudi sr				1928-31
	9	N.S.Mitchell-Innes				1934-37
	9	M.P.Donnelly				1946-47
Most Wkts – Season	70	I.A.R.Peebles		(av 18.15)		1930
Most Wkts – Career	182	R.H.B.Bettington		(av 19.38)		1920-23

UNIVERSITY MATCH RECORDS

Highest Total	610-5d		Cambridge	2005
Lowest Total	32		Lord's	1878
Highest Innings	247	S.Oberoi	Cambridge	2005
Best Innings Bowling	10-38	S.E.Butler	Lord's	1871
Best Match Bowling	15-95	S.E.Butler	Lord's	1871

Match Doubles: P.R.le Couteur (160 and 11-66 in 1910); G.J.Toogood (149 and 10-93 in 1985)

INDIAN PREMIER LEAGUE 2009

Owing to security concerns, following the terrorist attacks in Mumbai and Lahore, the second IPL tournament was held in South Africa between 18 April and 24 May. The first IPL tournament was won by Rajasthan Royals in 2008.

	Team	P	W	L	T	NR	Pts	Net RR
1	Delhi Daredevils	14	10	4	–	–	20	+0.31
2	Chennai Super Kings	14	8	5	–	1	17	+0.95
3	RC Bangalore	14	8	6	–	–	16	–0.19
4	Deccan Chargers	14	7	7	–	–	14	+0.20
5	Kings XI Punjab	14	7	7	–	–	14	–0.48
6	Rajasthan Royals	14	6	7	–	1	13	–0.35
7	Mumbai Indians	14	5	8	–	1	11	+0.30
8	Kolkata Knight Riders	14	3	10	–	1	7	–0.79

1st Semi-Final: At SuperSport Park, Centurion, 22 May (floodlit). Toss: Deccan Chargers. **DECCAN CHARGERS** won by six wickets. Delhi Daredevils 153-8 (20; T.M.Dilshan 65, R.J.Harris 3-27). Deccan Chargers 154-4 (17.4; A.C.Gilchrist 85, A.Mishra 3-19). Award: A.C.Gilchrist.

2nd Semi-Final: At New Wanderers Stadium, Johannesburg, 23 May (floodlit). Toss: Royal Challengers Bangalore. **ROYAL CHALLENGERS BANGALORE** won by six wickets. Chennai Super Kings 146-5 (20). Royal Challengers Bangalore 149-4 (18.5). Award: M.K.Pandey (Royal Challengers Bangalore, 48).

FINAL: At New Wanderers Stadium, Johannesburg, 24 May (floodlit). Toss: Royal Challengers Bangalore. **DECCAN CHARGERS** won by 6 runs. Deccan Chargers 143-6 (20; H.H.Gibbs 53*, A.Kumble 4-16). Royal Challengers Bangalore 137-9 (20; P.P.Ojha 3-28). Award: A.Kumble. Series award: A.C.Gilchrist (Deccan Chargers).

TEAM RECORDS
HIGHEST TOTALS

240-5 (20)	Chennai v Punjab	Mohali	2008
222-3 (20)	Kolkata v Bangalore	Bangalore	2008
221-3 (20)	Punjab v Rajasthan	Mohali	2008

LOWEST TOTALS

58 (15.1)	Rajasthan v Bangalore	Cape Town	2009
67 (15.2)	Kolkata v Mumbai	Mumbai	2008

BATTING RECORDS
500 RUNS IN A SEASON

Runs			Year	M	I	NO	HS	Ave	100	50	6s	4s	R/100B
616	S.E.Marsh	Punjab	2008	11	11	2	115	68.44	1	5	26	59	139.7
572	M.L.Hayden	Chennai	2009	12	12	1	89	52.00	–	5	22	60	144.8
534	G.Gambhir	Delhi	2008	14	14	1	86	41.07	–	5	8	68	140.9
514	S.T.Jayasuriya	Mumbai	2008	14	14	2	114*	42.83	1	2	31	57	166.3

MOST RUNS IN IPL CAREER

Runs			Years	M	I	NO	HS	Ave	100	50	6s	4s	R/100B
931	A.C.Gilchrist	Deccan	2008-09	30	30	1	109*	32.10	1	6	48	105	144.8

HUNDREDS

Score	Balls				
158*	73	B.B.McCullum	Kolkata v Bangalore	Bangalore	2008
117*	53	A.Symonds	Deccan v Rajasthan	Hyderabad	2008
116*	54	M.E.K.Hussey	Chennai v Punjab	Mohali	2008
115	69	S.E.Marsh	Punjab v Rajasthan	Mohali	2008
114*	48	S.T.Jayasuriya	Mumbai v Chennai	Mumbai	2008
114*	73	M.K.Pandey	Bangalore v Deccan	Centurion	2009
109*	47	A.C.Gilchrist†	Deccan v Mumbai	Mumbai	2008
105*	54	A.B.de Villiers	Delhi v Chennai	Durban	2009

† A.C.Gilchrist reached his 100 in a record 42 balls.

MOST SIXES IN AN INNINGS

13	B.B.McCullum	Kolkata v Bangalore	Bangalore	2008
11	S.T.Jayasuriya	Mumbai v Chennai	Mumbai	2008

HIGHEST STRIKE RATE IN A SEASON (Qualification: 100 runs or more)

R/100B	Score	Balls			
204.34	188	92	B.B.McCullum	Kolkata	2008

HIGHEST STRIKE RATE IN AN INNINGS (Qualification: 25 runs, 300+ strike rate)

R/100B	Score	Balls				
385.7	27*	7	B.Akhil	Bangalore v Deccan	Hyderabad	2008
306.2	49	16	Yuvraj Singh	Punjab v Rajasthan	Mohali	2008

BOWLING RECORDS
20 WICKETS IN A SEASON

Wkts			Year	P	O	M	Runs	Avge	Best	4w	R/Over
23	R.P.Singh	Deccan	2009	16	59.4	1	417	18.13	4-22	1	6.98
22	Sohail Tanvir	Rajasthan	2008	11	41.1	–	266	12.09	6-14	2	6.46
21	A.Kumble	Bangalore	2009	16	59.1	1	347	16.52	5- 5	2	5.86

MOST WICKETS IN IPL CAREER

Wkts			Years	P	O	M	Runs	Avge	Best	4w	R/Over
38	R.P.Singh	Deccan	2008-09	30	111	2	859	22.61	4-22	1	7.74

MOST WICKETS IN AN INNINGS

6-14	Sohail Tanvir	Rajasthan v Chennai	Jaipur	2008
5- 5	A.Kumble	Bangalore v Rajasthan	Cape Town	2009
5-17	A.Mishra	Delhi v Deccan	Delhi	2008
5-24	L.Balaji	Chennai v Punjab	Chennai	2008

MOST ECONOMICAL BOWLING ANALYSIS

O	M	R	W				
4	1	6	0	F.H.Edwards	Deccan v Kolkata	Cape Town	2009
4	1	6	1	A.Nehra	Delhi v Punjab	Bloemfontein	2009

MOST EXPENSIVE BOWLING ANALYSIS

O	M	R	W				
4	0	59	1	R.P.Singh	Deccan v Kolkata	Hyderabad	2008
4	0	58	0	Mashrafe Mortaza	Kolkata v Deccan	Johannesburg	2009

CHAMPIONS LEAGUE TWENTY20 2009

The inaugural Champions League Twenty20 tournament took place in India between 8 and 23 October. Twelve teams took part in the tournament, having qualified from their domestic Twenty20 competitions: three from India's IPL, two each from Australia, England and South Africa, and one each from New Zealand, Sri Lanka and West Indies. The teams were divided into four groups of three, with the top two going through to the league stage. England's representatives were Somerset and Sussex. Sussex were eliminated in the first stage, losing their decisive match to Eagles in a one-over eliminator.

LEAGUE A

Team	P	W	L	T	NR	Pts	Net RR
1 Trinidad & Tobago	3	3	–	–	–	6	+1.38
2 New South Wales	3	2	1	–	–	4	+1.84
3 Eagles	3	1	2	–	–	2	–1.11
4 Somerset	3	–	3	–	–	0	–2.00

LEAGUE B

Team	P	W	L	T	NR	Pts	Net RR
1 Victoria	3	2	1	–	–	4	+0.91
2 Cape Cobras	3	2	1	–	–	4	–0.22
3 RC Bangalore	3	1	2	–	–	2	–0.11
4 Delhi Daredevils	3	1	2	–	–	2	–0.40

1st Semi-Final: At Feroz Shah Kotla, Delhi, 21 October. Toss: New South Wales. **NEW SOUTH WALES** won by 79 runs. New South Wales 169-7 (20; C.J.McKay 3-27). Victoria 90-9 (20; M.C.Henriques 3-11). Award: D.A.Warner (New South Wales, 48).

2nd Semi-Final: At Rajiv Gandhi International Stadium, Hyderabad, 22 October. Toss: Cape Cobras. **TRINIDAD & TOBAGO** won by seven wickets. Cape Cobras 175-5 (20; J.P.Duminy 61*). Trinidad & Tobago 178-3 (19.2; D.J.Bravo 58*). Award: D.J.Bravo.

FINAL: At Rajiv Gandhi International Stadium, Hyderabad, 23 October. Toss: Trinidad & Tobago. **NEW SOUTH WALES** won by 41 runs. New South Wales 159-9 (20; R.Rampaul 3-20). Trinidad & Tobago 118 (15.5; S.R.Clark 3-21). Award: B.Lee (New South Wales, 48, 2-10 and 2ct). Series award: B.Lee (New South Wales).

TOURNAMENT RECORDS

Highest total	213-4	Trinidad & Tobago v Eagles	Hyderabad
Lowest total	84	Cape Cobras v Delhi Daredevils	Delhi
Highest score	104*	A.G.Puttick	Cape Cobras v Otago	Hyderabad
Most runs	224	J.P.Duminy (ave 112.00)	Cape Cobras	
Highest partnership	121	P.J.Hughes/D.A.Warner	NSW v Trinidad & Tobago	Hyderabad
Best bowling	4-17	C.J.D.de Villiers	Eagles v.Somerset	Hyderabad
Most wickets	12	D.J.Bravo (ave 15.83)		Trinidad & Tobago
Most economical	4-1-8-1	B.Lee	NSW v Sussex	Delhi
Most expensive	4-0-59-0	A.Mishra	Delhi v Bangalore	Bangalore

WOMEN'S TEST CRICKET RECORDS

1934-35 to 1 March 2010
RESULTS SUMMARY

	Opponents	Tests	E	A	NZ	SA	WI	I	P	SL	Ire	H	Drawn
													Won by ... *Drawn*
England	Australia	44	8	10	–	–	–	–	–	–	–	–	26
	New Zealand	23	6	–	0	–	–	–	–	–	–	–	17
	South Africa	6	2	–	–	0	–	–	–	–	–	–	4
	West Indies	3	2	–	–	–	0	–	–	–	–	–	1
	India	12	1	–	–	–	–	1	–	–	–	–	10
Australia	New Zealand	13	–	4	1	–	–	–	–	–	–	–	8
	West Indies	2	–	0	–	–	0	–	–	–	–	–	2
	India	9	–	4	–	–	–	0	–	–	–	–	5
New Zealand	South Africa	3	–	–	1	0	–	–	–	–	–	–	2
	India	6	–	–	0	–	–	0	–	–	–	–	6
South Africa	India	1	–	–	–	0	–	1	–	–	–	–	–
	Holland	1	–	–	–	1	–	–	–	–	–	0	–
West Indies	India	6	–	–	–	–	1	1	–	–	–	–	4
	Pakistan	1	–	–	–	–	0	–	0	–	–	–	1
Pakistan	Sri Lanka	1	–	–	–	–	–	–	0	1	–	–	–
	Ireland	1	–	–	–	–	–	–	0	–	1	–	–
		132	19	18	2	1	1	3	0	1	1	0	86

	Tests	Won	Lost	Drawn	Toss Won
England	88	19	11	58	52
Australia	68	18	9	41	23
New Zealand	45	2	10	33	21
South Africa	11	1	4	6	6
West Indies	12	1	3	8	6†
India	34	3	6	25	16†
Pakistan	3	–	2	1	1
Sri Lanka	1	1	–	–	1
Ireland	1	1	–	–	1
Holland	1	–	1	–	1

† *Results of tosses in five of the six India v West Indies Tests in 1976-77 are not known*

TEAM RECORDS
HIGHEST INNINGS TOTALS

569-6d	Australia v England	Guildford	1998
525	Australia v India	Ahmedabad	1983-84
517-8	New Zealand v England	Scarborough	1996
503-5d	England v New Zealand	Christchurch	1934-35
497	England v South Africa	Shenley	2003
467	India v England	Taunton	2002
455	England v South Africa	Taunton	2003
440	West Indies v Pakistan	Karachi	2003-04
427-4d	Australia v England	Worcester	1998
426-7d	Pakistan v West Indies	Karachi	2003-04
426-9d	India v England	Blackpool	1986
414	England v New Zealand	Scarborough	1996
414	England v Australia	Guildford	1998

| 404-9d | India v South Africa | Paarl | 2001-02 |
| 403-8d | New Zealand v India | Nelson | 1994-95 |

The highest totals for countries not included above are:

316	South Africa v England	Shenley	2003
193-3d	Ireland v Pakistan	Dublin	2000
108	Holland v South Africa	Rotterdam	2007

LOWEST INNINGS TOTALS

35	England v Australia	Melbourne	1957-58
38	Australia v England	Melbourne	1957-58
44	New Zealand v England	Christchurch	1934-35
47	Australia v England	Brisbane	1934-35
50	Holland v South Africa	Rotterdam	2007
53	Pakistan v Ireland	Dublin	2000

The lowest innings totals for countries not included above are:

65	India v West Indies	Jammu	1976-77
67	West Indies v England	Canterbury	1979
89	South Africa v New Zealand	Durban	1971-72

BATTING RECORDS
1000 RUNS IN TESTS

		Career	M	I	NO	HS	Avge	100	50
1935	J.A.Brittin (E)	1979-98	27	44	5	167	49.61	5	11
1594	R.Heyhoe-Flint (E)	1960-79	22	38	3	179	45.54	3	10
1380	C.M.Edwards (E)	1996-2009	18	33	3	117	46.00	3	8
1301	D.A.Hockley (NZ)	1979-96	19	29	4	126*	52.04	4	7
1164	C.A.Hodges (E)	1984-92	18	31	2	158*	40.13	2	6
1110	S.Agarwal (I)	1984-95	13	23	1	190	50.45	4	4
1078	E.Bakewell (E)	1968-79	12	22	4	124	59.88	4	7
1030	S.C.Taylor (E)	1999-2009	15	27	2	177	41.20	4	2
1007	M.E.Maclagan (E)	1934-51	14	25	1	119	41.95	2	6
1002	K.L.Rolton (A)	1995-2009	14	22	4	209*	55.66	2	5

HIGHEST INDIVIDUAL INNINGS

242	Kiran Baluch	P v WI	Karachi	2003-04
214	M.Raj	I v E	Taunton	2002
209*	K.L.Rolton	A v E	Leeds	2001
204	K.E.Flavell	NZ v E	Scarborough	1996
204‡	M.A.J.Goszko	A v E	Shenley	2001
200	J.Broadbent	A v E	Guildford	1998
193	D.A.Annetts	A v E	Collingham	1987
190	S.Agarwal	I v E	Worcester	1986
189	E.A.Snowball	E v NZ	Christchurch	1934-35
179	R.Heyhoe-Flint	E v A	The Oval	1976
177	S.C.Taylor	E v SA	Shenley	2003
176*	K.L.Rolton	A v E	Worcester	1998
167	J.A.Brittin	E v A	Harrogate	1998
161*	E.C.Drumm	E v A	Christchurch	1994-95
160	B.A.Daniels	E v NZ	Scarborough	1996
158*	C.A.Hodges	E v NZ	Canterbury	1984
155*	P.F.McKelvey	NZ v E	Wellington	1968-69

‡ *On debut*

FIVE HUNDREDS

			Opponents								
		M	I	E	NZ	SA	WI	IND	P	SL	IRE
5	J.A.Brittin (E)	27	44	–	3	1	–	1	–	–	–

HIGHEST PARTNERSHIP FOR EACH WICKET

1st	241	Kiran Baluch/Sajjida Shah	P v WI	Karachi	2003-04
2nd	235	E.A.Snowball/M.E.Hide	E v NZ	Christchurch	1934-35
3rd	309	L.A.Reeler/D.A.Annetts	A v E	Collingham	1987
4th	253	K.L.Rolton/L.C.Broadfoot	A v E	Leeds	2001
5th	138	J.Logtenberg/C.van der Westhuizen	SA v E	Shenley	2003
6th	229	J.M.Fields/R.L.Haynes	A v E	Worcester	2009
7th	157	M.Raj/J.Goswami	I v E	Taunton	2002
8th	181	S.J.Griffiths/D.L.Wilson	A v NZ	Auckland	1989-90
9th	107	B.Botha/M.Payne	SA v NZ	Cape Town	1971-72
10th	119	S.Nitschke/C.R.Smith	A v E	Hove	2005

BOWLING RECORDS

50 WICKETS IN TESTS

Wkts		Career	M	Balls	Runs	Avge	Best	5wI	10wM
77	M.B.Duggan (E)	1949-63	17	3734	1039	13.49	7- 6	5	–
68	E.R.Wilson (A)	1948-58	11	2885	803	11.80	7- 7	4	2
63	D.F.Edulji (I)	1976-91	20	5098†	1624	25.77	6- 64	1	–
60	M.E.Maclagan (E)	1934-51	14	3432	935	15.58	7- 10	3	–
60	C.L.Fitzpatrick (A)	1991-2006	13	3603	1147	19.11	5- 29	2	–
60	S.Kulkarni (I)	1976-91	19	3320†	1647	27.45	6- 99	5	–
57	R.H.Thompson (A)	1972-85	16	4304	1040	18.24	5- 33	1	–
55	J.Lord (NZ)	1966-79	15	3108	1049	19.07	6-119	4	1
50	E.Bakewell (E)	1968-79	12	2697	831	16.62	7- 61	3	1

† Excludes balls bowled in Sixth Test v West Indies 1976-77

TEN WICKETS IN A TEST

13-226	Shaiza Khan	P v WI	Karachi	2003-04
11- 16	E.R.Wilson	A v E	Melbourne	1957-58
11- 63	J.M.Greenwood	E v WI	Canterbury	1979
11-107	L.C.Pearson	E v A	Sydney	2002-03
10- 65	E.R.Wilson	A v NZ	Wellington	1947-48
10- 75	E.Bakewell	E v WI	Birmingham	1979
10- 78	J.Goswami	I v E	Taunton	2006
10-107	K.Price	A v I	Lucknow	1983-84
10-118	D.A.Gordon	A v E	Melbourne	1968-69
10-137	J.Lord	NZ v A	Melbourne	1978-79

SEVEN WICKETS IN AN INNINGS

8-53	N.David	I v E	Jamshedpur	1995-96
7- 6	M.B.Duggan	E v A	Melbourne	1957-58
7- 7	E.R.Wilson	A v E	Melbourne	1957-58
7-10	M.E.Maclagan	E v A	Brisbane	1934-35
7-18	A.Palmer	A v E	Brisbane	1934-35
7-24	L.Johnston	A v NZ	Melbourne	1971-72
7-34	G.E.McConway	E v I	Worcester	1986
7-41	J.A.Burley	NZ v A	The Oval	1966
7-51	L.C.Pearson	E v A	Sydney	2002-03
7-59	Shaiza Khan	P v WI	Karachi	2003-04
7-61	E.Bakewell	E v WI	Birmingham	1979

HAT-TRICKS

E.R.Wilson	Australia v England	Melbourne	1957-58
Shaiza Khan	Pakistan v West Indies	Karachi	2003-04

WICKET-KEEPING AND FIELDING RECORDS

25 DISMISSALS IN TESTS

Total			Tests	Ct	St	
58	C.Matthews	Australia	20	46	12	1984-95
43	J.Smit	England	21	39	4	1992-2006
36	S.A.Hodges	England	11	19	17	1969-79
28	B.A.Brentnall	New Zealand	10	16	12	1966-78

EIGHT DISMISSALS IN A TEST

9 (8ct, 1 st)	C.Matthews	A v I	Adelaide	1990-91
8 (6ct, 2st)	L.Nye	E v NZ	New Plymouth	1991-92

SIX DISMISSALS IN AN INNINGS

8 (6ct, 2st)	L.Nye	E v NZ	New Plymouth	1991-92
6 (2ct, 4st)	B.A.Brentnall	NZ v SA	Johannesburg	1971-72

20 CATCHES IN THE FIELD IN TESTS

Total			Tests	
25	C.A.Hodges	England	18	1984-92
21	S.Shah	India	20	1976-91
20	L.A.Fullston	Australia	12	1984-87

APPEARANCE RECORDS

25 TEST MATCH APPEARANCES

27	J.A.Brittin	England	1979-98

12 MATCHES AS CAPTAIN

			Won	Lost	Drawn	
14	P.F.McKelvey	New Zealand	2	3	9	1966-79
12	R.Heyhoe-Flint	England	2	–	10	1966-76
12	S.Rangaswamy	India	1	2	9	1976-84

ENGLAND WOMEN'S TEST MATCH RESULT IN 2009

At County Ground, Worcester, 10, 11, 12, 13 July. Toss: Australia. Result: **MATCH DRAWN**. Australia 309 (J.M.Fields 139, R.L.Haynes 98, K.H.Brunt 6-69) and 231 (A.J.Blackwell 68). England 268 (B.L.Morgan 58) and 106-3 (C.M.Edwards 53*).

WOMEN'S LIMITED-OVERS RECORDS

1973 to 2 March 2010

RESULTS SUMMARY

	LOI	Won	Lost	Tied	No Result
Australia	237	182	49	1	5
Denmark	33	6	27	–	–
England	243	133	100	2	8
India	178	93	80	1	4
International XI	18	3	14	–	1
Ireland	104	33	68	–	3
Jamaica	5	1	4	–	–
Japan	5	–	5	–	–
Netherlands	87	18	69	–	–
New Zealand	237	124	106	2	5
Pakistan	71	13	57	–	1
Scotland	8	1	7	–	–
South Africa	78	33	40	1	4
Sri Lanka	74	37	36	–	1
Trinidad & Tobago	6	2	4	–	–
West Indies	72	30	39	1	2
Young England	6	1	5	–	–

TEAM RECORDS

HIGHEST INNINGS TOTALS

455-5 (50)	New Zealand v Pakistan	Christchurch	1996-97
412-3 (50)	Australia v Denmark	Bombay	1997-98

LOWEST INNINGS TOTALS

22 (23.4)	Netherlands v West Indies	Deventer	2008
23 (24.1)	Pakistan v Australia	Melbourne	1996-97
24 (21.3)	Scotland v England	Reading	2001

BATTING RECORDS

2000 RUNS IN LOI

Runs		Career	M	I	NO	HS	Avge	100	50
4844	B.J.Clark (A)	1991-2005	118	114	12	229*	47.49	5	30
4814	K.L.Rolton (A)	1995-2009	141	132	32	154*	48.14	8	33
4064	D.A.Hockley (NZ)	1982-2000	118	115	18	117	41.89	4	34
3943	C.M.Edwards (E)	1997-2010	134	125	17	173*	36.50	4	31
3836	M.Raj (I)	1999-2010	120	107	30	114*	49.81	2	32
3690	S.C.Taylor (E)	1998-2009	114	108	16	156*	40.10	8	19
2919	H.M.Tiffen (NZ)	1999-2009	117	111	16	100	30.72	1	18
2844	E.C.Drumm (NZ)	1992-2006	101	94	13	116	35.11	2	19
2777	A.Chopra (I)	1995-2010	121	106	21	100	32.67	1	18
2630	L.M.Keightley (A)	1995-2005	82	78	12	156*	39.84	4	21
2357	L.C.Sthalekar (A)	2001-2010	97	89	18	104*	33.19	2	15
2201	R.J.Rolls (NZ)	1997-2007	104	91	3	114	25.01	2	12
2121	J.A.Brittin (E)	1979-1998	63	59	9	138*	42.42	5	8
2091	J.Sharma (I)	2002-2008	77	75	7	138*	30.75	2	14

HIGHEST INDIVIDUAL INNINGS

229*	B.J.Clark	Australia v Denmark	Bombay	1997-98
173*	C.M.Edwards	England v Ireland	Poona	1997-98
168	S.W.Bates	New Zealand v Pakistan	Sydney	2008-09
156*	L.M.Keightley	Australia v Pakistan	Melbourne	1996-97
156*	S.C.Taylor	England v India	Lord's	2006
154*	K.L.Rolton	Australia v Sri Lanka	Christchurch	2000-01
153*	J.Logtenberg	South Africa v Netherlands	Deventer	2007
151	K.L.Rolton	Australia v Ireland	Dublin	2005

HIGHEST PARTNERSHIP FOR EACH WICKET

1st	268	S.J.Taylor/C.M.G.Atkins	E v SA	Lord's	2008
2nd	262	H.M.Tiffen/S.W.Bates	NZ v P	Sydney	2008-09
3rd	244	K.L.Rolton/L.C.Sthalekar	A v Ire	Dublin	2005
4th	224*	J.Logtenberg/M.du Preez	SA v Ne	Deventer	2007
5th	188*	S.C.Taylor/J.Cassar	E v SL	Lincoln, NZ	2001-02
6th	139*	S.J.McGlashan/N.J.Browne	NZ v SA	Bowral	2008-09
7th	104*	S.J.Tsukigawa/N.J.Browne	NZ v E	Madras	2006-07
8th	85*	S.L.Clarke/N.J.Shaw	E v Sc	Reading	2001
9th	73	L.R.F.Askew/I.T.Guha	E v NZ	Madras	2006-07
10th	43	A.Sharma/G.Sultana	I v E	Sydney	2008-09

BOWLING RECORDS

100 WICKETS IN LOI

Wkts		Career	M	Overs	Runs	Avge	Best	4wI
180	C.L.Fitzpatrick (A)	1993-2007	109	1002.5	3023	16.79	5-14	11
141	N.David (I)	1995-2008	97	815.2	2305	16.34	5-20	6
120	J.Goswami (I)	2002-2010	105	835.1	2600	21.66	5-16	4
107	L.C.Sthalekar (A)	2001-2010	97	735.5	2702	25.25	4-20	1
102	C.E.Taylor (E)	1988-2005	105	856.4	2443	23.95	4-13	2

MOST WICKETS IN AN INNINGS

7-4	Sajjida Shah	Pakistan v Japan	Amsterdam	2003
7-8	J.M.Chamberlain	England v Denmark	Haarlem	1991
7-24	S.Nitschke	Australia v England	Kidderminster	2005
6-10	J.Lord	New Zealand v India	Auckland	1981-82
6-10	M.Maben	India v Sri Lanka	Kandy	2003-04
6-20	G.L.Page	New Zealand v Trinidad & T	St Albans	1973
6-32	B.McNeill	New Zealand v England	Lincoln, NZ	2007-08

WICKET-KEEPING AND FIELDING RECORDS

100 DISMISSALS IN LOI

Total			Career	LOI	Ct	St
133	R.J.Rolls	New Zealand	1997-2007	104	89	44
114	J.Smit	England	1993-2007	109	69	45

SIX DISMISSALS IN AN INNINGS

6 (4ct, 2st)	S.L.Illingworth	New Zealand v Australia	Beckenham	1993
6 (1ct, 5st)	V.Kalpana	India v Denmark	Slough	1993
6 (2ct, 4st)	Batool Fatima	Pakistan v West Indies	Karachi	2003-04

40 CATCHES IN THE FIELD IN LOI

Total			LOI	Career
45	B.J.Clark	Australia	118	1991-2005
41	D.A.Hockley	New Zealand	118	1982-2000
40	J.Goswani	India	105	2002-2010

FOUR CATCHES IN AN INNINGS IN THE FIELD

4	Z.J.Goss	Australia v New Zealand Adelaide	1995-96

APPEARANCE RECORDS
120 APPEARANCES

141	K.L.Rolton	Australia	1995-2009
132	C.M.Edwards	England	1997-2010
121	A.Chopra	India	1995-2010
120	M.Raj	India	1999-2010

100 MATCHES AS CAPTAIN

			Won	Lost	No Result	
101	B.J.Clark	Australia	83	17	1	1994-2005

PRINCIPAL FIXTURES 2010

CC1	LV County Championship (1st Div)
CC2	LV County Championship (2nd Div)
F	Floodlit
FCF	First-Class Friendly
LOI	NatWest Limited-Overs International
40L	ECB 40 League

T20	Friends Provident T20
IT20	Twenty20 International
[T20]	Other Twenty20 Match
TM	npower Test Match
UCCE	Univ Centre of Cricketing Excellence

Mon 29 March – Thu 1 April
FCF	Abu Dhabi	MCC v Durham

Sat 3 – Mon 5 April
FCF	Cambridge	Cambridge UCCE v Surrey
FCF	Derby	Derbyshire v Loughborough UCCE
FCF	Durham	Durham UCCE v Lancashire
	Chelmsford	Essex v Leeds/Bradford UCCE
	Bristol	Glos v Cardiff UCCE
FCF	Oxford	Oxford UCCE v Northants

Fri 9 – Mon 12 April
CC1	Chelmsford	Essex v Hampshire
CC1	Birmingham	Warwicks v Yorkshire
CC2	Cardiff	Glamorgan v Sussex
CC2	Leicester	Leics v Northants
CC2	The Oval	Surrey v Derbyshire
CC2	Worcester	Worcs v Middlesex

Sat 10 – Mon 12 April
FCF	Durham	Durham UCCE v Notts
FCF	Canterbury	Kent v Loughborough UCCE
	Taunton Vale	Somerset v Cardiff UCCE

Thu 15 – Sun 18 April
CC1	Chester-le-St	Durham v Essex
CC1	Manchester	Lancashire v Warwicks
CC1	Nottingham	Notts v Kent
CC1	Leeds	Yorkshire v Somerset
CC2	Derby	Derbyshire v Leics
CC2	Bristol	Glos v Northants
CC2	Lord's	Middlesex v Glamorgan
CC2	Hove	Sussex v Surrey

Thu 15 – Sat 17 April
FCF	Oxford	Oxford UCCE v Hampshire
	Kidderminster	Worcs v Leeds/Bradford UCCE

Wed 21 – Sat 24 April
CC1	Chester-le-St	Durham v Hampshire
CC1	Chelmsford	Essex v Lancashire
CC1	Canterbury	Kent v Yorkshire
CC1	Nottingham	Notts v Somerset
CC2	Derby	Derbyshire v Glamorgan
CC2	Bristol	Glos v Sussex
CC2	Northampton	Northants v Middlesex
CC2	Croydon	Surrey v Worcs

Wed 21 – Fri 23 April
FCF	Cambridge	Cambridge UCCE v Leics

Sun 25 April
40L	Chester-le-St	Durham v Hampshire

40L	Chelmsford	Essex v Yorkshire
40L	Cardiff	Glamorgan v Somerset
40L	Bristol	Glos v Derbyshire
40L	Canterbury	Kent v Warwicks
40L	Leicester	Leics v Notts
40L	Northampton	Northants v Middlesex
40L	Croydon	Surrey v Lancashire
40L	Worcester	Worcs v Sussex

Tue 27 – Fri 30 April
CC1	Manchester	Lancashire v Kent
CC1	Taunton	Somerset v Essex
CC1	Birmingham	Warwicks v Hampshire
CC1	Leeds	Yorkshire v Durham
CC2	Lord's	Middlesex v Glos
CC2	Northampton	Northants v Derbyshire
CC2	Hove	Sussex v Leics
CC2	Worcester	Worcs v Glamorgan

Sun 2 May
40L	Southampton	Hampshire v Notts
40L	Canterbury	Kent v Durham
40L	Manchester	Lancashire v Glamorgan
40L	Lord's	Middlesex v Essex
40L	The Oval	Surrey v Unicorns
40L	Birmingham	Warwicks v Leics
40L	Scarborough	Yorkshire v Northants

Mon 3 May
40L	Leek	Derbyshire v Essex
40L	Manchester	Lancashire v Somerset
40L	Leicester	Leics v Durham
40L	Hove	Sussex v Unicorns
40L	Worcester	Worcs v Surrey

Tue 4 – Fri 7 May
CC1	Southampton	Hampshire v Notts
CC1	Canterbury	Kent v Warwicks
CC1	Manchester	Lancashire v Somerset
CC1	Scarborough	Yorkshire v Essex
CC2	Leicester	Leics v Worcs
CC2	The Oval	Surrey v Glos

Wed 5 – Sat 8 May
CC2	Hove	Sussex v Middlesex

Wed 5 – Fri 7 May
FCF	Durham	Durham UCCE v Durham
	Cardiff	Glamorgan v Cardiff UCCE

Fri 7 May
40L F	Northampton	Northants v Derbyshire

Sat 8 May

40L	Nottingham	Notts v Kent

Sun 9 – Tue 11 May

FCF	The Oval	Surrey v Bangladeshis

Sun 9 May

40L	Chelmsford	Essex v Glos
40L	Cardiff	Glamorgan v Worcs
40L	Taunton	Somerset v Unicorns
40L – Hove		Sussex v Lancashire
40L	Birmingham	Warwicks v Durham
40L	Leeds	Yorkshire v Derbyshire

Mon 10 – Thu 13 May

CC1	Chelmsford	Essex v Kent
CC1	Southampton	Hampshire v Somerset
CC1	Nottingham	Notts v Durham
CC2	Cardiff	Glamorgan v Northants
CC2	Bristol	Glos v Leics
CC2	Lord's	Middlesex v Derbyshire

Mon 10 – Wed 12 May

	Weetwood	Leeds/Bradford UCCE v Warwicks
FCF	Leeds	Yorkshire v Loughborough UCCE

Wed 12 –Fri 14 May

FCF	Cambridge	Cambridge UCCE v Sussex

Fri 14 – Sun 16 May

FCF	Chelmsford	Essex v Bangladeshis

Fri 14 May

40L F	Southampton	Hampshire v Warwicks
40L F	Lord's	Middlesex v Glos

Sat 15 May

40L	Taunton	Somerset v Sussex
40L	Leeds	Yorkshire v Netherlands

Sun 16 May

40L	Bournemouth	Unicorns v Glamorgan
40L	Grace Road	Leics v Scotland
40L	Lord's	Middlesex v Netherlands
40L	Nottingham	Notts v Hampshire
40L	Birmingham	Warwicks v Kent
40L	Worcester	Worcs v Lancashire

Mon 17 –Thu 20 May

CC1	Canterbury	Kent v Durham
CC1	Nottingham	Notts v Hampshire
CC1	Taunton	Somerset v Yorkshire
CC1	Birmingham	Warwicks v Lancashire
CC2	Cardiff	Glamorgan v Glos
CC2	The Oval	Surrey v Middlesex
CC2	Worcester	Worcs v Derbyshire

Tue 18 – Fri 21 May

CC2	Northampton	Northants v Sussex

Wed 19 – Sat 22 May

FCF	Derby	England Lions v Bangladeshis

Fri 21 May

40L F	Cardiff	Glamorgan v Surrey
40L	Amstelveen	Netherlands v Essex

Sat 22 May

40L	Edinburgh	Scotland v Notts
40L	Birmingham	Warwicks v Hampshire

Sun 23 May

40L	Chester-le-St	Durham v Kent
40L	Arundel	Unicorns v Sussex
40L	Bristol	Glos v Northants
40L	Manchester	Lancashire v Surrey
40L	Amstelveen	Netherlands v Middlesex
40L	Edinburgh	Scotland v Notts
40L	Bath	Somerset v Worcs

Mon 24 – Thu 27 May

CC1	Chester-le-St	Durham v Kent
CC1	Southampton	Hampshire v Yorkshire
CC1	Manchester	Lancashire v Essex
CC1	Taunton	Somerset v Warwicks
CC2	Derby	Derbyshire v Glos
CC2	Leicester	Leics v Glamorgan
CC2	Northampton	Northants v Surrey
CC2	Hove	Sussex v Worcs

Tue 25 – Thu 27 May

FCF	Oxford	Oxford UCCE v Middlesex

Thu 27 – Mon 31 May

TM1	Lord's	ENGLAND v BANGLADESH

Sat 29 May – Tue 1 June

CC1	Nottingham	Notts v Essex
CC1	Birmingham	Warwicks v Durham
CC1	Leeds	Yorkshire v Lancashire
CC2	Cardiff	Glamorgan v Surrey
CC2	Leicester	Leics v Middlesex
CC2	Worcester	Worcs v Glos

Sun 30 May

40L	Southampton	Hampshire v Scotland
40L	Derby	Derbyshire v Netherlands

Mon 31 May

40L	Canterbury	Kent v Scotland
40L	Northampton	Northants v Netherlands

Tue 1 June

T20	Hove	Sussex v Somerset

Wed 2 June

T20 F	Chelmsford	Essex v Kent
T20	Leicester	Leics v Derbyshire

Thu 3 June

T20 F	Southampton	Hampshire v Kent
T20 F	Lord's	Middlesex v Sussex
T20	Birmingham	Warwicks v Northants
T20	Leeds	Yorkshire v Derbyshire

Fri 4 – Tue 8 June

TM2	Manchester	ENGLAND v BANGLADESH

Fri 4 – Mon 7 June

CC1	Southampton	Hampshire v Essex
CC1	Tunbridge W	Kent v Notts
CC1	Birmingham	Warwicks v Somerset
CC2	Lord's	Middlesex v Northants

CC2	The Oval	Surrey v Leics

Fri 4 June
T20	Chester-le-St	Durham v Lancashire
T20 F	Cardiff	Glamorgan v Glos
T20	Worcester	Worcs v Yorkshire

Sat 5 – Tue 8 June
| CC2 | Derby | Derbyshire v Sussex |

Sun 6 June
| T20 | Chester-le-St | Durham v Worcs |

Tue 8 June
T20 F	Cardiff	Glamorgan v Hampshire
T20 F	Northampton	Northants v Leics
T20	The Oval	Surrey v Glos

Wed 9 June
T20 F	Derby	Derbyshire v Warwicks
T20	Tunbridge W	Kent v Sussex
T20	Manchester	Lancashire v Northants
T20 F	Lord's	Middlesex v Somerset

Thu 10 June
T20 F	The Oval	Surrey v Essex
T20	Worcester	Worcs v Notts
T20	Leeds	Yorkshire v Durham

Fri 11 June
T20 F	Chelmsford	Essex v Glamorgan
T20	tbc	Glos v Sussex
T20 F	Southampton	Hampshire v Somerset
T20	Canterbury	Kent v Middlesex
T20	Manchester	Lancashire v Leics
T20 F	Northampton	Northants v Worcs
T20	Nottingham	Notts v Derbyshire
T20	Birmingham	Warwicks v Durham

Sat 12 June
| T20 | Taunton | Somerset v Surrey |

Sun 13 June
T20	Derby	Derbyshire v Durham
T20	Cardiff	Glamorgan v Sussex
T20	tbc	Glos v Kent
T20	Southampton	Hampshire v Surrey
T20	Lord's	Middlesex v Essex
T20	Nottingham	Notts v Worcs
T20	Birmingham	Warwicks v Lancashire
T20	Leeds	Yorkshire v Northants

Mon 14 June
| T20 | Chester-le-St | Durham v Leics |

Tue 15 June
| T20 | Richmond | Middlesex v Glamorgan |
| T20 | Nottingham | Notts v Lancashire |

Wed 16 June
T20	Taunton	Somerset v Essex
T20 F	Hove	Sussex v Glos
T20	Birmingham	Warwicks v Notts

Thu 17 June
| T20 F | Derby | Derbyshire v Notts |
| T20 F | Lord's | Middlesex v Surrey |

T20	Leeds	Yorkshire v Lancashire

Fri 18 June
T20	Chester-le-St	Durham v Yorkshire
T20	Leicester	Leics v Northants
T20	Taunton	Somerset v Glos
T20 F	The Oval	Surrey v Kent
T20	Hove	Sussex v Hampshire
T20	Worcester	Worcs v Warwicks

Sat 19 June
LOI	Edinburgh	Scotland v England
T20 F	Cardiff	Glamorgan v Essex
T20	Bristol	Glos v Hampshire
	Lord's	Middlesex v Australians

Sun 20 June
T20	Chester-le-St	Durham v Notts
T20	Beckenham	Kent v Somerset
T20	Manchester	Lancashire v Warwicks
T20	Leicester	Leics v Yorkshire
T20	Northampton	Northants v Derbyshire
T20	The Oval	Surrey v Sussex

Mon 21 June
| T20 F | Derby | Derbyshire v Worcs |

Tue 22 June
LOI F	Southampton	England v Australia
T20	Manchester	Lancashire v Durham
T20	Nottingham	Notts v Northants
T20	The Oval	Surrey v Hampshire
T20	Leeds	Yorkshire v Worcs

Wed 23 June
T20	Bristol	Glos v Essex
T20	Beckenham	Kent v Surrey
T20 F	Hove	Sussex v Glamorgan
T20	Birmingham	Warwicks v Leics

Thu 24 June
LOI	Cardiff	England v Australia
T20 F	Lord's	Middlesex v Kent
T20	Leeds	Yorkshire v Notts

Fri 25 June
T20 F	Chelmsford	Essex v Surrey
T20 F	Southampton	Hampshire v Glos
T20	Leicester	Leics v Lancashire
T20	Nottingham	Notts v Durham
T20	Taunton	Somerset v Sussex
T20	Birmingham	Warwicks v Derbyshire
T20	Worcester	Worcs v Northants

Sat 26 June
| T20 F | Cardiff | Glamorgan v Middlesex |
| T20 | Northampton | Northants v Durham |

Sun 27 June
LOI	Manchester	England v Australia
T20	Bristol	Glos v Middlesex
T20	Southampton	Hampshire v Essex
T20	Nottingham	Notts v Warwicks
T20	Hove	Sussex v Kent

T20	Worcester	Worcs v Derbyshire
T20	Leeds	Yorkshire v Leics

Mon 28 June – 1 July

CC1	Chester-le-St	Durham v Warwicks
CC1	Manchester	Lancashire v Yorkshire
CC2	Chesterfield	Derbyshire v Surrey
CC2	Bristol	Glos v Middlesex
CC2	Worcester	Worcs v Leics

Mon 28 – Wed 30 June

FCF	Canterbury	Kent v Pakistanis

Mon 28 June

T20	Taunton	Somerset v Glamorgan
	Northampton	India A v New Zealand A

Tue 29 June

T20 F	Chelmsford	Essex v Sussex
	Northampton	England Lions v New Zealand A

Wed 30 June

LOI F	The Oval	England v Australia

Thu 1 July

T20 F	Southampton	Hampshire v Glamorgan
	Leicester	England Lions v India A

Fri 2 July

T20	Chesterfield	Derbyshire v Leics
T20	Chester-le-St	Durham v Warwicks
T20	Bristol	Glos v Glamorgan
T20	Canterbury	Kent v Hampshire
T20 F	Northampton	Northants v Yorkshire
T20 F	The Oval	Surrey v Somerset
T20 F	Hove	Sussex v Middlesex
	Leicester	India A v New Zealand A
[T20]	Chelmsford	Essex v Pakistanis

Sat 3 July

LOI	Lord's	England v Australia
	Hove	Sussex v Bangladeshis
[T20]	Northampton	Northants v Pakistanis

Sun 4 July

T20	Chesterfield	Derbyshire v Lancashire
T20	Chelmsford	Essex v Hampshire
T20	Canterbury	Kent v Glos
T20	Leicester	Leics v Notts
T20	Taunton	Somerset v Middlesex
T20	The Oval	Surrey v Glamorgan
T20	Leeds	Yorkshire v Warwicks
	Worcester	England Lions v New Zealand A
	Lord's	Oxford U v Cambridge U

Mon 5 – Thu 8 July

CC1	Chelmsford	Essex v Notts
CC1	Southampton	Hampshire v Kent
CC1	Leeds	Yorkshire v Warwicks
CC2	Northampton	Northants v Glamorgan

Mon 5 July

IT20	Birmingham	Pakistan v Australia
T20	Manchester	Lancashire v Worcs
	Lord's	Middlesex v Bangladeshis

Tue 6 – Fri 9 July

FCF	Oxford	Oxford U v Cambridge U

Tue 6 July

IT20	Birmingham	Pakistan v Australia
	Worcester	England Lions v India A

Wed 7 – Sat 10 July

CC2	Arundel	Sussex v Glos

Wed 7 July

T20	Leicester	Leics v Worcs

Thu 8 July

LOI F	Nottingham	England v Bangladesh
T20 F	The Oval	Surrey v Middlesex
	Manchester	Lancashire v tbc
	Worcester	A XI Final

Fri 9 July

T20 F	Cardiff	Glamorgan v Surrey
T20	The Oval	Kent v Essex
T20	Manchester	Lancashire v Yorkshire
T20 F	Northampton	Northants v Warwicks
T20	Taunton	Somerset v Hampshire
T20	Worcester	Worcs v Durham

Sat 10 July

LOI	Bristol	England v Bangladesh
T20	Uxbridge	Middlesex v Hampshire

Sun 11 – Tue 13 July

FCF	Chester-le-St	Durham v New Zealand A
FCF	Leeds	Yorkshire v India A

Sun 11 July

T20	Chelmsford	Essex v Somerset
T20	Canterbury	Kent v Glamorgan
T20	Manchester	Lancashire v Derbyshire
T20	Uxbridge	Middlesex v Glos
T20	Northampton	Northants v Notts
T20	Arundel	Sussex v Surrey
T20	Worcester	Worcs v Leics

Mon 12 July

LOI	Birmingham	England v Bangladesh

Tue 13 – Sat 17 July

TM1	Lord's	PAKISTAN v AUSTRALIA

Wed 14 July

T20	Chester-le-St	Durham v Derbyshire
T20 F	Cardiff	Glamorgan v Somerset
T20	Manchester	Lancashire v Notts
T20	Birmingham	Warwicks v Yorkshire

Thu 15 July

T20 F	Chelmsford	Essex v Glos
T20 F	Northampton	Northants v Lancashire
T20 F	Nottingham	Notts v Leics

Fri 16 – Mon 19 July

FCF	Manchester	India A v New Zealand A

Fri 16 July

T20 F	Derby	Derbyshire v Northants
T20 F	Cardiff	Glamorgan v Kent
T20	Bristol	Glos v Somerset

T20 [F]	Southampton	Hampshire v Middlesex
T20	Leicester	Leics v Durham
T20 [F]	Hove	Sussex v Essex
T20	Birmingham	Warwicks v Worcs

Sat 17 July
T20	Nottingham	Notts v Yorkshire

Sun 18 July
T20	Derby	Derbyshire v Yorkshire
T20	Chester-le-St	Durham v Northants
T20	Chelmsford	Essex v Middlesex
T20	Bristol	Glos v Surrey
T20	Southampton	Hampshire v Sussex
T20	Leicester	Leics v Warwicks
T20	Taunton	Somerset v Kent
T20	Worcester	Worcs v Lancashire

Mon 19 July
40L [F]	Hove	Sussex v Worcs

Tue 20 – Fri 23 July
CC1	Chester-le-St	Durham v Lancashire
CC1	Chelmsford	Essex v Yorkshire
CC1	Taunton	Somerset v Kent
CC1	Birmingham	Warwicks v Notts
CC2	The Oval	Surrey v Northants

Tue 20 July
40L [F]	Derby	Derbyshire v Glos

Wed 21 – Sun 25 July
TM2	Leeds	PAKISTAN v AUSTRALIA

Wed 21 – Sat 24 July
CC2	Derby	Derbyshire v Worcs
CC2	Swansea	Glamorgan v Leics
CC2	Uxbridge	Middlesex v Sussex

Fri 23 – Mon 26 July
FCF	Southampton	India A v New Zealand A

Sat 24 July
40L	Manchester	Lancashire v Unicorns

Sun 25 July
40L	Chester-le-St	Durham v Notts
40L	Kidderminster	Unicorns v Worcs
40L	Swansea	Glamorgan v Sussex
40L	Canterbury	Kent v Hampshire
40L	Leicester	Leics v Warwicks
40L	Lord's	Middlesex v Yorkshire
40L	Northampton	Northants v Essex
40L	The Oval	Surrey v Somerset

Mon 26 July
T20		Quarter-finals 1 & 2

Tue 27 July
T20		Quarter-finals 3 & 4

Thu 29 July – Mon 2 August
TM1	Nottingham	ENGLAND v PAKISTAN

Thu 29 July – Sun 1 Aug
CC1	Southampton	Hampshire v Lancashire
CC1	Canterbury	Kent v Essex

Thu 29 July
40L	Cheltenham	Glos v Yorkshire

Fri 30 July – Mon 2 August
CC2	Cheltenham	Glos v Glamorgan

Fri 30 July
40L	Schiedam	Netherlands v Derbyshire

Sat 31 July
40L	Glasgow	Scotland v Durham

Sun 1 August
40L	Schiedam	Netherlands v Yorkshire
40L	Glasgow	Scotland v Warwicks

Tue 3 – Fri 6 August
CC1	Basingstoke	Hampshire v Durham
CC1	Canterbury	Kent v Somerset
CC1	Leeds	Yorkshire v Notts
CC2	Leicester	Leics v Derbyshire

Tue 3 August
40L [F]	Manchester	Lancashire v Sussex

Wed 4 – Sat 7 August
CC1	Southend	Essex v Warwicks
CC2	Cheltenham	Glos v Worcs

Wed 4 August
40L [F]	The Oval	Surrey v Glamorgan

Thu 5 August
40L [F]	Lord's	Middlesex v Northants

Fri 6 – Tue 10 August
TM2	Birmingham	ENGLAND v PAKISTAN

Sun 8 August
40L	Chesterfield	Derbyshire v Yorkshire
40L	Exmouth	Unicorns v Somerset
40L	Southend	Essex v Northants
40L	Colwyn Bay	Glamorgan v Lancashire
40L	Cheltenham	Glos v Middlesex
40L	Southampton	Hampshire v Durham
40L	Canterbury	Kent v Leics
40L	Nottingham	Notts v Scotland
40L	Guildford	Surrey v Sussex

Mon 9 – Thu 12 August
CC1	Manchester	Lancashire v Durham
CC1	Taunton	Somerset v Hampshire
CC2	Chesterfield	Derbyshire v Northants
CC2	Colwyn Bay	Glamorgan v Worcs
CC2	Lord's	Middlesex v Leics
CC2	Guildford	Surrey v Sussex

Wed 11 August
40L [F]	Leeds	Yorkshire v Glos

Thu 12 August
40L [F]	Nottingham	Notts v Warwicks

Sat 14 August

| T20 F | Southampton | Semi-finals and FINAL |

Mon 16 – Thu 19 August

CC1	Chester-le-St	Durham v Yorkshire
CC1	Nottingham	Notts v Warwicks
CC2	Cardiff	Glamorgan v Middlesex
CC2	Northampton	Northants v Glos
CC2	Worcester	Worcs v Surrey

Mon 16 August

| 40L F | Taunton | Somerset v Lancashire |

Tue 17 August

| 40L F | Southampton | Hampshire v Leics |

Wed 18 – Sun 22 August

| TM3 | The Oval | **ENGLAND v PAKISTAN** |

Wed 18 – Sat 21 August

CC1	Colchester	Essex v Somerset
CC1	Canterbury	Kent v Lancashire
CC2	Horsham	Sussex v Derbyshire

Fri 20 August

| 40L F | Cardiff | Glamorgan v Unicorns |

Sat 21 August

| 40L | Edinburgh | Scotland v Hampshire |

Sun 22 August

40L	Chester-le-St	Durham v Warwicks
40L	Wormsley	Unicorns v Surrey
40L	Colchester	Essex v Derbyshire
40L	Canterbury	Kent v Notts
40L	Rotterdam	Netherlands v Northants
40L	Edinburgh	Scotland v Leics
40L	Horsham	Sussex v Somerset
40L	Worcester	Worcs v Glamorgan
40L	Scarborough	Yorkshire v Middlesex

Mon 23 – Thu 26 August

| CC1 | Scarborough | Yorkshire v Hampshire |

Mon 23 August

| 40L F | Bristol | Glos v Essex |

Tue 24 – Fri 27 August

CC1	Nottingham	Notts v Lancashire
CC1	Taunton	Somerset v Durham
CC2	Leicester	Leics v Surrey

Tue 24 August

| 40L F | Derby | Derbyshire v Middlesex |

Wed 25 – Sat 28 August

CC1	Birmingham	Warwicks v Essex
CC2	Derby	Derbyshire v Middlesex
CC2	Northampton	Northants v Worcs

Wed 25 August

| 40L F | Hove | Sussex v Glamorgan |

Thu 26 – Mon 30 August

| TM4 | Lord's | **ENGLAND v PAKISTAN** |

Thu 26 August

| 40L | Rotterdam | Netherlands v Glos |

Fri 27 – Mon 30 August

| CC2 | Hove | Sussex v Glamorgan |

Sun 29 August

40L	Chester-le-St	Durham v Scotland
40L	Chelmsford	Essex v Netherlands
40L	Southampton	Hampshire v Kent
40L	Nottingham	Notts v Leics
40L	Taunton	Somerset v Surrey
40L	Worcester	Worcs v Unicorns

Mon 30 August

40L	Derby	Derbyshire v Northants
40L	Colwyn Bay	Unicorns v Lancashire
40L	Bristol	Glos v Netherlands
40L	Leicester	Leics v Kent
40L	Nottingham	Notts v Durham
40L	Birmingham	Warwicks v Scotland
40L	Worcester	Worcs v Somerset

Tue 31 August – Fri 3 September

CC1	Chester-le-St	Durham v Notts
CC1	Liverpool	Lancashire v Hampshire
CC1	Birmingham	Warwicks v Kent
CC2	Bristol	Glos v Derbyshire

Tue 31 August

| 40L F | Northampton | Northants v Yorkshire |

Wed 1 September

| 40L F | The Oval | Surrey v Worcs |

Thu 2 September

| 40L F | Chelmsford | Essex v Middlesex |
| | Taunton | Somerset v Pakistanis |

Sat 4 September

40L	Chester-le-St	Durham v Kent
40L	Liverpool	Lancashire v Worcs
40L	Leicester	Leics v Hampshire
40L	Lord's	Middlesex v Derbyshire
40L	Northampton	Northants v Glos
40L	Taunton	Somerset v Glamorgan
40L	Hove	Sussex v Surrey
40L	Birmingham	Warwicks v Notts
40L	Leeds	Yorkshire v Essex

Sun 5 September

| IT20 | Cardiff | **England v Pakistan** |

Tue 7 – Fri 10 September

CC1	Chelmsford	Essex v Durham
CC1	Canterbury	Kent v Hampshire
CC1	Nottingham	Notts v Yorkshire
CC1	Taunton	Somerset v Lancashire
CC2	Leicester	Leics v Glos
CC2	Lord's	Middlesex v Worcs
CC2	The Oval	Surrey v Glamorgan
CC2	Hove	Sussex v Northants

Tue 7 September

| IT20 F | Cardiff | **England v Pakistan** |

Fri 10 September

| LOI | Chester-le-St | **England v Pakistan** |

Sat 11 September		
40L	tbc	Semi-finals
Sun 12 September		
LOI	Leeds	**England v Pakistan**
Mon 13 –Thu 16 September		
CC1	Chester-le-St	Durham v Somerset
CC1	Southampton	Hampshire v Warwicks
CC1	Manchester	Lancashire v Notts
CC1	Leeds	Yorkshire v Kent
CC2	Cardiff	Glamorgan v Derbyshire
CC2	Bristol	Glos v Surrey

CC2	Northampton	Northants v Leics
CC2	Worcester	Worcs v Sussex
Fri 17 September		
LOI^F	The Oval	**England v Pakistan**
Sat 18 September		
40L^F	Lord's	FINAL
Mon 20 September		
LOI^F	Lord's	**England v Pakistan**
Wed 22 September		
LOI^F	Southampton	**England v Pakistan**

TEST MATCH CHAMPIONSHIP SCHEDULE

Months indicate the start of a series. Number of Tests in brackets.
All series involving Zimbabwe are subject to confirmation.

2010	May	**England hosts Bangladesh (2)**
	Jun	West Indies hosts South Africa (3)
		Zimbabwe hosts New Zealand (2)
	Jul	Pakistan hosts Australia in England (2)
		England hosts Pakistan (4)
	Aug	Australia hosts Bangladesh (2)
	Sep	South Africa hosts Zimbabwe (2)
	Oct	Pakistan hosts South Africa (3)
		Bangladesh hosts New Zealand (2)
	Nov	**Australia hosts England (5)**
		India hosts New Zealand (3)
		Sri Lanka hosts West Indies (3)
	Dec	New Zealand hosts Pakistan (2)
		South Africa hosts India (3)
		Bangladesh hosts Zimbabwe (2)
2011	Apr	Bangladesh hosts Australia (2)
		West Indies hosts Pakistan (2)
	May	**England hosts Sri Lanka (3)**
		West Indies hosts Pakistan (2)
	Jun	Australia hosts Zimbabwe (2)

	Jul	**England hosts India (4)**
	Aug	Zimbabwe hosts Bangladesh (2)
		Sri Lanka hosts Australia (3)
	Sep	Zimbabwe hosts Pakistan (2)
	Oct	South Africa hosts Australia (3)
		Bangladesh hosts West Indies (2)
		Pakistan hosts Sri Lanka (3)
	Nov	India hosts West Indies (3)
		Australia hosts New Zealand (2)
	Dec	Bangladesh hosts Pakistan (2)
		Australia hosts India (4)
		South Africa hosts Sri Lanka (3)
		New Zealand hosts Zimbabwe (2)
2012	Jan	**Pakistan hosts England (3)**
	Mar	New Zealand hosts South Africa (3)
		India hosts Pakistan (3)
		West Indies hosts Australia (3)
	Apr	Pakistan hosts Bangladesh (2)
		West Indies hosts New Zealand (3)
	May	**England hosts West Indies (3)**

DUCKWORTH/LEWIS – A BRIEF EXPLANATION

The Duckworth/Lewis (D/L) method has been around now for 12 years and it is generally accepted as being a very fair method for resetting targets in interrupted one-day matches. However, ask a typical cricket fan as to how the calculations are done and the fallback excuse of not being good at maths at school is frequently trotted out. But if you can work out how much tax you have to pay on your net income then D/L calculations are well within your grasp.

You may well have heard that the D/L method is based on the idea of resources – these are the combination of wickets and overs that a team has for its innings. However, it's not just the numbers of these that matter; it is also their relative value – wickets and overs have different relative importance as an innings progresses. For example, having lots of wickets in hand without overs left in which to use them is of little value, just as if lots of overs remain they have little value if there are no wickets left with which to use them. In conducting their innings, teams need to manage their twin resources in order to maximise the total they set or maximise their chances of winning the match. Through some not behind-the-scenes mathematics and statistical analysis of hundreds of matches, Duckworth and Lewis have produced a table that represents the average percentages remaining of their twin resources of a 50-over innings. In the extract of the table supplied you will see that teams start with all 50 overs and 10 wickets – and therefore 100% of their resources. As an innings progresses a team receives its overs, loses its wickets and thereby consumes its resources. The table works always in overs left – in that way it can be used for matches that are shorter than 50 overs – and tells us what percentage of their combined resources remains.

Wickets lost:	0	2	4	6	9
Overs remaining:-					
50	100.0	85.1	62.7	34.9	4.7
40	89.3	77.8	59.5	34.6	4.7
30	75.1	67.3	54.1	33.6	4.7
25	66.5	60.5	50.0	32.6	4.7
20	56.6	52.4	44.6	30.8	4.7
10	32.1	30.8	28.3	22.8	4.7
5	17.2	16.8	16.1	14.3	4.6

Suppose that a team has batted for 45 overs and has lost 6 wickets. With 5 overs left, for 6 wickets lost the table shows it has 14.3% of its resources remaining. If its innings is now terminated, these resources are lost and it has had available for its innings 100 – 14.3 = 85.7% resources compared with the 100% for a complete 50-over innings.

These figures came into play in a crucial Group match of the 2003 World Cup in South Africa. Against the host nation, Sri Lanka scored 268 in their 100% resources of 50 overs. Rain began to fall and abandonment looked likely at the end of the 45th over of South Africa's innings. Charts of the D/L method were consulted and the relevant figure was obtained through the comparative resources of the two teams. The calculation was 268 × 85.7/100 = 229.676. This meant that in order to win SA needed to reach 230 by the end of the 45th over if the match were abandoned. A score of 229 would be the score to tie.

How would South Africa know this? You will have seen the D/L par-score displayed on scoreboards. These numbers come from the par-score sheet that is distributed during the interval to team camps, match officials and the media. The par-score is given for the end of every one of the combinations of overs left and wickets lost (and even on a ball-by-ball basis). This sheet is clearly labelled as the score needed to tie. In the World Cup match the SA camp told the batsmen, Boucher and Klusener, that they needed to get to 229 by the end of the over. Thanks to a six from Boucher off the penultimate ball of the over, they achieved this – and to avoid losing his wicket, which would have raised the par-score, Boucher blocked the last ball. Play was duly abandoned at the end of the over but the dismay in the SA camp was palpable when it was finally realised that the 229 the batsmen had been told to score was in fact the score to tie and not to win the match. So a tie it was and the misreading of the clear information available led to the elimination of the host nation from the tournament.

Whenever a stoppage occurs within an innings, the table provides the information by which to calculate the resources lost. Suppose that there are 20 overs left with only 4 wickets down and a stoppage reduces the innings by 10 overs so there are now only 10 overs left on the resumption. You will see from the table that the team went off with 44.6% resources left and came back with 28.3% left. The stoppage would have cost it 44.6 − 28.3 = 16.3% of its resources so that it would have available 100 − 16.3 = 83.7% resources for its innings if there are no more stoppages (but if there are, the resources available are further reduced in the same way) and, in most cases, the target comes from reducing the first innings score in proportion to the resources available as in the World Cup example.

Sometimes teams start with fewer than 50 overs either due to a shorter match competition, such as the Pro40 or Twenty20, or due to a delayed start. For a 25-over innings, for instance, teams start with 66.5% resources compared with a 50-over innings. Although they have half the overs they still have all 10 wickets and therefore more than half their resources – the table says about two-thirds compared with a 50-over innings. Any loss of overs would reduce this further in the same way and using the same figures as in the table.

So you see that it really is simple to calculate targets following interruptions during the second innings. The method is simply to adjust the first innings score in proportion to the resources available to the two teams – rounding up to win and one fewer to tie.

A distinctive feature of the D/L method compared with previous methods of adjusting targets is that it compensates the team batting first for stoppages within its innings – its batting strategy has been based on the full 50 overs and so to have it curtailed is usually a disadvantage. The D/L method usually sets an enhanced target, that is, a target which is quite a few runs more than the team batting first scored. This has the effect of compensating it for the unexpected shortening of the first innings and the advantage that the team batting second has from knowing in advance of its shorter innings.

How this is achieved, together with further detailed descriptions of the Duckworth/Lewis method and some frequently asked questions, can be found at the Cricinfo website: www.cricinfo.com/db/ABOUT_CRICKET/RAIN_RULES/ and a booklet is available from Acumen Books at www.acumenbooks.com/ducklew.htm.

One of these FAQs concerns the effect that powerplays have on D/L calculations. Data on powerplays are not yet sufficient to do a thorough analysis, but the logic is similar to the old 15-over rule on which there are plenty of data. These show that the greater runs scored in these overs are consistent with what is expected from the D/L method for the overs and the *wickets* used up in those periods of more attacking fields. Consequently it is unlikely that the powerplays have any significant effect on D/L target calculations. But the situation will be kept under review.

Although rain is usually the cause of stoppages and D/L adjusted targets, interruptions have occurred for several other causes including sandstorms, snow, floodlight failures, crowd disturbances and, on a few occasions, due to the sun!

Cases at the higher levels of the game usually run to 80-100 per year and the total usage is approaching 1000 since the method's first use on 1st January 1997 in which England lost to Zimbabwe when they would have won by the old, unfair average run-rate method.

There have been some advances in the methodology since January 1997. With higher totals being more prevalent, and the introduction of Twenty20 matches which fit well into the D/L system, teams need to score a bigger percentage of their runs in the earlier stages of their innings than those suggested by the standard tables. Consequently, higher scores lead to the need for the table to be adjusted and this needs the computer to do the calculations. Whereas what is now known as the Standard Edition, using a single table of resources as described here, is used at lower levels of the game where computers aren't necessary or available, the higher levels of the game now use the more advanced computerised version called the Professional Edition. In this edition, the computer in effect produces a different table of resources for every match, but thereafter the calculations are the same as described here.

FIELDING CHART

(For a right-handed batsman)

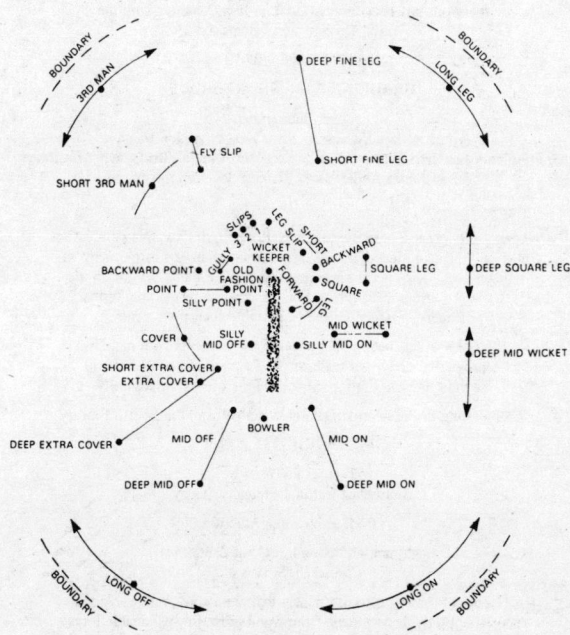

First published in 2010 by

HEADLINE PUBLISHING GROUP

Cover photographs:
(*Front*) Andrew Strauss © Scott Heavey/Action Images
(*Spine*) The Ashes Urn © Marylebone Cricket Club, London/Bridgeman Art Library
(*Back*) James Anderson © Richard Sellers/Sportsphoto

1

Cataloguing in Publication Data is available from the British Library

ISBN 978 0 7553 1747 9

Typeset in Times by
Letterpart Limited, Reigate, Surrey

Preface by Mike Atherton

Printed and bound in Great Britain by
Clays Ltd, St Ives plc

HEADLINE PUBLISHING GROUP
An Hachette UK Company
338 Euston Road
London NW1 3BH
www.headline.co.uk
www.hachette.co.uk